# The Death of an Industry.

by

## Michael Thomas

Published in 2004 by Colben System Pte. Ltd.
65 Joo Koon Circle, Singapore 629078

ISBN: 981-05-2395-5

## About the Author.

**Michael Thomas** was born in the Rhondda Valley and started his career as a National Coal Board apprentice. He later became a colliery Electrical Engineer responsible for all electrical systems at the mine. Awarded a Coal Board scholarship, he graduated from the University of Wales with a degree in Electrical Engineering.

During his working life he occupied a variety of management positions concerned with the generation and application of power world wide in a series of large-scale international projects. Latterly, he was Manager of Electrical Systems for a German company represented in Singapore and Technical Director for a Singapore company. He has given seminars on power quality and carried out power analyses for a number of concerns in various countries.

Now retired, he lives with his wife and son in Germany.

# CONTENTS

# PREFACE.

*Eternal Vigilance is the Price of Freedom.*

Slogan on the banner of Tower colliery NUM lodge.

Once there was a whole region epitomised by a single word – coal. Virtually the entire population worked, either directly or in a support function, to produce and feed this raw material into the gaping maw of urban development and the burgeoning industries upon which modern society was built. The clichéd Welshman was a troglodyte from another, subterranean, world. His face, pitch black with coal dust, was crowned with a belamped helmet, by whose light he was able to hew the black gold, between periods of singing his heart out as one of a mass of other, similarly benighted, souls. Behind this grotesque travesty lurked an element of truth, for the society in which the Welsh miner lived was as mono-economic as it was possible to be.

Exigencies of the time made it possible for a variety of individuals to get-rich-quick, tearing out the energy riches that lay beneath the original pristine beauty of the hills and glades, crowned to the north by rugged, imposing ridges. In so doing they created a new society in the suddenly cramped, dirty valleys. Exploitive and ruthless, when the whim of market forces deemed it necessary, this society would reject those who served it. The countervailing hatred produced a visceral radicalism that would persist to the bitter end, only temporarily assuaged by the passage of the industry into public ownership at the end of the Second World War.

Initially, coal was again king as Britain and the world recovered from the conflagration of war, only to see its throne usurped by newcomers on the energy scene. This again resulted in a countervailing movement on the part of organised labour, one that would culminate in the longest, most intense and widespread industrial unrest in British history. From that point on, what was seen in Government circles as the political imperative of breaking the industrial power of the miners influenced, and became intertwined with, the other objective of establishing market supremacy together with its handmaid globalisation. Rejection of social justice and corporatism as prime objectives, combined with the doctoring of a so-called "free" market, enabled the massacring of the industry and the emasculation of union power.

Even in the 1960s, the 200 year long presence of South Wales coal mining was all encompassing, not only because of the many pits still working but also due to the shells of abandoned mines which littered the valleys together with their accompanying detritus, not to mention the ubiquitous slag heaps that dominated the hills. With the sole exception of Tower colliery, which is still a living, breathing entity, the deep mining tradition in Wales now makes its presence felt only in museums, the Rhondda Heritage Centre and the fading scars on slowly greening hills. Whereas remnants of the Greek and Roman civilisations, after approximately two millennia, still lie scattered all around where they once held sway, the lost civilisation of Welsh coal has proven to be more transitory. An ancient Greek or Roman, returning to earth by some miracle, might have less difficulty in finding traces of his heritage than a returnee to South Wales. It is no doubt all to the good but, although the final closures were less than 15 years ago, it is as if a giant broom has swept away all remnants, with some of them fortunately being caught up in the handful of mining museums and heritage sites.

In the 1940s and 50s, both Government and Coal Board were confidently predicting a thriving coal industry lasting for the next 100 years. In the 21st. century, with oil and gas prices increasing, coal mining outside Europe is expanding. So what happened here - bad geology? bad labour relations? new and better fuels? concern for the environment? inability to adapt? Globalisation? short sightedness? or just political vindictiveness? All of these had a role to play, but each pit was very much an individual entity and the mixture could vary considerably from case to case.

Having grown up in the Rhondda, the archetypal Welsh coal mining valley, and having spent some of my formative years in mining, I have always been interested in the forces shaping the industry that moulded both me and my home town, in particular those changes that occurred during my own lifetime. Twenty years after the traumatic miner's strike of 1984-85, which changed British history, and ten years after the unique take-over of Tower colliery by its miners, now is an appropriate time to look back on those events and how things turned out. An introduction to the more distant past is essential, since the ethos and traditions of coal mining had been built up over 200 years.

The decline of the industry also did not happen in isolation, but was the result of national and international geo-political movements. In writing this book I have tried to deal both with such larger considerations and also with individual pits and coalfaces, getting behind the superficial rhetoric of interested parties to consider the questions in detail why? how? where? and when?

As a basis I have used information as listed in *Documentary Sources* and *Bibliography* below, as well as personal discussion with individuals. These are referred to in *Acknowledgements*. In addition, there is input from my

own experience in the industry. As an illustration of general trends I have referred to certain individual pits, with continuing reference to the developing strategic situation, both nationally and internationally. It is hardly possible to give a comprehensive history since each of the hundreds of pits had its own tale to tell.

When the dream of public ownership was finally realised, Vesting Day in 1947 was greeted in the coalfields with jubilation and hope for the future. It was a hope not to be realised, as over the next decades the industry was swept hither and thither by the cataclysmic changes taking place, nationally and world-wide. Nowhere was this to be more apparent than in the South Wales coalfield. This book tells the story.

---

# List of Diagrams.

# List of Illustrations.

# Chapter 1

## DEATH AT WORK - THE LAST EXPLOSION.

*"What has happened to our miners?*
*We don't see them any more,*
*This, our valley town was booming,*
*Not so many years ago"*
G. L. Davies, Llantrisant.

**THE ENVIRONMENT.**

Crouching beneath dripping grey skies, the surrounding hills crowd in on elongated grey strips of terraced houses, arranged in an echeloned hierarchy, each strip trumping the other, for the nineteenth century drive for accommodation had forced each successive terrace further up the hillside. The South Wales valleys are narrow but this one is narrower. This is Clydach Vale, a cul-de-sac off a cul-de-sac, a dead end. It is a side valley, a secondary twig, joined to the main branch of the Rhondda Fawr at Ton-y-Pandy. Nestled within the enveloping hills, and tucked in at the furthest point, is the Cambrian colliery, the sole reason for Clydach Vale's existence. Here, on the valley floor, a cluster of red brick buildings huddle around the duplicated pit headgear, a symbol of meaning and life for this backwater. One shaft opens directly to the atmosphere. The second is accessible only by means of an air lock. Adjacent to this a giant fan, electrically driven, moans with an incessant, subdued moan. Above the fan house, a thin spume of water vapour shimmers as the air is thrown out through a vertical venturi funnel. From this Spartan industrial settlement a single rail track, dedicated to coal alone, snakes its way along the mountainside, eventually descending from the Glamorgan uplands to link up with the main line at Llantrisant in the Vale of Glamorgan. Within the compacted sidings of the colliery yard, trains of coal wagons are shepherded together by a clanking, puffing tank engine, a railway buff's dream.

The wheels atop the black painted steel frameworks still rotate. A banging and clattering of pit top activity echoes as coal, men and supplies are wound. Singularly unimpressed by such activity and in symbiotic contrast to the presence of heavy industry on the valley floor, on the hillside scattered white dots of sheep munch stoically. In the tenuous sunshine of a late South Wales spring, maturing lambs would normally be gambolling and frisking around their mothers.

Today however, there is no sunshine. Today, as they so often do, rain clouds have rolled in from the Irish Sea, boxing in the valley and emphasising the predominant, uninviting grey. Clinging to the surrounding hills with the tenacity of glue, the clouds let their sputum drip over the terraced streets with depressing longevity. In this world of dampness, the grey sandstone of the terraces, their grey slate roofs, and the grey of the dominating rocky outcrops, shimmer dully in the reduced light capable of penetrating the murk.

While the woolly denizens of the hills above are lost in the mist and, between munching, huddle together for warmth and protection against the all-penetrating damp, their colleagues below, an urban underworld of sheep, hang pointlessly around, pathetic orphans of the storm. Later in the week, before garbage is collected, the more disreputable elements among them will rise early, to nudge over dustbins and scatter their contents over the pavement. Potato peel and other edible remains make a pleasant change from just grass, grass and more grass. Today however, misery personified, they huddle in doorways and below garden walls, oblivious to the raincoated figures of passing humankind, cursing the weather. That participation by sheep in community life, once so typical of the valleys, is now a thing of the past. Nowadays, action by the local council has put a stop to animal immigration.

One day fortune, and the sun, will smile again. Its rays will penetrate the freshly washed atmosphere, evaporating the grey depression. On the mountainside, greens, browns and yellows of bracken, trees and grass will emerge. Seen from the moorland crests, its light will highlight the verdant vale of Glamorgan to the south and the dark blue water of the Bristol Channel beyond. Life, and the world, will bloom again. Before that day dawns however, a tragedy has been ordained.

**It is noon, on Monday 17 May 1965.**


## MINING LIFE.

Only slightly below the mist, the scattered, utilitarian red brick buildings cluttering around the pit head-gear are dominated by the pithead baths/canteen. In the latter, a few grizzled, blue-scarred veterans, together with the occasional fresh-faced apprentice, tarry over a mug of tea. It will be two hours yet before the pit discharges their comrades of the morning shift, which will then disintegrate into a steam-obscured mass of naked flesh. Like a slippery shoal, they will tarry in the steam and Rabelaisian repartee of the raucous shower area as they hurry from their dirty clothes lockers to their clean clothes lockers and then out into the freedom of a Monday afternoon, into the real world. Some will seek out an individual, white-tiled cubicle to enjoy the soap and hot water removing the sweat and grime. These will be serenaded by groups of less introverted souls in the open shower area, formed up in circles to wash each others' backs, while belting out their ad hoc choral work.

On Saturdays, before making their way home, where the wife or "mam" will have dinner ready, the maintenance men like to tarry over a pint in a local hostelry. In the Bush, the Central, or the Clydach Vale they will look forward to the prospect of a "good night" on the forthcoming evening, while relaxing in the afterglow of the morning's achievement, its mental and physical effort still fresh in their minds. Character-ised by a lively, quick wit, so typical of the South Wales miner, their intercourse is a fricassee of mutual banter, penetrating character analysis and technical discussion. Stories are told, and the specialist work in their subterranean world, beyond the experience of today's existence, relived. Discussed will be strata characteristics, hydraulic versus friction roof supports, lower versus higher control voltages, etc., etc. However, that was Saturday and this is Monday. Weekdays are dedicated to production.

Prior to the massive pay increases which followed the 1972 and 1974 strikes, few miners could afford cars at that time and so, at about 2pm and for the second time that day, a convoy of red double-decker buses will discharge a complete shift at the pithead baths. The buses will then form in line, to collect their homeward bound colleagues. The latter, freshly scrubbed and with large highlighted eyes, where soap would be too uncomfortable to remove the grime from black-rimmed eyelids, will greet the subdued, normal looking incomers. Status reports will be handed over.

Soon, the incoming replacements will be transformed into helmeted, belamped miners, before being lowered into that world of men, that stygian underground factory whose tentacles extend, octopus-like, for miles. A world unknown except to the initiated awaits them, an underground network of intake and return airways, airlocks, fans, narrow-gauge rail tracks, conveyor belts, haulages, substations and coalfaces. Here work and King Coal rule, while comradeship dominates, a comradeship masked by acid, penetrating repartee and sexually laden banter. Cambrian's ethos is abrasive, with snide remarks about the size of one individual's nose being countered by ridicule of the exaggerated self-esteem on the dance floor as held by the other, the "Fred Astaire of Clydach Vale". This mask of superficiality hides the fact that each man has been evaluated, and judged by his peers. This is a team effort, in a dark, claustrophobic environment. There is mutual dependency in the avoidance of danger. Many of those destined to leave the industry later will come to miss this comradeship, as they will the sense of individual contribution. Men in pits work in small groups, sometimes on their own, where personal initiative is required. Rather than frightening, to many it is exciting and challenging, and preferable to standing on a production line.

In those days, before general issue of the standard, orange-coloured overalls, a pirate crew would emerge from the dirty clothes changing area. In dribs and drabs the motley band, bedecked in a variety of self procured blue overalls, scarves, worn out lounge suits, sports coats and army surplus, stroll across to the pithead. Helmets of the youngsters among them are individually decorated with stickers and lightning flashes, plus painted-on nicknames. They rest jauntily on the back of their heads. The lads rue their lot for having to work an afternoon shift, thereby missing out on any meaningful social life for the duration of the week. From bed, after eating, to work then from work, after eating, to bed. Their cap lamps are unhooked. At cables' end they dangle casually at waist level as the lads stroll and swear their way over to the pit-top or to the surface workshops. Conversation will dwell on the latest rugby match or the previous Saturday night's revelry. Then, the main streets of Treorchy and Ton-y-Pandy would have swarmed with local hedonists, out for a spree. By this time, the chapels and the workingmen's libraries, where Marxism and the soul were once predominant, have had their heyday, to be replaced by "booze and bingo". Clubs, pubs and the Italian cafes, the "Braccis" will have done good trade.

Typically, the weekly dance-floor punch-up at Judges Hall in Ton-y-Pandy will be discussed. Mixed up in the imbroglio this time could have been the lads from Aberdare or the Black boys from Cardiff who, with unfair tricks such as flattery and little gifts, seemed to have an uncanny knack of charming away the women. Those of more refined tastes will dwell on the "good night" they had at the Library dance hall, the "Dog and Muffler" workings men's club, the NCB social club, or a host of other hostelries. Mining was more than just a job, it was a way of life, and if the pit talk is about "the club", the club talk will have concentrated on the pit. Jokes will have been made about the amount of dust in the atmosphere and the need to consume more liquid for its suppression.

## CAMBRIAN COLLIERY.

Everybody is aware that this whole montage is a scene that might shortly be relegated to history. After nationalisation of the industry in 1947, Cambrian had continued to flourish. Indeed, even in the previous few years, extensive reconstruction had been carried out. Started in 1959 and completed in 1964, just one year previously, the investment was planned to be written off over a working life extending to 1992. It had all been a disappointment. Annual production, instead of increasing from 321,671t to 403,200t had in fact fallen to 297,000t. Instead of converting a financial loss of 3s 5d per ton into a profit of 10s per ton as planned, the results had in fact deteriorated, with a loss per ton (after interest) of 18s 8d. Anticipated reserves in the Pentre seam, upon which Cambrian's future had been predicated and which had served as justification for the investment, had proven to be illusory. As the coalfaces advanced the 3-foot (0.9m) section of coal in this seam, which had shown good sales potential and which had been easy to work, was becoming increasingly thinner, split in the middle by an unexpected band of hard rock. Of the hoped-for reserves, 60 per cent had been sterilised thereby.

Up-to-date coal ploughing techniques imported from Germany, hydraulic supports on the coal faces, improved ventilation, increased underground haulage capacity, new electrical winding engines for the shafts, new workshops and administration block, plus improved coal handling and market preparation facilities, all were being brought to naught. The workforce faced the looming prospect of either leaving the industry or being transferred to other, higher output collieries. Of the previous 816 men, 250 had already been transferred. Another 300 would soon follow.

## HELP FROM THE PAST.

The colliery's sorry financial results notwithstanding, improved ventilation in the Pentre seam had at least been an unqualified technical success. The workings were now several kilometres from pit-bottom. The distance involved, and hence the airflow resistance, had proven to be a problem for the main ventilation fan on the colliery surface. This had to drag an adequate quantity of air from the downcast shaft through the intake air roadways to the working districts, then back along the return air roadways before exhausting via the upcast shaft. To solve this problem, an opportunity had presented itself. The workings were now approaching the disused Maindy colliery. This was situated in another "cwm", or cul-de-sac valley off the main Rhondda, at Ton-Pentre. Now, utilising this relic of the past, which in the nineteenth century was one of the first collieries to be sunk in the upper Rhondda, the ventilation problem of machine mining in the latter twentieth century was solved.

Maindy had closed as a production unit in 1948. Its history nevertheless was noteworthy.

In 1866, here at Maindy, David Davies of Llandinam and his partners were staring bankruptcy in the face as, after 15 months of shaft sinking and the expenditure of over 38,000 pounds, no coal had been found. On Saturday morning, March 3 of that year, he was forced to pay off his men. According to his biographer, his farewell speech was short and to the point;

"Well boys, I am sorry to tell you that I cannot go on here any longer. I am very sorry, for I believe there is some grand coal here and that we are close to it".

On completion of payment he observed, "That leaves half a crown in my pocket", to which one man shouted, "We'll have that too". David Davis tossed it towards him saying, "Take it", before walking away contemptuously. After his departure the men discussed the position. They decided to give David Davies a weeks' work for nothing, a decision which would lead to an almost fairy tale ending.

On March 9, 1866, six days later, the two foot nine seam was struck at a depth of 197 metres, some of the finest steam coal in the world. Shortly afterwards the four foot was met at 210 metres and the six feet at 231 metres. Other sinkings followed and the Ocean Coal Company was founded, elevating David Davies to one of the great entrepreneurs of the Victorian age.

Now, a main return airway, 1570 metres in length, had been driven through from the Cambrian to one of David Davies's old shafts. Not only was the length of this return airway considerably less than the distance to the Cambrian upcast shaft, but a new and technically advanced extraction fan on the Maindy surface had solved all ventilation problems. The old fan at Cambrian itself remained, to ventilate workings in the deeper Nine Feet and Bute seams, but these were closer to the shafts, hand worked and with less than half the output of the Pentre seam. With its mechanisation and investment, it was in the latter that the future lay. Appropriately, nowhere else could one find a place so well ventilated as the Pentre seam of Cambrian colliery. Indeed, in terms of personal warmth and comfort, the volume of airflow tended to be excessive. It was consequently common knowledge that the Pentre seam, and the P26 coalface in particular, was virtually gas free.

On 11th. January 1965 the P26 had been completed, making it the newest face in the pit.

## DRAMA.

On 17 May 1965, some 2,743metres from pit-bottom and within the P26 district, a routine drama was being enacted which was to have far from routine consequences. Two groups of men were each striving to achieve their own objective, of which the other group was unaware. It would prove a fatal combination.

### Group One.

The first group were tasked with extending the conveyor system for coal transportation, a regular necessity as the face advanced. The specific job in hand was to bring into position the drive head for an additional belt conveyor, to be installed on the next weekend. Mining equipment is invariably heavy-duty and its transportation along the 8-foot (2.44m) high roadway, already occupied by the existing conveyor, was going to be associated with sweat and toil. In this case however, an opportunity presented itself that appeared god-given.

While intake airways are used to transport coal out, return airways are employed to transport supplies in. In this case, the intake-gate road, where the drive head was to be installed, passed directly over the main return airway to Maindy. It was along this latter airway that supplies were brought inbye. (Inbye is a mining term, meaning away from the shaft and towards the working districts. Outbye means the opposite). This roadway crossover was constructed as an air bridge, so as to isolate the two ventilation streams from each other. Through this air bridge however a penetration could be made, large enough to lift roadway support rings, electric motors, gearboxes and conveyor sections from one roadway up into the other, close to the point where they would be installed. This would significantly ease the task of transporting the new equipment into position (refer to Fig.1).

The disadvantage associated with this was a reduction in district ventilation. Some incoming air would inevitably take the route of least resistance and short-circuit directly from the intake into the main return airway, without having first traversed the coalface. However, there was no doubt in the minds of those concerned that with such first class ventilation, even with the penetration open, the factor of safety was more than adequate. In addition, the penetration was normally kept sealed in any event. It was only fully opened on the intermittent occasions when bulky supplies needed to be brought through. All of this was a temporary expedient that had now become accepted practice. Since the temporary solution worked, the driving of a permanent connection for supplies, complete with air lock, had been stopped. Other production-related work had been accorded higher priority.

Not appreciated by anybody was the fact that, when the crossover penetration was opened, as much as 80 per cent of the normal ventilation flow to the P26 coalface was being lost. Also not appreciated was that geological movement had induced roof fissures in the return-gate road from the face, near its junction with the main return airway. These extended to seams above and provided a passage for gas to migrate from these seams into the P26 return-gate. Such methane gas, trapped in the coal seams for millennia, oozes out as a normal feature of coalmining operations. Unlike at the coalface itself, there was no legal requirement for gas content to be measured on a regular basis at this point. With a ventilation flow that was now no more than minimal, this gas would migrate uphill towards the face tail end, against the ventilation stream.

Unaware of the threat they were creating, the first group of men applied themselves to their task - open the airbridge, then lift the conveyor drive head from the main return roadway up into the P26 intake gate road, finally bringing it into position.

**Group Two.**

While the above task proceeded according to plan in the access roadways, a second group of men was heavily engaged on the P26 coalface itself. For them the week was starting badly. The 3 feet (0.9m) height of the coalface was at the minimum extension range of the hydraulic supports employed. These supports had to be moved on as the plough did its work and the face itself advanced at an average of 1.52m per production shift. With such a low height it was proving difficult to disengage them from the roof. (Refer to Fig.2). The supports were in the process of being replaced with a shorter version. In the meantime, rate of withdrawal and then re-extension was erratic. This non-uniform advance along its 176m length had resulted in the face not forming a straight line but rather more of a flattened-out "S". Consequently, more strain was put on the continuous chain that hauled the plough back-and-fro along the armoured flexible conveyor (AFC), extending along the entire coalface length.

By 9 am that morning, the plough haulage chain had already broken. After some hours of struggle in a space 54cm in height, on top of the AFC, cursing, sweating, horny-handed men, dedicated in spite of themselves, had succeeded by practical skill and their own physical strength in splicing the break.

At 11 am there was relief when the plough once more slithered and scraped and jerked along the side of the AFC, ripping at the thin vein of the Pentre seam and transforming it into a black river flowing, at last, past the satisfied miners. Their relief was short-lived. Within fifteen minutes, the black river had dried up once more, this time due to a failure in the coalface signalling system. Without communication between miners, the whole enterprise was impossible. The production team had to know if and where the plough was stuck fast, when repair work was necessary, when the roof required additional support, when a pump had failed causing water build up, etc. etc. Resources had to be directed as appropriate. Without a coalface communication system, transfer of such information under cramped conditions and with a high ambient noise level, was impossible. Production once more came to a standstill. There was more delay as electricians crawled through the coaldust and black, glutinous mud where dust had mixed with water ingressing from the strata. Frustrating all attempts at cleaning, this ooze penetrated between the fibres of one's clothing and stayed there, like a black, permanent dye.

At approximately 12 noon, the fault was eventually found. The OK was given and once more noise and motion reigned as the earth gave up what it had taken millions of years to produce. Another surge of production, but for a period of minutes only.

At 12.15pm, the déjà vu of frustration as the plough once again stopped, again to the chagrin of the electricians. This time there was an electrical problem with the plough haulage motor at the tail end, which would not operate. The overman, Glyn Price, had instructed the plough to be hauled up to the main-end. In the absence of the tail-end motor to haul it back, there it remained.

Shortly after 12.15pm, two electricians gave a short "Good morning" to Mr. R.C. Jones, supervising the installation of a new haulage for supply transportation in the return gate road. They had been in such an environment, on a similar mission, countless times before and there was no stopping for the usual banter as they hurried up the 8-foot high (2.44m) roadway, with its unmistakable musty, dank aroma of return air.

Being a new face, the white blossoming of mould had not yet taken root on the timbers between the steel ring supports and these supports still stood erect, not yet crushed and distorted by geological pressure.

Both electricians were in their early twenties. Assistant Engineer Gerard Davies was accompanied by Electrician-of-the-Mine Ronald Gregson. The former, of big shambling appearance and silent, almost brooding, demeanour had been brought up by his sister, having lost his mother early in life. He enjoyed the reputation of being something of a hotshot, with a good career in front of him. He had made his name as district electrician for the previous, and successful, P21 face. The lack of any significant electrical problem on that face had attracted attention. The second man was a keen sportsman and the friendliest of young men, giving the lie to his stocky, rather pugilistic appearance and the brusqueness with which attempts to penetrate his personal space were rejected. Both men were recently married, Ron Gregson being in addition the proud father of a six-month-old baby girl. Their destination was the electrical switchgear, controlling equipment at the tail end of the face. Squat, heavy metal boxes, bolted together, and from which emanated a wirr-warr of cables, they provided energy for the mechanized muscle power that tore away at mother earth. The switchgear was situated within yards of the coalface itself. In the vicinity of the gear, looming in the light of the cap lamps, were some of the production team. They waited, while the electricians went into their well-tried routine.

## DISASTER.

This third stoppage found the deputy, Mr. T.E. Davies, ensconced on the face. That morning the repeated breakdowns had delayed his second safety inspection of the district.

At 12.40pm, and 37m from the main end, two figures, also with rubber kneepads and cap lamps on their helmets, scuttled out of the blackness like clumsy lizards, one behind the other. The beam of the deputy's cap lamp penetrated the claustrophobia between the hydraulic roof supports, arranged like some metal forest in triple rows, each 2 feet (0.6m) apart. It highlighted the agitated face of colliery manager Mr. E.J. Breeze, and that of Mr. L.J. Williams, Undermanager responsible for all underground workings in the Pentre seam. Below their helmets, the sweat of exertion had streaked the black faces. The repeated and prolonged stoppages were a matter of concern, and they were persistent with their enquiries.

Compressed within the less than 3-foot (0.9m) height, in the hydraulic forest between the armoured conveyor up against the coal and the collapsing waste left where coal had been extracted, a conference was held. Almost eyeball-to-eyeball, the exaggerated redness of his lips highlighted the exaggerated whiteness of his teeth as the manager's complaints issued forth. It was just one damn thing after another and the production time they were losing was just not acceptable.

At 12.45 pm the lizard-like conference disbanded and they scuttled away in opposite directions. With the manager's exhortations on his mind, T.E. Davis continued along the face to the intake airway. From here he would phone the other end, where the problem was, and try to hurry them along. The other two continued on to the source of the trouble. Maybe their personal intervention would "ginger things up".

Heavily engaged in replacing the hydraulic roof supports on the face with the more suitable and shorter type, Mechanic-of-the-Mine Mitchell had delayed his lunch break until after management had passed by. Although entitled to such a break he had judged it, under current circumstances, undiplomatic for the management team to be confronted with men sitting down off the face, relaxing with their sandwiches. Now that the Manager and Undermanager had passed by he judged the time to be opportune, and left the face, unwittingly escaping thereby the jaws of death about to clamp shut, the luckiest man alive on that fateful day.

Meanwhile, after twenty minutes of fruitless trying and with production still at a standstill the electricians would have been experiencing desperation. Already at the end of the previous week an intermittent problem with the tail-end plough motor had been experienced. Now it was back again with a vengeance. Later investigation would reveal that the cable plug at this motor had been slightly perturbed, interrupting the low-voltage proving circuit, which monitors the cable for correct connection. This perturbation had been caused by debris brought down by explosives from the ripping lip close by, where the 2.44m height of the roadway met the 0.9m height of the coalface.

Such a fault, particularly when intermittent, is notoriously difficult to find. It can only be done by means of a step-by-step process of elimination. The whole procedure had a drawback however, annoying in the extreme when under pressure of time. This was the time involved in obtaining internal access to the electrical panel controlling the plough motor. So as to contain all sparking within the enclosure, flame-proof switchgear is constructed of 13 mm thick steel. Following electrical isolation, ten bolts had to be unscrewed and then the steel cover removed. Once access was obtained and checks completed, the same procedure was required in reverse to effectively re-seal the enclosure. According to regulations, only then could the panel be re-energised and an attempt made to re-start. When repeated adjustments are necessary, this open-and-close procedure would have to be carried out a number of times, frustrating in the extreme when under pressure of time.

The small group of men, huddled around the switchgear at the P26 tail end, laboured on, confident in the knowledge that here the quality of ventilation was unsurpassed. Here, an explosive atmosphere was out of the question. Here the panel could be operated with the access cover removed, enabling a better insight into its workings and a correspondingly reduced time to rectify the fault. It was that flowing river of coal that justified their existence, and that river was now at a standstill. Management were in the district and they were not happy. Anxiety would have set in. In complete ignorance of the gas, which now, slowly and unseen, had slunk invidiously against the normal flow of ventilation up to the electrical switchgear and had already achieved a thickness below the roof down to switch level, the electricians, as part of their test procedure, simulated a start signal from the plough operator.

At 12.55 Kenny Davies, plough operator at the tail end, answered a phone call from the Deputy T.E.Davis, who by then had reached the main end of the P26. Kenny, a young man in his early twenties and living alone with his mother in the village, would ascertain the position from the electricians and then phone back. It was a phone call that never came. The satisfying "clunk" of the electromagnetic contactor as it closed, switching power through to the plough motor, was the last thought ever registered by those bending in front of the open control panel.

In the roadway at the other end of the face, the force of the blast blew the deputy T.E. Davies and those around him backwards off their feet. Lamps were smashed and helmets lost while swirling coaldust saturated the air, blocking all light from those lamps remaining and reducing visibility to no more than one foot (30mm). Along with the blast, which lasted for 2 or 3 seconds, came extreme heat. The shocked cries of men shouting, "Which way do we go?" penetrated the stygian blackness. Someone shouted that they should follow the conveyor and men groped their way along its side. Although the hearing of some would be affected for months afterwards, some men registered instructions by the deputy to stay put until the dust cleared enough to see. When it eventually did, in the light of those cap-lamps still operating, the Deputy knew that those colleagues on the coalface were beyond assistance. Smoke was oozing out of the face into the roadway and human groaning could be heard, continuing for some minutes. The shocked survivors listened helplessly, standing in confusion while surrounded by dust. For those miners on the face not killed by the explosion itself, the gases of combustion in such a confined space would snuff out all life. Any attempt to render assistance was to invite death oneself, since no breathing apparatus was available.

Further down the intake-gate, Mechanic-of-the-Mine Mitchell had had his lunch break rudely shattered by being blown into the side of the roadway. He now came forward, to be confronted by a scene of chaos. Glyn Price, the overman, was another man forcefully cast aside by the unseen hand. He also came forward. A desperate phone call was made for the mines rescue brigade and all help that could be given. Before its arrival, the overman, deputy and others in the intake-gate road who had survived the explosion, attempted to undertake their own rescue.

Realising the impossibility of going onto the face from the intake end, with smoke and gases oozing out, they made tracks back down the intake roadway, in the direction of fresh air. At the temporary opening in the air bridge, they descended the ladder into the Maindy heading return, which was clear of dust. After proceeding towards the junction with the P26 return-gate, the overman penetrated into this roadway for ten metres or so, before being wisely prevailed upon by his colleagues not to proceed further. The sight of bodies lying, and the presence of smoke and dust further inbye, forbade further progress. A haulage worker, Mr. T. Reece, lay in the Maindy heading return with serious injuries resulting from blast. First aid was rendered by the deputy and a stretcher party assembled to carry the injured man out. The transformer supplying electricity to the district was switched off.

# RESPONSE.

At 1.05pm The Dinas Mines Rescue Station was alerted. Within fifteen minutes the team was at pit-top. Police, ambulances and the fire service followed. Sirens and flashing blue lights, plus the sound of engines racing up the long, steep hill through Clydach Vale brought people to their doors in alarm. A sense of disaster soon hung in the air and small groups of women congregated on doorsteps, holding hands and gazing uneasily up towards the colliery. While people of the village, in teeming rain, climbed the hill and assembled at the colliery entrance, nervously waiting for news, police and surface workers, expressionless but with a subdued frenzy, cleared the No.1 pit-top area for stretchers and other emergency stores. Other rescue teams arrived, festooned with flexible tubing and the other paraphernalia of underground breathing apparatus. The survivors were wound to the surface, Mr. T. Reece carried on a stretcher and swathed in bandages. All were calm and in control of themselves. An ambulance tore across the bridge to the pit-top and then down the hill, its blue light flashing.

At 2.10pm the rescue team from the Dinas station arrived in the affected district and at 2.20pm entered the face from the main-gate end. The press would later seize on a statement by one of the rescue team describing the scene that confronted them, "Hell with the lid blown off".

At 3pm dust in considerable quantities still hung in the atmosphere. This eventually cleared and the sad task of removing the bodies commenced. Post-mortems were to show that of the thirty-one fatalities, twenty-five had died from carbon monoxide poisoning. All were burnt, with skin condition varying between pink and bright crimson, depending on proximity to the point of ignition. Fourteen had died on the face, with the remainder in the return gate. Further outbye, where the blast effect had been at its most vicious, four men had died as a result of multiple injuries. Here, in addition, two men had died from multiple injuries plus carbon monoxide poisoning.

On the surface, remaining ambulances gradually moved away as the realisation dawned that the initial small band were the sum total of those miners in the district who had survived. More relatives arrived from further afield to join the subdued, agonising wait in the mist and rain. After hours of waiting, some of those newly widowed were taken home by the last ambulances to leave.

As the pit-head vigil of those waiting in agony for news came to an end, it was replaced by a mass outpouring of silent grief. This grief, and the resulting devastation of the close-knit local community, was felt, not only throughout the mining valleys but also in the entire country. There was a strong empathy with mining folk and shock at the working conditions, plus the realisation that mining disasters were not just confined to the past. In a nationalised industry and in the latter part of the twentieth century they could still happen. A relief fund was set up, with donations received from all parts of the UK and from Europe. The fund was not without controversy. No one begrudged anything to those who had lost their loved ones, but what about those miners who continued to die regularly but singly or in pairs? For them there was no fund.

For two days, 21 and 22 May 1965, life in the valley came virtually to a standstill as the funerals were held. The community and the whole brotherhood of miners mourned, united in comradeship. For most of the deceased there were massed funerals. On the Saturday morning, at the Assembly Hall in Clydach Vale, a lay preacher, Mr. Albert Gregory, who had himself worked at the Cambrian until forced to give up because of dust disease, conducted a service that was relayed over loudspeakers to a congregation of thousands. Inside the hall, "Cwm Rhondda", "The Lord's my Shepard" and "In the Sweet Bye and Bye" were sung in the unique, soulful, emotionally shattering tones of a Welsh male voice choir. In the stunned, heart-broken stillness that followed, the coffins were carried reverently to the waiting hearses and the sad procession began. Down the narrow, twisting hill, up which the rescue services had previously raced, 5,000 people marched behind the coffins and the motorised processions.

Struggling along with them were many whose own health had been broken by dust and disability, a common feature of the Rhondda scene. The weather showed no appropriate respect. The rain continued. One English reporter from the national press felt called upon to write, "Incredibly, people still want to continue living here". Bareheaded nevertheless, the procession proceeded several miles to the cemetery at Trealaw, through streets lined with a grieving multitude assessed at over 22,000. From all over South Wales they had come, to give a special miner's farewell to comrades, who had shared a common danger. The slow crawl of countless cars and coaches were followed by the steady tramp of thousands in an eerie, almost total, silence.

This was to be the last of the massed miners' funerals, which for approaching two hundred years had been a disturbingly regular feature of South Wales life. The set-faced multitudes, the measured tread of thousands and the Welsh voices singing "Cwm Rhondda", echoing around the bleak valley and through the driving rain, were to be the swansong of this grim aspect of industrial history.

There were some individual services. Mr. Breeze, the manager, was interred at Ton-y-Revel. Among those in attendance was the squat, bulldog figure of Gerald Blackmore, Area General Manager. He would later emigrate to North America, becoming Chief Executive of a leading coal-mining company there. The suggestion would be floated at government level that an offer be made for him to return, to take over chairmanship of the National Coal Board itself. All of that was in the future. Now in the Rhondda, even his immense drive and determination to bring the area into the black would be defeated, by Mother Nature and a workforce scarred by history. Pit after pit would continue to disappear.


## AFTERMATH.

In September 1966, eighteen months after the disaster, the Cambrian finally closed. With the end of the Cambrian went not only the vibrant life of the local community. Closure meant the end of a living memorial to one of the most significant events in South Wales labour history. This was the last pit to survive of the Cambrian Combine where, in 1910-11, the great strike and associated Ton-y-Pandy riots spelt the death knell of the traditional miners' leadership of the liberal and chapel school. Henceforward, it would be the young Turks of socialism that were to set the tone for mining trade unionism in South Wales.

Each colliery had its own ethos, transcending its raison d'etre as a producer of energy. The ghosts of Cambrian's past guided the labour movement and still had an influence on men's minds. The events of 1910-11, when Home Secretary Winston Churchill felt called upon to deploy units of cavalry and infantry to the Rhondda Valley, "in support of the civil power", had left a permanent impression on the outlook of valley folk. At that time, pitched battles were fought between striking miners and the police, heavily reinforced by constables from the rest of Great Britain. In hand-to-hand fighting the powerhouse of the Glamorgan colliery at Llwynypia was held as a fortress by police on the night of 7th November 1910 against strikers incensed by the use of blackleg labour, employed to keep the pumps and ventilation going. In the nearby Ton-y-Pandy square, after the battle at the powerhouse, heavy rioting had continued throughout 8th November 1910.

The old powerhouse building was now an NCB central workshop, for the maintenance and repair of mining machinery. It was here that the burnt and blackened electrical equipment from the P26 was investigated, and the source of ignition ascertained.

On May 21/22 1965 large crowds again gathered in the square. This time they stood in silent respect as the massed funerals of the Cambrian deceased snaked through the narrow, tortuous crossroads, the final drama of underground mining tragedy in South Wales.

Her Majesty's Inspector of Mines, following investigation into the disaster, was to say that the poor construction of the air bridge and the way that it was used were, "deplorably bad practice, which should not have been tolerated by anyone having responsibilities for the safe working of the mine". Of the electricians, the inspector said that one could understand, but not excuse, the temptation to avoid the tedious process, when repeated adjustments have to be made, of always having to replace bolts before applying power. There would be an advantage in the use of single-bolt fixing for the covers of gate-end switchgear. Practical assistance could be given by providing adequate means for the testing of switchgear operation and suitable instruments for the tracing of external faults.

In 1992 a memorial service took place on the site where the colliery had once stood, its existence in the meantime having been totally obliterated by a 280-acre land reclamation scheme. Mr. Neil Kinnock MP officially inaugurated a memorial garden, with a pithead wheel as its centre point. Present were many of the widows and families of those who had died, together with local dignitaries. The site was dedicated to those who had died in the 1965 disaster and also in the disaster of 1905 when the same number of miners were killed.

The names of those killed in the 1965 explosion are:

| Name | Age | Occupation |
| --- | --- | --- |
| Ronald Arnold | 48 | Deputy |
| Earnest John Breeze | 38 | Colliery Manager |
| Ernest William Burnett | 46 | Chargehand |
| Peter Calvert | 40 | Repairer |
| James Channing | 46 | Post Erecter |
| Albert William Colcombe | 44 | Team Captain |
| Raymond John Daniels | 34 | Stableman |
| Gerrard Wayne Davies | 24 | Assistant Unit Electrical Engineer |
| Kenneth Davies | 26 | Plough Operator |
| David Evans | 28 | Post Erector |
| Ronald Flower | 45 | Repairer |
| Ronald Gregson | 28 | Electrician |
| David Alfred Griffiths | 43 | Repairer |
| Thomas Hann | 42 | Transfer Point Attendant |
| Richard William Hucker | 32 | Repairer |
| Ivor Jacobs | 45 | Post erector |
| Henry Lee | 56 | Roadman |
| Leonard May | 33 | Post Erector |
| Ivor Morgan | 32 | Post Erector |
| Arthur James Newman | 46 | Post Erector |
| Vivian Nicholas | 51 | Post Erector |
| Harold David Pope | 50 | Overman |
| Donald Price | 42 | Stableman |
| Evan Luther Rees | 48 | Post Erector |
| Richard John Roberts | 55 | Repairer |
| Gwilym Thomas | 28 | Assistant Stableman |
| William Isaac Thomas | 33 | Post Erector |
| Edmund William Williams | 51 | Repairer |
| Leslie James Williams | 54 | Undermanager |
| Sidney Williams | 47 | Post Erector |
| Trevor John Williams | 27 | Post Erector |

In addition, Thomas Rees, 62 years of age, was seriously injured.

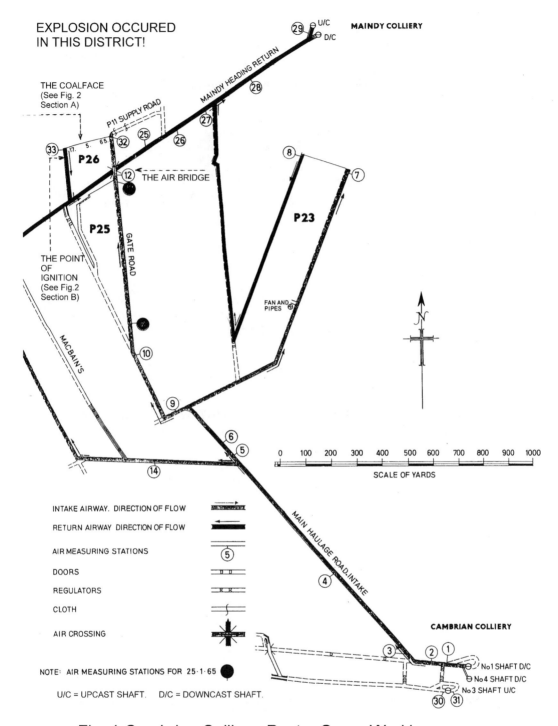

EXPLOSION OCCURED IN THIS DISTRICT!

MAINDY COLLIERY

THE COALFACE (See Fig. 2 Section A)

MAINDY HEADING RETURN

P11 SUPPLY ROAD

THE AIR BRIDGE

P26

P25

GATE ROAD

P23

FAN AND PIPES

THE POINT OF IGNITION (See Fig.2 Section B)

MACBAIN'S

N

0 100 200 300 400 500 600 700 800 900 1000

SCALE OF YARDS

INTAKE AIRWAY. DIRECTION OF FLOW

RETURN AIRWAY DIRECTION OF FLOW

AIR MEASURING STATIONS

DOORS

REGULATORS

CLOTH

AIR CROSSING

MAIN HAULAGE ROAD. INTAKE

CAMBRIAN COLLIERY

NOTE: AIR MEASURING STATIONS FOR 25·1·65

No1 SHAFT D/C
No4 SHAFT D/C
No3 SHAFT U/C

U/C = UPCAST SHAFT.     D/C = DOWNCAST SHAFT.

Fig. 1 Cambrian Colliery: Pentre Seam Workings.

11

# (A)

## TYPICAL SECTION THROUGH COALFACE

WASTE

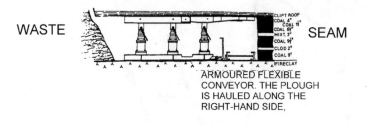

SEAM

ARMOURED FLEXIBLE
CONVEYOR. THE PLOUGH
IS HAULED ALONG THE
RIGHT-HAND SIDE,

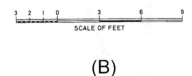

SCALE OF FEET

# (B)

## SECTION THROUGH RETURN AIR ROADWAY IN PROXIMITY OF ELECTRICAL SWITCHGEAR

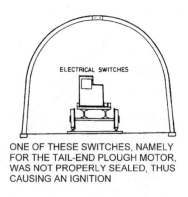

ONE OF THESE SWITCHES, NAMELY
FOR THE TAIL-END PLOUGH MOTOR,
WAS NOT PROPERLY SEALED, THUS
CAUSING AN IGNITION

Fig. 2 Cambrian Colliery: P26 Coalface and Roadway Sections.

# FIG. 3 WORLD ENERGY TRENDS
*Energy demand*
## (From IEC)

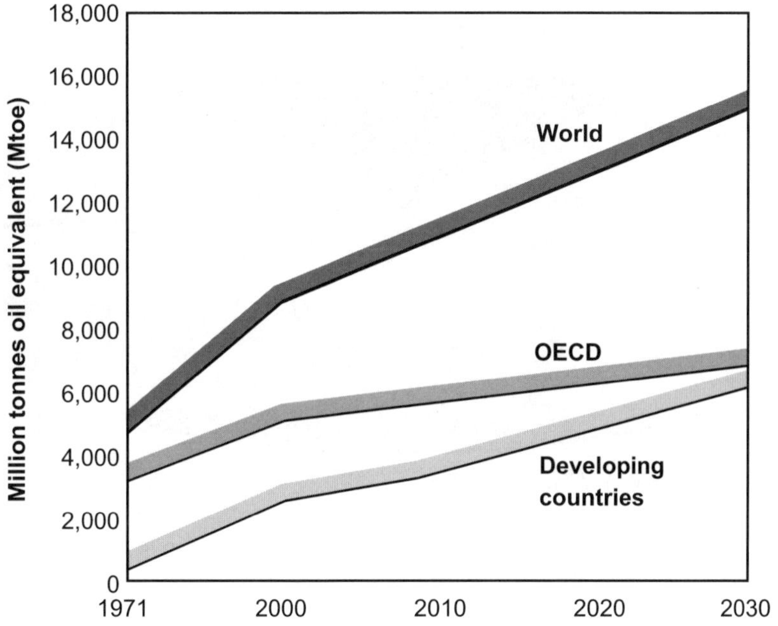

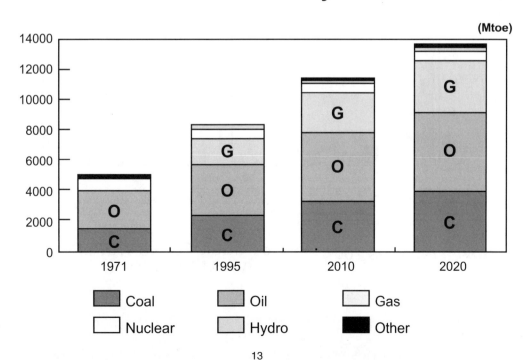

# FIG. 4 WORLD ENERGY DEMAND
## (WORLD COAL INSTITUTE)

## Outlook by Fuel

# FIG. 5 (World Coal Institute)

## *Proven reserves of fossil fuels worldwide*

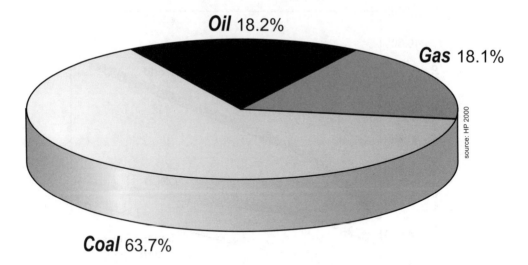

**Oil** 18.2%

**Gas** 18.1%

source: HP 2000

**Coal** 63.7%

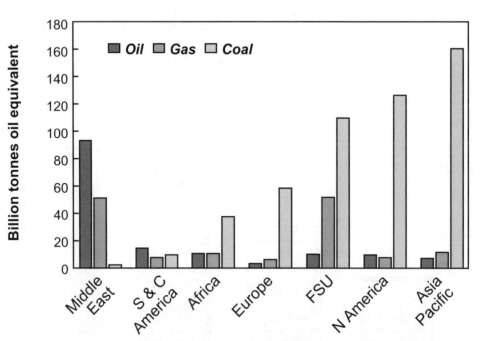

*Proven reserves* 2001    FIG. 6 FOSSIL FUELS WORLD-WIDE
(World Coal Insitute)

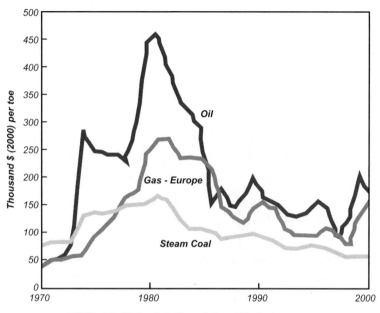

FIG. 7 (World Coal Institute)

# FIG. 8    THE SOUTH WALES COALFIELD

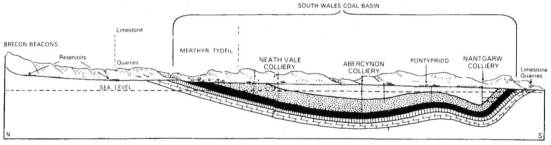

Section through coalfield.
Note that the seams slope gently in the north, steeply in the south and bulge towards the surface at the Pontypridd anticline.

*Source:* H. J. Savory. *A Geography of Wales*, 1968.

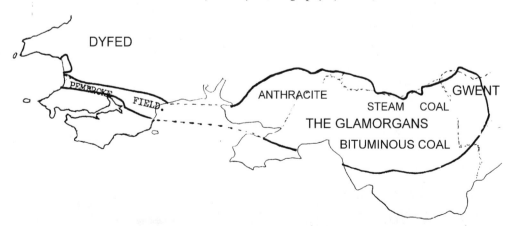

THE TYPE OF COAL VARIES FROM ANTHRACITE IN THE WEST TO STEAM COAL IN THE EAST AND CENTRAL AREAS; TO BITUMINOUS IN THE SOUTH

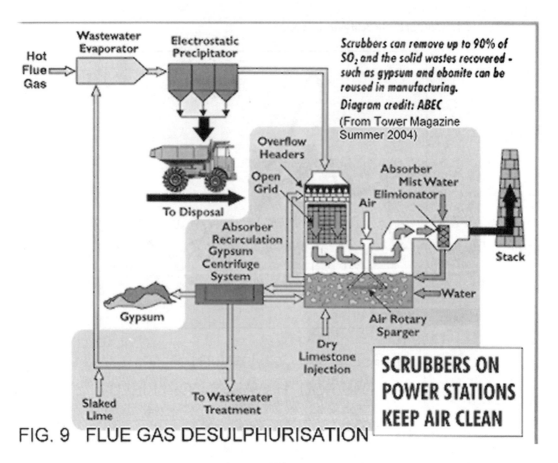

FIG. 9   FLUE GAS DESULPHURISATION

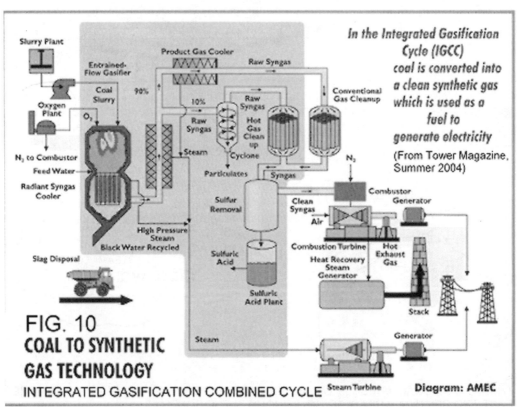

FIG. 10
COAL TO SYNTHETIC
GAS TECHNOLOGY
INTEGRATED GASIFICATION COMBINED CYCLE

# Chapter 2
## WHY COAL?

*"Then our streets were full and busy,*
*Shops were crowded every day,*
*All our menfolk then were mining,*
*Bringing home a good week's pay".*
G. L. Davies, Llantrisant.

At the time of the Cambrian disaster, British coalmining was still the third largest in the world, after the United States and the Soviet Union. It was among the most technically advanced anywhere and was operated as a state-owned industry by the National Coal Board (NCB). With approximately 600,000 employees this was then the largest industrial undertaking in Europe. It was however an industry subject to enormous economic pressure, with decline staring it in the face. The next forty years would see traumatic events, technical, economic, social, political and military. These were to be revolutionary and their effects in South Wales were profound. In the valleys, a complete, mining based civilisation was to be swept away. Headline-making events and discoveries, social conflict, technological developments, industrial and political wheeling and dealing, far away places with strange sounding names, all were to play their role in the national regicide of King Coal, whose resilience world-wide would nevertheless surprise many. Before proceeding with this story of coal, an analysis of its role in the overall scheme of things is appropriate.

### THE IMAGE OF ENERGY.

It is still only the recent past when British domestic culture required a "living fire". Without such a focal point, no home would be complete. There was magic and fascination in the conflagration, warmth that was felt psychologically and not just physically. Like some druid's ceremony, the reminiscing of one's elders in a darkened room lit by exposed flames, slowly drawing back into a static reddish glow as volatile gases were consumed, hang ethereal in the memory. Agitated shadows danced on the wallpaper while those, to whom stoking was both an art form and a pride, assiduously positioned the replacement lumps. When done with skill, the long, flickering red and yellow flames would increase the heating effect and reduce the useless and polluting unburnt smoke which otherwise would ascend the chimney and write a less than salubrious signature in the sky above the rows of terraced houses.

Such romanticism came at a price, and not only financial. Over a period of time, dust and smoke gradually darkened the room, while effort was involved in both igniting the fire and in clearing away the ash. The "home fires", which were to be "kept burning", a vision so evocative in the mind's eye of the public, were to be replaced as a vision of domestic bliss with cleanliness and convenience. Gas, with the discovery of large new indigenous reserves and with the development of appropriate technology, was able to shed its image of Victorian street lighting and Jack the Ripper's London. "Fanny by Gaslight" and "the gasworks" were consigned to history, being replaced in popular imagination by "modern high-speed gas" The death knell was thereby sounded for the large scale domestic use of coal. The energy picture as a whole is however many faceted.

### THE ROLE OF ENERGY.

Energy is the elixir of human society, with an importance that cannot be overemphasised. In man's primitive stage he could meet from his own efforts the basic needs of food, clothing and shelter, with an adequate amount of energy being provided by his food consumption alone. Since then, more sophisticated desires, which have now become necessities, have had to be satisfied. Such demand is not simply related to the size of a community but also to the stage of its development, i.e. its standard of living. From the industrial revolution onwards, mankind's use of energy has been used directly by the individual only to a very limited extent. Most is required by society, to power its machines, vehicles and the various processes that provide its goods and services. The environment must be illuminated, and heated or cooled as appropriate. Power-driven systems are essential, for the transport, manufacture and communications which developed societies demand and which developing societies aspire to.

As society advances, secondary energy as opposed to primary energy, continues to gain in importance.

### Primary energy.

This originates from direct utilisation of the sources existing in nature (e.g. fuel such as coal, oil, natural gas, etc.).

### Secondary energy.

This is mainly electricity, but also includes manufactured gas. Secondary energy is produced from primary sources. Electricity is the secondary source most dominant and convenient. It has become the form of energy most essential for human welfare. Its dominance is increasing, as consumers use less and less primary energy directly. It has the advantage that any of the primary energy sources may be used as a basis for its production.

At the beginning of the twenty-first century the energy sector of the UK represents around 4 per cent of Gross Domestic Product (GDP). However, this 4 per cent is an essential input for the remaining 96 per cent.

In 2002 the World Energy Outlook, published by the International Energy Agency (IEA) projected that world energy demand will grow by two-thirds over the next thirty years. Most of this growth will occur in developing countries, with a third of it in China and India alone. At present, the average citizen of these countries consumes just one seventh of the energy used by the average OECD citizen.

One of the main threads in history is man's search for sources of primary energy to supplement his own capacity - his use of animals, wind power, water power and heat.

For centuries wood provided the major source of such heat. The metal-working forges of antiquity and in the Middle Ages were based on the use of charcoal, a wood derivative. In Europe settlements were small, and surrounded by forest. Coal was already known in Roman times, with exploitation of the more obvious outcrops. Its importance was however minor. The abundance of timber tended to make it superfluous. Its use as a domestic fuel was limited in an age where most people used wood or peat, and there were few industrial applications. After the Romans left it remained largely unused for a considerable time; there is no mention of it anywhere in the Domesday Book.

### KING COAL.

Two developments gave a spur to mining. Firstly, there was the growth of towns. Here, in the new and cramped urban environment, the citizens no longer had access to wood for fuel. This was bulky to transport, expensive and in great demand. Along with wood, coal was the only fuel that could be handled, stored and transported in bulk, but its energy density was much greater than that of wood. So-called "sea coal", from seams exposed at the Durham coastline, were exploited first, since quantities could easily be transported to London by ship. In South Wales, already by the fifteenth century there were a number of simple mines. These were either "levels", basically short tunnels dug into a hillside, or "bell pits" so-called because the working space spread out like a bell from the bottom of a single short shaft. Winding in such shafts was by means of a horse and windlass system. When the space reached a point where it was in danger of caving in, the pit was abandoned and another sunk nearby.

The second factor that encouraged development of coalmining was the growth of industry, particularly from the time of the industrial revolution, which started in the late eighteenth century. Initially charcoal was used for the iron industry, but to smelt a ton of iron using this method an acre of forest had to be felled, resulting in their rapid disappearance. Coal was ruled out since components within it contaminated the iron. In 1709 came the breakthrough. Abraham Derby heated up coal out of contact with air. This drove off the volatiles and produced coke, excellent for the smelting of ore. From 1760, and for one hundred years, the greatest consumption of South Wales coal would be for the smelting of iron ore.

Further impetus came with the development of the steam engine, first for working pumps and then providing the power for factories and railways. Outcrops could no longer meet demand and shafts were sunk to access lower seams. Small coalfields were worked in Somerset, Gloucester, Kent and North Wales. The major UK coalfields were in the English Midlands, Yorkshire, Northeast and Northwest England, the central belt of Scotland, plus South Wales.

In the 19th Century, British coal mining was the largest industry of its kind in the world.

The first commercial development of coal in the United States was relatively late, namely in the 1830's, in Eastern Pennsylvania. From then on however, North American production exploded. Throughout the industrial revolution and into the second half of the twentieth century the most important source of primary energy in the world was coal. The rapid industrial growth in some areas of the USA and in Europe was due in no small measure to the availability and cheapness of this fuel. To the "black diamonds" of the time, there was no serious alternative; anthracite to heat the homes and factory boilers, steam coal to drive the ships on the oceans and the railway trains on the continents of the world, coking coal to smelt the international avalanche of iron and steel.

Between the two World Wars, in the field of marine transportation, coal was replaced by oil. However, application of the latter fuel remained largely confined to transport.

The rule of King Coal was to last until well after the Second World War. Only then would new usurpers challenge its role on a significant and increasing scale.


## THE USURPERS.

### Oil.

This has its origins in the algae and other low level organic matter that settled in the primeval swamps. Its presence in the earth's crust had been known for centuries. Significant usage, however, did not begin until the mid-nineteenth century. At this time James Young invented a process to recover oil from shale, a clayey rock with organic matter embedded in it, and for nearly a hundred years oil was obtained in Scotland by this means.

The birth of the oil industry as we know it is usually associated with a well drilled in Pennsylvania by one "Colonel" Drake, towards the end of the nineteenth century. Instead of brine as expected, from the well came gushing forth crude oil. From then on, the deliberate prospecting for oil, extending into mountain ranges, sub-zero temperatures, deserts and under the sea, has never looked back. Initially seen as a new source of lubricants and lamp oil, invention of the internal combustion engine ensured mushrooming of the industry. For this application oil was, and continues to be, the only economically suitable fuel.

The economic boom following the Second World War resulted in a demand for energy which coal was unable to satisfy. Political problems in Iran were an additional incentive to search for new sources of oil. Much more was found than the experts predicted. It was not only cheap to produce but easier to handle and cheaper to transport than coal. As a result, significant inroads were made into the latter's markets, so much so that oil now became the primary fuel. Its continued headlong advance seemed inevitable. Massive price rises, forced upon the world by OPEC in the 1970's, stopped this growth in its tracks and resulted in much fuel saving, particularly of oil.


### Natural Gas.

This has similar origins to oil and is frequently found together with liquid petroleum. Initially seen as an embarrassment, it was flared off in large quantities. Its use as a fuel was limited by the technical impossibility of transportation beyond its immediate source. All this was changed in the twentieth century with the development of suitable compressors, together with long distance pipelines of large diameter and operating at high pressure. Such pipelines could be either submarine or onshore and supplemented the transport of liquefied natural gas in ocean-going tankers.

Improved exploration and production facilities for hydrocarbons generally, particularly in offshore waters, significantly increased the quantities of gas available. Gas fields exist which are disassociated from oil. In general, with increasing depth and hence temperature and pressure, the more gas and the less oil is present.

As the cleanest fossil fuel, and the one most convenient for fixed installations, market penetration of gas depends on the amount and location of reserves available, together with the capital cost of accessing such reserves. Gas demand has grown quickly and is projected to grow significantly more, especially in the field of power generation.

## Nuclear Power.

This is a child of the latter half of the twentieth century. The fission (splitting) of the nuclei of uranium-235 or plutonium atoms in a controlled chain reaction releases energy in the form of heat, together with radioactivity. In terms of exhaust emissions, it is very clean. The limited quantity of fuel required is also an attraction. In the heady days of the 1950's a glowing future was foreseen, with "energy so cheap it will be given away". The "Atoms for Peace" programme announced by President Eisenhower, with its idea of beating swords into ploughshares was a concept that was to funnel 90 per cent of the entire UK power industry investment into this single technology.

How are the mighty fallen! In practice, the enormous capital investment required to contain and control the associated lethal radioactivity has confined the civilian use of nuclear power to large-scale, base-load, electricity generating stations. Here, corrosion has proven to be an issue. The eventual decommissioning of such stations with their radioactive core, together with the on-going problem of treating and storing for thousands of years the radioactive spent fuel, further increases the investment required. In addition to the financial aspects, fears concerning safety, in particular with regard to cancerous and genetic deformity, have brought this energy source, once seen as a panacea for the future, down to earth.

## THE LOW CARBON ECONOMY.

The 4 - fuel economy of coal, oil, gas and nuclear power is, at the beginning of the 21st century, in the process of undergoing a radical change, namely into a low carbon economy. The motivating factor is an increasing concern being felt with regard to climate change. The consensus of scientific opinion now maintains that not only are human activities resulting in an increase in mean global temperature but also that the consequences of such an increase could be severe. There is worldwide recognition that global warming is in fact an increasing problem. The pollution caused by the burning of fossil fuels, combined with a parallel interest in conserving resources, has resulted in energy conservation measures, such as improved insulation of buildings and low consumption vehicles, together with more effective use of the energy consumed. In addition, the increasing use of renewable sources (wind, water, solar power, biogas) has been added to the energy agenda.

This objective of reducing climate change has resulted in environmental policies not only motivated by a desire to control local pollution. They are also influenced by global and international factors, including international agreements.

These agreements include targets for the reduction in greenhouse gases. As with the glass of a greenhouse, such gases surrounding the earth allow the passage of high frequency solar radiation through to the earth's surface, where it produces heat. The low frequency heat radiation that results remains locked in however, unable to escape. The result is a good temperature for growing in one case and global warming in the other. The majority of industrialised countries have accepted the Kyoto Protocol of 1997. This has as its objective the reduction of greenhouse gas emissions by an average of 5.2 per cent below 1990 levels, to be achieved by the year 2012. This consensus however is not shared by some sectors of industry, particularly in the United States, resulting in that country's withdrawal from the agreement in 2001. The US accounts for one-third of the 1990 overall emission benchmark. Greenpeace has pointed out that Exxon-Mobil, the world's largest oil company and a major contributor to George W. Bush's election campaign, has been one of the major forces lobbying against Kyoto ratification in the US.

By 2004, 119 states had ratified, accepted, or acceded to Kyoto. Of the 37 industrialised countries which agreed to the Kyoto emission targets, only 5 had not yet ratified:

- Australia.

- Lichtenstein.

- Monaco.

- Russia.

- United States.

In the absence of US ratification, only a Russian signature could make the treaty legally binding, since the protocol must be ratified by at least 55 countries, which together account for at least 55 per cent of the 1990 global emissions. By 2004, current signatories accounted for only 44.4 per cent of these emissions, hence the key role of Russia.

On 23 October 2004, the Russian parliament voted to ratify the Kyoto International climate Change Protocol, leaving it just months away from coming into effect. Even if this was only a political quid pro quo for the EU supporting their own application to join the World Trade Organization, the way now seems clear for the Kyoto Protocol to become part of international law.

For those countries affected, differentiated targets are envisaged, recognizing that each country must address climate change, based upon its own energy profile and circumstances. So as to facilitate their economic improvement, developing nations and most countries of the former East Bloc are not faced with such a commitment. For the European Union to meet its overall target, individual member's targets have been laid down as follows:

| EU Member | Percentage reduction (or allowable increase) |
| --- | --- |
| Austria | -13 |
| Belgium | - 7.5 |
| Denmark | - 21 |
| Finland | 0 |
| France | 0 |
| Germany | - 21 |
| Greece | +25 |
| Ireland | +13 |
| Italy | - 6.5 |
| Luxemburg | - 28 |
| Netherlands | - 6 |
| Portugal | +27 |
| Sweden | +4 |
| Spain | +15 |
| United Kingdom | - 12.5 |

What seems increasingly certain to make an impact is the emission-trading scheme of the European Union. This allows those countries producing less greenhouse gases than their allowable limit to sell their shortfall to those countries that are in excess, resulting in the overall target being met. Such commercial considerations might well accelerate the drive for clean energy.

## Renewable sources of energy.

The drastic consequences of environmental pollution and global warming, combined with the depletion of fuel reserves while energy demand continues to grow, have brought renewable sources to the fore. These are sources that not only do not pollute but, in addition, do not involve the consumption of finite resources. Usually they have their origin, if not directly then indirectly, in the sun's radiation.

The only renewable source to date that has made any significant contribution on a worldwide scale is hydroelectric power. This in effect converts solar radiation into electricity. The immediate source of energy is the rainfall, brought about in turn by the action of the sun's heat in evaporating the oceans. An adequate flow of water is required, from a higher to a lower level, in combination with the engineering necessary to control this flow. Geographical conditions must be capable of producing an adequate head of water, as for example in Austria. Here the Danube falls 150 meters between the German and Slovakian borders, giving it the character of a mountain stream and making it ideal for energy production. Along its 320-kilometres length within Austria, nine hydroelectric plants produce a quarter of the country's electricity. Additional stations within the Alps result in approximately 70 per cent of Austrian electricity being produced by waterpower.

Electricity from non-hydro renewable sources is the fastest growing generation category. It is, however, a percentage increase from a very small base. The prediction of the International Energy Authority (IEA) is that by the year 2020 it will still represent less than 1 per cent of world generation. Within the European Union, non-hydro renewable energy contributes significantly more than the world average. By the year 2010 this contribution is forecast to be 11.5 per cent. Against the sustainable nature of the energy and its low emissions must be set the generally high cost, its intermittent availability and potential siting problems. If poor people in developing countries have to wait for renewable energy they may well have to wait a very long time. Non-hydro renewable sources are:

- WIND

- BIOMASS

- SOLAR

- GEOTHERMAL

- TIDAL

Currently, wind is the renewable energy most favoured. This is in spite of the fact that the effective utilization of wind power units is abysmal. Compared with their theoretical output, i.e. continuous output at full load, in Germany utilization is an average of only 16 per cent, in Denmark 21 per cent, in the UK it is about 25 per cent, which is regarded as being good. The best installations have a utilization of about 40 per cent. In terms of popularity, wind is followed by biomass. Solar or photovoltaic sources are many years away from being economically viable on a significant scale. Geothermal energy has been harnessed extensively in Iceland, but overall its application is geographically very limited.

At first sight, wave and tidal power from the ocean is an attractive resource. Not only is it clean and available in unlimited quantities, but unlike solar or wind power it is less subject to climatic irregularities. The moon's gravitational force ensures that the tide rises and falls twice a day, storing great amounts of energy as it flows in and out. Tidal power stations, consisting of a huge dam or "barrage" across a river estuary or between a group of little islands can capture this energy. As the tide flows through turbines incorporated in the barrage, electricity is generated. For such a plant to be effective however tides must be predictable, with a difference between high and low water of at least 5 metres. Very few locations around the world have been identified as suitable because of the conditions that have to be met. In addition, the plant can only generate when the tide is flowing. This is only about 10 hours per day and this might not occur when electricity is at its most desirable. Consequently, an alternative source of power is necessary for the remainder of the time.

The world's first tidal power plant has been in operation since 1966 at the enclosed estuary of the Rance River in Brittany, France. Here the difference between low and high tides averages 8.17 m, peaking at 13.5 m during the equinox. The structure consists of 24 turbines, while the barrage also supports a dual carriageway that links both sides of the estuary, thus serving as vital infrastructure for the region. Today, La Rance is still by far the largest tidal power plant, producing 240 MW. The next largest plant, in Annapolis, Canada produces only 20 MW.

Over the last 20 years the concept of "tidemills", i.e. underwater turbines without any associated barrage has been explored. These are, in effect, underwater windfarms. Seawater, with a much higher density than air, provides an enormous economy of scale. Since the turbines are under water, maintenance of all tidal systems is difficult. Their biggest disadvantage however is the enormous cost. Funding for such stations has been difficult to obtain.

Wave energy, as opposed to tidal energy, is very difficult to capture because of its diffused nature and the wide range of conditions to contend with - a single device must bear the brunt of powerful waves and storms, yet also be effective in mild conditions. As the wind blows over the ocean, a massive amount of potential energy is transferred to the water. Energy is stored in this way until released in the coastal shallows and beaches. To date all attempts to design and deploy cost effective devices have met with limited success.

In the 1940's, the Japanese were the first to experiment with wave energy. Although the concept has not made much headway, various ideas have been tried. In one, the wave-driven rise and fall of water in a cylindrical shaft compresses the air inside, thus forcing it through air turbines. In another, a series of "ducks" connected in a chain rise and fall according to wave motion. The relative motion between the "ducks" is utilised to drive a pump. This in turn drives an hydraulic motor, thus producing electricity. A third idea is to funnel the waves into a tapered natural or artificial channel. The wave level rises along the taper and spills into an elevated reservoir beyond the narrow end of the channel. The water then flows back to the sea through a turbine, generating electricity in the process.

The increasing inroads made by such sources as above do not alter the fact that, to date, man's energy overwhelmingly originates from heat generated from the primary sources of coal, oil, natural gas and nuclear power. Of these, the fossil fuel contribution is predominant.

## Fossil fuel.

This is the name given to organically based sources of energy obtained from within the earth's crust (coal/oil/natural gas). These alone provide currently 80 per cent of the world's energy needs. The following table shows the primary energy mix on a percentage basis, both worldwide and for Europe alone, as given by the International Energy Authority (IEA). Relative consumptions at the beginning of the twenty-first century are compared with those of thirty years previously. These percentages are of a total energy demand that has continued to increase:

| Fuel | World %age consumption in year | | European %age consumption in year | |
|------|------|------|------|------|
| | 1970 | 2000 | 1970 | 2000 |
| Coal | 24.9 | 23.5 | 31.5 | 15.4 |
| Oil | 45 | 35 | 58 | 41.5 |
| Natural Gas | 16.2 | 20.7 | 6 | 23 |
| Nuclear | 0.9 | 6.8 | 1.5 | 15.4 |
| Renewables (incl. Waste+ Hydro) | 13 | 14 | 3 | 4.7 |

## FUEL COMPARISON.

Compared with coal, its competitors in the generation of heat for mankind are all new "kids on the block".

### Oil

ADVANTAGES:     - Convenient.

                 - Easy to transport and store.

                 - For transportation, no effective substitute.

DISADVANTAGES:  - Carbon intensive.

                 - Price volatility.

                 - Geographic concentration of resource.

                 - Vulnerable to disruption and geopolitical instability.

                 - Transport risk.

In addition to the political unreliability of the areas where most oil reserves are concentrated, the rate of finding new reserves has declined sharply. No new major oil fields have been found since 1976 and a growing world economy is confronting a resource in limited supply. In particular, the economic boom in China accounted for 37 per cent of the growth in world oil consumption during the years 2000-2004. Additional sources of oil, such as the Canadian tar sands, can be exploited, but at significant cost.

### Natural gas

ADVANTAGES:     - Convenient and efficient.

                 - Fuel of choice for many uses, e.g. residential heating.

DISADVANTAGES:  - Carbon intensive.

                 - Expensive and difficult to transport and store.

                 - Dedicated and inflexible infrastructure.

                 - Price volatility.

                 - Geographic concentration of resource.

While no single technology is the clear winner economically in all countries, gas-fired electricity generation has become an attractive near-term option where gas is available and cheap. Over the next couple of decades, it stands to make the biggest inroads into this market.

The high efficiency of Combined Cycle Gas Turbines (CCGT), which is in the range 50-55 per cent, plus their low emissions, makes them particularly attractive for generating electricity. Even the most modern coal-fired power stations have an overall efficiency of only about 45 per cent. In addition they are associated with a higher level of exhaust emission. CCGT is a recent development (towards the end of the twentieth century). The high temperature exhaust from a gas turbine generator set provides heat for the production of steam. This in turn powers a steam turbo-generator, thereby producing additional electricity. Such systems are not only relatively cheap; they can also be constructed quickly. The wide range of sizes available enables capacity increments to be more closely matched to the growth in load.

Typical investment costs for gas-fired generation are approximately 560 $/KW, as opposed to 1,230 $/KW for coal (Scott, 1999). However, when a comparison of international mine investment costs versus pipeline costs is included in the equation, capital charges for the total system are about equal.

When generating an equivalent amount of electricity, a CCGT plant emits half the carbon dioxide of a traditional coal plant, around a quarter of the nitrous oxides, and negligible amounts of sulphur dioxide and particles. In addition, there is no ash. It must be said, however, that as little as 60 per cent of the greenhouse emissions from natural gas occur at the point of combustion. The remaining 40% occur elsewhere in the production chain, i.e. venting/flaring at the wellhead, stripping and venting during processing, leakage during compression, transmission and distribution, plus the gas consumed in processing and compression. Methane, the main component of natural gas, is itself a greenhouse gas with a global warming potential of 23 times that of carbon dioxide. Equally, the liquefaction of natural gas to make it transportable by sea (as LNG) requires large amounts of energy.

Of total gas reserves, 37 per cent are located in the former Soviet Union and 33 per cent in the Middle East. At present over half of the world's natural gas reserves are in the hands of just two companies, Gazprom of Russia and the Iranian National Gas Company.


## Nuclear Power

ADVANTAGES:          - No emission of greenhouse gases.

                     - Negligible restraints on fuel supply.

DISADVANTAGES:       - Highly capital intensive, resulting in dubious economics.

                     - Public acceptability can be a problem.

                     - Question mark concerning waste disposal.

                     - Decommissioning is complicated, costly and prolonged.


The claim of nuclear power to be an environmentally friendly source of energy has been undermined and not only by the lack of any satisfactory solution to the problem of waste elimination. The local media in Ireland draws attention to marine contamination of the Irish Sea as a result of discharges from the Sellafield plant of British Nuclear Fuels Ltd. The incident at Three Mile Island in America and, first and foremost, Chernobyl in the Ukraine have highlighted the dangers which potentially lurk and which have wilted the former glamour. Germany, Italy, Austria and Sweden have formally renounced nuclear power and plan to phase out their reactors. France alone, with 75 per cent of their electricity generated by such means, remains firmly wedded to the concept. Nowhere in the world have new nuclear stations been financed within a liberalised electricity market.

In 1990, the UK generation industry was privatised, but nuclear plant liabilities represented too great a risk for potential investors.

In 1994, the Prototype Fast Breeder Reactor at Dounreay in the extreme north of Scotland was shut down, the first British atomic power station to close.

In 1995, a 17 M pound contract was awarded to design, build and commission a plant just to dispose of the sodium coolant used at Dounreay. The removal of sodium residues is not expected to be complete before 2007. The former Energy Minister Tony Benn, who blocked further application of the fast-breeder reactor, has estimated a period of 100 years to finally clear up the mess and decontaminate the site (ref The Benn Diaries).

In 1996, the most modern stations were privatised as British Energy. The remainder stayed in government hands, as part of British Nuclear Fuels Ltd.

In 2002, the privatised British Energy was only able to avoid bankruptcy by a government grant of 650 million pounds.

In 2003 the UK had 90,000 cu. metres of processed radioactive waste in stock, in a form suitable for long-term storage. This quantity is expected to increase by a further 1.6 M cu. metres by 2120. The half-life of this waste (i.e. the time required for radioactivity to reduce by 50 per cent) varies between tens of years and up to hundreds of thousands of years, or even millions of years.

Unlike the early, halcyon days, staff in the nuclear industry tends to be aging. To encourage young engineers, statements have been made that the industry still offers good career prospects in waste disposal and in the decommissioning of existing plants.

In 2004 there was some hope for the nuclear lobby. Finland, with its total lack of energy resources, announced that it would build the first nuclear plant in Europe for over a decade. China, struggling to sustain its economic growth of 10 per cent per annum, needs all the energy it can get irrespective of source. It plans to build 13 reactors.

## Coal.

ADVANTAGES:          - Abundant supplies from many geographically separate sources.

                 - Cheap and safe to use.

                 - Easy to transport and store.

DISADVANTAGES:       - The most carbon intensive fuel.

                 - High carbon content poses challenges for greenhouse gas reduction.

                 - Extensive anti-pollution measures necessary.

In contrast to the newcomers above, coal is a very ancient industry. More recently it was the indispensable basis of the industrial revolution, which would radically and permanently change the way of life for mankind. Not for nothing is Blaenavon in South Wales and the coal mine "Zollverein" in Essen, Germany, classed as World Cultural Heritage Centres by UNESCO.

By the beginning of the twenty-first century, the vast increase in energy requirements worldwide has absorbed the contributions of newer alternatives without the abdication of King Coal. Both in developing countries, such as India and China, as well as in developed countries, such as the United States, coal is used in increasingly large quantities. In North America, 90 per cent of the fossil fuel reserves are coal. With the sole exception of Europe, growth in consumption is projected for all regions of the world.

Today, the market for coal is dominated by electricity generation. Of the total world coal production, 60 per cent is used as a fuel in thermal power stations. Coal currently provides fuel for 39 per cent of the world's electricity generation (twice as much as the next largest source). This application is projected to grow to 60 per cent of total generation by 2030.

Of the industrial users, steel works use about 15 per cent of world production, using coke made from coal plus coal injection to smelt iron ore in blast furnaces. Of the world's steel production, 70 per cent is produced this way. Cement plants consume about 5 per cent of world production to produce clinker, the basic component of cement. The remaining 20 per cent of total world production includes general industry and residential users, nowadays concentrated in China and in some parts of Eastern Europe.

In the last hundred years world-wide production has increased considerably; there has also been a radical change in the contributions of various countries. By the century's end, two newcomers, Columbia and Indonesia, were making significant contributions. Indonesia had risen from virtually nothing within a very short period of time. In stark contrast, from being second only to the United States, the UK had slipped to a position near the bottom of the table. In the USA, coal production is on a long term rising trend. There are major mining operations in 27 out of the 50 states, with Wyoming alone producing over 340 Mt per annum. Proven reserves are adequate for 250 years. Approximately 40 per cent of the output is from deep mines with the rest from opencast. This total production corresponds to 25 per cent of primary energy demand, with 50 per cent of US electricity being generated in coal-fired power stations. With generation from nuclear fuel and gas declining, seven eighths of their coal production is used for this purpose. Plans are afoot to significantly increase production.

Over the past 20 years in the USA there has been a big move towards larger and more efficient mines. Overall productivity has risen from 2.74 tonnes of coal per miner per hour to 5.5 tonnes. This has meant a large number of pit closures and job losses in the industry, with depression in the traditional coalfields. The number of mines has declined from 4,424 to 1,828. Of these, approximately half are deep mines and half open cast. The coal website of the US Government promotes the mining industry very vigorously, stating that deep mining is now as safe as a job in a supermarket. It states, "Mining has a lower rate of injuries and illness per 100 employees than the agriculture, construction or retail trades". Experts writing for the website explain how dust is kept to a minimum and vaunt the effectiveness of roof supports plus the quality of the safety equipment with which miners are supplied. Current policy documents of the US Government refer to energy from coal as being essential, affordable and increasingly clean.

With regard to black coal production, a comparison of the situation prevailing before the First World War, compared with the beginning of the twenty-first century, is given in the following table:

| Country | Production in 1911 (Mt) | Production in 2002 (Mt) |
|---|---|---|
| China | - | 1,171 |
| USA | 435 | 899 |
| India | 12 | 310 |
| Australia | 11 | 238 |
| South Africa | 7 | 225 |
| Russia | 26 | 169 |
| Poland | Divided between Germany, Russia, Austria/Hungary | 102 |
| Ukraine | Included in Russia | 81 |
| Indonesia | - | 79 |
| Kazakhstan | Included in Russia | 71 |
| Columbia | - | 45 |
| Germany | 158 | 35 |
| UK | 272 | 30 |
| France | 38 | 3 (Eliminated in 2004) |
| Belgium | 23 | - |
| Austria/Hungary | 16 | - |
| Japan | 16 | - (Only 2 collieries) |
| Canada | 10 | 38 |
| Spain | 4 | 8 |
| New Zealand | 2 | 4 |
| Other countries | 16 | 192 |
| Total world production | **1,046** | **3,700** |

In 1991, the US position as the world's largest producer was supplanted by China. However, the USA still produces 24 per cent of the world total, with an output in 2003 that had risen to just under one billion tonnes.

By 1997, China was employing 7 million people in approximately 80,000 mines (many of these mines however are very small or seasonal). In recent years, their economic boom has resulted in a reduction in the amount of their coal available for export. Coal has even been imported.

Nowadays, about 13 per cent of coal production is traded internationally, with East Asian countries being the main recipients. Malaysia for example plans five coal-fired power stations, each over 2,000 MW. The first of these was commissioned in 2002. They will be a major market for Indonesian coal..

The ratio of reserves to the rate of production is currently over 200 years, as opposed to 65 years for gas and 41 years for oil. Worldwide therefore, coal remains the fossil fuel having by far the largest reserves. Proven coal reserves have increased by over 50 per cent in the past 2 years. Unlike oil or gas, these reserves are much more evenly distributed throughout the whole world, in politically stable regions and with major exporters on every continent. This results in coal being less susceptible to politics and war, and subject to strong competitive pressure that minimises cost. Lower production from one supplier can easily be substituted by additional production from another.

International coal prices have a strong track record of stability, especially in comparison with other fossil fuels.

## COAL GEOLOGY.

Some 310 million years ago, in the coal-forming Carboniferous period, high-level tree and plant life existed across Europe in the form of swampy, tropical forests. In that steaming world, plants were storing the energy of the tropical sun. The process of photosynthesis converted carbon dioxide from the atmosphere into living plant matter and oxygen. As the trees and plants died they built up a layer of organic matter that, in time, would subside due to the movement of the earth's crust beneath. This resulted in flooding and an eventual covering with sediment. Starved of oxygen, the buried vegetation, still containing carbon, would rot and peat was formed. Marsh gas (methane) was generated and remained trapped within the organic matter. Continuing seismic movements over millennia would repeat the cycle as the land surface rose and fell. As the peat was buried deeper and compressed, the water was driven out. From this common organic matter, first the soft brown coal (lignite), still with a high water content, and then hard coal was formed.

When compressed, a peat thickness of about 100 metres would result in a coal seam of about 10 metres thickness. The applied temperature and pressure increased with depth of burial, resulting in a higher calorific value of the coal. Anthracite is the culmination of this sequence. Difficult to set alight, it burns smokelessly, with a heat more intense and enduring than other coal. Such seams are the earliest to have been formed, and have a carbon content of up to 98 per cent. In general the following stages occur:

| Type of fuel | % age carbon | % age hydrogen | % age oxygen |
|---|---|---|---|
| Peat | 60 | 6 | 34 |
| Brown coal (lignite) | 67 | 5 | 28 |
| Bituminous coal | 76-80 | Volatile matter 14-20% | |
| Steam coal | 80-90 | Volatile matter 8-14% | |
| Anthracite | >93 | Volatile matter 3-8% | |

As a result of the above process, sheets of coal were produced in series, one above the other at different levels. The individual sheets (seams) of coal were separated from each other by an intervening strata of shales, sandstones, mudstones etc. Such separation between individual seams is typically about 15 metres thick. The total thickness of the coal measures within a coalfield can reach to a depth of 2,000 metres in some areas of Europe.

In South Wales, the coal measures are divided into upper, middle and lower. The listing below is not exclusive, but the main seams in these sections (taken in descending order) are as follows:

Upper Measures.

   - No.1 Rhondda.

   - No.2 Rhondda.

   - No.3 Rhondda.

Middle Coal Measures.

   - Gorllwyn.

   - Two Feet Nine.

   - Four Feet.

   - Six Feet.

   - Red Vein.

   - Nine Feet.

   - Bute.

Lower Coal Measures.

   - Yard.

   - Seven Feet.

   - Five Feet.

   - Gellideg.

Towards the end of this Carboniferous period the quantities of sediment became greater and very sandy, with the result that the coal seams in the later, and upper, part of the sequence are fewer and much further apart. This is known as the Pennant formation. It is these measures that were worked by means of levels into the hillsides, whose entrance scars may still be seen. In latter years, the coals of the Upper Measures have been of little consequence.

Following the coal seam formation, great disturbances occurred. Some 280 million years ago, as a result of continental drift, Africa crunched into the mass of Europe, which at that time was united with America. The Alps were raised while the coal formations were split. Some were pushed deep underground while others were heaved up, to be eroded away completely. This resulted in the coalfields, as seen today, being scattered over a wide area and at greatly differing depths. Some were re-buried by the Jurassic seas, such as that of Kent. In such cases newer rocks cover the geology of the carboniferous (coal forming) era, which consequently is not apparent at surface level. Of these "hidden coalfields", some have only recently been discovered, such as the large coalfield lying beneath Oxfordshire. The Eastern part of the Notting-hamshire coalfield, in latter years the most productive in Britain, was also hidden and only thoroughly explored and developed after the Second World War.

The immense force from the south, resulting from continental drift and referred to above, compressed the South Wales coalfield. A large fault developed in the centre, known as the Noel Gilau fault. This deepened the western part while raising the eastern section. The seams in the southwest were thus thrown down by more than 460 metres. Westwards into Pembrokeshire the strata was acutely crumpled and distorted. In addition to such major folding, other breaks in the strata occurred across the entire coalfield, roughly along north-south lines. As a result of this process coal seams no longer lie in continuous sheets as when originally laid down but have been cut into sections by so-called fault lines, thrown up or down relative to each other. In the centre of the coalfield, compression buckled the sediments into a series of arch-type folds, or anticlines, and bowl-type folds or synclines. Further complicated breaks took place east to west, causing belts of rocks and coal seams to snap and slide on top of one another. This often gives rise to double sections of coal for limited distances, known as thrusts, while in other sections the seam simply disappears. Such cases are known as washouts. Over millions of years, denudation of the land surface has caused many coal seams to be simply washed away. Configuration of the underground strata bears no relationship to the surface appearance, which owes its structure to erosion and to glacial activity.

Other continents also broke apart and drifted about the earth's surface. For the most part, however, they were not involved in the violent coming together of plates that produced the great mountain ranges. Consequently, in such cases, the ancient deposits of bogs and deltas on each fragment remained uncontorted. For the most part they remained largely exposed, suffering erosion. This removed their cover, which was not replaced by later marine sediments. The result was thick and flat-lying coal seams, not far below the surface.

## COAL TRADE.

### Globalisation.

It is therefore a fact of mining life that while planning, equipment and methods of work have a considerable effect upon the cost and magnitude of production, Mother Nature still holds the trump card. It is to a great extent the accident of geology that determines the success or failure of mines. It is not the quality of European coal that is in question but the depth, thickness and disturbed nature of the seams there, and hence the cost of winning it. Europe is a zone where the edges of continents have collided and deformed, resulting in much of its coal being buried deep, in faulted seams. Continental landmasses such as Queensland or New South Wales in Australia are not only undeformed, leaving the sheets of coal relatively level and intact, but erosion has removed the overburden, leaving these seams near the surface where most of them can be mined opencast. Where underground operations are necessary they tend to be shallow drift mines, working thick, continuous seams, complete with roof and floor strata that are firm.

The potential for economic production at a particular colliery depends on:

- Seam thickness.
- Seam accessibility (depth, nature of overlying strata, inclination etc.).
- The degree of geological faulting.
- Water ingress and the amount of gas present.

Folding and faults, produced during the period when the Alps were raised, confuse the seams in regions such as South Wales. As a consequence it is here that the coal tends to be the most expensive, with maximum effort being required to win it. Typically, while in Queensland 400 men with open cast excavators produce 4Mt of coal per annum (10,000t per man), in South Wales in the early 1980's, 23,000 men were struggling to produce 7Mt (about 304t per man). While some good areas do exist, in general the seams here are deep, thin and confused by folding and faults. The mining communities of Western Europe, with South Wales as a prime example, were to suffer under this poor hand, dealt to them by nature.

In the rigid continental heartland of Eastern Europe the geology is more benevolent than that near the periphery of the continent. In the Midlands and North of England, the geological situation also improves. Here the seams dip gently away from the Pennines under the North Sea.

One feature of the late twentieth century is an unprecedented internationalisation in the markets for coal. One buzzword, which came to the fore during this period, was "globalisation". International agreements, such as the General Agreement on Tariffs and Trade (GATT), along with the founding of the World Trade

Organization (WTO) in 1995, have facilitated this movement considerably. What for some is a panacea for economic growth and a road to the optimum, most cost-effective production, is for others the maximisation of profits by multi-national companies while simultaneously allowing them to escape both their social responsibilities and the control of democratically elected governments.

Be that as it may, there is now a departure from any self-centred economic view of the world. Capital can be transferred between countries within minutes, while long established corporations, typically associated with a particular nation, are now in the hands of international shareholders. Labels such as "Made in England" have become irrelevant when the reality is: Made by such and such a corporation, "Somewhere in the world". Traditionally, industries grew up around local coalfields, where energy was available. Today, an increasing awareness of the "global village", together with market liberalisation, has resulted in Nature's blessings being made available worldwide, including to those industrialised countries that traditionally relied upon their own indigenous energy resources.

More and more, price competition on an international scale is replacing geographical proximity and political integration as the prime factor in determining a source of supply. South Wales experienced an early precursor to this tendency. With new methods of making steel the manufacture of wrought iron declined. For this steel manufacture, imported iron ore was more suitable than local ore. The clay iron-stone seams in the local coal measures, so important in the early days of the industrial revolution, were replaced as raw material by ore from Labrador and West Australia. The consequence was a relocation of the industry, from the northern outcrop of the coalfield to new steelworks built on the South Wales coast. Now, it is great ore carriers from abroad that feed the indigenous metallurgical industry.

## Movements of Coal.

The oil price shocks of the 1970's produced a concomitant scramble for cheaper fuel. The resultant cross border flow of capital and know-how enabled worldwide access to thick, unfaulted and easily accessible seams of coal. There was massive development of coalfields previously dormant and of those that, at the most, had been exploited for purely local needs. Large bulk carriers, with the dimensions of crude oil tankers, were constructed to reduce freight rates and to transport with equal facility either coal or metallurgical ore. Large-scale coal handling facilities were built in both exporting and importing nations. The international logistics chain proved to be highly efficient and flexible, capable of allowing this world seaborne trade to grow according to international needs. Previously, worldwide trade in coal had been restricted by small ships in inadequate numbers, as well as lack of port facilities.

Between 1973 and 1995, there was a doubling in world coal trade. The International Energy Authority (IEA) forecasts a further doubling by 2010, as low cost producers take advantage of market space created by closure of the heavily subsidised domestic mining industries, especially in Europe. Against this background, Japanese capital built up the massive fields of Queensland while Japanese coalmining itself virtually disappeared. By 1998, only two collieries remained in that country. Japan is the world's largest importer of coal. East Asia generally is one of the two main coal-importing regions, Europe being the other. Traditional export sources have been Australia, the USA and South Africa with, to some extent, Poland. Joining the exporters in recent years have been Columbia, Indonesia and China. About 15 per cent of coal production is traded internationally, as opposed to 20 per cent of natural gas. This trade is in high calorific hard coal for power generation, as well as coking coal.

Between 1970 and 1996, Australian production increased fourfold, to 195 Mt. This made it the world's fifth largest coal producer and, with 70 per cent exported, the largest coal exporter.

In 1996, of Australia's exports, 47 per cent went to Japan, 14 per cent to South Korea and 11 per cent to Europe.

In 1997, from the third largest exporter, South Africa, 54 per cent went to Europe and 37.1 per cent to Asia.

After Australia the world's second largest exporter is the USA, despite the fact that its mining industry is mainly orientated towards home consumption. The USA is the second largest coal producer after China.

At the beginning of the twenty-first century, the world price of coal is effectively set by the level at which United States producers find it attractive to export.

While, at a "super pit" in the Midlands of England typically 1,000 men produce 1 Mt of coal per annum, at the Bella Vista open cast site in the western USA state of Wyoming, to take just one example, 250 men produce an annual output of 12 Mt. This helps explain why in the United Kingdom and in Germany production continued to decline while imports increased. Relegated to history were the coal-mining industries of Belgium, the Netherlands, Italy, Portugal and Austria. Production in France was phased out in 2004.

Indonesia and Columbia are both new on the world market. In contrast to developments in Europe, between 1980 and 1996, during the massacre of coalmining in the UK, the former increased its production from 0.3 to 45 Mt, with 75 per cent exported to Japan, Taiwan and South Korea. In 1995 alone, Indonesian production increased by 27 per cent. Columbia has three-quarters of the reserves available in Latin America with more than seven billion tonnes of proven high-quality coal. The country is home to the world's largest opencast coal mine, Cerrejon Zona Norte (CZN) in Guajira province. This produces 19 Mt tonnes of power station coal per annum. Exploitation of neighbouring deposits could eventually boost annual output of this single complex to as much as 40 Mt.

In 2001, Columbian coal exports rose to 40 Mt, up from 36 Mt in the previous year, thus overtaking coffee in importance and making it the second most important export after oil. Their Vice-Minister of Mines predicted that, by the year 2008, exports would exceed 70 Mt. These developments, together with the associated ports and railways, have been driven primarily by the multi-nationals Broken Hill Propriety of Australia, Exxon and Glencore International of the United States, plus the Anglo-American Corporation of South Africa. Europe is the prime export market, with inroads being made into the southern United States. There is a high and increasing demand around the world for power station coal. With pressure on South African production, and as output declines in Germany and the UK, increased exports to the European Union are foreseen.

The potential for west European coal to compete against world market prices is bleak. Although consumption there has fallen by nearly one-third, Europe's imports have nevertheless grown by 20 per cent over 10 years. Germany alone imports about 20 Mt of about 120 Mt consumed. In addition, low-cost gas, particularly for power generation, is a formidable competitor. There is increasing pressure to reduce subsidies to the domestic coal industry, although in Germany and Spain some production will continue to be supported on social and regional grounds.

## CLEAN COAL TECHNOLOGY (CCT).

As well as "globalisation", another buzzword inherited from the late twentieth century is "environment". Increased public and political awareness has resulted in the current international debate, and regulations aimed at reducing emissions on a global scale. Throughout history, an increase in the consumption of energy implied, ipso facto, a concomitant increase in the standard of living. Nowadays a new "zeitgeist" is abroad, with a new objective, to decouple economic growth from increased energy use and the associated pollution.

The efficiency of energy usage varies considerably. In the most developed, environmentally conscious countries, future economic growth is expected to bring in its wake a much lower proportional increase in energy demand. In Germany for example, the success of energy conservation measures is shown by the fact that between 1979 and 1988 total consumption of primary energy declined by 6 per cent, in spite of a 20 per cent increase in the gross domestic product in real terms. In that country for the foreseeable future, no significant increase is foreseen in the level of primary energy consumption.

In 2003 Exxon/Mobil forecast an overall reduction of 7% in Germany's energy requirements by 2020, underlining that country's continuing status as one of the most fuel efficient economies.

# The Image of Coal.

As the fossil fuel associated with the highest level of emission, the issue of pollution is a particular challenge to coal. There is no doubt that coal suffers from a serious image problem, both public and political. The word conjures up, not only miners in peril but grimy pit towns and belching chimney stacks. Its competitors, such as the nuclear industry, have not been slow in vilifying the fuel. Behind the image, sufficient truth exists to warrant concern. Unless used in such ways that the sulphur is captured, high sulphur coal is an environmental disaster. Eastern Europe offered enough examples of this. Not only will inefficient combustion and inadequate pollution control have a negative effect on the environment but the systems which convert coal's energy content into electricity are not yet as efficient as those which burn natural gas. This results in a double handicap since, in addition to its intrinsic polluting effect, more coal-based energy has to be consumed in order to produce the same amount of electricity.

On the other hand, coal is an abundant fuel. The resource will still be available after the major oil and gas fields are depleted and will have to supersede them as a source of chemicals, as well as fuels. Whatever happens in the next decades, coal will be needed in years to come. Many countries have no option but to burn coal now, sometimes of very low quality, while others already use it to produce liquid fuel for transport. In addition to all of this, in the event of supply problems, it is prudent to have a range of energy sources available within the national mix. There are cost implications but coal can be burned cleanly. It can also be burned efficiently. Perhaps the real question should be not whether to burn coal at all but rather, how it should be burned?

Pressure is on for the introduction of flue gas treatment and for clean combustion technologies for coal. Coal-fired electricity generation is the largest source in the UK, not only of carbon dioxide ($CO_2$) but also of sulphur dioxide ($SO_2$) and nitrous oxides ($NO_x$). All of these have been targeted for significant reduction by European Union directives.

During the 1980´s, acid rain caused by $SO_2$ and $NO_x$ was a major concern, epitomised by the widespread and well-publicised demise of trees. Burners were modified to meet the $NO_x$ target by means of staged combustion. The requirement of the European Commission for a 60 per cent reduction in Sulphur Dioxide ($SO_2$) emissions by 2003, compared with 1980 levels, was met by employing combination of the following:

    i)   The importation of low-sulphur coal.

    ii)  Back fitting of flue gas desulphurisation (FGD) to existing coal-fired power stations.

    iii) Replacement of coal-fired generating capacity with gas fired stations.


The relative attraction of these methods obviously depends on the associated economics.

By 2003, the target of a 60 per cent reduction in $SO_2$ emission had been met in the UK. This removed acid rain from the agenda.


# Greenhouse Gases.

Still very much on the agenda is the issue of greenhouse gases, mainly carbon dioxide ($CO_2$), plus the associated climate change. Reduction in $CO_2$ emission is at a premium. The proportion of various gases, making up the overall greenhouse gas emission, is as follows:

    - Carbon Dioxide ($CO_2$):    80%

    - Hydrogen Carbide ($CH_4$):   13%

    - Nitrous Oxide ($N_2O$):     4-5%

    - Other gases:          2-3%

The UK government has decided on a 20 per cent reduction in its CO2 emissions by the year 2010, compared with 1990 levels. This is above requirements of the Kyoto Protocol and involves among other things:

- Suppliers being obliged to obtain 10 per cent of electricity from renewable sources, subject to the cost to consumers being acceptable (in 1999 renewable energy comprised 2.8 per cent of UK supply).

- Doubling the capacity of Combined Heat and Power (CHP) systems to at least 10,000 MW(e). In the year 2000 a record 500MW of CHP came on line. These systems utilise the heat that results from the generation of electricity in thermal power stations. Instead of going to waste as is normal, this heat is used for district heating schemes or for process heating in industry.

In June 2000, a Royal Commission report called on the UK government to set even higher targets for renewable and CHP generation, with the objective of reducing CO2 production from fossil fuels by 50 per cent in the next 50 years.

The technical challenge to the coal industry, and the importance of political will, is graphically illustrated by the case of Denmark.

In 1995, that country, which has no indigenous resources of fossil fuel, produced 93 per cent of its electrical power in coal-fired stations burning imported coal. This accounted for 40 per cent of total primary energy. Such a level of coal consumption was the result of a decision made on cost grounds, following the oil crises of the 1970's. Scandinavian cleanliness is apparent in the high degree of pollution control already in place. In the late 1990's, the government announced that, so as to meet its Kyoto targets, no further coal-fired stations would be licensed. Existing stations would be gradually phased out There would also be considerable investment in renewable energy and increased efficiency. Even today, a detached house in England or Wales, built to the latest standards, consumes nearly 20 per cent more energy than an equivalent house in Denmark.

By 2003, as a result of government policy, guaranteed minimum prices for renewable generation in Denmark proved to be so attractive that 21 per cent of electricity was produced from wind energy, compared with an official target of 16.5 per cent. The intention had been to increase this contribution to 50 per cent by the year 2030.

In 2002, in Denmark, election of a conservative Government threw the renewable camp into a period of uncertainty. Much of the subsidies for green power were removed, with the Government seeing carbon dioxide credits as a means of meeting its Kyoto obligations. This enables a country to contribute to its own contractual reduction in carbon dioxide emission by investing in reductions elsewhere. In the Danish case, Polish wind farms were being considered as a serious option.

The coal industry is well aware of the challenge facing it. So-called Clean Coal Technologies (CCT) exist and are developing. Such concepts are going to be needed if this resource is to realise its full potential in the future. Modern combustion and emission control technologies are now widely adopted in developed countries. These include flue gas washing for sulphur removal, and lower temperature burners plus Selective Catalytic Reduction (SCR) to reduce nitrous oxides (NOx). In addition, fabric filters or electrostatic precipitators are used to reduce particles, The capital and operating costs of emission control depend heavily on the physical characteristics of the fuel, such as sulphur content and ash content, plus fly ash electrical resistivity.

Such existing emission control does not however remove carbon dioxide from the exhaust, and carbon dioxide forms the bulk of the greenhouse gases currently being produced. Therefore, in addition to emission control as above, output of carbon dioxide must be significantly reduced. In general terms, the denser the fuel the higher the carbon content. This in turn results in a higher production of carbon dioxide per unit of fuel energy. At present, in supplying 39 per cent of the world's electricity, coal contributes about 10 per cent to the enhanced green house effect. One-third of all worldwide emissions of carbon dioxide ($CO_2$) emanates from power stations.

For a given amount of electricity generated, the amount of CO2 produced depends on the fuel used and the plant efficiency. When using coal two approaches are possible, either improve the efficiency of coal utilization or remove the carbon. The former results in less coal being consumed, and hence less emission for the same output.

## Improved efficiency (First approach).

1) Super-Critical Pulverised fuel Combustion (SCPFC). For conventional electricity generation, the pulverised fuel (pf) used has been ground in the power station to a consistency resembling talcum powder. Multiple burners then blow it into the furnace, where it behaves almost like a gas. Plants of this type have efficiencies in the range 36-38 per cent. By increasing steam conditions above the critical point of pressure, i.e. in excess of 240 bar (3,528 lb/sq.in) and temperature in excess of 538 degrees C, overall efficiencies of above 45 per cent have been achieved in Denmark, Germany, the USA and Japan. By increasing temperatures and pressures still further it is expected that efficiencies above 50 per cent are possible. For this to be done, new materials, which can withstand such temperatures and pressures, are under development.

2) Pressurised Fluidised Bed Combustion (PFBC). Here the burning coal is kept in an animated state by air injection through a bed of the fuel, in which steam generation tubes are immersed. The steam so produced is utilised by a steam turbo-generator. Such combustion under conditions of atmospheric pressure is well proven. Increasing the pressure under which combustion takes place improves efficiency and reduces emissions. The hot exhaust gas is cleaned, and then fed to a gas turbine/generator set. This results in electricity additional to that generated by the steam turbo-generator. Approximately 15 per cent of the power is generated in the gas turbine and 85 per cent in the steam turbine. The company ABB Carbon, which has built plants in Sweden, Spain and the USA, has spearheaded commercial use of this technology. The flagship development is in Stockholm, where two PFBC units, each with its own gas turbine, supply a common steam turbine. Electricity produced totals 135 megawatt, while 224 megawatt of reject heat is used for district heating in the city.

## Carbon Removal (Second approach).

This may be done either pre-combustion or post-combustion. The former method is less technically challenging than the latter.

1) Integrated Coal Gasification Combined Cycle (ICGCC). This involves the pre-combustion removal of carbon. CO2 is still produced as a result of combustion, but reduced to the level associated with gas firing. A relatively new technology, this is just on the threshold of its technical and economic potential. Coal is gasified on site using oxygen, often with steam. The main stages in the process are as follows:

- Slurry, consisting of coal and water, is pumped into a gasifier where it is mixed with oxygen. The coal is converted into a gas (syngas), plus a residue of solid slag.

- The syngas is then treated to remove impurities. Most of the pollutants associated with fossil fuels can be captured, including carbon dioxide and sulphur.

- The cleaned up gas is burned as a fuel in a gas turbine, in place of natural gas. The main combustible components are carbon monoxide and hydrogen.

- Waste heat from the gas turbine is used to produce steam. This in turn generates additional power via a steam turbine.

2) Carbon Dioxide Capture and Storage (CCS) involves the post-combustion removal of carbon. This technology removes all CO2, even that resulting from the combustion process, but is much less developed than the pre-combustion alternative (ICGCC) as above. It is unlikely to make much practical impact in the short term. In this case, coal is burnt normally and the carbon dioxide so produced is removed from the exhaust gases. Gas so removed will be disposed of by means of subterranean storage.

Such capture and disposal of carbon dioxide, so-called "carbon sequestration", is the key to the continuing large scale use of fossil fuels in a future world largely free of greenhouse gases.

Depleted oil and gas fields have considerable potential with regard to the long-term storage of the carbon dioxide sequestrated under point 2). Geological formations known as deep saline aquifers have the greatest capacity. Deep, unminable seams of coal offer an additional, but limited, possibility. Permanent, leak free storage involves a number of technical issues that have yet to be resolved. There are however more than 60 research projects worldwide, involving an investment of 70-80 M US$ in 2001. Funding will increase in future years, especially in the United States.

Typical efficiencies and emission levels of present day thermal power stations, using various fuels and combustion technologies, are as follows:

| Fuel | Efficiency (%) | $CO_2$ emission (kilogrammes per megawatt hour) |
| --- | --- | --- |
| Brown coal | 30 | 1,250 |
| Black coal with conventional pulverised fuel (pf) firing | 36 | 900 |
| Black coal (SCPFC) | 46 | 704 |
| Black coal (ICGCC) | 46 | 600 |
| Natural gas (CCGT) | >50 | 400 |

The use of gas therefore significantly reduces, even if it does not eliminate, the $CO_2$ problem. The future demand for coal worldwide will depend upon two factors. One is the outcome of competition, based upon price, between coal and gas in power generation. The other will be government policy adopted in order to meet requirements of the Kyoto Protocol on Climate Change.

The quantity and availability of coal assures its future as a major player on the world energy scene, subject however to clean coal technology and to price. Development of clean coal technology offers good export potential for the more technologically advanced countries, since the largest consumers of coal have no practical alternative to that fuel. Economy is the watchword. The costs will probably come down but currently carbon removal from coal by means of ICGCC involves a plant that is 70 per cent more expensive than one for conventional burning.

For any radical new technology, it is not expected that plant suppliers can offer guarantees to fully compensate for the risks. Consequently, power supply companies would have to carry most of the costs associated with under-performance. To entice them to move away from steady development of the existing and well proven pulverised fuel (pf) firing they would need to see a potentially considerable commercial benefit. Such compensating benefits would probably be the result of incentives offered by the state.

## COAL PRODUCTION.

Coal may be worked either by opencast or by underground mining, depending on the depth of the seams.

### Opencast.

Where the coal is almost at surface level, opencast is by far the cheapest method. It is an exercise in excavation, rather than in mining. First the overburden is removed, usually by means of dragline excavators. The coal so exposed is then worked by mechanical shovels and carried away by trucks. For the working of soft brown coal, once the seam is exposed a bucket-wheel excavator operated by one man may shift tens of thousands of tonnes per day.

During operation, an opencast site imposes a significant scar on the landscape. In Australia, excavations are up to 60 m deep and in Columbia up to 100 m. Between three and seven times as much overburden has to be shifted as coal removed. At least in western, developed countries, on completion of the site the overburden is reinstated and the site landscaped. This increases the cost of the operation, which nevertheless remains one of the cheapest forms of energy production. Sometimes the excavations are flooded on completion, resulting in a lake area for recreation.

Open cast has been extensively used throughout the world, where vast areas of virgin coal seams exist in unpopulated areas. Such conditions manifestly did not exist in the UK. Consequently the technique was always thought of as being inapplicable to this country. During the Second World War however, crippling shortage of coal supplies proved an incentive to reconsider the position.

In 1942, Sir Albert Braithwaite MP, director of a large civil engineering company, pressed this method upon the British Government as an emergency wartime measure and open cast mining began under direct Government control. It proved to be very successful, producing nearly 15 Mt per annum at its peak. After nationalisation of the mining industry it remained under direct government control.

In 1952 responsibility for opencast coal mining was transferred from the government to the NCB. Profitability ensured its survival, also in periods of coal surplus. The general impression remained however that this was an exceptional measure, designed to meet a crisis situation.

In 1958, the Defence Regulations were finally terminated. These had provided compulsory rights to enter land and win coal by opencast methods. Henceforward, with the Opencast Coal Act of that year, authorisation was required, including the planning conditions deemed appropriate for working and restoration. Granting of planning permission is now the major restraint. This reflects the generally held perception of an environmental threat, resulting in widespread local opposition.

Underground mining is associated with significantly more capital investment, operating costs, manpower and risk than is the case with open cast. Here there are two basic methods of working the seams. One is Room and Pillar while the other is called Longwall.

## Room and Pillar (sometimes called Pillar and Stall).

This method of underground working involves a series of narrow drivages, driven parallel to each other in the seam. These drivages are then crossed, at more or less ninety degrees, with a series of other drivages, thus forming a grid. The result is a series of oblong coal pillars, formed between the drivages. These pillars may be partially or completely shaved away. The degree of extraction depends upon the necessity to support the surface, and/or the extent to which geological conditions will allow the roof of the extracted seam to remain unsupported.

The size of pillars having to be left behind increases significantly with depth. Since by international standards UK mines are deep, room and piller application is limited if a high percentage of the reserves is to be extracted. This system requires the minimum amount of work on access roadways within the seam. Since it is characterised by a number of small production teams, one for each narrow drivage, co-ordination and esprit-de-corps within such teams tends to be high, reducing absenteeism. Mechanisation takes the form of so-called continuous mining machines, each advancing on its own narrow front.

## Longwall Advancing.

This is a later development, which gradually tended to replace room and pillar. It involves taking out the complete panel of coal to be extracted by working an elongated face advancing on a broad front. The coalface is served by a roadway at each end. As extraction proceeds and the roadways extend, they are supported on the face side, i.e. extracted side, by packs of stone. These roadways are then maintained in condition so as to provide for ventilation, plus the transport of coal outbye and the haulage of supplies inbye. Longwall working results in a much higher percentage of coal being extracted than is the case with Room and Pillar since, with the latter, blocks of unworked coal almost always have to be left behind so as to support the roof. In addition, longwall ventilation is straightforward and more efficient than that required by the extensive grid of Room and Pillar working. Operation requires discipline and co-ordination among all members of the production team, since the face must advance as a complete, coordinated whole. The typical length of such a face is 200-300 metres.

## Longwall Retreating.

This is a combination of the two preceding systems. As with Room and Pillar, drivages are worked in the seam and supported by the unworked coal on each side. However, there are only two such drivages, leaving a single large pillar between them. These pillars are then extracted in a single ongoing operation, working back towards the main trunk roadways from where the drivages were started. Where this system can be adopted it may combine the advantages secured by each of the other two systems, while avoiding their disadvantages. Prior to the start of production, the face roadways are driven out to their full extent within the seam. They are then progressively abandoned as the face retreats back to the starting line. The advantages of such a system are:

- Pre-exploration of the seam to be worked.
- No necessity to pack the roadway sides as the face advances (unproductive work).
- No roadway repair as with an advancing face, where the extraction on one side tends to produce geological pressure on the roadway.
- No separate construction of "stable holes" at the face ends (these provide room for a power-loading machine to move over, prior to its taking the next cut).
- Higher installation standard for the roadway conveyor, which is also less liable to damage. This results in a higher level of reliability.

## At the Point of Production.

In traditional hand working of coal, the collier would cut timber as necessary to provide for his own local roof support. Using his craft he would win the coal in his own "stint" by the use of pick and shovel. If necessary he would first undercut the coal before bringing it down by the use of wedges or explosive placed into "shot-holes" drilled into the coal. The first coalface machinery was confined to such undercutting and was compressed air, later electric, powered.

Nowadays, where it can be applied, longwall mining offers the lowest cost available. Power loading of coal is virtually universal. The power-loading machine will cut coal off the seam in such a way that it is automatically loaded onto an armoured flexible conveyor (AFC). This is installed along the entire length of the face and also serves to mount and guide the power loading machine. The AFC shifts coal from the power loader to the main roadway conveyor system for transport outbye.

Modern coalfaces require a high level of capital investment (approximately 12 million pounds sterling at late-1990's prices). A team of about ten men will operate each face. Recent policy in the UK is to invest in so-called Heavy Duty (HD) equipment. This involves an uprating of equipment power and reliability. The increased face lengths have necessitated this and also the greater depths/high pressures under which European faces tend to operate. HD equipment has also resulted in faster advance. This means not only greater output but also better roof control since the strata has less time to settle. Mechanical/electrical breakdowns have been reduced to an average total delay of typically 13 per cent of working time. This applies to the whole of the face system (Power-loader/AFC/roof supports). One strip of coal from a face, 275 metres long and 2 metres high will yield 465 tonnes run-of-mine coal (i.e. coal which has yet to be washed, separated from dirt/rock and graded in size).

After a coalface has reached the end of its allocated panel of coal, recovery and relocation of the equipment to a new face is undertaken. This is a prolonged procedure, normally requiring 10-16 weeks in the UK. Actual time involved depends upon the deteriorating condition of the roadways, plus availability of the replacement face and also historical custom and practice. Most collieries employ a specialised crew for face salvage work.

When compared with its competitors coal remains labour intensive, so the output per man is critical. Some labour costs in world hard coal industries are given below (International Energy Authority):

| COUNTRY | 1985 (US $ per tonne) | 1995 (US $ per tonne) |
|---|---|---|
| Germany | 39.9 | 86.6 |
| Poland | 11.9 | 19.5 |
| Australia | 8.52 | 10.6 |
| USA | 7.8 | 4.8 |
| South Africa | 2.9 | 3.4 |

Nowadays, only mechanised mining can produce coal at the necessary level of productivity and cost. There is however a problem with this concept. Human beings and hand working are flexible. Machines cannot so readily adapt to changing circumstances and geological variations, endemic in some parts of the world. Hydraulic supports are laid out with a fixed stroke. Power-loading machines are designed and installed to cater for a limited range of coal thickness. If Mother Nature does not play ball, if seam thickness changes significantly, if the roof strata is friable and/or the floor soft, if seam continuity has been broken by faults, with the different sections thrown up or down by prehistoric forces, a long and undisturbed production run is not possible. Such a run is necessary, to amortise capital investment of the installation. Add in the question as to the probability of water and/or gas ingress and the determining factor of geology becomes apparent. Unlike a factory, the ability of man to determine the environment within a mine applies to a certain extent only.

## Overview.

Since the Second World War, within the span of a single lifetime, the energy scene has changed out of all recognition while the wheel of coal industry organization has turned full circle. From an emphasis during the post-war period on the simple production of energy, almost at any price, the theme at the beginning of the twenty-first century is energy conservation, energy efficiency, and energy that is clean and renewable. An economy that was once the powerhouse of the greatest empire the world has ever seen, and a major exporter of coal, has now become a major importer of the same. Indigenous exploitation of the resource, under conditions of private enterprise, was replaced by public ownership, which managed supply as a public service. Later, with the industry reduced to a mere shadow of its former self, the return was made to privatisation as part of the "turbo-charged capitalism" resulting from the Thatcher era. This latter wind of change was to blow away indigenous energy provided by national communities, each with its unique and thriving local culture.

The shibboleths of "charity begins at home" and "where there's muck there's brass" have been replaced with the watchwords of "globalisation" and "environment". The blackleg workers of earlier years, who caused the labour movement so much grief, have had their role usurped by the servants of industries in other countries, beyond the reach of local trade unions. Coal is currently mined in over 50 countries, with some seven million people being employed. Of these, 90 per cent are in the developing world (World Coal Institute 2002).

Instead of national politics, heavily influenced by the indigenous sub-culture of mining, the political background to energy supply has shifted overwhelmingly to the world of diplomacy and international relations. Now, an international world of market forces and the realities of power, plus environmental treaties, set the tone. Specifically, four main things have changed:

    i)   International trade has increased.

    ii)  Electricity markets have been deregulated.

    iii) Mining productivity has increased greatly.

    iv) Shipping costs have been reduced.

On the technical side, the sole supplier of energy, initially produced by the muscle power of an army of men supported by horses, would then be sustained by technology, introduced and financed following state ownership. This well-meaning attempt to optimally serve both the nation and the industries employees would in turn also be toppled, culminating finally in a fully mechanised and trimmed-down operation where fiscal considerations rule. King Coal has been usurped from his once dominant throne, with the product being currently regarded as one commodity among several in the highly competitive global energy market of the early twenty-first century. This new situation, characterised by the virtual disappearance of British coal mining as a factor of any economic significance, is the culmination of a saga extending over several hundred years, during which time the industry was always at the forefront of social, if not always technical, developments. The "leitmotiv" of Welsh coal serves as a microcosm, a story of interest in its own right but also reflecting the overall macroeconomic picture.

# Chapter 3
## THE LEGACY

*"People shopping, people walking,*
*People, people everywhere,*
*Coming, going, stopping, talking,*
*Some just standing on the square".*
G.L.Davies, Llantrisant.

Between the bare and wind-swept mountains of the Brecon Beacons National Park to the north, and the gentle Vale of Glamorgan to the south; between the verdant agriculture of Pembrokeshire to the west and that of the English border counties to the east, lies a heavily dissected plateau. These dissections, known as "The Valleys" and gaping between intervening high moorland, once comprised one of the major coal-mining areas of the world. The topology is in sharp contrast to all other British coalfields, which have flat or gently undulating surfaces. Associated in latter years with recession and general economic decline, this area was a source of wealth for Victorian entrepreneurs, accounting at one time for one-third of the total coal exports of the world. The rise of the area from backwater to economic powerhouse was within the span of a single lifetime, as was its subsequent decline.

## THE BEGINNING.

Daniel Defoe was the son of a London merchant, a political activist and author of many works, including the world famous novels Robinson Crusoe and Moll Flanders. He was also an acute observer of contemporary British life, at a time when the country was experiencing the birth of new kind of economy, a transition to the world's first industrially based, mass consumer society. When in his travels around Great Britain he stumbled into South Wales, the area as a whole was still untouched by any such development.

In his work "A Tour Through the Island of Great Britain", completed in 1726, Defoe's impressions were as follows:

"Entering Glamorganshire from Brecknok, we beheld a ridge of horrid rock and precipices between; over which if we had not had good guides we should never have found our way. Indeed, we began to regret our curiosity in going out of the common road, as not having met with anything worth the trouble; and the country looking so full of horror we thought to have given over the enterprise and have left Wales out of our circuit. However, after a day and a night engaging thus with rocks and mountains our guide brought us down into a moist agreeable vale opening to the south and a pleasant river running through it called the Taaffe. Following its course we came to a famous spring of warm water called Taaffe-well. Four miles further we passed through the ancient city of Llandaff and in the evening arrived at Cardiff, a Welsh mile beyond it".

All of this was to shortly change. Thirty years later, in 1757, the Hirwaun ironworks opened, forcing works of man upon the isolation imposed by the "ridge of horrid rock and precipices" and starting a coal-rush into the adjacent Cynan valley. When Defoe was making his journey Cardiff was just a small market town but Merthyr Tydfil, bypassed by Defoe and then the largest town in Wales, was in the genesis of becoming the "iron capital of the world". Here, along the 1-mile wide strip of the coalfield's north outcrop, between Hirwaen and Blaenavon, ironstone was found. In addition there was a simultaneous presence of limestone, required as a flux to carry away impurities from the molten iron, plus fire clay, suitable for the lining of furnaces. The many streams in the area provided water. All this attracted the great iron works of the industrial revolution and by the mid-nineteenth century this area of South Wales became the iron-making centre of the world.

This first industrialised society needed more and more coal and, for a while, its main market would be the smelting of iron. With seams outcropping along the valley sides, coal could be won without deep mining, which in those early days was technically impossible. From this northern outcrop the seams dip gently into the depths, to re-emerge steeply inclined at the southern edge of the coalfield.

Just as the iron industry flourished along the north crop, along this southern outcrop there was a simultaneous development of the copper-smelting industry. By the mid-nineteenth century, the concentration of copper works in the lower Swansea Valley was producing over half the world's output. There was no copper ore in South Wales but, since 4.5 t of coal were required to smelt one ton of ore it was cheaper to bring the ore to South Wales from Cornwall and North Wales rather than transport large quantities of coal. At Neath and Swansea the coalfield lies close to the sea, making these excellent locations to bring in the ore by ship.

## THE COALFIELD.

The South Wales coalfield is the largest continuous coalfield in Britain. It is free of any covering of deposits newer than the coal measures themselves. The only concealed parts are those under-sea sections in the bays of Swansea, Carmarthen and St. Brides. The coalfield itself has the form of an elongated pie-dish, an oval basin, 90 miles (144 km) east to west. Its greatest width north-south is 21 miles (34 km), with most of it averaging about 15 miles (24 km). This reduces to a mere 4 miles (6.4 km) at the handle of the pie dish in the extreme west, in Pembrokeshire. The region is characterised by a high plateau area, dissected by numerous deep and often narrow valleys. From all sides, the coal seams dip towards the middle of the coalfield. Along the greater part of the northern outcrop the seams dip gently. On the southern crop the beds rise steeply and in many places are highly disturbed, making them difficult to work.

It would be natural to assume that the deepest seams are to be found at the centre of the coalfield. Anticlines, or folding of the strata upwards, have however brought the seams here nearer to the surface, making them more accessible. A special feature of the coalfield is the variety and quality of its coal, making it unique in the UK. The reason for this is not fully understood. There are three basic types, each of which met a market need. Coal ranges from the best anthracite in the west (4.5 per cent volatile matter), to bituminous in the south and east (35 per cent volatile matter). Anthracite is a very slow burning coal, smokeless and with little flame, while bituminous coal is suitable for coking. Between these two types, geographically as well as in terms of carbon and volatile content, is a form of coal that proved so good for raising steam in boilers that it became known simply as "steam coal". At the boundaries between coal types, this change in characteristic may be sudden, even within the area of a single colliery "take". The total coalfield reserves were divided as follows:

- 48% steam coal.

- 30% bituminous coal.

- 22% anthracite.

Coal itself, occurring in sheets or seams of variable thickness, makes up no more than 4 per cent of the total depth of the coal measures. These are grouped into the upper, middle, and lower measures. In general, the best gas and house coals are found in the upper measures, coking coal in the middle and thick seams of steam coal in the lower measures. As explained above, the same seam can exhibit different characteristics in different parts of the coalfield. In later years, operations were concentrated in the middle and lower coal series, with 10 to 12 workable seams at a typical colliery (although only a small number of these would be exploited at any one time).

## COALFIELD DEVELOPMENT.

The great period of British coal was within the reigns of Queen Victoria and Edward VII. As the industrial revolution rolled on, the initial demand of the iron industry was followed by the "coal-rush" of the nineteenth century, with its associated unbounded capitalism. This tore apart the bucolic environment of sheep and small farms in Defoe's "moist agreeable vale" and in all such vales. The tentacles of exploitation and development crawled inexorably through the valleys. By the beginning of the nineteenth century demand was enormous, with the graph of coalfield output still climbing. In addition to inland consumption there was a hungry export market to be served.

In 1841, the census of that year records Wales as being the first nation in the world to have a higher proportion of its workforce employed in industry rather than agriculture (National Museum of Wales).

By 1850, in this, the world's first industrial nation, coalfield output had increased to about 60 Mt per annum.

In 1851, the same year that coal was struck in the upper Rhondda by the 3rd Marquess of Bute, an Admiralty report declared South Wales steam coal to be the most suitable for the Royal Navy. Now, demand really took off. Other coalfields might argue that their coals should be blended with Welsh coal but, for the Royal Navy, only the best was good enough. Britannia ruled the waves and, during this period, it did so based upon Welsh coal. "Admiralty" coals, due to their smokeless quality, helped to protect the vessels by making their presence less conspicuous. They also contained more energy per unit volume, a significant factor in the limited space of a ship. This insatiable demand for steam coal for bunker purposes at sea became a dominant factor. In addition, there came the expanding industrial areas of France, plus the railways of Italy, Spain, the Balkans, Brazil and Argentina. Based upon the quality of Welsh steam coal, a flourishing export trade grew up, eventually consuming the lion's share of output.

Thus developed a great archipelago of pits, scattered across the coalfield, isolated and confined within its own home valley and with each the centre of its own local village. Less than a mile apart from each other as they often were, nevertheless, each pit had its own ethos, loyalty, working atmosphere and sometimes even mining technical jargon. The network of railways linking with these pits rivalled London's suburbia in its density. They were built as part of the "railway mania" that characterised Victorian Britain. Unlocking as they did the wealth of even the smallest valley, multiple tracks followed the rivers to the south, connecting with the rest of the country and the great coal exporting ports of Cardiff, Barry, Swansea and Newport. During this period, the mid- nineteenth century, approximately one third of world coal exports originated here.

To take just one example of the new development, the Rhondda grew from a pristine rural area with 1,998 people in 1851 to a crowded industrial complex in 1911, housing a population of 152,781. At that time second only to the United States of America as a magnet for immigration, on the floors and lower slopes of the narrow valleys a British wild west was imposed, with an economic importance comparable to the great oil centres of the world today. The new immigrants walked, cycled or rode in search of economic improvement, some from rural Wales, some from nearby England. Many others came from further afield, such as Scotland, Ireland and from all over Europe. They were housed in the string after string of grey sandstone terraced houses that were springing up, clinging to the valley sides.

Within just sixty years, continuous terraces of such workmen's cottages linked together the 53 large collieries along the Rhondda valley's 13-mile (21 km) length, trampling the emerald meadows and polluting the sweet-smelling air. Where, just decades previously, a Sabbath stillness had reigned, now it was the panting of steam engines, whirring of machinery, grating of coal screens and hammering of smithies that set the tone. The once clear Rhondda River ran like ink. Now a contaminated gutter for the colliery screens and washeries it swished around the blackened stones and mud banks that punctuated its length. In place of the isolated shepherds and farm workers, thousands of miners now walked to work in droves, to return at shift's end black as pitch. Once home, the daily bathing ritual in a portable enamelled bathtub in front of the open living room fire, was universal. One of the duties of the wife, or "mam" was to boil the water, ready for the warrior's return.

Thus grew up a "mono-industrial society", to the maximum extent possible, with over 70 per cent of the male workforce employed in the mines. Of the remainder, those employed in transport, brickworks, coal carbonisation plants, breweries and retailing were there to serve the coal industry and its employees. Even in the steel and tinplate areas of South Wales, coal mining remained the major employer. No significant manufacturing or service sector was developed during this period. Since mining is an extractive industry and inherently transitory, the inevitable result would be a society built on shifting sands.

Dominating and containing all this activity stood the hills, with their sporadic cliffs. Stripped of their woodland beauty they now stood rugged and bare, except for sheets of bracken, punctuated with immense heaps of colliery waste. The mountains forced a symbiotic relationship upon the society that they enveloped for, unlike other industrial areas, the valley floor, which had the highest population density in England and Wales, was elongated and narrow. All settlement lay in close (if vertical) proximity to the open moorland above. On these slopes, during spring and summer time, the sheets of thick, fresh, green bracken provided cover, a boon to courting couples and for children playing hide and seek. Its aroma would forever stay in their unconscious mind, ready to trigger recollections of childhood escapades. In autumn, with the bracken now brown and lifeless, farmers would burn it off. These flickering caterpillars of flame would form multiple slashes, dancing through the lengthening periods of darkness. Along the elongated mountain crests, sparsely grassed and the domain of sheep, plus some semi-wild ponies, emptiness and isolation ruled, all activity below attenuated to just a gentle murmur.

## COMMUNITY.

Among these mountains, giving emotional warmth and security to the people and which confined and sheltered them from the outside world, as well as isolating each valley from the next, a community of communities was created. Engendered by living together in narrow valleys, and working together in the claustrophobic confines of a mine, a common spirit, strong and pervading, existed. Epitomised by front doors kept open to the street outside, it was enhanced by a common history of suffering and a struggle against exploitation. There were no other communities quite like these. It was not only the intimate proximity between nature and "dark satanic mills". Whereas other towns might have suburbs or districts with individual characteristics, in this microcosm individuality could extend to particular streets. Local class differences were far less crass than was the case in England since, in the narrow valleys, isolation between the various strata of society was geographically impossible.

Nestled within this retort traditions and folklore developed with, in the absence of any alternative, an intense loyalty to mining. In contrast, the coalfields of the English midlands, in their flat open landscape, were closer to the heart of British industry and agriculture. People moved in and out of mining as employment opportunities changed. The tendency there was for less visceral involvement and more rational materialism. Within the valleys the intimate knowledge of, and interest in, individuals (and their business!), plus the pervading humour and sense of belonging was a foundation on which the social and political "genius loci" was to be built. The thirst for knowledge and education, plus the respect in which it was held, explain the plethora of Miners Institute libraries that sprung up all over the coalfield. Rich in socialist literature, they were virtually unique for a society whose daily bread was earned by brawn rather than brain. Within each valley there was still room for local traditions and in particular, local personalities, who sometimes played a deterministic role. There was never any shortage of real "characters", at all levels of society.

Against this epic background it was indeed so often individuals, and their achievements, that would set the tone. Already before the economic explosion, after describing Caerphilly as a few straggling cottages surrounded by rude and uncultivated mountains, Daniel Defoe wrote;

"About eight or nine miles north of this place, a few years ago, a very remarkable bridge was built over the Taafe. It consists of one arch (perhaps the largest in the world) the segment of a circle; the chord is 140 feet; the keystone, from the spring of the arch, is 34 feet high. The architect was William Edward —— He is now, or then was, a Methodist preacher. Had the remains of such an arch been discovered among the ruins of ancient Greece or Rome, what pains would be taken by the learned antiquarians to discover the architect; whilst honest William Edward, if living, remains unnoticed among his native mountains".

Subsequent years were to throw up a host of individuals and their achievements, which would remain unnoticed among their native mountains. In the absence of any Welsh Hollywood, any local "Dream Factory" to produce an appropriate epic, stories of the coal and railway barons, and those who opposed them, remain remote from public imagination. The example of just one Croesus of his day, David Davis, is the stuff of popular drama. A self-made man who became the leading railway contractor in Wales, in 1866 he stood within a hair's breath of bankruptcy as a result of his investment in shafts at the Maindy colliery and in Cwmparc, only to be saved at the last minute by discovery of the lucrative Rhondda no. 3 seam. He then went on to build his own Vale of Glamorgan railway and docks at Barry, in competition to the Taff Vale railway and Cardiff docks. These latter were the property of his great rival, the 3rd Marquess of Bute. This gentleman, though certainly more financially astute than the contemporary King Ludwig of Bavaria would, in is own limited way, mirror the latter's obsession with castle building. Having, together with his architect William Burges, converted Cardiff Castle into a Roman fort with a pseudo-gothic fantasy along the west wall, he looked for fresh ruins to conquer. These he found close to Defoe's "famous spring of warm water called Taaffe-well". Here, on a crag within the narrow rift gorge in which nestles the river Taff, were the mysterious ruins of Castell Coch, the Red Castle.

In 1871 the site was cleared and Burges and his patron created a romantic turreted construction, reminiscent of the castles along the Rhine, the Moselle and the Loire. This being so, there had of course to be a vineyard, and so one was created, the biggest British vineyard in modern times and marketing the first British-made wines since the Dissolution of the Monasteries along with their monkish vineyards, in the time of Henry the Eighth. The wine proved acceptable, in spite of Punch's comment on the first offering, that it took four men to drink one bottle - two to hold the victim down and one to pour it down his throat. A series of damp summers just prior to the First World War put an end to the enterprise. All of this was very remote from those toiling to create the wealth that the Marquis was so lavishly spending.

# STRIFE.

## The Seeds of Conflict.

The entrepreneurs who initially developed the coal industry were a product of their times. Believing in competition, but with a class loyalty that precluded a ruthless survival of the fittest, they set out to get cheap coal. Initially, with capital resources limited, as soon as a mine was sunk the cry was for output, and namely with men's hands not machinery. Any planning was strictly short-term, with no thought being given to long-term social consequences. Some of the coal-owners held their mineral rights under limited, short-term leases. They had to move fast to get the coal out quickly. As production rose steadily throughout the nineteenth century and into the twentieth, the sole motivation was to maximise quick profits. Regardless of long-term interests, or the social costs involved, the phenomenal growth of the coal industry had been based upon the cheapest possible methods. In contrast to other industries of the day, e.g. engineering, shipbuilding, textiles, of a rise in productivity there was no sign. As a result, when demand seemed insatiable and profits high, more and more miners were employed. Among these, along with choral singing, brass bands, religious revivals, amateur dramatics and carnival, another tradition, that of political radicalism, grew.

The great capitalists would be matched by other great figures, home grown. Those who were to achieve national prominence all had something in common, namely a concern for social justice combined with a visceral left-wing radicalism. One of the few areas in Britain where the Communist party would have a hold was the South Wales coalfield. The first General Secretary of the National Union of Mineworkers, Arthur Horner, plus his successor Will Paynter, were both Communist party members from the Rhondda mining community. South Wales was the main power base of Arthur James Cook, General Secretary of the NUM's forerunner, the Miners' Federation of Great Britain. It was he who led the miners during the traumatic national strike of 1926.

William Edward and his bridge at Pontypridd might have been unsung in his day but, by the time the twentieth century came to an end, the nature of news media had changed. This would enable worldwide transmission of the unique miner's takeover of Tower Colliery and illustrate that, in South Wales, not only socialist thinking but also the effort of individuals still had a role to play.

The industry's appalling safety record resulted in an everyday experience of death and human suffering within the closed communities, all in the service of capitalism and the social order of the day. The steady drip of accidents, many of them fatal, and the ongoing effects of dust related disease were punctuated by the occasional massacre of an underground explosion. This combined with the stark contrast between great fortunes made by certain individuals and the material lot of the miners, to spawn a concern for social justice that became endemic. Conflict between rapacious capitalism and a burgeoning labour movement was inevitable. Initial attempts to form miners' associations were matched by a determination on the part of the owners to smash them.

In 1869, the Amalgamated Association of Miners began in Lancashire. This was the first union to achieve any success in the fight for improved working conditions and a decent wage.

In 1873, in defence of the status quo, the South Wales Coalowners Association was formed, consisting of 85 companies owning 200 mines. This body built up a united front against the unions, opposing increases in miners' wages and trying to get more production out of the workers. Wages were by far the highest component of the coalowners' costs. Consequently their best method of increasing profit was to keep wages down as much as possible. A particular concern of South Wales coalowners was that output per collier there was significantly less than in other British coalfields. The men maintained that this was due to the difficult local conditions. For example, four times as many pit props were required for roof support here as in other coalfields. The owners on the other hand attributed the lower output to an attitude on the men's part of, "Sufficiency is enough". The men, so they said, were not prepared to maximize their output during the whole time that they were in work, presumably preferring to conserve their strength and reduce the pressure on older comrades. An ongoing drive for profit, combined with continuous haggling and argument over price lists, was the order of the day.

In 1875, a strike by the Amalgamated Association of Miners was resisted fiercely by the coalowners, who brought in strike breakers from Cornwall and the English Midlands. The result was bankruptcy and dissolution of the union. This led in that same year to a method of payment being introduced called the "sliding scale". It ruled out collective bargaining and tied wage levels to the seam concerned and the net selling price of coal which, depending on market forces, could slide up or down. Despite this set back, attempts to form unions persisted.

## Mabon.

In 1877, in the Rhondda Valley, the Cambrian Miners' Association was formed. It began its efforts under the inspired leadership of William Abraham (known by his Welsh Bardic name of "Mabon"). An impressive personality and a fine figure of a man, heavily built and with a full black beard, he was a renowned orator in both English and Welsh. Blessed with a fine tenor voice and a great supporter of Eisteddfodau, he had been known to re-establish discipline at a disorderly union meeting by cutting loose with a Welsh hymn. The other tenors, plus baritones and basses, would then join in with their own lines, all aggravation temporarily forgotten. He was to become a towering figure in serving the miners' cause and remained so for a full half-century. For thirty-five successive years, from 1885 onwards, he was to represent the Rhondda in parliament.

As vice-chairman of the joint Sliding Scale Association with the coal owners, Mabon was able to influence relationships between the two sides. The chairman of this Association was Sir William Lewis, "last of the industrial barons" and representative of "the old feudal spirit". Mutual respect between the two men was such that Lewis employed Mabon's eldest son as a clerk in his office. Bizarre as this may seem, Mabon had already witnessed the destruction of one trade union, the Amalgamated Association of Miners in 1875, and had no desire to repeat the experience. Determined to avoid conflict and maintain jobs, he vigorously supported the sliding scale. This policy of "identity of interest between master and man" was the policy of Mabon and it found resonance among the coal owners. This enabled miners' representatives to have a place in the councils of the powerful, albeit that their role was limited to the application of a fixed procedure. Such negotiation as there was occurred mainly at local level. Mabon was able to secure some concessions for his members, including modifications to the sliding scale and a holiday on the first Monday of every month, "Mabon's Monday".

Aided by relatively stable prices for coal and commodities at that time, the sliding scale gave South Wales 17 years of industrial peace, albeit peace with little more than a modest sufficiency for the average collier. It implied a permanent upper limit on remuneration and left their standard of living dependant upon the vagaries of supply and demand. Mabon might argue that, "Half a loaf is better than no bread" but more radical souls were now emerging. They argued for a minimum wage, irrespective of prices. The selling price of coal, and hence colliers wages, might well go down, but the cost of living not necessarily so.

Be that as it may, standards of living in the 1880's and 1890's did increase, and were attractive enough for the thousands of immigrants from rural Wales and elsewhere, who settled in the characteristic terraces rapidly filling the long, narrow valleys. Average earnings for South Wales miners in 1891 were 6 shillings six pence per shift. This was twice what agricultural workers in Glamorgan were being paid.

In 1889, the Miners Federation of Great Britain (MFGB) was formed, and their policy was a minimum wage. A bitter struggle developed between the young brigade, who wanted to scrap the sliding scale and join the MFGB and those, such as Mabon, who wanted to maintain the scale while forming a confederation of miners' trade unions. This was to be achieved by allying Mabon's Cambrian Miners Association with other similar associations already existing in South Wales.

In 1893 and 1898, strike action was taken when demands for increased wages clashed with a reduction in the price of coal. In both cases the military was brought in to intimidate the miners and in both cases the miners had to accept the owners' terms. The latter strike was particularly bitter and lasted six months before the miners were starved into total surrender, having to accept in addition the loss of "Mabon's Monday". By now even Mabon had become convinced that unity was strength, and that the days of the Sliding Scale and of district unions were numbered.

Following the 1898 defeat, the South Wales Miners' Federation (SWMF) was formed. The fight was taken up for a general minimum wage, as well as for an eight-hour working day. The older leadership still hoped to accomplish this by means of peaceful negotiation and conciliation. Although some progress was achieved, in the eyes of the younger activists this approach was outdated and inadequate. According to their assessment, class war, politics and use of the strike weapon was the only approach to which the employers were likely to respond in any meaningful way. Throughout the central area of the coalfield, particularly in the densely populated Rhondda Valley, these views gained in popularity.

In 1900, Keir Hardy, the first Member of Parliament for the fledgling Labour Party, was elected for Merthyr Tydfil.

By 1902, Lord Aberdare would write:

"The men are suspicious and believe that what is advantageous to the master must be injurious to the men —— the Aberdare collieries are worked at a cost nearly fifty percent above those in the north".

In spite of that, the quality of the coal, its high calorific value, kept demand high. These were boom times.

Between 1901 and 1911 South Wales absorbed immigrants at a faster relative rate than anywhere in the world apart from the USA: 129,000 people moved into the area.

Between 1908 and 1914 the Rhondda developed into the industrial relations storm centre of the coalfield. This became a characteristic that it would never lose. The increasing dominance of combinations among coal owners, and their vertical as well as horizontal integration, increased their power. This was seen as a threat and increased support for the younger union leaders. Mabon would face growing opposition from such men as Charles Stanton, miners' agent for Aberdare, who castigated:

"the faint-hearted, over-cautious, creeping, crawling, cowardly set who pose as leaders but do not lead (and) are responsible for the rotten condition of things today".

By now, socialist ideas had been firmly implanted into the mind of the younger South Wales miner. From their ranks attempts were made to dispose of the existing union leadership, broadly of the Liberal and Chapel school, who were associated with policies of conciliation and arbitration.


## Tonypandymonium.

Matters came to a head in the long and historic Cambrian strike, one of the bitterest conflicts in the history of coal industry industrial relations. This evolved into a complexity of issues, personalities and ideologies. At face value, in terms of the results achieved, the initial dispute that triggered the strike was not only a complete failure but a complete vindication of "Mabonism". However, the Cambrian conflict proved to have indirect results. These were both far-reaching and epoch making.

In 1909, there was a reduction in the working day from ten to eight hours, which tended to reduce both output and earnings. In an attempt to maintain both output and their profits, the owners put pressure on wages and on those workmen whose potential they regarded as being less than optimal. To a great extent, the collier was a hostage to fortune. If the roof was brittle and dangerous, if the section of coal thin and hard to work, even superhuman efforts would produce an output perhaps only one-third of that possible with a good roof and a thick section of easily worked coal. A man might have to toil in water, while the stone roof above thin coal seams had to be ripped away so as to make headroom for horses. This stone was then packed behind workings to support the roof where coal had been removed. Previously, if the collier's output and hence his wages were low due to such poor conditions, the colliery company would often pay an allowance to compensate. Concerned about the high wage bills in South Wales, the large coal combines now refused to pay such allowances. Matters came to a head at the Ely Pit in Pen-y-Graig, Central Rhondda. On developing the Bute seam the Cambrian Combine offered a price list of 1 shilling and nine pence per ton to the men. They in turn wanted two shillings and six pence per ton, stating that it was a particularly bad seam.

On 1 September 1910 the owners of the Cambrian Combine locked out, not only the 80 colliers who were in dispute with them, but all of the 880 or so men employed at the colliery.

In October 1910, the men rejected a compromise negotiated by Mabon.

On 1 November 1910, after a coalfield wide ballot, the South Wales Miners' Federation decided against a coalfield wide strike. Instead they called out on strike all of the 12,000 men employed by the Cambrian Combine, promising financial support. This was the first occasion that all collieries belonging to a particular owner had been specifically targeted. Since the Cambrian Combine was not just any owner but the apotheosis of the movement towards owner combination the gauntlet had therefore been thrown down. Its boss was the fighting D.A. Thomas, the man who later became Viscount Rhondda. This owner's combination was now up against the outstanding example of workers combination at that time. Mabon was becoming effectively sidetracked as Noah Ablett and the other hot-eyed socialists badgered and manovered the SWMF into an eyeball-to-eyeball confrontation with the "capitalist monster".

To nip such insubordination in the bud, the Monmouthshire and South Wales Coal Owners Association agreed to indemnify the Cambrian Combine against any losses incurred during the strike and not to employ the strikers in any of their pits. The capitalist version of combination and progressiveness, and the socialist version of the same, glared at each other in the form of repression versus revolt. When the owners used imported blackleg labour, under police protection, to keep the pumps and ventilation going at the Glamorgan Colliery, Llwynypia, matters came to a head. Incensed strikers determined to get into the powerhouse and stop the pumps. Thus started the "Ton-y-Pandy riots", the most memorable civil disturbances in Great Britain since the struggles for human rights in the early nineteenth century. The mid-Rhondda Fawr would see riots of a scale not seen in Wales since the Chartists were crushed at Newport in 1839.

During the night of 7 November 1910, around the powerhouse of the Glamorgan colliery, stone throwing began. Windows shattered, while strikers began to tear up the wooden fence around the colliery. The police had occupied the building and now, out of the shadows, they formed up to counter the threat. In the background and in command was the equestrian figure of Chief Constable Lindsay of Glamorgan. Boots clattered and commands were shouted as the ranks assembled. In a powerful, motionless, threatening silence the police stood stock still while the strikers girded themselves for a charge, but the police charged first.

Broad-shouldered and burly, their initial advance was slow, with mechanical precision; their domed helmets making them look gigantic. Then, after closing with their opponents, they leaped at the strikers with dervish yells. Truncheons on one side and pick handles on the other evoked their tribute and considerable casualties resulted. Eighty policemen were injured, with the number of casualties among the strikers being unknown. Such baton charges were to become a feature of the dispute, with one man, Samuel Rays, being killed by a police beating.

The rioters were pushed back to the nearby Ton-y-Pandy Square. Here during the following day, in the narrow confines in and around the square, mayhem continued as police and strikers continued to fight it out. There were further baton charges. Some mounted police were dislodged and beaten on the ground as sharpened broom handles were plunged into the horses' sides. Windows were smashed and shops looted, where traders were thought to have sympathised with the authorities. Notably left undamaged was the chemist shop of Willie Llewellyn. He had played as winger for the Welsh rugby team during their victory in 1905 over the All Blacks.

In response to highly agitated reports from Chief Constable Lindsay, in addition to 1,500 police rein-forcements from Cardiff, Swansea, Bristol and London Winston Churchill, then Home Secretary, dis-patched 200 cavalry plus two companies of infantry to the area, all units being furnished with live ammu-nition. General Nevil Macready, later a Commander-in Chief in Ireland during the IRA campaign for independence, was placed in overall command of these forces. The military was ordered to delay their arrival by several days, to allow the police to restore order first, if that was at all possible. The infantry was held at Swindon and the cavalry at Cardiff. The central station at Cardiff resembled a military headquar-ters in miniature as General Macready and his staff took over the stationmaster's office.

The presence of the military on the streets was a provocation, and was to cause great bitterness, but the situation stabilised. In the event, Winston Churchill was able to report to the House of Commons that order had been restored, "without recourse to the lethal weapons which the troops possess". He would never be forgiven by the Rhondda for the implication that difficulty in establishing order would indeed have en-tailed such recourse. As late as 1978, when Churchill's grandson asked about miners' pay in the House of Commons, James Callaghan, then Prime Minister, hoped that, "Mr. Churchill will not pursue the vendetta of his family against the miners of Ton-y-Pandy for a third generation".

In a subsequent report, General Macready queried whether the situation had really been so desperate, for which opinion he was castigated in certain sections of the press. They objected to his querying of Chief Constable Lindsay's judgement. The latter had been the man on the spot. In those days of unapologetic class distinction, officialdom was much influenced by the coal owners. Lindsay had evicted the pickets, turned the powerhouse into a police fortress, and had been the mounted "Roman Centurion" behind the frightening blue phalanx.

On 26 November 1910, rioting again occurred, in the manner that was to typify the disturbances. From a meeting at the Mid-Rhondda field in Ton-y-Pandy, some thousands of men marched to Pen-y-Graig, as a protest against "blacklegs" being employed at some of the Cambrian Combine collieries. On arrival at Williamstown the men were cheered by local women but were blocked at the gates of Ely Colliery. The police had received prior warning and were concentrated here in strength. An attempt to rush the police cordon and make an opening was frustrated. The situation remained tense as, in the vicinity of Saron Chapel, angry men distributed themselves among vantage points on the hills overlooking the colliery. The spark that would initiate further conflict was not long in coming. As one of the "blacklegs" working at the colliery wished to cross Penrhiwfer Bridge, his escort of policemen found themselves involved in an ambush. Men and boys, who had been in hiding behind some buildings, commenced a fierce onslaught with stones. As the constables retreated the assailants left their position, following up their advantage. Some of the rioters were armed with pick handles, while women replenished the stock of missiles with stones carried in their aprons. Eighteen police were injured. A series of baton charges were then made, resulting eventually in the streets being cleared.

The situation was stabilised when a squad of Somerset Light Infantry, under a Captain Paterson, was brought up from Pontypridd. They marched to the crest of a hill above the colliery, complete with fixed bayonets and live ammunition. According to newspaper reports, this seems to have had a deterring effect upon the malcontents.

The tumult continued, with further incidents at Clydach Vale, Blaenclydach, Ton-y-Pandy and Pen-y-Graig. As the strikers developed their tactics, phalanxes of police in the main streets were subject to flank attacks from groups of marauding stone throwers in the connecting side streets. They knew the layout of the back lanes better than the truncheon-wielding bobbies who counter-attacked, straining up the, to them, alien gradients. Incidents occurred where incensed policemen chased fleeing strikers into the terraced houses. There were many arrests and Will John, chairman of the Cambrian strike committee, was singled out for a severe sentence at the Glamorgan Assizes.

Leonard Llewellyn, General Manager of the Cambrian Combine, had left three hundred pit ponies un-derground, instead of bringing them up for strike-time grazing on the mountains. Great public sympathy was evoked for these animals, allegedly abandoned by the men. Repeated enquiries by George III as to their welfare added to the newspaper concern. The strike continued amid a welter of discussions, leaflets, manifestoes, pamphlets and newspapers.

On 25 March 1911 a ballot of the strikers rejected a return to work by 6,041 votes to 309.

On 16 June 1911, the Cambrian Strike Manifesto was issued and indicates the growth of the dispute, as seen by many on the strikers' side, into a crusade against the capitalist system:

"Through all the long dark night of years,
The people's cry ascendeth,
And earth is wet with blood and tears
But our meek suffering endeth.
The few shall not forever sway
The many toil in sorrow.
The powers of hell are strong today
Our kingdom comes tomorrow.

Fellow workers, we need your support in this strenuous struggle and the support of every man and woman who is prepared to make his or her sacrifice to put an end to Capitalistic despotism and to do battle for the cause of industrial freedom".

In his volume, "The Good Patch", H.W.J.Edwards was later to refer to, "Tonypandy's little war, which so unjustly gave Tonypandy the name of Tonypandymonium". He went on, "Rhondda (became) a byword for red politics". Influence of the Cambrian Strike Committee on the South Wales Miners' Federation increased. This effectively condemned to failure all attempts at compromise, by both the SWMF and the Miners' Federation of Great Britain. Indeed, Rhondda members of the Executive proceeded to up the anti. By mid-1911, the SWMF were demanding, not just appropriate wage rates in the Bute seam at the Ely colliery, but a general minimum wage, first in abnormal conditions and later to be extended to every colliery workman in South Wales.

On 12 June 1911 a meeting of South Wales delegates called for the MFGB to declare a general stoppage, with the object of securing a minimum wage. Failing this national action, the SWMF should itself declare a stoppage in its own area to secure this end. A rift developed between South Wales and the MFGB, since the latter still regarded the dispute as a purely local affair. In its June 1912 meeting it decided to "accept no further responsibility in this dispute". The resolution on the minimum wage was ruled out of order and its weekly contribution of 3,000 pounds towards the strike was terminated. This did not alter the determination of the Cambrian workmen. The strike continued.

On 25 July 1911 the last riot occurred, when 37 policemen were injured.

By the end of August 1911, the tenth month of the strike, strike pay was reduced again. Men and their families were becoming hungry and desperate. Eventually, intense suffering throughout the mid-Rhondda area forced the men back to work on the terms negotiated by Mabon the previous October, before the strike began.

On 1 September 1911, the pits restarted and were back in full production by October. Of the strikers, 3,000 were not re-employed. These events became part of the folklore of Rhondda life, emotional scars remaining until the final end of the mining industry there.

**The Radicals Take-Over.**

As a postscript to the strike, the three South Wales officials on the Executive of the MFGB were all voted out and replaced by younger socialists. Practically one-third of the miners in South Wales were from the militant Rhondda districts. The influence of the Cambrian lodges resulted in acceptance of their policies by the SWMF This body was in turn the largest constituent unit of the MFGB.

Mabon, seeing which way the wind was blowing, retired on grounds of ill health. For decades he had dominated South Wales mining unionism and this was the end of an era. When he eventually died, it was with more capital and directorships than his former trade union colleagues found acceptable.

On 11 October 1911, the principle of an individual minimum wage for all miners became the official demand of the MFGB.

On 1 March 1912, negotiation having failed, the first national strike of British miners began. The Liberal government was forced to intervene and on 19 March the Minimum Wage Bill was introduced in Parliament. Agitation in the Rhondda Valleys during the Cambrian strike had come to fruition.

In 1912, a grouping called the Unofficial Reform Committee produced a pamphlet called "The Miners' Next Step". Its authors had been intimately involved in the mid-Rhondda disturbances of 1910-11 and were dissatisfied with both the leadership style and the organization of the SWMF. Advocated was not only a minimum wage of eight shillings for a seven-hour day but also industrial democracy, with workers' control and ultimately ownership of the mines. In the section on policy, the pamphlet said, among other things:

I)      The old policy of identity of interest between employers and ourselves be abolished, and a policy of open hostility be installed ——

XII)    That a continued agitation be carried on in favour of increasing the minimum wage and shortening the hours of work, until we have extracted the whole of the employers' profits ——

XIX)    That our objective be to build up an organization that will ultimately take over the mining industry and carry it on in the interest of the workers.

These "syndicalist" activists argued that the British economy depended upon coal. Without it there could be no production, no exports, no navy and hence no great power status. Parliamentary activity created leaders, but inevitably separated these from the people they were supposed to represent. What was needed was a union focused on the reality of its own power. This would be achieved by the replacement of district organizations with a single South Walian executive, consisting of twenty-four elected members. There was of course a paradox here. To increase grass roots power, power had to be taken away from the grass roots.

Also advocated was adoption of the "irritation strike" (i.e. taking steps to reduce production while remaining at work). This method was held to be more effective than a conventional strike since, for minimum loss on the part of the workforce, it would eventually ensure the ruin and liquidation of the employers. These revolutionary proposals were widely discussed in South Wales and became well known to miners throughout Great Britain. Ultimately though, although the essential reforms of the SWMF which it proposed were carried out, the grander aims enunciated came to nothing.

In 1913, a continuing series of great mining disasters culminated in the explosion at Senghennydd, when 439 men lost their lives. Such disasters further inflamed opinion among the men. Henceforward, driven primarily from the central area of the coalfield, the general impression would be that only industrial warfare was capable of wringing concessions from the coalowners.

## At the Zenith.

In 1913, at the end of a century characterised by the advance of steam power, production reached its all-time peak. Nationally, 287,430,000 tons were produced from 3,000 working pits in Great Britain. The same year also saw the South Wales peak of 56,830,072 tons, produced from 620 pits. The number of people employed in the UK mining industry at that time was 1,107,000. The largest empire in history, "the empire upon which the sun never sets", had been built and sustained by the growth and profits that they had helped to produce. South Wales's flourishing export trade supplied more than 10 per cent of the entire world market at that time. Cardiff, as the main shipping port of the main exporting coalfield, had all the ethos of economic dynamism that later the oil ports of the Persian Gulf were to acquire.

## THE ROAD DOWNHILL.

### The Great War.

The disaster of the Great War effectively killed off the export trade. This was critical for South Wales, which had been built up on exports to a considerable extent and was the main exporting coalfield in the UK. In 1913 for example, 35Mt were exported out of a total production of 57Mt. Although employment in the British coalfields increased to an all-time peak of 1,250,000 in 1923, by then the business was already on the slide. Since that time, coal in Britain has undergone an uninterrupted period of decline.

The Great War and its consequences were to dominate industrial life in the South Wales coalfield for the next twenty-five years, with industrial relations being poisoned even further. A small minority group, largely members of the Unofficial Reform Movement of South Wales (who had produced the pamphlet "The Miners Next Step"), vehemently opposed the war. The war itself produced a great demand for coal. Munitions factories, foundries, iron, steel and tinplate works, all required more energy. The Admiralty increased its purchasing of South Wales steam coal from 1,5 Mt annually in peacetime to 15 Mt.

The Royal Navy needed coal but, due to the manpower requirement of the forces, there was a shortage of miners to produce it. This resulted in a strong bargaining position for the latter. There was a sharp rise in the price of food and a general awareness that, due to the demand for South Wales coal, the coalowners were making record profits. Traditional markets on the continent had been closed to South Wales coal but war industries, and in particular the Admiralty, were absorbing all that could be produced. Companies were charging up to 50 per cent more for coal since the outbreak of war and high dividends were being paid. During the six years up to 1914, the average annual profit of Lewis Merthyr Collieries was 98,000 pounds. In the interim annual report at war's end, profits of 418,807 were declared. In addition, financial reserves had increased by 220,000 pounds.

In July 1915, the coalowners' refusal of a new wage agreement resulted in a strike by 200,000 South Wales miners. Only this coalfield was involved, but without Welsh steam coal the Royal Navy could not sail. The press, the Government, and even the Miners Federation of Great Britain opposed the strike. A storm of chauvinistic abuse descended on the Welsh miners, with the suggestion being widespread that German agents were manipulating them. The Daily Express published a poem entitled, "The Kaiser's own Black Guards":

> "They've captured England's coal supplies.
> The life-blood of her fleet.
> They'll stop her works and factories.
> Their triumph is complete.
> They're better friends to me than my own Guards will ever prove.
> For all my vast battalions could not make so fine a move.
> As their occupation makes them black I'll show them my regards.
> By giving them the title of,
> "The Kaiser's own Black Guards".

The Government declared striking unlawful but their threat to imprison strikers was brought to nought by solidarity among the men. How could a workforce of over 200,000 be locked up? The Minister of Munitions, the Welshman David Lloyd George, settled the strike on the Government's behalf, granting most of the SWMF's demands.

In 1916, to ensure security of supply following continuing disputes, the government took over control of the South Wales coalfield.

In February 1917 the whole of Britain's coal industry was brought under government control. The Board of Trade regulated on a national basis output, distribution, prices, recruitment, wages, labour conditions and hours of work. There was however no control of profits, which continued to remain high during the period of state control.

In 1919, a Royal Commission into the coal industry was set up, under the chairmanship of Mr. Justice Sankey. This issued a number of recommendations, one of which was that coal and other important industries should remain under government control.

## False Dawn.

With the war's end came expectation that the previous expansion would simply continue. There was indeed a short-term boom, resulting from the re-start of industry at home and abroad, together with the temporary elimination of the French and German coalfields. The bubble then burst.

In December 1920 the export price of South Wales coal slumped from 80 to 40 shillings per ton. The profit of Lewis Merthyr Collieries in that year was 1,197,693 pounds. By the following year it had fallen to 150,027 pounds.

By February 1921, each ton of coal produced in South Wales was losing on average 18 shillings and 1.5 pence.

In March 1921 the Government relieved itself of responsibility for the industry, which was suddenly handed back to the owners with no provision for radical reform and against a recommendation of the Sankey Royal Commission. The owners' attitude to this recommendation had been that if they were not to be left in complete executive control then they would decline to accept responsibility for carrying on the industry. Thus, if the miners were given any effective say in affairs, the coalowners would decline to co-operate. Either that or the proposed miners share in control would be ineffective and a mere sham. Failure to accept the Sankey recommendation was regarded as a betrayal by the miners, whose lot was now to be significantly worsened by the world economic situation. The shaky foundation of the South Wales economy was to be brutally exposed. With its export orientation the coalfield was particularly sensitive to global economics. In the meantime other mining industries had developed, in the USA, India and Japan. These were more local to some of the traditional nineteenth century markets. Consequently these, in North America, South Asia, plus the Middle and Far East, had already shrunk. Now in addition, the reparations policy of the Versailles treaty, requiring that Germany "atone for its sins" by the provision of subsidized coal exports, had a devastating effect. In particular, such reparations to Belgium, plus France and Italy, cancelled important markets. On top of everything, South Wales coal remained more expensive than that from other British coalfields, as the following figures for 1921 show:

| Coalfield | Price per Ton |
| --- | --- |
| Yorkshire | 18/3d |
| Durham | 19/10d |
| Scotland | 20/9d |
| South Wales | 23/9d |

## Lock-Out.

In the 1920's wages comprised typically 71 per cent of the industry's total costs. The coalowners were faced with declining markets, plus world prices out of all proportion to the cost of production. Believing that under Government control wages had increased too much anyway, their reaction was to decide upon a series of drastic wage cuts. Those who refused to accept them were locked out.

From April to June 1921, there was a national coalfield stoppage. On 15 April, "Black Friday", railway-men and other transport workers withdrew their support and opted for conciliation. Under emergency powers, introduced during the Great War on a temporary basis but since extended, troops were sent into mining districts to restore order. The strike ended in a miners' defeat and a reversion to district wage bargaining. Wages were slashed; price-lists were cut; privileges were taken away; victimisation became rife; some pits never reopened.

By this time, four groups of allied companies controlled approximately three-quarters of the total output of the South Wales Coalfield. The tendency of coalowners to form combinations was already there prior to the First World War. It had increased since. In his book "The Condition of the Working Class in Britain", written in 1933, the Communist writer Allen Hunt said, "to journey in South Wales is not to journey from one county or one valley to the next but to travel from territory to territory of one or another of these combines". This process would continue.

## Past the Prime.

Of the 25 pits left in the Rhondda upon nationalisation, 14 were owned by Powell Duffryn and 8 by the Ocean Coal Company. The rational for such amalgamation was ostensibly more economic operation, due to better working methods and concentration of output. There was indeed a concentration on medium size mines (250-1,499 men employed), to the cost of both smaller and larger units. If larger collieries did remain open, manpower was slashed to medium size levels. This applied particularly to the large complexes of the Rhondda Valleys. For example, before the First World War, the Cambrian colliery at Clydach Vale employed 4,505 men, the Glamorgan Colliery at Llwynypia 3,307, while Ferndale Collieries Ltd. had 3,261 men at Ferndale plus 3,193 at Tylorstown. All of these figures were slashed.

While manpower was reduced, of modern mining methods there was little to be seen. There was some progress in the introduction of pneumatic picks and in the use of conveyors, both at the coalface and in its immediate vicinity. These replaced the horse-drawn, 30 cwt "drams" in this area. Previously, if the height was not adequate for horses and drams, the "boy", working as an assistant while being trained and paid pocket money by the collier, would drag the coal in a metal container to a point where it could be loaded. Nevertheless, by 1938 only 26 per cent of South Wales coalfaces were undercut by machine, compared with a British average of 59 per cent.

It was not just the fact that machinery was less flexible than manpower in the highly faulted strata. The low-wage, hire-and-fire economy of the time, plus the unpredictable nature of the export market, argued for the employment of an extra pair of hands, rather than to make a substantial investment in coal-cutting machinery. The mines themselves had been laid out so as to provide quick profits in the 1880's and 1890's, not for high efficiency under the intensively competitive conditions of the 1920's and 30's. During the First World War the rush to keep supplies flowing further denuded the more accessible, richer seams. To enable more difficult seams to be worked there was a crying need for investment. What actually happened was that men were laid off and less productive collieries ruthlessly closed down, with consequent dereliction. Social conscience, such as landscaping of the derelict sites, did not belong to the "zeitgeist" of the time.

In 1923-24, the industry experienced a fortuitous revival, when collieries once again worked full time. This was due to a prolonged coal strike in the USA, combined with the French occupation of the Ruhr. This abruptly stopped competition from that important coalfield.

Towards the end of 1924 however, this temporary industrial boom collapsed. Then began for the valleys a period of unremitting depression, persisting until the outbreak of the Second Word War in 1939.

In 1925, there was a return to the gold standard. This increased the value of the pound, making exports more expensive and compounding the problem of the Versailles reparations policy. Some countries, such as Poland and Germany, subsidised their exports so as to obtain foreign currency. The USA replaced South Wales as a supplier to South America, while other former customer nations were developing their own fuel resources. Between the two world wars, expansion of coal mining capacity worldwide outstripped the product's demand. In order to reduce the glut of steam coal, many mines were closed. Included among these was the Universal Colliery at Senghennydd, notorious for the 1913 disaster. The mine had been acquired in 1928 by the Powell Duffryn Mining conglomerate, which then promptly shut it down.

In contrast to the decline at home, much of the foreign expansion was more mechanised and rationally laid out than in South Wales. As an example, the Zollverein Colliery at Essen in the Ruhr became operational in 1932 and was hailed as a "wonder of rationalisation". Equipped with the most modern technology available to heavy industry at that time it yielded an output of 12,000 tonnes per day, four times the production of the largest contemporary collieries. Until its closure in December 1986 it was to remain Europe's leading producer of coal. The Bauhaus architectural movement inspired its surface layout and it is now an UNESCO cultural heritage site. Such large-scale planning, which characterised the development of many continental coalfields, was hindered by the multiple and divided ownership of the old-established British coalfields.

In addition there was competition from alternative fuels, in particular the substitution of oil for coal in the world's shipping. After the First World War the Admiralty switched completely to oil and by 1930 its order of coal was down to 182,000t, an eighth of its pre-war level. The proportion of coal-powered shipping worldwide fell, from nearly 90 per cent in 1913 to under 55 per cent in 1932. Greater efficiencies were also being made in the use of fuel. All of this sounded the death knell for the economic "Golden Age" of South Wales coal. What stood out was the high cost of production and low productivity in that coalfield compared with its competitors.

## General Strike.

In July 1925, determined to improve the fortunes of the industry as they saw it by reducing the price of coal, the coalowners terminated current wage contracts and required wage reductions, combined with an extra hour on the working day. The miners refused, resulting in further government intervention. While the Government paid the owners a subsidy to offset the losses they claimed they were making, a Royal Commission met to enquire into the running of the industry.

In 1926 the Commission reported that the coal industry was badly in need of reorganisation. Once this was carried out, it believed that the miners should accept some wage cuts. The coalowners insisted on large and immediate wage cuts while the Miners' Federation of Great Britain, under the leadership of the Welsh miner Arthur James Cook, fought these proposals under the slogan, "Not an hour on the day, not a penny off the pay".

On 30 April 1926, miners who refused to accept the owners' terms were locked out and the King signed a proclamation declaring Britain to be in a "state of emergency".

Between 1 - 9 May, 1926, the miners were joined by all other unions in the country, who supported them in the first and only general strike that the United Kingdom has ever known. The government and their supporters sensed an extremely radical situation and their propaganda spoke of a "red revolution". It was less than ten years since the communists had taken over Russia and shaken the world.

After nine days, the nerve of the Trade Union Council broke. They had only been playing at industrial brinkmanship, full-scale revolution was not on the agenda. They called off the general strike, arguing that the Government now wanted to negotiate a settlement to the dispute. Angry at what they considered a betrayal, the miners fought on alone. After a further six months, as with all of the previous major confrontations, the miners were eventually starved into surrender.

By Monday, 29 November 1926, work had been resumed in all of the important coalfields except South Wales, Yorkshire and Durham. Within days these had also returned. Never, in the history of British or other trade unions, had there been such a struggle.

On 13th December 1926, the Conciliation Board Agreement was dictated by the South Wales coalowners to the beaten men. There was no mercy shown in victory. Wages were drastically reduced and the working day was extended to the pre-First World War duration. Ruthless victimisation by the employers when pits re-opened stoked the fires of hatred, with results that would be felt for decades to come. Non-unionism became rife and encouraged by owners. Alternative, employer friendly unions were founded. Accompanying all the misery to come there was to be an ongoing struggle between the South Wales Miners' Federation and company unions. This reached its height in 1934 and was to plague the South Wales Miners' Federation until the extinction of such alternative unions, shortly before the Second World War.

## Depression.

Many mines did not re-open and South Wales became an acutely depressed area. The lack of any forward planning and the laissez-faire concentration upon a mono-economic structure, based upon coal alone, had come home to roost. To exacerbate the region's woes came the worldwide economic collapse of the late 1920's and 1930's, combined with additional loss of markets resulting from the 1926 struggle. Particularly in the central area of the coalfield there was an absence of alternative employment, such as agriculture or other industries. Here the "soup kitchens" became etched in popular memory.

In 1927 the first "hunger march" against unemployment left South Wales for London. The number of miners employed in Rhondda collieries alone fell from 39,177 in July 1927 to 19,873 in July 1936. The Rhondda Valley, or "Heartbreak Valley" as it became known, had reached its population peak of 169,000, in 1924. Between 1921 and 1931 it suffered a decline in population of 13.1 per cent. By the time the next census was held, in 1951, the population had decreased by an additional 23 per cent.

In these years of depression the anthracite area, in the west of the coalfield, faired much better than the rest of South Wales. During this period, demand for anthracite coal for use in central heating systems was growing and here were to be found some of the finest reserves in the world. Production rose from 3,199,330 tons in 1921 to a peak of 6,133,934 tons in 1934. For the rest of the coalfield however, deep depression was the ongoing tone. During his visit to the valleys Edward VIII made his famous remark "Something must be done", but nothing effective ever was.

In 1938, Government increased their involvement in the industry by nationalising mining royalties. Henceforward the owners would receive, instead of profits, agreed compensation from the Government

In September 1939, it was the outbreak of the Second World War that finally provided effective economic relief. Unemployment was reduced as munitions factories were set up in Hirwaen, Bridgend and Treforest. Energy production was essential to the war effort and mining became a reserved occupation.

In May 1941, the Essential Works Order prohibited a man from leaving his work without permission from the National Services Officer.

In 1942, as in 1917, the government once again assumed complete control over the coal industry. In their white paper the government stated "the organization now to be established will continue pending a final decision by parliament on the future of the industry". Whatever that decision might be, unlike after the First World War there was to be no precipitate return of the industry to the coalowners and traditional methods of working. However, decline of the industry in South Wales was not halted by wartime demand. Exports were again virtually wiped out. In particular the fall of France was the cause of some additional pit closures.

Between 1938 and 1944, the number of Welsh miners fell from 136,000 to 112,000. In the same period, output dropped from 35.3 Mt to 22.4 Mt, a decline regarded as excessive.

From 1944 on, so-called "Bevin Boys" were recruited, after the Minister of Labour Ernest Bevin. They were meant to make up the shortage resulting from so many miners having left the industry for the forces and war-related industries. In the same year the National Union of Mineworkers was formed, replacing the local miners' federations. World war or not, 80,000 miners went on strike nationally. The belief was still abroad that only militancy could bring improvement. As the post-war world approached, burdens of the past hung heavy. In the country as a whole there was a feeling that the old social system had not only failed but was fundamentally unjust. Radical change was called for.

In the 1945 general election this feeling expressed itself in a landslide victory for the Labour Party. It swept into opposition the Conservative Party, and the towering figure of Winston Churchill, the wartime leader. The inheritance of the South Wales Coalfield as it entered this new phase in history was a bitter one. Visceral hatred of capitalism, particularly in the coalfield's militant centre, had been weaned over a century of conflict. The industry itself was technically out of date, with minimal mechanisation. The valleys were scarred with the detritus of an industrial rape. Profits had been torn out of the land. The installations of the past together with their industrial excrement, namely the great waste heaps, lay unwanted and untended. Littered between the pits that still functioned lay the corpses of economic defeat. Chimneystacks, cold and grimy, stuck their grubby fingers to the sky. Scattered around them lay desolation. Boiler houses with no boilers, workshops with no tools or workbenches, railway tracks with the sleepers lying rotting and useless, the rails themselves long since removed for scrap. The focal point was that epitome of the valleys, the twin pit headgears, solid, foursquare astride their shafts, gaping open but unused. The wheels at their apex stood unmoving, locked in rusty bearings with the ropes long removed, or hanging sluggishly redundant. Behind them the empty engine houses, with a cloying smell of axel grease still hanging in the air.

For the youngsters of the village these sites were an adventure playground. One could climb, hide, romp and imagine the industrial wreckage as being a castle to be conquered from a rival gang. One could throw bottles down the shafts and time the whistle, before the final echoing smash. These derelict ruins however had once been living, vibrant entities where men lived, laughed, died, suffered and strove. Each had had its own character, tradition, comradeship and personalities. For those who had worked there they formed a never to be forgotten chapter of their lives. Their names roll off the tongue like the battle honours of a regiment: Ynisfeio, Abergorki, Nantdyrys, The Scotch, Swamp Pit, and so on. Evocative names, behind which lie a wealth of stories, never to be told.

# Chapter 4

## BRAVE NEW WORLD

*"No longer are our shops open,*
*Groups of men just stand around,*
*Without work they're lost and idle,*
*In their pockets, not a pound".*
G. L. Davies, Llantrisant.

*"Utopia is tomorrow's reality".*
Victor Hugo.

During the course of the Second World War, the need for a rational and planned approach to the country's problems had become apparent. This was combined with an increasing awareness of the inequalities and injustices of pre-war society. Sections of the press, and the documentary film unit of the Ministry of Information, suggested that a better future lay in a more radical approach, namely state intervention and planning. A series of subjective and emotional documentaries were produced, in which a future, full of hope, was represented. This was a holy mountain, which if climbed, would eliminate the miseries endemic in current society. One such documentary; Wales-Green Hill, Black Mountain (1943) ends with a glance at the recent past:

"Remember the procession of old young men,
From dole queue to corner and back again,
Nothing in their pockets, nothing now to eat,
Lagging from slagheap to the pinched back street.
Remember the procession of old young men.
It shall never happen again".
Finally, with a Welsh choir in the background;
"Out of the huddle of slum and valley must come the clean broad roads and the clean white houses".

## THE BEVERIDGE REPORT.

In December 1942, the Beveridge report appeared. It laid down a blueprint for social insurance as part of Britain's post-war renaissance. It referred to five giant evils, which stood in the way of progress:

IDLENESS, WANT, DISEASE, SQUALOR and IGNORANCE were afflictions that hitherto had afflicted the mass of the population. Of these five giants, in Beverage's opinion the largest and fiercest was idleness. To slay these giants, the proposal was for a free health service, child allowances, and full (i.e. 90% or more) employment. This would be funded by the state and by industry. The Labour Party endorsed unequivocally the proposals. Over six hundred thousand copies of the report were sold and a contemporary opinion poll revealed that 86 per cent of the population was in favor of Beveridge's recommendations. Although the Labour Party would make the running, following the Second World War the Conservative Party would also take on board as basic policy the triple concepts of:

- Full employment.
- Welfare state.
- A mixed economy.

## PLANNING.

The people of the South Wales valleys had seen the true face of unrestricted "Capitalist Freedom". It had revealed itself as the freedom of the few to exploit the many; the freedom to build up one-dimensional societies based on a single product, with nothing in the pipeline to take up the slack when that product suffered recession or, inevitable with an extractive industry, became worked out. There had to be a better way. That way was planning. The war seemed to give ample evidence that the full potential of the nation's inventiveness could only be achieved through planning. Diligent planning had made a success of the massive combined operations, such as the invasion of Europe. If such concepts could only be applied to the economy! The result must surely be superior to the uncoordinated effort resulting from a multitude of small independent groups. Those who had won the war were entitled to more than just a chance in a lottery called life.

The war had shown that state initiative and enterprise could draw out what was latent within individuals, with the result being victory. Over and above this, when public ownership replaced the old private coal owner, strikes might well become a thing of the past. Differences of opinion could be settled in a civilised manner around a table, between men and management at every level. The future belonged to state initiated planning, expressed through corporatism - an extra parliamentary cooperation between entrepreneurs, combines and state bureaucracy.

## THE REID REPORT.

In September 1944 the government set up a Technical Advisory Committee into the coal mining industry (the Reid Committee). The industry's technical backwardness, and record of poisonous labour relations, stood in contrast with an obvious requirement for adequate and economic energy supplies in the post-war world. The committee consisted of six eminent mining engineers under the chairmanship of Sir Charles Reid. Its terms of reference were. "To examine the present technique of coal production from coalface to wagon and to advise what technical changes are necessary in order to bring the industry to a state of full technical efficiency".

### Malaise at Home.

In the spring of 1945 the committee reported its findings to the Ministry of Fuel and Power. The report made clear that the patient was in a highly diseased state. Only radical surgery, in the form of major technical and organisational innovation, was capable of bringing the industry into the modern world.

The committee also analysed the circumstances that had led to this state of affairs. The long individualistic tradition of coalowners, operating in a large number of small, self-contained units, did not encourage major and radical development. Managers were not encouraged to visit other countries. Other than that required for day-to-day supervision, technical staff were not employed. For decades prior to the Great War of 1914-18 there had been virtually no change in the technical operation of the industry. The legacy of this was a host of mines, not easy to reconstruct so as to meet current requirements.

Customs and practices had developed which were coalfield specific. On the personnel side, sons had traditionally followed fathers into mining; often there was little choice. The only training received was the experienced gained when working as a collier's assistant, often to a father or elder brother. The collier's trade was one of handcraft, with its own traditions and customs. The gradualness of the little change that had occurred, combined with fear of unemployment resulting from the industry's traumatic past, had produced an attitude where the introduction of machinery was regarded with misgiving, if not open hostility.

Before the introduction of machine mining, each collier had his own working place, in much the same way that an allotment holder has his own plot. He worked his plot in his own way, with little interference, and had to live on what he got out of it. His responsibilities included not only hewing the coal and loading it into trams but also separating it from rock, the erection of such timbering as was necessary to support the roof, plus the maintenance of his working place in a safe and orderly condition.

### Elsewhere they do it Better.

Reid and his committee made comparisons with foreign coalfields. In the UK, the fact that mineral rights were in private as opposed to state hands had often resulted in leaseholds and consequently working areas that were unduly small or awkwardly shaped, depending entirely on the configuration of the surface estate. In other European coalfields, governments had distributed such rights on a more logical basis. These other coalfields however were not regarded as having any intrinsic geological advantages. The USA however was a different matter. Here nature had conferred a number of significant blessings, namely:

- The depth of seam was seldom greater than 1200ft. (366m).

- The seams were usually level, of convenient thickness and free from geological faults.

- The coal was of good quality and generally free of rock and dirt.

- The roof of the seam was often sufficiently strong to stand without support for lengths of 25ft. (7.6m) or so.

- The floor of the seam was not liable to heave upwards.

- With certain exceptions, gas emission was low.

- Very little water was encountered.

- Spontaneous combustion of coal was rare.

In addition to the above, mechanisation was a state of mind. In a culture of the survival of the fittest, machinery installation was seen as a proper corrective where competition was impaired.

Leaning heavily on the layouts employed in the geologically similar European mines, the report proceeded to make a number of radical technical recommendations. It also emphasised that a pre-requisite for such radical change was the provision of an appropriate organisational structure. Coalfield or, at the very least, area responsibilities were envisaged. The advantages of such a concept would be:

- An integrated training scheme for the industry as a whole.

- Central workshops for the maintenance and repair of machinery, serving a whole group of mines.

- An optimum area wide pumping/ drainage concept, not limited to individual leased areas.

- It would no longer be necessary to sterilize valuable areas of coal, so as to form barriers between individual leased areas.

- Some existing leases could be worked to better advantage from another mine.

- Investment in surface plant and shafts could be more readily justified if the area of coal to be worked was decided on techno-economic grounds, and not just on the basis of who had bought up individual areas of coal.

## Conditions for Success.

Technical suggestions alone were however inadequate. In the report's final chapter, "The Conditions for Success", the committee make clear that the recommendations made could not be carried out with the industry organised as it was at that time. In the words of the report, "The employers as a body have been prepared neither to accept the principle of the survival of the fittest nor fully to abandon their traditional individualism. In relation to their own undertakings the short view has too often prevailed —— We have come to the conclusion that it is not enough to recommend technical changes which we believe to be fully practicable, when it is evident to us as mining engineers that they cannot be satisfactorily carried through by the industry organised as it is today ". The report goes on, "It is evident to us that it is not possible to provide for the soundest and most efficient development and working of an area unless the conflicting interests of the individual colliery companies working the area are merged together into one compact and uniformed command of manageable size, with full responsibility, financially and otherwise, for the development of the area. It is essential however that geological, geographical and other technical considerations should be the determining factors. An authority must be established which would have the duty of ensuring that the industry is merged into units of such sizes as would provide the maximum advantages of planned production, of stimulating the preparation and execution of the broad plans of reorganisation made by these units, and of conserving the coal resources of the country. The existence of such an authority, endowed by parliament with really effective powers for these purposes, is, we are satisfied, a cardinal necessity".

In other words, what was being proposed was the establishment of a wide-ranging and hierarchical structure, so as to create order out of chaos and to prioritise both management and investment needs.

In 1945, the newly elected Labour government had no doubts as to what form this authority should take. Their doctrine was public ownership of the pillars of the economy. In the figurative as well as the literal sense, it was to be "Power to the People".

## REGIONAL SURVEY.

In addition to the Technical Advisory Committee, which reported in 1945, the Ministry of Fuel and Power also initiated regional surveys, with the object of clarifying the state of each British coalfield. These regional surveys reported in 1946. As well as describing the current situation, they gave an assessment of coalfield reserves and made recommendations as to the future course of action.

### Current Situation.

The current situation in South Wales was highlighted as follows:

1.1)  At the outbreak of hostilities in 1939, the industry had still not recovered fully from the disorganising influences of the first Great War.

1.2)  The profit/ loss (+/-) per ton of coal in South Wales versus the UK average during the war and pre-war periods was given as below (in current pence):

   1930: In SW +2p versus +4p UK average.

   1933: In SW -2p versus +3p UK average.

   1936: In SW -1p versus +11p UK average.

   1937: In SW +5p versus +15p UK average.

   1939: In SW +11p versus +19p UK average.

   1944: In SW +12p versus +18p UK average.

1.3)  A striking feature of the coalfield was the very wide range of different types of coal mined. They varied from low volatile anthracite to high volatile gas coal. Eighty-five per cent of the British anthracite reserves were in South Wales.

1.4)  Weight for weight, the coals offered a higher calorific value than those mined in some of the other British coalfields.

1.5)  Inland sales of coal had remained largely constant, in the range 19-20Mt. In 1913, at the historical peak of both national and South Wales production, 22Mt had been sold inland. In 1944, 21Mt had been sold inland.

1.6)  However, as the premier exporting coalfield, South Wales had suffered heavily following the considerable reduction in this export trade. SW exports were typically 37 % of the UK total.

   In 1913 - 37 % of UK total.

   In 1919 - 50 % of UK total.

   In 1926 - 39 % of UK total.

   In 1938 - 37 % of UK total.

   Although the percentage of UK total exports remained high, in absolute terms exports and ships bunkers from South Wales declined as follows:

   In 1913 - 35Mt.

   In 1939 - 17Mt.

   In 1944 - 1.6Mt.

1.7)  In 1931 South Wales was overtaken by Yorkshire as the highest producing coalfield in the UK, with a production of 40.6Mt. South Wales output, as a percentage of total UK output, was as follows:

In 1900 - 17.5 %.

In 1913-24 - approx. 18-20 %.

In 1926-30 - approx. 18.5 %.

In 1937-39 - approx. 15.5 %.

In 1943-44 - approx. 12 %.

1.8) Of the 176 collieries in production, 46 were regarded as having an extended output potential, up to the year 2044 and beyond. In addition to this, two of the collieries that had been temporarily closed, and were capable of being reopened, were regarded as having a similar output potential.

1.9) So as to more easily reach the most important lower coal measures, collieries had been constructed on the valley floor.

1.10) The upper coal measures were limited in scope. They had been worked to a very small extent, mainly by means of a few small private levels into the side of the mountain.

1.11) At the coalfield's northern fringe, the so-called "North crop", the seams dip gently downward from the surface. This facilitates mining, particularly open cast and shallow drift mining. In the latter case, instead of shafts, the seams are reached by means of inclined tunnels, or "drifts", from the surface.

1.12) At the southern fringe, or "South crop", the seams rise steeply. This results in only a narrow area of surface coal. In addition, the steep inclination of the seams underground renders mining in this area difficult.

1.13) In Pembrokeshire, at the extreme west of the coalfield, the geological structure was exceedingly complicated, with intense folding of the strata.

1.14) Its long history notwithstanding, there were areas of the coalfield which were still undeveloped. Communications in these areas were inadequate. This applied particularly to the anthracite region of the west. Here there were small, mainly drift mines only. The proportion of face workers (38.16 per cent) was less than that for the coalfield as a whole (43.58 per cent). In 1944, the output per man-shift in this area was 13.34 cwt (0.68 tonnes), as opposed to 18.60 cwt (0.94 tonnes) in the coalfield as a whole.

1.15) The average annual output per mine in South Wales had remained static for some time, as shown below:

In 1920 - 180,000t

In 1930 - 209,000t

In 1938 - 209,200t

1.16) The number of people employed had declined as follows:

In 1900 - 147,652

In 1913 - 233,800

In 1920 - 271,516 (its all time peak value).

In 1930 - 172,991

In 1938 - 136,116

In 1944 - 112,337

1.17) The percentage of coal undercut by machine was considerably less than that for the country as a whole. This was attributed to the difficult geology of South Wales, plus the difficulty there of negotiating price lists for new methods. (Note that machine cutting at this stage meant undercutting the coal only, so as to make it easier to bring down by explosives or picks. Loading of the coal onto a face conveyor was done by shovel. Mechanical loading was a later development).

In 1930, coal undercut by machine = 10 % in SW (vs. 30 % as UK average).

In 1944, coal undercut by machine = 32 % in SW (vs. 72 % as UK average).

1.18)   Due cognisance was given to the objections made concerning colliery refuse tips. These arose as a result of their unsightly appearance and their tendency to spontaneous combustion.

**Reserves.**

On the subject of reserves, the report made the following points.

2.1)   The total amount of coal already extracted from South Wales amounted to approximately 3,000Mt.

2.2)   Within areas already leased to coalowners, reserves of workable coal were assessed as being 5,500Mt.

2.3)   Within areas not at present leased, workable reserves were estimated at 2,500-3,000Mt. These figures included substan- tial reserves within the thinner seams, 12in.-24in. (0.3-0.6m) thick.

2.4)   The report went on to state, "It can be confidently expected that the 1938 level of output (35Mt) can be maintained for a least a hundred years from the coalfield as a whole".

2.5)   The largest undeveloped areas were the South crop, Pembrokeshire and the Anthracite region of the west. Dealing with these in turn:

SOUTH CROP: Within this area resided some of the principal reserves of good quality gas and high volatile coking coal. The steeply inclined seams, however, and complex geological structures, which were imperfectly understood, presented considerable mining difficulties.

PEMBROKESHIRE, and also the seams beneath Carmarthen and Swansea Bays, were subject to extensive geological faulting. This area was unlikely to contain significant reserves of workable coal.

ANTHRACITE REGION: To date, seam access had been mainly via drifts working southward from the North crop. South of this was a relatively unexplored area. This appeared to possess a geological structure that would lend itself to the development of new collieries.

**Future Policy.**

Recommendations were made as to what future policy should be:

3.1)   "A substantial increase in the export trade is essential, not only for the purpose of ensuring the future prosperity of the industry in South Wales but also as an important factor in meeting the needs of the economic life of the nation. We suggest therefore that there should be close collabora- tion between all interests in the coal industry and the government in effecting national and interna- tional arrangements".

3.2)   "There is evidence that the increase in productivity achieved by mechanisation has been less in South Wales than in other areas. We feel that a considerable increase in the scale of mechanisation is essential if the efficiency of the industry is to be improved. This cannot be achieved by the installation of machines alone; the success of such a policy will finally depend upon good planning and the effective co-operation of all concerned, and the factors which retarded progress in the past must be overcome".

3.3)   "The application of coalfield machinery of the type and on the scale now envisaged will require the use of electricity instead of compressed air, which is the chief form of power used for coalface work in this coalfield".

3.4)   "The problem of underground water in the coalfield as a whole and especially in certain parts is one which must receive serious consideration as it not only affects the present working of coal- mines in the field but will have an increasingly prejudicial effect upon the safe and economical working of the remaining reserves of coal".

3.5)   Pumping and drainage accounted for 8 pounds and 37 pence per ton of coal sold. (This is a significant amount when compared with the figures given in item 1.2 above, for the overall profit/ loss per ton).

3.6)   The main cause of manpower wastage was pneumoconiosis. "We desire to emphasise the extreme urgency of this problem".

**East Midlands.**

As a contrast, the report on the East Midlands (Nottinghamshire) coalfield was much less characterised by the statistics of decline and technical backwardness. As the report indicates, this region
would in future prove to be the main centre of the British coal-mining industry.

4.1)     Although the western part of Nottinghamshire and North Derbyshire had been worked for more
         than 100 years, East Nottinghamshire had been developed much more recently.

4.2)     Some of the large, more easterly, pits only began to produce coal between the wars.

         For the region as a whole production had been holding up well, into the Second World War as the
         following figures for saleable output show:

         In 1930 - 32Mt.

         In 1935 - 29Mt.

         In 1937 - 34Mt.

         In 1939 - 34.7Mt.

         In 1942 - 38Mt.

         In 1944- 35.7Mt.

4.3)     To date, the market had been largely house coal for inland consumption. This was subject to fluc-
         tuating, i.e. seasonal, demand.

4.4)     Increased output was possible from the hitherto undeveloped eastern section of the coalfield.

4.5)     Alternatively, a 25 per cent increase in production could be achieved by the end of the century,
         simply by increasing manpower. A 50 per cent increase was well within the realm of possibility.

4.6)     The Eastern area was largely unexplored ("complete ignorance east of the proved area"). How-
         ever, the coalfield was very rich, with a considerable programme of exploration required to deter-
         mine the eastern limits.

4.7)     Unlike the South Wales report, which made prognostications of production up to the year 2044,
         that for the East Midlands regarded 2004 as being the extreme limit of the enquiry. Any forecast
         beyond this was regarded as being subject to too many unknowns.

4.8)     Nevertheless, the report stated, "A great share in the future of the coalmining industry in Britain
         must be borne by this region". Proven reserves to date were approximately 6,000Mt.


## CHANGE AT LAST.

At the end of the Second World War the crisis in the coal mining industry was probably more critical in
South Wales than anywhere else, particularly in the isolated, single-industry valleys. The region's economy
remained narrowly based, dominated by the traditional nineteenth-century industries of coal and steel.

Between 1937 and 1946, mining manpower in South Wales had declined from 135,901 to 107,624 and
production from 37,773,000 tons to 20,950,000 tons. The region faced the new post-war world with every
appearance of an ageing coalfield. Of the 300 or so collieries still in existence, only 176 were still in
production. All but one were over 25 years old. Many were small and unprofitable. Only 36 per cent of
production was cut by machine. On the personnel side, in spite of improvements in wages and conditions
during the war, it was difficult to recruit young men for a workforce still embittered as a result of its
treatment by the coalowners.


## Nationalisation.

In 1946 the Coal Nationalisation Act was passed. As far as the mineworkers themselves were concerned,
thus was realised one of their long-standing aspirations.

In his evidence given to the Royal Commission on the industry in 1919, James Winstone, President of the
SWMF, was one of those arguing in favour of nationalisation:

"Men would feel they had control or some control over their own energies, and they were not merely at the will and direction of another being. They would be in a better position than the horse which they have to drive or the machine that they have to attend. As I have said on a previous occasion, it is that desire that cannot be crushed that is making itself felt in the ranks of labour at the present time, and has given rise to more unrest than anything else".

In addition, Arthur Horner, the first General Secretary of the National Union of Mineworkers, had written:

"The aims we set ourselves many years before in The Miners Next Step were thus more imperative than ever after the 1926 strike. So I went back (to work) realising that we had to start a period of organisational rebuilding leading to the creation of one miners' union and the nationalisation of the mining industry".

The fulfilment of that other great aspiration of the mineworkers had already occurred in 1944 when the old, loose association of local miners' federations was replaced by the National Union of Mineworkers. The former concept had been a source of weakness, rivalry and disunity for the best part of a century. This radical shake up, of both the industry and its associated trade unionism, created a general atmosphere of euphoria among both officials and men. Arthur Horner did express some reservations. He thought that the union's constitution, as finally agreed to, emasculated its strength. There was still too much autonomy allowed for individual areas. Each of these continued to maintain a separate legal identity within an over-all federal structure. As a good communist he doubted the new Board's ability, or willingness, to resist the "pervasive erosion" of market forces. However, even he supported a policy of full cooperation, so as to ensure that the Labour Party's great nationalisation experiment should be given the maximum chance to succeed.

Management's attitude was rather more ambivalent. Philip Weekes, later to become Director of the South Wales Area of the National Coal Board was, in 1946-47, the young manager of Wyllie Colliery, belonging to the Tredegar Iron and Coal Company. Interviewed in 1981, he would describe the worries he had felt 35 years earlier when confronted with the impending prospect of nationalisation:

"I was quite convinced that on January 1 1947 I wouldn't really be a colliery manager and I'd have a revolutionary committee running the pit and I'd be a sort of professional advisor —— I wanted change desperately, I felt it was right, but I feared for my own position in the set-up. I didn't want a complete revolution. I wanted some evolution. I hadn't thought things through very clearly, but on balance I thought it was good".

William Cleaver, a young Rhondda Undermanager in 1947, was also ambivalent:

"I wasn't politically tied to it but industrially I was tied to it because I thought it was the only sensible solution". On the workers' side however there was no doubt and Cleaver went on to describe the first three months of nationalisation, January - March 1947, as being "one of the greatest sort of hwyl (Welsh: meaning high emotion) periods I've ever seen".

Vesting Day, 1 January 1947, was greeted in every pit with speeches and a sincere feeling that this was the dawn of a new era. The ceremony at Lady Windsor Colliery at Ynysybwl, near Pontypridd, was typical:

"To J.E. Morgan, as being the oldest workman present as well as the oldest local Federation official, was given the privilege of hoisting the flag of the National Board to symbolise the taking over of the colliery.

Before doing so he reminded the audience that 50 years previously nationalisation of the mines had been the dream of a few visionaries who were then considered cranks. However, today the vision had become a reality, fraught with tremendous possibilities for those engaged in the industry, and for the prosperity of the nation as a whole".

The hope was for the final demise of the old era, an era where men had come to feel treated as economic pawns rather than human beings worthy of respect. If nationalisation was meant to do anything it was to create an atmosphere in which workers were treated with the dignity they deserved. Management by fear was to be replaced with management by consent.

**Reality.**

Among the miners, a feeling of goodwill towards what was now their industry was to persist for some time, albeit diluted by reality and by some socialist frustration in their own ranks. It would not be possible to change the world at the flick of a switch. Inevitably, if slowly, the euphoria died down. There was bitterness about compensation to the former coalowners (assets of £375 M nationally, on which interest had to be paid), and about the level of interest paid by the industry on capital borrowed. Some NUM lodges complained that nationalisation should have included the lucrative coal distribution trade, as well as the manufacture of mining equipment. There were complaints that the industry was being overloaded with appointments. Later, Hugh Gaitskell, Minister of Power, would announce that the "honeymoon" in the mining industry was over while "NC bloody B" soon became a common expression within mining communities.

Management still managed, including many who put more trust in the stick rather than in the carrot. Of workers' control, as demanded in the revolutionary pamphlet of 1911, "The Miners' Next Step", there was no sign. Policy would be set at the centre. The technical backwardness of the coalfield lingered on, allowing the continuation of hard physical labour. Piecework remained the norm, allowing the continuation of pithead wrangling over money and price lists. This had been a monotonous feature of life before Vesting Day and the management face, with which one argued, remained the same.

Inevitably, those in possession of the relevant experience would run the industry. Inevitably, there were therefore clear elements of continuity, in management, policy and personnel. Also inevitably, senior management in such a large organization would play the game of office politics. The big winners were ex-Powell Duffryn men. There was some logic in this. This company had been premiere among the previous coal owners, being the largest coal company in Great Britain. They had dominated the eastern coalfield and had strong links, at directorship level, with the leading anthracite companies in the west. With the new imperative being to unite notoriously diverse and geographically isolated management and workforces, "PD men" seemed to secure a majority of the new plum positions, followed by the Ocean Coal Company. As a consequence, their influence continued, or even extended, octopus-like, across the coalfield.

By contrast, each Divisional Board chairman was chosen from outside the industry. Nevertheless, in South Wales, this appointment was received with an equal lack of enthusiasm. One of the post-war problems of Prime Minister Clement Attlee was what to do with senior ranks of the armed forces upon demobilisation. They certainly had experience in working within large, structured organizations. What they lacked, however, was experience in mining generally and in industrial relations particularly. Initially such lack of experience would loom large. Noticeable by its absence was also experience in marketing issues. This latter deficiency however would not come to the fore until a decade later. The NUM were quick to realise the deficiencies, as did the mining engineers in charge of the new organization.

Lieutenant General Sir Goodwin-Austin, as chairman of the new South Western Divisional Board, might have been a good military man. What he certainly was not was the type of candidate acceptable to anyone who had dreamt of nationalisation as being on the road to a future socialist utopia. When, during the autumn of 1946, all appointments were announced, there was some disquiet. In December of that year, prior to the initial honeymoon and in something of a lovers' spat, the South Wales Area Executive of the NUM declared its "no confidence" in Goodwin-Austin and in his deputy Aeron-Thomas. This latter gentleman was from a small company background in the anthracite region. The union declaration was reversed, following pressure from the NUM national leadership. Goodwin-Austin himself did nothing to allay the misgivings however when, at a Powell Duffryn Sports Committee dinner in April 1947, he showed crass insensitivity by deploring attacks on "some very fine masters in the coalfield before the Board came". This was at a time when the miners were still jubilating over the fact that the detested coalowners, finally and not before time, had been confined to the dustbin of history. As a final, stiff-upper-lip flourish regarded as patronising, the new Chairman was quoted as saying, "We are all butties now".

Will Paynter, later to succeed Arthur Horner as General Secretary of the NUM, would describe him as:

"Some kind of general who had spent all his time in the Himalayas climbing mountains. Either him or his son had a mountain named after him. He had no mining background and we all considered that he knew nothing about coalmining". As to T.S. Charlton, a Yorkshireman appointed as Production Director to the new Divisional Board, he was dismissed by Paynter as being "too lazy to spit"(except he didn't say "spit").

By the mid-1960's, over 50 per cent of the nation's capital investment was in government hands. Not only that, it was also vital investment, which in turn triggered off investment in other industries. However, "Great Britain Ltd." was far from operating like a well-oiled machine. The great combined operations of wartime, which had been such an inspiration, did not translate well into a peacetime environment, neither in terms of their military discipline, nor in terms of their lack of financial constraint. The treasury tendency is to hold back investment, since money borrowed is raised by taxation and all governments want to lower taxes rather than raise them. There was a reluctance to raise money directly from the city for nationalised projects.

People who ran the state enterprises at the top were appointed by their Minister under an Act of Parliament. These people were however subject to watching and controlling briefs, by Cabinet, by the Ministers themselves, and by a variety of civil servants. In practice Ministers rotated regularly, often after a period too short for them to be able to master their briefs. Civil servants also rotated, and were in a position where they could exercise influence without being called to public account for decisions made.

In the energy sector, the statutory function of the Ministry of Power was to exercise a co-ordinating role. Its internal organization, with a division for each fuel - coal, electricity, gas, nuclear and oil, rendered this task difficult. Each Division became just the mouthpiece of the respective industry, fighting its own corner.

Nominally, the various fuels had to compete on price. The mining industry however was to complain constantly that the cost of miners redundancy, of unemployment, attracting new industries, and the loss of capital investment in the pits shut down was never included in the total sum. Policies were made either on the assumption that the present situation would continue indefinitely (e.g. first the shortage of coal, then the era of cheap oil), or that money should be poured into new technology on the basis that, eventually, the day of the great pay- off would one day dawn (e.g. nuclear power). Effective and long-term financial control would fall victim to a "Flavour of the month" strategy.

## Goodwill

Nevertheless, in spite of all this, a new atmosphere was undeniable. There was a marked improvement in labour relations. This was the period of Arthur Horner's greatest influence. Life-long communist and one of the leading lights in the 1926 general strike and lockout in South Wales, now as first General Secretary of the NUM, he showed immense political skill in being able to co-operate with the National Coal Board while fully representing the interests of the union. Until his retirement in 1959, his creative inspiration and commitment helped sustain and support this major nationalisation project of the social democratic Labour Government. Will Paynter who succeeded him, and who served until 1968, was cast in the same mould. Local disputes there would be - but no national strike would occur until 1972.

Undeniably, there was a steady improvement in wages and conditions. Following Vesting Day the long-awaited five-day week was introduced. A training programme for new entrants was devised which set an example to the rest of British industry. By the early 1950's the British miner was at the top of the industrial wages league.

With 800,000 employees, almost 110,000 of them in South Wales, the NCB was now the largest employer in the country. The Reid Committee report, in addition to dealing with technical challenges, also drew attention to the debilitating effects of the labour relations then prevalent:

"The problem of securing full co-operation between the employers and the workmen is the most difficult task the industry has to face. Unless this problem is solved, the value of our technical recommendations will be greatly reduced". The report goes on, "We consider that certain rights to which we have suggested the mineworker is entitled must be balanced by a recognition by him of certain duties".

In 1951, the NUM again showed its early goodwill in helping the NCB through its most difficult, early years. It agreed to allow back into the industry all those with pneumoconiosis who satisfied two medical examinations. That this was judged necessary is an indication of the manpower shortage at the time, and of the ongoing demand for coal.

# Chapter 5
## MONEY, MONEY, MONEY

*"Class distinction had reared out its fat belly among*
*higher officials of the Coal Board, who wore wedding rings*
*and drank whisky and hoped to buy a drink*
*for the General manager"*
Menna Gallie, in "The Small Mine" (1962).

**THE PLAN.**

The 1945 report of the Technical Advisory Committee had ended with the clarion call:

"A great pioneering task awaits the employer and the mining engineer, which is nothing less than the rebuilding of the industry on the most modern lines".

The short-termism of the coalowners pre-war had combined with bad trade and short time working. In addition, the Second World War had resulted in other, higher priorities for public money. Exploitation of reserves was carried out purely according to the exigencies of the national emergency, at the cost of any long term planning. All this had combined to produce a crying need for investment. It was this, along with political and social principles, which had been the major rationale behind nationalization of the coalmining industry.

When peace finally dawned the industry was exhausted. Health and safety was inadequate. To improve the efficiency of production, mechanization and new methods of working had to be introduced. There was a need to open up new reserves. In a situation where for example underground roadways frequently had to take indirect routes, so as to avoid certain private estates on the surface, mine layout was far from being optimal. From now on, rationalisation would be the watchword. All of this required a level of capital investment far beyond what the individual colliery companies could generate. The technical situation now changed radically, with an incoming flood of capital resulting in a bonanza for mining engineers.

The Technical Advisory Committee had made the following recommendations with regard to Mines Layout, Production Techniques and Organization.

### Mines Layout:

- In new or re-modelled mines, locomotive haulage to be employed. For this, strategic roadways, straight and level and driven in the strata as opposed to following the seam, should be employed.

- The drivage of roadways should be mechanised.

- Trunk conveyor systems to replace rope haulages.

- Man-riding facilities to be installed, so as to minimise travelling time and maximise production time at the coalface.

- For inclined seams, the continental system of horizon mining should be adopted.

- Winding arrangements should be reviewed.

- Mechanical cleaning of all output, with the sizes of coal standardised and reduced to about six in number.

- A general reconstruction of surface plant to be undertaken at the majority of mines. The advice of an architect should be taken.

- There should be complete electrification of mines.

- The use of electricity underground should be extended. Standard voltages should be selected and lightweight switchgear for use at the coalface should be developed.

- There should be an improvement in underground lighting, especially at the coalface.

- Specialist ventilation officers should be appointed at mines.

## Production Techniques:

- There should be more mechanical cutting and loading of coal, with the development of associated roof support systems at the coalface.

- On longwall faces, scraper chain conveyors should be used.

- Due to the fact that it offers the highest output per manshift, room and pillar working should be used wherever possible. As a second choice, retreat longwall should be employed.

  (Note that subsequent developments in technology would result in longwall working being the most economic in today's world. Retreat working was proposed as long ago as 1870. It was very rarely used due to its requirement for a higher initial capital outlay than faces working on the advance, combined with an associated delay in reaching full production. It was 120 years after its initial proposal that this method of working became standard in South Wales).

## Organization:

- A thorough reorganisation of the industry, approaching the problems on a coalfield rather than on a mine-by-mine basis.

- Long-term planning by a full-time planning staff.

- Extension of the engineering function, with a planned maintenance programme, colliery and central workshops, plus the employment of qualified engineers having technical responsibility.

- A nation-wide training and education scheme covering all necessary practical and theoretical aspects. This should be associated with a career structure such as to attract young men of ability from all classes of society and from all parts of the country.

On Vesting Day, 1 January 1947, the South Western Division of the National Coal Board, with headquarters at Llanishen in Cardiff, came into existence. It was tasked with the Board's objectives for the South Wales coalfield, along with the two small coalfields of Somerset and the Forest of Dean. These latter two combined supplied only 5 per cent of the Division's output. The industry as a whole was organised into five echelons of management. Each of these had a line-and-staff concept, translated into management and technical specialists:

  i)   National board.

  ii)  Divisional boards (eight in total). These corresponded approximately to the main UK coalfields.

  iii) Areas (seven in the South Western Division).

  iv)  Groups (typically three or four collieries per Area).

  v)   The collieries themselves.

Areas in the SW Division were as follows:

Nos. 1 (Swansea), 2 (Maesteg), 3 (Rhondda), 4 (Aberdare), 5 (Rhymney), 6 (Monmouthshire), 7 (Somerset plus the Forest of Dean).

## POST WAR WORLD.

### The New Era.

In 1947, when the industry was taken into public ownership, 90 per cent of the nation's primary energy requirements were still being met by coal. With the exception of road, air and marine transportation, this fuel met all energy requirements, both industrial and domestic. The largest surviving pits (958 throughout the UK) were nationalised. Of these, 222 were in the South Western Division (of which 176 were still producing). Another 400 tiny ones throughout the UK, including more than 100 in South Wales, continued to operate privately under licence. Manpower nationally was down to 700,000 (103,000 in the South Western Division) from a peak of 1,250,000 in 1923. National production, from its high water mark of 300 Mt tonnes in 1913, was down to 200 Mt.

The cost of this takeover by the state was £375 M, as compensation to the former coalowners, and on which interest had to be paid. In addition, £260 M in loans were obtained, this being capital necessary to modernise the industry. The selling price of coal however was fixed low by the Government. This was intended to assist British industry although it did nothing to encourage the concept of energy economy.

The country generally was bankrupt and down at heel. The post-war world, with its need for economic growth and increased mechanisation, generated in Britain an increased energy demand. This demand the industry proved incapable of meeting, in spite of introducing Saturday morning working. There were periodic "energy crises" by which was meant the "coal gap", that is a shortfall in domestic production.

## Coal at Any Price.

Immediately upon nationalisation the fuel crisis reached its most acute point. The winter of 1947 proved to be one of the worst on record, with a long sustained blizzard hindering the whole country. Combined with the scarcity of fuel and power, industry was paralysed as a result. In the absence of any serious rivals, coal became a seller's market, with the miners being urged on to greater efforts. The country needed energy. The countries on the continent were shattered by war and also short of energy, with their own coal industries being in no position to meet the demand. There was political pressure to provide coal for export, but this could not be done without closing down some industry at home.

In the event, some coal was exported to the continent, but only at the expense of importing American and Polish coal soon afterwards at high prices. The cost of this was debited to the Coal Board, to the tune of £70 M over the years. As a result of all this, coalmining was viewed more as a public service than as a business. The return on investment was not even a subject for discussion. From the beginning of the Second World War in 1939 up to nationalisation in 1947, and then through to 1957 when competition first began to bite, the pressure on the coal industry was to get coal at any price - maximise output. The question of cost never arose. With coal in short supply and rationed the marketing department was in effect nothing other than a coal allocation department. It was not until the late 1950's that the industry really had to start selling its products, by which time the marketing art had long been forgotten, or at least had lay dormant, unused for about twenty years. On the government side the objective of minimising fuel shortage was pursued by measures taken to provide adequate manpower, plus the avoidance of price rises resulting from any undue increase in miners' wages.

During the 1940's and 50's, with the national economy effectively tied to a single fuel, policies were pursued to prevent alternative male employment from locating on the coalfields. As a secondary effect this meant that, before the closure programmes started cutting deep and the hedonism of the 1960's took root, the miners' lodge and its officials continued in their role as a source of leadership, authority and cohesion within the community. They stood alongside the minister of religion as a figure of respect although, in many cases, mutual respect between the representatives of "morally sterile Communism" and "religion as the opiate of the masses" could be somewhat circumscribed.

## INVESTMENT.

### Quality is the Key.

During the Second World War the government had set up the National Coal Charges Fund. An acute shortage of energy meant that production would have to be subsidised, even if pits were being worked at great loss. Under this arrangement every colliery made a financial contribution and was entitled to draw on it according to need.

In 1946 the South Wales coalfield paid £13 M into the fund and received almost £20 M, a subsidy from the more profitable coalfields of more than £6.6 M. The South Wales contribution to national production had increased from 19.7 per cent in 1913 to 20.5 per cent in 1918. It had then fallen back to 11.7 per cent in 1945. In spite of the subsidy, by 1955 it was still only 11 per cent.

This notwithstanding, upon nationalisation the coalfield was slated for one of the highest levels of capital investment for any coalfield in the country, in spite of the fact that its expected rise in production was one of the lowest. Investment in South Wales was far higher than its proportion of total UK production would suggest. With 16 per cent of the NCB employees, it was slated to receive 21 per cent of the national budget. The determining factor in this level of investment was the superb quality of South Wales coal. The coalfield has the largest reserves of the best coking coal in the UK, which was in extremely strong demand. In addition, it produces virtually all of the naturally smokeless fuels (low volatile steam coal, plus some of the finest anthracite). These would form an essential part in the movement towards clean air. Apart from a small deposit in Scotland, UK anthracite is confined to the extreme west of the South Wales coalfield, between the Vale of Neath and the Gwendraeth Valley. It was this unique quality and variety of South Wales coal that attracted the investment. Between 1948 and 1953, nearly £32 M were invested in the Cardiff region alone.

The coalfield was judged to have considerable reserves remaining, second only to Yorkshire in the coalfields of the UK. The Ministry of Fuel and Power survey, published in 1946, had indicated that in spite of its long history of coal production, reserves existed in South Wales sufficient to last for up to 200 years.

The first National Plan for Coal (that in the early 1980s was the fourth) was drawn up in 1950. It envisaged an annual production of 240 Mt, to be achieved by means of an investment of 520 M pounds. This production target was never met. The highest NCB output was achieved in 1955-56, when 228 Mt were produced from all sources (i.e. deep mines, open cast, plus small private mines). Imports had to be rushed in, to the tune of 17 Mt. The Plan for Coal was revised upwards, with a new target of 250 Mt by 1970. So as to meet this, capital investment was to be more than doubled. South Wales output was included in this planned increase in production, from 20.5 Mt in 1945, to 23.8 Mt in 1955 to 26 Mt in 1965.

## Anthracite.

In particular the anthracite region in the west was undeveloped. The area had languished in relative isolation from the rest of the coalfield. The industry here had grown at a much slower pace than the central valleys. Collieries and communities in West Wales were much smaller, with clean, open, semi-detached villages instead of the cramped terraces. This was also an area where the Welsh language remained strong. Ties with local agriculture were so close that some men divided their work between mining and working on their own small-holding, or labouring on a farm. The result was a way of life quite different to the central and eastern valleys.

Due to the exceptionally fractured geological conditions in the anthracite area, outcrop slants rather than deep mines predominated. The region was typified by a plethora of small drift mines, strung out along the coalfields northern fringe. These drifts would follow the inclination of the seam, down from its outcrop. Many of these drifts had reached excessive lengths of a mile or more, resulting in slow and cumbersome transport of coal, men and supplies along steep, uneven rails. Twice as many men were involved in transportation and other tasks as were involved in production. In addition, there was a long history of difficult industrial relations.

In 1947, while average annual output per employee in the South Wales coalfield was 245.5t that in the Swansea Area was 199.2t. The alternative job on a farm or smallholding, which many miners held, diluted the mining ethos. The quality of workmanship tended to be less than in the exclusively mining orientated central and eastern valleys. Some questionable management practices had also grown up, such as men being paid water money for conditions of minimal water, or even no water at all. Another example was job and finish (men could go home early, as soon as they had finished a set task).

In the 1920's overseas markets for this prime fuel had rapidly developed, with Swansea the main point of export.

In 1934 anthracite production had reached its peak (6,134,000 tons), up from its 1913 figure of 4,833,000 tons. In contrast, this latter year had seen annual production peak in the industry nationally and in South Wales as a whole.

By the start of the Second World War output had dropped to 5,559,000 tons. The war then killed the export trade.

By nationalisation in 1947 output was down to 2,986,000 tons, produced by 17,500 men in 40 pits.

By the early 1950's the anthracite area was incurring the heaviest losses in the United Kingdom and was proving to be a considerable financial burden on the National Coal Board. The future looked perilous. Then, with the anthracite area teetering on the brink of extinction, salvation came in the form of the Clean Air Act. The regular occurrence of "smog" in the cities of Great Britain was no longer politically acceptable. Smokeless fuel was now at a premium. The growth of central heating and heat storage cookers also increased demand for slow-burning, smokeless fuel. Suddenly, the country could not get enough of Welsh anthracite. The upper coal measures however, close to the surface, were largely worked out and the older drifts were coming to the end of their useful lives. It proved impossible to cope with demand.

In 1954, major investment in the anthracite region commenced. Two major new pits were planned to exploit the virgin, deep lying seams of prime anthracite that could not be worked economically by the traditional drifts. These were Cynheidre at Pontyates in the Gwendraeth Valley, sunk to a depth of 730 metres, and Abernant near Pontardawe, sunk to a record depth for South Wales of 820 metres. As many as eight seams would be worked at Cynheidre and workable reserves were estimated at 60 Mt of high-grade anthracite. The main seam worked at Abernant was the Red Vein, at a depth of about 366 metres, but the shafts extended to just below the Peacock Seam, so-called because of its greenish-blue sheen and regarded as among the finest anthracites in the world.

The size of the take at Abernant would grow to eight square miles, with 44 miles of underground roadways and 10 miles of high-speed belt conveyors. The uniqueness and scope of each of these super-projects were epitomised by the domination of the surrounding countryside by the twin tower mounted winders directly above each shaft, replacing the traditional headgear.

In 1954, in addition to these two "super pits", the Brynlliw deep mine, closed since 1927, was reconstructed and reopened. The original shafts and headgear were reused but investment still totalled £4.8 M, for deepening the shafts, equipping no.2 shaft with skip winding, plus driving several thousand metres of new roadways for locomotive haulage.

There were also two new drift mines, Trelewis and Pentreclwydau. The associated immigration of management talent from East Wales to handle all of this was met invariably with the standard jibe of the anthracite workforce, "there cometh the wise men from the east".

## Amenities.

Between 1947 and 1955, capital expenditure in South Wales totalled £51 M, in collieries and associated activities. The Ocean Coal Company, at Deep Navigation colliery in Treharris, had constructed the first pithead baths in South Wales in 1916. Men were charged 6p a week for use of the facilities. Now they were to become universal and free, although it was not until the 1950's that the daily ritual of miners bathing in front of the living room fire finally died out.

New recruits to the industry would not just receive the benefits of pithead baths. Their training had been changed out of all recognition. Previously a lad would start as assistant to a collier, frequently his father or elder brother. This latter would pay him "pocket money" out of his own wages. Working in family groups ensured that experienced miners could look after the safety of the younger members until they had the experience to look after themselves. From now on, recruits would receive a methodical training, as well as a standard wage. Starting at an area training centre on the surface he would progress to a training coalface underground. The youngsters would then be divided into separate streams for further training, depending on their speciality (face workers, engineering apprentices). Once a week there was a full day's attendance at a local technical college. At every NCB colliery there was a training officer with an office, to administer the scheme and to deal with trainees problems. For potential management there would be advanced training schemes with residential courses and a range of experience at various collieries and workshops, as well as secondments outside the industry. For suitable candidates, miners' welfare scholarships and university scholarships were possible. For those lads who had missed their chance in school, the industry now opened the door to further education at all levels.

## Style.

It was the appearance of "modernism" in the surface buildings of new and rebuilt collieries, not just confined to pithead baths, which brought home the new era to those outside the industry. The Reid Committee had recommended architectural input for surface reconstruction. Combined with landscaping, the buildings for coal preparation plants, workshops, offices and electric winding engines would set a new tone. The following years would see trend-setting creations, such as the great tower mounted winders of Abernant and Cynheidre in the 1950`s. These replaced the standard pithead gear and ground level engine house, the cliché of South Wales mining. On the top platforms of these new, 47-metre high, enclosed structures a large electrically driven, multi-rope, pulley suspended the cages on winding ropes forming a continuous loop. This dispensed with the traditional heavy winding drum, with its considerable inertia. Apart from the weight of coal being raised, the whole system was now in balance, resulting in faster response times and reduced energy consumption. Herr Koepe, an engineer working for the Krupp concern in Germany, had developed this "new" system 100 years previously. The importation of such ideas was one of the results of nationalisation.

Mardy, at the head of the Rhondda Fach, was reconstructed in 1948-53 around cubic winding engine houses having continuous glazing and roof lights, more reminiscent of the Bauhaus movement in Germany than anything previously built in Britain. This was the first major project in South Wales, with an investment exceeding £5 M. Nantgarw closely followed it, with an additional £5 M for colliery, coke ovens and by-products plant. Llanharan Colliery gave a lead to the country with the first introduction of horizon mining. In the case of both Nantgarw and Llanharan, plans were implemented that had been inherited from Powell Duffryn Ltd. In its last gasp before nationalisation and in a flurry of activity, this company had initiated schemes so as to justify maximum compensation handouts.

## Risk.

Included in some of the schemes adopted by the NCB were some very risky mining ventures that normally neither geologists nor mining engineers would have selected, had it not been for the extreme pressure on the industry to increase total capacity. Nantgarw was a case in point. The bituminous coals of the southern outcrop are soft and friable, with a high proportion of volatile matter (20-40%). This makes them good house and coking coals. However, the coal seams dip steeply in this area, making mining operations extremely difficult.

Between 1910 and 1915 two shafts had been sunk just north of the site of the famed Nantgarw pottery, down to the Bute seam. This was found at a depth of 856 yards (783m), making it the deepest pit in South Wales at that time. The original owners failed to overcome the difficult geological conditions that the mine presented.

In 1924 the pit was sold to the Taff Rhondda Company.

In 1927, after three years of struggling with adverse geology at the base of the Caerphilly syncline, they too abandoned the effort. After lying idle for a year, the pit was bought by the Powell Duffryn Steam Coal Company Ltd., who mothballed it.

In 1937, plans were made by the company to introduce horizon type mining systems but the Second World War delayed such new developments.

In 1946 the concept was approved by the Ministry of Fuel and Power, thereby influencing the compensation paid to Powell Duffryn upon nationalisation.

When the NCB took up the challenge of working this difficult area, Nantgarw had a total compliment of 4 men working underground plus 12 men on the surface, providing maintenance services. Nationalisation permitted additional areas of coal, not previously owned by Powell Duffryn, to be worked from the Nantgarw shafts. In addition to a completely modern surface, horizon mining was to be employed. This technique was imported from the continent and is particularly suitable for working steeply inclined seams. Coalfaces are at a gradient corresponding to the seam and are laid out between the main horizons, which are at different levels. The horizon roadways themselves would be straight and level and would be used by trains of mine cars hauled by battery locomotives, the only pit in the coalfield to use such motive power. By 1954, manpower had increased to 200 on the surface plus 820 underground.

In spite of the new mining methods, old mother earth still refused to co-operate and Nantgarw's subsequent history would prove to be disappointing, though not one that matched the brazenness of Rothes colliery, at Fife, in Scotland. Sunk at great expense and commissioned in 1946, just before nationalisation, this also rated for compensation to the former owners. Regarded as the showpiece of the Scottish industry, the Queen visited it and the new town of Glenrothes was, to a great extent, a dependency. In practice, before the final decision to shut it down, it proved to be a tremendous loss-maker. The pit's reserves proved to be heavily waterlogged, badly faulted and even, in some places, completely absent. Of the sixteen coalfaces opened on one level, fourteen had to be abandoned early. None of the new projects in South Wales would prove to be a disaster of quite this magnitude.

## Money for (nearly) Everywhere!

As early as May 1947, the annual report of the local NUM complained about undue concentration upon specific units, stating that the "backwardness of the industry is largely the legacy handed down from the ex-coalowners. The efforts of the Board in reorganising the industry are mainly connected with the projects at Llanharan, Ffaldau, Cwm, Nantgarw, Mardy and Cefn Coed collieries. Most of these undertakings involve the utilisation of huge capital sums, but we feel that the progress made at the other collieries is far from satisfactory".

After the initial programme however came forty-four other reconstructions. Twenty-one of these were on a major scale. There were to be six new large collieries, with two of them, Cynheidre and Abernant in the anthracite field, as referred to above. Whereas almost all of the existing collieries had been developed by means of roadways in the seam, the new developments were laid out for horizon mining. In most of the major reconstruction schemes a system of locomotive haulage roads, driven horizontally in the strata as opposed to following the ups and downs of the seam, was adopted. In addition to production orientated investment, each colliery was provided with surface amenities, such as baths, canteen, medical centre etc.

By the mid-1950's, the 222 South Wales collieries at nationalisation (including those no longer in production) had been reduced considerably. Nevertheless, there were still well over a hundred in operation. There had been an ongoing drumbeat, build up the coalfield's capacity so as to meet the persistent and increasing demand for coal. The concentration on bigger pits meant that manpower was holding up well, at around 103,000 (down from 108,000 at nationalisation). Over the same period the coalfield's production had increased slightly, from 21,337,500 tons in 1947 (11.4 per cent of UK production) to 23,025,400 tons (11.1 per cent of UK production).

Between 1956 and 1965, an additional £150 M of investment in the coalfield was planned. New capacity, to replace that lost through closures and also to increase production, was put at 6 Mt per annum.

In 1958, Abernant, rivalling Cynheidre in size and expense, opened in the anthracite region. In the same year, the first of the combined mine projects was inaugurated, with the merger between Coedely and Cwm. Henceforward, all of Coedely's coal would be wound at Cwm.

Also in 1958, a major reconstruction programme took off at Fernhill, at the head of the Rhondda Fawr, with £5 M pounds to be invested.

In 1960, production finally started at Cynheidre.

## "Sinkers".

All of this time, the transitory presence of "sinkers", the rootless, pirate-like crew of contract workers employed for the sinking of shafts and the driving of headings underground, made their presence felt in the valley communities with their large pay packets and their big spending, hard drinking ways. At the time, colliery surfaces became almost synonymous with building sites while underground contractors tunnelled furiously. For them it would prove to be a lucrative business.

In 1954, to increase the element of competition, the Cynheidre sinkings were awarded to a foreign company, Thyssen Schachtbau of Germany. They would remain working at Cynheidre as contractors until the mine finally shut down, 35 years later. Their friendly reception in South Wales, plus the technical and financial success of the project for them (if not for the NCB), persuaded them to set up a British subsidiary, Thyssen (Great Britain) Ltd., with headquarters at Bynea in Llanelli. They quickly grew to become a major player in the field of British mining contracting, particularly so in South Wales. This aspect formed more than 85 per cent of their turnover until the beginning of the 1990's. When, during this decade and as a sign of the times, their Bynea office would finally close, Welsh-German marriages and tri-lingual children (English-German-Welsh) were a personal manifestation of the significant presence they had had on the South Walian mining scene.

## Satisfaction.

By the mid-1950s the National Coal Board could look back with some satisfaction upon their technical and production achievements.

In 1945, output had reached its lowest point since its peak in 1913 (excepting 1926, the year of the general strike), with 183 Mt being produced by 696,000 employees.

By 1955, under nationalisation, deep-mined coal production had increased again, to over 210 Mt, with 704,000 persons employed. In addition there were an additional 11.4 Mt of opencast coal, produced by 9,544 employees. On the technical side:

In 1913, the combined capacity of electrical motors employed within the industry was 477 megawatt (195 MW on the surface and 282 MW underground).

By 1955 this had increased to 2,945 megawatt (1,256 MW on the surface and 1,689 MW underground). The number of horses had been reduced from 73,034 in 1913 to 12,516 in 1955.

## PROFIT AND LOSS.

### Cold Wind.

Financially however, the position was less sanguine. With competition from cheap oil now making its presence felt, a cold economic wind had started to blow. It would blow even colder.

On 22 May 1958, in a speech to colliery managers at Harrowgate, Sir James Bowman, Chairman of the NCB said:

"Emerging as we are from years of chasing the last ton, during which heavy costs have been carried from imported coal and uneconomic pits and our giving priority to the home market at the expense of premiums we could have earned on exports, we have a cumulative deficit and lack of reserves with which to finance special measures".

The cause of this deficit and lack of financial reserves was attributed to the following:

i)    Compensation to the former coal owners (on which interest had to be paid).

ii)   High interest rates on the capital raised to modernise the industry.

iii)  Payment for imported American coal.

iv)  Compensation payments for subsidence.

v)   Tax on operating profit.

vi)  Cabinet refusal to authorise price increases. Since nationalisation the NCB had made 10 such applications:

- 1 was refused outright.

- 4 were less than asked for.

- 5 had to be postponed.

74

Over and above these financial restraints, the simple overriding fact was that coal was by now heavily engaged in a battle with oil. This latter fuel was not only plentiful but cheap. To this the NCB had no adequate response. Pits started to close at a rate of knots.

## New Broom.

In 1960, Lord Robens replaced Sir James Bowman as NCB Chairman. As a new broom, his mantra would be an NCB output of 200 Mt per annum. This was not only his, but also the opposition Labour Party's objective at that time. While the "White hot heat of the technological revolution" would seduce the Labour Party once in power, Robens himself remained convinced that this output target would optimise both costs and the size of the industry.

In 1963, Robens achieved his target of 200 Mt. In January of the same year, he gave the Cadman Memorial Lecture to the Royal Society of Arts. He argued against the concept that reducing the industry's capacity would inevitably result in financial improvement. On the contrary, it was financially vitally important to maintain as big an industry as possible. The industry at that time was committed to £43 M per annum in standing interest charges, as well as about £185 M in other fixed overheads. On an output of 200 Mt per annum, standing overhead charges would therefore equal 22.5 shillings/ton. For a reduced output, the overhead cost per ton would inevitably rise, to 25 shillings at 180 Mt and to 30 shillings at 150 Mt. In addition to this, labour costs were relatively inflexible and would not come down in anything like the same proportion as output.

Robens also made the point that shutting down a pit virtually meant the loss of its reserves for all time. Unlike a factory, one could not close the front gate, put a lock on it and then re-open it some years later when it might be needed again. In a closed colliery, without regular maintenance, strata converges and water seeps in. Within a few months, or even weeks, nature can undo years and indeed decades of human effort. This did not mean, however, that no pit should ever be closed since, with the continuing rise in productivity, the same output could be maintained from a smaller number of producing units. As things were to turn out, as a result of competition and government policy the industry was unable to maintain an annual market of 200 Mt, with a consequent inability to stabilise prices.

In 1964, a pamphlet, produced by some groups within the NUM, criticised the Coal Board's accounts, and in particular the amount of interest that was being paid. Especially the subject of interest payments to the old coal owners was good fodder for the troops, guaranteed to produce a reaction in union circles somewhere between apoplexy and a severe heart attack. That year Lord Robens played down the subject in his address to the NUM annual conference. To a chorus of boos from the usual delegates from the usual coalfields, Robens pointed out that of the £41.5 M in interest that the NCB had paid during the financial year 1963-64, only 10 per cent was to the former coal owners.

- £4 M were to finance coal stocks.
- £1 M were to finance the Board's deficit.
- £32.5 M were to finance the borrowing for new pits and machinery, better health and safety, improvements to miners' houses etc.
- £4 M were interest to the old coal owners.

Robens hammered home the fact that no one lent money without interest, and that the Miners' Pension Fund collected more revenue from interest on its investments than from the miners' own weekly contributions.

Nevertheless, and also for Robens, interest payments were an issue. In the first six months of the financial year in which he made the above address, the NCB made an operating profit of £2 M. Interest payments totalling over £20 M during the same period had reduced this to a net loss of £18 M. Much of this interest was on capital invested as a result of a policy decision, taken in 1950, to increase capacity to 240 Mt per annum. Faced with the energy shortage at that time, the Federation of British Industry had regarded even this level as being too low. They urged a planned output of 270 Mt. No one had foreseen that vast quantities of cheap oil would become available seven or eight years later - temporarily as it turned out.

Also unforeseen was the millions of tons of business that would be lost to the nuclear power stations - without any commercial justification. As a consequence of this, a great deal of the investment made in the 1950's had turned out to be abortive. This capital however still had to be serviced.

In July 1965, £415 M were written off the NCB's capital debt. Robens regarded another capital reconstruction as being necessary within the next ten years.

In 1971, Robens left the Coal Board, finishing his last financial year with a tiny surplus. A succession of price increases had compensated for inflation and a sag in the ongoing productivity rise. In six of his ten years in office there had been a surplus after meeting all interest charges while, in eight of the ten, an operating profit before interest charges had been made. Open cast and non-mining activities such as by-products had consistently shown a profit. Over the previous decade the industry as a whole had earned profits totalling £290 M and had to meet interest charges of £342 M. This meant a net result of £52 M deficit after interest. This corresponded to 0.7 per cent of total turnover. It could have been a profit, if the social consequences of pit closure had not been a brake upon the shutting down of uneconomic production.

## Voodoo Economics.

It had always been intended that the NCB should pay its own way. Indeed, this requirement had been written into the Nationalisation Act. Lord Robens himself (or plain Alfred Robens as he then was), as Parliamentary Secretary to the Ministry of Fuel and Power in the post-war Labour Government, had been instrumental in the Act's introduction.

In 1948, he had spoken to the summer school of the National Coal Board at Oxford. The sentiments expressed were those from which he was never to deviate, in particular when he himself would lead the Board. In attendance were about five hundred miners, accountants, scientists, engineers, administrators and industrial relations experts. These summer schools were held in the early years as an attempt to make everyone feel part of a single organization, with a single purpose.

Robens pointed out that, during the first year of public ownership, more than £60 M had been added to the wage bill in terms of improvements in conditions. He welcomed this and said that there were claims for still better conditions that would have some day to be met. He went on;

"It should be clearly understood however, that the industry cannot look on the consumer as a milch cow and merely go on increasing the price of coal to cover the extra costs. That policy is quite indefensible. The winning of cheaper coal, whilst maintaining and even improving the standards of the workers in the industry, can come only from greater efficiency. Technical efficiency is only a matter of time —— Greater production gives lower overhead charges and provides a surplus leading to higher standards of life of those working in the industry and lower charges to the consumer. The prosperity of the miner and all who work in the industry is dependant on the prosperity of the industry itself. And as for the nation, an abundance of cheaper coal in these immediate months and years will help to end our shortages and help to secure a fuller and better life for the whole community".

When Robens eventually became Chairman of the Board, his task was to be made immeasurably difficult by the financial "never-never land" in which he was forced to operate. The Act of Parliament which constituted the National Coal Board laid upon it the legal obligation of:

"making supplies of coal available, of such qualities and sizes, in such quantities and at such prices, as may seem to them best calculated to further the public interest in all respects, including the avoidance of any undue or unreasonable preference or advantage".

The way this was interpreted restricted price discounting as a means of getting on board a particularly desirable client. In addition, at no time were the relations between the NCB and the gas and electricity industries on a proper commercial basis. The debiting of coal imports to the NCB account was not the only example of "voodoo economics" to which the coal industry was subjected. Long-term, "take or pay" contracts were extremely rare, with the NCB being a coal warehouse. Even the Central Electricity Generating Board (CEGB) was free to take or leave coal in accordance with its own short-term requirements. Should a big generating set go down the coal was left with the NCB, to stock and recover at its own expense. If the Coal Board had been a private company they would never have invested the vast sums that they did without a sales contact to justify the expenditure.

In 1958, as an example, the gas industry indicated that their requirement for gas making coal would be 27 Mt in 1965, with a possible 30 Mt being required by 1970. In fact, in the year ending March 1971 they took 3.4 Mt, with none at all shortly afterwards. Exploitation of North Sea gas was certainly justified, but the gas industry was able to walk away from coal without compensation of any kind. In a commercial world, termination of contract would have brought in its wake proper compensation for abortive capital invested. Thus the true cost of this fresh source of supply would have been revealed. Instead of that, the Coal Board was left holding two babies, redundant capital investment plus excessive manpower.

By 1972, "real term" expenditure on major capital projects had fallen to little more than a tenth of the level prevailing one decade previously. Nevertheless, niche opportunities for investment continued to exist. As well as Coegnant and Blaenant, £0.5 M were spent at Deep Navigation and £2.0 M at Merthyr Vale. In addition, £1,5 M was invested in the new drift mine of Treforgan in the Dulais Valley. These were however exceptions. Where investment did occur, new buildings appeared unambitious compared with their predecessors. The early architectural aspirations of the NCB gave way to cheaper designs, more suitable for an industry in relative decline. Instead of brick and concrete, corrugated covers over steel frames increasingly became the order of the day.

### New Dawn.

Following massive oil price increases and the successful miners' strikes of 1972 and 1974, the government rushed out in the latter year the "Plan for Coal". A glowing future was foreseen for the industry, reversing the long years of decline. A new investment in coal mining of £3,000 M was commenced, to replace large quantities of oil in the fuel-hungry future as foreseen. The oil price increases, however, not only resulted in a slowing down of the economy but also initiated extensive energy saving measures. This rendered untenable the demand assumptions made in the Plan for Coal. Reduced demand meant in turn higher unit costs. Not only had the wage increases resulting from the miners' strikes to be paid for but also the capital charges due to the new investment. This in turn had created a growing surplus capacity, along with excess production. It was a conundrum not easy to resolve.

### Which Accounting?

In the coming years, much would be made of losses incurred by the coalmining industry, both nationally and by individual pits. A generally accepted system of accounting would never be achieved. In particular, the allocation of industry-wide, or area-wide overheads to individual pits was a subject of controversy. A pit could be judged uneconomic and shut down, but the overhead charges that had resulted in the red ink would not be saved thereby. On the contrary, they would then have to be carried by the surviving units, increasing their costs in turn and thus making it more difficult for them to operate economically. Robens opinion, "Off the record", was that a colliery should not be closed if it was making a contribution adequate to cover its own avoidable operating costs.

In late 1984, an article in the magazine "Accounting" highlighted that not all were convinced of the rectitude of NCB accounting practices. It stated:

"Careful scrutiny of NCB accounts produce the conclusion that they fail to form an adequate basis for informed management decisions, since they are almost bound to be misleading in any attempt to identify the changes in future cash flows consequent upon particular pit closures".

In particular the article said that the different revenues that could occur, depending on the coals destination, had not been credited. The price of coal would be different, depending on whether it had been sold, transferred to other collieries (for blending), or produced for stock. In 1983/84, wages comprised 42 per cent of total costs. However, since in event of pit closure manpower would be transferred elsewhere, the variable costs saved by a closure decision would amount to only a fraction of total costs. The contribution made by the closed collieries' production may well have covered this fraction of total costs saved. Other items, such as the hire charge of plant from the area pool, plus area and national overheads, would remain to increase the burden on those collieries that remained in operation. Depreciation and/or interest charges for the use of fixed assets at a colliery were also contentious and subjective, dependent for example on size of reserves, maximum period of write-off, and whether expenditure was capital or revenue.

The NCB countered this article with a statement:

"The fact remains that the industry's costs exceed income by a substantial amount, with government grants in excess of £500 M per annum being required to balance the books".

The new and rosy future predicted for the mining industry in the 1970's was a consequence of the energy crisis of that time. This in turn resulted from the massive increase in the price of oil. The all-time peak was reached in 1980. Translated into 2004 prices this corresponded to $72 per barrel. Subsequently, new non-OPEC sources were found and the world found ways to make do with less oil. Although economic growth lead to a gradual recovery, as late as 1993 world oil consumption was only slightly higher than it had been in 1979. In the United States, oil consumption did not regain its 1979 level until 1997. As a consequence, its price had decreased significantly. By 1998 it had fallen back to $12. With such a price reduction the case for UK coal was undermined, justifying a further rundown of the industry. Since the mid 1990's however, world oil demand has again grown rapidly with China, and to a lesser extent India, now making their presence felt.

In October 2004, crude oil prices in New York rose to over $55 a barrel, a 13-year high and still climbing. There was also a significant hike in the internationally traded price of coal. Although the mining industry world-wide stood to gain from these developments, by this time UK coal had virtually disappeared.


## THE GERMAN EXAMPLE.

Although during nationalisation there were a number of years when the Coal Board was surviving as a result of government subsidies, at no stage was this officially recognised as being an acceptable state of affairs for the long term. Always such subsidies were meant to tide the industry over for a limited period only, until such time as it found its financial feet. The nationalisation act required the NCB to at least break even, and this remained the official objective.

Germany proved to be an object lesson, exciting the envy of left-wing supporters of the British coal mining industry while causing chagrin to free-marketeers. For the former, German subsidies were an example as to how the British Government should also proceed. The latter would eventually file a formal complaint with the European Union against German government support. In truth, the German industry would be subject to the self same macroeconomic forces as the British industry. At the end of the Second World War there were approximately 250 mines in the Ruhr coalfield.

By 1956, when cheap oil started to flow in earnest, mines in West Germany were down to a total of 140, employing 500,000 miners and producing 120 Mt of coal. However, while striving continually to improve productivity and minimise losses by means of a controlled run-down, the German Government would openly recognise that, without ongoing public finance, indigenous production stood no chance of withstanding competition. The end, namely keeping the industry in existence, was judged as fully justifying the means of state subsidies, both considerable and long-term.

Both of the major political parties, Conservatives as well as Socialists, supported the subsidies. There was a reluctance to put all one's energy eggs in a foreign basket. Having a local showcase for their wares also assists the indigenous mining machinery manufacturers. Local ethos is also significant here, with public acceptance of the fact that areas of their country should not just be allowed to run down, and that there is a valuable place in society for the "Kumpels" or "our lads".

In contrast to the thinking of leading British politicians from the same era, German Economics Minister of the late 1990's, Werner Mueller, is quoted as saying that out of inner conviction his heart lies with the German mining industry and that there must be and will be a viable deep-mined coal industry. The unions, fully aware of the precarious economics, have cooperated in rationalisation. In the post-war period, with energy at a premium, miners were the most highly paid workers. This is no longer the case, although their social provisions, such as retirement at age 55, are exemplary.

This policy of generous public spending was not something confined to coal mining alone. The "economic miracle" experienced by Europe's largest economy following the Second World War provided the means for a succession of liberally inclined and socially minded governments to build up one of the most generous social security networks anywhere. Germany's international posture was characterised by "cheque book diplomacy", while the country provided 25 per cent of the European Union budget. For this policy, engendered during the "sunshine days" of 5 per cent growth, the writing was already on the wall after the massive oil price increases of the 1970's.

From 1990 onwards the enormous costs of reunification, plus increased international competition resulting from globalisation, resulted in a lack-lustre economic performance. Developing countries were transforming into competitors while only China was showing long-term growth. Industry in the former German Democratic Republic had virtually collapsed due to its inability to compete, while that remaining operated with only 70 per cent of West German productivity. The consequence was a national economic growth close to zero and an unemployment rate of over 10 per cent. The level of budget deficit exceeded the 3 per cent maximum laid down by the European Union. It was touch and go whether the country would be subject to EU sanctions.

In a painful about-turn, cut backs now became the order of the day. Even then, coalmining was not singled out but had to suffer along with everyone else. In the general process of belt tightening, not only the mining subsidies but also health services, pensions, unemployment benefit, renewable energy etc. all felt the screw being turned.

In 2004 state subsidies to the German mining industry totalled 3.3 billion EUR, similar to that for wind energy. This corresponded to EUR 82,500 for every miner employed. An agreement with the European Union for the continuation of German coal subsidies was wrestled through against opposition. Subsidies would remain, but would be reduced by 7-8 per cent per annum. This EU agreement is valid until 2007. After that, re-negotiation will occur. There is now discussion as to how large the base contribution of indigenous coal should be. The expressed aim of the Conservatives and the Green Party is to eliminate coal subsidies by 2010. Should this occur, the result could well be a total cessation of deep mining in Germany shortly afterwards.

Also in 2004 however a world-wide shortage of coking coal resulting from Chinese economic expansion, and the effect of this on the German steel producers, increased public support for the maintenance of an indigenous coal mining industry.

Plate 1 The Valleys in Defoe's Day.
The Old Bridge at Pontypridd.

Plate 2 The Valleys as they later became.

# Chapter 6

## WHITE HOT HEAT.

*"Now our menfolk are not working,*
*Women too are on the dole,*
*Unemployment is accepted,*
*Now there is less need for coal"*
G. L. Davies, Llantrisant.

By 1958 the days of perpetual energy shortage, combined with coal's monopoly position, were over. From coal at any price, henceforward coal had to be produced competitively. Once it was cheaper or more convenient to use another fuel, sentiment would count for nothing. The consumers now had a choice and ultimately it was they who would determine the industry's size. The international oil industry was the first to call into question the all-encompassing power of King Coal.

### THE FIRST BLOW.

Already in 1914, oil's first major blow against coal had been struck. The Royal Navy, under Winston Churchill as First Lord of the Admiralty, started converting their ships from coal to oil firing. The latter had a higher energy density, requiring less storage space for an equivalent range. It could be easily pumped, instead of laborious manual handling. In addition, it did not produce quantities of ash, which also had to be handled and disposed of. Large-scale conversion of the marine industry from coal to oil became reality between the two world wars. By and large however, oil was confined to the realm of sea, road and air transportation, where its virtues are at a premium. This situation persisted until the mid-1950's.

The post-war economic recovery, and the subsequent economic boom, resulted in a demand for energy that had grown faster than coal could be mined. The international petrochemical industry proved flexible enough to make up the shortfall and the proportion covered by imported oil increased. Political problems in Iran were an additional incentive for the oil companies to seek new reserves elsewhere and large new quantities were found, far exceeding the predictions of the experts.

In 1957, oil really started to take off when increasing quantities became available from the Middle East and North Africa, produced at very low cost. The enormous Saudi Arabian fields, the largest in the world, began large-scale production in 1950. In the mid-fifties oil was found in Algeria and in 1959, vast new reserves in Libya. New refineries came on stream in the UK while developments in transportation, in particular the continually increasing size and quantity of the "super tankers", facilitated availability as well as reducing transport costs. For consumers, this alternative was not only cheaper than indigenous coal, it was also cleaner and more convenient to handle. The most dramatic market loss was in rail transport. The elimination of the fireman and the dead time involved in a prolonged period of steam raising resulted in an unanswerable economic case against the steam locomotive.

The smog that engulfed London and the Northern cities prompted the creation of "smokeless zones". At home, with increasing living standards, householders opted for oil-fired central heating, later to be replaced with gas.

From 1958 onwards, this glut of cheap oil resulted in a market pressure which coal was unable to withstand, with the result that demand fell back steadily. The decline in production lagged behind, resulting in ever increasing coal stocks. In the words of one wizened marketing man from the NCB, "Things are getting so bad now that I can't even look at an oil painting anymore, it's got to be charcoal". Charcoal notwithstanding, there was worse to come. The miners had always been full-blooded supporters of the Labour Party. The latter in turn had always shown itself sympathetic to the miners. The act of nationalisation itself was an expression of this common approach, but times were about to change.

# TECHNOLOGY AS POLITICS.

In 1960, at Labour's national study conference on energy and in a book by Harold Wilson, future leader of the party, New Deal for Coal, this mutual empathy was set to continue. The party committed itself to a minimum annual production of 200 Mt.

By the early 1960's the party had been in opposition for well over a decade and in the country as a whole there was a feeling of economic decline in the air. It was not only the party which needed rejuvenating, the nation did too. Growing up in Britain after the Second World War one had a sense of national exhaustion and poverty. The effects of this were brilliantly disguised for decades, particularly from Britain's own citizens. Why should there be any need to change - we had won the war hadn't we? The country felt it had a position to maintain in the world, a huge empire to administer and then dismantle. When the American Dean Acherson stated the obvious, that Britain had lost an empire but had yet to find a role, he was reviled. Not until the 1960's was it generally realised that the country had fallen behind. Questionable management, the poor quality of the goods produced, late delivery and union restrictions had all contributed to British industry losing out to competition This fact was coupled with a reluctance to admit any such thing. British politicians exaggerated Britain's role: Britain was Greece to America's Rome (Harold MacMillan). With regard to the European Community, naturally, Britain would slip into the leadership role. Only towards the end of the 1970's was sufficient energy and impatience mustered to begin the necessary revival.

In 1963, the Labour Party made a start. The speech by Harold Wilson, leader of the Labour Party, at the party's annual conference was dynamic. Its theme was "The white hot heat of the technological revolution". The intention was to convince the electorate that while the country at present, under the Conservatives, was ticking along on a single cylinder a new Labour administration would get all four cylinders firing. Wilson had ridiculed the Conservative leader Sir Alec Douglas-Home as "An elegant anachronism".

In contrast, in his "Message to the sixties", Wilson portrayed himself as being a human nuclear reactor. Images were invoked of a scientific and technological revolution, socialistically inclined, that would release an enormous amount of energy to create a world of unprecedented prosperity and leisure. It was public relations mumbo-jumbo, but it did reflect the "Zeitgeist" of the time. People who met Wilson felt that he really did intend to rejuvenate British society and the increasingly uncompetitive British economy. During the following year, Labour, with Wilson as Prime Minister, was elected to power.

In practice, Wilson's brave new technological world was more fantasy than reality. It was hamstrung by the inability of the British economy to perform, plus the lowly status of trade, industry and engineers when compared with finance and the law. This was reflected in the general thrust of the nation's education. The ongoing mud-wrestling match between management and unions epitomised the endemic problems of a class-conscious society. Nevertheless, so as to "to drag Britain screaming into the twenty-first century", technology's call would be heeded. A new Ministry of Technology was created.

# THE KING IS DEAD, LONG LIVE THE KING!

In 1964, in the same year as their election, the new Labour Government authorised a second nuclear power programme. While the first nuclear power programme was initially conceived at a time when coal was struggling to meet its commitments, this second programme would inevitably be associated from its very beginning with the loss of mining jobs. A 2,000 MW power station burns 5 Mt of coal per annum. At the time, that meant employment for about 10,000 men.

Extensive publicity immediately proclaimed that the electricity produced from this new British technology, based on Advanced Gas-cooled Reactors (AGRs), would be cheaper than that from coal-fired stations. In fact the programme involved the scaling up, by a factor of 20, of a small prototype. Problems of inadequate development were exacerbated by the disastrous decision to order three different AGR designs from three different consortia. Engineering expertise available was scarcely sufficient for one. Construction took twice as long and cost twice as much as expected. Extensive modifications to the central core proved necessary due to the potential for corrosion. Taken together, all this killed off the cherished dreams of an important export business.

As a commercial dud this second civil reactor programme in the UK mirrored the first. This first programme was based on the so-called magnox technology and had been announced by the Conservative Government in 1955. At the time it was not expected to be economic, a fact not revealed publicly until the release of cabinet papers in 1989. Only much later would it be revealed that, at a time when pits were being closed on economic grounds, if the full cost of development and of the long-term storage of nuclear waste were included, then nuclear power was significantly more expensive than coal.

For successive British governments, nuclear power was a priority, both in terms of national energy policy and in giving access to government research and development funding. Ever since the early 1950's, when nuclear power appeared on the scene as something futuristic, almost magical, it caught the imagination. Not only the lay public were impressed but also politicians and the electricity generation industry, plus the whole technical and scientific community. The prospect of almost unlimited energy from small quantities of material, all produced in a spotlessly clean environment by a new exotic technology, was clearly a wave of the future. Naturally, Britain should be in the forefront of this wave, not only for its intrinsic merits but also for the export potential that such futuristic technology would offer. This was all too good to pass by. In retrospect it was also all too good to be true, as advantages were exaggerated and disadvantages overlooked.

In a typical presentation, the protagonist would wave his spectacle case in the air and speak of the number of megawatts of electricity the equivalent volume of uranium-235 could produce. Simultaneously, a slide would project on the screen a photograph of St. Paul's cathedral with superimposed next to it a pile of coal, dominating the building. This represented the amount of fuel required if the equivalent amount of electricity were to be produced by the burning of coal.

Another half-truth, current at the time, was that Britain generated more electricity from nuclear power than any other country in the world, thereby indicating how technologically advanced the country was. Left unsaid was that none of the electricity so generated was competitive with conventional generation. The country had gone over the top, going straight into a massive building programme for a new, and still developing, technology. This not only consumed much needed capital, it also sterilised much capital already invested in the coalmining industry. It would also cause devastation in many mining communities.

In 1964, when the Labour party was elected after 13 years in opposition, coal for the last time still outstripped all other sources combined, providing 50.4 per cent of the nations primary fuel consumption. Traditionally the miners had always been Labour's staunchest supporters. Labour's stated policy in opposition, that coal production be maintained at a level of 200 Mt per annum, had been justified on the basis that this was the optimum size of the industry, bearing in mind the capital investment already made. Any reduction would push the industry into having to make price increases. Now they were in power, such statements became unsaid. Coal had become associated with a byegone era, a past that was both traditional and conservative. Harold Wilson's enthusiasm for technological change would shut pits at a faster rate than when the Conservatives were in office.

The new Minister of Power, Richard Marsh, won the respect of Lord Robens (one of the few Ministers of Power to do so). He would later leave politics to become Chairman of British Rail. When in the House of Lords he would refer to the devastation that his government's policies had created in the mining communities, inferring that perhaps the "white hot heat of the technological revolution" had been a little overdone.


## BONANZA!

In September 1965, came the first North Sea gas find. It came from the very first hole put down by British Petroleum. Unlike the meretricious attractions of nuclear power, North Sea gas would indeed bring significant advantages to the UK over the years to come. Initial publicity however magnified the undoubted attractions into the realm of a fairy tale. Banner headlines screamed "BONANZA", while newspaper articles would breathlessly describe how, "unknown for centuries, these islands of ours have been floating on a bubble of gas".

In 1965 the Labour Government's "Coal Plan" envisaged production falling from 200 Mt to 170-180 Mt by 1970. During the following four years, no fewer than 204 collieries were closed, almost one per week.

## TECHNOLOGY RULES! OK?

In March 1966 the Labour Government was re-elected. In June 1966, in a sign that all was not well in this new technological world, the country's first Minister of Technology, the ex-trade union leader Frank Cousins, resigned as a result of the government's industrial and incomes policy. Subsequent to his resignation he stated, "If I were to tell my members that I thought they should be sacked, they'd think I was crazy, and so would I". He was replaced by Anthony Wedgewood -Benn (Tony Benn), fresh from the position of Postmaster General, where he was in the middle of rejuvenating the Post Office. He now threw himself into the task of pushing British industry into a new technically and socialistically orientated future. Inspired by the "Atoms for Peace" programme, launched by President Eisenhower, Benn was inspired by the concept of "Beating swords into ploughshares". His responsibility for the nuclear power programme was predicated on what he was told, believed, and would argue publicly; that nuclear power was cheap, safe and peaceful. Included among his trusted advisors was obviously not a fellow Labour Minister from the previous generation, Lord Robens. He stated that the nuclear power programme was disastrously large for a new process. He continued to demand an independent inquiry into the true cost of nuclear power. Coal could compete he asserted, but not against the artificially low costs which were being made public. All such requests were turned down.

In the same months as Benn's take-over as Minister of Technology, spokesmen for the gas council were prophesying that the cost of gas to the consumer might fall to between half and two-thirds of the then current price. "Fanny by Gaslight" was consigned to history, to be replaced by a massive advertising campaign, extolling the virtues of "modern high-speed gas". Coal was hit with a double whammy. When natural gas from the North Sea started to flow through the national pipe network in the late 1960's, not only did a massive group of customers, the municipal and state-operated gasworks, disappear but gas also began to decimate coal directly in the domestic market. Government policy was to force the introduction of North Sea gas as quickly as possible, as well as supporting the second nuclear power programme. These two fuels were new and, it was assumed, must automatically be better than coal, which was old. As a result, hospitals, army camps and government-owned factories continued to reject coal for oil. The inevitable consequence was an acceleration of the pit closure programme.

In 1966, as a sop to the miners, the proposed closure of sixteen pits was deferred until the following year. This ploy was seen for what it was. It also resulted in that following year seeing the highest number of annual closures ever known. It created 12,700 compulsory redundancies, as the Board were unable to accommodate all of the men whose pits were closed but who still wanted to remain in mining.

## THE ENERGY WHITE PAPER.

In 1967 a white paper on fuel policy scaled back the coal production forecast for 1970 to 152 Mt (reduced from the estimate made two years previously of 170-180 Mt, itself a reduction from the original estimate for 1970, made in the early 1950's, of 250 Mt). It was anticipated that further swinging reductions would come. By 1975, output should be down to 120 Mt and by 1980 down to 80 Mt. The latter figure implied a total manpower figure of 69,000, reduced by 312,000 from the number then employed. These prognostications were based on the optimistic future for North Sea Gas, combined with the rose tinted spectacles through which nuclear power was viewed, all combined with the continuing glut of cheap oil.

In the same year as this White Paper came one of the major Arab-Israeli wars, but no significant alarm bells were rung. Already in 1960, OPEC (The Organization of Petroleum Exporting Countries) had been formed. In his book, Ten Year Stint Lord Robens gives credence to the Welsh miner who said, "Do you think the Arabs are for ever going to live in tents?" an analysis which proved in the event to be far more germane than those originating from "expensively briefed" and "disastrously wrong" civil servants. In retrospect, and referring to the fuel policy white paper of 1967, the NCB economist Dr. Schumacher would say:

"If, instead of getting all these experts together and using a computer-based model, the Government had asked the lady who cleans my office to do the job, she couldn't have been more wrong".

Blissfully unaware of the traumatic price rises which were to hit the oil industry in the early 1970's the White Paper of 1967 stated, "On the evidence available, it seems likely that oil will remain competitive with coal and that pressure to force up crude oil prices will be held in check by the danger of loss of markets —— The Government are conducting a thorough re-examination of ways of strengthening the security of our supplies. They nevertheless consider it right that regular supplies of oil at competitive prices will continue to be available and they believe that it would be wrong to deny to British industry the advantages that oil can bring". (This sanguine forecast was to be trashed by subsequent events. As a result of these, actual coal production in 1980 was not 80 Mt, as forecast by the white paper, but 121 Mt. Had the capacity still been available it could have been much more, since there were significant imports of coal at this time).

Following the white paper, a Coal Industry bill was introduced. It provided financial help to ease the social consequences of the industry's contraction. The coal burn at existing power stations was to be subsidised where alternative fuels were cheaper. This support would continue until 1971. To be sure, Labour's policies did write off a £400 M debt, banned coal imports, continued the fuel oil tax and introduced a redundancy scheme for those miners over 55. The effect of all this was however minimal. So-called advance factories were set up to bring light industry into coalmining areas as alternative employment. Many of them proved to be here-today-and-gone-tomorrow entities, while there was always a feeling that, "miners do not fit easily into pop factories" (to the extent that men were employed at all).

## CRYSTAL BALL GAZING.

In 1968, the Parliamentary Select Committee on the Nationalised Industries issued a report on the "Exploitation of North Sea Gas". It was cautious rather than wildly optimistic, while the future of the coalmining industry was not viewed in unduly pessimistic terms. Known reserves of natural gas were enough for twenty-five years and, in the opinion of the Ministry of Power, a consumption rate planned to result in depletion over this period was the right one. This consumption rate was 85 Mcu.m/day (equivalent to 91,400 t of coal), or three times the current consumption rate based on town gas. Since further discoveries were likely, the Gas Council were planning for a consumption rate of 113 Mcu.m/day (equivalent to 121,500 t of coal) from the mid-1970's. The report also made the following points:

- "The Ministry of Power think that in the near future the fuel displaced will be mainly oil but in the mid-1970's coal will be displaced to some extent by natural gas".

- "It will be necessary to study the economic advantages and disadvantages of taking steps to ensure that an over-rapid rundown now (of the coal industry) does not jeopardise the future efficiency either in terms of moral or recruitment"

- "Retaining the nucleus of a sound coal industry may be even more important in the long term. The possibility of further discoveries of gas not being made has to be catered for"

- "Even if further discoveries are made, the position when supplies of gas are becoming exhausted, possibly in 25 years, must not be lost sight of altogether".

- "Your Committee have welcomed the Ministry of Power's approach to the question of the exploitation of North Sea gas by economic analysis. They will be content if the future of the coal industry is judged by the same criteria".

The Ministry of Power was quoted in the report as saying that one of the major factors in the run-down of mining manpower was the industry's success in increasing productivity. This trend would be inevitable into the 1970's, for either productivity would continue to rise or, if this did not happen, it would be impossible to maintain the demand for coal. The Ministry expected that for the industry to stabilise by the mid to late 1970's it would have to become profitable. The nature of the industry as it currently was, and the skills to be expected of underground workers in the future, would be very different.

Lord Robens gave evidence to the Select Committee, stating, "We think we are going through the same phase the Americans went through in the 1940's. With the impact of competition from natural gas and oil, their coal was not required and so they cut their coal output very substantially, from approximately 500 Mt to less than 400 Mt. They were then left with their most efficient pits and in operating them they are now well over their 400 Mt and are reaching up to 500 Mt. By next year they will probably be on the way to 600 Mt. We are of the opinion this will happen to us. It should be borne in mind that the coal industry has carried a lot of very expensive coal because the users, principally the gas and electricity industries, put forward estimates of requirements substantially in excess of what they now say they want. One cannot close pits any more quickly than social consequences permit. In the next few years the high cost pits will go out —— We are therefore in the process of eliminating the high cost coal and concentrating output on the better pits. That is the exact phase through which the Americans went. When we have, by the early seventies, eliminated the high cost pits, with new techniques available to us by reason of the research that is going on in our industry, I see no reason why we should not substantially increase the amount of very cheap coal that would be competitive. Our serious worry is that plans now being made for power station generation would prevent this coal being used".

In 1969, the current Minister of Power, Roy Mason, gave as his reason for rejecting all calls for an inquiry into the cost of nuclear power as being the need to protect the miners' morale! He was satisfied that nuclear power was cheaper. Any examination would only prove his case. The result would be a foregone conclusion, killing the coal industry and shattering the miners' morale.

In 1971, oil beat coal into a clear second place. Between 1952 and 1972, UK coal production had fallen from 220 Mt to 140 Mt. The industry became primarily dependant on electricity generation. Here the mechanical handling systems as required with coal were but a small proportion of the overall capital cost. The process of technology substitution can be complex, and while the replacement of steam locomotives by diesel represented an outright loss for coal, electrification of the railways (for example the main east and west coast lines between London and Scotland) could be represented as "coal by wire". Although any of the primary fuels can be substituted for each other in the generation of electricity, in this area for decades coal was to reign supreme.

The figures for UK primary energy consumption up until this period are given below in million tons of coal equivalent (Mtce) as well as in percentage terms:

|  | 1950 |  | 1960 |  | 1970 |  | 1973 |  |
|---|---|---|---|---|---|---|---|---|
|  | Mtce | % | Mtce | % | Mtce | % | Mtce | % |
| Coal | 204 | 89.6 | 199 | 73.7 | 157 | 46.6 | 133 | 37.6 |
| Oil | 23 | 10.0 | 68 | 25.3 | 150 | 44.6 | 164 | 46.4 |
| Nat Gas | - | - | - | - | 18 | 5.3 | 44 | 12.5 |
| Nuclear | - | - | 1 | 0.4 | 10 | 2.8 | 10 | 2.9 |
| Hydro | 1 | 0.4 | 2 | 0.6 | 2 | 0.7 | 2 | 0.6 |
| TOTAL | 228 | 100 | 270 | 100 | 337 | 100 | 335 | 100 |

## WITHDRAWAL SYMPTOMS.

In the early 1970's, OPEC finally showed their teeth. It would become apparent to everyone that the world had become over dependant on cheap and plentiful oil. Oil prices were rising, rendering null and void the results of previous calculations.

In 1971-73, producing governments assumed control over the production and price of oil. This was to trigger a series of events that would drive up energy costs and place a stranglehold on the world's economy. Consumer nations were now to be faced with severe consequences, resulting from political action over which they had no control.

In 1974, there were additional oil-price increases, resulting from the Yom Kippur War in the Middle East. By this time, coal's share of the total British fuel market had dropped to one third. In an era of continually increasing energy demand coal's contribution, both proportionally and in absolute terms, had continued to decline. The massive oil price rises in the 1970's were however to put a brake on this development. For a time it seemed as if a new dawn had broken for the coal mining industry.

## THE CAT IS LET OUT OF THE BAG!

For nuclear power to come down to earth took rather longer than was the case with oil. In the early 1990's, when the electricity industry was privatised, the nuclear power cat was finally let out of the bag. Finally, with impending privatisation of the electricity generation industry, and with nuclear power up for sale, the real costs of the enterprise were exposed.

After years of official assurances that nuclear power was (or could be) the cheapest form of electricity generation available, when faced with the prospect of commercial discipline in the private sector, nuclear power (from both existing and proposed reactors) suddenly became expensive. In all of the initial nuclear power bally-hoo, not mentioned were the immense capital investment required in containing and controlling the deadly radioactivity, which is produced by the chain reaction in addition to heat. Capital amortisation is the largest cost component and this capital has already been spent. With such costs up front, and a limited turndown ratio, the stations are locked into an inflexible operating regime of continuous maximum output, irrespective of the actual cost of production.

In addition to the extremely high capital costs, not considered previously in the cost of generation was processing the radioactive spent fuel elements and then storing, for hundreds or thousands of years, the radioactive material. Also not considered previously was the cost of eventually decommissioning the radioactive core of the station.

The consequence of these revelations was a failure to find private investors prepared to take over the industry. A later, partial, privatisation was proved to be sustainable only by the receipt of extensive government subsidies. A levy on electricity sales was raised, partly to subsidise generation from renewable sources, but mainly to support nuclear power.

In 1989-90, the Parliamentary Energy Committee, in their fourth report "The Cost of Nuclear Power" stated:

"The nuclear industry has a long history of over-optimistic forecasts —— On the basis of evidence we have received, we are convinced that there has been a systematic bias in Central Electricity Generating Board (CEGB) costing in favour of nuclear power, both in ignoring risk and failing to provide adequately for contingencies and, in respect of investment, in putting forward "best expectations" rather than more cautious estimates. One result has been prejudice in investment decisions against non-nuclear generation. We believe the Department of Energy, as the CEGB's sponsoring department, must share the blame for this, since it apparently made no attempt to obtain realistic costings from the CEGB until it was seeking to privatise nuclear power —— One other aspect of nuclear costs deserves attention, namely the secrecy which has surrounded them —— The Department of Energy has done little or nothing to make information more available. The Committee regards a written answer on 15 December 1988 as the government's first public statement that the cost of electricity from the CEGB's nuclear stations exceeds that of coal-fired generation —— The (fossil fuel) levy is a huge subsidy to nuclear power totalling about £900 M a year, and will have substantial economic and social effects".

With regard to future investment in nuclear power, the report went on:

"In this context we are concerned by the decision that new investment by Nuclear Electric will be subject to the standard public discount rate of 8 per cent. This would mean a lower discount rate for investment in nuclear power than for investment in any other form of generation, and indeed any type of energy, despite the higher risk associated with nuclear power. It would effectively be a subsidy to new nuclear investment".

The first British nuclear power programme was based on the so-called magnox type of reactor. The report states;

"According to Lord Marshall the British magnox programme has probably produced more nuclear waste than all the rest of the world put together —— Magnox reprocessing costs increased five-fold in real terms in the ten years to 1988. The major reason was more stringent regulations concerning discharges and safety".

In the United Kingdom, 90 per cent of the research and development expenditure for power generation has been dedicated to nuclear power. It has been stated from within the industry itself that one thing has always dogged the British electricity industry, namely they become so excited whenever a new technology comes along as to put it into practice irrespective of cost.

The report by the Governments Trade and Industry Committee in 1993, "British Energy Policy & the Coal Industry" states:

"The European Commissioner for Energy emphasised the Commission's rule that state aid should not exceed 20 per cent of the energy used to generate electricity. The Commissioner noted that the UK has preferred to use that margin to protect the nuclear industry".

Until Finland broke the cycle, with an announcement in 2004 of a new construction, no new nuclear power stations have been built in either Europe or the United States for many years. Those operating still require government financial support to survive commercially. At present its two main advantages, no emission of greenhouse gases plus the small fuel requirement, are not enough to counteract its high cost and queries regarding safety. The potential for terrorist attack, along with alternative methods of combating global warming, raise further questions over its role in the twenty-first century.

In September 2002 the nuclear generator British Energy plunged into a financial crisis, being kept afloat only by means of a £650 M government bailout. In his campaign against the excessive size of the nuclear power programmes Lord Robens, NCB Chairman between 1960-71, had been vindicated, too late however to prevent a waste of investment for which the nation's infrastructure and social services were crying out. In addition there was the loss of tens of thousands of mining jobs, for the electricity generation market developed to the point where it meant life or death for the coal industry. Whereas in 1953, power stations consumed only 20 per cent of UK coal production, and the remaining market sectors (general industry, iron/steel, domestic, transport, commercial/public buildings) a full 80 per cent, by 1985 the situation had completely reversed. In that year power stations consumed 73 per cent and all remaining markets together 27 per cent.

Plate 3 Such scenes were well known into the 1950s, when pithead baths became universal.

# FIG. 11 PITS OF THE SOUTH WALES COALFIELD UPON NATIONALISATION

# FIG. 12 PITS OF THE SOUTH WALES COALFIELD IN 1983

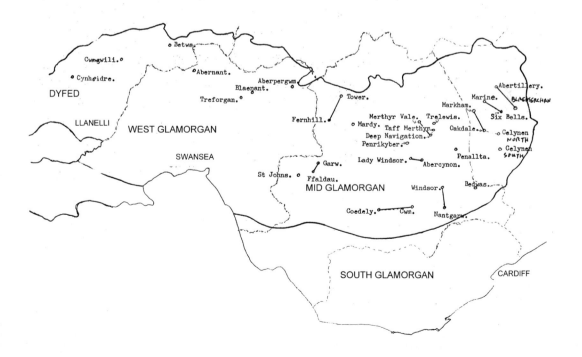

# PITS OF THE SOUTH WALES COALFIELD IN 1989

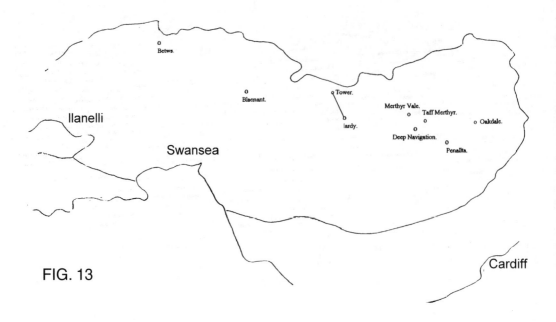

FIG. 13

# Chapter 7

## THE ODYSSEY OF DECLINE.

*Farewell the colliery worker, the muffler and the cap.*
*Farewell you Rhondda Valley girls, we never will come back.*
*The mines they are a-closing, the valleys all are doomed.*
*There's no work in the Rhondda boys, we'll be in London soon!*
Frank Hennessy, 1970's.

By the time of nationalisation, the number of mines in South Wales had already been pruned drastically, from almost 500 in the 1920's to 222. Of these, 176 were still in production. Of the remainder, many were used as pumping stations to de-water the workings of adjacent, active collieries. The subsequent fate of the South Wales pits is listed below.

Not listed are the small Forest of Dean and Somerset coalfields, which were included in the South Western Division of the NCB. The last pit in the former closed during 1960 and in the latter during 1973.

## PIT CLOSURES IN SOUTH WALES SINCE 1947.

| Year. | S.W. deep mined output (tonnes) / % age of total UK. | Total no. of SW miners/ % age of total UK | Collieries closed. | Location. |
|---|---|---|---|---|
| . 1947 | 21,679,967 t / 11.4% | 115,500/ 16.4% | Erskin. Blaenclydach. Llanmarch. Argoed Levels. Llanerch. Penrhys. Glenafan. | Blaendare. Blaenclydach. Brynmawr. Cynonville. Cwmnantddu. Port Talbot. Cymmer Afan. |
| 1948 | 22,840,702 t / 11.4% | 114,943 | Hook. Pwllgwaun. New Gellihir. Nantewlaeth. Islwyn. Maindy. West Blaina. Maerdy. Glanamman. Broadoak. Cwmneol. | Haverfordwest. Pontypridd Swansea Valley. Cymmer Afan. Afan Argoed. Rhondda Fawr. Blaina. Ammanford. Ammanford. Llanelli. Mountain Ash. |
| 1949 | 23,136,170 t / 11.2% | 110,225 | Cwmcynon. Llanerch Padarn. Blaendare. Tareni. Wernfawr. Werfa Dare. Glynogwr. Pontyberem. Brithdir. Penrikyber No. 3. | Mountain Ash. Abersychan. Pontypool. Swansea Valley. Ammanford. Aberdare. Gilfach Goch. Llanelli. Bargoed. Penrhiwceiber. |

| Year. | S.W. deep mined output (tonnes) / % age of total UK. | Total no. of SW miners/ % age of total UK | Collieries closed. | Location. |
|---|---|---|---|---|
| 1950 | 23,394,958 t / 11.2% | 105,931 | Rhiw Colbren No.2. Lucy No.5. Cilely. | Abertillery. Merthyr. Tonyrefail. |
| 1951 | 23,801,987 t / 11.0% | 107,420 | None closed. | |
| 1952 | 24,281,665 t / 11.1% | 110,300 | Garngoch No. 1. Talyclun Pwll. Trane. Nebo. | Fforest Fach. Pontarddulais. Burry Port. Tonyrefail. Rhondda Fawr. |
| 1953 | 24,145,006 t / 11.2% | 107,400 | Oaklands. Rhos. Pidwellt. | Bridgend. Onllwyn. Rhymney. |
| 1954 | 24,268,456 t / 11.1% | 107,100 | Trimsaran. Brynteg. Rock Vein. | Carmarthenshire. Severn Sisters. Glyn Neath. |
| 1955 | 23,482,541 t / 11.0% | 103,700 | Lucy Thomas. Mynydd Maen. Mynydd Newydd. Brynhenllys. Ynisarwed. Dare (combined with Park). | Merthyr. Pontypool. Fforest Fach. Upper Cwmtwrch. Resolven. Rhondda Fawr. |
| 1956 | 23,351,471 t / 10.9% | 103,700 | Crynant. Bedlinog. Pengam. Saron. Deakins Red Ash. | Neath. Merthyr. Gelligaer. Ammanford. Talywain. |
| 1957 | 23,500,830 t / 11.0% | 104,100/ 14.9% | Deakins Slope. Bwllfa Dare. Rock. Ystalyfera. Gelliceidrim. | Talywain. Aberdare. Blackwood. Swansea. Ammanford. |
| 1958 | 22,045,643 t / 10.7% | 99,600 | McLaren. Vivian. Naval. Glenhafod. Llandebie. Tirherbert. | Merthyr. Abertillery. Rhondda Fawr. Port Talbot. Carmarthenshire. Hirwaen. |
| 1959 | 20,443,231 t / 10.3% | 92,200 | Ty Trist. Aberbaiden. Cwmllynfell. Mount. Steer. Tydraw. Tir Pentwys. Glyn Tillery. Ferndale No. 5. Garth Merthyr. Glengarw. Pentre. | Tredegar. Kenfig Hill. Ystalyfera. Ammanford. Gwauncaegurwen. Rhondda Fawr. Pontypool. Pontypool. Rhondda Fach. Resolven. Blaengarw. Kenfig Hill. |

| Year. | S.W. deep mined output (tonnes) / % age of total UK. | Total no. of SW miners/ % age of total UK | Collieries closed. | Location. |
|---|---|---|---|---|
| 1960 | 19,537,792 t / 9.7% | 83,400 | Britannic. Carway. North Rhondda. Tylorstown. Rock. Hendy Merthyr. Rose Heyworth. Ferndale No. 9. Lewis Merthyr (combined with Tymawr). | Pengam. Kidwelly. Glyncorrwg. Rhondda Fach. Glyn Neath. Swansea. Abertillery. Rhondda Fach. Pontypridd. |
| 1961 | 18,398,540 t | 80,400 | Garn and Kay Slope. Maritime. Clydach Merthyr. Graig Fawr. Llanbradach. | Blaina. Pontypridd. Swansea. Crumlin. Caerphilly. |
| 1962 | 19,349,697 t | 79,000 | Gelli. Onllwyn No. 3. Great Mountain. New Cross hands. Llanharan. Blaenhirwaen. Elliot West. Aberaman. | Rhondda Fawr. Neath. Ammanford. Llanelli. Llantrisant. Llanelli. New Tredegar. Aberdare. |
| 1963 | 19,367,201 t | 77,000 | Severn Sisters. New Rockwood. Bryn Navigation. Cwmgwrach. Ffaldydre. Waunlwyd. | Neath. Taffs Well. Port Talbot. Glyn Neath. Resolven. Ebbw Vale. |
| 1964 | 18,827,020 t | 72,000 | Western. Onllwyn No. 1 Cwmgorse. Garth Tonmawr. Pochin. Nine-Mile Point. Wern Tarw. Daren. Varteg. | Nantymoel. Neath. Gwauncaegurwen. Port talbot. Tredegar. Ynysddu. Pencoed. Trebanog. Pontypool. |
| 1965 | 16,771,135 t | 64,000 | Rhigos. Glyncastle. Fforchaman. Felinfran. Wernos. Aberbeeg. | Aberdare. Resolven. Cwmamman. Swansea. Ammanford. Abertillery. |

| Year. | S.W. deep mined output (tonnes) / % age of total UK. | Total no. of SW miners/ % age of total UK | Collieries closed. | Location. |
|---|---|---|---|---|
| 1966 | 16,384,535 t | 58,000 | Pwllbach. Garngoch. Hafodyrynys. Risca. Albion. Duffryn Rhondda. Dillwyn. Park. Glenrhondda. Cambrian. Fernhill (linked to Tower). | Ystalyfera. Fforest Fach. Pontypool. Cross Keys. Cilfynydd. Cymmer Afan. Neath. Rhondda Fawr. Rhondda Fawr. Rhondda Fawr. Rhondda Fawr. |
| 1967 | 15,746,000 t/ 9% | 53,000/ 11.6% | Abercrave. Elliot. Pentreclwydau. Abergorki. Crumlin Navigation. International. | Swansea Valley. New Tredegar. Glyn Neath. Mountain Ash. Gwent. Blaengarw. |
| 1968 | 14,505,748 t | 48,000 | Newlands. Ynyscedwin. Wylie. Lindsay. Cefn Coed. National. Cwmcarn. Groesfaen. East. | Pyle. Ystradgynlais. Pontllanfraith Cross Hands. Dulais Valley. Rhondda Fach. Newbridge. Bargoed. Ammanford. |
| 1969 | 12,788,223 t | 40,000 | Pantyffynnon. Penllwyngwent. Llanhilleth. Avon. Mountain. Tirpentwys. | Ammanford. Ogmore Vale. Gwent. Abergwynfi. Gorseinan. Pontypool. |
| 1970 | 11,873,030 t | 38,000 | Waterloo. Glyncorrwg. | Oakdale. Cymmer Afan. |
| 1971 | 9,665,305 t | 36,000 | None closed. | |
| 1972 | 10,808,839 t | 34,000 | None closed. | |
| 1973 | 7,349,729 t/ 5.5% | 31,000 | Coedcae. | Abertillery. |
| 1974 | 8,631,767 t | 31,455 | Pentremawr. | Llanelli. |
| 1975 | 8,437,237 t | 30,483 | Ogilvie. Beynon. Glyntillery. Ammanford. Windsor (linked to Nantgarw). Ffaldau (linked to Garw). | Bargoed. Blaina. Pontypool. Ammanford. Bedwas. Bridgend. |

| Year. | S.W. deep mined output (tonnes) / % age of total UK. | Total no. of SW miners/ % age of total UK | Collieries closed. | Location. |
|---|---|---|---|---|
| 1976 | 7,785,000 t | 29,997 | Ammanford. | Ammanford. |
| 1977 | 7,445,560 t/ 6.9% | 28,965/ 12% | Bargoed. Caerau. | Bargoed. Maesteg. |
| 1978 | 7,624,876 t | 27,384 | Graig Merthyr. | Pontardulais. |
| 1979 | 7,600,000 t | 27,384 | Deep Duffryn. | Mountain Ash. |
| 1980 | | 26,356 | Big Pit. Fernhill section of Tower/Fernhill. Cwmgwili No. 1. | Blaenavon. Crosshands. Rhondda Fawr. |
| 1981 | 7,000,000 t | 25,328 | Coegnant. Deep Duffryn. Morlais section of Morlais/Brynlliw. | Maesteg. Mountain Ash. Llanelli. |
| 1982 | | 24,269 | Cwmtillery. | Cwmtillery. |
| 1983 | | 22,172 | Lewis Merthyr /Tymawr. Blaengwrach. Brynlliw. Britannia. | Pontypridd. Neath. Swansea. Pengam. |
| 1984 | 6,638,000 t | 22,071 | Wyndham/Western. | Ogmore Vale. |
| 1985 | 6,744,540 t | 19,293 | Celynen North. Celynen South. Blaenserchan. Bedwas. Markham. Treforgan. Aberpergwm. Penrikyber. Abertillery. St. John's. Garw/Ffaldau. Roseheyworth. | Newbridge. Newbridge. Pontypool. Caerphilly. Blackwood. Neath. Glyn Neath. Mountain Ash. Abertillery. Maesteg. Bridgend. Ebbw Vale. |
| 1986 | | 13,479 | Cwm/Coedely. Nantgarw. | Llantrisant. Taffs Well. |
| 1987 | | 10,200/ 8.9% | None closed. | |
| 1988 | | 9,421 | Lady Windsor /Abercynon. Abernant. Six Bells. | Ynysybwl. Pontardawe. Abertillery. |
| 1989 | | 6,924 | Cynheidre. Marine. Merthyr Vale. Oakdale. Trelewis. | Llanelli. Ebbw Vale. Aberfan. Oakdale. Trelewis. |

| Year. | S.W. deep mined output (tonnes) / % age of total UK. | Total no. of SW miners/ % age of total UK | Collieries closed. | Location. |
|---|---|---|---|---|
| 1990 | 5,125,000 t/ 4.7% | 3,697 | Blaenant. Oakdale. | Blaenant. Blackwood. |
| 1991 | | | Mardy. Penallta. Cwmgwili No. 2. Deep Navigation. | Rhondda Fach. Gelligaer. Ammanford. Gelligaer. |
| 1992 | | | Taff Merthyr. Betws New Mine (Management buy-out) FINALLY CLOSED IN 2003. | Gelligaer. Ammanford. |
| 1993 | | | None closed | |
| 1994 | 600,000 t / 1.0% | 500 | Tower (Workers' buy-out. Last deep mine open in South Wales) STILL IN PRODUCTION (2004). | Hirwaen. |

Far from being just a list of dry statistics, behind the litany as above is a wealth of human stories and the breaking up of communities, plus politics, finance and strategic thinking. Each closure was, to a greater or lesser extent, a microcosmic drama in its own right, while the macrocosmic background went through various phases. In general, five such phases can be identified.

## PHASES OF CLOSURE.

### Phase 1.

Between 1945 and 1956, although coalfield annual production increased from 20.7 Mt to 22.7 Mt, the number mines in the South Western Division dropped, from 222 (of which 176 were in production) to 155.

During this initial period of nationalisation many of the older, smaller pits were eliminated in the UK, as the first attempts were made to rationalise the industry. There were no artificial boundaries between collieries anymore and "takes" were optimised. Boundaries between collieries were now usually selected to coincide with major geological faults between the two sets of workings. In the absence of such major faulting the take for a single colliery could be enlarged, making other pits in the immediate vicinity redundant. In addition, quite a number of pits taken over by the NCB were functioning as little more than pumping stations, so as to relieve water ingress into nearby mines. They were never worked again and closed officially a year or so later. In such a case, the working mine would itself take over the pumping duty. These early closures occurred within the general climate of post-war optimism and increasing demand for coal. There was virtually no loss of manpower, since adjacent mines easily mopped this up. There was some occasional local resistance but nothing resembling a national, or even a coalfield-wide, movement.

### Phase 2.

Between 1957 and 1963, 51 collieries closed in South Wales.

In the late 1950's the harsh reality of competition from cheap oil intervened. Coal's share of energy demand went into a nosedive. Simultaneously, the effect of large-scale underground mechanisation made itself felt, as fewer units became necessary to produce the required output. Mines began to shut down at a rate approaching one per week. In this period the number of closed mines in the UK totalled 264, many of them by no means antique. No other coalfield in Britain suffered such a savage contraction as South Wales. Coal from the East Midlands, the cavalry division of the NCB, was a much more difficult marketing proposition due to its lower quality. It was nevertheless saleable, due to its lower cost. This was the result of significantly higher productivity in that coalfield. This in turn was due to more amenable geology, plus excellent industrial relations.

## Phase 3.

The period 1964-1971 saw 49 collieries close in South Wales.

This was initiated by the Labour government elected in 1964. In spite of commitments made to the coal industry when in opposition, their policy for a "new technologically oriented Britain" would prove to be devastating. The "white hot heat of the technological revolution" would add its weight to the ongoing assault by cheap oil. In addition to natural gas, nuclear energy was also pushed ahead, although every unit of electricity so produced was more expensive than the equivalent from conventional coal-fired power stations.

In 1960 there were still 83,400 miners in South Wales; by 1970 there were 40,300. Among the pits to close would be many where significant and recent capital investment had been made, and had not yet been written off.

## Phase 4.

During this period 25 mines were lost.

Between 1972 and 1984, coal as a whole was enjoying a renaissance. The ten-fold increase in the price of oil during the 1970´s had reversed the fortunes of the industry worldwide. Nevertheless, coal still had to operate in an economic environment. South Wales had the local high cost of production as a millstone around its neck, just at the time when involvement in coal production by the oil companies and the international trade in coal was taking off, bringing cheap coal to Europe. This showed itself in the loss of the speciality coal market, for example when the metallurgical industry started to import large quantities. It was markets such as these that had justified a higher selling price for South Wales coal in the past. Therefore, in this coalfield, pits continued to shut down.

## Phase 5.

From 1985 onwards came the fifth and final phase. This led to the industry's demise in South Wales, with the sole exception of opencast, plus Betws and Tower collieries.

Such was the result of the politically motivated massacre by the Tory Government, led by Margaret Thatcher, following the defeat of the miners in the 1984-85 strike. Behind the fig leaf of improved efficiency and market freedom, the selectiveness with which such concepts were applied exposed the vindictiveness with which the Government, and the hatchet men who were now running the industry, devoted themselves to the task.

## INDUSTRIAL RELATIONS.

## Problem Child.

From the beginning, within NCB circles South Wales was seen as a problem child. The NUM here was exceptionally militant, the geology exceptionally difficult and the financial losses exceptionally high. Years later in 1984, Lord Robens, previous chairman of the NCB, was to state:

"Every coalfield in Britain, with the exception of the East Midlands and Yorkshire, was a dead loser and I don't believe that South Wales or Scotland have ever made a penny profit for the National Coal Board". He would also write:

"If the industrial behaviour of the East Midlands miners had been as truculent as that of South Wales or Scotland, the coalfield could not have prospered".

The promotion of an East Midlands man to a position in South Wales had all of the dubious honour of a politician being appointed as Secretary of State for Northern Ireland. At the time of the Aberfan disaster the local Area General Manager was Mr. Thomas Wright, a native of the English Midlands. On being interviewed after the disaster by NCB Chairman Lord Robens and Production Director W. V. Sheppard CBE, Mr. Wright said that it was his experience in Wales that he could not make people do as they were told or make them work —— Generally, he (Wright) had thought long and hard about the events which had happened and could offer no explanation except that it was Wales and Welshmen (ref Aberfan, Government and Disasters).

Such statements expressed, without explaining, an underlying malaise. The closure policy and perceived remoteness of "the N.C. bloody B", plus conflict over price lists for wages based on output, all served with time to sour relationships. While trade union leaders came in as industrial relations officers (in the opinion of some just a case of the NUM kicking its dead wood upstairs) the attitudes of both management and men remained largely unchanged after nationalisation.

## Ghosts.

Always, lurking in the background of men's minds, were images of the past. What the miner-poet Idris Davies described as, "the ghosts of the slaves of the successful century", still stalked the mining villages. Most men were not even born, still less working, during the pre-war battles with the old coal owners, but that was not the point. During that period a culture had been created, into which they had been born and bred. The demeaning forelock-tugging obsequiousness, that all too often in former years was what stood between an employee and the poverty which redundancy would bring, plus the blight brought on small communities by death, injury and broken health for modest wages in the service of capitalism, continued to permeate the fibre of communities.

Varying in intensity between individual lodges and between different parts of the coalfield, a visceral hate, bitter and all pervading, hung in the collective memory. It dominated any political debate and, like some Olympic torch, was handed on from one generation to the next, and what a motivating thing it could be. It drove one on and gave strength in adversity. It gave clarity to the world and a black and white understanding of its rights and wrongs. The negative drive to curtail power and profits could not be turned around overnight, and not by transfer of the industry to public ownership. Such ownership, for the benefit of workers and people as it ostensibly was, maintained its traditional day-to-day characteristics. Management remained the same, risks remained the same and the pressure for production, production, production also remained the same. The introduction of pithead baths might have resulted in a concomitant disappearance of the blackened droves from the buses and streets of the valleys, thankfully wending their way home at shift's end. There was no equivalent disappearance from their hearts of the nagging corrosion that past injustice had wrought.

## Back to "Aggro".

At the onset of nationalisation there was a brief period of industrial relations quiescence among the South Wales miners. Until the beginning of the 1950's they were responsible for proportionally less production lost through disputes than most British coalfields. Then, with a few exceptions, from 1951 onwards they restored their reputation for industrial militancy.

In 1952, the biggest lodge in the coalfield, at Park and Dare combined collieries in the Rhondda Fawr, banned Saturday working as a political protest against the Conservative Government's economy measures. The Prime Minister at the time was Winston Churchill, re-elected after 6 years in opposition and, in spite of failing faculties due to advancing age, enjoying worldwide respect as an outstanding war leader - but not at Park and Dare. Their coalfield circular, calling on other lodges to follow their unofficial action, is indicative of the attitude prevailing:

"Churchill of Tonypandy fame doesn't listen to reason, the Warmonger is only impressed by ACTION. Let the Miners of Wales lead the people of the country into action, and show him that we are not prepared to have our living standards attacked to serve the interests of the Tories".

By 1966, although producing less than a tenth of total British output, South Wales was nevertheless responsible for over half the output lost through disputes. In assessing the future of an individual pit, attitude of the workforce could be a significant factor. This could vary considerably, with each unit a community in its own right. The degree of enlightenment or otherwise of the previous coal owners, the fervour and proselytising skill of left-wing activists, plus individual personalities past and present on both the management and union side, all entered into the equation. There were pits proud of their good labour relations, of which Lady Windsor in Ynysybwl, near Pontypridd, is an example.

On 4 November 1980, the manager, Mr. Glyn Pritchard, was quoted in the local press as saying:

"Our lads took grave exception to a recent description of Lady Windsor/Abercynon as a militant pit. We reject this inference, and I'm glad we have answered the comment in the most appropriate manner, by producing more coal". He went on to say:

"Traditionally this colliery has always had excellent relationships between management and men and has largely been dispute free". Such an exemplary record of good labour relations, combined with consistent profitability, was a major justification for the reorganisation scheme initiated in 1958, the same time as that at Fernhill, at the top of the Rhondda Fawr. As at Fernhill the objectives were:

i) Deepen shafts.

ii) Provide skip winding of coal.

iii) Drive new horizons below ground for locomotive haulage.

iv) Comprehensive reorganisation of the surface.


Workable reserves were assessed at 44 Mt, with the majority of this below the 9 ft. seam, which was the limit of the existing shaft depth. Good labour relations continued to be a characteristic of Lady Windsor and the reorganisation scheme was pursued to completion. In stark contrast at Fernhill they weren't and it was not.

Some pits, usually those such as Fernhill lying deep within the enclosed valleys at the coalfield's centre, were equally proud of their record as being "the ruination of management". For, as seen through the eyes of some, management was on the front line of worker oppression by the capitalists. The level of militancy at a particular pit would reflect the attitude of certain key members of the local NUM lodge for these could convince, or sometimes cow the workforce with the fear of being ridiculed as "bosses' men".

Managers themselves came to terms with this ethos and dealt with it in their own way. Some seemed hell bent on justifying their bogeyman reputation, with loud-mouthed ignorance being the main interpersonal skill in their repertoire. On the other side, it was not unknown for the wife of a colliery manager to be treated almost as an outcast in the local shops. The more notorious managers all had nicknames. There were many stories, some apocryphal, of the on-going aggravation, with two examples being given below:

At his first meeting with the Park Colliery lodge, manager "Tommy Echo" was informed, "You know that we in Park Colliery have the reputation of being the ruination of management, we'll take the wave out of your hair". To which the gentleman concerned patted his flowing locks while replying, "Well, many have tried but its still there".

So as to freeze recalcitrant colliers currently operating a go-slow, manager "Dai Dappy" (dappy is Welsh slang for crazy) increased the ventilation flow in the district concerned. After traversing the coalface and being confronted with a series of catcalls, he turned to holler, "You're all a lot of b——s, but I'll f—— the lot of you yet".

Dai Dappy had received his nickname following a course of treatment at a mental hospital, resulting in his famous retort, "At least I've got a certificate to prove that I'm sane, which is more than what you b—
—s have"!

## PLANNING AND PROSPECTS.

### The Hidden Agenda.

In early 1965 a meeting was held between the Minister of Power and the Secretary of State for Wales. The meeting brief, issued by the NCB South Western Division, summed up official thinking. Gone is the early euphoric optimism. Its negative outlook combined with the poor employment situation in Wales, plus the fact that mining was still the largest employer, explains its classification of "Secret". Excerpts give an insight into the Board's assessment of prospects in South Wales at that time.

General Background.

"Making forecasts for the South Wales coalfield is singularly difficult because of its geology. Although the characteristics of its rocks are similar to those of other British coalfields (i.e. the percentage of workable coal thickness and characteristics of associated sequences) the fault intensity is three to four times that experienced in the Midlands coalfields. This results from the coalfield being at the confluence of two major fault systems. The tectonic forces set up by these zones of rupture have resulted in the high fault intensity. This fault pattern and its effect on associated weak roof shales and coal seams is the prime limiting factor in the economics of mining in South Wales. In present working areas no material improvement can be expected in geological conditions; none of the virgin areas are likely to afford better mining conditions. Because of the geology, some parts of the South Wales coalfield are not suitable for modern intensive mining methods".

Investment.

With such a poor basis to work on, returns on investment were questionable:

"In other Divisions it is possible to take a view of the future within reasonably narrow limits - to estimate potential production, to erect a tentative forward closure programme; and to schedule further developments which will enable a required level of output to be maintained. Because of geological factors, referred to above, this is not possible in South Wales. Experience has shown that what appears to be the best investment opportunities may fail in the event. Collieries such as Nine Mile Point, Cambrian, Harry Stoke, Llanharan, Rhigos have been the subject of major capital schemes, which have failed. The new collieries, Abernant and Cynheidre, have encountered unexpected difficulties, which have led to changes of plans, and difficulty in attaining planned results. It is idle to pretend that the slate is now clean. Other collieries are in difficulties from which they may or may not emerge".

Future Prospects.

With regard to future prospects, it was stated that the main factor affecting the level of output was the cost of production. Nevertheless, the Board still expected current output to be maintained. Production in 1970-71 was expected to be 19-21 Mt.

Financial Performance.

Financial performance of the Division had been miserable:

"The losses sustained by South Western Division over recent years have been a considerable burden on the industry. In the fifteen months to the end of March 1964 the Division produced 24.4 Mt but at a loss before interest of 1,800,000 pounds or 1/6d per ton. In the half-year to September last (i.e. September 1964) the Division lost 2,060,000 pounds before interest".

Colliery Closures.

With regard to colliery closures:

"Wherever practicable we shall continue to close collieries which make no contribution to fixed charges. The uncertainties of mining, which affect South Wales particularly, are such that there may have to be closures of collieries that at present look like being economic producers for many years ahead. No firm programme of closures can therefore be formulated".

With regard to the 95 collieries operating in the Division at that time, the briefing went on to say:

"Subject to all the uncertainties, South Western Division might have some 65 collieries in operation throughout the 1970's, including some new units not yet in production. —— In the context of broad policy, pits are closed by exhaustion of reserves and by the customers. The industry is bound to suffer if the price of coal is high in relation to gas or oil. Individuals cannot be forced to buy what they do not want. Thus if by keeping heavily losing pits in production we are forced to increase prices, sales will fall and in the end there may have to be more closures than ever".

Manpower.

On the subject of manpower, the briefing pointed out that although total manpower was expected to decline as productivity increased, the present rate of rundown was excessive, with shortages in many parts of the Division. According to plan, the 1963-64 figure of 76,700 should be reduced to between 52,000 and 57,700 in 1970-71, that is a rundown of between 32-25 per cent. Currently, the level of voluntary wastage was 25 per cent above budget, whereas the level of adult and juvenile recruitment was 21 and 18 per cent below budget respectively. There were 2,000 immediate vacancies and the Division had a considerable housing programme in hand. This was to ease redeployment within the Division and to encourage trained miners to transfer from the North-east of England and Scotland. The general policy on manpower was expressed as follows:

"The whole idea behind the Board's plans for investment in new and reconstructed collieries was to enable these to take manpower from, and thus permit the closure of, old collieries that were uneconomic or bad geologically. The Board has spent some 90,000,000 pounds in South Western Division, reconstructing the industry to replace the capacity of old and uneconomic collieries. Closures and the redeployment of manpower to the reconstructed collieries are necessary if the Board is to get a good return for its investment. Mobility of labour within the industry must be maintained if the industry is to adapt itself to technological change. The present manpower shortage in South Wales means this is the best time for the closure of collieries which are uneconomic or whose reserves are becoming exhausted, as men can be redeployed with an absolute minimum of redundancy to more modern collieries. The Board will continue by the careful planning of individual closures and its redundancy and transfer schemes to make special efforts to ease the social effects of colliery closures".

Conclusion.

The briefing summed up by stating:

"In physical terms there is considerable flexibility in South Western Division. If manpower is available, the level of output will depend on the level of costs that can be supported. To a greater extent than in most Divisions flexibility depends on the timing of closures - the scope for attractive further new construction and reconstruction is limited. Subject to proving and economic assessment there may be scope for the construction of a few small new units in various parts of the South Wales coalfield."

With the exception of these few small new units therefore, the best that the South Wales coalfield could hope for was a prolongation of inevitable decline. The NCB would speak much about, "A secure future in long-life pits" but such supposedly long-life pits could not be guaranteed for their status could change, virtually overnight. Manpower was urgently required in such pits but only for the present, so as to optimise decline. The "flexibility" which the Division offered was no more than the ability to manipulate pit closures, with the transfer of associated manpower as the Board saw fit.

The above briefing could hardly be publicised as an inspiration for the new recruits that the Coal Board were trying to attract, nor for the 76,700 currently employed. Neither did it conform to the case for nationalisation as put forward by the SWMF to the Royal Commission in 1919:

"Men would feel that they had control or some control over their own energies, and they were not merely at the will and direction of another being".

The strategic imperative of redeploying manpower at the will and direction of the NCB, so as to further economies in production, might have been perfectly logical from the Board's point of view. It might also have been in accordance with the objective of the NCB to break even, as laid down by Parliament. For the South Wales miners, however, it seemed all too often as arbitrary manipulation by an authority as remote from them as any capitalist coal owner. The briefing as above implies a degree of short-termism with regard to individual closure decisions.

Not stated, but widely believed, was a tendency to close small pits, even if making a profit, so as to use the manpower to reduce (if not eliminate) the losses being made by the big pits. From an accountant's viewpoint, the overall financial contribution was thereby enhanced. Older pits were closed more rapidly than they otherwise would have been. If this had not been done, excess capacity, combined with the market contraction at the time, would have left the newer pits insufficiently depreciated.

## Nomad Miners.

Older and smaller pits might not fit into the NCB's economic view of the world. They were nevertheless, in many cases, the sole reason for a community's existence. People had grown up and had their roots there. No other industry has the comradeship of the mining industry and this applies especially to small mines and in particular to the enclosed valley communities. A transfer could be traumatic, with the loss of old comradeship and customs, sheltered employment for the disabled and the familiarity of the old pit. As colliery after colliery shut down, many miners were subjected to multiple displacements. Large units might in theory be more efficient but they often seemed impersonal to the men transferred, by NCB decision, from the warm and exclusive companionship of their regular "butties". This was why such manpower transfers had only limited success.

Between May and June 1951, the most serious disruption in South Wales since nationalisation occurred. The NCB wanted to transfer 87 miners from Wern Tarw colliery, at Pencoed near Bridgend, to Llanharan. This latter pit had received millions of pounds of investment, on the basis of reserves sufficient for 150 years work. The Wern Tarw men saw this as being one step towards closure. Although an official coalfield conference of the NUM decided not to support the lodge and the transfer went ahead, unofficial action brought out 15,000 miners, including the whole of the Dulais Valley in the anthracite area. Ironically Wern Tarw, which closed in 1964, outlived Llanharan, the official long-life pit with 150 years of work in front of it. This closed in 1962.

In another case, Nantgarw, in which £5 M had been invested in the 1940's and early 1950's, was proving to be something of a white elephant. In spite of pioneering horizon-mining techniques its output was only 100,000 tonnes per annum. It had a vast turnover of manpower. The seams, and hence coalfaces, were steeply inclined. In a method of working unique in South Wales, along these faces chutes rather than conveyors were the order of the day. In hand working the colliers would break off the coal which then slid down the incline. Each collier's "stent" was stepped back from the one below to prevent the coal so won from falling onto his colleague. Due to poor working conditions resulting from such difficult geology, between 1959 and 1960 over 1,000 men left the colliery. The NCB attempted to replace them by partial or full closure of older pits, transferring their manpower to Nantgarw.

In 1958, Naval Colliery in the Rhondda was shut down for this purpose, while a contraction was proposed for Park Colliery, thus enabling the transfer of an additional 350 men. On this latter occasion the tactic was vigorously opposed by the NUM, who were able to make a case for keeping the men at Park. Naval did shut down, with a high proportion of its workforce preferring to leave the industry rather than work in the dreaded Nantgarw.

On the break-up of their local, traditional environment, many men preferred to make a fresh start outside the mining industry if possible. Technical staff were proving difficult to keep anyway. While the position of mining in the overall pay scale was slipping steadily backwards, the apprenticeship schemes of the Board continued to enjoy a good reputation in outside industry. For technicians the possibility beckoned of work that was purely technical, without the considerable physical effort, risk and industrial relations stress of the pits.

For those who left the industry, all was not necessarily rosy. With the exception of technical staff, highly skilled miners are only highly skilled in mining. Outside, they may well be employed as a common labourer or as an unskilled assembly worker. This had a profound effect, not only on wages but also on self-esteem. Even technical staff would sometimes miss the comradeship and challenge of their recent past. On the social side, as pits closed miners' welfare halls, in order to survive, became clubs dedicated to bingo and drinking. The concept of "miners' welfare", with its emphasis on educational, sporting and cultural pursuits disappeared from the scene.

## Rhetoric.

The ostentatious reading of newspapers by South Wales delegates during the speech of the NCB Chairman to the annual NUM conference, accompanied by much noise and activity during the turning of pages, was one of the least intelligent methods of expressing the coalfield's case.

On 20 November 1964, at a meeting at Hobart House, NCB headquarters, the arguments were expressed more cogently by Mr. William Whitehead, South Wales Area President of the NUM. Will Whitehead had replaced Will Paynter as South Wales President in 1959, on the latter's promotion to National General Secretary. At this time he was regularly in the news, having become something of a media personality in South Wales. Later, in 1966, due to issues related with a rest home being built for South Walian miners in Cornwall, his union colleagues would turn against him. Glyn Williams would replace him as South Wales president. Both the rest home and Whitehead would disappear from the scene. The union would sell off the former while NCB Chairman, Lord Robens, would assist the latter with the offer of a post in industrial relations. Now, his lucidity and passion were still at their peak, albeit that his arguments would turn out to be in vain. The immediate issue was the closure of Rhigos (in the Upper Cynon), and Glyncastle (in the Dulais), plus the partial closure of Cambrian (in the Rhondda). Whitehead said:

"You are heading to disaster, for ruin in the South Wales coalfield if this policy is pursued, and that is why we are taking this opportunity of raising these three pits and the consequences which will follow from them. Take Cambrian; the Cambrian colliery is situated in Blaenclydach, a mining village. As a mining village it has already suffered enough. It is, I may say, a closely-knit community. The manpower is employed in Cambrian colliery and there are difficult conditions in that pit, as in others. Nevertheless, these men are cohesive. Maybe the discipline is not of the sort that the Board would require but they have played their part in the labour movement. The lodge in fact has a very good tradition and its tradition is, amongst other things, that for miners it is the premier lodge. There is a regard for Cambrian in the South Wales coalfield, amongst the men as well as everybody else.

The point we want to put is this; it may well be that the ways of the Board will prevail over the ways of the Union in this matter but we will tell you now the consequences of transferring these men. All that you will do will be to lose them to the industry. True, a small proportion will go to Lewis Merthyr and the other pits but you will not solve any problem, because what are your problems. You have problems at National, Lewis Merthyr, Tymawr, Lady Windsor, Cwm and Coedely collieries. All of these pits want manpower, so you transfer these men from Cambrian, but only a fraction of them will go. You solve therefore neither the Cambrian problem nor the problems at the other pits. We know that is going to be the result of your actions.

Now what is the history of recent years with regard to Cambrian? In 1959 the Coal Board closed Tydraw and a substantial number of men were transferred to Gelli colliery. As if they were contemplating running the valley out of existence, in 1962 the Board closed Gelli and transferred the men to Cambrian. In 1963-64 however, 250 men were transferred from Cambrian to neighbouring pits and now in 1964 it is proposed that a further 300 or so be transferred. Somebody said, and there is a measure of truth in this, that these men have become the gypsies of the coalfield because they have moved from Tydraw to Gelli, Gelli to Cambrian, Cambrian to where? You won't hold them, you will lose them.

That is Cambrian; we do not accept that all the reserves of coal are completed there. There are seams, which can be worked. In fact we say that in many of the English coalfields there are seams being worked of inferior quality to those being worked in Cambrian, yet you are still working them.

Now let us look at Glyncastle colliery. The Board decided to close Onllwyn 3, between 500 and 600 men. These were distributed over 26 pits and some of them went to Glyncastle. This is a pit with enormous reserves, probably there is not a pit in any British coalfield with the reserves of that quality coal, the finest quality, which Glyncastle has. This is not in dispute, no one around this table would be so foolish as to question whether there are reserves there of the finest quality anthracite coal. As a union, we recognised that we may fail in those other pits in the Dulais valley, but we try to look beyond the end of our industrial noses. We agreed that if the Board decided that they couldn't work those other collieries then we would recognise Glyncastle as a major receiving pit, so as to be sure that the men would be found employment. For many years Glyncastle made a profit. It only ceased to make a profit when the Coal Board experimented with new techniques. The answer will be given by the Board that it is the new demands in wages and so forth that has compelled it to make a loss but wages have been increasing since 1937 and it has continued to make a profit. It could still make a profit, it is a small pit with hardly any drivages at all and hardly any traffic at all. In fact I make a challenge that if the books are properly shown it is making a profit today. In these last weeks that pit could have made a profit because there are no haulage roads of any consequence to maintain. That is the position at Glyncastle".

The NCB reconsidered, and then confirmed their original decision to proceed with the above closures. Reasons given were, as usual:

- Capital investment was required to access new reserves.

- In view of geological problems being experienced, it was unlikely that such new reserves would be any more successful than the present area of work.

- It was the government's policy to hasten the closure of short life, uneconomic pits, especially where a long life colliery was nearby to absorb the men.


## Niche Opportunities.

The financial failure of all the big development projects eventually led to a school of thought on the part of senior management that South Wales's future, to the extent that it had one at all, lay in niche opportunities, with smaller pits of perhaps 500 men or so working limited takes and producing moderate outputs of superior coal. These would be in areas where the level of geological disturbance was not prohibitive.

The 1965 briefing of the South Western Division had stated, "Subject to proving and economic assessment there may be scope for the construction of a few small new units in various parts of the South Wales coalfield". Such small new units were indeed constructed. Most of these were drift mines in the anthracite area of the west. Here, colliery "takes" were characterised by small areas of relatively undisturbed coal, surrounded by deformed strata where successful working was difficult.

Working as they did the relatively easy seams close to the surface, capital investment in such projects was much less than with the big, deeper pits. With a high value product obtained with low manpower, backed up with extensive mechanisation and the automation of coal transport, they proved to be highly successful. First class profits were made. In the deeper seams, faulting and a propensity for gas outbursts would not allow such a rosy picture. A list of such "niche" projects is given below:


Cwmgwili, at Crosshands, Carmarthen.

In 1960, two drifts were driven into the Big Vein seam.

In 1970 a 150,000 pound scheme merged the mine with Lindsey colliery, which was another drift mine in the vicinity sunk in 1962. With a work force of only 379, an extremely high tonnage of anthracite was produced. Annual output in the late 1970's was around 126,000 tonnes. The mine was one of the few units to operate the room and pillar method of mining. Joy Loaders were employed to load out the coal, which had been won by explosives and/or hand working. This continued into the 1980's, the last example of such methods in South Wales.

Blaengwrach, at Cwmgwrach, near Neath.

There had been workings in this general area since 1814. A new drift was completed in 1962, thereby accessing the Six Feet seam. In the late 1970´s the colliery drove into the Nine Feet seam but was unable to prevail against difficult geology. The mine closed in 1983.

Treforgan, at Crynant, near Neath.

Driving of the two drifts, with a gradient of 1 in 3, commenced in 1963 and production started in 1966. Highly automated, very high annual output of much needed anthracite was produced from the Red Vein seam. Originally intended as a short life mine, Treforgan became one of the most profitable mines in the UK. Its performance slumped in the late 1970's, only to recover again later.

Blaenant, in the Dulais Valley.

Following the closure of Cefn Coed colliery in 1968, a short-lived drift operated for a few years in the vicinity. The new Blaenant Drift was then commissioned to work the No. 2 Rhondda seam. This drift was 605 meters in length, with a gradient of 1 in 3.7. The old Cefn Coed shafts were retained for service and ventilation. A modern manriding train carried 120 miners to their place of work in the production district. En route it crossed over the Dulais River on a covered bridge. This also carried the main trunk conveyor for the complete production. The mine had highly mechanised workings, with ten miles of underground roadways and three miles of high-speed conveyors.

Bettws New Mine, at Ammanford.

This was the last major mine to be sunk in the South Wales coalfield. Sinking began in 1974, to exploit an isolated area of reserves in the Red Vein seam where the 3 leaves of coal, which constitute this seam, come together. In this area, these formed a fairly thick section of about 1.5 m, in a good geological environment. Twin drifts were driven to the Red Vein seam, a distance of two and a half miles at a gradient that varied between 1 in 5 and 1 in 14. Initially, hard, water-bearing sandstone slowed down the rate of advance but construction was completed in the two and a half years allocated. Retreat mining began in the early spring of 1978. The mine was laid out to produce 500,000 t/a from two coalfaces, with a third in reserve. The workforce of 500 was composed of men from the closed Ammanford slant and Graig Merthyr mine. By 1983 it was the second most profitable pit in the country. The mine became a showcase, with low level, cream coloured surface buildings along with trees and landscaped tipping so as to blend into the rolling Carmarthen countryside. Together with Tower colliery, it was one of the only two working mines remaining in South Wales when the industry was privatised in 1994. It closed in 2003.

## MANPOWER AND MECHANISATION.
### Why Work 5 Days When I Can Live On 4?

Among those miners that remained in the industry, absenteeism, at an average of 17 per cent, was well above the national level. This aspect of the morale problem was particularly pronounced in South Wales, and especially on Mondays and Fridays. If a three-day pay packet was capable of meeting the weekly outgoings, which face-workers especially as the highest paid group often judged it to be, then for many miners the attraction of a long weekend was proving to be irresistible. The standard, knee-jerk, reply to the question by management, "Why do you only work three days in a week"? was, "Because I can't live on two"! The work was hard, and many of the underground workers were past their physical peak. Alternative, lighter work in the communities to which they were so attached was not available. Besides, they thrived on the comradeship and what other employer would tolerate an employee regularly taking unpaid leave at whim? In those pits judged to be longer life, manpower was anyway at a premium and the consequence of such absenteeism was to reduce effective manpower to even less than that shown on the books.

On Monday, 20 June 1962 there was absenteeism of 58 per cent in the Rhondda area. At Park Colliery, one of the Rhondda pits, it averaged 58 per cent for the whole week!

In the second half of 1966, average absenteeism for the South Wales coalfield was 17.5 per cent. In the Rhondda Valley it was 23.38 per cent, with 30 per cent not unusual. To make matters worse, it was mainly at the "sharp end" of production, at the coalface, where these men were missing.

## Mechanisation.

The only hope of providing a return on the considerable investment already made in pit infrastructure was to maximise output from such investment. This requirement, combined with the chronic shortage of manpower at pits, made mechanisation an imperative. It was, however. by no means an easily applied panacea. The degree of mechanisation in South Wales, as well as productivity, continued to lag behind the national average.

Already in 1919, Mr. E. H. Hann of the Powell Dyffryn company, had explained to the Royal Commission on the coal industry why so few machines had been introduced into South Wales mines:

"This slow progress is due chiefly to three things.

- Firstly, most of the coal seams contain slips or breaks every foot or two, and thus loosen the coal, a feature peculiar to South Wales.

- Secondly, the weight or crush is far greater at equal depths in South Wales than in any of the other fields, thus rendering far more face timber necessary and increasing the difficulty of safely maintaining the necessary space for the machine, likewise other troubles in the faces.

- Thirdly, the fact that small faults or dislocations are so much more numerous than in other districts and so frequently prevent the development of or interrupt the progress of a face.

- A less frequent trouble is the presence of water which, however, is sometimes absolutely fatal to the attempt to use the machines".

Even by the late 1950's only 9 per cent of South Wales coal was power loaded. The remainder was won with pneumatic picks or explosives and then shovelled by hand onto the face conveyor. Traditional manual methods were however flexible, which machine mining was not. With the introduction of mechanisation, time and again a limited return to traditional methods became necessary as weak roof strata broke up between hydraulic supports. This would necessitate additional and temporary timber supports being erected by hand in the affected area, slowing down the whole production process. Seam thickness would vary beyond the pre-planned range of both power-loader and hydraulic supports, sometimes to disappear completely or sometimes to be split into sections by an unworkable band of rock.

Time and again, machines would be installed, to work just a portion of the face only, and then perhaps not the full seam thickness. Attempts to produce on two shifts per day instead of only one would sometimes result in a rate of advance with which the roof would not co-operate, resulting in excessive pressure on the supports and/or falls of ground. In the past, cheap manual labour using skill, hand-tools and experience, could and did produce under these circumstances, with sweat and muscle power, coal that was economic on the market place. Wage rates and social expectations had advanced and those days were gone.

## Broken Dreams.

As often as not investment failed to bring results, with the big "glamour" projects failing to live up to the hopes they had originally kindled. There were many such broken dreams.

By 1958, Nantgarw was losing 22 shillings and eight pence for every ton of coal produced, while the saleable yield from total production was only 55 per cent.

Mardy, the first mine to be completely reconstructed in the South Western Division, is another example. The experience of just one coalface at Mardy can serve as being typical of many.

In 1968 the Y1 face was opened in the yard seam. Approximately183 metres in length it was fully mechanised, with the intake and return gate roads at each end being driven on some metres in advance of the face itself. These roadways were advanced by explosives, with the coal and spoil so produced being loaded out by gathering arm loaders of Joy manufacture. Between the two gate roads, a power-loading machine of the "trepanner" type worked the face. This would win the coal and load it onto the armoured, flexible chain conveyor that traversed the face. The typical seam section was 1 metre with a self-advancing hydraulic system for roof support, of a type specially designed for low, faulted and disturbed seams. With such a configuration and the quality of coal being worked, all seemed set fair.

Within weeks the face ran into geologically disturbed ground. One fault had been struck halfway along the face, and a second by the advanced heading of the return gate road. On the face itself, on both sides of the fault, prehistoric stress had broken up the ground and destroyed adhesion between adjacent levels of strata. As a consequence, in this area the roof was breaking up and falling in between the roof support beams. The result was a cavernous open space above the coalface. This had to be supported by wooden blocks, arranged in "chock" form on top of the regular hydraulic supports.

The roof was not the only problem, for the floor stratum was proving to be soft, causing bases of the supports to sink in. The leading edge of the support assemblies would then have to be dug out with pick and shovel and the way smoothed to enable these self-advancing supports to self-advance. Mechanisation was intended to reduce manual effort, but considerable manual effort was necessary to give mechanisation any chance at all. The caustic, all-pervading, humour was not to be done down, with everyone trying to trump the previous joke. Much was made of the vaunted characteristics of the roof supports (specially designed for low, faulted and disturbed seams, ha ha!).

If top and bottom were giving problems on the face, the coal seam in between also contributed to the general litany of woe. The section was not constant. In the fault's vicinity, the 1 m seam thickness reduced to 66 cm. At the fault itself, seam thickness reduced to 33 cm. This was much less than the cutting section of the machine. Fortunately, the machine was able to cut through soft shale above the coal. As well as varying thickness, instead of being laid out in a flat plane the seam exhibited a "wave-like" configuration, with the result that the power loader frequently cut into the roof and floor. To lower the machine's cutting horizon below its limited range, sections of the armoured face conveyor, on the side opposite to the face, would be jacked up and wooden blocks placed underneath, thus giving a tilting effect.

The fault at the return end had thrown the seam upwards, resulting in the return gate road, driven in the seam, now being at a higher level than the face itself. Consequently, to avoid a vertical step of several metres at the interface between return gate and coalface, the top and bottom strata in this area had to be continually cut away as the face advanced, thus resulting in a more manageable ramp interface. The whole saga was completed with problems experienced by the electrical system. These were:

- Difficulty in advancing the tail-end switchgear due to the step of several metres in the return gate-road, resulting from the second fault.

- Frequent failure of the signalling units along the face due to water ingress.


As the Y1 inched painfully forward, the whole picture is of local practical initiative combined with considerable manual effort, totally out of proportion to the production actually achieved. All of this was necessary to deal with problems extraneous to production but without whose solution production simply could not take place. Problems were occurring which theoretically just should not be there and, inevitably, output statistics were a disappointment.


## West is Worse.

If geology in the Rhondda valley area was bad, in the west, that is the anthracite field, it was worse. The two new ultra modern pits, Cynheidre and Abernant, developed to work the lower coal measures, soon encountered geology far more complex than anticipated. The seams proved to be highly disturbed, and very costly to work. They would never achieve the performance originally expected of them. Production rarely exceeded 50 per cent of that anticipated.

By 1972 at Cynheidre, 1,430 men were producing 472,000 tonnes/a from the only 2 seams found workable, the Big Vein (a combination of the seams known as 4ft.and Upper Gellideg elsewhere) and the Pumpquart (known elsewhere as the Lower Gellideg). The former was acceptable due to its thickness and the latter due to its relatively good geological characteristics. Attempts were made initially to work most of the seams present at the mine but such attempts were abandoned, either because they were too thin (<9cm) or because of poor geology (weak roof and/or in-seam disturbance). Cynheidre was technically first class but its geology was the worst in South Wales. Indeed, former Area Director, Mr. Phillip Weekes, called it the worst in Europe. Since by world standards Europe is difficult generally, that is saying something.

At Abernant, the other big anthracite mine, 1,020 men produced 365,000 tonnes/a. This mine was also technically first class and prime anthracite was produced from the Red Vein seam at a depth of 366 metres. The shafts, at a depth of 828 metres the deepest in the coalfield, actually extended down to the Peacock seam. So called because of its characteristic bluey-green sheen, this coal was described as, "The best anthracite in the world". However, geological difficulties combined with pressure at this depth meant that to mine it proved impracticable.

Both pits were subject to the phenomena of outbursts, i.e. high-pressure methane in the seam bursting forth on the coalface with explosive force and in a quantity sufficient to cause asphyxiation. In 1972 at Cynheidre, six miners died as the result of such an outburst. Water ingress compounded the problems. Large pumps, each of 450 KW rating, removed between 10 and 15 million gallons of water per week from the colliery.

An illustration of the general ethos of the western area, and the different experience of working shallow versus the deeper seams, is given by the example of Graig Merthyr colliery near Pontardulais. A drift mine, tucked away and hidden in a narrow and empty farming valley to the north of this village, it was accessible only by circuitous single lane roads. Two clanking tank engines, Austerity and Norma worked trains of Graig Merthyr coal along an NCB private line, down the valley to the coal preparation plant at Brynlliw colliery.

Largely Welsh-speaking, and strongly oriented towards the villages of Velindre and Pontardulais, a minimum of what went on at Graig Merthyr reached the outside world. Production statistics could not be hidden, but otherwise questionable records were submitted to the Area office of maintenance inspections ostensibly carried out, while unofficial incentives for work to be finished on time flourished. Such incentives would be typically the payment of "water money" where no work in water was involved, or overtime payments given to men who finished early.

Dewatering of the mine was assisted by the old Clydach Merthyr drift at Clydach, 7 miles (11.27km) to the north of Swansea. This drift closed in 1961, but was retained as a pumping station for Graig Merthyr. It could have been retained as an industrial museum. Not only did it have an underground blacksmith's shop in the Graigola seam, there were underground boilers too. These were thought to have been in operation until the late 1940´s. A drift from the boilers terminated at a stack in the side of the valley. Rising air from the boilers assisted the main ventilation, which was provided by an historic Waddle fan of 6 metres diameter, dating from 1880 and driven by a single cylinder steam engine.

Graig Merthyr had another surprising feature, this time natural. The large area of unsupported sandstone roof was unique. The roof of the Graigola seam was exceptionally strong. Graig Merthyr and Clydach Merthyr were the only mines operated by the National Coal Board to work with a roof needing little or no support. On being asked by an Inspector of Mines on one occasion, "Mr. Jones, what exactly is holding up this roof?" the Undermanager addressed could only reply, "It must be purely imagination".

About 605 men produced around 150,000 t/a, originally in the Graigola and Swansea Six Feet seams. Particularly the Graigola was close to the surface, while seam thickness was such as to enable miners to stand upright. Workings were room and pillar, with coal being won by hand and loaded out by means of gathering arm Joy loaders.

In 1969, as the shallower seams approached exhaustion, a 250-metre longwall face was opened in the Three Feet seam. This lay deeper and to the west of the take. For the men at Graig Merthyr this was a different world, with life suddenly becoming very hard. Absenteeism became a problem. Officials struggled to motivate men in this new fight for coal, bribing, bullying and cajoling those whose presence was due solely to the commitment to their village and the mining way of life. Certain individuals, at ease with physical hardship, became key men. On the face, no longer was it possible to remain dry and stand upright. In heights of 2 ft. (0.6m) there was inadequate space to crawl, and sliding became the order of the day. To compound the misery, heavy water ingress converted coaldust into a black glutinous slime that impeded progress. Along the armoured flexible conveyor the plough would rattle and grind, sometimes scooping up as much water as coal. Pumps, situated at intervals along the face, were essential, even if they did sometimes clog with coaldust. The result was the formation of miniature underground lakes, through which one had to slide if pump intakes were to be freed of obstruction.

In this wet, lizard-like existence, some men dressed in oilskins as protection against water while others objected to this additional confinement in an environment already extremely confined. Movement alone was itself hard work. With such restriction, coalface communication was at a premium. The initiative of the electrical department was taxed to its utmost in keeping alive a system of loud speaking telephones, never designed for submarine service.

On one occasion, Her Majesty's Electrical Inspector of Mines, after traversing the face, emerged pitch black with saturated and torn clothes over his bruised body. As a colonel in the Salvation Army his quiet verdict on the situation was:

"Yes, I do appreciate the difficulty of maintaining good engineering standards under such conditions but it's rather like preaching the gospel. You just have to keep plugging away".

In 1978, the unequal struggle ended and Graig Merthyr closed, due to exhaustion of reserves.

In the anthracite area at the time of nationalisation, 17,500 miners worked 40 pits.

By 1981, of the five anthracite mines remaining, Cynheidre and Abernant were deep mines. Betws New Mine, Aberpergwm and Blaengwrach were drifts. A total of 3,628 men were employed. Of these, 1,269 were at Cynheidre and 862 at Abernant.


## CHANGING STANDARDS.

Standards and expectations changed with time. To take Mardy as an example, the reserves of over 120 Mt quoted by the NCB at the time of Mardy's development, and sufficient for over one hundred years work, became a mere 7 Mt thirty years later. The question as to what constituted a reserve was no longer whether coal existed in the ground but whether such coal could be worked economically by machine mining, against a background of an energy market subject to increasing competition. The answer of the Coal Board and the Government during the late 1950's and through the 1960's was, in all too many cases, no!

Plate 4 Mining as it was.

# Plate 5 Mining as it is (a) Plan View of Plough Drive-End.
## (Normaly duplicated at other end of face).

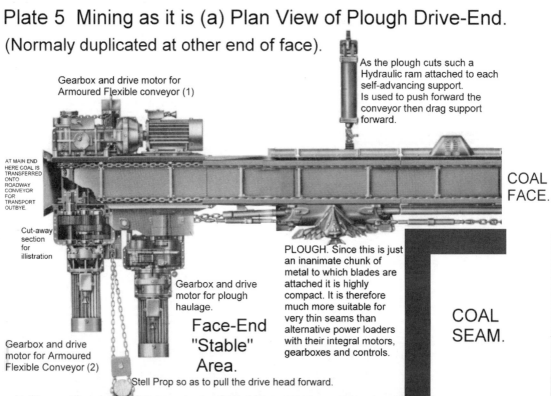

Gearbox and drive motor for
Armoured Flexible conveyor (1)

As the plough cuts such a
Hydraulic ram attached to each
self-advancing support.
Is used to push forward the
conveyor then drag support
forward.

AT MAIN END
HERE COAL IS
TRANSFERRED
ONTO
ROADWAY
CONVEYOR
FOR
TRANSPORT
OUTBYE.

COAL
FACE.

Cut-away
section
for
illistration

PLOUGH. Since this is just
an inanimate chunk of
metal to which blades are
attached it is highly
compact. It is therefore
much more suitable for
very thin seams than
alternative power loaders
with their integral motors,
gearboxes and controls.

Gearbox and drive
motor for plough
haulage.

Gearbox and drive
motor for Armoured
Flexible Conveyor (2)

Face-End
"Stable"
Area.

COAL
SEAM.

Stell Prop so as to pull the drive head forward.

# Chapter 8
## WHY US?

*Oh there's many a man that I've met in my day,*
*Who lived just to labour his whole life away.*
*Like a fiend with his dope or a drunk with his wine,*
*Some men are born for the work of the mine.*
Appalachian folk song.

## SHUT DOWN PROCEDURE.
### In Theory.

With a declining market and the consequent need to reduce capacity, closures were imperative, but which units should be closed and when? In practice the decision-making process could be messy and subjective.

From 1967, colliery closures were discussed between management and unions as part of the consultative committee procedure. These were regular meetings between the parties, held at both pit and Area level. Their function was to deal with general issues such as safety, productivity, manpower and any problems being experienced. Henceforward, if financial losses were high, the committee and higher officials would be warned that the results being achieved were such as to put the future of a pit in jeopardy. The unions would then be asked if they wished to carry out an inspection within the next six weeks. A so-called "jeopardy meeting" was then held. At this meeting it was NCB policy not to state that any decision had been made with regard to closure. Instead targets were given, so as to remove the pit from the jeopardy list. Any such removal however required the permission of national headquarters. The constituency MP would be informed by NCB senior management. A colliery would officially be placed in jeopardy at least 6 months before the date of closure. This period of notice could be prolonged. All closure decisions, including partial closures and mergers, except where less than 50 men were involved, were to be made by the NCB at national level. If the Board decided on closure, the NUM had the right of appeal. If a closure decision was made, official notice was normally given 3 months before the closure date.

### In Practice.

In practice, NCB internal opinion was often itself divided as to whether a pit had a future, whether investment could turn it around and if so how much investment and where. It could be possible for a pit to get out of bad geology by driving roadways into new, less disturbed areas. Entering into the equation was also the market for that particular type of coal, corporation policy, and attitude of the workforce. Each closure had its own story, and many left outstanding questions. The role played in some cases by lodge militancy and lack of co-operation appears to have attracted neither public attention nor investigative journalism, with an equal lack of interest being evoked by the fact that closures frequently occurred shortly after the completion of significant capital expenditure. Even if not discussed in the public domain, such waste was well noted by the miners themselves and reinforced their lack of respect for the organization for which they worked. The NCB planning department in particular bore the brunt of their irony.

In 1966, when Dyffryn Rhondda Colliery at Cymmer in the Afan Valley closed, Cementation Construction Ltd. was in the process of deepening the shafts. In the absence of acceptable cancellation terms the contract was fulfilled. Those locals aware of what was happening looked on perplexed as the shafts were finally deepened (would the colliery later re-open? Was this some Byzantine NCB plot just to scare the workforce?). There was no plot. After completion of the work the shafts were capped and the colliery surface demolished.

Also in 1966, Park Colliery at Cwmparc in the Rhondda Fawr was shut down, just two years after new roadways of a standard that impressed all who saw them were driven into an area of fresh reserves. In the new roadways one of the first automated conveyor networks in the Rhondda Area was installed, again of flagship standard. This was meant to ensure the colliery's future and those involved worked hard and with a will, so as to meet the tight deadline and secure the valley's prospects, often going home late and exhausted to collapse in sleep. When closure occurred so shortly afterwards it caused consternation, with the question being put, "What was the point of it all"?

In the latter quarter of 1968, National Colliery at Wattstown in the Rhondda Fach closed, shortly after £750,000 had been spent on improving underground transport so as to cater for increased output. In 1962, both winding engines had been electrified (they were previously steam driven). Such investment was normally written off over a period of 10-15 years. At the same time, additional investment had been announced for improvements to the coal preparation plant, and for underground development. The NCB stated publicly that they wanted to keep the National going but insisted on an assurance of "reasonable cooperation" from the 500 or so men working there. National belonged to the band of highly militant lodges. As a prerequisite for proceeding with the scheme, the NCB requested:

- That the day shift should be a production shift every week (to date the production shift had alternated between days and afternoons).

- Surplus surface workers (20-30 men) should be transferred to other collieries.

- For the transitional period being experienced, some underground workers, who were not registered as colliers, should be allowed to work coal.

The NCB stated at the time that the lodge's reaction did not represent the kind of cooperation being sought. Nevertheless, the investment was proceeded with.

On closure, the local press quoted the men as being "shocked", with one miner speaking of "a stab in the back". Another miner emphasised the amount of money invested in the colliery, saying, "It is a scandal that needs exposure". The prospect of finding alternative employment was regarded as slight, with great consternation being caused to older men, who inevitably suffered hardship.

The NCB quoted absenteeism, combined with lack of manpower, as the reason for closure, thus laying the blame squarely on the men themselves. Bill Woods, Lodge Chairman, would comment;

"We don't want to keep the National open because we like going down the pit. We'd rather work in a chocolate factory if we could only get one in the Rhondda" (Rhondda Past and Future, Introduction).

However, there were no chocolate factories, nor was it by any means certain that the men he represented would be happy working in them if there were!

**Closure Diplomacy.**

Until the end of the 1960's, NUM leadership at national, if not local, level accepted the logic of the closure programme and the rationalisation of the industry. During the "Ten year Stint" of Lord Robens as chairman of the National Coal Board there was a good working relationship between him and the Welsh communist Will Paynter, who was NUM General Secretary during this period. The latter's influence in the background, in his attempt to break the habit of having all South Wales closures automatically referred to the appeals procedure, is apparent during the flurry of such cases that occurred in the NCB West Wales area during 1967-68. This series of closures is also indicative of the interfaces between all five parties involved: NCB (national)-NCB (South Wales)-NUM (national)-NUM (South Wales)-Labour Government.

The first pits to be affected were Abercrave in the Swansea valley, Cefn Coed in the Dulais Valley and Pentreclwydau at Glyn Neath. Pentreclwydau was a new mine, developed to replace certain of the older drifts in the Neath Valley. In the NCB's opinion its workforce were not showing the commitment necessary to obtain acceptable results.

On 23 September 1966, at a meeting between the NCB and the NUM, the union rejected proposals for closing Pentreclwydau. This involved the transfer of 250 men to Blaengwrach and 60 to Aberpergwym, with the other 50 remaining to carry out salvage work. Instead the NUM presented their own plans, to continue developing and working fresh panels in the Peacock seam.

On 16 October 1966, the Board emphasised again that without a determined effort from all the men there was no hope of pulling the colliery around. Their proposal to reverse the fortunes of Pentreclwydau was accepted in principle by the colliery lodge. This included revised manning to secure bigger stents (i.e. the length of coalface worked by an individual collier) and re-allocation of tasks. Area officials would consider exact layouts. Also accepted by the union was the need for urgency, subject to the negotiation of satisfactory contract rates where none existed. It was now a question of getting things done.

On 9 December 1966, a letter was sent to the National Board from South Western Division. It stated, "Even now, these negotiations (i.e. for the new contract rates) have not been concluded —— as time went on, it became increasingly clear that the promised change in attitude was not materialising. —— the chances of improving the colliery's results slipped away". Pentreclwydau was therefore doomed, but there were still more closures to come.

On 16 January 1967, instructions were given to South Western Division from NCB headquarters, "The board have been concerned about the high losses incurred by a number of collieries. After reviewing these they have decided that Cefn Coed Colliery must be closed early in March 1967. Your Board (i.e. the S.W.Division Board) are to ensure that the Area Director-designate for West Wales puts the arrangements for this closure in hand without delay. It should be included in your Board's revised closure proposals".

On 17 January 1967, the very next day, the Division responded. Donald Davies (West Wales Area Director-designate) was most apprehensive about the effects of implementing the instructions as received. In the face of strong NUM resistance, the Divisional Board was already committed to, and heavily involved in, securing the successful closure of Abercrave and Pentreclwydau. The South Wales NUM had asked Will Paynter, their National General Secretary, to push for delaying the closures. With these negotiations going on it was neither desirable nor practical suddenly to confront the unions with the additional closure of Cefn Coed.

An NCB internal meeting was held at S.W.Division in Cardiff concerning the imminent closures of Abercrave, Pentreclwydau and Cefn Coed. It was stated that in total 1,700 men would be affected. Of particular concern was redeployment of the manpower at Cefn Coed. This would be difficult, especially in view of the high proportion of disabled men employed there.

On 27 January 1967, Hobart House (NCB headquarters, in London) replied to Donald Davies's letter as above, "The Board agree with your Divisional Board's view that it would not be opportune to put in hand the closure of Cefn Coed Colliery while negotiations for the closure of Abercrave and Pentreclwydau were proceeding. —— The early closure of Cefn Coed was however, inevitable. —— The Board decided that Cefn Coed should be closed within 3 months of the closure of Abercrave and Pentreclwydau".

On 7 March 1967, Lord Robens, NCB National Chairman, wrote to the S.W.Division concerning the subject of Pentreclwydau;

"In brief, while we know that the colliery has no possible future, it is most helpful to Paynter at this moment to get a deferment of this closure for three months. He hopes in this way to break the habit of having all South Wales closures automatically referred to the appeal procedure. —— he has undertaken that if at the end of a period of three months the general position of the mine and its prospects have not improved the union will accept closure without requiring a meeting at national level. In return we have agreed to defer the closure until the end of May. As we have to give a month's notice for the closure of the colliery this will mean issuing the notices at the end of April, unless there is a remarkable turn-round".

On 8 March 1967, a reply to Lord Robens concluded the issue, "Thank you for your letter of 7 March regarding the decision to defer the closure of Pentreclwydau. I fully appreciate the factors leading to this decision and hope that Paynter will be successful in reducing the number of appeals".

Abercrave and Pentreclwydau closed in 1967, subject to the agreed delays. (Following privatisation of the industry in 1994, Pentreclwydau reopened, only to close again at the end of the century).

In February 1968, the Labour Prime Minister Harold Wilson ventured into the lion's den and made a visit to South Wales, where pit closures were now in full swing. During the previous year the number of compulsory redundancies in mining had jumped to 12,900 nationally. This was more than six times the previous maximum. By this time, Ynyscedwyn had joined Cefn Coed on the closure list. In a good example of "stirring it up", just prior to Wilson's visit an NCB announcement informed the public that these pits would close the following month.

On the evening before the Prime Minister's departure, the Minister of Power issued a statement that the Coal Board had been wrong and premature in their announcement. The NCB had not followed proper procedure. While in Wales, Wilson backed up the Minister's statement, glossing over the fact that it was his government's energy policy that was forcing pit closures through at their current high rate. The NUM South Wales Secretary, Dai Francis, said the problem was that, "Lord Robens is in a political battle with the Government and Mr. Marsh, the Minister of Power". This was a correct assessment since Robens was at odds with the government over their White Paper on Energy in 1967, as a result of which large-scale pit closures were inevitable. Relations were at a low ebb.

While en route to Swansea, to view the situation on the ground, Wilson made a detour through Cefn Coed. Together with reporters and television crews, the miners assembled there, waving placards such as "Coal not Dole" and "Please Let Us Keep Our Jobs", were left standing as the Prime Minister's cavalcade drove straight through the village without stopping. Later he did speak with NUM representatives from the two pits, but to no avail.

Both Cefn Coed and Ynyscedwyn closed later that year.


## SOME CASE STUDIES.

### The Court of Star Chamber.

A tendency on the side of the local NUM to oppose automatically any and all closure proposals was matched by an equivalent tendency on the part of NCB planning to be "closure happy". Headquarters planning department would sometimes show exasperation at any reluctance, further down the line, to come to a closure decision. A series of memos would yap at the heels of such laggards. Any tendency to let matters slide was to be counteracted by agreed dates for coming to a decision, and this timetable was then to be adhered to. Reference to some examples in the NCB East Wales Area will help to illustrate the general picture. Like some industrial Court of Star Chamber, NCB Area Management operated a closure committee. These would sometimes act in a fashion seen as cavalier by other parties, with these other parties not being confined to the unions.


Markham Colliery, at Blackwood.

At the end of 1969, this pit was placed in jeopardy. The result was consternation within NCB marketing. A memo from this department at the time states;

"The coal concerned is a valuable rank 301a/204 coking coal for which the market demand is very strong. —— It is difficult to see the reason for placing the colliery in jeopardy. Certainly East Wales (Area) have not given any clear reason in their letter and I gather our regional marketing people were not consulted. —— There are other collieries in East Wales and elsewhere, with far worse results than Markham that are not being proposed for jeopardy status. —— Unless there are reasons not contained in the Area's letter I doubt whether we should put in jeopardy a pit which there can be little or no question of closing, at least on the basis of current results".

The "reasons not contained in the Area's letter" turned out to be the desire of production department to give the men at Markham a fright. In their opinion the men were not pulling their full weight, and were showing a reluctance to operate mechanised face techniques.

In 1985, 16 years later, Markham eventually closed.

Ogilvie Colliery, at Bargoed.

On 18 April 1969, a memo to the Area Closures Committee from planning department at headquarters condemned the pit. This stated, "A problem of dirty coal. Profitable working is impossible. Decision about closure can be taken at end-June 1969".

On 6 August 1969, at an accountability meeting between the National Board and East Wales Area, it was stated, "Ogilvie could well lose £600,000 this year and would never become profitable. Its closure would greatly assist the manning of other pits. It was agreed that the Board should be asked to put the pit into jeopardy immediately, with closure to be effected as soon as possible".

On 3 September 1969, the pit's fate was sealed with a letter from Hobart House in London (NCB headquarters) to East Wales Area, "Ogilvie to close in fourth quarter of 1969/70. Area must therefore place it in jeopardy before end of current quarter". This reads like, "We'll give him a fair trial before we hang him", for the concept of jeopardy was that no definite decision had been made, and that the pit still had a chance to save itself by meeting specific targets.

On 17 November 1969, the jeopardy meeting was held. Mr. Lister Walker, NCB East Wales Area Director, stated that steady progress was now being made in emerging from the difficulties at Ogilvie. The S.54 face would start off in about four weeks time and this additional panel would up production by 300-400 tons per day. In view of this very encouraging position, it was agreed that a further meeting be held, in early February 1970.

On 9 February 1970, the follow-up meeting was held. Mr, Glyn Williams, President of the South Wales NUM, stated that the transfer of men from McLaren to Ogilvie had been affected very smoothly and that this had undoubtedly improved the financial position. Mr. Walker, the Area Director, accepted that incorporation of the new men had been carried out smoothly. Unfortunately, serious difficulty had affected the S.60 and S.54 districts. In particular the latter was not performing and this had cancelled out the benefits expected at the previous meeting. All parties acknowledged that, in addition to geological problems, the present rate of absenteeism was having a crippling effect on results. The following was agreed:

a) The lodge committee, along with colliery management, would intensify their efforts to improve the absenteeism position.

b) The overall position at Ogilvie would be watched closely and that a further review meeting would be held at a date to be mutually agreed.

On 17 December 1970, Ogilvie was removed from jeopardy.

Five years later, the pit was again in trouble. This time a spirited defence by the lodge involved the lobbying of parliament by miners and intervention by local MP Michael Foot, Aneurin Bevan's successor in the constituency and future leader of the Labour Party. This party was now back in power following the successful national miners' strike of 1974. In spite of this, and the glowing future being forecast for coal as a result of the oil price rises, this time the closure went ahead. At the pit closure meeting, Michael Foot was subjected to severe barracking.

In 1975, Ogilvie closed.

Celynen South, at Newbridge.

On 31 October 1968, a letter from NCB headquarters to East Wales Area stated, "The Board have decided that Celynen South should close early in the March quarter 1968/69. Please inform of proposed closure date and when it will be announced". The Area requested deferment to 1969/70, when they would close it "at the earliest date consistent with the maximum redeployment of men".

In December 1968, in the year of its planned closure, men were transferred to the pit from Cwmcarn Colliery. This had the effect of increasing the Output per Man Shift (OMS).

In February 1969, the price of the high volatile coking washed smalls from Celynen South was increased to 10s/0d per ton. As a consequence of this, the pit was now in a profit-making situation.

On 30 April 1969, a letter to NCB headquarters informed them of the good news that the pit was now in the black, and giving the results expected for 1969/70:

Saleable output  -  216,000 tons

OMS              -  30 cwts (1.5t).

Profit           -  £36,000 or 3s/4d per ton.

The letter went on, "In view of these results and the continuing shortage of high volatile coking smalls produced at the colliery, it is suggested that Celynen South be taken out of jeopardy".

On 13 May 1969, the Area were informed that the Board were not prepared to agree to their request that Celynen South be taken out of jeopardy. Once the NCB had set their minds on closure, they had the bit between their teeth. The good results persisted however, and it was difficult to argue with success.

On 3 September 1969, grudgingly, Celynen South was removed from the closure list and taken out of jeopardy.

In 1985, sixteen years later, Celynen South eventually closed.


Abercynon, in the lower Cynon Valley.

This serves as another example of just how short-term and uncertain some of the negative assessments were.

On 6 August 1969, at an area accountability meeting it was stated, "Abercynon had been crippled by roof collapses, and it could be judged by the September/October results whether the pit should go into jeopardy".

On 21 October 1969, a letter from NCB HQ stated that Abercynon, together with Fernhill, was to close in the second quarter of 1970/70. In another example of insisting on a fair trial before the execution it went on, "The normal closure procedure would require that they be put in jeopardy in the fourth quarter of this year or earlier. Please let me know your Director's intentions".

In November 1969, the Director's report stated, "The colliery objectives for next year assume closure at the end of September 1970".

On 22 December 1970, instead of closure, the pit was removed from jeopardy.

In 1974 the pit, having survived, was a beneficiary of the capital investment program resulting from the 1974 Plan for Coal. In that year two parallel roadways were driven, one 920 metres and the other 1600 metres long, linking Abercynon with Lady Windsor Colliery in Ynysybwl on the other side of the mountain. High speed belt conveyors, remotely controlled from Lady Windsor, sped the coal into a 400 ton spiral bunker shaft, fitted with "nucleonic" capacity monitoring, the first of its kind in any British coalfield. All coal was wound at Lady Windsor for washing and blending, as preparation for the market.

In 1980, a further £1 M were invested in improving coal clearance, by the installation of skip winding in the Lady Windsor downcast shaft. Manufacturing of this system was carried out at the nearby NCB subsidiary, Tredomen Engineering. This money was in addition to the £3.7 M already invested so as to access new coal reserves to the west of the combined mine. Weekly production at the time was running at just over 9,000t.

In 1986 there was another boost, at the cost of Penrikyber Colliery, when the latter's reserves were allocated to Lady Windsor/Abercynon. Lady Windsor/Abercynon were noted for exemplary labour relations, a fact which did not save them from the post national strike slaughter.

In 1988, Lady Windsor/Abercynon closed.

Penallta, at Gelligaer.

Seen in retrospect this is another example of negative thinking, this time on the part of Area Management. It contrasts with their approach as described below to Nantgarw, for whose sake Penallta was planned to be sacrificed. Penallta was another pit that was able to save itself, albeit after a saga both difficult and prolonged.

Until the construction of Abernant Colliery in the 1950's, with a shaft depth of 828 metres, Penallta had the deepest shafts in the coalfield (No. 1 at 720 metres and No.2 at 694 metres). It had a typical Powell Dyffryn surface layout with an enormous central engine house for housing the winding engines, compressors and generators. Left over from the days of private enterprise, it had its own small power station of 5 MW capacity, connected into the NCB's (previously Powell Dyffryn's) own electricity supply grid in East Wales.

In 1966, a small reconstruction scheme costing £1.8 M was completed. Expected results however were not achieved.

By 1968, the pit had been a consistent loser for the previous 4 years. NCB computer analysis therefore selected this colliery as a suitable candidate for closure in the fourth quarter of 1968/69.

In April 1968, objections to closure were raised by the South Western Division on the grounds that not only was the colliery a substantial "contributor" (i.e. it covered its operating costs, thereby making a contribution to the industry's overheads), it would maintain this position for some years to come. The marketing position was also over-riding. In particular:

- Penallta coking smalls were the base coals for the GKN steelworks in Cardiff. It would be undesirable to cast general doubt on the ability to meet these requirements over the next 10-15 years.

- The supply of house coal to South Wales had been extremely critical during the previous year. With the impending closure of National Colliery, an important supplier, this would be tantamount to "throwing in our hand" and giving up that valuable trade. The area was relying on Penallta to see them through. It was suggested that an alternative closure to Penallta should be found.


On 22 July 1968, at an accountability meeting between East Wales Area and the National Board, it was stated that results had fallen to an all-time low, with an OMS down to 24.1 cwt (1.22t). and a loss of 34s/11d per ton.

On 12 November 1968, at a following accountability meeting, the views expressed were now much more sanguine;

"The Penallta type of coal was unique and Mr. Kellet (Chairman, NCB S.W. Division) suggested that they should look into a new area of coal. Lord Robens (Chairman, NCB National Board) said that they should treat this very cautiously but there was no harm in examining the possibilities". An action plan would be developed to increase face capacity at Penallta.

In January 1969, in spite of this new development, Penallta was placed in jeopardy.

On 18 April 1969, the HQ planning department stated in a memo to the National Board that this development into a new area of coal could well pay off.

On 7 May 1969, less than three weeks later, the same HQ planning department changed their opinion, stating "there was no prospect of the colliery breaking even and that it would have to close. —— I am satisfied that there is no hope for the colliery and unless there is a remarkable improvement, which I do not expect, the colliery will close in the second quarter of 1969/70 —— After much pleading by the union, it was agreed to hold a further meeting before the date of closure was announced".

This negative opinion on the part of the planning department was not shared, neither by the lodge, who were fighting hard for their pit, nor by local colliery management.

On 16 June 1969, at a meeting held between NCB Area Management and the South Wales NUM, both sides expressed their appreciation of the improvement achieved over the previous six weeks. The Area Director, Mr. Lister Walker, stated, however, that the rate of coalface advance was still inadequate, due largely to manpower shortage. If absenteeism could be reduced by a further 2-3 per cent there would be sufficient labour to meet all requirements. As it was, the results achieved had been due to taking men off development work for future production. All such work had been suspended completely. He refused to give any undertaking that, based on the results achieved, the colliery could be taken out of jeopardy or given a reprieve of at least six months.

Under heavy pressure from the unions, the Area Director did give an assurance that the colliery would not be closed, provided the results currently being achieved were maintained (it was making a small contribution to fixed costs, at an OMS of 25 cwt (1.3t)). This assurance had its origin in a statement made by Lord Robens, NCB Chairman, that any pit making a contribution, and with real prospects of continuing to do so, should not close. The statement had already been quoted fairly freely but, nevertheless, this commitment to the unions caused immediate consternation at NCB headquarters.

On 19 June 1969, as a result of this consternation, the Area Director felt called upon to write to the Board;

"There is no reason why the pit should not close within the period given by the Board if that is the Board's wish, whether the pit breaks even or not. I had been previously been told by Sir William Webber that any pit making a contribution would not close, and that is all that I said. If the pit does not maintain a profitable position it is still my intention to carry out the Board's instruction".

On 26 June 1969, an NCB internal memo to the Board Secretary dismissed the above explanation as a red herring and went on;

"The important thing is that he (i.e. the Area Director) should have cleared his lines with headquarters before giving any indication to the union that the colliery was likely to remain in production. I suggest — — a policy directive should be issued to areas so that any recommendations they make about closures are in line with national policy".

On 3/4 July 1969, further internal memos to the Board Secretary spoke of deferring closure until such time as the present temporary improvement in results ran out. Since this improvement had been obtained by completely suspending development work, there was a limited time that the colliery could go on.

On 29 July 1969, East Wales Area informed NCB Headquarters that Penallta's allocation of the general overhead and depreciation budget (i.e. the non-operating costs assigned to the pit) was £295,000 per annum;

"The future of the colliery is limited and at best has only 2-3 years life unless major development is undertaken. The results for June should be maintained for a few months if the men continue to cooperate fully, and it will be difficult to close in the light of these results. The Director would welcome advice on whether or not the colliery should be closed in accordance with the Board's instruction but suggests that the position should be reviewed in 3 months' time".

With regard to a plan to boost manpower at Nantgarw upon closure of Penallta:

"Experience in the past has shown that when men have been transferred from collieries working level seams, e.g. Wyllie, to the steep seams at Nantgarw they do not stay, so the effect of keeping Penallta open will not seriously affect Nantgarw".

On 3 September 1969, the pit was removed from the programme for immediate closure but remained in jeopardy.

On 19 June 1970, NCB national headquarters agreed that its jeopardy status be removed.

The colliery went on to achieve substantial success.

By 1979, all production was in the Seven Feet seam, with 13 kilometres of underground roadways and four kilometres of high-speed belt conveyors at work.

In late 1985, a heavy-duty, high-technology coalface was installed, along with skip winding of coal. This latter would increase shaft capacity by 33 per cent for the expected increase in production.

By March 1991, in the financial year just ended, 590,000 tonnes of saleable coal were produced for Aberthaw power station. This was achieved by retreat mining, based on a single face. Overall productivity was 6.62 tonnes per man shift, its highest annual average ever.

On 1 November 1991, almost 23 years after being placed in jeopardy, Penallta closed, one of the last mines in South Wales to remain working. The end was announced with a headline, "Bad Geology Brings November Closing Date". After saying that 86 years of mining had come to an end, the story led off, "Penallta's life as one of South Wales' most productive collieries, it secured a European record for coal winding in 1939, has come to an end because it has exhausted reserves that can be worked profitably".

## Favourites.

Some other pits, notably the "glamour" collieries of the glory days of capital investment, had a much easier time in convincing Area Management that they should stay open. Here, interpretation of prospects would tend to be optimistic, as opposed to pessimistic elsewhere. Justification of the capital already spent was no doubt a factor. In their cause, the interests of other pits were frequently sacrificed.

Nantgarw, at Taffs Well.

This had always been controversial and technically challenging, due to the steeply inclined seams. It was also something of a white elephant, with a massive turnover in personnel. By the late 1960s, Penallta was planned to be the latest pit in a series whose manpower was destined to be transferred there.

On 22 October 1968, the NCB informed East Wales Area:

"The Board have agreed that Nantgarw colliery should close by the end of the present financial year, subject to additional costs arising at Nantgarw coke ovens if the colliery were to close".

Losses in that year were £207,000, or 35s/8d per ton. In that same year, in a special review of the colliery by East Wales Area, the situation was outlined as follows:

- Although there was enough face room available for the pit to break even, absenteeism by the colliers was preventing this from being achieved.

- Of the 66 colliers on the books, with an absentee rate of 40 percent only 40 were working on any one day.

- This was enough to work one face with a production shift every working day. The other two faces had a production shift only every other day.

- With 10 more colliers working regularly, one of the two faces at present producing every other day could then produce every day. This would enable the pit to break even.

- This, however, would not cover the very heavy development expenditure required in due course, so as to maintain continuity of output for the future.

- Three colliers had recently resigned and a further three would be dismissed for excessive absenteeism. The prospect of obtaining the additional colliers required to increase output was very remote.

- The lodge had worked very closely with management to improve attendance, but so far to no avail.

- In addition to the above, the colliery was losing men. Since 25 March 1968 manpower had fallen from 559 to 514.

- In addition to its own output, the coal preparation plant was also washing the output of National Colliery.

On 12 November 1968, both Nantgarw and Penallta were a subject of discussion between Area, Divisional and National Management. Both pits it was said suffered from a shortage of face labour and absenteeism. This was the same accountability meeting in which the unique nature of Penallta coal had been referred to and at which the Divisional and National Chairmen considered the opening up of a new area at this pit. An action plan would be proposed to increase face capacity. The Area proposal however was quite different, close Penallta and transfer the men to Nantgarw, "With extra face labour, this pit could be profitable".

On 18 April 1969, with Nantgarw in jeopardy, a memo from HQ planning department to the East Wales Closure Committee was upbeat, "Good labour force. Four years' workings opened up. Should at least break even 1969/70". This "good labour force" happened to be plagued with an enormous turnover and absentee rate. This was the same planning department that had been so (unjustifiably) pessimistic about Penallta.

On 30 April 1969, a letter was sent to the National Board, explaining the Areas view on the future of Nantgarw. The March quarter results were as follows:

Operating loss    -    £18,862, or 10s/3d per ton.
(before interest).

Operating loss    -    £25,328.
(after interest).

"Of this loss, £9,679 was incurred in the month of February when colliery results were adversely affected by bad weather. The March quarter costs include a charge of £9,000 for overheads, and £16,000 for depreciation —— With the pending closure of Penallta colliery, men will be transferred to Nantgarw. Although the steep workings at Nantgarw are not popular, it is hoped that enough men will stay at Nantgarw so that it could make a small profit —— The Area Director recommends that this colliery should be given a further six months before deciding whether it should close or be taken out of jeopardy".

At this time, the non-operating costs (overheads) assigned to Nantgarw were £126,000 per annum. At Penallta they were £295,000. Nevertheless, at the latter, operating costs were still being covered. With the improvement of results at Penallta its closure so as to provide manpower for Nantgarw would have been politically difficult.

On 29 July 1969, as a consequence of Penallta not now being closed, East Wales Area amended the plan for Nantgarw:

"It is proposed to introduce longwall retreating at Nantgarw with self-advancing supports which should eliminate the need for extra men".

On 17 December 1970, the pit was removed from jeopardy.

In 1974, as a result of the 1974 Plan for Coal, investment was made available. In that year Nantgarw was linked underground with Windsor colliery at Bedwas. Henceforward, Windsor's coal reserves would be worked, thus allowing Nantgarw to break free from the difficult geology and steeply inclined seams with which it had always been plagued. All Windsor's production was wound at Nantgarw, due to the latter's efficient coal preparation plant. Losses continued, however, and by 1977 were over £1 M in that year alone.

In May 1978, installation of the F44 coalface, equipped with an Anderson Strathclyde power-loader of the ranging drum shearer type and on a chainless haulage system, transformed the situation. Output was raised to over 5,000 tons per week with a coalface OMS of 17 tonnes, the best ever achieved in Nantgarw/ Windsor and one of the best in South Wales. The result was a profit per month of over £40,000.

In 1978, an NCB press release stated, "Nantgarw/Windsor is one of the coalfields premier collieries, linked by a £1.75 M project. The colliery will exploit over 9 Mt of coking coal, which will keep the mine in business until well into the next century".

By 1981, the manpower distribution was; 101 on the surface, 131 on the coalface, 197 elsewhere below ground and 142 on development. The six feet seam was being worked with a section of 1.6-1.8m and the seven feet seam with a section of 1.45m. Coalface length varied between 144-200m. Both faces were equipped with self-advancing supports and power loaders of the ranging drum shearer type.

In 1985, in spite of making a good recovery from the 1984/84 miners' strike the colliery's luck ran out. In that year losses of £5 M were declared, with an additional £4 M in the first 6 months of 1986. British Coal attributed this continually declining output to worsening and uncertain geological conditions in the two production districts.

With the exposure of the coal industry to the full blast of international market forces, and the NUM's defeat in the 1984/85 strike, there would be no more second chances. The Area Director stated that, because of the colliery's uncertain geology, he could see no justification for continuing mining operations at Nantgarw.

In 1986, Nantgarw/Windsor closed.


## NEW PROCEDURE, NO CHANGE.

In 1972 the method of organising colliery closures was revised. The previous concept of "jeopardy" would disappear. The new system was called the "Colliery General Review Procedure". Every three months a meeting would take place between the NCB Area Director and senior representatives of the three unions concerned (NUM for the miners, NACODS for the officials and BACUM for management). Discussed would be the mining industry nationwide and the status of individual colliery units - their finances, markets, manpower, methods of work and geological difficulties. The accent was to be on constructive ways of improving results. If closure was in mind there would be a specific meeting on this topic within the next three weeks, involving the pit itself.

The Area Director would inform the National Board, who would authorise the Director to make a public statement on the issue. If a union did not agree to closure they had the right to make a technical inspection and study market prospects. They had one month to decide whether or not to ask for a national appeals meeting. The Director would report their views to the National Board and inform local authorities that closure was pending. Official notice of closure would be given 4 months in advance and the whole time frame was typically five and a half months.

In 1981, an NCB report on the functioning of the colliery review procedure in South Wales stated, "In the current round of colliery reviews in South Wales, 12 mines were identified for further examination due to high production costs. Collectively these collieries employ about 8,300 men and account for losses of about £35 M. In South Wales the number of mines set aside for detailed examination is understandably larger due to the historic and inherited problems, concerning age and geology, which are more acute than in many other parts of Great Britain".

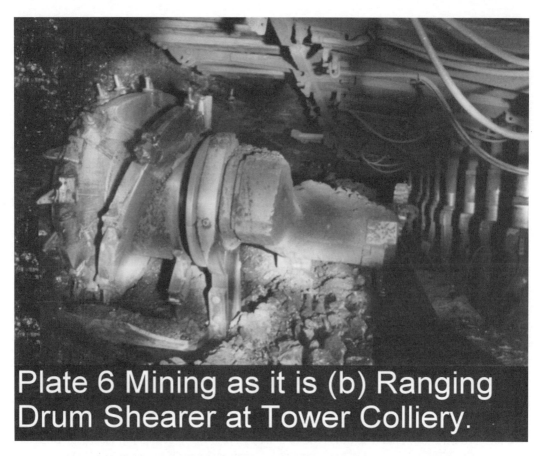

Plate 6 Mining as it is (b) Ranging Drum Shearer at Tower Colliery.

Such supports provide a continuous canopy along the entire length of the coalface. A coalface hydraulic system provides the operating pressure.

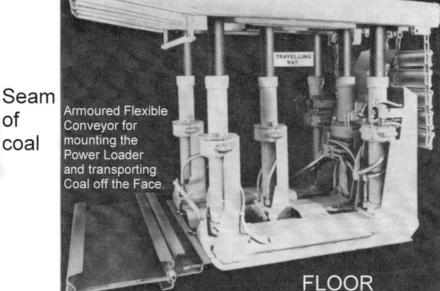

ROOF

Seam of coal

Armoured Flexible Conveyor for mounting the Power Loader and transporting Coal off the Face.

Behind the face in this area the roof is allowed to collapse into the waste.

FLOOR

Plate 7 Mining as it is (c). Typical Self-Advancing Support.

# Chapter 9
## DUST AND DISASTER

*"When I am an old man I hope to be able to go around
the mines of South Wales and not find
a single young man coughing, spitting and panting,
with nothing to do but wait for the undertaker".*
Charles Fletcher,
Director of Llandough Pneumoconiosis Unit (1950).

**SYMBIOSIS.**

In general, the decline of the mining industry was met with considerable opposition, particularly on the part of those employed in it. Apart from the fact that in many cases no alternative employment existed, there was also a positive side to the miner's lot, expressed by the following viewpoint:

"The pit makes a good citizen out of a man. The older men will turn a long-haired youth into a man. There's nothing like the atmosphere you get in a pit, there's comradeship - you can be cursing a man one minute but if there's a fall you are in there getting the rocks off him. You can tell a man off, but the next moment you are working together and it's forgotten. You don't get that in a factory - everybody is more selfish and you are always looking over your shoulder at some little Hitler of a foreman".

There was however a dark side. Miners have always been ambivalent about their industry, with such ambivalence often being felt within one individual. There was another viewpoint, and it hardly seems like the same industry that is being talked about:

"God did not make men for them to spend their lives working like moles underground. The social cost of mining should be counted in terms of the men who have been killed and injured, and those in the prime of their life who, because of pneumoconiosis, not only can't work but also can't climb stairs. The sooner all the holes in the ground are filled in the better. We don't want to go underground - we want alternative jobs".

In truth, the possibility of disaster is endemic in the very concept of underground coalmining. Danger lurks, in the potential for falls of roof, in the steady emission of flammable gas, the possibility of water ingress, plus problems in ventilation and the difficulty of installing and operating machinery in a dark, restricted environment.

Today, China is home, not only to the world's largest coalmining industry but also to the most dangerous. During the first 10 months of 2003, 7,000 miners were killed in that country. The world's greatest single mining disaster also occurred here, namely:

- Honkeik in 1942, with 1,572 fatalities.

This compares with:

- Courriers (France) in 1906, with 1,100 fatalities.

- Senghenydd (Wales) in 1913, with 439 fatalities.

- Barnsley (England) in 1866, with 361 fatalities.

- Blantyre (Scotland) in 1877, with 207 fatalities.

Between 1868 and 1914, as a UK average, one miner was killed and one seriously injured every 6 hours. South Wales, due to its gassy mines and difficult geology, was the most dangerous British coalfield.

In the year 1905, deaths from accidents in the collieries of South Wales amounted to 2.66 for every 1,000 employed. The figure for the United Kingdom as a whole was 1.35. Thirteen of the twenty-seven major explosions in the UK between 1890 and 1913 occurred in South Wales, with the loss of 1452 men in that coalfield alone. Between 1851 and 1960, one third of all fatalities in British coal mining occurred in South Wales, although its output and manpower were approximately just 18% of the total.

Against the background of a steady attrition rate due to general accidents and falls of roof, it was the underground explosion that dramatised and epitomised the dangers inherent in the miner's lot. Such events would evoke public sympathy that sometimes extended to financial contribution, which the considerable number of isolated casualties never did, although trauma for the individuals concerned was equally as great.

## EXPLOSIONS.

Explosions are invariably the result of methane being ignited. The effects are compounded if this gas explosion sets off a coal dust explosion. Gas in an explosive mixture is usually present locally, whereas coaldust is spread throughout the mine. The great danger is that a gas explosion will raise and ignite the dust into a self-sustaining chain reaction, capable of devastating the entire underground workings. Even after the invention of the safety lamp, of which Sir Humphrey Davy invented the most commonly used in 1815, gas ignitions were common. Only a minority of these involved fatalities, but that was bad enough. In the 100 years between 1837 and 1937, as a result of 71 fatal explosions in Welsh coal mines, 3,790 miners lost their lives. The breakdown of this figure is given below. The lower casualty figures tend to be where the explosion occurred on repair and maintenance shifts at the weekend or during the night, when fewer men were at work.

| Year. | Date. | Location. | No. of fatalities. |
|-------|-------|-----------|--------------------|
| 1837 | 10 May | Plas-yr-Argoed, Mold | 21 |
| 1837 | 17 June | Blaina (Mon.) | 21 |
| 1844 | 1 January | Dinas | 12 |
| 1845 | 2 August | Cwmbach | 28 |
| 1846 | 14 January | Risca | 35 |
| 1848 | 21 June | Victoria (Mon.) | 11 |
| 1849 | 11 August | Letty Shenkin, Aberdare | 52 |
| 1850 | 14 December | New Duffryn Colliery | 13 |
| 1852 | 10 May | Duffryn | 64 |
| 1853 | 12 March | Risca Vale | 10 |
| 1856 | 13 July | Cymmer | 114 |
| 1858 | 13 October | Duffryn | 20 |
| 1859 | 5 April | Neath Chain Colliery | 26 |
| 1860 | 1 December | Risca | 146 |
| 1862 | 19 February | Gethin, Merthyr | 47 |
| 1863 | 17 October | Margam | 39 |
| 1863 | 24 December | Maesteg | 14 |

| Year. | Date. | Location. | No. of fatalities. |
|---|---|---|---|
| 1865 | 16 June | Tredegar | 2 |
| 1865 | 20 December | Upper Gethin | 30 |
| 1867 | 8 November | Ferndale | 178 |
| 1869 | 23 May | Llanerch | 7 |
| 1869 | 10 June | Ferndale | 60 |
| 1870 | 23 July | Llansamlet | 19 |
| 1871 | 24 February | Pentre | 38 |
| 1871 | 4 October | Gelli Pit, Aberdare | 4 |
| 1872 | 10 January | Oakwood, Llynvi Valley | 11 |
| 1872 | 2 March | Victoria | 19 |
| 1872 | 8 March | Wernfach | 18 |
| 1874 | 5 April | Abertillery | 6 |
| 1874 | 24 July | Charles Pit, Llansamlet | 19 |
| 1875 | 4 December | New Tredegar | 22 |
| 1875 | 5 December | Llan Pit, Pentyrch | 12 |
| 1876 | 13 December | Abertillery | 20 |
| 1877 | 8 March | Worcester Pit, Swansea | 18 |
| 1878 | 1 September | Abercarn | 62 |
| 1878 | 11 September | Abercarn | 268 |
| 1879 | 13 January | Dinas | 3 |
| 1879 | 22 September | Waunllwyd, Ebbw Vale | 84 |
| 1880 | 15 July | Risca | 119 |
| 1880 | 10 December | Naval Colliery | 96 |
| 1882 | 15 January | Risca | 4 |
| 1882 | 11 February | Coedcae | 6 |
| 1883 | 1 February | Coedcae | 5 |
| 1883 | 21 August | Gelli | 4 |
| 1884 | 16 January | Cwmavon | 10 |
| 1884 | 28 January | Penygraig | 11 |
| 1884 | 8 November | Pochin Colliery, Tredegar | 14 |
| 1885 | | Naval Colliery | 14 |
| 1885 | 24 December | Mardy | 81 |
| 1887 | 18 February | Ynyshir | 37 |
| 1888 | 14 May | Aber, Tynewydd | 5 |
| 1890 | 20 January | Glyn Pit, Pontypool | 5 |
| 1890 | 6 February | Llanerch | 176 |

| Year. | Date. | Location. | No. of fatalities. |
|---|---|---|---|
| 1890 | 8 March | Morfa | 87 |
| 1892 | 12 August | Great Western Colliery | 38 |
| 1892 | 36 August | Park Slip | 110 |
| 1894 | 35 June | Cilfynydd | 276 |
| 1896 | 8 January | Tylorstown | 57 |
| 1899 | 18 August | Llest Colliery, Garw | 19 |
| 1901 | 24 May | Senghenydd | 82 |
| 1901 | 10 September | Llanbradach | 12 |
| 1905 | 10 March | Clydach Vale | 31 |
| 1905 | 5 July | Wattstown | 119 |
| 1913 | 13 October | Senghenydd | 439 |
| 1923 | 26 April | Trimsaran | 9 |
| 1927 | 1 March | Cwm, Ebbw Vale | 52 |
| 1929 | | Milfraen, Blaenavon | 9 |
| 1929 | | Wernbwll, Penclawdd | 7 |
| 1932 | | Llwynpia | 11 |
| 1934 | | Gresford, Wrexham. | 265 |
| 1937 | | Lovestone, Pembrokeshire | 7 |

Such a casualty rate contributed to the bitterness felt throughout the workforce. In the early days, accidents were generally attributed to miners' carelessness. The owners were not subject to any regulation until 1850 and even then it did not always work. Prior to the explosion at Cymmer Colliery on 13 July 1856, which killed 114, the South Wales Inspector of Mines had informed the owners that the ventilation was bad, but nothing was done. Always, safety regulations have tended to be retrospective, adapting to accidents and incidents that have already occurred.


## SENGHENYDD.

On 13 October 1913, during the same year that output and profits reached their peak, an explosion devastated the Universal Colliery in the village of Senghenydd near Caerphilly. With 439 fatalities, this is the greatest disaster ever experienced in a British mine. Michael Lieven has described the event in detail in his book Senghenydd.

At 8.10 am, after the initial activity of winding the morning shift, but before the flow of coal to the surface had gathered momentum, the 3 tonne cage suddenly shot out of the Lancaster shaft into the headgear like a projectile from a massive cannon, decapitating the man in charge of the pithead and bringing in its wake great clouds of enveloping dust.

The initial underground explosion was smaller than the one that had shaken the mine previously in 1901, but this time the blast gained in momentum and power as the shock wave raised accumulations of coal dust, which fed and sustained the conflagration. The accelerating eruption roared through miles of tunnels, derailing drams, blowing out timber roof supports, burning and/or burying those in its path. Following the initial blast and flame survivors saw a terrifying red glow penetrating the suspended smoke and dust. Timbers had been ignited and fires started. For the hundreds still alive underground the main danger now was neither the fire itself, nor the smoke nor the falls of rock nor the explosive methane gas released by the falls. It was the non-explosive but poisonous carbon monoxide, the product of combustion.

Back on the surface the manager, Edward Shaw, was engaged in casual conversation in the lamp room when the detonation shattered his morning routine.

In a classical example of the action man devoid of foresight, he would earn lasting respect in the community for his immediate and frantic activities to mitigate the effects of the disaster he had allowed to happen. Within seconds he rushed across the yard to ensure the ventilation fan was still working, gave orders to repair the damaged pithead and then proceeded to compound his previous "oversights".

Instead of ensuring that the rescue services were properly alerted, he immediately descended the apparently undamaged York shaft with a small band of men. The water pipes had been fractured. Shaw and his companions therefore used hand extinguishers to battle the conflagration that was consuming row after row of timbered supports. These flames would result in further falls of ground, and add to the carbon monoxide now filling the mine. In the smoke and fumes, breathing apparatus was essential if an adequate water supply was to be re-established. Falls of roof forced Shaw back. Finally admitting defeat, he returned to the surface. The rescue brigade from the Dinas station, just 13 kilometres away, arrived with their vital breathing equipment at about 11 am, three hours after the explosion. Shaw's spontaneous heroics had resulted in the loss of valuable time.

The underground fires, and the trauma, were to last for weeks, with an image running through much of the reporting that the mine was some kind of evil presence, "a monster gulping down his ration of human flesh". By recovering the bodies of their comrades, the rescue teams were in a way snatching back something from the monster of death and defying it. The main conflagration was near the base of the downcast shaft, which brought fresh air into the mine. This resulted in the gases of combustion being carried throughout the entire workings. The colliery had no means of reversing the air current, one of the "oversights" criticised at the enquiry. Here, the point was repeatedly made that the vast majority of fatalities resulted not from the explosion itself but from suffocation or carbon monoxide poisoning as a result of the fires. These had also isolated many men and prevented the rescue teams from reaching them. Had water been available and had rescue teams arrived on the scene faster, more lives might have been saved.

A previous explosion at the same mine in 1901 had already claimed 82 lives. It was accepted that coal dust had been involved in that explosion. In spite of such a salutary lesson, excessive coal dust remained, to be a major factor in the 1913 disaster. The source of ignition was never satisfactorily explained, although electrical sparking at signal wires was regarded as a possibility. This resulted in extensive research being initiated in the field of "intrinsic safety", the design of low current electrical equipment such as to ensure that any sparking is at an energy level too low to cause ignition.

Of the 436 deceased, only 72 bodies were recovered. The court verdict was accidental death. The company argued that they were not legally obliged to rectify all of the issues that in retrospect they were accused of. It was nevertheless generally accepted that, regardless of whether or not the company at that particular moment was technically within or outside the law, they had failed to take a number of necessary precautions well known to everyone inside the industry. With regard to the supply of water Richard Redmayne, who led the enquiry, said:

"I am convinced that had there been available at that time an adequate water supply, and had brigades of rescuers attacked the three fires — simultaneously, the fires might have been extinguished in a comparatively short time. I should have thought, in view of the fact that the colliery was such a gassy one, and as it had already been devastated by an explosion, that the management would have made arrangements for a supply of water adequate to meet an emergency of the kind that actually occurred".

On the subject of coal dust, the management was adamant that it was impractical to clear dust from the sides and roofs of the roadways. This was refuted by Redmayne, who did not consider its removal impractical. He concluded that the dust on the roof and sides was practically disregarded. He had no doubt whatever that coal dust existed on the roof, sides and timber in a dangerous quantity.

Redmayne seems to have liked Edward Shaw, the manager, as a person. There was special praise for his courage, and those of the other men, who had entered the mine within minutes of the explosion. Redmayne wrote that, "Mr. Shaw impressed me as an honest, industrious and in many respects, an active manager, and he gave his evidence in a clear and straightforward manner and assisted in the inquiry to the utmost of his power".

Nevertheless, his overall conclusion was that:

"Some of these breaches (of the Mines Act) — may appear trivial, but taken in the aggregate they point to a disquieting laxity in the management of the mine".

Shaw was found guilty of failing to keep proper records, of being unable to reverse the air current and failing to adequately clear dust. He was fined £24. At the time, a reasonable wage for a collier was regarded as being £1.30 per week. The company was found not guilty of any responsibility. Compensation was paid but the amounts claimed contested in many cases by the company.

Overnight, the small village of Senghenydd was left with 205 widows, 542 fatherless children and 62 old, dependent parents whose sons had gone forever. In a similar effect to the massacre of the "pal's battalions" at the forthcoming battle of the Somme, whole streets were devastated. In Commercial Street they counted 40 dead, in High Street, 33. Chapels were denuded of deacons while, three years later, the village rugby team would field a team of 13 under-sixteens - there were so few older players left.


# NATIONALISATION.

## Gas Ignitions.

After nationalisation the industry became a much safer place to work. Nevertheless, there was a continuing toll of accidents. There were a number of gas ignitions and some major explosions.

On 10 October 1952, at Bedwas Colliery, there was an example of a so-called non-major explosion, resulting in 1 death and 20 injured. The presence of a mildly explosive gas mixture had caused the flame safety lamp being carried by an assistant surveyor to extinguish. Repeated attempts to relight it resulted in a small particle of flint breaking off and becoming lodged in the external gauze of the lamp. This gauze isolates the heat of the flame from the external atmosphere. As gas inside the lamp ignited the lodged particle became heated, thus transmitting the heat through the gauze to the external atmosphere and causing the explosion.

The inspector was of the opinion that a more experienced man would have recognised the inability to relight the lamp as possibly being due to the presence of gas. Before persisting in his attempts at relighting he would first have withdrawn to another area.

All gas ignitions were traumatic, though not all had fatal consequences.

On 13 January 1954, just after 9.30am at Glyncorrwg Colliery in the Afan Valley, an ignition occurred on a face in the six feet seam. As the first sledgehammer blow was struck on a steel wedge, so as to secure a roof support, flame appeared at the point of impact. The tongue of flame shot out a few feet towards the coalface and then in the reverse direction, into the waste. From here, burning methane gushed back onto the face. Initially of such force as to move against the ventilation, the burning mass then returned with the air current. In its path were 32 men of which 24 were burned, 17 of them severely.

In the confusion, with men shouting and running, some with their clothes on fire, Glyn Thomas the overman, fortunately unharmed, saw the injured men safely off the face and telephoned the surface for assistance. Before the stricken men were brought out, local first aid was given, with burns dressed and morphia administered. The injured were taken to hospitals in Neath and Maesteg. The 17 severely burnt cases were then transferred to St. Lawrence Hospital Chepstow for plastic surgery. Nurses accompanied the journey and maintained plasma injections.

Roadways into the district were sealed off with plugs 5.5 metres thick, made of sandbags and reinforced with steel. Rescue teams wearing self-contained breathing apparatus monitored the situation. All persons were withdrawn from the mine for 24 hours.

On 24 January 1954, 11 days later, normal operation resumed. Air samples taken confirmed that two additional ignitions had occurred, subsequent to the initial one.

New knowledge was gained at the Safety In Mines Research Establishment in Buxton, Derbyshire. Here, extensive testing was carried out on the danger of incendive sparks occurring as a result of rusted steel impacting upon light alloy in the presence of methane.

On 6 September 1955, at Blaenhirwaen Colliery near Cross Hands, 16 miles NW of Swansea, 6 men were burnt to death and a further 13 injured. Of the fatalities, 4 died immediately and 2 later in hospital. These injured were also treated at the plastic surgery unit of St. Lawrence Hospital Chepstow. A sudden and abnormal outburst of methane had occurred about 1 minute before the explosion. This came into contact with a compressed air driven auxiliary fan, which contained pieces of stone blown in as a result of shotfiring. Friction between this stone and the rotating blades of the fan was the source of ignition.

In October 1966, at Taff Merthyr in Gelligaer, gas was ignited and there were 2 fatalities. A number of others were severely burned.

Major Explosions.

| | | |
|---|---|---|
| - 1956 | Lewis Merthyr | 9 fatalities. |
| - 1960 | Six Bells | 45 " |
| - 1962 | Tower | 9 " |
| - 1965 | Cambrian | 31 " |

In the former two cases, the source of ignition was a spark caused by falling rock impacting upon steel. In the latter two cases the source of ignition was electrical.

On 22 November 1956, At Lewis Merthyr, in the lower Rhondda Valley, an explosion occurred in the N4 district of the Two Foot Nine seam, resulting in 9 fatalities. Previously, on 9 November, there had been a fall of roof in the gate road, adjacent to the coalface. This was followed on 20 November by a second fall in the same area. These falls had resulted from the roof breaking up as a consequence of a fault in the strata. The effect was to create a large cavity above the roof of the roadway, 7.3m high and 4.9m in length. At the top of this cavity a seam of coal and a band of ironstone had been exposed.

The falls had displaced arches used for roadway support. On the day of the explosion, arches of 3m hight were being erected within the original and displaced 4.3m arches so as to afford protection against further falls. From the top of one of the latter a test had been made for gas within the cavity. None was found.

During the continuation of repair work there was another fall of stone. Most of this was in the form of a single rock weighing approximately 2 tonnes. This fell some 6m before impacting on one of the steel arches. The result was an incendive spark. This ignited gas that had accumulated in the apex of the cavity and had been brought down along with the fall. The conflagration spread immediately, extending 64m back up the gate road, 22.9m along the right hand face and 13.7m along the left hand face. It persisted for some time, enveloping those present in flame. The burns suffered were severe, with two fatalities on the scene and seven others later in hospital. Two died in East Glamorgan Hospital within 12 hours and the other five afterwards, in the Chepstow Burns Unit. Among those who died in hospital was Mr. Fox, the manager, who had been supervising the repair work.

The inspector's report said that the established method of roof support should not have been persisted with after its shortcomings had been exposed by the initial fall. It should have been modified to cater for the particular conditions being experienced. The fact that it was not led to the second fall. The deterioration in the strength and cohesion of the roof meant that such measures as were taken amounted to little more than the engendering of a false sense of security. In addition, cavities such as the one that occurred as a result of the fall should always be ventilated.

On 28 June 1960, at Six Bells Colliery in Abertillery, 45 men were killed at 10.45am, in a district within the Five-feet/Gellideg seam. As with all of the really big explosions, coal dust was the major factor involved, ignited by an initial gas explosion. The dust cloud raised had extended all the way back to pit bottom.

Immediately following the explosion, while survivors groped their way along pipe ranges through an atmosphere thick with dust, someone telephoned the surface. First reports were garbled and confused, and prevented an awareness of the enormity of the disaster. The manager instructed a deputy to go forward and investigate. On approaching the district, falls of roof blocked his way while the air was thick with coal dust. He telephoned the manager and informed him that, according to all appearances, an explosion had occurred. All men were then withdrawn from the mine and emergency services actuated.

Management descended to investigate, taking a canary with them. On testing for methane some way in they found 2 per cent in the general body of the air. A little further in the canary died. They then retreated to the main intake airway. Here they met the team from the Dinas rescue station. Severely hampered by falls of roof a systematic investigation was made of all roadways and coalfaces in the district. No survivors were found. Of the 48 men in the affected district at the time of the explosion all but three perished. Twenty- eight had succumbed to carbon monoxide poisoning and seventeen to the violence of the explosion. The survivors had been working in the outer part of the district and received only minor injuries.

It was not possible positively to determine the source of ignition but the inquiry's report of gave the probable cause, similar to Lewis Merthyr, as being a fall of rock. A quartzitic rock had fallen from a height of about 2 metres at a ripping lip exposed by shotfiring. Beneath this ripping lip, a canopy had been constructed to protect the conveyor. Impact of the rock onto a steel girder forming part of this canopy resulted in an incendive spark. Lyndon James, head of the NUM's safety department in South Wales concluded in his review;

"The road head was not properly supported; had it been, the fall that caused the explosion, if fall it was, should not have happened".

The gas explosion alone might not have caused any casualties, as there was nobody in the vicinity at the time. The explosion that ravaged the district was primarily one of coaldust, raised from the roadway by the initial gas explosion. The inspector's report concluded that sufficient stone dust barriers, suitably placed, might well have confined the extent of the explosion.

On 12 April 1962 at Tower, Joy continuous miners worked production headings in accordance with the "room and pillar" method of working. It was in such a heading, at 10.30am, that a gas explosion occurred in the N2 development drivage in the 9 feet seam. This was the worst accident in the long history of Tower Colliery. The force of the blast ripped down roof supports in the vicinity but no fall of roof occurred. Nine men lost their lives and there were nine injured, some seriously. The source of ignition was electrical.

As a consequence of the continuous miners' advance, electrical switchgear in the heading had been moved forward. The additional length of feeder cable necessary had just been installed. It had been pulled into position by a horse, using a wrapped-around chain. Where connected to the switchgear, the cable had been bent back upon itself. On re-energising, a short-circuit occurred at this point, just the place where it had been lashed with the chain. The resulting arc ignited gas in the vicinity. This gas had been allowed to accumulate since the auxiliary fan ventilating the heading had been without power during the time that the additional length of cable was being connected in circuit.

The inspector's report recommended that provision be made in future to ensure auxiliary fans continue running when other plant in such headings are shut down, and that such plant be automatically switched off should the fan stop. In addition, a more flexible type of cable should be used, and transported in a manner such as to ensure that it is not damaged. The inspector also made reference to the unavailability of an adequate number of qualified electricians. In common with other pits, persons had been trained, only to leave the industry upon attaining minimum qualifications.

On 17 May 1965, at Cambrian, as at Tower, the source of ignition was electrical. This was the last explosion in South Wales and 31 men were killed. It has been dealt with in detail in the first chapter of this book. Briefly, an air bridge had been rendered ineffective, thus causing a short circuit in the ventilation system. This in turn allowed a build-up of methane gas. Simultaneously, when dealing with an electrical fault on a tailgate switch, the electricians neglected to replace all of the bolts in the flameproof cover. This allowed gas to ignite, with the flame passing into the roadway and causing the explosion.

As late as 1960, 316 men were killed in the UK coal mining industry overall, and 1,553 seriously injured. For each of the previous three years there had been at least one major disaster (that is where at least 10 or so men are killed). At the start of Lord Robens' tenure as NCB Chairman a new safety campaign was initiated. A film for electricians, "Isolate and Check", included the Cambrian disaster as an example and was shocking in its effect.

- In 1961 there was a new low record of 234 deaths, but the trend did not continue.

- In 1962, 255 men were killed.

- In 1963 there were 250 fatalities.

- In 1964, a new low record was set, with 192 fatalities.

- In 1969/70, for the first time, the annual death rate was less than 100.


## Outbursts.

Cynheidre, near Llanelli, was to be the site of a particularly bizarre form of accident. The new mines in the anthracite area, in particular Cynheidre, were to prove themselves prone to sudden outbursts of methane. The reason is assumed to be a layer of impenetrable sandstone above the lower seams, thus prohibiting any release of gas pressure. The mechanism of outbursts is not fully understood. Since they do not occur at a depth of less than 270 metres it is assumed that mechanical stress on the coal seam plays a role. Usually a put-putting sound, similar to the two-stroke engine of a small motorcycle starting and accelerating, would provide an initial warning. An explosion-like release of gas would then follow, causing displacement of coal, rock and machinery, with great clouds of coal dust being ejected with the gas.

The amount of coal so ejected varied from a few tonnes to a thousand tonnes and was proportional to the amount of gas. The quantity of gas involved precluded any danger of explosion since it exceeded the mixture (upper explosive limit) for which an explosion is possible. With such great quantities of gas, the danger lay in suffocation. Fortunately, the threat existed for a limited time only, until the ventilation had carried away the slug of gas and the danger had passed.

Between October 1962 and 1971, 67 such outbursts were recorded at Cynheidre, fortunately without any loss of life.

On 6 April 1971, following such an outburst, six men died as a result of suffocation while 69 others suffered varying degrees of asphyxia. The outburst occurred at about 12 noon, at the face of a new drivage. The quantity of gas emitted was such as to overwhelm the auxiliary ventilation system in the drivage. The three men working there were killed. The fact that their bodies were found some distance from the working face where the outburst occurred suggests that they had had some warning and were trying to escape when they were overcome by asphyxiation.

As the gas burst forth from the drivage into the main ventilation stream other men were alerted, by a sulphurous smell followed by a cloud of dust and the rising flame on a safety lamp. One man reported an unusual buzzing sound, as if something was passing through the duct of a nearby auxiliary ventilation fan. Those that did not collapse unconscious rushed in the direction of the intake fresh air, heads bowed as close to the floor as possible since methane, being lighter than air, tends to rise. As the ventilation stream gradually cleared away the gas, those that had collapsed in unconsciousness began to recover. In addition to the three initial fatalities, three others did not recover. It was only when some of the men recovered consciousness that telephone calls were made to the surface and the emergency services alerted. On coming to, the first action of the undermanager was to speak on the district loudspeaker system and instruct everybody to get outbye to fresh air as soon as possible.

It was estimated that 14,000 cubic metres of gas had burst forth, bringing with it 407 tonnes of coal. The inspector's recommendations included compressed air lines with frequent breathing points, plus compact self-rescue breathing apparatus for every man. Following this recommendation, coalfaces at Cynheidre had air lines run along them to which, in such an event, miners could connect a face mask for emergency breathing.

Between 1980-85 there were a further 7 outbursts at Cynheidre. The above measure prevented additional fatalities on these occasions. Those listening to recordings of the affected miners, speaking via microphones integral to the facemasks, were taken by the low-key, sanguine nature of the conversation. A knowledge of the Welsh language was however necessary to understand what was being said.

## Safety First!

Mining does not have to be the cruel harbinger of human suffering that traditionally it so often has been. An acceptable level of safety is attainable. It involves a custom and practice incorporating the cumulated experience of more than a century. The pre-requisite is good engineering and relevant regulations, backed up by the discipline to enforce them. This means first and foremost self-discipline, plus a watchful eye on the youngsters.

The allure of turning a blind eye to regulations in the interest of production, with its short-term kudos, has always tempted, sometimes with disastrous results. The meretricious nature of such an allure is countered by statistics, showing that the safest pits, and the safest Areas, are also those with the highest productivity. Technical measures taken to increase productivity frequently went hand in hand with safety, the introduction of self-advancing roof supports, with their wide overhead canopies, being an example of this.

In 1987, the report of the Parliamentary Energy Committee into the coal industry claimed that British Coal was the safest deep mine industry in the world. During the previous five years the accident rate had remained fairly stable, as the following table shows.

| Year | Fatalities/serious accidents per 100,000 man shifts. |
|---|---|
| 1981-82 | 1.76 |
| 1982-83 | 1.78 |
| 1983-84 | 1.87 |
| 1984-85 | 1.52 |
| 1985-86 | 2.00 |

The Chief Inspector of Mines attributed the increase shown in 1985-86 to a loss of "pit sense", resulting from the yearlong 1984-85 strike.

As the industry shrank, it resulted in a greater concentration by ministry inspectors upon individual pits, increasing the general awareness of safety issues.

By 2001, for the second year in succession, there was no underground emergency situation in the UK that necessitated the use of any mines rescue team.

## DUST.

### The Problem.

Less obvious than explosions or accidents, but also invidious, is pneumoconiosis, the traditional miners' lung disease resulting from the inhalation of airborne dust. This builds up in human lungs, gradually reducing their efficiency. Unless detected early and the sufferer transferred to a dust-free job, it can disable a man, making it difficult for him to breathe. It can even kill him. The disease is usually quite slow to develop, with those certified being the victims of conditions they worked in many years ago. According to "Control of Dust in the Mine", published in 1959 by the Safety Department of the South Wales NUM, in 1950 four men died as a result of dust for every one by accident; in 1958 the ratio was five to one. In addition, it stated that the annual number of widows caused by dust disease in South Wales alone was 272. Due to the restrictive character of medical diagnosis at the time there were in fact many more widows, who were failing to qualify for benefit.

The lack of precise information as to the pathogenesis of the disease was an embarrassment to the engineers involved in controlling dust within the mine. Neither the size ranges nor the concentration of dust necessary to overcome nature's defence system could be adequately defined. Standards were adopted that were arbitrary, both with regard to the maximum concentration and also the size of dust particle allowed. These standards had no medical foundation, except to the extent that dust particles found in a man's lungs are normally below 5 microns in size.

Difficulties associated with dust in the mine are not confined to the practical problem of dust control. There is also the psychological problem of getting men to consistently and diligently apply known means of alleviation. Although for each man killed by a fall of ground about 10 would die as a result of dust inhalation, the former danger was direct and easy to appreciate. In the latter case it was not easy to associate the presence of dry dust on the floor of a mine roadway with death and disability. As a result, propaganda was necessary to ensure that all persons in the mine, as well as those concerned with its planning and equipping, would view every act and innovation from a dust control point of view. In practice, such propaganda was by no means continuous and not always effective.


## The History.

Also in this aspect of safety and health at work South Wales was particularly disadvantaged, especially in parts of the anthracite coalfield. The local hard coals, so desired by the markets, tended to exacerbate the effect of such dust upon sensitive lung tissue.

From 1931 to mid 1948, over 22,000 British miners were required to leave their work as a result of pneumoconiosis. Of these, 85 per cent lived in South Wales. A prolonged campaign for compensation by the Miners Federation of Great Britain was met by resistance from the coal owners. Lung congestion, breathlessness and attendant ills were diagnosed as "bronchial chest", with no compensation. Between the two world wars, mechanical coal cutters were gradually introduced. Without any water suppression they increased the production of dust considerably.

In 1934, in notable litigation concerning Tirbach Colliery in the Swansea Valley, the South Wales Miners Federation lost their case in the House of Lords.

In 1942, the Industrial Pulmonary Disease Committee of the Medical Research Council concluded that the disease commonly found in coalminers could indeed be caused by coaldust and rockdust. It suggested calling both "coal workers pneumoconiosis".

In 1943, the Coal Mines (South Wales) Pneumoconiosis Order enabled the Mines Inspectorate to direct managers to install dust suppression measures, should the inspectorate deem them to be appropriate. However, without such specific direction, managers were under no statutory obligation to provide such facilities. From this year onwards, coal miner's pneumoconiosis was regarded as a compensable disease. All miners so certified were suspended from employment within the industry. As compensation they received a lump sum or weekly payment (reduced if alternative work was obtained). Humane as it may sound, the modest nature of the payment and lack of suitable alternative employment resulted in the financial effect on the individuals, families and communities concerned being devastating.

In 1946, the Pneumoconiosis Research Unit was set up at Llandough.

In 1947, following pressure from Arthur Horner, General Secretary of the newly created NUM, the coal industry was subject to a legal obligation to minimise harmful dust.

In 1949 a programme of dust research was started at the Safety in Mines Research Establishment (SMRE).

In 1952, the Pneumoconiosis Research Unit at Llandough published the results of a survey of the Rhondda Fach. Of the entire adult population, 89 per cent had been X-rayed. Half of the working miners had the disease. Nearly one in five had progressive massive fibrosis, the most severe and deadly form. This was the result of tuberculosis infection of lungs already damaged by dust. Tuberculosis, of a form severe enough as to be infectious to others, was found in six per thousand males and seven per thousand females.

In 1953, a programme of field research into dust was started by the NCB.

In 1954 the Mines and Quarries Act, which became operative three years later, made dust suppression at mines a statutory necessity.

In 1959 a periodic X-ray scheme for miners was set up by the NCB.

In 1961 the South Wales Area of the NUM completed their own 13-year survey of the pneumoconiosis situation. The results were "startling", with the percentage of those having the disease being high every-where. The worst returns were 40 per cent at Elliot Colliery (New Tredegar in the Rhymney Valley), and 38 per cent at both Great Mountain Xolliery (Tumble in the Gwendraeth Valley) and Ferndale (in the Rhondda Fach). Another disturbing revelation was the number of those affected who were getting pro-gressively worse. Deep Duffryn colliery (Mountain Ash) was not unusual. Here, 213 miners had been certified as having the disease. Of these, 93 were subsequently reassessed as being progressive cases and 32 of them had died from the disease during the period of study. Of the 93 progressive cases, 47 of them were still at work. Other disturbing conclusions were that not only were methods of dust suppression entirely inadequate but that record-keeping of dust counts in the air was unsatisfactory.

## Dust Suppression.

In a coal mine the dust content of the air varies between very wide limits, depending on operations being carried out. Concentrations as high as 2,000 milligrams per cubic metre have been recorded when "cutting dry". This sort of figure would cause lung diseases, as well as a potentially explosive atmosphere. There are four basic approaches to control of the dust hazard:

i) Prevention of dust formation.

ii) Prevention of dust dispersal once formed.

iii)Rapid removal of the dust dispersed.

iv)The provision of individual protection (i.e. dust masks).

The "dry cutting" of a coalface had been illegal since 1950. However, the large-scale introduction of mechanisation meant that more and smaller dust was now being produced, since machines tended to smash up the coal more than hand working did. On the other hand, dust production was thereby concen-trated at one point, namely the power loader, and therefore easier to control, such as by water spraying. Dust suppression measures such as infusion were also making progress. In this case, water is applied under pressure to holes drilled along the coalface, thus wetting the coal prior to production.

In 1965 the NCB Mining Research Establishment gave the degree of reduction in the dispersion of respir-able dust, using three different methods of water application, as follows:

- Infusion (i.e. pre-impregnation of the coal) - 50%.

- Conventional, machine-mounted sprays - 25-40%.

- Pick face flushing - 60-70%.

With the former method, water percolates through the cleavage planes or slips in the coal seam. These slips are the result of movement associated with faulting. Dust is produced as a result of coal grinding against coal under great pressure. South Wales coals are predominantly dusty due to such slip dust, which results from the considerable local faulting. An additional source of dust is disintegration of the coal as it is being won. This cannot be treated by infusion, due to the inability of water to penetrate solid coal. Sprays at the point of production are the only defence against dust resulting from disintegration.

Studies have found that far less dust was produced if the power loader was hauled along the face at high speed, with the disc or drum mounted picks taking the largest possible bite at the slowest possible rota-tional speed. Regular pick replacement is important since blunt cutting edges produce excessive dust by crushing. In addition, the extra resistance results in slower haulage rates and pick penetration. Excessive dust dispersion would also result from cutting into the roof or floor of the seam. Such dust is much more fine, and consequently more dangerous. For mechanised cutting using discs or drums, the use of a cowl to confine the dust produced, combined with sprays properly placed within the cowl, has proven to be effective. Ploughing techniques are not so vicious in their action, resulting in less degradation of the product. However, coal still disintegrates at the point of production and considerable dust can be raised. Pre-infusion is a necessity. In all cases, roof control should be such as to minimise the pressure to which the area immediately in front of the coal face is subjected. Otherwise the seam will be crushed and preformed dust will become a hazard. Ventilation layout is determined by the method of production employed but basically the more air available to dilute the dust the less will be the hazard to health.

## Dust Measurement.

When it came to the payment of compensation, the NCB always seemed to be fighting a rearguard action, whatever statistics or standard of dust measurement was employed. With regard to an assessment of the danger, the position is complicated by the fact that a visual impression does not necessarily correlate with measured values. Although clouds of visible dust might cause concern, it was maintained that the smaller (maybe invisible) particles were the more dangerous, since these were less likely to be caught in the nasal passageways. In addition, a man could be certified as having pneumoconiosis without him ever having worked anywhere where the dust count was above approved standards. It was not possible to preclude the possibility of infection, even in atmospheres conforming to recognised standards. Clearly, something was wrong.

In March 1961, check sampling was introduced in South Wales. The aim was to check sample every face at least once per annum, a target that with only three samplers for the whole South Western Division was difficult to achieve. Over the years, check sampling consistently produced higher dust counts than routine sampling. The suggestion made (and denied by production department) was that the reason lay in the fact that routine sampling was carried out by those responsible for dust suppression measures.

For the year ending 31 March 1971, in the East Wales Area, 18.1 per cent of the routine samples (236 of 1,036) exceeded the latest standard of 8.0mg/cu.m. Of the check samples taken (about 10 per cent of the routine samples), 32 per cent exceeded this allowable maximum.

A routine sample, so the suggestion went, was only carried out when all dust suppression measures were in force. On a regular day-to-day basis, or during check sampling, this was not necessarily the case. The standards for dust sampling went through a series of revisions, as given in the following table:

| Year | 1944 | 1949 | 1956 | 1965 | 1970 |
|---|---|---|---|---|---|
| Standard | Interim standards, Monmouthshire SW Coal Dust Research Committee. Respirable dust, measured by Heywood Sedimentometer. | NCB approved conditions. | NCB sequential sampling scheme. | National Joint Pneumo. Committee (NJPC). Standards for "full shift" continuous sampling using Long running Thermal Precipitator. | NJPC standards using SMRE Gravimetric Sampler. |
| Maximum Allowable. | 0.4 g/1,000cu.ft. 14mg/cu.m. for anthracite mines | 800 particles 1-5 microns/ cu.cm. (steam + bituminous coal). 650 particles 1-5microns/ cu.cm. (anthracite). 450 particles 0.5-5 microns/ (stone work). | 850 particles 1-5 microns/ cu.cm. (steam + bituminous coal). 650 particles 1-5 microns/ cu.cm. (anthracite & mixed stone/ coal dust). 450 particles 0.5-5 microns/ (stone work). | 700 particles 1-5 microns/ cu.cm. (steam + bituminous coal). 500 particles 1-5microns/ cu.cm. (anthracite). 250 particles 1-5 microns/ (stone work). | 8mg/cu.m. for all coal work. 3mg/cu.m. for stone drivages. |

At the end of the 1950's, the number of new pneumoconiosis cases diagnosed annually in the UK averaged 2,800. By 1969 this was down to 624. The following table, based on information issued by the NCB, illustrates the effect of the greatly improved environmental conditions and dust suppression measures that were introduced. It gives the prevalence of all classes of pneumoconiosis at 149 collieries surveyed nationally in each of the given years.

| Year. | Incidence of Pneumoconiosis (% of men X-Rayed). |
|-------|--------------------------------------------------|
| 1959-63 | 10.5 |
| 1964-68 | 8.4 |
| 1969-73 | 8.2 |
| 1974-77 | 5.9 |
| 1978-81 | 3.8 |
| 1982-85 | 2.0 |

## The Board in Denial.

The above statistics however do not tell the whole story. Not included are those cases of emphysema and chronic bronchitis, both of which may be caused or exacerbated by factors other than the inhalation of dust, in particular by smoking. Since nearly all of those miners affected smoked, this fact enabled the NCB (later British Coal) to fight prolonged delaying actions against claims for compensation.

In 1991, eight former miners brought a case claiming compensation for such chest diseases.

In 1998, they finally won their case. A High Court judgement considered coal dust to be an independent factor in the causation of chronic bronchitis and emphysema. It was recognised that inadequate precautions at work had resulted in an exacerbation of chest complaints. The degree of respiratory disease is now regarded as being much greater than previously supposed, with almost all underground workers after 1954 being affected to some extent. In a landmark judgement, compensation was awarded and a precedent set. The ultimate pay out to all claimants will be the biggest personal injury settlement ever awarded in the UK.

Mr. Justice Tucker described British Coal's approach to the case as "messy and grudging". They had, he said, "wasted a substantial amount of court time". There was abundant evidence that British Coal officials had placed coal production above health and safety. They had failed to take reasonable steps to combat the effects of coal dust and had failed to encourage the use of respirators - available from the mid-1960`s.

The nationalised British Coal no longer existed but its liabilities were transferred to the Government, through the Department of Trade and Industry. This Department is responsible for administrating the compensation scheme and for paying all legal expenses related to a claim.

Peter Evans, from South Wales solicitors Hugh James, who fought the legal battle on behalf of one of the plaintiffs from the South Wales Area, said that the ruling was a "damning indictment of British Coal, at all levels and throughout its entire history". British Coal had put profits before people" and, "If it was a question of production or safety then, unfortunately and sadly for the miners, production tended to predominate —— they did much too little and much too late. They often paid lip service to the suppression of dust".

## ABERFAN.

### The Event.

On Friday, 21 October 1966, not only South Wales but also the whole world was shocked by an event as terrible as it was unique and unexpected. South Wales had become used to mining disasters, they had become part of the region's ethos. This, however, was something different. The victims were predominantly children, struck down, not by the dangers of underground working, but by the incursions of man into the landscape. The setting of the event was the Merthyr Valley, stretching north from Pontypridd. Hugging the eastern slope of the valley, the old Pontypridd to Merthyr road offered a view of the collieries on the valley floor and of the settlements themselves, nestling along the lower western slope. One of these settlements bears the name of Aberfan. It had grown around, and was justified by, the adjacent Merthyr Vale Colliery.

The waste heap of this colliery, sprawling along the crest of the western hill, dominated the village. At the time, with an annual UK production of 150 Mt of coal, 60-70 Mt of spoil were also being brought to the surface. Such "tips" as they are known locally, were as much a feature of South Wales as the ubiquitous pit headgear. Playgrounds for the valley kids, but otherwise unloved and ugly, nobody gave them much thought, least of all as it would transpire the NCB itself. Sometimes in the form of a perfect cone, like miniature volcanoes, sometimes extended and sprawling, they scarred and dominated the slopes and the crests of this once fair land, often perched precariously above the villages, hemming them in from above.

In spite of the nature of South Walian terrain, in spite of all the visual evidence as to its possibility, no significant thought had ever been given to the likelihood that such a tip might slide. Indeed, apart from the occasional heavy rainfall that brought black mud into some dwellings, thereby necessitating an annoying clean out and a change of carpet, the country had been spared any tip-orientated disaster. This was to be suddenly and brutally changed. The tip complex concerned had been extended across a mountainside spring, producing water at the rate of about 10,000 gallons per hour. Gradually, but unknown and insidious, the tip's base became waterlogged and unstable, unable to support the great mass above.

At 9.15am on Friday 21 October 1966, when it eventually slid, 107,038 cubic metres of semi-liquefied material first bulged from the tip and then came rushing down the mountainside in a great wave, emitting a roar like a jet aircraft while enveloping and smashing everything in its path. In the morning sunlight that bathed the mountain, the tipping gang could watch its progress as it crashed down into the mist that still hung in the village. Their own survival was an act of fate since, just at that time, they had left their normal place of work to go for a cup of tea. (Coincidentally, their survival also meant that the Mines Inspectorate was to play no role in the investigation. They only become involved when accidents occur to colliery employees). The occupants of two farm cottages became the first victims. Beyond lay the village, and Pantglas Junior School for the younger children. It was the last day of school before the half-term holiday. The children had just started their lessons after morning assembly. The school was engulfed, along with about twenty houses in the village. Of the 144 fatalities, 116 were children, mostly between the ages of seven and ten. Of these, 109 had died within the school itself. Five teachers were among the 28 adults who died. Of the 35 injured, 29 were also children.

By lunchtime an ugly black scar had defaced Aberfan. A black dagger of semi-liquid ooze had sliced through the village with its point aimed squarely at Pant Glas school. The village had been ripped into two sections by this obscene landslide of glutinous mud. The center section of the village no longer existed. As well as the farmhouses and the school, part of a row of terraced houses had also been swept away. On the fringe of this wasteland of black slime, half houses stood, their innards laid bare, their half-supported roofs sagging grotesquely. From the vicinity of where the school had once stood, a column of gray smoke ascended. Emanating from an open fire, which had suddenly become subterranean, it continued persistently to smolder over the next fateful day, a bizarre smoke signal in the sky of the tragedy that had occurred.

## The Response.

Its total unexpectedness notwithstanding, the emergency services, consisting of a loose organization of various police forces, civil defence, local authorities and ambulance brigades, responded well. Soon, across the whole site, the WVRS, Salvation Army and Red Cross distributed cups of soup, tea and coffee while a mortuary was set up in Bethania Chapel. Three of the surviving young teachers labelled the children, enabling parents to be taken immediately to the body of their own child. As the word spread around, parents and relatives arrived at the front door. They waited in a long, patient line to identify the little, blanket-clad figures. Adding to the confusion were contradictory radio appeals, for volunteers to assist and for people to stay away from the area. Eventually, 2,000 or so people worked at the grim task of recovering broken bodies from the glutenous black slime and of making the tips as safe as possible.

After 11am on the day of the disaster nobody was rescued alive, but it took nearly a week before all bodies were recovered. All roads leading to the incident became blocked with rescue workers vehicles, both official and voluntary. Under the circumstances, the two organizations capable of providing most of what was needed were the army, held back until rather late in the operation, and the NCB itself. The Board was able to provide lorries and earth-moving equipment, as well as all kinds of stores, shovels etc. From a base at the adjacent Merthyr Vale Colliery they had vital communication links with the outside world and were able to organise the mineworkers. These were the main instrument in the attempted rescue operations. Lord Robens, NCB Chairman, would be criticised for keeping an appointment on that first day of the disaster, to be installed as Chancellor of the University of Surrey. He went to Aberfan on the following day, later defending himself on the grounds that the initial priority was for solid practical help and not for VIP visits. Once there he would further blot his copy book by making a statement, motivated by a desire to protect his local officials but later shown to be untenable, that it was impossible for anyone to know that the tip had been built on top of a spring.

The Prime Minister, Harold Wilson, did make a short visit that first evening, causing some degree of disturbance but nevertheless doing his best to ensure that all necessary facilities would be made available. Richard March, Minister of Power, was also there, according to Wilson looking very ashen and worried about charges that were already spreading about negligence by the NCB and the warnings they had been given. George Thomas, the Welsh MP, was the VIP most affected. He had taken on the job of comforting the relatives and had attended the relatives' meeting, held by the Director of Education.

It soon became sickeningly clear, however, that all the resources, all the activity, all of the desperate commitment of both professionals and volunteers could not change one terrible fact. The children, and the adults, were gone. Night fell, but under hastily erected floodlights the tragedy continued. Its actors, half lit shadowy figures, flitted by in cameo roles. Local men, their eyes red with weeping and emotionally crushed, emerged from one terraced home to visit another. United in their grief, they comforted those who could not be comforted. The women were nowhere in sight. Locked in their cocoon of agony, even the short passage from one house to another seemed beyond them.

Soldiers of the Parachute Regiment, troubleshooters of the British army, were superfluous in their role of supporting the police in maintaining order. The chaos that prevailed was not of the willful, negative type with which they could have dealt. The police, firm but humane and low key, maintained a background presence. The centre stage was dominated by the toiling figures of everyman. Working under self-discipline and following the quiet instructions of unknown, shadowy figures, they formed the digging gangs and the long lines behind them, removing the spoil from buried victims. They strove for the unachievable, for the fact remained, the children, and the adults, were gone. Occasionally a victim would be located as, for example, a hand would be exposed. Sheets would be raised to afford some dignity to the black bundle that had, until so recently been alive and joyful, with a future to look forward to. After careful exposure a stretcher would carry another body, back to the temporary mortuary. As an example of the inadequacy of adequate resources, boxes of chocolates would be ripped open and their contents thrown by the fistful at the lines of toiling figures, on the off chance that some hunger could be stilled or some respite could be given thereby. Most of this 'manna from heaven" was ignored and simply trampled under foot.

The next day, Saturday 22 October 1966, heavy rain started at 2.30pm, causing some concern that the tip would slide again, engulfing some of the 2,500 rescue workers on the scene. Prince Philip was on his way and would report back to the Queen as to when during the next days her visit would be appropriate. Lord Snowdon, the husband of Princess Margaret, had gone spontaneously and was already there. On the following Tuesday, a still moved and shattered George Thomas MP would report to Wilson that of all the visitors Lord Snowdon had won the highest praise. Instead of just inspecting the site he had made it his job to accompany Thomas on his visits to bereaved relatives -holding the hand of a distraught father, sitting with the head of a mother on his shoulder for half an hour in silence. In another house he comforted an older couple that had lost 13 grandchildren - in another where they were terribly upset he offered to make a cup of tea, went into the kitchen and returned with a tray with cups for them all. He helped an older man persuade his son, who was clutching something in his tightly clenched fist, to open his hand. It was a prefect's badge, the only thing by which he had been able to identify his child.

On the following Monday, at an inquest on 30 of the children at Sion Methodist Chapel in Aberfan, the brave front of the people cracked, and there were harrowing scenes. There were shouts of "murderers" and "they have killed our children". The coroner of Merthyr, Ben Hamilton, tried to restore order saying, "I realise your grief is such that you may not be realising what you are saying". A father repeated, "I want it recorded - buried alive by the National Coal Board. That is what I want to see on the record. That is the feeling of those present. Those are the words we want to go on the certificate".


## The Tribunal.

Five days after the disaster, resolutions were passed in both Houses of Parliament, declaring that it was expedient to establish a tribunal. This was appointed by Cledwyn Hughes, Secretary of State for Wales. Its Chairman would be Sir Herbert Edmund Davies, one of Her Majesty's Lord Justices of Appeal, who was born within five miles of Aberfan. Evidence was taken in public on seventy-six days, the first sittings being held in Merthyr Tydfil and the later ones in Cardiff.

An unseemly argument would blow up in the press when the Attorney General, Sir Elwyn Jones, warned against the media conducting their own examinations. Intended to prevent the conditioning and leading of vital evidence, it was interpreted by the press as a gag upon free press comment.

On 3 August 1967, the report of the Aberfan tribunal was published. It was a devastating criticism of the NCB. The introduction stated;

"Our strong and unanimous view is that the Aberfan disaster could and should have been prevented". It went on "Blame for the disaster rests upon the National Coal Board". It was pointed out, "There was a total absence of tipping policy and this was the basic cause of the disaster. In this respect however, the National Coal Board were following in the footsteps of their predecessors. They were not guided either by HM Inspectorate of Mines and Quarries or by legislation". This was perfectly true but, as NCB Chairman Lord Robens would later point out, with two small and partial exceptions, no other country in the world had seen any need to make regulations about tips. One exception was Germany, where the Mines Inspectorate issued an order in 1964 governing the construction of colliery spoil heaps, but not, however, their siting. The second exception was South Africa. Here there was an Act that contained requirements covering slime dams.

The report went on to say:

"The basic cause of the Aberfan disaster was that for many years in the coal mining industry little or no attention has been paid to the siting, control, or management of spoil tips. It might be said that, for this reason, most of the men whose acts and omissions we have to consider have had, as it were, a bad upbringing. They have not been taught to be cautious, they were left uninformed as to telltale signs on a tip, which should have alerted them. Accordingly, if in the last analysis, any of them must be blamed individually for contributing to the disaster (and that, unhappily is the conclusion we have been drawn to regarding some of the National Coal Board employees and staff who appeared before us), for all of them a strong "plea in mitigation" may be advanced".

The tribunal found that the blame was shared (in varying degrees) among the National Coal Board Headquarters, the South-Western Divisional Board, and certain individuals. Severn NCB officials were named who, the report said, were in varying degrees liable to censure. These were either moved to "jobs of smaller compass" without reduction in pay or left in comparable or more senior posts.

The loyalty of Lord Robens, Coal Board Chairman, to his industry and his desire to protect his boys, who had been loyal servants of the Board, was not always appreciated. At Aberfan itself the tipping gang and its charge-hand were all bitterly reviled, and treated as pariahs. The report, however, made it clear that these men were absolved from all blame for the disaster. They were untrained in the assessment of such dangers, and were faced with a difficult situation. This would not be the only case of apparently unreasonable reaction on the part of emotionally stressed-out people, in the pressure cooker atmosphere of a small village and confronted with a myriad of additional problems outside their experience.

## The Aftermath.

Aberfan is a small, self-contained community, by British standards quite isolated. Pantglas was the village school, to which every family sent their children. In a community of 4,000, 144 deaths meant that everyone was bereaved, either through family or friends. The trauma was bound to be profound, compounded by the fact that men of the village worked in the colliery that had created the waste. They had supported the setting up of the NCB, the organization officially blamed for the disaster. As to the remains of the tip, day after day, sorrowing parents would still look up at it. Children refused to go to bed in rooms from which it could be seen. If they were cajoled into going to bed, they could not sleep.

Removal of the tip became a cause celebre in its own right, with the issue turning into a running sore that lasted three years. Official opinion was that the tip was now completely safe. It would therefore be unjustified to spend a million or so pounds on its removal. The Coal Board proposed a scheme, paid for by themselves, that included removing a good deal of the tip, plus landscaping, terracing, grassing and some tree planting on the lower slopes. This would, in their view, completely take away the menacing impression. The engineering was good, but it failed to address the emotional scars that the very presence of the tip, in any form at all, kept raw. A petition was signed by 500 villagers, pleading for complete removal. This daily reminder of their loss should be completely obliterated.

In April 1968, matters came to a head when 70 villagers burst into the Welsh Office demanding to see George Thomas, in the meantime Secretary of State for Wales. In what Thomas described to Prime Minister Wilson as, "One of the most harrowing and difficult meetings I have ever had", tip slurry was dumped on the table in front of him. The tyres on the Minister's car were slashed. Thomas left the meeting in tears and met Wilson the next day. The decision was made to completely remove the tip. There was some tough talking between the Prime Minister, the Chancellor of the Exchequer and a reluctant NCB, but the tips were removed.

The final tender price was £850,000. Costs were divided between the Coal Board, the Government and the villagers, using £150,000 from the disaster fund. Prime Minister Harold Wilson regarded the magnitude of the fund as being almost an embarrassment to its trustees. The latter contribution was, in his eyes, therefore fully justified. In the agony of the disaster's aftermath his representative, George Thomas, secured villagers' agreement. Thomas got a rough ride from some of them but pushed the line that he was not asking for any money contributed by the public, but only the accumulated interest. After years of protest the money was finally returned to the fund in 1997, this action being initiated by Ron Davies, Secretary of State for Wales at the time. Bethania Chapel, the makeshift mortuary, was rebuilt at the cost of the fund, since its members could no longer bear to worship there. Robens had rejected the request. While insurers wrangled, the ruins of the school and the wrecked houses remained for twelve months.

The press labelled the Aberfan Disaster Fund as "The second Aberfan disaster". It had been front-page news all over the world, and had brought in commensurate donations. As with the material resources made available at the time of the tragedy, financial compensation was the least that a sympathetic world could contribute. On the evening of the disaster, the Mayor of Merthyr, Mr. Stanley Davies, initiated a disaster appeal for funds. It quickly raised the unprecedented sum of £1.75 M (worth approximately £19.62 M in 1999). Officialdom was to be far less generous. Damages for injuring an adult or killing a farm animal are based upon an estimate of the earning capacity foregone. In the case of a child it is not. Hence the Coal Board's contention in 1966 that an offer to the parents of £500 for each child killed was, "a generous offer".

The saga of the Disaster Fund ensured the continuing presence of the press, with their notebooks, pads and questions, perpetuating the alien, unreal world in which the village now lived. There was a feeling that the press gained more satisfaction out of negative stories than positive ones. In this highly charged atmosphere, jealousies and problems were spawned, included in which was now the administration of a large sum of money. Questions arose; not only whether the fund should contribute to the cost of tip removal but also did so-and-so have the right to charge his holiday to the fund when he himself had not lost children but only lived in the proximity of the destruction? Should all of the money be distributed immediately or used for long-term investments? If distributed immediately then on what basis? So it went, on and on. Gradually, the tone of international press coverage changed, from one of sympathy to a portrayal of carping, small-mindedness.

The immediate tragedy receded into the past but the emotional overload remained, creating stress out of everyday life. Women who had sent their children to school on that day when they hadn't wanted to go suffered terrible feelings of guilt. Children felt guilty about being alive and did not go out to play for a long time. Those who had lost their own children couldn't bear to see the children of others. There was bitterness between families who had lost children and those who hadn't. How could some parents relax and enjoy the laughter of their children at a child's birthday party, knowing its effect upon neighbours who had lost their own? Indeed, were laughter and the enjoyment of life not themselves inappropriate and out of place in this small, goldfish bowl community?

In an example of closing the stable door after the horse has bolted, the NCB would survey all tips, treating them now as engineering structures. Particularly in South Wales, due to the local topography, they would be smoothed, capped, reinforced and drained. The expense and effort, unthinkable previously, to prevent recurrence of a disaster which had never happened before (and seen through pre-disaster eyes, probably never would happen) came rolling forth.

Following the report of the Aberfan tribunal, NCB Chairman Lord Robens felt called upon to tender his resignation to the Minister of Power, Richard March. In his letter Lord Robens said:

"It may be that the doctrine of ministerial responsibility does not strictly apply to me as Chairman of the National Coal Board, but I have spent all my life in public service and I feel bound by its rules. I have decided, therefore, that I must offer you my resignation".

The resignation offer was rejected; March saying in his reply:

"I am quite clear that I should not accept your offer. When you told me of your decision you mentioned the doctrine of ministerial responsibility, but I do not think such arguments can reasonably be applied to a chairman of a nationalised industry, nor do I consider that the conclusions of the tribunal are of a kind that call for your resignation. Nothing will ever erase from our minds the terrible tragedy of Aberfan, but we all have a duty to ensure that nothing like it can ever happen again, and I believe that in this, as in other aspects, your contribution continues to be important in the national interest".

Prior to March's reply, newspapers and the NCB had received numerous letters, the great majority urging Lord Robens to stay at his post. The National Union of Mineworkers appealed to Richard March not to accept the resignation. The letter, written on behalf of the union's National Executive Committee, and signed by General Secretary Will Paynter, said that Robens' departure in the midst of the difficulties associated with the reconstruction of the industry would be to the detriment of both the industry and the nation.

Plate 8 Old Colliery Surface. Cambrian 1910.
(Note amount of steam from local boiler plant).

Plate 9 New Colliery Surface. Cynheidre 1971.
(All electric pit. Note tower mounted winders).

# Chapter 10
## FIGHTING RETREAT

*"I was not prepared to just sit on the opposition benches
for ten years shouting, "resign".*
Lord Robens.

## A STAR IS (RE)BORN.

### New Broom.

Richard March's rejection of Lord Roben's resignation offer, as well as being in accordance with the expressed wishes of the NUM, was supported by public opinion. A Gallup poll in August 1967 recorded 74 per cent vs. 15 per cent that he should stay. Against the background of such a terrible tragedy, support for the chairman of the organization concerned may seem strange. There was a widespread feeling, however, that the disaster was an accident and that the chairman of such a large entity could not be held responsible for the detailed operation of every tip. In addition, Robens was not just any chairman. For years he had dominated the industry.

As a former Labour politician and government minister he knew exactly how and where to apply political pressure. A colourful character and a highly political animal, he was extremely good at manipulating the press. His role in the post-war coal mining industry was nothing less than historic, and was seen as such at the time. The defence of his boys after the disaster, not appreciated in all circles, epitomised his commitment to the industry and the people in it, during a very trying time. In short, under Roben's Chairmanship the Coal Board was managing decline very competently.

Throughout the Second World War, and for many years afterwards, coal was a commodity in short supply. It was not until the late 1950's that the industry really had to start selling its products hard. By then, markets were rushing away on the advancing tide of cheap oil. The NCB was over-producing and by November 1959 stocks had reached 36.2 Mt, the "Mountains of Mourne" as one miners' leader called them. In the intervening period, however, marketing was an art that had largely atrophied. This change in the energy market had long been predicted but, instead of rising to the challenge, the Board had every appearance of being cut adrift in heavy seas. From being heroes of the nation and indispensable providers of energy, miners now became unfortunate employees in an industry that destiny had condemned to inevitable decline. The malaise percolated through to the coalfields.

This attitude was now to receive a breath of fresh air. The aim nevertheless was to renovate and optimise, not to sweep away. Until the Thatcher Government came to power in March 1979, corporatism would remain the dominant post-war political culture. There was a bi-partisan policy to ban coal imports, which lasted into the 1970's. Even then imports remained limited, although the pithead price of coal in the USA was less than half its price in the UK.

### Entrance.

On 13 June 1960, a scoop headline in the Guardian heralded a new era, "NCB CHAIRMANSHIP FOR MR. ROBENS-LABOUR LOSING A 'STAR'". Almost overnight the mood at the NCB changed to one of proactive activity. The next ten years were to be characterised by a fighting retreat. Under the mantra, "There's no friend like an old friend", issue was to be taken with the inevitability of coal's decline. Behind the new ethos would be the dynamism, strategic thinking, public relations flair and firm belief in the concept of nationalisation that characterised one of the nation's leading centre-left politicians.

A trade union leader before entering politics, Alfred, "Alf" Robens was a senior member of the Labour Shadow Cabinet. He would later say, matter-of-factly, that if he had not taken the Coal Board job he would probably have ended up as Prime Minister. He was regarded as being odds-on favourite to succeed Hugh

Gaitskell, Labour Party leader at that time. He regarded the move to the NCB, however, as having being the right choice under current circumstances. His appointment to the House of Lords, as Lord Robens of Woldingham, ensured his connection with national politics. He would later say that politics would have been the only thing capable of tempting him away from the National Coal Board. An agreement with Gaitskell was to the effect that, if Labour won the next election, he would join the Government. Fate took a hand however and by the time the next election came around, which Labour won, Gaitskell had passed away. His premature death had been a surprise to everyone. Harold Wilson, his replacement as party leader, thus became Prime Minister. Wilson's reputation was as a shrewd political operator, but colleagues would later write about his sense of insecurity. Competition was the last thing he wanted. Roben's relationship with Gaitskell had been good, and the two had previously worked together at the Ministry of Power. From 1947, Gaitskell had been the Minister and Robens his Parliamentary Secretary, before himself being promoted to Minister of Labour in 1951. As a contrast, between him and Wilson coolness was the order of the day. From the occupant of number ten, therefore, no invitation came, and Lord Robens was to stay at the Coal Board for a total of ten years and nine months. Later, Roben's return to national political life was hardly assisted by condemnation of the National Coal Board in the Aberfan tribunal's report. During his battles with the Labour Government over fuel policy, it must have entered Roben's head that he could so easily have been a senior member of that Government himself, if not its leader.

Being at the Ministry of Power during the post-war Labour Government, Robens had lived through the drafting and introduction of the first experiment in nationalisation. Initially, his appointment to the NCB by Conservative Prime Minister Harold Macmillan sparked controversy from all sides of the political spectrum, where the tendency was to see it as a Machiavellian ploy to weaken the opposition. In addition, the industry itself was far from enamoured. The latter tended to think that one of their own should have got the job. Experience would prove them wrong and, for the duration of his chairmanship, both he and the National Coal Board were regularly in the headlines. Marketing was reborn and the industry had got its ideal "front man".

## Nationalisation Works!

Robens expressed his abiding political interests as being both mining and men at work. A Lancastrian himself he described mining folk as being the salt of the earth, although Welsh and Scottish miners were to blot their copybooks by their militancy, and the tendency of some of their delegates to ostentatiously read newspapers during his speech at the NUM annual conference. Nevertheless, the mining industry was something to which he was, and would remain, emotionally bound.

That background notwithstanding, he had no time for the concept that, for nationalised industries, profit should be a secondary consideration. His aim of breaking even during 1962, the second year of his tenure, was to be criticised by some colleagues as being an obsession. This aim was achieved, with a surplus of nearly £9.5 M , after the payment of £22 M in interest charges to the Ministry of Power. He would point out that the Coal Industry Nationalisation Act required the industry to break even, over a period of good and bad years. More than that, as a supporter of nationalisation, he set out to show that coal could be a model of efficient public enterprise. He agreed with Herbert Morrison when he said that it was vital national ownership show itself superior to private enterprise in all-round efficiency. Upon starting his remit, Robens immediately made three basic principles public:

- Decentralisation of the organization, in as much as only those matters which could not be dealt with in the coalfields should continue to be handled at the centre.

- No decentralisation on broad policies such as wages, and no return to the pre-war system of district prices and district wages.

- As a simple mantra, the industry should aim at a marketing target of 200 Mt per annum. He had previously used this figure in speeches and it was also something to which the Labour Party was committed. With production at that level, standing overheads would be roughly 22.5 shillings/t. With sales of 180 Mt they would rise to 25 shillings/t and at 150 Mt would increase to 30 shillings/t.

In addition to such public statements, he had made his views known in political circles that, in addition to substantial changes being required in the administration, the totally different energy situation obviously entailed an industry physically smaller than the one that the planners had proposed, and for which capital investment had been made. Such arguments on his part no doubt contributed to the Prime Minister's decision to appoint him. His strategic approach was based upon:

    i)   A massive sales campaign.

    ii)  The greatest mechanisation drive the industry had ever seen.

    iii) Complete reorganisation of the administration.

## SALES.

### Domestic.

The marketing campaign was sufficiently successful for Robens to be nominated jointly as "Marketing Man of 1964". New and attractive appliances were developed to burn coal smokelessly while providing central heating. By extolling the charms of a "living fire", on the domestic front the NCB was able to fight a prolonged rearguard action by means of continuous burners and smokeless fuel behind glass.

In response to the "high speed gas" campaign, Robens commented at a press conference that gas had been going at the same speed for years and that for him it was merely, "an old flame tarted up with a mini-burner". While the "living fire" sales campaign produced results, the competitors counter-attacked, stressing greater convenience and incorporating mock coal fires into their own appliances. So the battle continued.

### Industrial.

On the industrial front, Robens constantly plugged the theme, "It is not coal that is obsolete. It is the out-of-date equipment in which it is frequently burned that gives rise to the accusation that it is old-fashioned".

In 1966 the Coal Board launched an organization, Associated Heat Services, capable of designing and servicing district heating schemes, sometimes burning refuse as well as coal.

### Coal Distribution.

At this time, the controversial chairmanship of Dr. Beeching was revolutionising the railways. In cooperation between the Coal Board and British Rail, centralised, mechanised coal depots were developed, each serving a large number of merchants. This made it possible to work full trainloads from the collieries to such depots, eliminating four or five marshalling operations en route. By the use of automatic, mechanical means, the coal was unloaded virtually upon arrival, leaving the locomotive to pull out with the empties. The coal would then be stored locally, ready to serve the merchants.

In 1963 the first such depot was ready, at West Drayton in Middlesex. This served an area that had previously relied on 23 small distribution points, using ten times the number of wagons. Previously, coal was delivered in small numbers of wagons to multiple points. These had then been treated as coal warehouses, until emptied and returned.

For the power stations, coal's biggest customer, there followed a major co-operative effort between the NCB, British Rail and the Central Electricity Generating Board. Thus was introduced the "merry-go-round" train system, between pits and the power stations. Permanently-coupled trains load in minutes at creep speed, from overhead bunkers at the colliery. At the power station destination they unload equally speedily, with bottom doors in the wagons opening into hoppers beneath the rails. The trains make a number of round trips per day between pit and power stations, as far as fifty or seventy miles apart. They need never stop moving - hence the term "merry-go-round". This resulted in tremendous reductions in the number of wagons that the railways had to handle. It was recognised at the time as a breakthrough in freight haulage as far as the UK was concerned.

To handle coastwise shipments, mainly to power stations on the Thames and in the south, but also with exports in mind, the biggest bulk handling terminal in Europe was built at Immingham on the Humber. This was conceived together with British Rail and the British Transport Docks Board. Coal from "merry-go-round" trains would be discharged via conveyors to the stocking area. Here, a bucket-wheel arrangement would reclaim the coal and discharge it via conveyors into ships' holds at the rate of 4,000t per hour. For the first time in the long history of British exporting, coal trains would not have to wait for ships, and vice versa. Ultimately the British Steel Corporation joined in and the facility was extended to handle iron ore imports for Scunthorpe Steelworks.

## No Imports.

Pressure from the steel industry to be allowed to import coking coal was successfully checked, with the Conservative Government of the early 1960's imposing a total ban on imports. In South Wales alone, £46 M had been invested in pits specifically to supply the blast furnaces. An extensive stocking problem, as well as industrial unrest, was therefore avoided. Had the decision gone the other way, Robens would have demanded elimination of the 10 per cent protective tariff on steel, and freedom to ship around the spot markets of the world for the steel that his industry used.

## New Technology.

In the battle for markets, NCB laboratories involved in coal utilisation did significant work. This included the production of a smokeless solid fuel from ordinary bituminous coal, plus the blending of various coals as a substitute for the specific type of coal previously used to manufacture foundry coke. This was becoming in short supply.

The new concept of fluidised bed combustion was also advanced. This consists of a boiler where the water tubes are immersed in a bed of ash, formed from the combustion of finely ground coal. The ash bed is at great heat and kept in constant animation by the injection of combustion air. Excess ash is removed, and fresh coal supplied, on a controlled basis. The advantages are; lower capital cost, improved heat transfer, and the possible use of high ash coals, thus reducing the requirement for expensive preparation so as to reduce ash content. In addition, water tube corrosion was reduced and, perhaps the most important factor, sulphur from the coal was retained in the ash, instead of going up the chimney and causing pollution. While at home the Generating Board were lukewarm, in the USA on the other hand there was an outcry against pollution. This persuaded Robens to initiate personal discussions with Mr. Stewart Udall, United States Secretary of the Interior.

In 1969, Robens signed an agreement in Washington with the National Air Control Pollution Administration to exchange technical information on fluidised bed combustion. The following year he visited Washington again, returning with a contribution of a quarter of a million dollars towards the cost of research. Such Coal Board diplomacy was effective, but did not prove popular in British political circles, where Robens was regarded as acting above his station. For them, inter-governmental contacts would have been more appropriate. From his own experience in politics, Robens recognised a Gordian knot when he saw one. This one he determined to cut, thereby eliminating the associated bureaucracy, with its endless meetings of working parties and hours of consultation.

## Discount.

In 1967, the company ALCAN decided to power their new aluminium smelter in the North-East of England from their own power station, which would be coal and not nuclear powered. The station would be 30 per cent cheaper than nuclear on capital cost. In addition, in an uncharacteristic playing of market forces, the NCB would sell coal at a special price based on the forecast costs of the nearby Lynemouth Colliery. Not only was the argument of cheap nuclear power rejected, thus undermining the strategic thinking of the electricity generating industry, the Electricity Council also expressed their chagrin that coal should be sold to the aluminium smelter at a price cheaper than to them.

# MECHANISATION.

While Robens personally did not sell a ton of coal, his influence revolutionised the industry's approach to marketing. Similarly, he would revolutionise its approach to mechanisation.

In 1960, the labour content in the cost of producing a ton of coal was over 60 per cent. With annual wage increases a regular feature, productivity had to improve. Otherwise coal was going to price itself out of most markets. Mechanisation was already under way. Now Robens would turn it into a crusade.

## Off with the Old, On with the New.

In 1960, only 38 per cent of output was power-loaded. That is, coal both cut and loaded onto the conveyor system by means of a machine. In the East Midlands the figure was 62 per cent and in South Wales a mere 24 per cent. The national figure was already on the increase (up from 9 per cent in the early 1950's). This mechanisation drive would now go into high gear, resulting in 92.2 per cent power loading within the next decade. The basic machines were already available, having been conceived in the 1950's. What was not available at that time was a determination to depart from the known traditional methods and face the inevitable new problems which change would bring. After all, labour was not too difficult to come by, price pressures had not arisen and there was no central direction of planning. There was still an ongoing demand for big lumps for the domestic market and machine mining significantly increased the percentage of small coal. In addition, machine mining meant teamwork. This discounted the craft tradition of the collier and reduced the control he personally had over his immediate place of work. Traditionally, the collier had regarded his "stint" almost as his own allotment, where even the manager's writ did not run.

The new mines sunk after nationalisation were all conceived as having large numbers of hand-worked faces. Traditional coalfaces were supported with wooden props, in combination with wooden roof beams. The positioning of such supports, and working of the timber with his axe, was part of the collier's art. A belt conveyor was laid along the face while a team of colliers, working with pick and shovel, won the coal in their own individual "stints" and shovelled it onto the conveyor. Stint dimensions depended on seam height and conditions but a typical length would be 6 m, with an advance per shift of 1.2 m. Production was on one shift per day. On the "back shift" a turnover gang would come onto the coalface and advance the conveyor into the new space just cleared by the colliers. On the following day, the whole cycle would recommence. With the introduction of machines for undercutting the seam, coal-getting advanced from the sole use of pick and shovel. Assisted with explosives or pneumatic picks, this method allowed the coal to collapse and break up, thus making it easier for the collier to load it onto the conveyor.

In the 1950's a movement began in earnest to replace wooden props and beams with hydraulic props, in combination with steel roof bars. Such bars were cantilevered out over the conveyor, thus removing the necessity for a line of supports directly against the coal. This line of props between the conveyor and the coal had traditionally prevented it being pushed over as a unit. It had always been necessary to dedicate one shift in each production day to dismantling the conveyor then moving the sections over between the new lines of supports previously erected by the colliers. Finally, the conveyor would be reassembled in its new position. Removal of the line of supports directly adjacent to the coal enabled the so-called "prop-free-front". This had been a significant obstruction with regard to moving on of the conveyor as a single unit. With the elimination of this obstruction the way was opened for multi-shift working and full mechanisation.

Full mechanisation entailed the use of power-loading machines, in combination with an Armoured Flexible Conveyor (AFC) along the length of the face. Such power-loading machines are mounted on the AFC and travel along it, ripping off the coal while simultaneously loading it onto the conveyor. A variety of machine types exist - ploughs, hauled back and fro along the face side of the conveyor; trepanners, with a rotating head that cores out the coal or, by far the most popular, the ranging drum shearer. This machine travels along the top of the AFC and is equipped with one or two rotating spiral steel cutting drums. To these drums are attached small tungsten carbide tipped picks. The drums can be raised or lowered hydraulically, according to the cutting horizon.

From the 1960's on, the hydraulic prop system, where each support required manual pumping, was gradually replaced by self-advancing, multi-legged supports, all pressurised by a common hydraulic system that served the whole coalface. These "walking chocks" were so-called due to their self-advancing characteristic, as opposed to having to be individually manhandled over. Each such support is attached to the AFC by means of a hydraulic ram. Operation of a lever at each support extends this ram, thus allowing that section of conveyor to be pushed forward after the power-loading machine has made a cut. When each support has pushed forward its own section of conveyor, it is then lowered in its turn from the roof, by the operation of a second lever. The hydraulic ram is then retracted, thus pulling the support forward into its new position. Finally the support is re-extended to the roof.

The effect of this sequence is to snake first the conveyor and then the roof supports over, following passage of the power-loading machine. The space just cut by the machine is thus reoccupied by the AFC. The system works on the basis that only one support is disengaged from the roof at any one time. As the face advances, the roof behind is left to collapse into the waste. An additional advantage of the system is enhanced protection of the miner against falls of roof. Instead of roof bars, each chock is equipped with a steel canopy. This results in complete roof cover along the coalface length.

Subsequently, the whole cycle of cutting/loading - pushing over of the conveyor - advancing of the supports, is repeated. Nowadays, a performance of two or three strips in a shift, with typically 5 hours Machine Available Time (MAT), is normal.

## Preaching the Gospel.

For the coalface worker this was a new world. No longer would the creaks and groans of the timber speak to them constantly, giving them a continuous feel for the mine and its movement. As a first priority, however, management itself had to be convinced that mechanisation was the true path towards righteousness.

The Coal Board had a cadre of extremely competent staff, who knew thoroughly how to manage miners and how the work was done, although not necessarily how it could be done better. Colliery managers are men's men. No one may manage a pit unless, in addition to his technical education, he has acquired special qualifications. These include statutory obligations with regard to safety, plus a specified time in the pits with actual coalface experience. All managers during their qualifying training must have worked with men during the process of coal-getting.

Within nine months, either Robens personally or W.V.Sheppard, Director-General of Production, had addressed every one of the 682 managers, group managers and deputy managers concerning the new mechanisation policy. One-week courses were held at the NCB staff college at Chalfont St. Giles in Buckinghamshire. In addition, ongoing courses were held throughout the coalfields to bring home the technical details to men, many of who were more used to solving their problems with the application of brute force rather than scientific finesse. After one such presentation, on the relative virtues of closed versus open-loop control, and time-division versus frequency division multiplexing, one stunned wag was heard to declare, "I understood every word. It was just when they were all put together that I was f— lost".

## The Great Leap Forward.

In the push for mechanisation, the coalface itself was concentrated upon. This is the sharp end of production, as well as being the dustiest and most dangerous point. The Mining Research Establishment was making progress on the use of hydraulics, electronics and remote control in a mining environment, but in Robens' view too slowly. Following a meeting in his office with his leading technical men, Robens, with the vision of an outsider, made the decision to go for nothing less than a manless coalface, operated totally by remote control. Originally suggested as the Automated Longwall Face (ALF) this was vetoed by Alfred Robens as having too much of the cult of personality about it. What eventually emerged was the Remotely Operated Longwall Face (ROLF).

148

In 1963, by the summer, two such faces had been installed, at Ormonde and Newstead Collieries in the East Midlands. Cutting/loading of the coal, as well as advancing of the roof supports and face conveyor, was controlled from a console in the main gate road, some 60 metres back from the coalface. Later, each Division got its own ROLF. That for South Wales was installed at the end of the decade in Marine Colliery, in the east of the coalfield. It must be said that South Wales Area Management could not be accused of showing an excess of zeal or interest with regard to this new concept. The equipment lay around on the surface for an embarrassingly long time, with pointed questions on the subject being diverted with a blandness worthy of any politician.

The full ROLF system as originally conceived never did work properly. Catering for the number of variables present in the mining environment proved to be difficult. In addition, the systems were expensive to procure, operate and maintain. A major problem was automatic control of the cutting horizon within the seam. In practice there was an ongoing tendency for the cutting drum to drift up into the roof or down into the floor. A man had to accompany the machine along the face so as to intervene and avoid this problem, the solution of which proved to be immensely difficult. Many attempts were made at a solution, including a device that scattered gamma rays, but all to no avail. The full-blown automated version proved to be uncompetitive and manpower is still essential on today's longwall faces. However, the spin-off from this great leap forward was immense, for it brought in its wake considerable modifications and refinements to the techniques of coalface mechanisation and control.

More immediately successful was the automation of coal transportation and preparation, plus pumping and data acquisition.

In 1965, not content with initiating automation of the coalface, Robens' imagination let loose upon the world the first completely automated colliery. This was the new mine of Bevercoates in Nottinghamshire. As with ROLF it was a case of three steps forward and two steps back. As a politician, and with his flair for public relations, Robens knew the importance of images, and also knew how to grab the headlines. Not only "high speed gas" and the technological magic of nuclear power; coal too could contribute to the "white hot heat of the technological revolution". Journalists came from far and wide to see this new phenomenon, white-coated miners operating a fully automated pit.

A complete ROLF installation was prepared on the surface for display. Using coal imported from elsewhere, an automated coal preparation plant loaded into the creeping snakes of "merry-go-round" trains. Visitors could also view the mine control room. Here, from the surface, the complete ventilation system, underground conveyors and bunkers, coal preparation plant, plus manpower status were monitored and/or controlled. One surface craftsman, preparing to carry out routine maintenance work while dressed in standard blue overalls was told to clear off, "We're expecting visitors. You can't do any work here and besides, you're not wearing a white coat". Needless to say, the white coats did not survive the first day of genuine production. It was all rather exaggerated and done with an eye to public relations.

There were to be no more "great leaps forward". Nevertheless, the technical basis for the future had now been laid, and would serve until into the twenty-first century. At the coalface, hydraulics and electronics became watchwords. What would happen was that the concepts introduced and proven at this time were to be subject to an incremental but continuing development. Capacity, power levels, reliability, adaptability and operating convenience would be continually increased. In addition, there would be variations on the basic theme, such as speed control for conveyors, automatic actuation of the powered roof supports as soon as the power loader had passed and close range radio control of the power loader. This latter allowed the operator to position himself in the most judicious position, which was not necessarily directly adjacent to the machine itself. Overall control and monitoring of the mine would be refined into MINOS, the Mine Operating System.

### Family Squabbles.

These developments emphasised the importance of the mechanical and electrical engineering staffs, at all levels. These were not only responsible for a wide and complicated spectrum of their respective engineering disciplines but were charged with the duty of maintaining safe and continuous operation under harsh and potentially hazardous conditions. In addition they had to work underground, independently and sometimes alone. Between them and the mining engineers relations could on occasions be abrasive. For the latter, the NCB was virtually a monopoly employer whereas the former were in high demand throughout industry generally, the solid nature of their background being well recognised.

The Mines and Quarries Act of Parliament required a suitably qualified Mechanic-of-the-Mine, plus an Electrician-of-the-Mine, to be the engineers in charge. However, it also laid down that Colliery Managers and Undermanagers must be mining engineers. This left a feeling among technical staff that, rightly or wrongly, they were always in the position of being responsible to someone not appreciative, either of their worth or of their problems.

## More from Less.

A necessary concomitant to mechanisation and the big capital investments involved, was a concentration upon fewer but higher production coalfaces. Only by this means could an adequate return on investment be obtained. For each such installation a high level of production had to be achieved, and maintained. Gone were the days when, in event of problems occurring on a face, the Undermanager could significantly reduce his loss by simply re-allocating colliers to clean up spillage alongside the roadway conveyors. With outputs in excess of 1,000 t per day, many faces began producing as much as a reasonable size colliery only a short time previously. A large modern colliery, sunk after nationalisation, might have been planned to operate with eighteen or so hand-got faces. During the 1960's period it would have been operating with perhaps four or five mechanised ones. Later this would be reduced even further, to two, or even one. The coalface itself became a significant business undertaking in its own right. This revolutionised face management, with one-day conferences being held for the production team and the involvement of each man personally. Also included in the new system thinking was underground transport, and indeed the whole organization of the pit up to and including the coal washing and preparation plants.

Elsewhere underground, locomotive haulage and the growing use of trunk conveyor belts, plus the introduction of Freely Steerable Vehicles (FSV's) for the transport of supplies, made pit ponies redundant. In 1960 there were still 7,750 ponies working in the pits. By 1971 this number had dwindled to 620. By the mid-70's they were all gone. Thus ended the long and intimate relationship between the miner and his animal "butty". Garages, haulage engine houses and substations replaced the whitewashed stables underground, with their smell of hay and manure, and their sounds of chomping, snorting, and horseshoes scraping on a concrete floor. Instead of annual leave in some surface farmstead, plus vetinary service and working conditions checked by Her Majesty's Horse Inspector of Mines, care and attention took the form of the Planned Maintenance Scheme for the Mine, with its lubrication schedules, functional checks, insulation resistance measurements and parts replacement.

Along with the relationship between man and horse disappeared a wealth of yarns:

- Of the pony who, on delivering a load of materials near the coalface would then jump onto a moving conveyor belt to ride back out (untrue story);

- Of the horse that bolted while pulling in a new length of cable and, unimpressed by the shouting, arm-waving crowd running along behind, was only stopped when the cable pulled out a roof support, strategically sited at a bend in the roadway. With the cable now buried under a pile of rocks, further progress by the racing steed was only halted by the cable's elasticity (true story);

- Of the group of miners struggling to manhandle some item of equipment while a horse stood dolefully looking on in the background, quietly laughing to itself (apocryphal).

While high cost capacity was being run down, simultaneously those pits that survived were being transformed into the most mechanised in Europe. This contrast was epitomised by the Durham Coalfield in North East England. As the deep mines to the South West of this coalfield were closed down, those on the east coast were expanded, with new districts and faces being developed out under the North Sea. With typical Robens flair, local newspapers showed a photograph of him pointing out to sea where the future lay, as if indicating the New World. The caption encouraged the miners to drive eastward, "all the way to Norway".

During his ten-year tenure, Robens' team succeeded in wedding a reduction in total output to a steady increase in productivity. A deep-mined output of 184 Mt at a productivity of 305 tons per man-year had been converted into 133 Mt at 465 tons per man-year, an increase in productivity of nearly 52 per cent. From 24.9 cwt (1.26t) in 1957, national output per manshift (OMS) increased to 44.1cwt (2.24t) in 1971.

## ORGANISATION.

Apart from mechanisation, other more mundane production problems were to be grasped, quantified, and subjected to on-going study and improvement.

In 1964, method study had shown that coalface machinery was standing idle for much longer than it was actually running. On average there were only 2.5 hours of coal-getting on each shift, of the six or so hours that the men actually spent on the face. Even after making all allowances, there was still too much time being lost for no good reason.

### No More Piecework!

The technical revolution in the industry was also resulting in great changes occurring in the skill, responsibility and labour content of different jobs. Another target set by Robens was the elimination of piece-rates and their replacement with a standard wage. A system based on standard wages would enable wage costs (which were more than half of total costs) to be predicted more accurately. It would also facilitate job mobility, both within a pit and between pits and coalfields. There were other reasons too. Robens himself had a visceral dislike of the carrot and stick system, regarding it as degrading. His early life in the depression and his work as a full-time trade union official meant coming into contact with the losers under the system and not only the winners. As a result, the concept of piece-work was not something he could easily live with.

The NUM itself had long attacked piece-working as a factor that contributed to accidents. Miners were being pushed to produce as much coal as possible, to the neglect of safety. Management, by contrast, although in the process of changing, with younger men moving away from the old authoritarian ways into a more sympathetic and consultative style, still had doubts about taking away an incentive for men to give of their best. In the United States day wage conditions prevailed but, so the argument went, there was also motivation, namely the fear of being fired if one did not perform.

In March 1966, the NUM's National Executive accepted parity between the better-paid and less well-paid coalfields under the National Power Loading Agreement. Such parity was to be achieved within five years. This meant that, so as to enable less fortunate colleagues in unprofitable coalfields to catch up, it was necessary for the best-paid men to mark time with regard to pay increases. In some cases, even cuts in wages were accepted. The persuasive powers of the NUM and in particular of Will Paynter, their General Secretary, were taxed to the limit, but they achieved their goal. There was an immediate, and significant, reduction in the number of unofficial strikes, the main cause of which had been piece-work rates. The permanent abrasion at collieries, concerning allowances for this that and the other, about the rate to be paid for a new job, whether a man had been prevented from achieving a reasonable wage through circumstances beyond his control - all these arguments were confined to the past. Most of the spats that traditionally sapped the energy and swallowed up the time of management, union officials and men were swept away at a stroke. In the first year of the new arrangements, tonnage lost through disputes fell by 70 per cent. There was a further reduction during the following year.

### Changing the Harness to Fit the Horse.

From the beginning, Robens had regarded the five-tier management structure of the NCB as being a weak point. In his view, top management, as well as technical specialists, were too remote from what was actually going on in the coalfields. The Directors-General at Board level were responsible for the day-to-day management and administration of the departments that they headed, but had no authority to instruct the lower echelons. Their remit was only to "guide and advise". The Divisional Boards had a degree of authority but real power lay in the hands of the Area General Managers. However, the two levels of management above them, plus the two levels of management below them, diluted even their authority.

In 1965, in the autumn, the main principles of the new NCB organization were decided. Robens' strategy was to reinforce the Area General Managers (to be renamed Area Directors). Not only would the Areas themselves become much larger geographically, henceforward they would report directly to the National Board. In turn, individual collieries would report directly to them. Natural wastage, and early retirement of staff, would be big factors in the reduction of administrative personnel prior to the shake-up. Special permission had to be obtained to recruit from outside. A series of conferences and interviews were held to inform and to discuss with staff their place in the scheme of things. Transfers from the previous Group and Divisional levels, now to be eliminated, would reinforce area and colliery staffs.

In April 1967, in an exercise that Robens referred to as, "Changing the harness to fit the horse", the new organization was introduced. Staff numbers were thereby reduced nationally by 7,700, one sixth of the total. The five-tier structure, Colliery-Group-Area-Division-National Board thus became a three-tier structure, Colliery-Area-National Board. The number of Areas was reduced to seventeen, each with between 15-20 collieries. South Wales was reduced from the seven areas at nationalisation to two (later to be reduced to one). These were the West Wales Area, with headquarters at Tondu, and the East Wales Area, with headquarters at Ystrad Mynach. Among other things, the new organization brought investment decisions closer to the pits, with the result that they tended to be more relevant to the facts on the ground.

With the new organization came the concept of management by objectives. After prior discussion with the Area Directors, each Area was to be set objectives, in terms of output, sales and profitability. After consultation with colliery management, the Area Director, with the advice of his Business Planning Team, would in turn set objectives for the individual collieries. To achieve the objectives so conceived, both Area and colliery action plans were developed. These covered a period of eighteen months ahead and were updated on a quarterly basis. The initial tendency was for excessive optimism. It took two or three years before reasonably accurate estimates of the results to be expected were being turned in.

At national headquarters, what Robens described as a "plethora of committees" was abolished. There was some political infighting but by the time he left the Board had but two. These were the Board itself, which met monthly, and the General Purposes Committee. This met every week. At these meetings, Directors-General of departments, responsible for the implementation of Board policy, attended as advisors. Small working parties were set up for special projects, to be disbanded upon completion of their task. This brought the whole of the Board into close contact with every major decision and avoided the previous tendency to create "states within a state".

## Diversification.

Another weak point was that the Divisions were managing coke ovens and chemical plants. Since the Divisional Boards were pre-occupied with the problems of getting coal, ancillary activities were not getting the specialist management attention they required.

In January 1963, the Coal Products Division was created to manage the coke ovens, chemical and smokeless fuel plants, plus the North Sea gas activities of the NCB. Such NCB operations would be used as a basis for diversification into related commercial activities. They were to bring in £13 M of annual profit. Without this, coal prices would have had to be correspondingly increased. Such diversification included the following:

- Experience in drilling for coal off the Durham coast had provided the NCB with a technological base for joint operations with Gulf and Continental Oil in the North Sea. Their Viking field would supply about 15 per cent of the total UK gas market. In the Board's opinion, involvement by the nationalised industries in this valuable new resource would contribute to obtaining maximum benefit for the British economy.

- Benzole is produced as a by-product of coking plants. Additional refining of this chemical was undertaken by the NCB, in partnership with Dutch State Mines and a steel company.

- J.H.Sankey and Son Ltd., an old established builders' merchant, had been acquired by the NCB with 77 per cent of the equity. This provided them with a nation-wide chain of solid fuel appliance show rooms. Here the customer could obtain a full service under one roof, covering purchase, installation and easy terms.

- The NCB operated seven computer centres, involved in their huge and complicated pay-roll work as well as procurement etc. There was one in each of the major coalfields. Spare capacity was rented out to other commercial and industrial users.

## Communication.

Public Relations had previously been a responsibility of the Board Secretary. During reorganisation, in an act typical of Robens' style, it was made into a Department in its own right with its head directly responsible to him. He was thus able personally to look after what he regarded as one of the most important aspects of his job as Chairman.

Early in his Chairmanship the NCB publication Coal Magazine was replaced by Coal News. Whereas the former, as its name suggests, was a handsome magazine, the latter was a tabloid-size newspaper, published in local editions. In effect, Tatler was replaced by The Sun. A mixture of hard facts, breathless optimism (usually misplaced), feminine beauty and such things as a mineworkers' marrow-growing contest, Coal News proved to be highly successful in circulation terms, being read by the vast majority of the labour force. It was heavily criticised by certain sections of the NUM, ostensibly on the grounds of its superficiality. In one incident the lodge at Tower Colliery would join the historically dubious band of literature burners by organising a public incineration of the latest issue (It must be said that when, years later, a regular magazine was brought out by the workers-owned Tower Colliery it proved to be highly informative and of a much higher standard than Coal News).

Robens remained unfazed by such attack. He countered by saying that what really raised the spleen of the NUM leaders, or some of them at least, was that the Board now had a better means of communicating with their members than they had themselves. Such communication included the union's own views and activities. For complicated new wage agreements, Coal News would often include a pullout guide. If union leaders regarded this as going over their heads then it was up to them to improve their own methods of communication. Robens' standpoint was, "They may be union members but they are our employees. We have every right to communicate with them. And we have every intention of going on communicating with them".

# POLITICS.

## Office Politics.

In 1966, the then Minister of Power, Richard Marsh, appointed the strong-willed Cecil King, Chairman of the International Publishing Corporation, as a part-time member of the NCB. Marsh would be quoted as saying that the motive was to act as a brake "on the enthusiastic bulldozing of the Chairman of the Coal Board". To Marsh's chagrin, King went native, not only becoming an ally of Robens but publicly attacking Harold Wilson's leadership of the government and his handling of the economy. There were hints of a King-inspired plot for a coup d'etat against Wilson. Robens was known to share King's contempt for government ministers and his belief that a more business-oriented approach should be adopted to the running of the country - Great Britain Ltd.

By 1967, relations between Robens and the government were at their lowest ebb, as a result of the energy White Paper of that year. Ministers were muttering about Roben's "megalomania" and were smarting at some of his tactics, such as the briefing of Labour MP's at Coal Board headquarters. There was a belief that he would think nothing of selling his minister down the river. Why then did the government keep him on, particularly after his offer to resign following Aberfan?

The fact of the matter was that his spirited defense of the coal industry had resulted in him being a popular figure with the NUM. It was then an axiom of British politics never to take on the miners, the Church of England, or the Brigade of Guards. Only Robens, ministers felt, could shield them from the wrath of the NUM. A Robens outside the NCB, trashing the White Paper while expressing his bitterness towards the government in general and Harold Wilson in particular would surely have had the full support of the Daily Mirror, owned by his friend Cecil King. In addition, there was the lack of any suitable successor.

In September 1967, a draft note by the Minister of Power, Richard Marsh, stated, "His successor might therefore encounter some hostility. With the many serious difficulties that lie ahead of the coal industry, hostility between the chairman and unions would be a severe handicap". But times were to change!

### End of an Era.

In 1968, Will Paynter, General Secretary of the NUM, retired. He was replaced by the militant Lawrence Daly, thus ushering in a new age of confrontation and undermining one of the pillars of Robens' strength, namely the good working relationship which had existed between himself and the union.

In 1969, to Robens' displeasure, Cecil King's three-year term of appointment as member of the National Coal Board was not renewed. The days of Robens himself were soon to be numbered.

## DEPARTURE.

### Clipped Wings.

In 1970, Labour lost the election and the Conservatives were re-elected. A new Department of Trade and Industry (DTI) was inaugurated, which swallowed up the old Ministry of Power. A Coal Industry Bill followed that limited the Coal Board's activities, indeed reducing them below the statutory authority of the original 1946 Act. This new Bill enabled the Minister to issue a direction on all matters other than the mining of coal and its preparation for the market. It was made clear that government policy was going to be disengagement from industry, plus the "hiving off" of parts of the nationalised industries to the private sector. As the party of free enterprise, the Conservatives were generous in the lip service given to entrepreneurship. Such entrepreneurship did not however extend to nationalised industries. In particular, a recalcitrant baron such as Robens did not fit into their concept of the realm. There had been unease in Conservative circles concerning Coal Board activities. Their MP, Christopher Tugendhat, had expressed this in his previous capacity as journalist (Financial Times, 7 July 1969);

"Faced with a similar situation, most private enterprise companies would follow the same kind of policies as those of the NCB. But there is one big difference between public and private sector organization causing great and growing concern. In the private sector, companies can only diversify if their ideas are financially sound, whereas nationalised industries can often get hold of tax-payers money on easier terms".

### Pig in the Middle.

There was another thing, which would lead to bad odour between Robens and the new Conservative government. This new government, under Prime Minister Edward Heath, was determined to fight the country's economic problems, in particular inflation, by a strict prices and incomes policy. This would clash head on with the militancy now emerging from the, also new, NUM leadership. Robens found himself as "pig-in-the-middle".

On 27 October 1970, a memo to the Prime Minister informed him that Lord Robens regarded an overall wage increase of 12 per cent as being acceptable to the NUM. This was 2 per cent more than Robens had been authorised to make but, in Robens' judgement, this offer was essential to avoid damaging the NCB and its investments. He presented the government with two alternatives:

    i) He would inform the NUM that government intervention had prevented him from making the offer.

    ii) He would make the offer, and then see it rejected by the government.

The Department of Trade and Industry were informed that no legal powers existed which could prevent Robens from making the offer. Robens was told that he should take the second option, while ministers met to decide on the form of a public statement. On the above memo Heath scrawled the comment, "This is bad. L.Robens has let us down and gone back on his word".

There were those in government who viewed with unease the chairman of a nationalised industry taking the initiative in fighting his corner. The chairmen were there to push through government policy, and this policy at the time was not enamoured with public ownership.

In 1971, at the end of his second term as chairman, Robens was 60 years of age and quite prepared to finish his working life with a third term. Although a Labour man all his life, it was a Conservative government that had brought him to the NCB. Now, another Conservative government would lead to his retirement. At the Coal Board, Robens' entrepreneurial spirit had flourished, but now the brakes were to be put on.

The new Coal Industry Bill clipped Robens' wings and made it impossible for him to continue in position. In his own words, "In the world of builders there are two most important people. There is the architect whose task is to produce the plan to enable building to take place. Equally important is the demolition expert, whose job is to pull down and clear the site to enable building to begin. Both important, both essential, but I am by nature an architect not a demolition expert".


## Postscript.

The Robens' magic, with politicians and with the unions, had run its course but he was far from being a busted flush. He continued with his 21 year service as a Director of the Bank of England. He was also a well-known figure in both business and trade union circles. On his retirement from the NCB, the government appointed him to chair the new committee investigating industrial health and safety. The Aberfan experience notwithstanding, under his stewardship the NCB accident rate had declined by 22.4 per cent.

The committee reported in 1972 and its deliberations would result in the 1974 Act of Parliament, "Health and Safety at Work". It changed the basic philosophy from regulation by the state to "self ownership of safety". As opposed to a heap of regulations, perhaps no longer relevant and designed to eliminate risks obvious to those who drafted the law (often in response to a disaster), far better, thought the Robens committee, was a system whereby those who worked in an industry should co-operate in defining the main risks and how to minimise them. After all, the wealth of regulations incorporated in the Mines and Quarries Act had not prevented the Aberfan disaster, whereas intelligent forethought might have.

Robens would continue his career as industrialist, being lured in the early 1970's to become Chairman of the Vickers engineering group. Based in Tyneside, and with 35,722 employees, Vickers was one of the country's major companies. His salary at £30,000 per annum was regarded as modest, compared for example with F. D. Nicholson, the highest paid Tyneside industrialist. The latter gentleman, as Chairman of Vaux and Allied Breweries with 3,972 employees, clocked in with £52,121 per annum, in addition to his personal share dividend of £47,250.

In 1993, Robens's health broke when he suffered a stroke that confined him to a wheel chair, extremely frustrating for such an active man.

On 26 June 1999 he passed away.

Robens had held the line, as far as the NCB was concerned. In addition to furthering technical progress, financial losses and industrial disputes had been minimised. When he finally retired as Chairman of the National Coal Board, Matthew Coady wrote a profile in the Daily Mirror, "Miners' leaders, whatever their criticisms of Robens, would agree on the value of his work. Any other single individual, given the job of running down the industry, would have been faced with violent upheaval. Under his leadership this has not happened. The fight on this perhaps has been totally ruthless. His knowledge of Whitehall has taught him every trick in a sophisticated book. Civil servants have been harried, ministers lectured and press leaks deftly engineered to serve coal's cause". After his departure he deliberately kept a low profile on coal and energy matters. By 1974 however, with oil price rises starting to bite, he was publicly attacking government energy policies.

Robens' ethos would remain for some time. Deputy Chairman Derek Ezra, previously responsible for marketing, replaced him. With a reputation for being a cold fish, but totally sincere, he later became a Liberal peer. Ezra had already spent 24 years in the industry and would spend a further 11 as Chairman. He had joined marketing department in 1947 on leaving the army. Since there was at that time very little marketing to be done, he spent much of his early years with the industry on the British delegation to the European Coal and Steel Community. In this capacity, between 1952-66, he had spent 4 years in Luxemburg.

Norman Siddall in turn would replace Ezra. He too had worked under Robens, in the capacity of Chief Mining Engineer. He was known to have an enormous commitment to the industry. Both of these successors were successful in their own way, although later they would be confronted with the contempt in which Prime Minister Margaret Thatcher held the management of "this over-unionised industry". In retrospect, as a result of the "slings and arrows of outrageous fortune" that followed him, Lord Robens would have been justified if, on his departure, he had quietly whispered to himself, "Après moi le déluge"!

Plate 10  Caliper Brakes for Abernant Winder at Tredomen Central Workshops.
Such NCB Workshops were Engineering Factories in their own right.

# Chapter 11
## MILITANCY - AND TRIUMPH.

*"If we had insisted that Mr. Ezra, Coal Board Chairman,
stand in the middle of Piccadilly Circus with his trousers
down he would have done it".*
Member, NUM Executive.

### ROBENS' LEGACY.

### Consensus Rules-.

In 1960, after the appointment of Alf Robens, there were 698 pits nationally. At the end of his "ten year stint" there were 292. In the same period, from 583,000 people on colliery books the number had declined to 283,000. This was achieved with an absence of any concomitant industrial dispute. Alternative work was available in the economy. For those who wished to stay in the industry there were the flourishing central coalfields. These, Yorkshire, Nottinghamshire and the Midlands, saw an influx of displaced Scots, Welshmen, Lancastrians and North-Easterners as the industry elsewhere contracted. At the end of Robens' tenure, coal still provided 47 per cent of the nation's energy, while coal stocks had been reduced from 35 to 7 Mt (mostly suitable only for power stations). Against the pressures with which he was confronted, this was no mean achievement. Robens was to write (Ten Year Stint);

"Without the understanding and co-operation of unions and of the men themselves, this task could never have been accomplished. I shudder to think what the consequences would have been for the nation and the industry if it had been otherwise. A coal industry locked in industrial struggle would have brought the nation to its knees".

It could well have been different, for in the 1960s and 1970s both Tory and Socialist governments found themselves engaged in a battle of wills with organised labour. The tradition of mutual support between trade union movement and Labour Party became rather more ambivalent, when the latter achieved power and was confronted with economic reality. An inexorable rise in trade union power was a feature of post-war British history. Underpinned by a determination never to return to the injustices of the past, unions were to act on the lesson learnt in the "bad old days", that faced with rapacious management and a capitalist system, nothing could be expected that did not have to be fought for. Against this industrial relations background and the radical change outlined in previous chapters, the honeymoon period with the NUM lasted a surprisingly long time, particularly bearing in mind the militant antecedents of both Arthur Horner, the first General Secretary of the NUM, and his successor Will Paynter. Both of these were committed Welsh communists who spent their formative period in the dark depression years of the Rhondda Valley. This notwithstanding, the NUM had held back from ruthlessly exploiting their position when coal had been desperately scarce, especially during the immediate post-war Labour government. Arthur Horner used to say in those days that if the union had asked for the moon, the government would have to get it for them. However, both Horner and his successor Paynter wanted to make a success of nationalisation. They were prepared to loyally serve a succession of rightwing presidents and national executives and basically accepted the logic behind a smooth contraction of the industry.

### -Or Maybe Not!

The overall success of his chairmanship notwithstanding, the position was not quite as sanguine as Robens had written. Such an enormous contraction had indeed created stresses and strains. During the last two years of his tenure, fault lines were already opening up. His vision of an apocalypse, under his stewardship mercifully averted, would indeed come to pass. Gradually and pervasively, the feeling was spreading throughout the workforce that their almost total cooperation in the mechanisation, contraction, and rationalisation of their industry had not brought any commensurate reward in terms of pay and conditions.

Robens was proud of the fact that, under his tenure, NCB finances had been kept under control. For most years there had even been a small surplus. The Board was locked in a competitive struggle with cheap oil and committed by statute to at least break even. In addition, there was a policy of subsidising the loss-making coalfields so as to minimise social disruption. With wages forming over 60 per cent of NCB costs at that time, it was difficult to fit large pay increases into the equation. To make matters worse, highly publicised strikes by workers in other industries, for example dustmen in 1969, were paying off for the strikers, whether the settlements were inflationary or not. This was causing great bitterness among the miners. Inexorably, their relative position in the national pay scale was slipping backwards. A wage agreement for bus crews in Yorkshire gave women conductresses a minimum wage of £18 per week, considerably more than the NCB minimum for an adult male surface worker. Such publicity was eating away at consensus within the industry.

## THE WORM TURNS.

### Grass Roots Disquiet.

Throughout the late 1960's and early 1970's, such dissatisfaction was to find more and more adherents. The concept was challenged that low salary increases had to be accepted as the price for having a job at all in an industry which was dying, and which otherwise would only die faster. Men who had uprooted their families several times already, and were now reluctant to face further disruption, were especially open to this new spirit of resistance. If mining is a dying industry anyway, so went the new logic, starvation wages are not going to save it. If on the other hand society wants coal then society had better come to terms with the fact that, in this day and age, appropriate wages will have to be paid. This became a general feeling among the men, and many new groups sprang up to harry the official union leadership. This was increasingly seen as being passive and supine. One of the most active of these groups was in Yorkshire, the Barnsley Miners Forum. The initiator was one Arthur Scargill, face worker at Wooley Colliery and, in 1967, a twenty-nine year old NUM compensation secretary at the pit. Scargill and his fellow elected delegates would, more and more vociferously, express the growing dissatisfaction.

Delegates were invariably the most committed and left wing elements. Being regular members of the workforce and part-time union officials only, they were more in tune with popular sentiment than was the National Executive, whose members were highly paid and full-time. Members of the National Executive received benefits comparable with those of senior management. Each member received a free house that he could occupy until his death or the death of his wife (whoever died last). He had the opportunity to buy this house from the union at an artificially low price. His heating, lighting, telephone and rates were paid for by the union. He was given a car and benefited from a system of allowances that, for example, permitted him to claim three nights subsistence for a meeting that only lasted a day.

### Hand in Hand Corporatism.

The veteran General Secretary of the NUM was Will Paynter. Like Arthur Horner, his predecessor as General Secretary, Will Paynter was a communist and a product of the Rhondda Valley. A fiery and effective orator, he had been involved on the Republican side in the Spanish Civil War. His expressed aims were the changing and improvement of society as a whole. A traditional militant, he was nevertheless concerned that all action be kept within a constitutional framework so as to achieve maximum unity. He had been instrumental in the progress made towards eliminating piece-work in the mining industry and also in persuading miners in the more profitable coalfields they should forgo potential wage increases, so as to enable colleagues in other coalfields to catch up.

Between 1951 and 1959, Paynter had been President of the South Wales NUM. Shortly after becoming South Wales President he had countered, with a speech described as electrifying, an unofficial movement that had met in a Neath pub called "The Shakespeare". He wanted to know who was running the union. Was it the executive or was it the boys from "The Shakespeare"? A specially convened conference, at which this speech was made, "outlawed" the unofficial bodies.

In the spring of 1967, he addressed the problem of bad attendance at work in the South Wales coalfield by speaking to an audience of Monmouthshire miners. He told them that the record of absenteeism at many South Wales pits was nothing other than, "irresponsible, anti-social behaviour". He pointed out that the average rate in South Wales was higher than that for Great Britain and that this represented a corresponding loss of income to the coalfield. He asked;

"How many more pits will face precipitate closure because the will to save them is undermined by this couldn't-care-less attitude?" He followed up with, "If this attitude to work is not changed, what really is likely to be the response of manufacturers to government invitations to site industry here?"

In believing that an efficiently run nationalised industry was a pillar of society Paynter was of one mind with Lord Robens, who was to write;

"I believed too that it was not possible for a workman to behave as just an organised worker, concerned with just his own selfish wants as a worker, but that he must recognise that he was also a consumer and above all a member of the whole community". Both men thought that employees, and the community as a whole, would benefit only if the industry that employs them is efficient and prosperous. The fact was that industries were nationalised for the benefit of the community, not just for the people who worked in them, however urgently their conditions needed improving. All the benefits could not go to the worker. That was syndicalism, and neither the NCB nor the miners' leadership at national level were syndicalist, although at area and pit level many NUM officials certainly were.

## From Consensus to Confrontation.

In 1968, Will Paynter retired. Thus ended the almost team-like co-operation that had marked the relationship between him and Lord Robens. That co-operation had been a formal one, with an appreciation on both sides of the dangers associated with too close a relationship with the other camp. Nevertheless, both were old time socialists of the pre-war school, albeit one left and the other right of centre. Paynter's retirement now marked the beginning of the union's transformation, from a moderate and compliant partner in the strategy of the National Coal Board to the spearhead of leftwing opposition.

Elected as Paynter's successor was a Scottish former communist, Lawrence Daly. Daly had quit the party in 1956 over the Soviet invasion of Hungary, but had lost none of his radicalism. With 52.3 per cent of the national vote he comfortably beat his only opponent, the pragmatic and cautious Joe Gormley from the Midlands. Gormley was far from being a write-off; he later become National President and would strongly influence NUM policy throughout the 1970's. Nevertheless, Gormley would find himself more and more on the defensive and there was no doubt that with Daly the militants had made an important advance.

Indicative of the new ethos was a blistering pamphlet called "The Miners and the Nation". This Daly had written as part of his election campaign and it had struck a chord among the rank-and-file.. Whereas all previous NUM stoppages had been limited to, and were the result of, purely local disputes, this advocated industrial action on a national scale, to "secure a change in fuel policy", to "protect our mining communities from the worst effects of redundancy", and to "win conditions and rewards that would hold young, skilful and intelligent men in our modern coal industry".

## First Blood.

In 1969, one year later, the new spirit began to make itself felt. Eight pits in South Wales, plus all of those in Yorkshire, went on unofficial strike over the issue of surface workers hours. The mainspring for this action was in Yorkshire, which was now rivalling South Wales as the most militant coalfield. Lord Robens attributed this to the Welsh and Scottish miners that had been transferred there. Surface workers' wages had been on the union's agenda for years but nothing ever seemed to happen. Contrary to what is usually the case, miners earn their best wages when they are young and fit and suitable for the coalface. With advancing age, men move on to lighter work and eventually to surface work, with the result that many of these workers were worn out from long years of working underground. Social justice demanded better conditions for such men, but their case had never enjoyed any high priority on the part of the union leadership.

Picketing by the initial strikers caused stoppages to spread across the country. For a fortnight, 130,000 miners at 140 pits defied their leaders. The strike is largely forgotten now and its aims were limited, but surface working hours were reduced and to those taking part it was judged as being a success. In fact it was far more than just a success. Later to become known as the "October Revolution" it was a significant rehearsal for things to come and proved to be a sea change in rank-and-file thinking. Young miners, with no previous experience of serious industrial action, discovered there were ways of short-circuiting established procedure. They had felt their own muscles and smelt their own power. Pressure could be exerted in high places, bulldozing and if necessary bypassing their own elected representatives. The twenty-three year old Tyrone O'Sullivan had just become a lodge member at Tower Colliery. His union career thus started with a victory and, moreover, he had had a say in working conditions for the men. From that moment on he would describe himself as being "hooked".

In 1969, the same year and on the broader industrial front, the Labour government introduced a plan for the reform of trade union law. The document was called "In Place of Strife" and was intended to lead the way to industrial peace. Rarely has any name been so inappropriate, for its result was exactly the opposite. It was seen by the unions as an attack on their independence and, after a bruising confrontation, the government was forced to back down.

In June 1970, in an atmosphere of economic decline and industrial unrest, the Conservatives under Edward Heath replaced Labour as governing party. The promises were lower taxes, reduced government influence upon prices and wages, some privatisation, new laws to curb trade union power and an approach to the European Economic Community. With the exception of the latter, things did not go well. Tax reductions and cheap credit resulted in a boom that proved to be unsustainable. A growth rate of 7.4 per cent pulled imports into the country and pushed inflation upwards. The militant reaction of organised labour resulted in an average annual salary increase of 15 per cent, with no corresponding increase in productivity.

The miners, whose own productivity had increased significantly, whose pay demands had been modest, and who had co-operated in the run-down of their industry, looked on with the increasing frustration of reasonable men who see their reasonableness exploited. NUM statisticians reckoned that, over the two-and-a-half post-war decades, their ranking in the national pay league had declined from first to seventeenth. The abolition of piece-work rates, combined with extensive mechanisation, meant that in some cases men were working on coalfaces producing 3,000 tons per day for the same wages they received when that same face was producing 300 tons per day.

The miners' leaders were now themselves being led, by an unstoppable ground swell of opinion, building up among the rank and file. NCB Chairman, Lord Robens, had diverted criticism over the magnitude of the previous pay award with the statement, "But it's all that you asked for". The feeling spread that perhaps the time was now ripe to start asking for more!

### The Stakes are Raised.

Parallel to the rise of NUM militancy, indeed almost in step with it, was the rise of OPEC militancy. The oil producers of the Middle East had also come to the conclusion that they had been exploited for too long. The wellhead price of oil had not increased for ten years and it was cheaper than Coca Cola. Not only was revenue too low, their economic wealth was being drained away at a rate of knots, with no basis being created to replace it. There was also political dissatisfaction with the west over their one-sided support of Israel.

The 1970's would be characterised by the massive and traumatic rise in the price of crude oil, the result of a political decision by OPEC, the oil producers' cartel. This inevitably transformed the situation in coal's favour. In developments that were extremely judicious for the NUM, oil prices rose and, in the early 1970's virtually exploded. In 1973 the oil price quadrupled in three months, from $3 to $12 a barrel. This triggered a world recession. Barely had the economy recovered when a second oil shock, this time precipitated by the fall of the Shah of Iran in 1979, pushed prices up again, causing a second world recession. These developments would provide an ongoing backdrop to the events about to take place.

In July 1970, the NUM conference unanimously passed a resolution for pay increases all round. As an additional flourish a resolution from South Wales was carried, demanding strike action until the Board conceded the claim. South Wales also organised the picketing of negotiations and an unofficial meeting between the demonstrators and NUM leadership. At the conference, in a travesty of normal constitutional practice, the national leadership reported on the position to an assortment of malcontents camped outside, before reporting back to the areas via official channels. When the national membership were asked to vote, the question was not whether to accept the NCB counter offer but whether to accept the recommendation of the National Executive for strike action. Robens' tactic was to inform all miners by post of what the offer actually was. According to the current union rules, strike action required a two-thirds majority. The militants did their best, but this was not achieved. With an 83 per cent poll, only 55 per cent voted for strike action.

Lord Robens was to question the secrecy and ethics of the ballot, stating that in Scotland, 23,500 men at work on that day had produced 26,500 votes. In Wales, absence from work was almost 24 per cent. Thus 31,000 men at work produced a vote of 35,400. The votes were sent to the Electoral Reform Society, who would count them and declare the result. However, the papers had to be "straightened out" first. An unofficial count frequently took place while this was happening.

Following the ballot there were further negotiations, resulting in a modest increase in the Board's offer. Unofficial strikes broke out at many pits across the country. In Wales the stoppage became total. All but eight pits in Scotland were idle, and all of those in the Doncaster Area. As a precursor of things to come, picketing became rough and intensive. Yorkshire developed their own speciality, namely motorised columns of pickets which toured the county, intimidating those who turned up for work. If direct confrontation did not produce the desired result there was always the cars in the car park upon which the pickets could vent their spleen.

By this time, the Government was calling the shots. To fight the problem of continually rising prices, a Prices and Incomes policy had been introduced. Prime Minister Heath and Chancellor of the Exchequer Anthony Barber determined on a maximum pay increase for the miners of 10 per cent overall, to be distributed as the NCB saw fit. The NUM wanted 23 per cent. Robens initially judged a settlement of 8-9 per cent to be possible, certainly within 10 per cent.

By 7 September 1970, Robens had increased his offer to 10.4 per cent.

By 11 September 1970, the Robens offer had increased to 11.8 per cent. He confirmed to the Government his inability to achieve the 10 per cent limitation.

On 12 September 1970, a phone call to Robens from Whitehall insisted that the 10 per cent maximum apply.

On 27 October 1970, Robens communicated to the Government that a 12 per cent offer was necessary to protect the Coal Board's interests and that the union would settle on this basis. If the Government blocked this then they would have to take public responsibility (giving rise to the Heath comment referred to in the previous chapter, "This is bad. L.Robens has let us down and gone back on his word").

On 19 November 1970, there was a confrontation outside the NCB Area headquarters at Doncaster, between Robens and what he was to describe as, "A yarling mob"-crude, vulgar and unfit to lead the decent men he knew in the pits —— But for the presence of the police I believe they would cheerfully have murdered me". Robens' public allegations of communist influence in the NUM proved controversial. About eighty left-wing members of parliament signed a petition calling for his resignation as Chairman of the Board.

The day following Lord Robens' experience saw similar scenes outside the NUM headquarters in Euston Road London, where the National Executive were holding a meeting. In particular those members of the Executive thought to hold moderate views were subject to barracking and physical assault. Between 40-50 police were required to control the hostility. Following the failure of the strike ballot, the NUM membership voted on whether to accept the offer of the Board. In a 77 per cent poll, 158,239 voted for and 82,079 against.

On 5 January 1971, it was announced that Lord Robens did not wish to serve for a third term as Chairman of the National Coal Board. He would stay on for some months while his replacement, Derek Ezra, took over.

In July 1971, at the NUM annual conference of that year, a South Wales resolution was passed which reduced the majority required to sanction industrial action from two-thirds to 55 per cent of the poll. Such a poll would be called if the NCB response to the wage claim in that current year turned out to be unsatisfactory.

## THE FIRST NATIONAL MINERS STRIKE (1972).

### The Dam Breaks.

In 1971, there was a small setback for the militants with the election of the moderate Joe Gormley as NUM National President. Their candidate, Mick McGahey, the Scottish President, had lost by 92,883 votes to 117,663. Nevertheless, their policies, and a growing truculence in pursuing them, had taken hold. When the time came to negotiate the annual pay claim for that year, the stage was set for confrontation. The government was committed to an incomes' policy that sought to impose an eight percent limit on all pay awards during that year, with a maximum of 9 per cent for coal (their initial offer was 7 per cent). The NUM was looking for 17 per cent for face workers, 47 per cent elsewhere underground, and 44 per cent on the surface.

From the end of October 1971 there was an overtime ban in all coalfields. Facing as they were a definite possibility of the first national strike since 1926, the feeling in government circles was nevertheless sanguine. The NUM would not be able to sustain a strike beyond one month and, in addition, 9 weeks stock of coal at the power stations was a good defence.

In 1971-72, during the ice-cold winter of that year, the dam of the miners' frustration finally broke. During the month of November 1971 a rash of unofficial strikes caused great unrest in the Welsh mining communities. Matters were coming to a head.

On 2 December 1971, in a national poll of the miners, 58.8 per cent voted in favour of strike action (under the previous rules this would have been inadequate). In South Wales, 65.5 per cent of 29,249 voted in favour. There were further negotiations, which came to nothing. The government decided to stick by their pay policy and, if necessary, resist a strike "which would last between four to six weeks" according to a cabinet assessment..

On 9 January 1972, a national withdrawal of labour took place in what was the first official strike of the miners since 1926. On government instructions the existing pay offer was withdrawn by the NCB. In South Wales, all 50 collieries and 85 small private mines were at a standstill. Contrary to union instructions, safetymen were withdrawn at 7 pits (Blaenavon, Caerau, Coegnant, Cwmgwili, Fernhill, Garw and St. Johns). Ffaldau and Wyndham-Western joined these later. Five other pits had only partial safety cover. There was significant support from the dockers, who refused to unload imported coal. Railwaymen hindered oil supplies to power stations. Open cast sites continued to work but picketing prevented coal coming out and hindered supplies going in. The Transport and General Workers, the union on these sites, gave general support to the miners.

The strike lasted seven weeks and won the miners more than two-thirds of their massive pay demand. It put them back in the position of being the country's best-paid workers. It was won by consequent application of two revolutionary new concepts, which took the government by surprise and for which they were not prepared. Firstly, there was the mass application of "flying pickets", mobile bands from all coalfields, summating to thousands. Secondly, these were applied at non-colliery targets to enforce a systematic and well-planned strangulation of the nation's power supplies. NUM planning targeted all power stations, steelworks, ports, coal depots, and other major coal users. Motor transport was organised to bring the "flying pickets" to power stations and other strategically important points. It took a brave soul to cross a picket line consisting of thousands of hefty, determined men. Both of these winning strategies were identified as originating with the young union leader from Yorkshire, Arthur Scargill. Until then hardly known outside his own local Yorkshire area of Barnsley, now, at the centre of such apocalyptic events and with a natural feel for publicity, his name would become a household word throughout the land.

Arthur Scargill started work at the age of 15, in Woolley Colliery near Barnsley in his native Yorkshire. The next 20 years, before becoming full-time president of the Yorkshire miners, he spent working at the coalface. During this period he became one of the country's youngest union branch officials. At the age of 27, after 5 years on the branch committee, he was elected delegate. During the 1972 strike he was 34 years of age. In this same year, Scargill won the post of Compensation Agent for the Yorkshire NUM and shortly after a place on the union's national executive.

First as the man who arranged and executed the effective blacking-out of East Anglia and then as the "Hero of Saltley Gate", when this vast West Midlands gas works was shut down, career-wise he was on his way. At Saltley Gate, 1,000 police struggled for a week with 2,000 miners to keep the coke lorries moving.

The NUM gave advice to their members concerning their right to obtain social security benefit, in the absence of an incoming wage. This reduced to some extent the financial hardship involved in going on strike. During the seven-week conflict, some 53 per cent of the eligible miners' families received supplementary benefits - a higher proportion than in any strike before or since. Rents and the interest part of mortgage repayments were covered. Family allowances continued but were deducted from the total supplementary benefit to which a family was entitled. Free school meals could also be provided. Single or widowed miners without dependants also claimed emergency benefits on an unprecedented scale, something like one in eight of all single miners. Such emergency benefits included for example, rent payment where an eviction threat had been made. Union encouragement, plus the tight-knit nature of mining communities where everyone is facing the same problems, may explain these high take up figures. Under the circumstances there was no need to hide the "shame" of social security.

The Sunday Times calculated a weekly payout of £18,30 for a married man with three children receiving supplementary benefit and family allowance. This compared with a net weekly wage without overtime of £21.36 for an attendant at the pithead baths and £30.11 for a coal face craftsman. Picketing away from home kept the morale of the striking miners high. It was motivating and better than hanging around street corners.

At Tower Colliery (and only at Tower Colliery), the officials' union NACODS went on a one-week sympathy strike, in spite of their responsibility for safety. The South Wales Area Executive Committee had rejected calls for the withdrawal of safetymen and had instructed its members not to picket clerks at NCB offices. Over-enthusiasm did, however, result in angry scenes at the offices of Llanishen, Ystrad Mynach, Tondu and Pontarddulais. Safetymen were prevented from entering Penrhiwceiber Colliery as 300 pickets clashed with police. Windows were smashed at the homes of three Lewis Merthyr Colliery officials and officials generally were banned from the colliery club for the duration of the strike. Compared to what was to happen twelve years later, however, such aggravation was minimal.

On 9 February 1972, talks were reopened under the auspices of the Secretary of State for Employment. An improved offer (still within the pay policy guidelines) was made and rejected.

On 10 February 1972, the government set up a commission of enquiry into miners' pay. It was headed by Lord Wilberforce. On the same day, and following a request for solidarity by Scargill, 40,000 workers in scores of Birmingham factories downed tools. Ten thousand of them marched to the Saltley coke depot to support the miners already there. On occasions the confrontation would go beyond just vigorous pushing and shoving.

Confronted with this multitude of 12,000, the police were finally swamped and the plant shut down. Such a mass of determined humanity, rapidly applied at critical points, proved to be invincible. As a portent of political things to come, parallels were drawn by some with the storming of the winter palace by the Bolsheviks in the October revolution. Certainly the role of charismatic, revolutionary leader was ably, and willingly, filled by the young Arthur Scargill. Inebriated with the exuberance of his own verbosity, and nowhere happier than, with loud hailer in hand, addressing mass pickets in his clipped certainties on the themes of working class solidarity and (questionably) the cheapness of British coal, the next twelve years would see him develop into a prominent left-wing figure on the British scene.

By mid-February 1972, 14 major coal-fired power stations had ceased to deliver electricity to the national grid. The government announced that, with power stations picketed as they were and at the present rate of consumption, coal stocks were sufficient for two weeks only. A State of Emergency was declared and electricity cuts began. Factories worked just three days per week. One million people were compelled to take the corresponding time off work. Ministers were talking of calling in the troops to avoid a total industrial shutdown, expected within a fortnight. Offices were illuminated with candles and families told to heat one room only. The new energy minister, Patrick Jenkin, advised the nation to clean its teeth in the dark.

## Capitulation.

On 18 February, the Wilberforce Report was published. It said that there was a low pay problem. Miners' earnings had not risen as fast as for some other groups and the Midlands miners, in their high productivity pits, had been marking time so as to allow others elsewhere to catch up. He recommended pay increases. These were accepted by the NCB, and rejected by the NUM as inadequate. Negotiations then transferred to Downing Street. In direct negotiation with the NUM, Heath tried to hold the line at the Wilberforce recommendation. Aware of the strength of his position, General Secretary Daly would have none of it, saying that what last week had been a basis for negotiation had now become a basis for settlement. Heath caved in. The Wilberforce recommendations were improved upon.

On 24 February 1972, the Security Service reported to the Prime Minister on the possibility of Communist agitation being behind the strike. Their conclusions were:

- Traditional moderates in the NUM Executive and among the rank and file have adopted as militant a stand as the Communists.

- The Communists are neither in control of the NUM Executive Committee nor of a majority of the areas which together make up the union.

- The Communist Party has exploited this strike to the full and has given it wholehearted support (but) —— There is no evidence that the Party exercised a decisive influence on this strike.

On 28 February 1972, when the miners returned to work, they returned triumphant, with an average 24 per cent increase in pay, plus increased holidays and special bonuses. The Government had been taken by surprise by the solidity and violence of the NUM's action. Their intelligence on the feeling prevailing in the mining communities had proven totally inadequate. In addition to the new and revolutionary tactics employed, critical to the success of the strike was the unanimity of the miners themselves, combined with the high level of external support. Their cause had struck a chord with other unions and with the public at large. There was widespread sympathy for the miner, with a general feeling that the prevailing rates of pay in combination with hard working conditions underground resulted in him being in a manifestly under-privileged position. There was support, and not only moral support, from the general trade union movement. Dockers and railwaymen had refused to handle coal. Payment of supplementary benefits to strikers eased their hardship, at no cost to the NUM.

The inflexible nature of the government's pay policy meant that they could not afford defeat. The policy's success rested ultimately on the willingness to face make-or-break confrontations. This meant, inevitably, that one side or the other would be humbled. By siding with the employers in the cause of lower pay settlements, the government had forfeited its right to act as conciliator. Faced with NUM determination, the strike could only have been averted at the price of serious damage being done to the incomes' policy. Failure to win the strike, however, had also resulted in serious damage being done to the policy. It had also been demonstrated that militancy can pay, and how it should best be organised.

## The Arab Allies.

In 1973, Arthur Scargill won the succession to the Yorkshire presidency and the power obtained by OPEC was first exercised in a big way. Following the Yom Kippur Arab-Israeli war, a limited oil embargo was imposed due to western support of Israel.

In October of 1973, the next blow fell when OPEC doubled their prices. In December of that same year they struck again, when prices were redoubled. Oil demand fell, with a reduction in world economic activity.

On 8 December 1973, one year after the strike's end, Derek Ezra, Chairman of the National Coal Board, gave a lecture to the Institution of Electrical Engineers. Its theme was the future of coal as the backbone of electricity generation. It took place against a revitalised corporatist concept. Nationalised coal, national-ised electricity and the nationalised railways would work together. Jointly, they should be so planned as to optimally serve the nation. Mr. Arthur Hawkins, Chairman of the Central Electricity Board, led the discus-sion and gave expression to the new spirit that was abroad:

"Coal's dramatic change of fortune during the last twelve months reminds me of the story of Cinderella. It has gone, colloquially speaking, from rags to riches. Productivity per man-shift has reached a record level; a new spirit of co-operation between management and unions has manifested itself —— and Her Majesty's Government, in the guise of the good fairy godmother, has promised massive financial help".

He then went on to make his own industry's case:

"The electricity service in England and Wales does not exist just to burn fuel. It exists to serve nearly 19 million customers who want electricity on tap at the lowest possible price —— In the interests of the electricity consumer, we must always seek maximum flexibility in the use of power station fuel, and we shall reject dear fuels whatever they may be —— We have no doubt that nuclear is the fuel of the future for electricity generation. This is not to say, however, that we have shut the door on coal. On the contrary, we can and will increase our coal burn to record levels if the price is right —— We hope that the massive aid proposed under the Coal Industry Bill - up to £1,200 M over the next five years - will be used to bring about a viable coal industry at last and not be used as a stopgap to prop up uneconomic coal production. We also hope that the new co-operation between the coal unions and management has cleared the way for the complete rationalisation and thoroughgoing concentration on cheap coal production which are so es-sential to the coal industry's long-term well being".

Mr. Ezra for his part made one statement as questionable in hindsight as Mr. Hawkins was concerning the future of nuclear power:

"By the late 1980's natural gas can probably be discounted as a power station fuel of any consequence because of its need for other purposes". Otherwise, he saw coal, electricity and the railways forming a mutually supporting triad, to the great benefit of the nation:

"Coal, electricity and railways are already dependent on one another for a large part of their individual prosperity. Half Britain's coal output goes under power station boilers. Nearly 70 per cent of all electricity is generated from coal and about 60 per cent of the railways' freight traffic comes from coal, most of it going to power stations. Thus we have linertrains linking some of the most efficient collieries in Europe with some of the most modern power stations. About 6000,000 t of coal per week flow by this means into the 2,000 Megawatt stations in Yorkshire and the Midlands —— It is now a decade since we last sank a new pit, but we have hundreds of millions of tons of proven reserves in North Yorkshire and North Not-tinghamshire ready to be exploited and ideally situated for supplying new power stations —— There would be an improvement in the security of energy supplies since electricity generation would be solidly based on an indigenous source - British coal. Finally, there would be a substantial benefit to the balance of payments".

## THE SECOND NATIONAL MINERS STRIKE (1974).

### Don't Stop Now!

One year and one day after the lecture, a mere two years after the previous national strike, there was to be a rerun of the same. Inflation was again a problem, partly accelerated by increased food prices consequen-tial upon the 1973 entry of the UK into the European Economic Union.

Heath, the convinced non-interventionist, felt himself forced to hold fast to a rigid Price/Wages Policy. For major pay negotiations such as the miners' a detailed blow-by-blow account would be sent to the

Prime Minister's office. There was first a wages' freeze, and then a limit on annual salary increases to a maximum of £350. The miners would have none of it. They demanded twice as much.

On 19 February 1973, at the South Wales Area Conference of the NUM held at Bridgend, the mood was gung ho. The taste of blood was recent and addictive.

There was a 93 per cent vote for strike action, with the demand that this start immediately. The local president said that all necessary picketing would take place and that the trade union movement as a whole would be called upon for support. In addition to calling for the retirement age to be reduced to 60, a motion was unanimously passed to the effect that if NACODS (the officials union) did not strike in sympathy then the NUM would not work with them after the strike. It was decided that a letter be sent to NACODS informing them of this decision (in practice, the NUM at national level did not follow up on this threat).

On 16 July 1973 a private (and secret) discussion was held at Number 10 Downing Street between Prime Minister Heath and Joe Gormley, National President of the NUM. At this stage, sensitive telephone calls between Gormley and the Prime Minister's Office were made via the former's home telephone number and not via the NUM switchboard. Also present at the meeting was Sir William Armstrong of the civil service. The widening gap between Gormley's thinking and that of his executive committee is apparent in government notes made of the meeting:

- Gormley expressed his understanding that rising prices were the greatest single difficulty currently facing the government. They did however provide a readymade platform for the militants in his own union. Counting communists and fellow travellers, these now made up almost half of his executive committee. In these circumstances it was almost inevitable that wild resolutions would be passed. At least a decision at the union's recent conference to retain the ballot provided a useful sheet anchor against precipitate action.

- He did not think that there was much to be gained in increasing pensions or family allowances. To the extent that most miners did not tell their wives what was in their pay packets, this latter measure would assist the housewife. However, it was the men who decided whether or not to strike and they wanted to see something on wages.

- He saw a brighter future for the coal industry, and reported that he had had a useful talk about energy policy with the Secretary of State for Trade and Industry that morning. In this context he was anxious to get things right on the industrial relations side and was already talking with Mr. Ezra about the possibility of introducing productivity agreements. He considered Mr. Ezra as settling down extremely well, and likely to prove a very good Chairman of the National Coal Board.

- He had in mind two possible forms of productivity agreement, both of which were common in the Soviet Union. Consequently, his militants could resist them only with difficulty.

  i) A norm for each pit, with a bonus to everyone at the pit if this norm was exceeded.

  ii) An allowance above the national average for those prepared to work shifts. He thought that there was considerable scope for increasing shift work, with a view to using machinery for as much as 18-20 hours per day.

- In Gormley's view, the future lay in getting away from a nationally negotiated wage towards a national minimum wage, coupled with a pit-by-pit negotiation on productivity lines.

Personally, he favoured the participation of workers in management, provided trade unionists were prepared to accept management responsibilities. In his view, most trade unionists were not. In the present state of affairs, the difficulty was that workers' representatives on the board would be unwilling to take the rough with the smooth. In his personal opinion, as in the Soviet Union a leader of the mineworkers' union could emerge through management ranks.

Later that year in the autumn, when the NUM annual conference came around, Gormley was able to retain nominal control. In practice his room for manoeuvre was to be tightly constrained since the left, for the first time in the union's history, was within touching distance of an actual majority. There was a combination of communists such as Mick McGahey (president of the Scottish miners) and labour radicals like Arthur Scargill (in the meantime president of the Yorkshire miners). The tide was definitely running their way.

A national majority of 80.99 per cent supported the Executive in their call for a national strike. Never in the history of the NUM had the leadership been given such a show of support. Of the union's 23 areas, 22 supported the call. This compared with only 12 in the pre-strike ballot of 1971. Two areas, South Wales and Yorkshire, voted more than 90 per cent in support. Another ten registered more than 80 per cent. Some, such as the Midlands, Durham, and South Derbyshire moved for the first time into the militancy league, never ever having voted to strike before.

In October 1973, the effects of the six-day Arab-Israeli war enhanced confidence of the miners in victory. The consequential oil embargo resulted in shortages and a four-fold increase in price. The miners insisted on their demands being met. The government still determined to avoid setting a precedent, whereby those with the strength and will to damage the economy seriously could get their own way while the rest were held down. Capitulation meant that what remained of economic policy would be vulnerable to pressure, resulting in more industrial unrest rather than less.

To show that they meant business the miners introduced an overtime ban. This was the final straw for Heath, already worn down by the energy crises in oil, by the rate of inflation, a threatened railway strike, and the worst balance of payments deficit ever, all combined with the collapse of a power-sharing agreement in Northern Ireland due to a Protestant boycott. There was also an on-going dispute with the Electrical Power Engineers Association, concerning work outside normal hours.

On 13 November 1973, a state of emergency was declared. This was the second time in two years, in spite of the fact that there was no miners' strike on this occasion but only an overtime ban.

On 23 November 1973, Leader of the Opposition Harold Wilson wrote a personal letter to Prime Minister Heath;

"My soundings about coalfield opinion leave me with a strong and disturbing impression. We know the problem of militancy in the coalfields but I am impressed by the number of district leaders, of a very moderate persuasion, who are as militant on these present events as any of their colleagues".

Wilson went on to make a suggestion whereby the miners could be paid for the time they spent in the pithead baths at the beginning and end of every shift (typically 40 minutes in total). If the suggestion was taken up, then, as is the case in normal industry, miners would clock on immediately upon arrival at their place of work. The concept was not accepted, on the grounds that it would breach incomes' policy.

The government were well aware that during the previous strike the miners had enjoyed overwhelming public support. They were also of the opinion that one reason for the maintenance of this support was that the public had only began to suffer from the dispute as it was nearing its end, or had already ended.


## Who Runs the Country?

On 27 November 1973, an internal cabinet memorandum (ref Cabinet Paper CP(73)131) from the Secretary of State for Employment made clear what the Government thought the dispute was all about, and their unease concerning prevalent public opinion:

"It is now clear that this is a conflict between the Government and the NUM militants. But the general public is not aware of the constitutional importance of Daly's open challenge to the authority of parliament —— It might also be desirable, particularly if the NUM —— intransigently press their claim - to introduce urgently emergency restrictions on power consumption in order to highlight for the public the implications of the miners' action and the Government's resolve to conserve fuel supplies —— With a strike ballot in late January, ability to hold out would probably not extend beyond mid-February —— The Government could increase the pressure on the NUM to hold a ballot by intensifying the severity of the curtailment of energy consumption because of their (i.e. the NUM's) indefinite continuance of the overtime ban; and in what would then be a crisis situation with people being thrown out of work".

On 28 November 1973, the day following the above memorandum, Heath met the whole of the NUM Executive to explain the Prices and Incomes Policy as being something necessary for the nation. He also put to them the full implication of their position in seeking to go beyond the limits set by parliament. The omens were not good. NUM General Secretary Lawrence Daly had been addressing mineworkers meetings on the following lines:

"If Mr. Heath throws down the gauntlet, I hope the NUM Executive will have the courage to pick it up. I am confident you will have victory". Even less encouraging had been a "Dear Ted" letter that Edward Heath had received some days previously from J. Whelan, an executive member from the Notts Area:

"What Britain needs is an honest man, who at the same time could be Prime Minister. What a cheek and audacity you have to suggest that the miners are taking action against the people and the nation! If anyone is taking this kind of action it is you and your government. —— You have requested the pleasure of the company of myself and that of my colleagues of the NEC in order to discuss the ban on overtime and our wages claim. For myself I cannot in all honesty say that I am really looking forward to the event and I can only hope that it is not going to prove a propaganda stunt or a gimmick, at which your predecessor was most accomplished. If the occasion is to be a success we shall want to see the colour of your money".

After going on to harangue Heath and his government on their record, while eulogising the miners, the letter concluded:

"I hope when we meet on Wednesday 28th inst. you will have second thoughts and find ways and means of doing the sensible thing; give the miners what they deserve and need, a decent living wage, in your own interest and that of the nation".

No reply was made to the letter, though there was discussion in some government circles about the narrow horizon of these people, reinforcing opinion that they should indeed be "on tap but never on top". At the meeting, nothing was achieved. Both sides simply reiterated their positions.

On 29 November 1973, one day later, in a meeting with Sheik Yamani, the Saudi Oil Minister, the latter announced that total production had been cut to 75 per cent of the level in September (ref Cabinet Paper CP(73)134). There was no question of increasing production above this level until a satisfactory political solution of the Israeli problem had been found. In addition, further progressive cuts of 5 per cent per month would be applied.

By 3 December 1973, a 16 per cent shortfall in crude oil imports to the UK was forecast for that month, with 20 per cent in January (ref Cabinet Paper CP(73)136).

In December 1973, the three-day week was re-introduced. Television transmission ended at 10.30pm, so that people went earlier to bed. A general speed limit of 50km/hr. was introduced and coupons for petrol rationing printed. There were reminiscences about the home front during the Second World War. When the NUM finally held their ballot, to the Government's chagrin, the vote for a strike was overwhelming.

In spite of the vote, Heath determined not to cave in to the miners as he had done in 1972. He called a general election. It was to be fought on the issue of who rules the country, parliament or trade unions. Following an appeal by Heath, Gormley duly proposed that the strike be postponed until after the general election. Within the union there were calls for his resignation. The vote in favour of a strike had been overwhelming and of the 26 members of the union's executive, only 7-8 supported him. In this year, Emlyn Williams had replaced Glyn Williams as South Wales NUM President. Interviewed on the media, the former said that no choice existed, other than to support their members' wishes.

On 9 February 1974, the miner's strike finally began. Once again the miners enjoyed general public support. Compared with the previous strike, there was increased support from other unions. Transport workers also cooperated and the dockers refused to handle coal. Gradually, Heath's lead in the opinion polls disappeared. The government's attempt to make the public suffer this time, hoping that as a consequence they would then blame the miners for the inconvenience, had backfired. The country as a whole were not convinced by the government's analysis, or of the necessity for a general atmosphere of "Apocalypse now". It was Heath, not the miners, whom the public held responsible for their privations.

On 28 February the election was held. Labour won, with 301 seats against 296 for the Tories. A second general election, that same autumn, confirmed Heath's defeat and gave Labour a small, but absolute, majority. Within days of the Labour victory, Michael Foot, Secretary for Employment, authorised the NCB to negotiate a wage settlement "unfettered by previous government dictates". The treasury would foot any bill necessary to purchase an immediate return to work. This was the first time in their history that all of the miners' demands had been virtually met. These were heady days, with the humiliating defeat of 1926 being well and truly avenged. The miners accepted a pay rise of 35 per cent overall. The main items were:

- Face Workers: Claim for £45 per week as basic pay was met in full.

- Other underground workers: Claim for £40 per week basic pay was settled at £36.

- Surface Workers: Claim for a £35 weekly minimum was settled at £32.

## Recovery.

Unlike after the 1972 strike when restart of the industry was relatively painless, on this occasion and despite the shorter duration of only three weeks, it proved to be more difficult. This time around more safetymen had been withdrawn. Pits cannot simply be mothballed. The dangers of pits being left without any manning at all are, for example, pump failure resulting in flooding, sudden falls of roof resulting in blocked roadways and coalfaces, gas emissions, plus other features requiring a constant round of inspections. To a far greater extent, management themselves had had to take over such tasks.

## THE PLAN FOR COAL.

### Coal's Future Assured-!

By 1974 the effective five-fold increase in oil prices had transformed the energy landscape. A new Department of Energy was set up, replacing the old Ministry of Fuel and Power. This was intended to acquire and optimise in the country's interest, usage of the huge new oil revenues flooding in from the North Sea. It would also revitalise prospects for the coal industry, reversing the trend of on-going decline. Coal was now in the position of being the cheapest fuel and its main customer, the electricity generation industry, wanted every tonne the NCB could produce. Coal was being imported and Lord Robens regarded his original 1960 production target of 200 Mt as being vindicated. By now, however, the run-down in capacity forced on the industry had rendered this figure unobtainable.

In April 1974, the government published, with the tripartite agreement of the NCB, mining unions and Department of Energy, the 1974 Plan for Coal. This was meant to ensure coal's role in the future and the document was rushed out at high speed to placate and reassure the miners. It outlined the National Coal Board's proposals for long-term investment in the mining industry and received a warm welcome. For the miners' leadership it would remain their bible for the next decade. The plan committed the government to a massive programme of investment into new and existing pits. The objectives stated included the underpinning of long-term job security, the financing of better disability payments and pensions, plus the development of new markets, thus reducing dependence on the industry's dominating customer, the Central Electricity Generating Board.

### -Assured? Well, Maybe!

Contrary to its subsequent portrayal (one authority, Professor Derek Spooner, described it as being made "in the hysterical climate" of the time), the Plan for Coal was not an unrestricted bundle of goodies for everyone in the mining industry. It was based on certain assumptions, which under current circumstances did not seem unreasonable. Even allowing for the fact that certain of the assumptions made did not withstand the test of time, for those who read it carefully the plan already contained within it the seeds of future grief for South Wales and other so-called "peripheral" coalfields. This was not adequately appreciated, either at the time or subsequently. The Plan started off with a note of caution:

"The Board recognise that, although the new energy situation presents a new opportunity to British coal, this is not unconditional, and will be influenced principally by:

a) The growth in UK energy requirements.

b) The availability of natural gas.

c) The price relationship between coal and oil.

d) The power station building programme, particularly the rate at which nuclear power is expanded.

The Plan regarded each of these considerations as being subject to a great deal of uncertainty. Consequently, a range of possibilities was considered. Annual coal output for various scenarios was given as in the following table. Figures are in million tonnes of coal equivalent (mtce).

| Year | 1972/73 | 1985 (Low growth/high gas) | 1985 (High growth/low gas) | 1985 ("Central" estimate) |
|---|---|---|---|---|
| Total requirements | 336 | 400 | 490 | 430 |
| Natural gas | 38 | 100 | 70 | 80 |
| Nuclear/hydro | 12 | 50 | 50 | 50 |
| Coal+oil | 286 | 250 | 370 | 300 |

Coal was seen as being in direct competition with oil, with the division between them being a function of price, "If relative prices were favourable to coal clearly a substantial potential market would be available".

Completely misjudging the extent to which the multinational oil industry would now invest in the international production of coal, the Plan goes on:

"The Board do not consider it likely that large tonnages of cheap imported coal will be available on a continuing basis".

In a sentence that should have sounded alarm bells in South Wales and elsewhere:

"It is clear both that the central coalfields currently enjoy a significant competitive margin over oil and that the margin in favour of coal is modest in the peripheral coalfields. These factors indicate both the opportunities for coal and the need to recognise the great importance of cost control, and the selective basis for future investment". This point was emphasised in the conclusions, "Individual schemes will have to be treated on their merits, with investment concentrated on the expansion of output from the lower cost reserves".

With regard to individual markets:

- POWER STATIONS: These would remain the largest single market.

- COKE OVENS; With the planned expansion of British steel- making capacity, that industry was likely to absorb all of the coking coal which the NCB could make available.

- OTHER MARKETS: Smokeless fuels had better prospects of withstanding strong competition from gas.

The Plan goes on, "Provided that coal is able to keep its competitive advantage over oil, a reasonable range for demand in 1985 would be as follows":

Figures for the various markets are in million tonnes (Mt).

| Year | 1973/74(Before allowing for dispute) | 1985(Min - Max range) |
|---|---|---|
| Power stations | 75 | 80 - 100 |
| Coke ovens | 23 | 18 - 22 |
| Industry+others | 18 | 11 - 13 |
| Domestic | 14 | 7 - 9 |
| Exports | 3 | 4 - 6 |
| TOTAL | 133 | 120 - 150 |

On this basis the Plan continues:

"The Board would propose a plan towards the top of this range, involving broad stabilisation of the industry. It is recognised of course, that if coal costs were unfavourable in relation to oil, and energy growth limited, demand would be significantly less than indicated above —— any plan providing for overall stabilisation of the industry in the years ahead must embrace substantial additional output to offset losses through exhaustion". Such additional output was to be achieved by improved performance, and also by investment to:

a) Extend the life of existing pits by gaining access to new reserves.

b) Increase output levels at existing pits.

c) Open new mines.

A large exploration programme was to be initiated, and open cast production increased to 15 Mt per annum. In the summary it was stated that the Board's plans were based on investment in some 42 Mt of additional capacity by 1985, made up as follows:

i) 9 Mt from life extensions of pits, which otherwise were planned to close.

ii) 13 Mt of additional output from major schemes at existing pits.

iii) 20 Mt from new collieries (with the possibility of further opportunities in the light of continued exploration).

The necessary investment was initially estimated as being £600 M at 1974 prices. This was in addition to the £70-80 M per annum for normal ongoing capital expenditure. Over the next 5 years, £40 M would also be spent on new technologies to utilise coal.

Financing all of this from internal resources would be a problem for the Board. It would only be possible if market conditions allowed significant price rises. In any event, higher productivity was essential, with 4 per cent per annum judged as being feasible:

"The necessary advances in productivity can be secured only with the full co-operation of the work force". Even with this productivity increase, recruitment would have to average 28,000 per annum if output is to be stabilised. "Maximum recruitment efforts will be required in the central coalfields".

## New Dawn for South Wales.

The plan heralded a new dawn for the mining industry. Ten years of expansion were foreseen. The £600 M investment at 1974 prices became £3,000 M. Emphasis was put on the use of advanced, heavy-duty mechanisation and open cast expansion. The Plan made repeated reference to the "central" as opposed to the "peripheral" coalfields as having priority but, unlike South Wales, the central English coalfields have no anthracite, no prime coking coal and no low volatile steam coal. Since one of the Plan's objectives was to expand markets for coal, South Wales therefore could not be ignored completely. For this coalfield, £140

M were to be invested during the following 5 years for major modernisation projects. These entailed the streamlining of long-life pits, the location and logging of new coal reserves, the creation of new mines and the linking of established neighbouring pits underground, so as to form single, high-production units - Britain's guarantees for the fuel-hungry future, as the NCB publicity blurb stated.

Alone at the highly profitable Treforgan drift mine, £7 M were to be invested to open up new workings in the deeper Nine Feet and Bute seams, thus ensuring continuity once the Red Vein became exhausted in 1980. The new working depth was to be 700 metres. Later, an additional £1.24 M were to be spent. Output from the reconstructed mine was expected to be around 350,000 t/a from rapid retreat coalfaces.

At Cynheidre, where by 1979 only the Big Vein seam was being worked at a depth of 604 metres, drivages were planned to access the 12 Mt reserves in the Pumpquart seam, 183 metres below the Big Vein.

At Brynlliw, an underground roadway was driven under the estuary of the Afon Llwchwr to link up with Morlais Colliery. From 1977, all output from Morlais would be wound at Brynlliw.

Oakdale Colliery was one of the largest reconstructions. New skip winding equipment was installed in one shaft to wind the combined outputs of North Celynen and Markham Collieries, as well as that of Oakdale itself. Its central coal preparation plant on the surface was correspondingly uprated.

At Lady Windsor in 1974, two parallel underground roadways were driven under the mountain separating it from Abercynon Colliery. The two units thus became linked, with all coal raised at Lady Windsor for washing and blending. High-speed conveyors under remote control from Lady Windsor carried the coal into a new spiral bunker shaft of 400 tonne capacity, the first of its kind in any British coalfield. A new skip winding plant was also installed, as were major development drivages to open up additional reserves.

At Cwm Colliery, such drivages were also completed.

At Trelewis, a new drift was driven from the surface to access fresh reserves.

In 1983, at Betws New Mine, £12 M were allocated to extend the main access drifts through a major geological disturbance known as the Gardner's Fault. This had previously formed the boundary between the Betws take and that of Abernant.

By the early 1980's, ten major schemes had been completed in the South Wales coalfield.

All faces were to be equipped with power loaders and self-advancing supports, with the emphasis on heavy-duty equipment and higher horsepower. Computerised systems would transport the coal outbye. There was to be a corresponding development in coal preparation plants to cater for the many individual market requirements, along with a change in the product resulting from different mining methods such as types of machines and the nature of seams being worked. In South Wales, the flagship of the new coal era was to be a new drift mine to exploit the reserves of prime coking coal adjacent to the Margam Steelworks, at Port Talbot on the coast.

In 1975, an appreciation was made of the prospects at Margam. In the following investigation, eight boreholes were completed and a 41.4 km seismic traverse made. The results showed 8 seams of prime coking coal, of which 3 were workable. Of the UK reserves of prime coking coal, 84 per cent are in South Wales. Most of this is in the Margam area, close to its potential market, the steelworks. The concept was of high output (in excess of 1M tonnes per annum) produced by a couple of hundred men for a period of at least fifty years.

In 1978 a borehole was sunk near the proposed site for shaft sinking.


## COAL FOR THE FUTURE.

### Same Strategy, New Facts.

In 1978, four years after the Plan for Coal, the government policy on energy was updated. The new energy secretary, Tony Benn, published this revision to the "Plan for Coal" under the title "Coal for the Future". It broadly endorsed the overall strategy of the Plan for Coal, while revising the figures it contained.

True to the concept of planning, this consultative document attempted to set guidelines for a long-term energy strategy for the United Kingdom. It stated that in the twenty years prior to 1974 the UK had changed from a 2-fuel economy (coal+oil) to a 4-fuel economy (coal+oil+gas+nuclear). The paper stated:

"It is not sufficient to concentrate on achieving a low cost and secure energy supply in the present and immediate future. Energy policy is necessarily concerned with a long time horizon —— All estimates must be highly speculative". As an example, it took ten years to fully develop a new mine, while the investment cost of new mines and major projects had already increased by 50 per cent since the Plan for Coal. This increase was attributed to the lack of recent experience in estimating such projects.

In spite of maintaining the same overall concepts, there was a crass difference between "Coal for the Future" and the "Plan for Coal". Overall energy demand, instead of increasing as expected, had in fact gone down. The massive oil price increases had resulted in a worldwide reduction in economic activity. Consequently, it was not only oil consumption that had declined, but energy demand overall. In addition, the high cost had now made energy-saving measures attractive. The previous prediction of 150 Mt for coal sales in 1985 was lopped to 135 Mt.

## Keep Smiling!

However, the overall tone remained optimistic as far as coalmining was concerned. Indeed, the precipate fall in coal's relative (if not absolute) fortunes had been halted. The figures for UK primary energy consumption during the period are given below, in million tons of coal equivalent (Mtce) as well as in percentage terms:

|         | 1973 | | 1978 | | 1980 | | 1981 | |
|---------|------|------|------|------|------|------|------|------|
|         | Mtce | % | Mtce | % | Mtce | % | Mtce | % |
| Coal    | 133  | 37.6 | 120  | 35.3 | 121  | 36.7 | 118  | 37.4 |
| Oil     | 164  | 46.4 | 139  | 41.0 | 121  | 37.0 | 111  | 34.9 |
| Nat Gas | 44   | 12.5 | 65   | 19.2 | 71   | 21.6 | 72   | 22.7 |
| Nuclear | 10   | 2.9  | 13   | 3.9  | 13   | 4.1  | 14   | 4.3  |
| Hydro   | 2    | 0.6  | 2    | 0.6  | 2    | 0.6  | 2    | 0.7  |
| TOTAL   | 335  | 100  | 340  | 100  | 329  | 100  | 317  | 100  |

Oil, the arch enemy of coal, was now in full retreat and nuclear power was stable. While natural gas was making great strides, it was foreseen that this would be confined to prime applications, such as domestic heating. That it should one day seriously compete with coal in the field of power generation was not foreseen. As far as the future strategy for coal was concerned, the policy document concluded:

"Using the appropriate financial tests we should proceed with the creation of further new capacity in the coal industry, over and beyond the Plan for Coal, to come into production mainly in the late 1980's and 1990's. The industry needs to generate some 4 Mt a year of new and replacement capacity in the latter part of the century. We also need to ensure that there are ready markets for coal; in particular the electricity industry should continue to maintain the ability to burn large quantities of coal efficiently".

In 1979-80, the second steep rise in oil prices during the decade (a ten-fold increase in total) seemed to reinforce both the view of coal as the cheapest fuel for the future and also the basic philosophy of the 1974 Plan for Coal. Imports were now proving necessary to meet the requirements of the Electricity Generating Board.

**Towards the 21 Century.**

In April 1979, this rosy view of the future was driven home in an article in the IEE Journal entitled "Coalmining Towards the 21st Century". It was presented by Norman Siddall, Deputy Chairman of the NCB. He pointed out that in response to future production requirements, investment in the industry was climbing, from £7 M in the year prior to the 1973 energy crisis to over £450 M in the current year. The NCB's strategic objective was to achieve a production of 170 Mt by the end of the century. Only a high level of investment in new and existing mines would offset natural exhaustion and make this possible. Dealing with each of the main aspects in turn:

Opencast Mining: The future of bulk coal supplies lay inevitably with the big, deep mines, but opencast would remain a permanent and flexible part of the coal industry's economy. Such sites could be producing and contributing to target outputs within a maximum of three years after letting of the contract. That compared with a lead-time of ten years to develop a large deep mine. Although it represented just 12 per cent of the total, opencast output was many times more profitable than deep-mined coal. In addition, half of the anthracite and a significant proportion of the best coking coals came from opencast mining. The blending of some high-quality opencast coals with deep-mined output frequently created a mix more acceptable to other markets, e.g. power stations.

Mechanisation: This had enabled coalface productivity to increase fivefold over the last 20 years but with 94 per cent of all coal now coming from fully mechanised faces this rate of improvement was slowing down. The proportion of men employed at the coalface had fallen from 41 per cent to 29 per cent of the total work force. Installed power at the coalface had increased ten fold, to the 1,500 KW currently found on the largest faces. Production targets would not depend on any new technological breakthroughs. The process would be evolutionary not revolutionary. The first coalfaces equipped with the new, heavy duty, machinery were already installed in Yorkshire. One of them, at Kellingley Colliery, had a designed output of 1 Mt per annum, as much from a single face as from many large collieries currently operating. For further increases in overall productivity the Board were looking to a wider application of remote control and automation, for which a vigorous research and development programme was under way.

New Mines: The average age of existing mines exceeded 70 years. Many were very old and would reach the end of their productive lives before the end of the century. By that time Britain would probably need some 30 entirely new mines, as well as having to prove fresh reserves of capacity for the continuing long-life pits. By the turn of the century about two-thirds of annual output would have to come from new sources. The great advantage of this situation was that production could be planned on a scale that provided for the most efficient use of both manpower and capital resources.

Exploration: During the previous 20 years drilling for coal had been minimal but between 1974 and 1978, over 500 deep holes (in excess of 500 metres) had been drilled. These were not only to prove the workability of known reserves but also to discover hitherto unproven, though suspected, deposits in virgin areas. The aim was to create a 50-year "cushion"- a reservoir of fully proven and accessible seams that would enable the industry to plan its production schedules and capital investment programme well in advance. Not only were new deposits being found, the quality of the 2,000 Mt of new reserves found in the previous 4 years and considered workable by new mines was better than those currently being worked. These newly discovered seams were thicker, less faulted, shallower and more consistent. They were equal to anything that the industry had mined in the past.

Exploration had now began to move outside the established coalfields to explore thoroughly any extensions found, and to locate entirely new coalfields. These might be in parts of the country that had never seen coalmining before. The final outcome would be the complete mapping of all the nations coal deposits, a remarkable undertaking and one of overwhelming value in planning the British economy.

Environment: In this new golden age of coal, the environment would not be sold short. Omelettes are not made without cracking eggs and coal cannot be mined without bringing out waste. However, with good will and the right resources it was possible to alleviate its effect and frequently use the product to advantage. Between 5-10 Mt per annum of mine waste was being sold as base fill for major civil engineering works. If this was not possible, it would no longer to be left in ugly piles to simply disfigure the landscape. Profiling and grading could ensure that the heaps blended into the surrounding topology. Careful removal of topsoil before the start of tipping meant that a fertile cover could be finally laid over the graded waste, on which grass or crops could be sown and the land returned to its previous use.

The Future: It was in the nature of pits that the larger and newer perform better than the older and smaller. Consequently, the key to the industry's future lay in new collieries of large capacity. It was on these that the greater part of the industry's development had to be concentrated.

Such promising prospects for highly productive new mines in the near future had already emerged at Margam in South Wales, Thorne in Yorkshire, Daw Mill in the Midlands and Musselburgh on the Firth of Forth.

Selby: The first of these new opportunities was at Selby in the Vale of York. An outstanding success of the exploration programme, it would be the jewel in the crown of the NCB. The world's biggest and most advanced deep-mining complex was being developed, equipped with the most efficient machinery and expected to win 10 Mt of coal per annum at a productivity rate four or five times the current national average.

Everything about Selby was superlative. At a cost of £1.3 billion, it was one of the largest deep coalmining projects ever undertaken anywhere. A "take" of 110 sq. miles would be worked by 5 pairs of satellite shafts sunk at strategic points throughout the coalfield to provide access for men and materials and for ventilation purposes. These would be linked by some 124 miles of underground roadways. All production would be conveyed to the surface by two long inclined drifts at Gascoigne Wood. For the first time, the whole life of a mine would be planned on paper before a single lump of coal had been won. They already knew how every part of the "take" would be mined, in what sequence, and over what period. Approved in 1976, Selby would begin production in 1983.

It was not part of Mr. Siddall's brief to dwell on difficulties, but accessing the seams at Selby was not proving easy. Water ingress was a problem and new consolidation methods for the shafts had to be devised. The coalfield was controversial generally, with local Tory, land-owning gentry being less than enamoured by the prospect of non cap doffing, horny handed miners, with their wild ways and alien politics, invading their bucolic idyll. The feeling was mutual and, despite subsidies, few miners made the transfer to the newly built estates near the colliery. Most remained in their own pit communities, preferring to commute.

To pacify the locals there was to be no hint of dark satanic mills, or of pit wheels whirling on traditional headgears. Red brick towers would surround low level winding gear. Of traditional coalmining, above ground and to the outsider, there would be no sign. Stringent restrictions allowed mining to be carried out in the Barnsley seam only. Even here, according to the IMC Ltd. Colliery review, "An application to work reserves to the east of the river Derwent aroused significant local opposition". In that politically and environmentally sensitive area, the rural fear of the dreaded slagheap was always a problem, although confined to Gascoigne Wood, where all production was brought to the surface.

Mr. Siddall concluded his article by saying that the value of research had been recognised, and had been co-ordinated with plans for developing the industry along modern lines. The nature of coalmining in the 21st century would depend upon the research and development currently being undertaken.

In reality the future would be determined primarily, not as the result of the research and development programme, but by an event that had occurred in March 1979, just one month before Norman Siddall's article. This "deus ex machina" was a vote of confidence in parliament which, following the "Winter of Discontent", the Labour government lost. The result was a general election, with an ignominious loss of power for the Labour Party. "Coal for the Future" would prove to be the last throw of that administration's thinking on energy policy, while Siddall's article would prove to be the swansong of British coal's new era. Henceforward a cold wind would blow, eventually to sweep away the mining industry almost in its entirety.

In a report inaugurated by the incoming Conservative administration, the 1978 paper on energy policy was written off as "uncertainty combined with wishful thinking". Of the concepts proposed in that paper, none were to survive the Thatcher revolution.

Arthur Horner
First General Secretary
of the NUM

Philip Weekes OBE
NCB Board Member,
South Wales Area Director,
First Chairman of Tower Colliery.

William Abraham (MABON)
Leader of the Cambrian
Miners' Association.

Lord Robens
NCB Chairman
1960 - 71

# Plate 11  Some Personalities.

# Chapter 12

## ATE.

- *Firstly, the great and the gifted achieve the pinnacle of their success.*
- *Secondly, Ate, the goddess of mischief, induces them to commit the folly of exceeding what is reasonable in an orderly universe.*
- *Thirdly, the tragic hero thus commits the sin of Hubris, that arrogant self-confidence which, more than anything else, excites the hostility of the gods.*
- *Fourth and finally, Nemesis, the goddess of retribution, inevitably wreaks divine vengeance upon the moral transgressor.*

(The classical tragedies of ancient Greece).

The latter quarter of the twentieth century would witness a tragedy, in which the once great UK coalmining industry would be irrevocably struck down.

### POWER TO THE WORKERS!

The events of 1972-74 left the miners walking on air, conscious of a new place in the sun. Decades later, in a newspaper article written in 2004, Tyrone O'Sullivan of Tower Colliery would describe the situation thus:

"From 1972 until 1974, working people had never been so powerful. For the first time in 200 years working people forced governments to listen to them. It had not worked in the Merthyr rising, it had not worked in 1926 - but it did in 1972-74. The institute of Government feared the power of the unions - and the NUM was the vanguard of the unions, the most powerful union of all" (Pontypridd Observer 1 April 2004).

This was a heady change after all the years of decline. Not only had the miners demonstrated their industrial muscle, they had made clear to all the key role that King Coal still played in keeping the country going. The previous conventional wisdom had been turned on its head. Coal's reduction from the 90 per cent of national energy supply in 1950 to 40 per cent in 1974 had been regarded as indicative of a dying industry, one whose glass was already half empty. Events had demonstrated that 40 per cent of the total energy requirement of the country was still a critical mass. When this included 80 per cent of the indispensable production of electricity, then in fact mining's glass was well and truly half full. In addition, it seemed to many that the miners and their industry were a major line of defence against OPEC and the rapacious sheiks of the Middle East.

In 1974, the Lord Mayor's Show in London gave expression to the general euphoric atmosphere. The procession featured a float full of coal, piled as high as a double-decker bus and escorted by burly colliers.

Harold MacMillan's maiden speech in the House of Lords was also emotionally supportive. A Tory grandee, he was the former Conservative Prime Minister who had appointed Lord Robens. During service in the First World War he had commanded a platoon composed of Durham miners. Apparently they had earned his lasting respect. Now, he criticised his own party's government in their handling of the miners. As a "one nation Tory", he would express sadness at conflict with "the best men in the world". He warned that no government could afford to take on the Church, the Brigade of Guards, or the Miners.

### NEVER AGAIN!

#### Plans.

Lurking in the background, however, on the political right wing, a rather more jaundiced view was prevalent. The miners might maintain that the strikes had been non-political, only confined to wages and condi-

tions, and that Heath through misjudgement had defeated himself. This was not the way that these apocalyptic events were incorporated into Tory thinking, particularly into the thinking of their leadership. For
them the episode constituted a flagrant abuse of industrial power and a challenge to democracy itself. As
time went on, this bitter resentment throughout the Conservative Party was exacerbated by the firmer hold
established by the left within the NUM and by the aggressive pronouncements of Scargill on the class war
and the obscenity of capitalism.

Following the Tory defeat in 1974, Margaret Thatcher replaced Edward Heath as leader of the opposition Conservative Party in February 1975. One of her prime objectives was to ensure that the extra-parliamentary flouting of government decisions by the deployment of trade union muscle could never happen
again. Lord Carrington, Energy Secretary in the Heath government and hence in the thick of those earlier
battles, was invited to identify the key lessons which needed to be learned. A parallel enquiry, under the
rightwing MP Nicholas Ridley, took a hard look at the nationalised industries. The former report was
sober. Due to their command over sophisticated new technologies, there had been an irrevocable shift in
the balance of power to the shop floor. This applied particularly to the fuel and power sector. Here, groups
like the miners and the electricity workers now had ample ability to throttle the political and economic life
of the country.

The Ridley Report on the nationalised industries saw the world through quite different eyes. A new start
should be made. Henceforward, state corporations should be forced to make their own financial way in the
world. They should be subject to the rigours of the competitive market and cut free from treasury subsidies. Management should be better paid, more highly motivated and freed from ministerial involvement
in day-to-day affairs. Subsidies would only be approved if ministers could properly cost and justify them
to a sceptical treasury.

It was recognised that such a policy would inevitably lead to large-scale layoffs and the closure of
uneconomic plants. Opposition was expected and would have to be dealt with. Depending on the level of
trouble they might cause, industries were grouped within three classes.

- Water, sewage, electricity, gas and the health service were areas where the government might
  well stir up a hornets' nest.

- Coal, railways, docks and garbage collection fell into an intermediate category.

- Buses, air transport, education, steel and telecommunications would be the easiest to deal with.


Contrary to conventional wisdom, the Ridley team expressed confidence that victory in such a conflict
could be won. An appendix to the report made proposals as to how such a challenge could be met. To a
great extent, the strategy recommended was in fact the one actually employed when the day of conflict
finally dawned. As a summary of these recommendations:

a) Above-average wage claims could be paid to the "vulnerable" industries. If necessary, economic
   justification could be made by rigging the figures for return on capital.

b) The battle should be on ground chosen by the Tories in a field they thought they could win
   (Ridley at that time suggested railways, British Leyland, the civil service or steel).

c) Every precaution should be taken against a challenge in electricity or gas. However, since there
   was little prospect of redundancy in these industries, conflict here was unlikely.

d) The greatest deterrent to any strike would be financial hardship for the strikers. To this end,
   social security payments should be terminated for those on strike. The union itself would be
   compelled to finance them.

e) Create a large mobile squad of police, suitably equipped and organised to uphold the law against
   violent picketing.

f) The most probable battlefield would be the coal industry. In view of that, the following measures
   should be taken:

- Build up maximum coal stocks, particularly at the power stations.

- Make contingency plans for the import of coal.

- Encourage the recruitment of non-union lorry drivers by haulage companies, to help move coal where necessary. "Good non-union drivers" should be recruited to cross picket lines with police protection.

- Introduce dual coal/oil burning at all coal-fired power stations as quickly as possible.

## Cooperation.

While, within the inner circles of the Conservative party, options were evaluated and plans made, Derek Ezra, Robens' replacement as NCB Chairman, continued with his corporate policy. In particular, and in spite of the national strikes, the Board developed a close relationship with the union leaders, especially Joe Gormley, National President of the NUM. In a form of worker participation, regarded by Ezra as being in advance of current thinking, a Joint Policy Advisory Committee was set up. This was a vehicle for discussing all Board policies with the union leaders.

## VANGUARD NUM.

### Overconfidence.

While Joe Gormley continued to advocate moderation, within the ranks of the NUM overconfidence was the order of the day. Gormley felt compelled to warn in public that his lads had broad shoulders, and felt like champions. His art of the possible involved obtaining the best terms and conditions, subject to the constraints of reality. Under the subsequent leadership, awareness of these constraints was to be replaced by the vision of a socialist utopia, with the belief that this could be achieved being based upon past success. With an ability to see only their own point of view, the militants were blind to the fact that a significant section of the country was not with them in regarding union/NUM rule as being an ideal state of affairs. The scene was set for tragedy.

At the 1976 annual conference of the NUM, even the militant Lawrence Daly, national General Secretary, pleaded with delegates to tone down their increasingly bitter criticism of Labour ministers. The NUM, said Daly, "must avoid a situation where the people we shall be facing across the negotiating table will be the Michael Heseltines of the Conservative party". It was a situation that, in the then distant future, would become bitter reality. Before the next confrontation, due to health problems, Daly would leave the scene. Joe Gormley, his co-protagonist in 1972 and 1974, would continue on his diplomatic course.

In the view of the NUM left, no pit should be closed except on grounds of exhaustion. This flew in the face of NCB and government policy. The fact of the matter was that in virtually all cases of closure coal was still left in the ground. Subject in some cases to capital investment, this coal could also be worked. According to the NCB and government, the determining factor was not whether coal could still be worked but whether it could be worked economically. The miners became exposed to the charge that what they were proposing was nothing less than an alternative commercial philosophy, radical, selfish and self-centred. This view was expressed by The Times newspaper, in one of its leading articles during the 1984-85 strike:

"It symbolises the division between two philosophies - one that seeks to run pits, regardless of costs, as a kind of occupational therapy for miners; the other which wants to apply the usual commercial criteria to pits, as all other industrial enterprises do, particularly in the harshly competitive field of energy".

The writer, Raymond Williams, expressed an alternative view:

"The miners' strike (1984-85) is being expressed as the last kick of an old order. Properly understood, it is one of the first steps towards a new order. This is especially the case in the emphasis they have put on protecting their communities. Here is another keyword, which needs to be understood. What the miners, like most of us, mean by their communities is the places where they have lived and want to go on living, where generations not only of economic but of social effort and human care have been invested and which new generations will inherit. Without that kind of strong, whole attachment, there can be no meaningful community".

On 10 December 1978, Peter Evans, Chairman of Deep Duffryn lodge, put it more succinctly at a public meeting against the proposed closure of his pit, "We've taken a hundred years to build these communities, you can't kill them overnight".

## Ourselves Alone.

Previous miners' leaders, from such militants as Arthur James Cook, who lead the disastrous national strike of 1926, to Arthur Horner and Will Paynter, both members of the Communist Party, had never sought to promote their cause by means of a blind, unwavering defiance of the rest of society. The left wing of the NUM, however, could not forget the "betrayal" as they saw it by the Trade Union Congress in their quick settlement of the 1926 general strike, which had been initiated in support of the miners. The negotiations associated with the 1972-74 strikes were carried out independent of the TUC. This tendency to keep the established mandarins of the trade union movement at a distance, if not indeed to treat them with disdain, would not assist the miners later, when they needed all the help they could get. There were additional dangers, potentially fatal, in this new "in your face" stance of the miners' leadership. Unity and public opinion, major strengths of the miners in the 1972 and 1974 conflicts, were now subject to a question mark, as Gormley's style of the art of the possible was abandoned for more ambitious targets.

The previous overwhelming public support, engendered by modest wages, tough working conditions and a desire to support British miners as opposed to Arab sheiks, could no longer be taken for granted. This was because the issue now at stake was no longer just wages and conditions but the demand that jobs be maintained and pits be kept open, in the face of NCB opinion that it was uneconomical to do so.

To convince the country as a whole that there were valid reasons to maintain a virile domestic coal industry, one that had already shown its commitment to modernisation and productivity, required a skilled public relations campaign. The continued existence of such an industry would ensure the prosperity of long-established communities and would provide a buffer against the vagaries of oil pricing, with its sensitivity to global demand, war and Middle Eastern politics. The emotional commitment of the Japanese to their rice farmers, or the Germans to their own coalminers is supported by such rationale. The German attachment to their "kumpels" (mates) would need more than the attraction of cost-saving measures, possibly short-term anyway, to break. However, the term "spin doctor " was not yet in general circulation and certainly enjoyed little credence with the NUM leadership, whose hot-eyed socialist rhetoric could only have a jarring effect upon the traditionally middle-of-the-road British body politic.

Ate continued her work as, the stance of his National President notwithstanding, President of the Yorkshire miners, Arthur Scargill, denounced the "social contract" (cooperation and consultation between union leaders and government, in association with wage restraint) as a "social con trick" and derided "maximum restraint". The Labour government felt itself forced to accept such concepts when faced with continuing economic weakness and the oil price-induced world recession. Also demanded by Scargill was a large wage increase for face-workers. Inescapably, the miners were becoming identified as the shock troops of the trade union movement and the target for an ultimate showdown.

## REALITY.
### Demand Down -.

As the 1970's advanced, the shortcomings of the 1974 Plan for Coal became apparent. The vast increase in UK energy demand as predicted simply did not materialise. Britain's total energy requirements, which were "bound to increase", according to the earlier plan, actually dropped by nearly 10 per cent in three years. The fact was that the massive increase in oil prices had triggered off a worldwide recession, reducing demand for energy overall. In addition, the new cost awareness regarding energy matters was resulting in extensive energy saving. This showed itself in such things as improved insulation for buildings and energy-saving schemes for industry. The forecasts were sharply pruned. The proportion of the nation's energy supplied by coal had indeed increased slightly since 1974, but an increase in sales was quite another matter. Although the undermining of coal by oil had been halted, both of these fuels now found total consumption declining.

Neither the "Plan for Coal" nor the follow up "Coal for the Future" involved any significant positive step to increase the UK market for coal. Indeed, the latter paper talked about increasing the contribution of nuclear power. There could have been a halt on the construction of nuclear power stations (thereby saving the country much-needed capital). The railway system could also have been electrified. This would have involved capital expenditure but saved significant imports of oil and replaced them with "coal by wire", since electricity generation was predominantly coal-fired. No such measures were taken; instead the glowing future foreseen for coal had been predicated upon the blind faith that overall energy demand was bound to increase.

## -And Costs Up.

What did increase was the cost of indigenous coal. Not only had the wage bill gone up enormously but the planned improvement in productivity failed to materialise. In addition, since the considerable capital investment involved in the Plan for Coal could not be financed from the NCB's own resources, money had to be borrowed. This resulted in a corresponding level of interest charges having to be paid, supported now by a reduced level of sales. The charges were distributed throughout the industry and proved to be another millstone around the neck of those pits still struggling financially, including the South Wales coalfield.

## The Oil Companies Move In.

The Plan for Coal assumed that the current demand for coking coal would be maintained. Indeed, it stated that the British steel industry would take every ton that could be produced. In practice, the British steel industry was fighting for its life against stiff foreign competition in a worldwide recession. This particular market for coal had been slashed by more than half. Since South Wales was by far the biggest producer of coking coal in the UK, this coalfield was particularly hard hit. The following table takes the year 1980 as an example:

| Markets | Plan for Coal. (Estimate for 1980) (M tonnes) | Actual 1979-80 (M tonnes) | Actual 1980-81 (M tonnes) |
|---|---|---|---|
| Power stations: | 83 | 85 | 83 |
| Coke ovens: | 22 | 12 | 9 |
| Other inland: | 25 | 25 | 21 |
| Exports: | 5 | 3 | 5 |
| TOTAL NCB SALES: | 135 | 125 | 118 |

In addition to less steel being produced, more and more coking coal would be imported, not only because it was cheaper but also its lower sulphur content was better suited for the production of high-specification steel.

This was another aspect that had not been foreseen. Events would show that the massive oil price rises had been a double-edged sword as far as indigenous mining were concerned. They had indeed held out the prospect of a new lease of life for the coalmining industry. Such a prospect was, however, not confined to UK coal alone. The 1970's would see dramatic changes to the international trade in coal, a low cost high volume commodity. The enormous expansion of steel production in Japan and around the Pacific Rim encouraged the exploration of new coking coal deposits in Australia. It also transformed South Africa into a major exporter. This coal was increasingly mined in large opencast sites and was characterised by high quality and low price. Surpluses were offered for sale in Europe, on terms difficult to refuse. Following the trend in the steel and foundry industries, electricity generation was also looking increasingly towards the international coal market. Their requirement was for steam coal, which is purely for the generation of heat. This is cheaper than the high specification coals for coke production.

International oil corporations saw the opportunities and now became energy companies, diversifying into coal production. New, enormous, export-orientated mines (mostly opencast) were opened up in the USA, Australia, South Africa and Columbia. Subsequently these were followed by Venezuela and Indonesia. One commentator, Malcolm Edwards, was jaundiced in his appreciation of this development. In his view, the oil companies had:

"moved into coal just as robustly as they had moved into heavy chemicals in the 1960's and with even more disastrous results —— too large, too fast, too grand to listen, far too optimistic about the response of the market. All these overnight cuckoos crowded into a very small nest".


## The Plan for Coal Revised.

Against this market background, not only had NCB productivity failed to increase but also "old and inefficient capacity" had not been phased out at the rate of 3-4 Mt per annum as envisaged. As a result of all these developments, the "Plan for Coal" and its revisions became to be regarded as passé by both the Government and the NCB (although not by the NUM, whose bible it was to remain).

Notwithstanding the above, the general strategic thrust of the Plan for Coal still applied, namely:

- Reduce dependence of the economy on oil.

- Continue exploration and increase capacity at existing and new mines, so as to replace the capacity at older, less productive pits.

- Satisfy appropriate financial tests, so as to justify investment in such new or replacement capacity.

- Increase the output of lower cost coals (including opencast).

- Increase productivity, as an absolute priority.

- Emphasis to be put upon retreat mining subject to the right geological conditions, in particular roadway stability over a reasonable period of time.


## THE BENN ERA.

### The Man -.

Since 1975, the Secretary of State for Energy had been Anthony Wedgwood Benn (latterly Tony Benn), doyen of the Labour Party's left wing and one of their leading front men. Pressure by industry and the city on the Prime Minister, Harold Wilson, to remove him as Secretary of State for Industry had resulted in his demotion to the Energy Portfolio. Denis Healey, right wing Chancellor of the Exchequer, was locked in combat with Benn for party leadership. As political infighting between left and right for the soul of the party raged, knives came out and the clash of steel echoed through the corridors of power. It was Healey who would eventually triumph. Not one to mince his words, he would associate Benn with "feudal socialism" as described by Marx and Engels in the Communist Manifesto of 1848:

"always ludicrous in its effect, through total incapacity to comprehend the march of modern history". Since Benn was the man chosen to head the government's most technologically orientated departments, being in turn Postmaster General, Minister for Technology, Secretary of State for Industry and then Secretary of State for Energy, the charge of "total incapacity to comprehend the march of modern history" was a bizarre verdict indeed.

No one doubted the sincerity with which Benn advocated workers' rights and the cause of socialism. His support for workers' control and the avoidance of redundancy was epitomised by his positive approach to the sit-in at Upper Clyde Shipbuilders. There were, however, many in the country, including from among the ranks of his own party, who questioned the practicality of his approach. His published diary quotes his Russian interpreter on 5 September 1960 as telling him, "You are an idealist underestimating the forces against you and you will be due for disappointments".

## - And His Times.

Since his period as Minister of Technology in the first Harold Wilson Government, information acquired by Benn, together with the exposure of misinformation, would cause him to reconsider his earlier positive view on nuclear power and the consequent run-down of the coalmining industry. The previous protestations of Lord Robens, NCB Chairman and one-time Labour minister, had not had such an effect. On inheriting a Peerage Benn automatically became disqualified to represent his constituency and therefore lost his seat in Bristol. Following a determined fight to renounce the peerage he was then able to be elected once more as MP, this time for Chesterfield, a mining constituency. Later he would become an honorary member of the NUM, with membership number 001. He would continue his pro-miners stance until the end of his political career.

Benn's conversion to coal's cause notwithstanding, being more philosopher than technocrat, there was still no attempt by his Department of Energy to obtain realistic figures concerning the actual cost of nuclear power. This was an ongoing feature of the department, both before and after Benn's tenure, and it would be criticised by the Parliamentary Energy Committee in 1990.

On 7 December 1977 Benn addressed the NUM conference at the Royal Hotel in Harrogate. The conference, he said, was historic. It would pioneer the future of nationalisation and the mining industry. There were three possible ways forward:

i)  Meaningless consultation, which didn't involve any serious transfer of power. This was just window dressing and should not be accepted.

ii) Instead of fighting for socialism, just waiting passively until it was provided.

iii) Benn's preferred approach, which was a step-by-step transition to full workers control.

Audience response was muted. For the right wing he had gone too far while the left were angry that he had intervened in the ballot on productivity schemes (he had spoken in favour).

On 27 April 1978, according to his diaries, Benn informed Mick McGahey, President of the Scottish NUM and Deputy National President, that he would inform the Coal Board they could not close pits without the miners' consent. He would give instructions that closures must be agreed with the NUM. If the Board felt that they had a case then they would have to satisfy the union. "I am determined to leave a structure like this behind me to ensure that they can't start a closure programme after I have left without reopening the whole matter".

By 1978, matters were coming to a head for the coalmining industry. There was an element of Mr. Macawber about the government's approach. Unwilling either to adopt the focused and ruthless approach of their successors or the open policy of subsidies as practiced in Germany, they seemed to rely on something turning up. This something was a massive increase in energy demand, which never materialised. Benn's inclination was for subsidies, which was not something that his colleagues in government, least of all Chancellor Healey, were prepared to countenance.

## Financial Black Hole.

On 18 August 1978, a letter was sent from Sir Derek Ezra, NCB Chairman, to Secretary of State Benn. It referred to the "serious financial problems" with which the Board were faced, in particular "the heavily losing coalfields which are imposing an increasingly heavy burden on the profitable central coalfields". With regard to the former coalfields, inward capital investment as foreseen by the Plan for Coal was compounded by heavy losses on the revenue account. This resulted in a cash flow that was horrendously negative. The letter goes on:

"While the problems of Scotland are serious, those of South Wales are even more so and have led to losses of frightening proportions which, unless further drastic action is taken, will continue to escalate — — Faced with a possible cash requirement this year of £80 M (anticipated losses plus investment in South Wales alone), which the Board cannot afford to fund, the Area Director has been obliged to re-examine investment plans, in particular the major investment at Margam, and the revenue resources available for heavily losing collieries". The Board saw only two alternatives, of which the first was rejected:

    i)  Widespread closures and a cut-back on investment, which in view of the special qualities of South Wales coals (particularly anthracite and coking) can only lead to significant increases in imports.

    ii)  A package of measures based on government support over a five-year period. During this time a combination of closure of high cost capacity, coupled with mergers and an agreed investment programme (on the Scottish model) would bring the Area into a healthier position.

Tony Benn replied, recognising the very serious nature of the problem and calling for a meeting between the Department of Energy and the Coal Board to discuss the situation.

On 20 September 1978, the meeting was held at Thames House South. Area Director Phillip Weekes highlighted in particular the position of Abernant and Mardy. Each of these was losing over £3 M annually. If these pits were closed, large-scale redundancies would be an inevitable consequence. Strenuous resistance was therefore to be expected. Sir Derek Ezra was unable to put a figure on the financial requirements of the coalfield over the next five years, but deep mines were currently operating at an annual loss of £40 M while the profit resulting from open cast was down to £2 M.

Tony Benn indicated that the government wanted this problem approached on a tripartite basis (government, management, unions). He would discuss the problem with the South Wales NUM during the following week. Sir Derek Ezra repeated his previous suggestion that the NUM be asked as to whether they wished to have Area Director Weekes present at the meeting (The Area Director was the one who managed the coalfield and who had immediate responsibility for policy. It is perhaps significant, and indicative of the relationship with the unions as pursued by the government and Benn in particular, that the suggestion had to be made by Ezra, and then repeated by him.).

Mr. Benn urged Sir Derek to draw public attention to the subsidies received by the German coking industry and their coal industry in general. If this could become a major public issue it would assist his discussions in Whitehall. The fact that this was raised as an issue is also an indication of the way Benn's mind was working.

In November 1978 the Coal Industry Tripartite Group (Sub-Committee on the South Wales Coalfield), was inaugurated by the Department of Energy under Secretary of State Tony Benn. This was a joint effort, by management, unions and the government, to address the problems of the industry in South Wales.

In 1979, the outbreak of the Iran/Iraq war resulted in a further oil price increase of 250 per cent (a tenfold rise in a decade). This underpinned the pro-coal attitude of the government and the confidence of the NCB. However, as far as South Wales was concerned, there was still a rub. Coal had to remain competitive, albeit now at a higher level of price. The basic problem in this coalfield was that cost of production had to be reduced at a rate far exceeding that in any other part of the United Kingdom. A Coal Board note of the time states:

"The inherent characteristics of the coalfield and in particular its difficult geology, together with the age of the workings and the exhaustion of the best seams, have to a large extent determined the high cost structure of the South Wales Area".

On 7 March 1979, a meeting was held at the Department of Industry between the following:

- Coal Board Chairman, Derek Ezra.
- Chairman of British Steel, Charles Villiers.
- Secretary of State for Industry, Eric Varley.
- Energy Secretary, Tony Benn.
- Minister for Mines, Alex Eadie.

On the grounds that the NCB could not provide coking coal of an adequate quality, Villiers wanted to sign long-term contracts on behalf of British Steel for such coal to be imported from Australia. Tony Benn regarded this as meaning 10,000 mining redundancies in South Wales, plus massive financial losses for the NCB. Varley asked Villiers to reconsider, who responded that that would be unbusinesslike and would constitute political interference. Varley's request was totally ignored and the import programme gathered momentum. Benn would lament to his diary how weak he felt himself to be before such "public sector barons".

On 30 March 1979 the Tripartite Group, set up by Benn in the previous November, issued their report. Its terms of reference had been:

i)   To ensure exploration and exploitation of coal for the benefit of the nation.

ii)  To ensure the utilisation of mining skills to the maximum extent and the maintenance of job opportunities.

iii) To put the coalfield on a financially viable footing.

The basic problem, which the report did not solve, was the dichotomy between the last objective and the other two. Similar to the 1978 Government Paper "Coal for the Future", also under the aegis of Tony Benn, it was basically pro coal and was full of good intentions. Similar to "Coal for the Future" it was more general than specific. Noticeable was the lack of focus, and specifics as to precisely how the financial viability, to which the report referred, was going to be achieved.

The report stated;

"To achieve progressive financial viability within a period of 5 years, i.e. by 1983/84 —— The Sub-committee sees 3 main areas for decision and action if financial viability is to be achieved:

1.1) Programme of investment.

1.2) Programme to deal with losses on current operations.

1.3) A willingness by the Government to provide a measure of financial support to help sustain the coalfield in the period during which financial viability is to be achieved.

Their recommendations were:

2.1) Further financial help for the coalfield.

2.2) Continued investment and financial help on a sliding scale over a five-year period.

2.3) The phasing-out of some older capacity.

2.4) Replace the ageing ovens at the Aberaman phurnacite plant with the new, cleaner ANCIT process.

Their summary of the situation over the previous twelve months was:

3.1) Both output and productivity had increased by 9 per cent. However, financial results had fallen back due to deterioration in performance at pits that were normally the backbone of the coalfield, i.e., Oakdale, Blaenant, Taff ) Instead of lifting from stocks as planned, so as to assist cash flow, the stocking of coal had recommenced. This was an immense financial burden.

3.2) The world recession had resulted by the end of 1979 in a reduced demand for steel, plus a reduction in world coal prices and a strengthening in the value of the pound sterling.Merthyr, and Trelewis.

3.3) In October 1979, British Steel announced their intention to import cheaper foreign coal at the expense of South Wales coal. This was followed by their decision to reduce capacity in South Wales by 50 per cent. It was only an NCB grant of £22 M that maintained their supplies into Llanwern Steelworks, plus some additional supplies for Shotten and Scunthorpe. This would protect a market of 1.2 Mt until the end of 1980. In 1979-80, the same sector took 1.75 Mt.

Prospects for the immediate future were viewed as follows:

4.1) Assisted by the oil price rises, the demand of the Central Electricity Generating Board (CEGB) had increased by 900,000 tonnes and this was expected to hold good, provided prices did not rise above inflation.

4.2) Subject to price, South Wales sales of 9 Mt were projected for 1980-81, with an additional 0.5 Mt going into stocks (in 1979-80, sales had totalled 10 Mt, including 400,000t being lifted from stocks).

The survival of the coalfield depended on:

5.1) Containing production costs, especially for power station coal, so as to retain an important market worth 3.5 Mt per annum.

5.2) Continued financial support, so as to win back British Steel Corporation (BSC) contracts.

5.3) A reduction in the crippling stock levels, currently 5 Mt in South Wales.

It was emphasised that the National Board of the NCB had not asked its South Wales management to make profits in the next few years, or even to break even. The objective was to reduce losses to a level that could be carried by other coalfields. In the current financial year this meant reducing costs so that losses for deep mines would be about equivalent to those of 1978-79 (approx. £19 M).

## DIFFICULT CUSTOMERS.

### Squaring the Circle.

The beginning of the 1980's was to prove devastating for South Wales. As we have seen, official thinking, even if unpublicised, was that South Wales was condemned anyway, by its difficult geology, to a role of permanent decline. Even the optimistic Plan for Coal in the wake of the 1974 strike, and the sympathetic government paper in 1978 "Coal for the Future", talked about the future of the industry as being in new pits with good seams and capital intensive production. The highest levels of the Coal Board saw the future as belonging to large new pits, working seams that were rich and largely undisturbed. Experience since nationalisation had taught that the tortured geology in South Wales allowed only limited, niche opportunities. "Super pits", à la NCB strategy, were out of the question. South Wales still had many relatively small and very high cost mines operating. According to current philosophy, these had to be replaced with new or reconstructed capacity. This concept, however, had had a questionable history in South Wales. The Plan for Coal referred to the necessity of closing down between 3 and 4 Mt of uneconomic capacity per annum to provide opportunity for the new, more efficient capacity being created by the massive investments. Paragraph 16 said:

"(The industry) will keep production costs —— down to a minimum and so preserve the competitive margin essential to sustain the greater demand for coal that can now be envisaged". In Scotland, and first and foremost in Wales, such control of production costs was not happening.

## Union Concern.

The NUM were astute enough to sense the gist of what conclusions the NCB were drawing from all of this. During the late 1970's, visits by the local NUM to, and contact with, Notts and Yorkshire had convinced them that their area was being written off. The disproportion in capital investment was too obvious to be overlooked and the delegates felt that their coalfield was being short changed. Creeping uncertainty was setting in. Their fears were well founded, as the trend in the following table shows:

| Year | 1974 (prior to strike) | 1978 | 1984 (prior to strike) |
|---|---|---|---|
| No. of Welsh miners. | 31,000 | 27,384 | 22,071 |
| S. Wales output (tonnes per annum) | 8,632,000 | 7,624,876 | 6,638,000 |

## Steel.

The euphoria of the mid-1970's was rapidly slipping away. A major factor in the new malaise was that a major local market was in the process of turning its back. Proximity to large reserves of prime coking coal was one reason for the development of a steel industry in South Wales. Indeed, this region has by far the largest UK reserves of such coal. This fact was a major justification for the considerable investment in the coalfield following nationalisation. It also made this coalfield particularly sensitive to the steel industry's fortunes. About one-third of coalfield output was in the form of coking coal, to smelt iron ore in the blast furnaces. Now the steel industry was itself declining.

The worldwide reduction in economic activity following the oil price increases affected large-scale consumers of steel such as construction, plus the manufacture of cars and machinery. In addition to this, much of the money that had flowed to the oil states had been reinvested by them in new steel industries, primarily in developing countries. These, being brand new and equipped with the latest technology, posed formidable competition for the reduced markets remaining.

## Electricity Generation.

At this time the relationship between the two biggest state-owned industries, NCB and Central Electricity Generating Board (CEGB) was also gradually being transformed into one that was more antagonistic. A constant underlying theme of CEGB policy, amounting almost to an obsession, was that they should not be in the pocket of any single large supplier. The CEGB did not exist just for the purpose of burning British coal. More pressure was being put on the NCB to control both quality and price. A series of "Joint Understandings" governed coal supply to the CEGB. Although non-contractual, these formed a basis for joint intent as far as pricing and operations were concerned.

In 1979, the Joint Understanding required the NCB to "use their best endeavours to supply 75 Mt per year of suitable coal". The CEGB also identified three major management changes that they considered the NCB should undertake:

i) Improve the quality and consistency of coal supplied.

ii) Reduce costs and pass on the reduction to coal users.

iii) Introduce a rational pricing policy for coal sold for electricity generation.

The NCB failed to reduce its costs and prices, resulting in tension between the two industries.

In October 1979, the facts on the ground were rubbed in when the largest coal rains ever seen in South Wales began to run - taking American or Australian imported coal from Cardiff or Newport docks to Didcot power station in Oxfordshire. This lies adjacent to the South Wales-London main line. Each train comprised 45 automatic-discharge wagons with a total payload of 1,350 tonnes. This new phenomenon, coal being imported into South Wales to be sent to England, must have had David Davies of Llandinam, founder of the Ocean Coal Company, spinning in his grave. The limited success of the previous year, where between 1977-78 exports from South Wales ports had increased from 807,000 tonnes to 969,000 tonnes, had proven to be no more than a flash in the pan.

## BROTHERLY DISCORD.

### Productivity Agreements.

Meanwhile, sterling remained weak and the national economy continued to deteriorate, partly as a result of the oil price increases.

By 1976, inflation had reached 28 per cent. Sterling was in crisis. Chancellor of the Exchequer, Dennis Healey, regarded himself as being forced to accept a credit from the International Monetary Fund to the tune of three billion pounds sterling. The price was an introduction of austerity measures, including major cuts in public expenditure. This stabilised the pound, but people continued to demand more than the country could afford. Under the tight incomes' policy adopted by the 1974-79 Labour government, almost the only officially accepted way for a group of workers to win extra pay awards was by means of "productivity agreements".

In 1978, the NUM succumbed to the Siren voices from within their own ranks and accepted the concept of local productivity bonuses. Joe Gormley, their National President, had for years been advocating them as a means of securing the future of the industry. However, as the miners of South Wales fought to preserve their coalfield, the key question would be - to what extent could they now count on the support of their colleagues in the central, profitable coalfields?

As foreseen by some at the time, in particular by the South Wales Area of the NUM, this decision was to undermine national unity, the achievement of which was one of the reasons for their resounding victories in 1972 and 1974. Such unity had been one of the prime objectives of the earlier miners' leaders and had never been realised in their day. A major basis for such unity had been the national wage agreements of 1956 and, in particular, 1966.

Traditionally, coalface wages had been calculated on a piece-work basis. The pay for particular tasks and "stints" was the subject of intense local bargaining. Due largely to the range of geological conditions, there was a corresponding variation in the amount of effort required for a given level of production. Consequently, such rates were anything but standard. This was a key factor in preserving the regional autonomy that characterised the old pre-war Miners Federation. Subsequent to nationalisation, it was carried over into the quasi-independent area rulebooks.

The advent of widespread mechanisation, with the resulting changes in working practices, resulted in the National Power Loading Agreement of 1966. This virtually eliminated piece-work and for fully mechanised, that is "power loaded" coalfaces, gave a standard wage structure throughout the industry (the relatively few conventional, hand cut faces remained on piece-work rates). With mineworkers in Britain now on the same pay rate, this resulted in a unity and common interest that had never previously been enjoyed. However, since the concept was basically an "averaging out" across the whole country, there was some disquiet on the part of those men who would now have to accept smaller pay increases, thus enabling their colleagues in less productive areas to catch up. Particularly in the high-profit areas like Nottinghamshire, a demand arose for the reintroduction of incentive payments. The more militant members of the NUM executive saw the dangers and fought hard to discourage this divisive move.

## Ballot Overturned!

In 1977, in a nationwide pithead ballot, there had been a majority of 110,634 to 87,901 against any reintroduction of incentive payments. This result notwithstanding, those who saw potential earnings slipping away were not prepared to accept defeat. A significant number of men, particularly in Nottinghamshire, indicated that for them the choice was money first and foremost, with unity a long way behind. Joe Gormley lent his support.

In January 1978 there was a series of local insurrections and area votes against the result of the national ballot. In the face of bitter opposition from the South Wales Area of the NUM, the result of the national ballot was overturned by the union executive. The NCB was happy to encourage this movement as a means of increasing productivity in the industry. They canvassed heavily on the issue while "Coal News" sang its praises. As a background to the debate it should be understood that although the pick, shovel and pit pony were no longer tools of the trade, British mining still remained a labour-intensive industry. Great progress had been made and between 1947 and 1973 output per man-year had increased from 269 to 464 tonnes. Now, after the miners' strikes and the 1974 Plan for Coal, productivity had more or less stuck fast for a decade. In spite of considerable investment, far from increasing at 4 per cent per annum, regarded as essential by the Plan for Coal, between 1974 and 1978 productivity actually decreased, from 2.3 to 2.2 tonnes per man shift. Only in 1982/83, after the reintroduction of productivity payments, did output per man-year rise above 500 tonnes.

This flouting of ballot results and conference decisions by the National Executive Committee incensed the militants. It is interesting to note that those who had done their best to overturn the result of the 1977 national ballot on productivity payments (namely Nottinghamshire) were the same men who, in the course of the 1984 national strike, would complain the loudest about the absence of such a ballot on that occasion. This was something not lost on the men of South Wales and the other, lower productivity coalfields.

In South Wales the union attempted to salvage something from the wreckage and introduce an area productivity scheme. The Board would have none of it. Phil Weekes, the Area Director, informed the union that he had orders from the National Board that on no account could he make an agreement on an area basis. The union officials left the meeting in disgust, but only productivity deals on a pit basis could be negotiated.

## "Damn Traitors!".

Nottinghamshire had lived up to its reputation for back-stabbing. It had always been the object of suspicion and envy by the rest of the coal industry. This most productive British coalfield lacked an all-pervading mining culture. Traditionally, alternative jobs had been available. In South Wales there never had been other jobs available, on anything like the required scale. After the great six-month miners' lockout, which followed on the short-lived General Strike of 1926, the Notts men, under the leadership of George Spencer MP, negotiated their own return to work. A.J. Cook, miners' leader at the time, addressed a Federation conference in October 1926:

"I hope this conference will treat Mr. Spencer as they would a blackleg. Mr. Spencer is a blackleg of the worst order. A conscious blackleg. I want to say here that Notts has been more responsible for the present position we are in —— than any other district —— While we are fighting, Mr. Spencer is prepared to accept a reduction and advocated a district agreement in his own district".

George Spencer was promptly expelled from the Miners Federation of Great Britain, to form one month later, a "non-political union" - the Nottingham and District Miners Industrial Union. Encouraged by the owners, who often victimised activists in the Miners Federations, this remained a rival to the MFGB until just before the Second World War. Nottingham's reputation as potential betrayers dates from this experience. For the Notts men, with their rich, profitable pits and a future that seemed assured, high productivity bonuses seemed set to guarantee a good standard of living for the long term. The area therefore fell back on its tradition of hard-headedly putting its own interests first. Men now strove to earn the new and enticing bonuses available with a high production of coal.

# THE WINTER OF DISCONTENT.

Meanwhile, in the country as a whole, economic turmoil continued. Chancellor of the Exchequer, Denis Healey, felt himself obliged to comply with IMF prompting. Later, in House of Lords retirement, he would say that the belt-tightening advice he received at this time was exaggerated, and that in retrospect the consequent provocation of the working population had been unnecessary. Be that as it may, an attempt by the government of James Callaghan to make the unions a partner in solving the country's economic problems failed, ship-wrecked by the inability of senior trade union leaders to impose discipline on all of their members. The situation assumed every appearance of spiralling out of control and culminated in a series of simultaneous strike actions, the so-called "winter of discontent". This at the time seemed to atrophy the normal functioning of British society.

In July 1978, Prime Minister Callaghan proclaimed a 5 per cent limit on pay rises over the next twelve months, misjudging the groundswell of opposition building up on the shop floor. It triggered off a lem-ming-like rush on the part of the trade unions. Local activists, whose roles had been severely curtailed by three years of income policies agreed to by their national leaders, now rebelled. Those same national leaders proved unable, or politically unwilling, to hold them back. The consequent mass suicide during the following winter terminated the post-war era of consensus, and led to the elimination of trade unions as a force to be reckoned with in British politics. One after the other and night after night a series of left-wing trade unionists on the picket lines, often bearded, in duffle coats and huddled around braziers, would explain to the media the anomalies that the incomes' policy was responsible for, how much they hated industrial action and how it had been a last resort. However, now they had been forced to take this course they were going to see it through.

Reporting of the general chaos suffered when, before Christmas, action by the Association of Broad-casting Staffs blacked out BBC television. In January there were four 1-day strikes by train drivers. These coincided with severe blizzards, resulting in chaotic travelling conditions. Between February and April, clerical and executive civil servants carried out widespread action, affecting even the staff at number 10 Downing Street. The car industry went on strike and won 17 per cent. The fire brigade followed with 22 per cent, bakers with 14 per cent, heating technicians with 30 per cent and lorry drivers 22 per cent. Not to be outdone, and following a series of sporadic local stoppages, the public service employees declared a 24-hour general strike. Schools were closed and rubbish remained uncollected. In Liverpool the dead remained unburied because the gravediggers went on strike. They settled in February 1979 with a pay rise of 9 per cent.

In March 1979, as a result of such industrial mayhem, the government lost a vote of confidence in parliament. In the subsequent general election the Conservatives under Margaret Thatcher were returned to power. The Winter of Discontent had resulted in trade unionism being branded with the mark of Cain in the public eye. The policies, introduced by Labour in 1945 and sustained by subsequent Conservative governments, had thus come to a messy end. The death knell was sounded for old-style trade unionism and state intervention to prevent unemployment, while the very ethos of a welfare state was left hanging by a thread. Labour had always been regarded as the party of the trade unions. Consequently, as a direct result of the industrial unrest above, the party was dispatched into a wilderness of irrelevance and internal strife. It would take eighteen years before they finally emerged. When they did eventually emerge, they were to prove as disenchanted with the concept of trade union influence on government as their immediate pred-ecessors had been.

Plate 12  Nantgarw Reconstruction in 1951. The Colliery is on the Left and Coke Ovens on Right. To Service such Capital Expenditure Other Mines were Sacrificed.

Plate 13  Mardy Underground. Red Horizon Roadway in 1951. Trains of Mine Cars are Hauled by Diesel Locomotives. (In Nantgarw the Locomotives were Battery Powered).

# Chapter 13

## DEUS EX MACHINA - BUT DELAYED

*Deus ex machina (A god from the machine).*
*If the plot becomes so complicated that it appears incapable of resolution,*
*the playwright simply summons up intervention in the form of a divinity,*
*which appears suddenly on stage.*
(The drama of ancient Greece).

### THE IRON LADY.

In mid-1979 the Conservatives under Margaret Thatcher replaced Labour. By the time she came to power the battle lines had already been drawn. The "tea and sandwiches at no.10" scenario, which had become a standard means of intercourse between senior trade union leaders and British prime ministers (including the Conservative Ted Heath) now became anathema. The new Prime Minister saw trade union power as being the single most important reason for Britain's post-war economic decline. She had made no secret of her views, and of her conviction that the macro economic aims of trade union leaders were not only fundamentally wrong but also were far in excess of their station in society. She was not alone in this. In 1969, the government of Harold Wilson was forced to think again when they attempted to introduce legal controls upon the application of trade union power. Subsequently, Edward Heath introduced a new legal framework and pay controls, only, as we have seen, to go down to defeat in 1974 in an election fought largely on the issue "Who's running the country?"

Thatcher was capable of U-turns, but only for short-term tactical reasons. While still in opposition she was quoted as saying that people who believed in consensus were, "quislings and traitors". Her way of constructing a government was expressed in typical frankness to The Observer. It was:

"to have in it only the people who want to go in the direction in which the Prime Minister wishes to go —— It must be a conviction government. As Prime Minister I could not waste time having internal arguments". In Thatcher's view, and that of her advisors, the road taken in 1945 had led inexorably to the ongoing malaise of old industries, sluggish growth, the candle-lit winter of 1973-74, and the IMF loan of 1976. It had culminated in the "Grand Finale" of institutionalised proletarianism, the "Winter of Discontent". Corelli Barnett expressed this right-wing radical view of the world in his book The Audit of War. The post-war welfare state, so the argument went, had produced a "segregated, sub-literate, unskilled, unhealthy and institutionalised proletariat, hanging on the nipple of state materialism".

This was a sea change in mainstream thinking, for, ever since the great depression of the 1930's, socially conscious economic concepts had dominated the thinking of democratic governments in Europe, both of the right and of the left. With Alan Walters as economic advisor, who in turn was influenced by the "guru of monetarism", Professor Milton Friedman of Chicago University, this custom and practice was now to be rejected by Thatcher. Henceforward, it was to be the rough-and-tumble of a free market that was to set the tone. The nation's economic health was going to be restored by a stringent dose of such policies, including privatisation of the nationalised industries. However, this would not be just a return to the discredited, class- and confrontation-ridden past. This new designer version of capitalism would not be confined to an aristocratic elite. Its saving grace would be that everyone could and should participate. She would later write:

"Britain under my leadership was the first country to reverse the onward march of socialism. By the time I left office, the state-owned sector of industry had been reduced by some 60 per cent. Around one in four of the population owned shares. Over six hundred thousand jobs had passed from the public to the private sector. It constituted the greatest shift of ownership and power away from the state to individuals and their families in any country outside the former communist block".

The alternative view of the world was that this was just another way of proposing, "dog eat dog" and that a divided society would be the result. In any event, the concomitant effect of such a philosophy was a decline in influence of the trade unions and the poor, plus other left wing or vulnerable interest groups. These were the very people to whom British politicians had been paying increasing attention since the Second World War.

In April 1978, Thatcher told the Bow Group "Some fear flying pickets more than they fear the law". In her eyes, the thugs and bullyboys on the picket line were the very antithesis of "freedom", which was the right of an individual to configure his or her existence as they wished and in accordance with their abilities. In her view, the coalmining industry had come to symbolise everything that was wrong with Britain, being over-unionised, protected and monopolistic.

In 1979, her convincing electoral victory had given her a mandate to right what was in Thatcher's view a fundamental distortion of economic life and to eliminate what she had referred to as, "the enemy within". Such an approach from "the Iron Lady", cold war warrior, put her on a collision course with an NUM leadership even more radical than the team that defeated the previous Conservative government in 1974. They too were determined to fight for "freedom", the freedom to have a job and the freedom to continue living in one's own home community while enjoying a good standard of living. In South Wales, when she came to power, under the slogan "Close a pit and kill a community", there was an ongoing campaign to save Deep Duffryn Pit in Mountain Ash. The miners generally were not involved in the "winter of discontent" which had brought down her immediate, socialist predecessor. However, as in a conventional war where the protagonists are in possession of nuclear weapons, the miners' presence lurked in the background. With their deeply engrained subculture they were "shock troops of the labour movement", the ultimate weapon.

## FIRST MOVES.

### Softly Softly.

The nature of the protagonists, and the recent history of the country, made some kind of showdown inevitable but the miners required careful handling. The time was not yet opportune for a confrontation. During Thatcher's first year of office, there were no moves that provoked conflict.

In November 1979, and in spite of ministerial objections that it was too high, the NCB offered a "special case" pay rise of 20 per cent. The NUM executive advocated rejection of the offer and a national strike. They were forced to back down when, in a national ballot, the offer was accepted by the membership. The government was now welcoming developments in the international coal trade. Buyers were encouraged to use this market. There was a commitment to the expansion of nuclear power, in which Thatcher firmly believed. In something quite out of character, even when nuclear power was shown later to be unviable in a private enterprise environment, one of her core beliefs, she still stuck to her nuclear power guns (because Britain was supplying plutonium from its nuclear power stations for the American atomic weapons programme, as Tony Benn alleges?).

In December 1979, the third nuclear power programme was announced. This would be based upon Pressurised Water Reactor (PWR) technology from the United States. It was to comprise 15 gigawatts of generation capacity and was to cost £15 billion (at 1979 prices). Significant opposition, on the grounds of environmental protection, reduced this programme. In fact only one of the planned PWR stations was completed. This was Sizewell B in the mid 1990's, and that only after an epic public enquiry.

### The Screw is Turned.

In 1980 the anti was raised, as the government initiated the following significant policy moves:

- The new Employment Act. This removed all legal immunity from pickets, except those engaged at their own place of work, or at most with their employer's first supplier or first customer. "Secondary picketing" of other industries thus became illegal, as did "sympathy strikes" and a closed shop for trade unions.

- Social security rules were amended such that any claimant who was on strike was deemed to be receiving financial support from the union. This was to be the case even if no actual union payment was being made. Consequently, the overall level of benefit to strikers and their families would be sharply reduced.

- The Coal Industry Act was revised so as to require the NCB to break even without any operating subsidy, latest by the financial year 1983-84. It was clear that this latter requirement could never be achieved merely by abandoning unsafe or physically exhausted pits. It would thus be necessary, for the first time since the drastic rundown of the 1960's, to start looking hard at the realities of economic performance.

The government paper "Coal for the Future" and the Tripartite Report on the South Wales coalfield, both under the aegis of the left wing Minister of Energy, Tony Benn, had as their basis a planned approach to achieving social objectives. That as much of the coalmining industry as possible should survive was implicit. This concept was now replaced by a penetrating analysis of financial reality. The follow- up was a determination to see through conclusions judged necessary to achieve fiscal probity, unpleasant though the effect of such conclusions might be. Shortly after the change of government, Coal Board Chairman, Derek Ezra, expressed his extreme concern to South Wales at their recent output levels in relation to budget.

On 17 September 1979, a letter was sent to Ezra in reply, giving reasons for South Wales's difficulties. These were:

- An unusual number of petty strikes and walkouts, plus delays in settling bonus rates on key faces. This deterioration in attitude was seen as a reflection of the ongoing campaign against the closure of Deep Duffryn Colliery.

- There had been an unofficial strike at Oakdale Colliery, which lasted 4 weeks.

- A number of collieries had encountered quite exceptional and unforseen geological difficulties.

The year 1980 would prove to be climactic. At the time however the position did not seem entirely negative. Skillful investment of £140 M in the more successful South Walian pits during the five years following the Plan for Coal had brought production in a number of them up to record-breaking levels. Of the British prime coking coal reserves, 84 per cent lay in the South Wales Coalfield. British Steel was the coalfield's biggest customer and, looking to the future, closure of the older high cost pits would be counteracted by a projected £160 M investment in a new drift mine at Margam. This would produce coking coal for the adjacent Margam Steelworks. Problems being experienced by the British Steel Corporation were, however, to prove devastating. This lucrative market was hit by the international recession and by competition from the new steel industries springing up around the world. Activity in this vital industry was consequently reduced.

## Enter MacGregor.

The appointment of Ian MacGregor as Chairman of the British Steel Corporation (BSC) was indicative of the new era. It was a move in keeping with the revised government approach to nationalised industries. Ian Kinloch MacGregor was the apotheosis of a transnational meritocrat. A Scot, with a degree in metallurgy from Glasgow University, he started work in the family concern. As milestones in his career:

- By 1940, after four years of industrial experience on the Clyde, he had made a sufficient name for himself to be summoned to the United States to assist in the technical aspects of UK armaments procurement, concentrating mainly on tanks. His attraction towards American capitalism and their way of life resulted in him staying on in that country when the war was over.

- In 1969, as Chairman of the AMAX metallurgical corporation and after a series of diversifications, he took it into the coalmining business. Further diversification, into oil and gas production, followed.

- In the late 1970's, while still with AMAX, he became re-involved in the industrial affairs of the UK as non-executive director of British Leyland, advising and counselling that sick company on the change from a labour intensive to a capital-intensive economy. Among other things "Red Robbo", the infamously militant shop steward, was fired.

- By 1980, he had become one of the most expensive and sought-after business brains of his time. Currently a partner in the merchant banker Lizard/Freres, that company was paid an annual fee of £1.8 M for his services to British Steel.

A high priest of globalisation and the capitalist revival, Ian MacGregor would later, as chairman of the National Coal Board, cause the miners even more grief. Now under his overlordship the steel industry, in addition to slashing manpower and reducing output, followed the logic of market forces and opted increasingly for cheaper coking coal from the United States. BSC was also becoming increasingly unhappy with the high sulphur content of much of the local deep-mined coal. This added cost and increased the problems of producing high-specification steels. These were becoming more and more necessary in the highly competitive markets.

The decision at the end of the 1970's to import coking coal as a cost- saving measure was a body blow to the South Wales Coalfield. Globalisation, and the cold wind of international competition, was starting to be felt. Under pressure from the government to restructure, the formula worked out by the British Steel Corporation was that they would only use indigenous coking coals if the NCB could offer them competitively, taking into account both price and the quality specification. Previous government restrictions on imports were loosened up. This meant death for a significant number of pits. It also killed off the new coking coal mine adjacent to the Margam Steelworks. Capital investment in this project would have been high (£200 M in 1981), as were interest charges. This was at a time when the Board was striving to reduce its negative cash flow into the coalfield. Against the background of a severe contraction in the British steel industry, combined with low freight rates for imported coal, any benefits when compared with imported coal would have been marginal.

South Wales coal always had been more expensive. Its saving grace was its high quality and the willingness of specialist consumers to pay premium prices. The ability of its bituminous coal to be converted into coke was an example of such quality, as was the prolonged burning characteristic of anthracite. With the erosion of such markets, steam coal for electricity generation became predominant, and here low cost heat content is what matters.

## THE STIRRINGS OF RESISTANCE.

### Steel and Coal.

In early 1980 the South Wales NUM announced that they had become aware of a Coal Board plan to initiate a further round of closures in their area, five almost immediately and a further seven within two years. Restart of the closure programme revived the possibility of "nomad miners", that industrial equivalent of the Wandering Jew and anathema to a society where community affiliation was predominant. A movement started to join the steelworkers in a combined fight for jobs. One of Ian MacGregor's priorities had been to slash significantly the steel industry payroll. The result was strife, with a 3-month long strike by steelworkers against redundancy.

In February 1980, Mr. Peter Thomas, lodge chairman at the Nantgarw coke ovens, expressed the feeling at a conference of South Wales Area delegates in Porthcawl. He was quoted as saying that if South Wales miners wanted to safeguard their livelihoods then action must be taken:

"There's no option left to us. If we accept things as they are our valley communities will just be decimated —— We need a national miners' strike to smash the Tory government before they do too much damage". At the conference the area executive recommended industrial action in support of the steelworkers. To the militants' great chagrin, the coalfield strike as proposed was voted down. Some, who also feared a consequent lack of support when their own day of need dawned, regarded this as betrayal of their fellow trade unionists.

The militants were to be again disappointed by a second failure to initiate strike action, this time over the pit closure issue. There were 4,000 votes for and 22,000 against. Miners' leaders blamed Coal Board interference, such as a comment in the press of "bloody madness" by Area Director Phil Weekes on the eve of the ballot. An additional factor was the reluctance of the men to see South Wales go it alone. The NCB had also denied that any such closure plan existed. Such denials were to become routine. To paraphrase Winston Churchill, "Truth is sometimes so important that it has to be protected by a cocoon of lies".

## Lewis Merthyr/Tymawr.

The logic behind NCB reluctance to divulge the whole truth and nothing but the truth became apparent later, in the determined struggle against closure put up by Lewis Merthyr/ Tymawr. Resistance blossomed from the moment that their planned fate became clear to them. These two pits were situated in Trehafod, at the entrance to the Rhondda Valley. They worked the Four Feet and Upper Nine Feet seams and since 1958 had been linked underground. All coal was wound at Tymawr with supplies going down Lewis Merthyr. The latter pit had previously voted for the strike against closures while Tymawr was overwhelmingly against.

In May 1980, the attitude of the Tymawr men changed when a closure announcement for their own colliery was suddenly issued - too suddenly according to the NUM. The colliery had served the coking coal market and hence had become extremely vulnerable. Of the 700 miners, 350 would not be offered alternative employment. Tymawr was the last pit in South Wales to be worked predominantly by hand. The lodge argued that attempts at mechanisation had not been pursued with the necessary determination, and that financial losses had been exaggerated by the inclusion of a one-off, £400,000 contribution to landscape the tip. As the productive Four Feet seam approached the end of its life attempts were made to work the Upper Nine Feet seam with a fully mechanised coalface. Power loaders of the shearer type were introduced but, according to the NCB, all attempts at mechanisation were defeated by geological conditions. Seams directly above and below the Upper Nine Feet had already been worked and this made the strata there extremely unstable, making the use of powered roof supports almost impossible.

There then started an abortive and divisive struggle within the union to save the pit. The local NUM regarded urgent action as being necessary to correct the situation. The men at Lewis Merthyr/ Tymawr were prepared to put up a terrific fight and this they did. Led by Des Dutfield of the Lodge, who later would become South Wales Miners' President, their pit would become a cause celebre for the South Wales NUM.

## Economic Sense?

The exigencies of economic life might be quoted as a justification for closure, with free trade and globalisation the lodestones to be followed as a means of achieving the most cost-effective production, but there was another yardstick involved. What about those displaced thereby, with no corresponding work to go to? What about the break-up of established communities? Was globalisation all that it was cracked up to be if in its wake previously productive resources, including people, were left lying fallow? Such resources, so went the theory, could then be devoted to alternative objectives, more efficient than the original. In practice, and all too often, such alternatives were not available, belonging more to the realm of economic theory than to reality. Recognition of this fact has blocked the economic rationale of converting Western Europe into a vast prairie and of allowing unrestricted food imports. Instead, the preservation of farming communities and the existing countryside has remained stubbornly on the agenda. To those seeking work, Norman Tebbit, cabinet minister in the current government had given the advice, "Get on your bike". If by that he meant that those seeking work should be prepared to move home then who would buy their house in a depressed area?

As far back as 1 February 1959, at a general meeting of the Fernhill Colliery employees, Ronald Griffiths, lodge president at the time, summarised the union's attitude. The struggle against pit closures, he said, was:

"one where the union was fighting for the right to work, which meant struggling against the basis of the capitalist system of society where men were only allowed to work provided they maintained the level of profits".

Much later, the chairman of Tymawr lodge, Mr. David Hughes, put it another way:

"If we can retain our jobs then we can retain our little villages in this valley. Should we go into a recession of coal then what happens to our communities? Let us give some consideration to our up and coming children".

## SECRETS.

### Memoranda.

On 12 June 1980, a reply was made by the NCB to articles in the South Wales newspapers, Evening Post, Argus, and Echo. It said:

"There have been assertions that anything from 6 to 21 collieries in South Wales are about to close, and these are quite absurd. The future prospects of the industry do depend, however, on our ability to bring our costs down so that we can become more competitive and sell our coal at prices our customers can afford. Our long-established colliery review procedure is part of the management/trade union discipline for taking stock and taking action on our increasing costs. Unless we observe these procedures the situation can only get worse".

On 5 September 1980 a report, classified secret, was sent to Coal Board Chairman, Derek Ezra, and the Secretary of State for Wales by Phillip Weekes, NCB South Wales Area Director. It concerned policy for the Area and confirmed what the NUM had suspected and what the Board had known. It tallies exactly with NUM accusations, made at the beginning of the year and denied by the NCB at the time, that 5 pits were to close as soon as possible and a further 7 later. Excerpts from the report are:

"The importance of coking coal for some 1.6 Mt deep-mined output cannot be too strongly stressed. Without that a further 5 pits, which would otherwise be "ongoing capacity", employing over 4,000 men would have to go —— We must continue to pursue with determination the elimination of "hopeless capacity" - 12 collieries producing 1.6 Mt/a collectively account for a loss of £50 M per annum —— To the extent that any of this capacity remains, then its output will be at the expense of ongoing collieries because of the limited total size of the Area market. I know the Board will not contemplate producing for stock purposes only —— This turnaround in the Area's financial position can only be achieved if we stick rigidly to the strategy of removing the hopeless capacity. It will not be an easy task, bearing in mind the NUM attitude, and there could well be some form of industrial action while we restructure the Area. —— I know that you feel that we should not indicate any lack of enthusiasm or determination in tackling the issue. I am, incidentally, convinced that our task would be eased considerably if Government can be persuaded, separately from the Board's overall investment strategy, to give us a green light for Margam".

On 5 December1980, following a meeting between the Coal Board and the Secretary of State for Wales, a secret NCB internal memorandum was prepared, confirming the way ahead. For the union, had they known, it would have confirmed their worst fears. The punch line read:

"in the light of continuing deterioration in the industry's market and financial position both locally and nationally —— for the longer term South Wales can sustain only about 6.4 Mt of deep-mined output, assuming continuing development of good capacity and stabilisation of the market at about present levels. This implies a more substantial restructuring of the coalfield than was envisaged at the time of the Tripartite Review in 1979".

A study by the Area Director worked out specific consequences for the coalfield. It meant a contraction in the Area by 1986, from the current 35 pits employing 25,700 men to 18 pits employing about 16,000 men. The twelve biggest losers in the Area should be subject to an accelerated closure programme. This went way beyond Lewis Merthyr/Tymawr. Included on the Area Director's list were such "glamour projects" as Mardy and Abernant, both in areas of particularly high unemployment. In the situation existing at the time this was political dynamite. The social consequences of such a rundown were appreciated by the NCB, who proposed government financial support for the programme. There would still be investment in the coalfield, totalling £25 M annually and aimed at improving the prospects of long-life pits. The new Margam project might be reconstituted, albeit for power station fuel instead of coking coal. This would involve higher output and less elaborate coal preparation facilities on the surface. The Area director argued for the new Margam project on the grounds that it would be a significant moral booster in a picture that was otherwise characterised by total decline. He concluded his study:

"It is nevertheless difficult to escape the conclusion, based on several years of difficulty and frustration, that a wide contingency margin needs to be attached to any plan for improving prospects in the South Wales Coalfield".

## Welsh Coal is Best?

It was true that the South Wales coalfield produced a range of products unique in the UK and that, if the coalfield shut down, any continuing demand for these would have to be imported. Anthracite for domestic heating was unique and boilers at the massive Aberthaw power station had been specially designed to burn low-volatile Welsh coal. In addition, the steel industry would continue to require supplies of coking coal and this was produced locally. However, anthracite could be replaced with gas while Aberthaw and the vast Margam Steelworks lay directly on the coast. With deep-water facilities at each of these sites, suitable coal could be imported - at a price cheaper than indigenous production. The facts on the ground were that the coking coal market was in the process of collapsing and the main steam coal market, Aberthaw power station, was experiencing technical difficulties, resulting in only two of the three generator sets being operational.

In 1981 an "Anthracite Strategy Review" carried out by the NCB South Wales Area highlighted the salient points of working these high revenue, but extremely difficult seams. Sales were virtually confined to the domestic heating market, with price locked to gas, its cheapest rival. Meeting such competition implied high productivity. With such bad geology this was only possible in small takes within the upper coal measures. As a way ahead, the review concluded:

i) Select the best geology, with the best productivity expectations.

ii) Utilize as far as possible existing investment (shafts, main roadways, coal preparation plants etc.).

iii) To sink a new mine is extremely expensive. On the whole, productivity achieved to date does not justify such expenditure.

iv) One should not be over-ambitious regarding output targets. These should be conscious of market outlet requirements at all times.

There were 7 anthracite mines: Abernant, Aberpergwm, Betws, Blaengwrach, Cwmgwili, Cynheidre, and Treforgan. Of these, only Betws made a profit. In the previous 3 years it had cumulated £4.3 M, against gross losses in the other anthracite mines of £71.8 M. Significantly, Betws worked the upper measures, where the intensity of geological disturbance was lowest.

After their coming to power in 1979, the new Conservative government imposed a strict External Financing Limit on the nationalised industries (see following section). One result of this was a new closure programme proposed for South Wales.

On 13 February 1981, a press release of the National Coal Board stated:

"Due to continued high costs of production and the sharp drop in markets caused by the worldwide recession, 5 South Wales pits have been nominated for closure. These are:

- Lewis Merthyr/Tymawr.
- Coegnant.

- Brynlliw/Morlais.
- Brittania.
- Aberpergwym.


They employ 2,800 men, of whom as many as possible will be transferred to alternative jobs in the numerous secure and reconstructed collieries in the coalfield —— In just over a year the coalfield's coking coal market had fallen by more than 1 Mt because of the British Steel Corporation's (BSC) slimline. In spite of higher exports, more sales to power stations and industry, the area's losses had escalated rapidly, because it was no longer possible to secure premium prices —— This year the coalfield was facing an overall loss of £80 M and this deficit would exceed £100 M next year, when the South Wales Area would consume almost one quarter of the cash available to the NCB as a whole, for less than one twelfth of the output. — — The Area Director (Mr. Phillip Weekes) had been obliged to take fresh account of collieries, which because of age or major geological difficulties had exhausted their realistic reserves and could not, in any foreseeable circumstances, make a contribution to the area's future. Much of the coal from South Wales collieries was being sold at very considerable discounts and measures had to be taken to correct the imbalance of production and markets".


## THE LADY IS FOR TURNING.

### The Government Shows Its Teeth.

Although South Wales was an extreme case, the coal industry nationally was experiencing problems. These now came to the fore. As part of their drive for privatisation, and the elimination of loss making industries, one aim of the Conservative government was to achieve a coal industry that was self-financing.

In 1979, this financially orientated approach had led to a tight External Financing Limit (EFL) being imposed on nationalised industries. The object of this was to limit government subsidies. In a situation of sales recession and of output exceeding demand, the NCB saw an accelerated closure programme as being the only way of meeting the government's diktat. NCB chairman Sir Derek Ezra outlined to Joe Gormley and the NUM executive his plans for responding. The fate of particular collieries would have to be decided by the areas concerned.

The South Walian response was to issue the press release as above, dated 13 February 1981. Nationally, twenty-three pits plus 13,000 jobs were involved, and the NUM leaders reacted furiously. Contrary to what was to happen later in 1984, there were immediate, unsolicited pledges of massive support, from the seamen, transport workers, steelworkers and railwaymen. Bill Sirs of the steel workers' union and Sid Weighell of the railwaymen both said that they could not rule out the possibility of a general strike unless the cabinet quickly forced the NCB to back down.

Both militants and moderates on the NUM Executive agreed unanimously on a seven-day ultimatum to the government: either bail out the coal industry and shelve the shutdown proposals or, if they proceeded, there would be a poll of the members for strike action. In this event, a solid, ballot-backed, national strike was a near certainty. In spite of Gormley's impassioned warnings that precipitate action might be putting jobs and the union at risk, South Wales did not bother to wait for the ultimatum to expire. Here, where five pits had been threatened with closure, all of the miners walked out for a one-week total strike. This time, fired in particular by the Lewis Merthyr/Tymawr issue, South Wales did go it alone. Emlyn Williams, President of the South Wales NUM, expressed what it was all about:

"I wouldn't call it a strike, I would call it a demonstration for existence —— The miners in South Wales are saying, we are not accepting the dereliction of our mining valleys, we are not allowing our children to go immediately from school to the dole queue. It is time we fought".


### A Battle We Cannot Win.

On 16 February 1981, at a meeting with the Department of Energy, Margaret Thatcher was appalled. The government had inadvertently entered into a battle that it could not win. Stocks at power stations were simply not sufficient. All the government could do was cut its losses and plan for the future when, with adequate preparation, victory might be possible. Defeat in a coal strike would have been disastrous. Her reading of NCB management attitudes caused her confidence in them, never very high, to take another blow:

"Far from acting as management might be expected to do, the NCB Board was behaving as if it shared the interests of the union representing its employees". So much for the identity of interests of all those employed in the industry, and the common cause between management and men, which Ezra and Gormley epitomised and of which both were so proud.

On the same date as the above meeting, which was a Monday, three collieries began strike action, Coegnant, St. Johns and Brynllew/Morlais. There was also a conference of South Wales miners' delegates, as a result of which, within 24 hours, all other collieries were out. There was some support in other parts of the country, although it was a long way from being a national strike. All 26,000 miners in South Wales downed tools, plus the 3,000 in Kent. They were to be followed by all of the 18 pits in Scotland, plus 4 in Durham, 2 in Yorkshire and 1 in North Staffordshire.


## Flexibility and Bluff.

On 23 February 1981, one week later, all collieries resumed normal work. Unprepared at this point in time to face a major dispute, the government backed down before expiry of the seven-day countdown. All the threatened mines were reprieved and what Gormley called "A hell of a lot of money" was to be made available to the industry. He continued, "The National Coal Board's closure plan has been withdrawn completely". One of Margaret Thatcher's famous quotes, made from a public rostrum was. "The lady's not for turning". The so-called U-turn was embarrassing for her and her government, but they had lived to fight another day.

On the miners' side there was little triumphalism. Mr. Jack Collins, NUM Area Secretary for Kent said, "We are dealing with cunning people and for the present the Kent miners have a guarded mistrust of the new situation". In South Wales a second delegates' conference was held, which called off the strike. The decision was not unanimous. Many of the miners' leaders were of the opinion that the government's guarantees were not solid enough; in particular there was no provision for any independent arbitration. In their eyes the government was only playing for time, so as to build up its defences against any move by the . miners in future. A showdown with Thatcherism was inevitable. It had merely been postponed and would now have be fought under less propitious circumstances. In his speech at the conference in Bridgend, Tyrone O`Sullivan of Tower Colliery spoke about coming back with a basket of goodies, only to discover there was a hole in the bottom, and the basket was empty. As to the decision to call off the strike, he suggested that the assembled delegates all look under their seats since they must have pissed themselves with fear, he could smell it at the rostrum. Nevertheless the union, including the South Wales leadership, accepted the placatory package offered "as a first instalment". What could have been achieved if a more determined stand had been made on this occasion is one of the "what if's" of history.

The package accepted consisted of £50M worth of grants for industrialists willing to convert back to coal, plus an increase of £10,000 (making a total of nearly £36,000) in the compensation offered to pit workers taking early retirement. There was also a £200M cash injection to cover the cost of withdrawing the closure programme and of compensating those customers who had gone abroad in search of cheap coal and who were now forbidden to bring it in. This particularly affected the Central Electricity Generating Board. They had signed a contract with Australia and were now forced to let the deliveries pile up in Rotterdam, ultimately to some 3Mt.

As for Margaret Thatcher, she wrote in her book The Downing Street Years:

"I concentrated attention on limiting the financial consequences of our retreat and preparing the ground so that we would never be put in such an awful situation again —— We would have to rely on a judicious mixture of flexibility and bluff until the Government was in a position to face down the challenge posed to the economy, and indeed potentially to the rule of law, by the combined force of monopoly and union power in the coal industry".

# CHANGING OF THE GUARD.

## A Knighthood For Moderation.

On 8th December 1981 the fire-eating Arthur Scargill won by 70.3 per cent the vote to replace Joe Gormley, who was shortly to retire. The latter had walked a thin line between moderation and militancy. Under his leadership the devastating and successful national strikes had been initiated while, in spite of an economy that was worsening and an increase in productivity much less than that forecasted, employment had been sustained and wage levels increased. On the face of it this was a good enough record for a trade union leader. Nevertheless, he had constrained the unfocused, shoot-from-the-hip fervour of many of his activists and had eased through, in spite of a national ballot to the contrary, a productivity incentive scheme in accordance with Coal Board wishes. Gormley had never been the left's man and now, as his moderating influence disappeared from the scene, he became Lord Gormley, peer of the realm. The leftist camp would accuse him of selling out the miners for a knighthood.

Notwithstanding the defeats that the establishment had suffered at his hands, obviously Gormley's type of wheeling and dealing had not been totally repugnant to them. He had fought a rearguard action against growing left wing influence, and not totally without success. A grace and favour bonus, invented by him, was not something that would exactly undermine executive support for his policies (Spectator, 11 August 1984). This was paid as a pension supplement to members of the National Executive. It had the distinctive feature that its rate, and whom it was paid to, was at the discretion of the NUM President, that is Gormley himself. Gormley had delayed his retirement, thereby ensuring that Mick MacGahey, his Vice-President and also President of the Scottish miners, would just exceed the maximum age of a candidate to replace him. Since 1974, MacGahey had also been Chairman of the Communist Party of Great Britain. If Gormley hoped thereby that after his departure militant influence on union policy would be limited he would be sadly disillusioned. Arthur Scargill was young, and raring to go.

## Strike Lads, Strike!

The new president started as he meant to continue, with a call for immediate strike action over a 23 per cent pay claim. This was rejected by national ballot. Within 3 months of his election, Scargill was to call yet again for national strike action, this time to save Lewis Merthyr/ Tymawr. The result was a second ballot defeat.

## There Is No Such Thing As An Uneconomic Pit.

At this time he visited South Wales and, at a meeting with Area Director Phillip Weekes, left no doubt concerning the new NUM policy, namely that there was no such thing as an uneconomic pit, only pits which had been starved of investment. He would support the South Wales NUM in their view that no pit should be closed where reserves existed. Weekes countered that when any pit closed there was always some coal left in the ground and that the economics of extraction had to play a role. When Weekes happened to look away, Scargill winked at local NUM Secretary George Reece, who was present, and asked whether any hit list existed of pits to be closed. In reply he received the party line that there was no such thing. Reviews would be carried out in accordance with performance and reserves.

The new NUM thinking saw things differently. To them it was just Coal Board policy and their accounting methods that determined whether a pit was uneconomic or not. At the meeting there was disagreement over the practicality and economics of developing new areas, particularly around Cynheidre, under Swansea Bay and the deeper seams of the Rhondda Valley. NUM thinking on these matters, as seen through Coal Board eyes, was so much "pie in the sky". In particular, cost limitation was not on the NUM agenda. In the words of one wag, coal would continue to be produced, even if it had to be taken away in Securicor vans for storage in the local bank!

# WHERE'S OUR SHARE?

## Discussion.

On 10 January 1983, local NUM concern about lack of investment came to a head at a meeting dedicated to that topic and to recruitment. It was held in Hobart House, NCB national headquarters. By this time, NCB investment in South Wales was £600 per miner; in Yorkshire the figure was £39,000. Shelving of the new mine at Margam was regarded as a betrayal by the NUM. Emlyn Williams, South Wales NUM President, led the union delegation that met the National Coal Board. In the chair was NCB Chairman Norman Siddall, recently appointed to replace the retired Derek Ezra. Those present included Area Director Phillip Weekes. The meeting commenced with Emlyn Williams making a strong plea for investment. The union made specific proposals but the Board's reply was clear in outlining the basic problems in which the coalfield found itself. They were however singularly opaque in explaining their strategy on how to deal with them. As outlined above, this strategy had been worked out over two years previously, but on this not a single word was lost at the meeting, no doubt understandable in view of the sensitive politics involved. It had in any event been thrown out of gear by the 1981 confrontation. Abernant and Mardy for example, instead of closing would survive, Abernant until 1988 and Mardy until 1991.

Mr. Siddall explained that the Board did not have any preconceived notion of what individual areas should have, but capital resources were not unlimited. Decisions were taken on the basis of maximising return on investment for the Board as a whole. South Wales's problem was that its difficult geology unfortunately resulted in production costs being higher than other coalfields. Higher proceeds were therefore necessary if the coalfield was to pay its way. High production costs combined with weak prices in the market place resulted in the critical financial position in which the coalfield now found itself. The Board had to have regard to the Area's record of sustained heavy losses when considering the opportunities available for capital investment.

For the past 8 years, ever since the Plan for Coal, investment in South Wales had run at an average of £40 M per annum. Currently, however, the coalfield's negative cash flow of well over £100 M per annum was proving a disincentive. The markets were proving extremely difficult. In particular the steel and foundry coals, which had been the main source of income, had gone into rapid and serious decline. It was true that South Wales coal had many special qualities, but it was not marketable at any price. The British Steel Corporation, which currently bought 1.4 Mt/a from the coalfield, was a case in point. At the moment the coal was sold at a price far below production cost because otherwise it would not be sold at all. An early advance on Margam was not likely. The project was marginal in financial terms the last time the Board looked at it and since then coking prices had collapsed. He could not hold out any false hope.

Mr.Cowan (NCB) said that one of the fundamental problems in South Wales was that the average cost of production had risen by 80 per cent in the last 5 years. It was essential to reduce production costs.

Mr. Thomas (NUM) said that the Area was in a Catch 22 situation, whereby they were told that they could not have capital funds until results improved yet results would not improve until they had capital funds.

Mr. Dutfield (NUM) said that if the Board were sincere and serious in getting the best performance out of South Wales they would be putting definite proposals to the NUM rather than the NUM making proposals to the Board. He maintained that many pits were being crippled through the Board's policies, but the South Wales mineworkers were prepared to fight for their future. It was clear that men were not being recruited because the Board hoped to transfer men from closing pits to fill vacancies. They would prefer to discuss the nature of the coalfield without having to resort to industrial action. However, they could not rely on discussions because of the number of promises that had been broken by the Board.

## Decision at Tymawr.

On 22 February 1983, a stay down strike commenced at Lewis Merthyr/Tymawr (Des Dutfield's pit). On this Monday morning shift, 15 men stayed underground, plus 13 men in the afternoon. Sympathy strikes were held at Mardy, Penrikyber, Tower and Nantgarw. The Abercynon men held a meeting, and decided against taking action. On the same day, a colliery review meeting concerning Tymawr was held at the NCB offices in Llanishen, Cardiff. The chairman, Area Director Phillip Weekes, emphasized that the average advance per shift of the N92 face over the last 8 weeks had been 8 inches (20.3cm), resulting in an output of 65 tonnes per shift (at this time the best faces in the country were measuring their output in 1,000's of tonnes per shift). For a modern, fully-mechanised face, complete with expensive self-advancing supports, this was totally unacceptable.

There was a hard core of 12 or so pits in the area on which he hoped to build a profitable coalfield. The Board had already invested substantial capital in pits such as Lady Windsor and Nantgarw, which were in possession of good reserves. Although these pits were losing money now, the Board understood the position. They needed additional manpower for development, so that their full potential could be exploited. In conclusion, Mr. Weekes payed tribute to the men and officials in Tymawr who had worked well under extremely difficult conditions. Following the meeting, a memo from Area Director Weekes stated:

"After a further detailed assessment of the situation, I have reached the conclusion that the remaining reserves are not technically workable and that further development in any seam at Lewis Merthyr/Tymawr would not be justified. In my opinion, therefore, the colliery should cease production by July 1983. Alternative employment will be made available for all men who wish to transfer to other collieries".

On 25 February 1983, the following Friday, the Area Executive's call for coalfield strike action in support of Lewis Merthyr/Tymawr evoked a patchy response, with 55.4 per cent of the coalfield voting for and 44,6 per cent voting against. Six pits went on strike with safety cover: Mardy, Penrikyber, Trelewis, Britannia, Celynon North, and Tower. A further three went out with no safety cover: Lewis Merthyr/Tymawr, St. Johns and Coedely. During this same month, a conference of South Wales NUM delegates called for industrial action over the lack of investment.

## IMPENDING STORM.

### The Government Prepares.

Meanwhile, ever since the government's retreat in 1981, and as a preparation for what was coming, the NCB was being encouraged to over-produce. The Generating Board was asking, and getting, a premium to make more storage space available.

By February 1983, over 50M tonnes were stacked up, corresponding to half a year's output (this compares with the 36.2 Mt "Mountains of Mourne", which had caused such concern in 1959, when coal consumption was much higher). For the first time the government ensured with coal what it always had done with oil, namely that there was a strategic reserve available. Unlike the case with oil, however, this was not financed by the government, but by the NCB. In addition, the Generating Board had invested in a cross-channel link with the French electrical supply industry (EdF). This resulted in the routine import of French (largely nuclear) power into the UK, equivalent to 6 Mt of coal per annum. Approval for this had actually been given by Tony Benn, as Energy Minister for the previous Labour Government. As a convert to the miners' cause, he would later justify this action by maintaining that the link had actually been set up for the export by wire of British coal to France.

In March 1983, the appointment was announced of Ian MacGregor as Chairman of the National Coal Board. He would take up his duties in September, on completion of his tenure as Chairman of the British Steel Corporation. As opposed to the £1.8 M annual fee that Lazard/Freres had received for his BSC services, this time the fee would be a mere £1.5 M. This was defended by the Energy Secretary, Nigel Lawson, on the grounds that although it was a great deal of money," It is only the amount that the NCB is losing every day".

### Tymawr - the End.

On 14 March 1983, production came to an end at the mechanised N 92 face of Lewis Merthyr/ Tymawr. In spite of being equipped with expensive, self-advancing supports, it had been consuming one tonne of timber as additional roof support for every 10 tonnes of coal produced. Production continued elsewhere in the pit by means of hand working in the Four Feet seam.

On 17 June 1983, Lewis Merthyr/ Tymawr finally closed. In the NCB list of closures, the reason given is "Remaining reserves not technically workable".

The industry as a whole had shown itself unwilling to face any national confrontation, in particular over the Lewis Merthyr/ Tymawr issue. As a consequence the Welsh miners regarded themselves as being let down by their Midlands colleagues. South Wales men, canvassing in Nottinghamshire for support, were surprised by the difference in attitude prevailing there, as compared with that on their home turf. Mutual incomprehension was the order of the day as emotional appeals to protect communities and secure employment for the children failed to break through the dourness of those whose concern was limited to a continuation of the weekly wage packet, and the short-term financial benefits if loss-making collieries were closed. This indifference to the problems of others was to emerge again in the 1984-85 strike, when the majority of the Nottinghamshire men remained at work. The Welsh miners saw the "I'm all right Jack" mentality, which so upset them, as a vindication of their earlier opposition to the concept of local productivity bonuses.

On the other side of the coin, resentment within union ranks, on the part of the Nottinghamshire miners, remained a considerable force. Between nationalisation and 1970 the Scottish mining industry had lost about £190 M after meeting interest charges, despite the benefit of a positive price differential over most other coalfields. In the same period, South Wales lost about £145 M. In comparison, the East Midlands pits had accumulated a surplus after interest of about £265 M. Without being subsidised by such excellent results, the Scottish and South Wales coalfields could not have survived. The losses and the low productivity in the latter two coalfields, however, rarely inhibited industrial action. Such action was taken over a great many issues that, in the East Midlands, would have been settled amicably.


## Right versus Left.

South Walian experience of economic rationalisation, at the beginning of the 1980's, would be continued, and extended to the coal industry nation-wide. In spite of skirmishing, plus an extensive programme of privatisation, a head-on clash with the unions had been avoided during Margaret Thatcher's first term in office (1979-83) but, with the exception of short-term strategisms as above, the lady really was not for turning. Her characteristic, single-minded determination was not about to give up the principle of thoroughly shaking out British industry, any more than it would balk at facing down a host of IRA hunger strikers, or waging war against General Galtieri of Argentina. The latter conflict would prove to be a watershed. Thatcher's industrial policies had been causing pain and polls were recording her as the most unpopular Prime Minister since the Second World War. Her unexpected total victory in an unexpected war changed all that and resulted in a previously unexpected election victory.

In June 1983 the general election was held, with the "Falklands Factor" playing a significant role. In a wave of patriotism and national pride, Thatcher and the Conservatives were swept to a landslide majority of 141 seats in the House of Commons. The English mining constituencies also showed a definite shift to the Tories. To emphasise the yawning philosophical gap between her and her opponents the manifesto of the Labour Party, "The longest suicide note in history" according to Gerald Kaufmann MP, was classic socialism, with more public ownership and a reinforcement of the welfare state. During their four years in opposition the Labour Party had moved significantly to the left. As for the NUM, for the first time in their history, of the twenty-four voting members of the executive, the left was now in a majority. On the Government side, Nigel Lawson was promoted to Chancellor of the Exchequer and replaced as Energy Secretary by Peter Walker.

The consequences of Thatcher's election victory for the coal industry would prove to be bleak. Her Government would now show that it meant business. The Conservative Campaign Guide claimed that the Government had "maintained an understanding and flexible approach" to the problems of the coal industry, but noted a disappointingly slow growth in productivity - 20 per cent lower than the levels promised in the 1974 Plan for Coal. It said that much of the shortfall was due to the fact that "old and inefficient capacity" had not been phased out at the rate that the plan envisaged. Consequently, the least profitable slice of deep-mined capacity had notched up losses of £250 M during the year 1981-82. However, there were signs that the need for improved performance was being grasped. Notably, there was the double rejection of Mr. Scargill's calls for strike action, both over pay and over the recent closure of Lewis Merthyr/ Tymawr.

## Counting the Pennies.

At the time of MacGregor's appointment, the government had also initiated a new study into the coalmining industry, to be carried out by the Monopolies and Mergers Commission (MMC). The NUM had refused to cooperate. Unlike the previous studies, under the aegis of Tony Benn, this report was by accountants.

In June 1983, the MMC report was submitted to the Secretary of State for Trade and Industry. It was immediately accepted by the government. The report made sober reading. Between 1972-82 there had been only two years (1976-78) where deep mines had made a profit (£31.9 M for the first year and £0.3 M for the second). Otherwise losses had been compensated for by opencast production. Of the deep mines, only 22 out of 170 had consistently covered their operating costs. As an average over the six-year period 1976-81 as studied by the Monopolies Commission, a bare fifty or sixty had done any better than being able to break even. At that time wages formed 48 per cent of total costs, with materials, repairs and external contractors forming 26 per cent.

Results in the previous three years had been as follows:

| Year | Deep Mines Profit(loss) in £M. | Opencast Profit(loss) in £M. | Total Profit (Loss) in £M. |
|---|---|---|---|
| 1980-81 | (107) | 157 | 50 |
| 1981-82 | (226) | 157 | (69) |
| 1982-83 | (151) | 179 | 28 |

Deep mine operating figures for 1981-82 are given below, on an area-by-area basis. These include the effect of the one-week strike in South Wales plus social costs and grants, but not regional grants.

| Area. | Operating Collieries. | Manpower. | Saleable Output in Mt. | OMS in t. | Cost/t in £. | Surplus (loss) per tonne in £M. | Total surplus (loss) 1976-82 in £M. |
|---|---|---|---|---|---|---|---|
| S. Wales. | 33 | 24,800 | 7.6 | 1.47 | 58.8 | (13.2) | (304.4) |
| N. East. | 22 | 30,400 | 13.4 | 2.07 | 42.8 | (3.8) | (133.1) |
| Scottish. | 14 | 18,300 | 7.2 | 2.00 | 42.6 | (5.5) | (130.8) |
| Western. | 21 | 21,500 | 11.1 | 2.45 | 40.5 | (1.4) | (99.4) |
| S. Yorks. | 17 | 16,300 | 7.2 | 2.22 | 40.3 | (0.8) | 41.0 |
| N. Yorks. | 14 | 14,800 | 8.3 | 2.80 | 37.2 | (2.7) | 37.1 |
| Barnsley. | 16 | 15,000 | 8.4 | 2.71 | 37.4 | (1.8) | (64.1) |
| Doncaster. | 10 | 15,900 | 7.1 | 2.27 | 39.4 | (2.9) | (77.8) |
| S. Midlands. | 17 | 16,100 | 8.6 | 2.52 | 36.2 | (2.7) | (20.7) |
| N. Derbyshire. | 11 | 12,000 | 8.5 | 3.33 | 33.8 | 0.1 | 7.1 |
| S. Notts. | 11 | 15,300 | 8.5 | 2.68 | 36.0 | (2.6) | (43.4) |
| N. Notts. | 14 | 18,100 | 12.3 | 3.17 | 32.1 | 3.1 | 256.0 |
| TOTAL | 200 | 218,500 | 108.2 | 2.4 | 39.5 | (2.6) | (635.4) |

In the year 1981-82, of the 33 South Wales pits, only two had made a profit. These were Betws New Mine, with a profit of £10.5 per tonne and Deep Navigation, with a profit of £5.4 per tonne.

The following is an example of the losses being incurred by some pits:

- Tymawr/Lewis Merthyr:     £83.9 /tonne.
- Tower:     £33.2 /tonne.
- Mardy:     £24.6 /tonne.
- Cynheidre:     £24.1 /tonne.
- Abernant :     £20.8 /tonne.

The report compared production statistics in the UK with those in Germany (the German policy of heavily subsidising their mining industry was not dealt with).

| Country. | Number of collieries. | Output per annum in Mt. | Underground manpower. | Output per underground man/hour in t. |
|---|---|---|---|---|
| Germany | 38 | 95 | 122,000 | 0.531 |
| UK (All pits) | 200 | 108.81 | 174,000 | 0.392 |
| UK (38 highest output pits) | 38 | 43.24 | | 0.588 |

The collieries in Germany were much larger and some work practices were better organised; for example, faces could work continuously due to the overlapping of shifts. This was to cater for the travelling time to and from the coalface. In general the 38 German pits were not more efficient than the best 38 of the UK pits. However, the Germans had obviously been much more successful than the UK in shedding uneconomical capacity.

The report summarised, "We consider that as a result of a tendency to be optimistic about physical and market related factors, the NCB has tended to over-estimate the prospective revenue and under-estimate the prospective costs which a colliery will experience following investment ——— We note that much investment has gone into collieries which are either unprofitable or of doubtful potential profitability ——— Very large sums of public money are needed to maintain the coal industry. The NCB has received regular and increasing support from the government, including deficit grants to cover losses and other grants for purposes including help in meeting the costs of the reduction in capacity".

- In 1979-80, grant aid was £251 M, including a deficit grant of £159 M.
- In 1980-81, grant aid was £254 M, including a deficit grant of £149 M.
- In 1981-82, grant aid was £575 M, including a deficit grant of £428 M.

Interest on loans from the treasury for the financing of new and redeveloped capacity was a major component in the deficit grants required. In the previous two years, money borrowed for this purpose was as follows:

- In 1980-81, £586 M.
- In 1981-82, £902 M.

In 1983-84 the External Financing Limit for the NCB equalled £1,130 M. This was the largest of any nationalised industry and indeed was 40 per cent of the total for all of these industries together.

Concerning the issue of large-scale redundancy, the authors of the report did not regard it as being part of their remit to recommend detailed government policy. However, it was made clear that to mop this up measures would have to be taken in affected areas. Such large-scale redundancy would be an inevitable consequence of any meaningful attempt to rectify the situation. From the point of view of industry finances, there was no alternative other than to terminate any concept of energy production as being a public service. The imperative was to ruthlessly shed uneconomic capacity.

Such "dead wood" was, however, precisely in those areas where alternative employment was the most difficult to find. In the once proud giants of the industry, Scotland, the North-East of England and, first and foremost South Wales, red ink was flowing heavily. The regularly profitable mines were increasingly concentrated in the counties of Yorkshire, Derbyshire and Nottinghamshire, with Yorkshire being held back to some extent due to bad labour relations. In addition, most of the most promising seams for future development were located in these same counties. With any consequent application of fiscal policy, this was where the centre of gravity of British coalmining, and the future, would have to lie.

At the dawn of the 1984 miners' strike, the fiscal situation of the South Wales coalfield was bleak, as the following statistics for the pits in that area show:

| Colliery. | Manpower employed. | Weekly output in tonnes. | £ per miner per week. | | Profit or (Loss) per tonne in £. |
|---|---|---|---|---|---|
| | | | Revenue. | Profit or (Loss). | |
| Abernant. | 835 | 3,830 | 273 | (74) | (16.2) |
| Aberpergwm. | 317 | 1,169 | 223 | (165) | (44.7) |
| Abertillery New Mine. | 448 | 2,190 | 226 | (126) | (25.8) |
| Bedwas. | 599 | 3,556 | 259 | (126) | (21.2) |
| Betws New Mine. | 683 | 11,141 | 994 | 223 | 13.7 |
| Blaenant. | 698 | 6,871 | 255 | (156) | (15.8) |
| Blaenserchan. | 421 | 2,793 | 306 | (90) | (13.6) |
| Celynen North. | 570 | 3,042 | 257 | (129) | (24.2) |
| Celynen South. | 470 | 1,685 | 167 | (213) | (59.5) |
| Cwm/ Coedely. | 1,274 | 9,453 | 358 | (58) | (7.8) |
| Cynheidre. | 1,033 | 3,832 | 243 | (121) | (32.6) |
| Deep Navigation. | 772 | 7,582 | 425 | 78 | 5.9 |
| Garw. | 689 | 3,073 | 208 | (172) | (38.5) |
| Lady Windsor/ Abercynon. | 1,116 | 8,575 | 304 | (91) | (11.9) |
| Mardy. | 773 | 2,808 | 208 | (133) | (36.7) |
| Markham. | 595 | 4,692 | 377 | (31) | (3.9) |
| Marine. | 640 | 7,743 | 530 | 71 | 5.9 |
| Merthyr Vale. | 664 | 5,343 | 410 | (34) | (4.2) |
| Nantgarw. | 638 | 3,754 | 282 | (171) | (29.1) |
| Oakdale. | 867 | 6,753 | 373 | (59) | (7.5) |
| Penallta. | 645 | 5,413 | 343 | 8 | 0.9 |
| Penrikyber. | 649 | 3,146 | 236 | (99) | (20.5) |
| St. Johns. | 881 | 3,354 | 169 | (153) | (40.2) |
| Six Bells. | 487 | 3,587 | 320 | (74) | (10.0) |
| Taff Merthyr. | 681 | 7,570 | 446 | (1) | (0.1) |
| Tower. | 655 | 3,286 | 267 | (50) | (10.0) |
| Trelewis. | 296 | 3,819 | 442 | (185) | (14.3) |

Each "millstone around the neck of the industry" tended, however, to be the heart and focus of its own long-established community. The main purpose in life of such a community, and sometimes the sole source of jobs and income, was the production of coal. It was therefore no surprise that the abrupt attempt to impose regular business standards upon an industry previously run in the public interest would be confronted by resistance, both radical and far-reaching. Under the banner of "Coal Not Dole" the fight was taken up for such communities, against globalisation and against marginalisation of the working class movement. For a while there was to be a lull before the storm, but both parties knew that a storm was coming.

Plate 14 Mardy Colliery Surface.

Plate 15 The Duke is Introduced to Officials at Fernhill.

David John Hughes (2 from R) would later become an effective manager of Fernhill.

Plate 16  Fernhill - the Unfinished Symphony. The old surface has been demolished and the new will never be completed.
(The closest headgear is for No. 5 shaft with No. 4 behind).

Plate 17  Fernhill Site Today (The Original Fernhill Surface is on the left and North Dunraven on the right).

# Chapter 14

## HUBRIS.

*"Great events and personalities in history repeat themselves,*
*the first time as tragedy, the second time as farce"*
(Karl Marx, quoting Hegel).

## THE GLADIATORS.

### Virtue Versus Righteousness.

The first great victory of the miners was followed in quick succession by a second, when Prime Minister Edward Heath went down to defeat in a general election fought on the theme, "Who runs the country?". From the miners' viewpoint, this political aspect was incidental, the strike being fundamentally concerned with pay and conditions. The third time round involved a different dimension. This time an overt political challenge was made to the right of the National Coal Board to make management decisions in furtherance of the Tory government's policies. It was a conflict therefore primarily about ideology, transcending the issues of pay and conditions, with which strikes have traditionally been associated. Indeed, the subject of difficult working conditions, pushed so hard during the previous national strikes, was now a non-issue for the NUM. What would be the logic in fighting to keep pits open while simultaneously trumpeting how unpleasant it was to work in them?

Whatever the strike's result it was bound to be epoch-making, either opening the door to globalisation and untrammelled market forces, or to a resurgence of trade union power and a controlled economy. The two leading protagonists were colourful, and as diverse as their policies. Margaret Thatcher, the first woman Prime Minister in the UK was a "commitment politician", emotionally committed, as she would see it, to releasing the fresh air of capitalist freedom and "rolling back the powers of the state". The forthcoming NUM action, in her eyes, was nothing less than "insurrection" which, for the future of the industry and of the country had to be defeated. Arthur Scargill, on the other hand, had dedicated himself to "rolling back Thatcherism", an object which was inevitable, "provided we remain united". While enjoying the "high" of being both media star and standard bearer of extra-parliamentary opposition, he was able to attract great loyalty among those who saw the welfare state and the socialist achievements of British society, instead of being further developed, whittled away by an unfeeling, dog-eat-dog orientated government.

As the two opponents squared up, on the right was an apostle of market forces, flushed with victory in the Falklands War and firm in the belief that she had a parliamentary majority to further the market economy. On the left was a Marxist revolutionary, equally firm in the conviction that his mass pickets, with their unbroken record of success, could be the vanguard of the socialist revolution. On the one side a conviction that the coal industry should conform to the dictates of the market place and that the freedom of an individual to seek his own material well-being was paramount. In one of her oft-quoted statements, "There is no such thing as society". On the other side an equally strong conviction that the industry should be run to further the interests of a society fit for the workingman, in particular for the benefit of his union members and the communities in which they lived. Joint action for communal good was the mantra.

The scene was thus set for a battle of the titans, each of the protagonists fully convinced of their qualification to wield the flaming sword of righteousness. It would be a fight to the death, with the loser being cast into the political wilderness forever. It was to turn into one of the most significant events in post-war Britain for, had things turned out differently, the country's history would have been different. It was to have far-reaching economic, political and social implications for decades to come.

On 4 July 1983, at the annual conference of the National Union of Mineworkers, Arthur Scargill spelt out his philosophy in unequivocal terms:

"I am not prepared to accept policies proposed by a government elected by a minority of the British electorate (in spite of its 141 seat parliamentary majority). I am not prepared to quietly accept the destruction of the coalmining industry, nor am I willing to see our social services utterly decimated —— This totally undemocratic government can now easily push through whatever laws it chooses. Faced with possible parliamentary destruction of all that is good and compassionate in our society, extra-parliamentary action will be the only course open to the working class and the Labour movement". The battle lines were forming up! Not everyone, not even among left-wingers, signed on to such rhetoric, and there were alternative views:

"If elements of the left claim the right to bring down a democratically elected Tory Government then right wing extremists are vindicated in bringing down a democratically elected Labour Government. In which case, what is the point in having elections at all"?


## MacGregor Comes On Board.

On 1 September1983, after a tenure of just one year, Norman Siddall retired as Chairman of the National Coal Board. Siddall was a mining engineer who had spent his life in the UK mining industry and who had come to prominence under the Robens' regime. In the world of behind the scenes king-making, the name of Gerald Blackmore had been put forward as replacement, by none other than Ian MacGregor, Chairman of British Steel and doyen of the new world capitalists. Blackmore was also a mining engineer who had risen within the NCB. During the Robens' era he was Area General Manager of the No. 3 (Rhondda) Area in the South Westen Division. In 1965 he had stood among the mourners at the graveside as Mr. Breeze, the manager of Cambrian Colliery, was laid to rest. Subsequently he had left the NCB and emigrated to Canada. Currently he was Chief Executive with a US coalmining company. This suggestion of MacGregor was blocked. Instead, against the tendency of industry insiders to repel all boarders, his own name was pushed through by Prime Minister Margaret Thatcher, plus Chancellor of the Exchequer Nigel Lawson. His immediate boss, Peter Walker, the Secretary of State for Energy and a leading cabinet "wet" was, and would remain, less than enthusiastic about the appointment.

Fresh from his three-year savage pruning of British Steel and its preparation for privatisation, Ian MacGregor now commenced another three-year term, this time as Chairman of the National Coal Board. The new incumbent was twenty days short of his seventy-first birthday and so, on the face of it, well past retiring age himself. He was however healthy, active and self-confident. Silver-haired and deceptively avuncular, he was fully convinced that his abilities as a manager were at their peak.

The MacGregor magic would now be applied to free the coal industry from an endless succession of government grants. His remit was to create a state of financial balance by 1987-88. This was four years later than the government's original target but still a daunting mission. In the current financial year the NCB would record an operating loss of £410M. This was excluding interest charges that totalled an additional £467M. This meant that, in order to keep it in the black for that year alone, an £875M grant from the government would be necessary.

As with Robens, the appointment was political and, as with Robens, MacGregor would have a direct line to Downing Street. There, any political resemblance ended. Whereas Robens had been appointed to make a success of nationalisation, MacGregor's objective was to prepare the ground so as to wipe it off the face of the earth. A vignette included in Robens last address to the NUM annual conference, at Douglas in July 1970 (see Ten Year Stint), perhaps illustrates the difference in background philosophy between the two men. Robens recalled a visit he had made to the United States as junior minister at the Ministry of Fuel and Power. He had met John L. Lewis, the then President of the United Mineworkers of America. Robens argued with Lewis that, although mechanisation and technical progress were obviously desirable, if they were not planned in association with other outlets for the labour no longer required, there would be great domestic and social problems. Robens continued, "Mr Lewis, let me put a hypothetical case to you. Suppose a mine operator said to you: "Mr. Lewis, I have some new machines that will be put into the mine next month and instead of employing 2,000 men I shall want only 500 to turn out the same amount of coal". What would your reaction be?"

Lewis answered, "I would say to the mine operator, O.K., get on with it". When asked about the 1,500 men who would be put on the road he just shook his great shaggy head and laughed into Roben's incredulous face, saying with a roar, "The great expanding American economy will take care of all those boys, and in the meantime I shall want another dollar or so a shift for those that remain". Robens was not entirely convinced at the time. Subsequently he would see some of the human results of mining industry rationalisation in the USA, namely the ghost towns, and the flotsam and jetsam of humanity existing from the soup kitchen that the great expanding American economy had not taken care of. Robens made it clear that on this issue his sympathies did not lie with John L. Lewis.

In stark contrast, it was against just such an American background that MacGregor's reputation as a successful coal man had been won. In 1981 he had been awarded the John Fitz Medal of the American Institute of Mining, Metallurgical and Petroleum Engineers for his, "Distinguished Leadership of the American Mining Industry" (previous recipients of the award included Marconi and Alexander Graham Bell).

His reputation rested upon two things:

Firstly, under his stewardship, coal output of the AMAX corporation had trebled in 10 years to 40Mt, raising it from 11th to 3rd among American coal producers and producing a third as much as the entire British coal industry at that time. The company possessed 11 open cast and one deep mine, with the latter producing 2.5Mt per annum. He was to say that, with the availability of liquid petroleum and natural gas likely to decline, coal had potentially a better future than any other business with which he had ever been associated. That was why in America he had got into the business in the first place. There was however an indispensable prerequisite to all of this - the price had to be right.

As a second characteristic, throughout his career he had exhibited an unyielding opposition to the influence and activities of trade unions. In the recent past he had been victorious in a 2-year dispute with the United Mineworkers of America. Whereas traditional mining areas in the US, such as the Appalachians, are strongly unionised, newer areas in the south and northwest are largely not. Consequently there are problems concerning health care and pension rights. These benefits are paid by the mining companies and not by the state, with many companies finding ways and means of avoiding such costs. There is no National Health Service in the US and many miners have no cover at all. During the first three months of 1975 the huge new open cast mine of the AMAX Corporation at Gillette, Wyoming, was closed by strike action. The pickets were fighting for a cents-per-ton pension contribution from the company. MacGregor judged that, since the men were already earning good money, they would not back a strike for pension rights only, since they would lose wages for a cause that would not increase their current standard of living. After company negotiation with the local "real red-blooded western sheriff" who was to call out a posse in their support, plus the judge who was a "nice orderly old American lawyer", the instigators were run out of town and dispatched back east whence they came. The strike was broken. Although the mine was subject to picketing for a further two years, at the end of the day it was the United Mineworkers of America that had to admit both defeat and a loss of influence in the vast coal measures of the Middle West. No one seemed more capable than this man of blowing Scargill out of the water.


# THE RUN UP.

## Girding their Loins.

The miners' executive regarded this change of regime at the top of the NCB as a certain sign that they would soon have a real fight on their hands. To the NUM it was clear how MacGregor would approach his task. In his previous tenure at British Steel, between 1980 and 1983, one aspect of his performance was to reduce the payroll, in the teeth of trade union opposition, from 166,000 to 85,000. Judging from this track record, Scargill drew the obvious conclusion, "We have consistently warned that this man's mission is to savagely butcher the British coal industry". In an interview, MacGregor himself stated that changes would be "evolutionary, not revolutionary". He regarded himself not as a butcher, but as a plastic surgeon. As to whether the human aspect of the cuts in the steel industry payroll disturbed him, "There is no way, with poor economics you can guarantee a social environment". A sound economic environment had to come first.

## The "Hit List".

In the month of his appointment, MacGregor informed the government he intended to cut the workforce by some 64,000 over three years. His evaluation of market prospects at that time was for a deep-mined output of 90 Mt per annum plus 5 Mt of open cast. Current annual production was about 115 Mt. He saw no future in maintaining uneconomic capacity, turning out coal that the country did not need at costs that it could not afford. The "uneconomic tail" of the industry had to go. In his view he was there to put things right, and had only three years in which to do it. During a tour of his new domain, shortly after his appointment, the men in Bilsdon Glen Colliery in Scotland were informed, "Perform and you have a future, don't, and you have no future, it's as simple as that".

Scargill had long claimed, based upon NCB documents in his possession, the existence of an NCB "hit list", consisting of seventy-five pits slated for closure. A special session of the House of Commons Energy Committee was called to get at the facts. The NCB conceded that the documents were genuine but were merely a review of economic performance, not a basis for actual decision-making. Scargill expressed much scepticism, correctly, since in the current climate poor economic performance implied the threat of closure. The term "hit list" was no doubt overly dramatic, a typical Scargillism. Nevertheless, by simple logic, the government insistence that the coal industry pay its way led inevitably to the shedding of loss-making capacity. All indications were, however, that his members were not yet ready to accept the threat's reality. The NUM agreed, with reluctance, to accept the closure of Cardowan in Scotland and Brynlliw in South Wales, both high up on the list of loss-making pits.

At the time there were 171 pits in the UK and 180,000 mineworkers. When challenged on a television interview as to whether Arthur Scargill was correct in his assertion that MacGregor's aim was to reduce the industry to 100 pits and 100,000 men, the Prime Minister replied, "Mr. MacGregor's aim, and the Government's aim is to produce a good, profitable coalmining industry". In retrospect those figures of Scargill hardly appear as the doomsday scenario they seemed at the time!

## Overtime Ban.

On 30 September 1983, MacGregor responded to the NUM's demand for a "substantial" pay rise with a "first and final" offer of 5.2 per cent. Five more pits were added to the closure list. In protest at both the size of the offer and the unabated intention to slim down the industry, branch and lodge representatives gathered from all over the country voted with impressive unanimity to call an all-out ban on overtime working. That same weekend, MacGregor told a meeting of colliery clerical staff, meeting in Wallsend-on-Tyne, that they and their colleagues had better brace themselves "to get out of the hopeless places" that could never contribute to coal's prosperity, or even survival.

On 31 October 1983, the overtime ban took effect. The unity of this ban was maintained throughout, even in those pits that did not strike for a single day. In fact, it was still being widely observed weeks after all the men finally went back to their jobs. The measure, however, proved to be highly divisive within the NUM's own ranks. This was due to the fact that a relatively small group of craftsmen and specialists were financially the prime sufferers. The significance of overtime in coalmining is that repair work and mechanical preparation, involving primarily this relatively small group, is normally done at weekends. This enables production to start with the first shift on Monday and continue without interruption throughout the week. The men concerned had become used to a life style based upon such regular overtime payments, which they would now lose. The overtime ban was the result of a ballot, the majority of whose voters would not personally be involved in the overtime issue. As time went on, however, and production suffered, bonuses were also cut for production workers.

In December 1983, MacGregor re-submitted his plan to the government. He had decided to accelerate the programme, aiming to cut the workforce by 44,000 over the next two years. In the coming year he proposed 20,000 redundancies. This would involve the closure of around 20 pits while annual capacity would be reduced by 4 Mt. He urged extending the existing redundancy scheme to include miners under the age of 50. The terms agreed with the Government was a two-year scheme whereby a lump sum of £2,000 would be paid for each year of service.

## Confidence.

Not yet aware of the full details, the NUM looked on suspiciously. Among the militants, confidence was high as the following interview with Tyrone O'Sullivan, lodge secretary of Tower Colliery, shows (ref. South Wales Miners' Library, tape AUD/60). The interview was recorded prior to the 1984 strike. Union policy on the pit closure issue was restated during the interview:

"The Board can make a pit unviable through no investment, or mis-investment. As long as there is coal underground we should work it. No pit is unviable truthfully. We can produce the cheapest coal in Europe. We can make our pits viable and that should never be accepted as a reason for closure". With regard to tactics:

"However violent the police become, miners are 288,000 strong, physical, well-organised people. Whatever is put on the road against them will not stop them. They're the most active members of picket lines anywhere. When you see the organization we've got there's nothing in this country to touch it, it's brilliant. We can get men on the road. It costs a lot but we are not afraid to spend. If they make one wrong move they'll have the country on their backs and I hope we are the cause of it. I don't care what police they put against us, or even the forces, which I don't think they will put against us. I know we are strong enough and we'll defeat them. Our men are working hard every day of their lives; they can take on the police. If they want to close a picket down, they'll close it. They are not white-collar workers or timid men. They'll take on any police or picket. If they want to close a place down they'll close it down, they are physically strong enough, 80 per cent of my pit are physically strong men. There is no way they can stop us once we are marching, NO WAY! We'll overwhelm them like ants. However many they put on a picket line, we can put as many".

In spite of the bravado, the interview did make some concession to the need for national unity. Support from railwaymen and dockers was stated as being essential for any national strike over closures. Damage had been done to such national solidarity since the miners did not support the steelworkers during their own redundancy dispute. This was a tactical mistake. The interview continued;

"If they don't forgive us we are in trouble, but 288,000 miners can put up a fight themselves. ——— Ninety-five percent of pits would not cross picket lines, I would bet £100 on it, absolutely certain".

The specific case of Nottinghamshire, which in the event would turn out to be a joker in the pack, was not referred to. That all miners might not be as gung-ho for the cause as he was himself was recognised by Mr. O'Sullivan, who stated that 40 per cent were naturally radical while another 40 per cent were always reluctant. The remaining 20 per cent, however, were floating and could be swayed:

"If you don't lead the men strongly the men will not go on strike, they will always find an excuse not to. Men do not want to lose their bonuses by going on strike". The strikes of 1974-74 were an exception. Then the men forced the leadership into action.

On this occasion, the omens for militancy were not good. After several years of intermittent illness, Lawrence Daly, the NUM General Secretary, retired. In an electorate of 191,000 members, the left-wing candidate, Peter Heathfield, scraped home with a majority of 3,516 votes. It was a less than wholehearted endorsement of the conflict that was to come. His opponent, John Walsh, had campaigned on the basis of "less aggro and more results" and also that a ballot of the membership be a necessary precondition before the taking of any serious industrial action.

## Times Change!

Notwithstanding the ardour of the miners' leaders, there were this time significant differences compared to the situation prevailing at the time of the 1972 and 1974 conflicts. As a consequence of these differences the outcome on this occasion, unlike the quick and decisive victories of the early seventies, was more akin to the charge of the Light Brigade. As per the accusation sometimes levelled against generals, the miners went into action still trying to fight the last war. This time round Government, Police and Generating Board had all taken on board the lessons of the previous decade and were determined never to be made fools of on that scale again. Ten years had gone by, enabling the preparation of contingency plans and, in the case of Government, the introduction of appropriate legislation. In addition, a completely different spirit was abroad in the land, namely:

- Since the last national strike, the miners had become used to a standard of living that compared very well with other industries. With 3 million unemployed in the country at that time, there was much more to lose. Not every miner was happy with the thought of putting at risk that which he had already won. In Nottinghamshire, where a majority of the miners continued to work, such sentiments were felt particularly strongly. MacGregor's strategy of materialism was to resonate. The lure of the family saloon car, the holiday in Spain, plus mortgage payments for the semi-detached would undermine solidarity, essential if the militants were to succeed.

- Compared with 1972 and 1974, social security payments to strikers had been drastically curtailed. Wives and children were entitled to claim social security but now benefits were calculated on the basis that £15 per week strike pay was being received from the union, which would never be the case. The industrial action fund of the union totalled a mere £40,000. This had been kept separate from other assets since February 1972, as a defensive move against the possible legal consequences of the Industrial Relations Act. The previous strikes had been of short duration. In addition, although there was no jam, social security had ensured that there was at least enough cash for their bread. Now, a prolonged strike would mean real poverty.

- The police had learned from experience. Britain had no national police force but 52 local forces, each headed by a Chief Constable having operational control. Authority was divided between the Home Secretary, Chief Constables and local police authorities (made up of local councillors and magistrates). Prime among the new weapons forged as a result of the 1972 mass picketing and crowd control debacle was the National Reporting Centre of the police. This was housed in London and, using improved communications and intelligence, was tasked with matching police requirements at the various points of confrontation with the number of officers each local force could make available. There is no doubt that this played a key role in blunting the picket weapon. It enabled the concept of mass picketing to be countered by an adequate mass of policemen, although great and bloody were to be some of the battles. As the strike proceeded, more and more of the financial burden of such policing was borne directly by the Government.

- Coal stocks, both at pits and at the power stations, were at an all time high and this was combined with temperatures that were rising as summer drew on. The subsequent winter would also prove to be mild.

- Suppliers of power station materials were only given contracts if they were prepared to deliver through picket lines. As a last resort, arrangements were made to fly materials in by helicopter.

- Strikes judged to be illegal, namely those not supported by a ballot of union members and also sympathy strikes by workers not directly affected by the dispute, were now forbidden by law, on pain of union funds being sequestered. Other key unions, e.g. power workers, transport workers and dockers, would therefore think twice about sacrificing themselves on the miners' behalf. Indeed, the South Wales miners had themselves recently refused to come out in sympathy with their local steel industry, involved in their own protest against redundancy.

- The memories of the "Winter of Discontent" hung heavily in the public consciousness and had not been forgotten by the media. Later, miners' leaders would complain bitterly about media lack of support, if not down right antagonism, but this had not happened in a vacuum. Their colleagues in the trade union movement had already ensured, by their actions in 1978-79, a basic public distaste for industrial action. This contrasted sharply with the early nineteen-seventies, when public support for, "the lowly paid miner" was widespread and profound.

## THE STRIKE BEGINS.

### The Bait.

In February 1984, MacGregor was jostled to the ground by demonstrating miners at a Northumberland colliery. It was an early foretaste of the violence that would later be released.

Although the conflict was expected, the time and place of its initiation was a surprise. In retrospect, it is seen as being a most inopportune timing for the miners' cause, being too early in the year. As a result of the overtime ban, coal stocks at the power stations, although still considerable, were decreasing. By the time winter came around they might well have been down to a level low enough to cause concern if the strike was to be a prolonged one. Margaret Thatcher would later write:

"In dealing with the coal industry you must have the mentality of a general as much as that of an accountant, and the generalship must often be Fabian rather than Napoleonic".

In his book The Enemy Within, Ian MacGregor gives credence to the belief that the government and NCB deliberately provoked the strike, at a time most opportune for them. He quotes himself, in a conversation with the Prime Minister, as saying:

"It seems obvious that if Scargill is heading for a confrontation, first of all he will try to prevent the further accumulation of coal stocks in the next year, then challenge us with a set of demands we can't meet as the next winter comes on —— Therefore Prime Minister, I think we should realize this and try, if a confrontation comes, to make sure it happens at a time suitable to us rather than to him".

The Prime Minister, looking puzzled, asked, "How can you manage that? It seems you are going to dictate when this strike is going to happen".

"That will be part of my job. We have to face the fact that the miners' leaders will almost certainly use any attempt to put the industry in order as an excuse to launch an assault on the NCB and, through us, on your government. We have to be totally prepared for that contingency".

In March 1984, Scargill took the bait. The spark occurred with such an "attempt to put the industry in order". The National Coal Board announced that they would bring forward closure of the pit Corton Wood, in South Yorkshire. This was regarded as breaking an earlier NCB commitment to the community and antagonised the NUM. The economic case for closure at that time was questionable. The Monopolies and Mergers Commission report had indicated that the receipts at Cortonwood were £44.3 /t, with operating costs £50.5 /t, thus giving a loss of £6.2 /t. However, the fixed cost element (other operating expenses, overheads, depreciation) lay between 17.2 per cent and 23.1 per cent of the unit cost of £50.5 /t. This component would not be saved as a result of the decision for closure. The mine was therefore making a contribution of between £2.49-£5.45 /t to NCB operating performance ("Accountancy" magazine, late 1984).

The NCB issued a rebuttal of the magazine article, stating that, "Future production and marketing prospects have to be considered, e.g. limited reserves remaining and likely increase in unit costs as final exhaustion approached, plus output being stocked as no market exists". (Author's note - It should be noted that the production and marketing problems referred to were future, not current, while policy at the time was anyway that coal stocks be increased)!

In the case of Lewis Merthyr/Tymawr, the attempt to escalate the overtime ban into a full strike had failed. This occasion was different. Corton Wood was in Scargill's home territory, for months the main recipient of his speeches and rallies. Inaction would have implied loss of face. A ballot of his 66,000 Yorkshire members had already given him 86 per cent approval for a resolution which read, "Are you in favour of giving the NUM Yorkshire Area authority to take various forms of industrial action (including strike action, if necessary) to stop the closure of any pit, unless on the grounds of exhaustion?"

Scargill announced that Corton Wood was just the beginning of another closure wave. In spite of the fact that it was still early spring and that energy consumption would not peak for some time, now was the time he chose to stand and fight. As he led his miners over the top there would be retrospective quotations of General Ludendorff, referring to the British Expeditionary Force in 1914, "Lions led by donkeys".

## Playing Games with the Rule Book.

On 5 March 1984, at a meeting of the Yorkshire area council, the vote was for strike action. A call was made on all other areas, and other unions, for immediate support. Half the local pits joined in with a will. The militants had a problem, however. Since becoming president, Scargill had already initiated, and lost, two ballots calling for a national strike. It was unlikely that a third such call would be any more successful on this occasion.

Previously, Rule 43 in the union rulebook had governed all national disputes. This laid down that a "national strike shall only be entered upon as a result of a ballot vote of the members". The previous two-thirds majority required had already been reduced in July 1971, but a 55 per cent majority was still required to get a national strike off the ground (later this was reduced again, to a simple majority). Scargill therefore adopted a ruse. He fell back upon paragraph 41 of the union rulebook. The object of this rule was to enable purely local issues to be dealt with locally, subject to a veto by the National Executive over industrial action in individual areas. It allowed local strikes to be initiated by individual pits or areas, even without a ballot being taken, subject to approval having been first sought and granted at National Executive level. Technically, therefore, there would not be any national strike, just a nation-wide series of simultaneous area strikes. These did not require a ballot, merely approval by the National Executive. Logically, such a situation should mean a whole series of area negotiations between the NUM and Coal Board locally, not national negotiations involving the National President. This, however, was not what the NUM leadership had in mind, made clear by Scargill's public calls at this time for all miners in the country to stop work.

Rule 41 therefore facilitated the stratagem whereby the minority of militant pits could push a national strike upon their less than enthusiastic colleagues. The key to success lay in trade union solidarity. Those units on strike would picket their non-striking colleagues, relying on such solidarity to bring out the latter in sympathy. As things were to turn out, such solidarity would be patchy. Centrifugal forces, which had developed amongst the miners since the last strike, would become all too apparent. In the tiny North Wales Coalfield the situation was epitomised when, of the two pits there, Bersham joined the strike while Point of Ayr continued to work throughout.

Rule 41 had never, on any previous occasion, been used as a constitutional platform to justify a national stoppage. When Scargill briefly canvassed the idea during the Lewis Merthyr/Tymawr discussions of 1983, the remainder of the executive had ruled it out of court. The whole strategy hinged on the sentiments expressed in one of Scargill's fiery speeches at the beginning of the strike;

"We're in a fight to save our jobs and our pits and I don't care what arguments you advance, I don't care what statistics you put forward, I don't care what rules and democracy you quote, there is one rule in this union's rulebook and there is one rule in the whole of the trade union rulebook in Britain that supersedes every other - when workers are on strike you don't cross picket lines".

In the absence of any democratic process, picketing, instead of being a means to win over minds, became a means of coercion. In the absence of a ballot, the only way of spreading the strike was by muscling men out. It would prove to be the case that it was only muscle that could keep them out.

On 7 March 1984, Mick McGahey, president of the Scottish miners who had immediately followed the Yorkshire walkout, said:

"I want to make it clear, we are not dealing with niceties here. We will not be constitutionalised out of a defence of our jobs. Area by area will decide, and in my opinion it will have a domino effect". By skillful application of Rule 41, striking areas could receive national approval on an individual basis. They were then free to picket the non-striking areas. This was the "domino effect" and the strike rolled on throughout the UK.

On 8 March 1984, the National Executive met. Emlyn Williams, the South Wales president, moved endorsement of the Scottish and Yorkshire requests for recognition of their strike calls under Rule 41. This was carried. Picketing now became crucial, as striking miners spread throughout the country, so as to convince their colleagues that withdrawal of labour was the path of righteousness. Local ballots were held throughout the country, as Area after Area insisted on having one. The experience of South Wales was typical. Only six pits downed tools, the remaining twenty-one voted to ignore the strike call. They had not been supported over Lewis Merthyr/Tymawr, why should they now strike over Cortonwood? Emlyn Williams, who had set the whole official process in motion, was moved to reflect, "I've been leading the South Wales miners for twenty-five years and never before encountered a rejection like this".

## Manipulation.

Until such time, however, as the union leaders could vote in a new membership, they would either have to accept the wishes of the membership they had or opt for manipulation. They opted for manipulation. Emlyn Williams, the same Emlyn Williams who in 1974 had said that they had no choice other than to accept the wishes of the membership, would now turn a blind eye as activists organised enough pickets from the six Welsh collieries on strike to bring out the whole coalfield. It was a grotesque travesty, of democracy and of constitutional trade unionism.

Twenty years later Tyrone O'Sullivan would justify his actions, being quoted as saying, "The fact was that within the National Union of Mineworkers there were too many non-mineworkers to pass a strike vote". By this he meant that of the 225,000 or so NCB employees, 45,000 were white-collar workers. These allegedly did not have the motivation to fight closures. In addition, many of them were just wives providing a second income. Apart from the implication that, "All animals are equal but some are more equal than others", the fact was that the great majority of his own South Wales miners had rejected strike action.

On Sunday 11 March 1984, union men from the six pits on strike, including Tyrone O'Sullivan, the Branch Secretary of Tower Lodge and Kim Howells, Union Research Officer in South Wales, met at the Ambulance Hall in Hirwaen. At Tower the vote had been 99 per cent in favour of a strike and Tyrone O'Sullivan would become chairman of the Cynon Valley Strike Committee. He would forever insist that, were it not for the strike, pits would have closed immediately and that the strike sustained the position of pits in the South Wales coalfield for a number of years.

Tower would be one of the most active collieries, in terms of putting pickets in the field. At the meeting, maps were studied, all collieries located and plans made. They then returned to their own villages and booked the buses, which the following morning would be filled with pickets. Local mores were such as to readily accept the Scargill doctrine, that whatever the legal niceties "you do not cross picket lines". The spirit of 1911 and of 1926 was still abroad. The feeling was still endemic that without mutual support, individuals, including the weak and infirm, are exposed to the arrogance of power. If they scatter when conflict looms, they are lost. Those who queried the downing of tools before working class solidarity had been proven at the ballot box were faced with the prospect of becoming a "scab". A pamphlet, written by a certain Jack London, made it clear what a "scab" was:

"After god had finished the rattlesnake, the toad and the vampire, he still had some awful substance left with which he made a scab —— A scab is a two-legged animal with a corkscrew soul, a waterlogged brain, a combination backbone of jelly and glue. Where others have a heart he has a tumour of rotten principles. When a scab comes down the street, men turn their backs, the angels weep in heaven and the devil shuts the gates of heaven to keep him out —— Esau was a traitor to himself; Judas Iscariot was a traitor to his god; Benedict Arnold was a traitor to his country.

A STRIKE BREAKER IS A TRAITOR to his god, his country, his wife, his family and his class.

A REAL MAN NEVER BECOMES A STRIKE BREAKER".

An alternative definition was never circulated:

"A scab is someone who participates in a vote, in which the majority are for strike action, and then refuses to honour the decision. If you are denied the right to vote, it's impossible to be a scab".

By Tuesday 13 March 1984, all but 30 of the 171 pits in the UK had been picketed into submission. Two days later, only 11 were working normally.

## THE STRIKE GETS SERIOUS.

### Poverty.

Initially, on the part of the union rank and file, confidence reigned. After all, they had won the two previous battles. Any euphoria that there might have been, however, was soon brought down to earth, as regular pay packets were replaced by social security payments, now significantly reduced on the basis that men were receiving strike pay of £15 a week from the union. This would never be the case, although those on picket duty (and only those on picket duty) did receive a contribution from union funds (later to be sequestrated) of £2 per week. Dependants alone were eligible to claim social security, not the men themselves, a problem for those who were single. For married couples with children, the art of living on five pounds per week was to be developed over the months ahead. At this time, the weekly take home pay of a typical face worker in South Wales was £98 (including bonus).

Not every relationship was to survive the strain. While many men were out fighting for a cause and sometimes spending long periods away from home on picket duty, it was the women who, in unaccustomed loneliness, had to come to terms with day-to-day living. For some men who stayed at home, it became a terrible thing to watch the wife approach a nervous breakdown through the worry of mortgage repayment and other bills, while continually having to say "no" to children who had previously never been without. In most cases building societies and other creditors showed leniency, but even then it involved a reduction and not an elimination of repayments, while increased contributions were being built up for the future. As weeks became months and the months clocked up, with no end in sight, savings evaporated. Cars were sold and endowments cashed in. With building society letters threatening legal proceedings for repossession of the family home, with the wife in floods of tears on the telephone, begging creditors to hold off, many miners would question the cause for which they were being asked to suffer.

Fund raising initiative was to be taxed to the limit, and charity was to prove indispensable. The rattle of the miners collection bucket became familiar on the streets of British towns. Even if Scargill as a personality was anathema to some people, they could still be moved by the plight of an individual striker. By and large, the miners retained their image as good-hearted, rough diamonds, macho men of the soil. Among others, support was provided by racial and other minorities, plus the National Union of Students with, in the words of one commentator, miners being presented on university campuses like the noble savage in "Brave New World". The women's role was critical. Without their support at home the strike could not have been sustained. In many cases they played not just a supporting but a leading role. A group of women emerged who were able to go anywhere, to speak, fund-raise or picket. A group of Maerdy women went to Oxford, where the Oxford Miners Support Group was formed. It raised a considerable amount of finance to feed the miners. Among the areas that also formed miners support groups, which helped the strike fund, were Islington, London and Poole in Dorset.

Soup kitchens reappeared from the history books as miners' wives organised food centres based in the miners' welfare halls. Here, numerous meetings would also discuss the latest situation report on demonstrations, picket-line strategies and food parcel distribution. The three ultra-militant pits in Kent would have it easier in this respect, due to their proximity to the great catchment area of the metropolis, with its booming economy and vocal support from "Red Ken" Livingstone, of Greater London Council fame.

### The Government Reaction.

On Wednesday 14 March 1984 in the evening, David Jones, a young Yorkshire miner of Welsh background, collapsed and died in a crush of fellow pickets near Ollerton Pit in Nottinghamshire. He would have been an example of the outside influence that, in the view previously expressed by Lord Robens, was perverting Yorkshire's moderate soul. The day was to be fateful for another reason.

Earlier, at 3pm in the afternoon, MacGregor had had a meeting with the Prime Minister, plus Energy Secretary, Peter Walker and Home Secretary, Leon Brittan. The extent of the strike and Scargill's methods had taken them by surprise. Peter Walker had previously advised the Cabinet that the miners had never initiated a national strike without a ballot. Consequently they were unlikely to on this occasion. The widespread nature of the strike, and how this had been achieved, was totally unexpected. MacGregor was boiling with righteous indignation. According to his own account (The Enemy Within), he put it as vehemently as he could:

"Prime Minister, I am sorry to have to say this, but I never thought I would be sitting here in the UK, wishing I had a bunch of good untidy American cops out there. Because, whatever else you can say about them, if someone points out to them a law is being broken then they go and do something about it. Unhappily, I must tell you that our British police don't seem to have the same conviction about their job. This aspect of the fight is not between the NCB and the NUM. It is between men who want to work and a bunch of thugs who are trying to deprive them of that right, yet the law-enforcement machinery seems to want to keep out of it".

He suggested that, if this were America, the authorities would have called out the National Guard by now. There was a rather sharp reaction that this was not America and such a move, calling out the military, would be political dynamite. MacGregor went on:

"Well, you've got to do something, because you are dealing with a well-rehearsed and organised rebellion here. You know, from what Scargill has said, that he is out to topple the government. If it goes on, I fear he will succeed".

To MacGregor's delight, he found he was preaching to the converted. After all, in the eyes of the Conservative leadership, the NUM had in the past, and were now in the process of repeating, nothing less than the undermining of a constitutional state. Thatcher made her attitude clear on a number of occasions, "This is an attempt to substitute the rule of the mob for the rule of law, and it must not succeed".

Motivated as they were perceived to be by an alien ideology, "The Enemy Within" would indeed be fought, by focused application of the civilian security apparatus of the state. There would later be allegations that things went beyond this, from the use of soldiers in police uniform (see The Benn Diaries, 4 November 1986), to MI5 destabilisation of the NUM leadership (refer to Seamus Milne's book -The Enemy Within - the secret wars against the miners). Much later, in 1993, the MPs Tam Dalyell and George Galloway would table a motion in the House of Commons, noting the use of NUM Chief Executive Roger Windsor as an agent of the Security Service during the strike.

To date, there had been very little actual violence, although the threat of potential violence had contributed to the strike's effectiveness. Now, violence would become real and would escalate, as the pickets' determination that working miners should not get through ran into police determination that they should. Before it was all over there would be a second death on the picket lines, as well as thousands injured and arrested. Never before had squads of riot-trained police been required on such a scale.

On Thursday, 15 March 1984, the day following the above meeting, Home Secretary Leon Brittan told the House of Commons:

"Any attempt to intimidate those who wish to go to work is a breach of the criminal law. The mere presence of large numbers of pickets can be intimidating. The police have a duty to prevent obstruction and intimidation —— A major co-ordinated police response, involving police officers throughout the country, has been deployed to ensure that any miner who wishes to work —— may do so".

The National Reporting Centre at Scotland Yard was quickly activated. Police tactics developed over the previous decade were now to bear fruit. The first units of police from outside the coalfield were already on their way to Nottinghamshire.

**Reason.**

Phillip Weekes, the South Wales Area Director, tried reason. On 23 March 1984, he issued the following press release:

"In the last 2-3 weeks many damaging and wildly incorrect statements have been attributed by the media to NUM leaders and not denied by them. For example, it has been said that the Board plan to annihilate at least 1/3 of the coalfield within 12 months, and to reduce it to about 6 pits over the next 8 to 9 years. That is not true —— Despite the overtime ban from 1 November, South Wales made very good progress in 1983-84. Productivity improved and our costs were reduced. If there had been no strike we would have improved our financial performance by something like £25 M compared with the previous year —— Our markets are uniformly strong. The emergence of Aberthaw B as a successful, modern and large power station has meant that not only anthracite and coking coal but also steam raising coals have been in demand. As a result, coalfield stocks have fallen by well over 1 Mt in 1983-84 —— Four collieries, Bedwas, Penrikyber, St. Johns, and Treforgan are currently the subject of review procedures —— Celynen South is expected to exhaust economic reserves in the latter half of 1884-85. The underground linkage of Mardy and Tower, and the closure of Mardy surface has already been agreed with the lodges concerned, as has the absorption of Blaenserchan into the Marine complex —— The Board will complete their arrangements in respect of all the above-mentioned collieries with no compulsory redundancies. The Board has no other proposals for closure or merger in 1984-85 —— It is not Board policy to reduce output from South Wales pits. On the contrary, I shall wish to enter into discussions with the NUM as soon as normal working is resumed, not only on the redeployment of men from some or all of the collieries referred to above, but also on ways and means of increasing output from continuing pits to at least 7 Mt per annum —— Finally there is the question of Margam New Mine. If the present dispute can be quickly settled, if we can get back to normal working, if I can demonstrate to the Board that we have well laid plans in South Wales for achieving an output of 7 Mt per annum from our continuing pits, then I believe I shall be in a strong position to press once more for Margam. Nothing would give me greater pleasure than to be able to do so".

Phillip Weekes was trusted in the coalfield and subsequently would do his best to save what could be saved. However, he could be, and in the event was, overruled by MacGregor. Relations between the two had not yet deteriorated to the point to which they would subsequently sink. His current opinion of the Board Chairman was confided to his diary in the entry of 13 March 1984:

"MacGregor has now been with us for about 8 months. His reputation came before him but at first he appeared to be a shrewd fellow, who handled Board meetings well. Always laconic with press and TV - easy to chat to - a splendid double-handed handshake, the arm on your shoulder, a ready smile with his mouth, but not with his eyes. However, he is there and he is beloved by our leaderine".


## Miners' Solidarity?

Their initial lack of enthusiasm notwithstanding, once the strike had commenced South Wales was to show that it had lost nothing of its traditional spirit of working class solidarity. Support was to remain virtually total, with strikebreakers, the so-called "scabs", few and far between. No need here for use of the ultimate weapon in Scargill's armoury, the massed picket. By this time flying pickets were illegal but, illegal or not, they made their presence felt, mainly in Nottinghamshire. Here the desire to continue earning good money in a coalfield regarded as being largely secure took precedence in the eyes of many over any nebulous concept of unity and union folklore. What motivated them were their financial commitments, and the lifestyle to which they had become accustomed. Here the strike motion had not only been rejected, the instruction by the area executive to respect picket lines was also widely ignored. A high proportion ignored the crowds, missiles and abuse, forcing their way, with heavy police support, into work.

The lack of a ballot gave the Nottinghamshire miners the moral authority to continue working. It also gave the legal authority for individuals to take on the union in the courts, winning their cases and hurting the NUM financially. Union officials might have walked off the job but the vast majority of the ordinary branch members were going in every working day. Its twenty-five working pits guaranteed that the greatest concentration of power stations in the country, along the Trent Valley, would never miss a shift. One local union official summed up the county's basic attitudes:

"I don't want to be in a position where I'm all right Jack, but I don't want to be in a position where we are ordered what to do. It's like feeding the people of Ethiopia; everyone wants to do it, but you don't take the last crumb off your own table. You give your surplus, but you don't inflict hardship on yourself". This attitude was to bring down on them the full fury of the massed flying pickets.

## Violence.

Irresistible force was to be confronted with an immovable object as, apart from a few days at the beginning of the strike, nearly 25,000 Nottinghamshire miners opted to continue working. MacGregor claimed later that in the first seven months more than 7,000 people were arrested for offences connected with the dispute (most of these on the picket lines or for attacks on property); 790 police officers were injured, 65 of them seriously; two working miners committed suicide; two died as a result of picket line violence and 255 were injured.

With time, picketing became more determined and behaviour more extreme. There were no Marquis of Queensbury rules, and both sides played dirty. It was generally felt that local police tended to handle a situation more calmly and professionally than forces drafted in from elsewhere. In particular the metropolitan police had an aggressive reputation. Between periods of picket line duty, police and strikers might pass the time with a game of soccer but, gradually and on both sides, there was a fatalistic acceptance of the violence. Police dogs and snatch squads for the snatching and arresting of leading rioters were used, while the NCB decided that anyone arrested while on picket duty would be fired.

In effect, the police sealed off the Nottinghamshire Coalfield. In a highly questionable restriction of the individual's freedom of movement, for days at a time parts of the county became virtual no-go areas. Would-be visitors ran a gauntlet of roadblocks and spot traffic checks. According to the chief constable, in the first twenty-seven weeks of the strike, 164,508 "presumed pickets" were prevented from entering the county. Whoever they were, they either turned back when ordered or faced immediate arrest. Those who got through, mainly from South Wales and Yorkshire, hid up in strikers' houses, like resistance fighters or prisoners on the run, often venturing forth at night to attack the families, homes and property of men who had chosen to work. Intimidation in the villages went hand-in-hand with the barrages of missiles and abuse at the pit gates. There were frequent ugly scenes. In the end, police discipline and their sometimes questionable rough justice would win through.

At Gascoigne Wood, part of the brand new Selby complex nestling in the Vale of York, the rural surroundings enabled a bizarre twist to be given to the chaos. Some of the pickets, apparently brought up on a diet of "Wagon Train" and "Bonanza" released all the cattle from adjacent fields and, using their latent cowboy skills, stampeded them with accompanying whoops and cries towards the riot-shielded blue line. Those cops who did not also fancy themselves as rodeo artists scattered for cover. It was said that not all of the excrement lying on the road afterwards came from the cattle.

Security forces of the state were one of the few groups upon which the Thatcher regime had smiled, as far as salary increases were concerned. These were now combined with considerable overtime payments. With earnings typically 2.5-3 times their normal salary, the regime, and the strike, were to prove a financial boon for the police. It was not unknown for NUM branches to receive sardonic letters of thanks from groups of coppers who, when parked in their transit vans as the pickets drove past, would sometimes wave pay cheques at their impoverished foe. "Keep on strike boys, because my bank balance is incredible" was a typical comment. The pickets had nothing to counter with, other than taunt the police with the rhetorical question of what their wives were up to in their absence.

# THE BATTLE FOR STEEL.
## Strategy, what Strategy?

With a warm early spring and record stocks, any early interruption to the supply of electricity was discarded as unrealistic by the miners' leaders, despite anguished criticism from many rank-and-file strikers, particularly those from South Wales. However, the steel industry was also a potential target, and there was the possibility of support from other unions.

Already in the early days of the strike the decision was made to concentrate maximum effort on cutting deliveries to the four biggest integrated steel complexes, Margam and Llanwern in South Wales, Ravenscraig on the Clyde, and Scunthorpe in Lincolnshire. Margam and Ravenscraig, however, were adjacent to deep-water ports, with adequate facilities for unloading both coal and iron-ore directly from the ships. There was an additional problem. Faced with crumbling markets and international competition, steel was in decline. In the opinion of many, shutting it down was less likely to bring swift victory than to put even more steelworkers and miners on the dole. In addition, the miners had not supported the steelworkers in their own battles with Ian MacGregor when that industry was being run-down. With total non-cooperation from the steel unions, and sharp divisions throughout the rest of the labour movement, effective action was replaced by endless confrontation and some of the bitterest clashes of the strike.

On 3 June 1984, Phillip Weekes made an entry in his diary concerning the first of a series of clandestine meetings he would hold with the NUM leadership in South Wales:

"Just over a week ago I took South Wales NUM officials George Reece and Emlyn Williams to a secret lunch at St. Mellons Country Club (outside Newport). They promised to keep things on an even keel, safety men in all pits, minimum picketing and, above all, our coking coal would continue to flow into the Llanwern Steelworks. Well, my comrades kept their promises until Scargill interfered. Emlyn was saying publicly, we will look after the Llanwern Steelworks because I run NUM policy in South Wales (but) Scargill and co. made him backtrack. The boys were virtually forced to check the flow of coking coal to Llanwern".

Cooperation was now seen as collaboration and orders were given to picket the Margam Steelworks. Margam itself had its own deepwater port but coal and iron ore brought in here were also transported by road to Llanwern. In South Wales the first real clashes between police and pickets occurred, as daily convoys of 40 lorries or more roared along the M4, escorted by police motorcyclists plus a police vehicle leading and trailing the convoy. The South Walian police were proud of their low key stance. The issue would be treated as a traffic problem, rather than one of civil disorder.

Months later, as the aggravation increased, there would be a new dimension. Windscreens were smashed and other damage inflicted by a deluge of stones and other missiles hurled by strikers emerging from undergrowth along the motorway, while rocks, pieces of metal and wood were rained down from bridges over the M4. For the moment, however, Phil Weekes remained sanguine, writing in his diary:

"The South Wales police have been superb, largely due to the Deputy Chief Constable Viv Brookes, with whom I have been in close communication and who is respected by the NUM. Between the sensible approach of Viv, the South Wales NUM leadership and our management, South Wales has been a vicar's tea party compared with England and Scotland".


**Conflict at Orgreave.**

In mid-June 1984, far from the "vicar's tea party" of South Wales, violence and aggravation reached its peak in the battle of the Orgreave coke works. Here, NCB coal was "coked" in huge ovens, ready for use in the blast furnaces of Scunthorpe Steelworks forty miles away. It was here that the battle for steel was fought, in the literal sense of the term, and won by the authorities. Behind the scenes, internal NUM differences on strategy were beginning to appear. The mass picketing of Orgreave was a case in point. George Reece, General Secretary of the South Wales NUM, would later maintain that South Wales had opposed this action, on the grounds that it was not worth the effort. There were only two days' of coal supply there and anyway the plant would be bypassed, "but to get this across to Arthur was an impossibil-ity, he was locked into the 1972 era". After the fêting he had received in Yorkshire Scargill was riding the crest of a wave, "Arthur believed he could walk on water" (SWML AUD/573).

There was no chance that shutting down Orgreave would damage the country's economy. It would, however, be a victory in the battle of wills. With success proving elusive, closing the plant down would be a public display of NUM superiority and might weaken the opponents' resolve. It had of course the poten-tial to backfire if things did not go according to plan. It was meant to be a repeat performance of Saltley

Gate, twelve years earlier. Instead, it was a vindication of the National Reporting Centre. This proved to be a formidable entity, flexible and effective. Especially the left would see it as an undermining of the local autonomy of British police forces and the beginning of a kind of national force to handle riots and civil disturbance. What it proved was that the days of the invincible flying picket were over. Mass could and would be met with equivalent mass.

The Chief Constable later stated the police presence as being 4,600 officers and 40 horses, together with dogs. Some observers judged it as being up to 8,000, facing 10,000 or so pickets. Scargill had made public calls for pickets from all over the country to beef up the presence at Orgreave. En route, as they encountered police checks, there was a surprising reversal of normal procedure. On this occasion, instead of being turned back, they were directed to proceed and informed how to get there. In the cauldron awaiting them, ten years of preparation by the authorities finally bore fruit. Flying pickets were met with flying squads of police. According to many strikers they included soldiers in police uniforms: "They were there to fight". On the police side, military terminology was the order of the day. The absence of numbers on some uniforms would arouse suspicion elsewhere, not just at Orgreave.

The initial carnival atmosphere turned into pushing and jostling as the first lorries approached. Determined, and armed with a host of assorted missiles, the pickets confronted phalanxes of police in riot gear, both mounted and on foot and banging their shields in a well- rehearsed attempt to break morale. Then, in a change from just defensive tactics, the police lines opened and the cavalry charged through. Faced with the prospect of being run down or clubbed by the martial phalanx storming towards them, the miners broke and ran, scattering in fear before tons of onrushing horse meat. With tactics refined in Northern Ireland, "Snatch Squads" followed up, grabbing ringleaders from the mass and carting them, struggling, away. Miners who reacted, incensed at the manhandling of their colleagues, were themselves roughed up in turn. Some of the most dramatic images of the whole confrontation were when pictures of Scargill, directing his legions like some loud hailer toting Napoleon at Waterloo, gave way to scenes of thousands of strikers fleeing across open fields, pursued by the baton-wielding cavalry of mounted police. Scargill himself was arrested and received a blow to the back of the head, inflicted by the police he said; accidentally as he slipped and fell down a bank according to the police.

As the cavalry returned to the police lines, to the applause of their colleagues on foot, the rout of the miners was complete. When the final accounts were totted up, the bloodstained heads, broken limbs, blighted lives and long prison sentences arriving out of Orgreave turned out to have been in vain. British Steel was able to report that the output for the year, far from falling, had exceeded expectations.

## LETTER WRITING.

In the same month as Orgreave, June 1984, MacGregor wrote a "Dear Colleague" letter to all employees. It went on;

"Your Future in Danger.

I have been accused of planning to butcher the industry. I have no such intention or desire. I want to build up the industry into one we can all be proud to be part of. But if we cannot return to reality and get back to work then the industry may well be butchered. But the butchers will not be the Coal Board —— This is a strike which should never have happened. It is based on very serious misrepresentation and distortion of the facts. At great financial cost miners have supported the strike for fourteen weeks because your leaders told you this:

- That the Coal Board is out to butcher the coal industry.

- That we plan to do away with 70,000 jobs.

- That we plan to close down around 86 pits, leaving only 100 working collieries.

IF THESE THINGS WERE TRUE I WOULD NOT BLAME MINERS FOR GETTING ANGRY OR FOR BEING DEEPLY WORRIED.

<u>BUT THESE THINGS ARE ABSOLUTELY UNTRUE.</u>

I state that categorically and solemnly. You have been deliberately misled".

Also in June, it was not only MacGregor who had been busy preparing letters. NUM General Secretary Peter Heathfield wrote to the general secretaries of all the main power unions, asking them to respect NUM picket lines. Crippling of the electricity generating industry was a tactic that had previously proven decisive. This time around, and in contrast to the previous national strikes, picketing at power stations was both sporadic and desultory. On this occasion the picket army was fully committed elsewhere, trying to turn around the recalcitrant members among their own ranks. Heathfield's request was bizarre; that all power stations be considered as picketed, even in the total absence of any miners at the entrance gate. A deafening silence was the main response.

## KEEPING THE LIGHTS ON.

### The Generation Mix.

A repeat of the 1972 experience, with the shutting down of generating stations or even the inflicting of major power cuts, would have been equally traumatic for the nation. With the strike lasting longer than expected, and looking as though it would extend into winter, the Generating Board expressed concern that, if the supply position could not be improved, power cuts would be inevitable during the period of high electricity demand. Government ministers monitoring the situation suggested that stronger measures were necessary, including the possible use of troops.

Electricity generation is far and away the biggest customer for coal. In the last full pre-strike year, 81.8 Mt were burned. At that time, Britain had fifty-five coal-fired power stations, representing some fifty-five percent of generating capacity. There were sixteen oil-burning plants (23 per cent) and thirteen nuclear stations (14 per cent). For cost reasons, in recent years the pattern had been to rely on coal for 80 per cent of actual electricity production. Nuclear power ran continually at their rated load, while the prohibitively expensive oil contribution was used for peaks and emergencies. The trick during the strike was to change this pattern. Some limited success was achieved by running with reduced system reserve, increasing purchases from private generators and running peak-load gas turbine generators for much longer than their design periods. Such measures were marginal, however.

### Oil to the Front!

Normally, generating plant is brought on stream in the order of cost-effectiveness; now a computer programme named endurance was written to switch the whole focus of CEGB operation from cost efficiency to coal stock preservation. Nuclear capacity was in any event normally run close to full load. The use of gas for power generation was limited at that time, but oil-fired generation was increased to maximum output, despite the fact that oil was twice as expensive as coal and coal stocks were at an all-time high. The two newest oil-fired stations, Grain and Littlebrook in southeast England, went into high levels of overload. With fingers crossed all round, the 660 MW sets were run at 10 per cent above their nominal rating for months on end. At every coal-fired station where it was possible to burn more oil together with the coal, this was done. Oil-fired plants that had been closed were brought back into service, with staff drawn from other stations. Elderly components within such plants were hurriedly adapted. Large coal-fired stations in strike-bound areas and not receiving coal supplies were modified to burn oil. They could not supply anything like full load but their assistance was vital. Operation of the national grid system, whereby normally large amounts of power flowed south from the concentration of coal-fired stations in the north, was reversed, since all of the large oil-fired stations were in the south.

### Coal Keeps Coming!

These changes brought the coal contribution down to 50 per cent from the normal 80 per cent. Notts' decision to keep working filled a full three-fifths of this 50 per cent. The remaining 20 per cent came from stocks, open cast, imports and those other scattered pits still producing. It was just about sustainable and was sustained, though highly vulnerable to picketing and diverse acts of god. Those coal-fired stations deep in the most strike-bound regions of Scotland, Yorkshire and South Wales sat quietly ticking over through the summer, ready to commit their remaining stocks when winter really started to bite.

## The Day of the Juggernaught.

The rail unions were giving strong support to the striking miners. Consequently rail transport, the usual method of moving coal from working pits to power stations, was only a shadow of its former self. This problem was countered by a massive turn to road transport, with hundreds of contractors being engaged. With the help of local authorities and police, routes were arranged through quiet country lanes and villages, to the chagrin of local inhabitants. It took time to build up the fleets of lorries and their drivers had to be given protection against assault, both during overnight stays and on journeys through picket lines. By the time that the new operating regimes were in place, coal stocks had fallen by 6 M tonnes. By the summer they were falling only moderately and by mid-summer hardly at all.

## Coal Sneaks Ashore.

Although of infinitely less importance than oil, sea-borne coal continued to get through. Polish coal, carried in Russian ships, benefited from a long-standing mutual arrangement between British and Soviet dockers. Larger vessels, particularly from the United States, faced the problem of finding suitable berths where they would not fall foul of the Transport and General Workers Union. The trick was to land at Rotterdam and tranship onto small coasters. These would then set off to some backwater jetty, so remote that the miners and their allies had never heard of it. Obscure dots on the British coastline would now find themselves transformed into centres of international trade.

## Recalcitrant Power Stations.

An additional problem was that the staff at four coal-fired stations, Aberthaw and Uskmouth in South Wales, plus Brighton and Didcot, supported the striking miners. Staff here refused initially to use the coal and then to maintain the equipment for handling it. Initially, it was judged unwise to risk full-scale conflict by forcing coal deliveries on them, or building up their oil burn. They were therefore reserved for use during the winter peaks. If this problem could not be solved there would still be power cuts in the cold winter months. Starting in November, coal deliveries were forced through. Night and day, convoys of juggernaut lorries led and flanked by police cars and motor cycles, crossed the Severn Bridge into South Wales and, with accelerators hard down, raced along the M4. Other police closed the slip roads to ensure unimpeded progress. They then returned empty for another load. After prolonged persuasion, and pressure on recalcitrant staff, the stations were brought back to normal operation, in the case of Didcot not until 20 January 1985.

## We Did It!

When it was over, the Generating Board had kept the lights on, at a cost to the taxpayer of more than £2 billion, mostly from the increased oil burn. The reduction in coal burn was 40 Mt, resulting in an extra cost of £50 per tonne of coal saved. Although expensive, it did not result in a massive rise in the price of oil, which many oil companies had predicted in the early days of the strike. Every effort had been made to control the level of oil prices by refusing the highest quotations. This had been a gamble but it worked.

## OTHER UNIONS.
### Verbal Solidarity.

For those attempting to enlist the support of other unions, the missing ballot proved to be a millstone around their necks. During the September 1984 Congress of the Trade Union Council, John Lyons of the power engineers faced shouts of "scab" and "Tory swine" as he warned the delegates that "The electricity supply industry is not, and never has been, available to solve industrial disputes external to it, not even for the miners". However, in a front of solidarity, the Congress as a whole was fulsome in its support. A motion was passed to great acclaim, promising total support for the NUM, a major fund-raising drive, and detailed discussions about blacking all NCB products, or substitutes for them. Eric Hammond of the electricians said, "Either this means a complete cessation of civilized life, or it doesn't mean what it says and it is a con trick on the miners". Civilised life continued, it did not mean what it said. Union leaders in general, particularly those on the TUC council itself, were aware that their membership was not composed of the revolutionary material that Scargill would have liked them to be.

The left had been contemptuous of Gormley for his right-wing inclinations but, in terms of achieving working class solidarity, it was he who had brought home the bacon. In the strikes of 1972 and 1974, and in the confrontation of 1981, effective support from other unions had been brought on board. It was the new left-wing messiah who would alienate potential rescuers. He had never shown much regard for any of them and earlier in the dispute had shown every inclination of keeping them out of it. The result was that he was neither liked nor trusted.


## Sacrifices.

The National Union of Seamen and the rail unions made the biggest sacrifices. The former loyally rejected coal cargoes, while the latter maintained a broad, but never total, ban on coal movements to the end. In both cases their efforts were brought to naught by the ease with which it proved possible to find alternative means of transport. At sea the work switched to foreign flags over which the union had no control, while the railwaymen merely saw a large slice of their industry's basic trade switch over to the roads.

Road haulage was a key factor. Although independent owner-drivers were responsible for many of the lorry journeys which resulted, a substantial majority were members of the Transport and General Workers Union, working in open defiance of their union guidelines. Particularly in Nottinghamshire and the Midlands, where it would have been most useful to tie down coal stocks, drivers, and also workers at the power stations, took the view that with 34,000 miners working there was little reason for them either to defy management or to pass up lucrative jobs, especially since the NUM had not held a national strike ballot.

On 10 July 1984, a national dock strike broke out and gave the government a considerable fright, as well as giving heart to Arthur Scargill. It was, however, over a breach of rules for the use of non-registered labour in the docks, and not in support of the miners. It ended 11 days later, with hundreds of irate lorry drivers stranded a Dover being instrumental in the strike's demise.


## WHAT DOES "BENEFICIAL" MEAN?

## Semantics.

Also in July, the NCB and the NUM each produced a written draft of an agreement on which they would be prepared to end the dispute. With the dock strike and with winter yet to come, the NCB was under pressure. During negotiations between the parties, agreement was reached on all issues, except one. This concerned the justification for pit closures. Even here, both parties agreed that pits could be closed when they were physically exhausted or when geological difficulties were so bad as to compromise safety. The only substantial point of disagreement concerned the inclusion or exclusion of a single word, "beneficial". The NUM draft provided for collieries to be shut down when there were no further reserves, "that are workable or which can be developed". The NCB formulation expanded this central phrase to read, "that are workable or which can be beneficially developed" . Therein lay the quintessence of what the whole dispute was about.

MacGregor wrote a circular letter to the country's miners, pointing out that agreement had been reached on all points except one. He maintained that the NUM were saying "pits should be kept open even when they were of no benefit to the industry, while the NCB could not sanction a policy which might harm the industry". As he summed up, it was, "a small but significant point". It was also the point on which the talks broke down. When asked on television what was meant by "beneficial" in the context of mines staying open, MacGregor replied: "Beneficial to the community of those who work in the industry, beneficial to the mining communities, beneficial to the community of people who live in Britain".

It was the case, and was quoted by the NCB in negotiations, that the Coal Industry Nationalisation Act of 1946 gave them clear responsibility, not only to operate the industry effectively but also to make a profit. It is an open question as to whether that key word, "beneficial", could have been negotiated to include, not only the profit-and-loss account of the NCB but also macro-economic factors and the social costs incurred in the event of pits being closed, involving redundant miners, their communities and associated industries. It was, after all, the maintenance of communities that the strike was supposed to be all about. An extensive lobbying and public relations campaign by the NUM to that effect could well have produced results. The possibility of this happening was sufficiently strong for Margaret Thatcher to write later she had been alarmed at the prospect and that (horror of horrors) a settlement on these lines would have given Scargill the opportunity to claim victory. In any event, the offer made that July was the best the NUM would receive during the course of the dispute.

## NUM Unease.

It was not only Margaret Thatcher who thought that Scargill was within a hair's breath of victory. In an interview 2 years after the event George Reece, General Secretary of the South Wales NUM since 1976, would talk of differences in strategy, even at this relatively early stage in the conflict (ref SWML AUD/ 573). According to Reece, "The strike could have ended in July". He spoke of a paper, prepared in South Wales and sent to the union's national office, which analysed the situation. According to this analysis, coal stocks were adequate to last until mid-1986, a conclusion the Government and the Generating Board were themselves coming to at this time. There was therefore no chance of a Government, or an NCB, surrender. The Communist Vice-President of the union, Mick MacGahey of Scotland, submitted a similar paper and regarded the compromise offer made by the NCB as an acceptable outcome. To Reece's chagrin, neither paper was even discussed by the National Executive.

Through to the bitter end, neither side would budge one iota from their respective stands, on whether pits could be closed if they continued to lose money or whether they should continue in operation as long as there was coal in the ground.

## DEFEAT FROM THE JAWS OF VICTORY.

### Isolated incidents.

On 16 August 1984, the unthinkable happened. A single miner in South Wales actually turned up for work. The token picket at Ffaldau Colliery in the Garw Valley was taken off-guard as Monty Morgan, an Englishman who had moved to Betws, strolled through and sat in the pit canteen, alone. All hell then broke loose as his workmates rallied support and hundreds of miners, bitter and betrayed, arrived at the pit, to be met by hundreds of policemen. There was violence as the men tried to get through and the police struggled to stop them.

At shift's end, Monty Morgan emerged inside a colliery bus, besieged on all sides by chanting miners. His arrival home, at Heol Glannant in Betws, was greeted by more police and more strikers. There was an all night vigil outside his home and at dawn police and strikers assembled in the street once more, set for another confrontation. Word eventually emerged that he was now prepared to honour the strike and would not try to go to work.

Several days later he once more surprised everybody by turning up for work again. His one-man action did not persist and it remained just that - nobody else was tempted to break the strike.

On 23 August 1984, dock workers walked out and the Transport and General Workers Union called a second national dock strike in protest over an incident at Hunterston in Scotland. Here, British Steel Corporation workers had been used on board the Ostia to unload coal necessary to maintain the Ravenscraig steel plant in production. In Scotland, public opinion was strongly opposed to any action that threatened the future of Ravenscraig and this dock strike caused the Government much less concern than the first. At the beginning there was considerable support from registered dockers, but the majority of ports remained open. The strike was called off on 18 September.

## Once More "Beneficial" - or Something Similar.

On 14 September 1984, negotiations between the NCB and NUM were again resumed, with a similar offer being made to the one in July. These also came to within a hair's breath of a solution, but again collapsed, once more over the single word "beneficial". Convoluted attempts were made to talk around it. "Beneficial" was replaced with a formulation whereby pits should be deemed exhausted when, following examination by both NCB and NUM mining engineers, "further investment of human and financial resources could not be justified" - but all to no avail.

It is highly questionable whether any corporation, either private or state-owned, or any government, irrespective of political colouring, could ever accept the concept that coal had to be extracted at a particular mine, at all costs and at any cost. By rejecting the offer, and insisting on such an absurdity, Scargill was able to snatch defeat from the jaws of victory. As time went on and "General Winter" was unable to cause even a hiccup in the normal life of the country, the negotiating stance of the Board hardened and the NUM's best opportunity slipped away.

On 27 September 1984, an evening TV news programme would see Crown Prince Hassan of Jordan tell Arthur Scargill, who replaced him as interviewee, *"The problems of a few million people in the Middle East are a mere bagatelle in comparison with the problems of your coal industry"*.

## THE MOST DANGEROUS MOMENT.

### The Deputies Provoked.

On 29 September 1984 came the most dangerous moment for MacGregor and the Government. Suddenly, another problem presented itself that the NCB could well have done without. The pit officials' union NACODS (National Association of Colliery Overmen, Deputies and Shotfirers) voted by a majority of 82.5 per cent for strike action. By law, no work could be carried out underground unless a statutorily qualified official known as a deputy supervised the district concerned. He was responsible for the local management and, first and foremost, with his training in first aid, gas detection and emergency procedures, for safety within that district. In the absence of such officials then, irrespective of the wishes of the workforce and the remainder of management, according to the Mines and Quarries Act of 1954, the pit could not legally operate. They therefore had absolute power to shut down the industry should they so decide.

NACODS fully shared the NUM's anxiety over the pit closure programme. There was, however, one important difference between the attitude of the two unions. The deputies fell well short of supporting the miners' total rejection. Their criticism focused more narrowly on the NCB's long-established Colliery Review Procedure. In theory, these "consultative" arrangements ensured agreement by all parties to any particular shutdown. Both NACODS and the NUM felt that this process had degenerated into a rubber-stamp exercise. The Board made its proposals and then effectively acted as judge, jury, appeal court and hangman in its own cause. NACODS at least recognised the possibility of reform. If acceptable improvements could be agreed, there might be a basis for compromise.

In practice, throughout its whole existence, with responsibility inculcated into their history and training, NACODS had been the most moderate of unions. The requirement in their rulebook for a 66 per cent majority for any strike action made it even less likely. What had brought such a moderate group of men to make such a radical move?

Six weeks previously, the personnel director of the NCB had made the statement that those junior management officials who were unwilling to be bussed into their pits, if necessary under police escort, would no longer be paid. Under guidelines developed for the 1972 and 1974 strikes, any such official subject to harassment, or an intimidating picket line, was free to return home, telephone the colliery manager to explain the situation and continue to draw full wages. The difference on this occasion was that those previous strikes had been total. Now there were a significant amount of miners who were breaking the strike. Even in the more stubborn coalfields the Board was encouraging miners to trickle back. There was little sense, however, in setting up armoured bus convoys and massive police escorts to get a handful of colliers to the pithead if there were then no supervisors and safety men to take them underground. In addition, safety examinations were becoming more urgent as a growing number of coalfaces were confronted with the prospect of flooding, fire and general collapse. This logic was unlikely to have been lost on the officials. The pre-requisite was that the Board approached them with some degree of finesse, and an appreciation of their situation. The lack of any such finesse and appreciation was a provocation, which brought matters to a head.

## MacGregor Loses Touch.

MacGregor himself seemed incapable of appreciating the critical importance of deputies. He was contemptuous of their status, regarding it as anachronistic and something which members of the general workforce could be trained to do. He was equally contemptuous of NACODS as he was of all trade unions, and of their General Secretary, Peter McNestry, in particular.

MacGregor remained gung-ho, apparently unaware of the danger and firm in the belief that NUM strike-breakers in Nottinghamshire were numerous enough, and also so inclined, to pressurise any striking deputies there to return to work. He had secretly met some Nottinghamshire miners who had written to him, criticising both the strike and NUM tactics.

Peter Walker, the Energy Secretary with whom he had never got on, and with whom tension not infrequently emerged, was incredulous. MacGregor quotes him as saying, "You mean you're prepared to let them go on strike?" On recept of an affirmative answer, the response was, "You must be out of your mind!" It was not the only occasion when Walker would consider MacGregor out of touch. The latter also thought that the strike would end when financial hardship started to bite the strikers. That they should have aims over and above the purely material was something he found difficult to grasp. Walker's concerns were communicated to the Prime Minister, Margaret Thatcher, leading to what MacGregor describes as the only direct order given by her to him during the entire course of the dispute. While the government had laid down the strategic direction, day-to-day handling of the strike had been left to him. In an atmosphere very different to previous meetings, his expressions of confidence that the NACODS dispute was not critically important were cut short by the Prime Minister, "Well, I'm very worried about it. You have to realise that the fate of this government is in your hands, Mr. MacGregor. You have got to solve this problem". The month to come would see matters rise to a crescendo.

## LAW AND LAWLESSNESS.

### The Judge Moves In.

In early October 1984, following a court case instigated by two Midlands miners who objected to the strike, Mr. Justice Nicholls ruled that the whole dispute must be treated as unofficial since, in the absence of a ballot, it had been illegally called. Scargill and his executive publicly rejected this decision. With Scargill in his seat, attending the Labour Party conference and in full view of the media, a writ for contempt of court was served on him. The union was fined £200,000. It was also ordered to purge its contempt by accepting that the strike had been unconstitutionally declared. This it refused to do.

### Murder Most Foul.

One week later the Conservatives held their own party conference at Brighton. There was a speech from the platform by a Young Conservative type who, unbelievably, declared himself to be a miner, a working miner or, "as some people call me, a scab", but the conference would go down in history for another reason.

On 12 October 1984, in the evening, an IRA bomb devastated the Brighton Grand Hotel where leading lights of the Conservative party were staying. There were fatalities and serious injuries but Margaret

Thatcher escaped unharmed. The next morning, with a definite air of invincibility, she came out fighting, insisting that the conference continue.

## NACODS Fobbed Off.

On 23 October 1984, within thirty-six hours of the threatened NACODS strike, a deal was reached using the Advisory Conciliation and Arbitration Service (ACAS). It was conciliatory with regard to the deputies' requirements. There was to be the possibility of early retirement, with a pension. The key item was that the existing procedure, under which pits had been abandoned in the past, would be re-examined in the light of extensive demands for improvement. These NACODS had already debated, agreed and tabled. Only later would it dawn on NACODS that what they had got was different to what they thought they had got at the time. MacGregor would later describe it as a solution that avoided giving away the store, although one which added frustrating steps to the process of shutting down a pit. The key thing was that NACODS was happy and the government had been let off the hook. Scargill had never put much faith in his temporary allies anyway. He shrugged it off as a temporary setback, but far worse was to come.

## The NUM Is Skint.

On 25 October 1984, Mr. Justice Nicholls ordered sequestration of all the NUM's assets. As well as defiant non-cooperation, the court's directives produced the revelation that most of the money had been deliberately squirreled away abroad. The court's response to this was to put all NUM finances under the control of an officially appointed receiver. In practice, there proved to be such difficulty in tracking down the funds that it was even possible the sequestrators might not have been able to cover their costs. Accordingly, the government agreed to indemnify them against any loss. The government was also involved in trying to obtain maximum co-operation from the governments of Ireland and Luxemburg, where NUM money had been lodged. By the end of January some £5 M had been recovered.

NUM power to finance picketing and other strike activities within the UK had been severely curbed by the court's verdict. This finally brought the NUM leadership themselves to court but their appeal failed. From 1 December 1984 they effectively lost control over the union's affairs. Their financial straits were to push them into questionable and, as it turned out, highly damaging actions. Behind the union scenes, differences in policy continued, e.g. over legal action and the organising of people to gather support abroad.

## SPIN.

### Shaking Hands With The Devil.

On 28 October 1984, the Sunday Times reported that Arthur Scargill had made direct contact with the Libyan leader, Colonel Gaddafi, in search of funds to bolster the union's haemorrhaging finances. Scargill had acted through the NUM's chief executive, Roger Windsor. Years later left-wing MP's would table a motion before the House of Commons claiming that Roger Windsor had been an agent of MI5. At the beginning of October, Scargill (travelling under an alias "Mr. Smith") had visited Paris together with Windsor to meet representatives of the French trade union, the CGT. Present at the meeting was a Libyan, whom Scargill would later claim to be a representative of Libyan trade unionists. Later, there was a follow-up visit to Libya by Windsor.

The union had been canvassing for, and was receiving, international donations from other trade unions. The German trade union movement was inclined to help alleviate hardship but suspicious of Scargill's policies. IG Metall, for example, provided finance via the Metal Workers' and Transport and General Workers' Union for the direct purchase of food, thus bypassing the NUM leadership. Others, including the Soviet miners, were not so particular. These latter donations in particular excited the extreme displeasure of Margaret Thatcher, who raised the issue with Soviet President, Mikhail Gorbatchov.

In the case of Libya, Scargill had gone over the top. For the government, it was a gift from heaven. This was the same year that Woman Police Constable, Yvonne Fletcher, had been killed in the centre of London by shots fired from the Libyan People's Bureau, their current name for the embassy. This apparent willingness to deal with a backer of international terrorism proved to be an extremely damaging misjudgement and laid Scargill open to establishment attack. Together with the lack of a ballot, plus the ugly scenes on the picket lines, this story could not fail to result in a rapid and widespread erosion of public support.

On 31 October 1984, another round of negotiations between the two parties broke down, and for the same old reason. The gap concerning pit closures was proving impossible to bridge. Behind the scenes, Labour Party leader Neil Kinnock and Stan Orne, his spokesman on coal affairs, attempted to mediate with a suggestion that "beneficial" be defined as including the national interest. Kinnock states that, within hours, MacGregor accepted the suggestion, only to have it rejected by Scargill. Orne told Kinnock, "Scargill is unlike any trade unionist I've ever met, he doesn't believe in negotiation. What do trade unions do if they don't negotiate"!

## Charisma; And Lack Of It.

Initially, Arthur Scargill had dominated the media, always ready to provide "good television" with a plausible quote, or a new shock to rock the audience. Bernard Ingram, Margaret Thatcher's Press Secretary, would later describe MacGregor on the other hand as, "The antithesis of the modern public relations man". On one occasion, MacGregor's attempt to confound reporters by appearing with a paper bag over his head left his supporters speechless. In contrast to the cheeky chappie, chat show charisma of his opponent, he was not at ease in the media circus and, with his dead pan, monosyllabic answers to reporters' questions, tended to come over as Old Man Grump. He did not suffer fools (or those he regarded as fools) gladly. His cohorts tended to be almost equally dour. With time, professional public relations expertise was brought in, while advertisements and press releases were issued, all presenting the NCB version in a more positive light.

A new NCB spokesman was found, North Yorkshire Area Director Michael Eton, with an easy, pipe-smoking, TV charm. He had been instrumental in developing the new pit at Selby. Following a meeting with him on a visit to Yorkshire the previous month he had been proposed by Margaret Thatcher as a national spokesman for the NCB. In public he came across as sympathetic, capable of debating effectively with Scargill on TV. In their search for another hero, the media immediately lionised him. This was much to the chagrin of his cohorts in the industry, who saw their youngest Area Director become a star overnight. They determined to bring him down to size. MacGregor, who regarded him as being too easygoing, also did not share media speculation about Eton's glowing future. Later, the strain of being front man for policies over which he was being denied any control, plus the hectic media and social whirl, all exacerbated with a bout of flu, resulted in Eton's collapse and departure from the NCB.

This NCB hiccup notwithstanding, the miners were losing the public relations battle. Scargill remained a one-man band, with his tune progressively discordant in the public ear. Like General Galtieri of Argentina and the IRA, he would prove how lucky Margaret Thatcher had been in the enemies ranged against her. Denis Healey wrote that he was probably the only public figure in Britain more disliked than Thatcher herself, and commanding far less respect.

Both sides were to criticise alleged media bias against them but now there was a growing feeling in the country that Arthur Scargill was indeed an anti-democratic "enemy within". This was encouraged in certain quarters. A BBC TV news report of the battle at Orgreave showed police cavalry charging the miners. It showed stones being thrown first, before the cavalry charge. The impression was thus given of a riot that the police were forced to control. At the subsequent trial, Scargill subpoenaed the police video, which had a time-code on it. This showed the cavalry charging first, before any stones had been thrown. In May, Scargill's photograph on the front page of The Sun, coincidentally with his hand outstretched and under the headline "Mine Fuehrer", was a classic of the genre. The printers' union refused to print the issue, regarding it as being a calculated attempt to bring down a fellow trade unionist.

# BACK TO WORK GATHERS MOMENTUM.

## The Moses Way.

On 1 November 1984, the strike was still largely solid, excepting those areas that had not been in from the beginning, namely the counties of Nottingham, Leicester and South Derbyshire, plus one or two isolated pits. Scotland had 366 men back, mainly at the big Lothian Colliery, Bilsdon Glen. There were also a tiny handful of mavericks in every coalfield. The exception was South Wales, where the strike was total. It was in the course of this month, the eighth of the strike, that the drift back to work really began.

Area Director Ken Moses of North Derbyshire initiated a well-planned campaign. It was taken up by the NCB nationally and gradually began to show results. It involved letters to individual miners, advertisements, secure telephone numbers, personal contacts and sometimes a visit by the manager. More and more lone individuals, at the end of their tether due to financial hardship, family responsibilities, or overwhelming distaste at the way the strike was being run, were prepared to take the plunge and, escorted by massive police resources, face the aggravation. The first man returned at Corton Wood where, eight months previously, the strike had began. To increase the pressure, attractive Christmas bonuses were offered to those who would return to work beforehand.

This tendency was encouraged by the NCB as a second front, since it forced Scargill to dilute his Nottinghamshire army so as to confront the "scabs" elsewhere. The need to canvass for financial support was, to some extent, already diverting the pickets. Stratagems were adopted such as fitting curtains to the minibuses and taxis taking men to work. This was to prevent the NUM knowing how many men were returning. It also enabled the use of decoy taxis, carrying nobody. This was meant to keep pickets at their home units and away from the real centres of the return to work.

Dafydd Wigley, Plaid Cymru MP, wrote to the South Wales Area Director querying the back-to-work policy of the Board. Given the close nature of the valley communities, it was certain to result in social discord and personal unhappiness. The Welsh Council of Churches also questioned the morality of encouraging men to take a step guaranteed to ensure future opprobrium, both for themselves and their families. Reluctant to face the intimidation involved in a direct confrontation with the pickets, miners wishing for an end to the strike had approached justices of the peace and ministers of religion. No one wanted to be the first to go back. The fear of potential violence and the certainty of being outcast and alone, walled up in the community of a narrow valley to which they were deeply attached, was a strain few would countenance.

Nevertheless, even in South Wales, the NCB continued in its attempt to get men back to work. Letters were sent to individual addresses, from the Area Director concerning general issues and the colliery manager on concerns specific to the pit. They reminded miners that South Wales did not support the strike, that by a majority of 14,000 to 6,000 the miners in that coalfield had voted in March to continue working. Suggestions were made that it was not the majority who voted to work, but the minority who had picketed their colleagues out of work who were the real scabs. The Area Director pointed out that, whereas in the previous year Llanwern Steelworks took nearly 1Mt of coal from Oakdale, Marine, Six Bells, Abertillery, plus North and South Celynen Collieries, all of its coal was now imported. Newport and Swansea had exported 1.25Mt, but traditional customers had turned elsewhere. Aberthaw Power Station had taken a record 3,5Mt. Its output was being replaced by oil and nuclear fuel.

All such attempts largely came to nothing. MacGregor, in his book The Enemy Within, would explain why:

"Typically when a man came through the gates the pickets would tell them that that was the end of their normal lives. No one would ever speak to them again; no one would drink with them. Their wives would be ostracized, and nobody's children would play with theirs. When the strike was won they would never work again and until then they would be hunted down and abused, or worse, wherever they went. Tough, grown men would arrive inside the gates ashen-faced and shaking, and some would be physically sick. Union officials were able to keep their hands officially clean, while instigating the intimidation".

The abuse, threats, spitting, other humiliations, damaged cars and houses, all belonged to the pickets' armoury nation-wide. However, a man who decided to return to work in Scotland was very much more on his own than a man who lived in Nottinghamshire, or next door in Derbyshire, while a South Walian attempting the same would become a tortured soul indeed.

## The Weekes Way.

Area Directors won kudos with MacGregor according to their commitment to, and success with, the back-to-work movement. Philip Weekes, the South Wales Director and a valley man, tried other methods.

Weekes himself had been the subject of a written complaint by the Managing Director of British Benzol Carbonising plc, addressed to the Department of Energy with a copy to Ian MacGregor. The letter refers to "undiplomatic actions which are in my view either stupid or mischievous". Mr. Weekes's crime had been consorting with pickets, "including drinking cups of tea —— whilst sitting in their car". Mr. Weekes denied drinking tea with strikers since, "they didn't offer me any". A reply was sent to British Benzol by The Department of Energy:

"What you have chosen to interpret as consorting with strikers might equally well be seen as the prudent maintenance by NCB management, as opportunity offers, of lines of communication with those on strike. That seems likely to be of benefit to all concerned. I am confident that the sinister overtones you attach to the incident are unwarranted".

Ian MacGregor, however, seemed less and less interested in maintaining such lines of communication. Total victory was his aim, and this was appearing more and more likely.

On 19 November 1984, showing that his methods were not confined to just drinking tea with pickets, Phillip Weekes communicated to his diary, "I pressurised Emlyn Williams and George Reece to start turning the NUM's Executive. They must lead the South Wales miners back before the union is broken —— — and none of us want that".

On 20 November 1984, although soup kitchens in the mining communities were in top gear, as an indication that much of the country, including non-unionised workers, had interests other than fighting the class war, the privatisation of British Telecom resulted in a plethora of applications for shares. The attractions of capitalism and of a "privatised share-holding democracy" were starting to make inroads beyond city wiz kids. By this date, the number of collieries in the country wholly stopped had fallen from ninety-three to forty-seven. Even in stubborn, determined South Wales, the first sixteen men went back. One of these at Marine Colliery, influenced by his wife, was motivated by the desire to give his two daughters of 6 and 13 years of age a decent Christmas. The suggestion by a lodge member that his girls could keep warm by lighting a candle and dancing around it left him singularly unimpressed. According to a letter from his wife, his first day at work resulted in a visit by the lodge chairman, who allegedly said that if he worked the next day, pickets would be sent to smash up his home. The wages that he had just earned should be donated to the union. Bigger issues were at stake, transcending the basic human desire for a harmonious and happy family life.

## FREE COLLECTIVE BARGENING BY RIOT.

### Beatings and the Noose.

The NUM withdrew safety cover at pits where any scab returned. Violence, both on and off the picket lines, increased commensurately as those committed to the strike tried, in frustrated desperation and growing hatred, to stop the slide. In addition to incidents at colliery gates, there were a number, some involving violence, outside the homes of working miners. Feelings were running high. The excessive brutality of one side provoked counter-violence on the other. Which side was which in that equation was, of course, in the eye of the beholder. During this period, the working miner Michael Fletcher, of Pontefract Yorkshire, was badly beaten in his own living room by a stick-welding mob, while his wife and children cowered upstairs. Nineteen men were arrested for the crime. Supporters of the strike would allege that they too had been subjected to violence, not only by the police but also in Nottinghamshire by working miners, and that media bias had prevented such cases being reported. Such allegations did not strike a general chord. There were no scenes on television of poor pickets being abused by masses of working miners having to be held back by the police.

During this month a massive rally for supporters of the strike was held in the Aberavon Lido, on the South Wales coast. It started in classic Scargill style, as he punched out his words before a mass of striking miners and their families from all over the South Wales Valleys:

"I am not prepared to condemn the actions of my members, whose only crime is fighting for the right to work, fighting to save their pits , their jobs and the mining communities —— When you look back you'll look back with pride and you'll say to your son or your daughter, in 1984 I took part in the greatest struggle in trade union history. I fought to save your pit, I fought to save the jobs, I fought to save this community, but in doing so I preserved my dignity as a human being and as a member of the finest trade union in the world. I am privileged to lead you. I salute you. The miners, united, will never be defeated".

Later there was consternation, and disquiet rustled through the audience. There were shouts of "get him off", "rubbish", and "we want action now", as Norman Willis, General Secretary of the TUC, failed to fulfil his allotted role. In a sober presentation, which contrasted with Scargill's histrionics, Mr Willis condemned the violent excesses that had been committed on the picket lines. Angry men leapt to their feet on being told that any miner who resorted to violence while on picket duty would be wounding the case of their fellow miners rather than damaging the resolve of their opponents. The screaming chorus of boos and catcalls reached a peak as he said:

"Violence creates more violence and out of that is built not solidarity but despair and defeat —— I have marched proudly before many miners' banners and I know that there will never be one that praises the brick, the bolt and the petrol bomb".

Emlyn Williams, South Wales NUM President, looked even more po-faced than usual, Peter Heathfield, National General Secretary, slumped forward cheek in hand, while Scargill raised his eyes to the roof to show what he thought of the sentiments being expressed and to watch the final flourish - a noose was lowered from the ceiling to dangle in front of Mr. Willis. The "jarling mob" à la Lord Robens was alive and well. Disquiet with the TUC was not confined to the rank and file. Emlyn Williams would express on TV his deep disappointment with support being received. In spite of Scargill's glowing reception at the TUC national conference, financial contributions were a mere trickle.

## Death Takes a Hand.

On 30 November 1984, the most notable individual act of violence throughout the strike brought things to a crescendo. In South Wales, two young strikers dropped a concrete post from a bridge across the Heads of the Valleys Road onto the taxi carrying a working miner from Rhymney to Merthyr Vale Colliery. This killed outright the driver David Wilkie. The fact that David Wilkie's girlfriend was eight months' pregnant at the time, and that he had two children from a previous marriage, stirred up national coverage. The miner, in the back seat, escaped without injury. Due to heavy police and picket clashes at the colliery, the taxi had been escorted by three police vehicles. There followed a massive manhunt, with 120 detectives and dog-handlers making house to house inquiries in the Merthyr area. This led to the arrest of the two perpetrators.

In early 2004, in a TV documentary on the miners' strike, Kim Howells, Member of Parliament and a transport minister made a confession. At the time of the strike he was employed as research officer for the South Wales NUM and was a leading organiser of the picketing:

"I remember feeling physically sick after I heard he died after action taken by some of our members. I thought: hang on, we've got all those records we've kept over in the NUM offices (at Sardis House in Pontypridd), there's all those maps on the wall, we're going to get implicated in this —— and I remember thinking, I've got to get to that office and I've got to destroy everything, which I did. I've never told anybody that before".

Since this involved the destruction of potential evidence in a death inquiry, the confession resulted in a statement from the South Wales police that they were liasing with the crown prosecution service as to whether any offence had been committed. Mr Howells, however, insisted that with regard to the death he had nothing to hide. He had merely destroyed the NUM order of battle, rather than have it all carted off by the police. Information destroyed included such things as strength and location of pickets, plus their accommodation.

In December 1984, Arthur Scargill was found guilty of two charges of obstruction while picketing. He was fined £250 and ordered to pay £750 costs following a scuffle outside Orgreave Coke Works on June 18.

## Still No Progress.

On the 5th and 14th of December, and independently of the NCB and the NUM, direct talks were held between the TUC and Peter Walker, Secretary of State for Energy. These annoyed MacGregor who was not informed in advance. He saw a slow-down in the return to work if men sensed that the strike would end soon anyway. Relations between him and Peter Walker became strained to the point of unpleasantness. In the event, the talks came to nothing. TUC mediation continued, but this time with NCB involvement.

At Cortonwood in Yorkshire, where the strike had began, the pickets manning "The Alamo", a do-it-yourself fortress of concrete blocks and wood at the colliery entrance, had dwindled away from a peak of approximately two hundred at the start of the strike to a derisory six or so. In the Yorkshire Area, Scargill's heartland, the back-to-work movement was under way. Nationally, the figure was 69,000. A motion from the Yorkshire Woman's Council submitted to the Labour Party National Executive Committee, calling for a national strike, found but small support from a few left-wing members.

## THE LAST BASTION.
### Rank and File Morale.

By this time, South Wales had clearly emerged as the last bastion of serious resistance. Of the last twenty-six pits in the country without a single miner signing on, twenty-one of them were here. History and the exceptionally close nature of the mining communities, plus the fact that all to often there were virtually no jobs for a redundant man to go to, had resulted in a level of local support unmatched in any other coalfield. In the valleys there were many who thought that if the colliery closed, they would be out of work for the rest of their life. In addition, there were their sons to think about. Now, even here, cracks were beginning to show.

It was at this time that the veteran Will Paynter died. Successor to Arthur Horner, he was the second General Secretary of the NUM following nationalisation, and his death symbolised the passing of an era. His funeral provided the opportunity for an oration reaffirming community and internationalist values. As a convinced Communist, these were things he had struggled for throughout his life, his main thrust being the necessity to change society, meaning society as a whole. Whether he considered this compatible with the current concentrated focus on keeping all mines open, allegedly in the interest of mining communities, is not recorded. In common with Arthur Horner, as well as longer-term changes in society he had aimed at immediate improvement in people's conditions in the form of achievable goals. For this he had never considered it necessary to unleash such mayhem.

Christmas would prove to be the straw that finally broke the camel's back. That would be the occasion on which morale finally collapsed. Not because it was a dismal flop, for the reverse was the case. As a culmination of effort and the pinnacle of hope and joy it turned out better than expected. Communities racked with worry about debt and the repossession of their houses were at least united in their detestation of the police, the Department of Health and Social Security, plus the media. In this "blitz spirit" every effort was made to make Christmas for the kids a heart-warming success. Adverts were placed in The Guardian and The Mirror by London socialists. Soon, pop stars and religious leaders put their names to the appeal. A significant contribution was made by SOGAT, the printers' trade union. Countrywide efforts to raise cash and donations raised about £400,000. Generous donations of toys flooded into the distribution centres. The aftermath was a brutal contrast, with nothing more to look forward to, only the deadening realisation of impending despair. With no prospect of even a flicker in the country's energy supplies there was no hope anymore, only the certainty of even more hardship, with surrender at the end of the line.

## The Organisers Wobble.

On 1 January 1985, in such an atmosphere of New Year hangover, 5-6 members of the "unofficial left" within the South Wales NUM met at their favourite hideaway, the Brynffynon pub at Llanwonno, near Ynys-y-bwl. A coincidental call by a reporter to the home of Kim Howells during the latter's absence enabled this information to be elicited. After putting two and two together, a lead story appeared in The Times the following day, under the headline:

"MILITANTS ATTACK SCARGILL FOR LACK OF INITIATIVE"

It was to be just a start.

On 6 January 1985, a regular meeting was held between Arthur Scargill and his "kitchen cabinet", a selected fifty or so broad-left activists. This group, parallel to the National Executive, had acted as his principal advisory body and sounding board throughout the strike. This time there were two items on the agenda, each of which would guarantee disruption within the union. One was to terminate the 41-year-old federal structure, in which the areas had separate legal identities. This measure would end their jealously guarded autonomy. Instead there would be "a single national organization to embrace all workers within the British coalmining industry". The second proposal was for nothing less than the expulsion from the union of Nottinghamshire, the second largest area. The NUM was now on course for a split from which it would never recover. Margaret Thatcher would later write disparagingly of the "comradeship of mining". Of this she had seen little sign.

On 10 January 1985, the NUM Executive agreed to Nottinghamshire's expulsion. A delegate conference confirmed it on the 29th. Roy Link was the number three NUM man in the Nottinghamshire area. He had already crossed swords with Chadburn and Richardson in the area and with Arthur Scargill. Six months later, after the strike, he would lead the coalfield out of the NUM and help form the new Union of Democratic Mineworkers. This was to be inaugurated with its base in the Nottinghamshire Coalfield, where it swept the board. This at least filtered out the "betrayers" from the mainstream NUM and acted as a safety valve for the hatred that would otherwise have eaten away at the union like vitriol.

At the beginning of the month, of the 173 pits nationally, coal was being produced at 71 of them. In 47 pits, production was proceeding normally. Work was being done at a further 71 collieries. In only 31 was the strike still solid. Of the NUM workforce, 37 per cent were back at work. By the month's end it would be 43 per cent. Of the Yorkshire miners, Scargill's own, 5,000 or so had already gone back to work.

On 17 January 1985, during two weeks of very cold weather, the highest electrical demand of the winter occurred. This was met in full, without even a voltage reduction. Coal stocks at the power stations, which at the beginning of the strike stood at 50 Mt, had only fallen to 36.5 Mt. This was a further blow to the already tottering morale of the striking miners. They were fast losing heart and the success of the Central Electricity Generating Board in meeting these peaks marked the beginning of the end of the strike. In the South Wales area of the NUM the feeling was growing that politics at the top was taking precedence over union interests. There were complaints over Scargill's centralism and authoritarianism. The over-the-top-and-charge-the-machine-guns stubbornness was achieving nothing except further suffering. In an interview the following year, George Reece would say, "We failed in not supervising Arthur properly. We let him have his head" (SWML AUD7573) . Instead of South Wales being allowed to exploit their contacts in Nottinghamshire, friends were turned into enemies.

## POLITICS.

### At the Top -

Behind the scenes other political, influences were at work. The Labour Party was struggling back from the political wilderness at this time. Its previous shift leftwards, with the associated election manifesto, referred to by Gerald Kaufmann as "The longest suicide note in history", had made the Labour Party unelectable. In the intial stages of the movement that would later culminate in "New Labour", Neil Kinnock, now leader of the party and a South Wales MP, was active in moving the party back to the right. Kinnock was to fight and win a battle to expel from the party the notorious Marxist councillors of Liverpool. These had given both financial and physical help to the picketing miners and were one of several millstones around the party's neck. In particular, Kinnock was highly conscious of the electoral curse which affiliation with Marxist-inclined trade unionism had proven to be. Arthur Scargill and what he stood for were the epitome of this handicap. Kinnock would say that as a result of the strike and its aftermath, British politics did not return to normal until 1986, one year before the next general election. This was too short a time in his view to implant in the electorate's mind the concept that Labour was a responsible and constructive party of government.

In 2004, in an interview, Kinnock would say about Scargill:

"I detest him. I did then, I do now and it's mutual, he hates me too (but) I would much prefer to have his savage hatred than just the merest hint of friendship from that man". He would also say:

"My huge mistake of course was not at a very, very early stage to resolve the dilemma by saying "if these decent people are going to even fight a draw, let alone win, they're going to have to do it on the basis of a democratic vote —— It's the greatest regret of my whole life; that I didn't make that view public from the very earliest stage".

Kinnock was concerned that any public denunciation of the strike itself would enable Scargill, following his inevitable defeat, to claim that victory could have been theirs, if only the Labour Party had not withdrawn their support.

At that time, both Kinnock and the trade union movement found themselves unable to say in public what they really thought of Scargill's behaviour, although not only the TUC General Secretary but also Kinnock himself were howled down for attacking the violence of some of the miners' pickets. As a miner's son representing a miners' constituency, he found himself in a particularly difficult position, at a time when he had not yet had a chance to establish his authority as party leader. The result was that he came across as ineffective, failing to stand for anything.


## - And at the Bottom.

Just as Scargill's local involvement had played a key role in Yorkshire, being the crucible from which the strike had emerged, now Neil Kinnock's local involvement would edge South Wales along the road of finally giving Scargill the "coup de grace". Schemes were afoot to end the strike and so assist in rescuing Labour from the political wilderness.

Secret meetings were held. NUM Research Officer Kim Howells, one of the activists who had got the strike off the ground against the wishes of the majority and who had played a major role in organising pickets, now took a different tack, continuing his penchant for the Brynffynon. No longer in existence, this was an isolated pub at Llanwonno, near Ynys-y-Bwl. In these idyllic surroundings the possibility was raised of returning to work without victory. Enveloped within undulating, forested countryside, this was a hostelry more used to welcoming the surreptitious trysts of extra-marital love affairs. One meeting would also be characterised by emotion, but without the background violins. Having made Tyrone O'Sullivan, his lodge secretary and another of the coalfield's "unofficial left", aware in advance, Glyn Roberts, an activist from Tower Colliery, turned up. Robert's impassioned outburst that such unofficial goings-on were against union policy and therefore out of order terminated the proceedings, which continued at another time, if not another place. Now, Howell's opinion of Scargill more and more mirrored Kinnock's. He would later describe him as "A great mob orator, but I don't think he was that bright really".

Howells and his fellow activist from day one, Tyrone O'Sullivan, would part philosophical company. Whereas the latter would remain on the barricades of left-wing thinking, the former would move into the Labour Party mainstream. Initially Dr. Howells would work in the media and write an arts series, taking over as Labour Member of Parliament for the Taff constituency in 1989. In 1997, upon Labour's return to power in that year, he was promoted to junior minister for consumer affairs. In June 2003 he became a transport minister and later a minister for education.

Gradually this possibility, of returning to work without victory, was to gain more and more momentum. Later, in February, Kim Howells floated the idea in a radio interview. This incurred Scargill's wrath and Dr. Howells was temporarily suspended from the union. His criticism of Scargill became forthright: not only was the man intransigent but his picketing tactics were proving counter-productive. In this Howells was not alone. George Reece, the South Wales Area Secretary, had been bred in Fernhill, at one time arguably the most strike-prone pit in the country. He himself had been a long-term supporter of using the strike weapon as a defence against closures. Now, exposed to the realities of a wider world, even he felt called upon to warn the National President. Without a quick settlement, the pressure for a return to work, even without an agreement, would become irresistible. Emlyn Williams, the South Wales President, had already intimated that, without a resolution, South Wales might not be the last area returning to work. Ill feeling between different factions within the union was growing steadily. The diverging priorities between the union in South Wales, both leaders and rank and file, and Arthur Scargill were to widen even further.

On 25 January 1985, the television news programme "Wales Today" issued the following report:

"The miners' union said today that the negotiations (between the NCB and the NUM nationally) have to produce an honourable settlement between the two sides. If that doesn't happen then the South Wales miners, in an unprecedented move in this dispute, say they'll be prepared to consider whether or not to call off the strike unilaterally in this area —— At a South Wales miners' delegate conference today, the need to settle was at the top of their list of priorities. It is the first time that the local leadership have indicated publicly that it will consider pulling the plug on Scargill".


## The Church Intervenes.

The Wales Congress for the Support of the Mining Communities, a diverse combination of Plaid Cymru, the Labour movement and the Welsh churches, had used its considerable influence in keeping the strike solid, at a time when it was visibly eroding elsewhere. Now they were expressing concern about the effect the strike was having on families, creating disagreement, social tension and the potential for long-term scars. The Congress was ready with strong encouragement when the Welsh pitmen's leaders, now deeply doubtful about the negotiating strategy of their National President, decided to initiate a search for some new way to break the negotiating deadlock. The Presbyterian Church of Wales met both the NUM and NCB to sound out the possibility of mediation. Lord Tonypandy (George Thomas) and Lord Cledwyn Hughes were mentioned as potential mediators. The best idea on offer was an elaboration of the independent review body, negotiated by NACODS.

On 30 January 1985 a meeting, initiated by South Wales Area Director Phillip Weekes, was held between the Welsh Council of Churches and the National Coal Board. The object was to find a basis of compromise. With the strike on the way to collapse Ian MacGregor, who was in attendance, felt no incentive to do any such thing. In his view, when faced with extreme demands, no compromise was possible. The delegation put emphasis upon the creation of an Independent Review Body. This would examine long-term energy policy and the needs of both producing and receiving communities. It would assess the total cost of a colliery closure on society as a whole. Included in total cost would be the intangibles of personal and inter-personal happiness. MacGregor remained unimpressed. Who would form this independent body? In practice most of the suggested parties had their own constituency and their own agendas (e.g. nuclear power, coal and electricity industries, government and the community). Consequently, they were unlikely to be truly independent. The meeting ended inconclusively.


## Management Increases the Pressure.

On 4 February 1985, a circular went out to all South Wales miners from area management, with the object of organising wavering souls to return as part of a group. It was pointed out that pits were deteriorating and customers were making alternative arrangements. Contrary to the assertion that a management plan existed to annihilate the coalfield, there never was any such plan, but the union was leading them along a path that would achieve just that. In practice, the much-vaunted "solidarity" of South Wales miners meant that they had been brought out on strike although 60 per cent of them had voted against it. The preamble ended with the statement, "At the end of the day it's your coalfield. It's your choice". As a final incentive it was pointed out that the tax year ended on April 5. Those who returned to work before then would pay no tax on earnings prior to that date.

On 12 February 1985, Phil Weekes made another entry in his diary.

"At their request I met with the South Wales NUM officials Emlyn Williams, George Reece and Terry Thomas. I started the meeting very solemnly by saying that as far as the South Wales coalfield was concerned, all was now lost. They had not led the South Wales coalfield back although there were thousands at work in Scargill's area. I had no doubt that Thatcher and MacGregor would eventually put their feet on our necks. They went into a routine as to why they couldn't go down in the history books as the men who broke the strike. I told them that their public image was more important to them than the future of the South Wales Coalfield. At last, Emlyn said he would stir things in the NUM National Executive".


## THE BITTER END.

### Take it or Leave it.

On 17 February 1985, the TUC submitted final proposals for ending the strike. These were the result of TUC negotiation with all parties as well as meeting the government, including the prime minister. They were unable to dent the NCB's stipulation that, while a revised review procedure was acceptable, they, the NCB, not arbitration would have the final word in deciding whether a pit was uneconomic or not. The proposals stated, in summary:

- The parties will concentrate on the future success of the industry and commit themselves to reconciliation and restoration of relationships.

- The NUM recognise that it is the duty of the NCB to manage the industry efficiently. The NCB is firmly of the view that the interests of all its employees are best served by the development of an economically sound industry. The NCB recognises that the NUM represents and advances the interest of its members and their employment opportunities.

- The parties undertake that immediately upon a return to normal working, discussions will commence upon the revised Plan for Coal, such revision to be completed within six months.

- The parties accept the need to modify the existing Colliery Review Procedure. Following a return to normal work there will be urgent talks about the early establishment of a modified procedure and about the constitution, membership and role of the Independent Review Body, which is to be incorporated. Until then, existing procedures are to apply.

- All parties are committed to give full weight to the view of the proposed Independent Review Body.

- Pits, which are exhausted, or facing severe geological difficulties, will be closed by joint agreement.

- In the case of no further reserves existing which can be developed to provide the Board, in line with their responsibilities, with a satisfactory basis for continuing operations, either party may request for a modified Colliery Review Procedure. In such a case, the review will be carried out before the Board takes its decision as to whether or not the colliery will be closed.

- At the end of this procedure the Board will make its final decision.


For the NUM this last point was a killer, and the proposals were rejected out of hand three days later. It was this issue on which the strike had been fought and now, after nearly twelve months of struggle, it was still there.

By 25 February 1985, of the 20,000 or so Welsh miners, 270 had returned to work. Cynheidre, with 93, and Celynen South, with 37, were the main centres.

## Mardy Quits!

On 26 February 1985, Mardy, last pit in the Rhondda and the "Little Moscow" of the 1920's, a symbol of iron-hard resistance for generations, voted to return to work. Their decision was made without consulting Scargill. These had been Arthur Horner's finest, those of whom he wrote after the 1926 trauma, "They would never have given in. Right to the end there was not a whisper of defeatism among —— the members of Mardy lodge. If the whole coalfield had stood as firmly as Mardy we could have won". The scions of those men were made of similar stuff, for not a single man had broken the strike, but even here they had had enough. All they wanted now was to go back to work, but with dignity, not as "scabs" escorted by police through picket lines. For the strike overall, their decision signified the death knell.

## Enough is Enough!

Among the increasingly desperate and poverty-stricken membership, feelings of frustration and pointlessness were building up into a pressure to return to work under any circumstances, if not with an agreement, then without one. This would leave everything unresolved, but with the national leadership still insisting on death or glory there seemed no alternative. With glory unattainable and death unacceptable, the idea took on a life of its own. Emlyn Williams would say, "We are going back with no agreement. Better that than signing a document which closes this coalfield".

The strike was to end as messily as it had begun. For the next few days, every miners' lodge and branch in the country that were still on strike were locked in debate. The Durham miners' leadership expressed the general ethos, "It is unreasonable on humanitarian grounds to call upon the membership to endure still further pain and sacrifice to themselves and to their families in loyalty to the union".

It was a South Wales resolution that had officially started the national strike. Now it was a South Wales resolution that would end it. Traditionally the most militant coalfield in the UK, they were about to earn Scargill's disfavour. At a packed conference in Porthcawl, the decision was made to return to work. Emlyn Williams, South Wales Miners' President, put on as brave a face as possible. He called for a "coordinated, orderly return to work" saying: "We came out as one and we will go in as one".

On 27 February 1985, the magic figure was reached, with more than half of the NUM members now back at work. This was a statement as effective as any anti-strike ballot.

On 1 March (St David's Day), the entry in Phil Weekes diary reads:

"After 10 at night, George Reece telephoned. "If we go back to work on Monday", he said conspiratorially, "will you give us a meeting on the same day to discuss the dismissals which have taken place during the strike?" Naturally I agreed straight away".

On 3 March 1985, a conference of union delegates was held in Congress House of the TUC. The NUM Executive had been split 11:11 on whether the strike should continue and Scargill had refused to use his casting vote. Now, on that Sunday morning, Terry Thomas moved the South Wales resolution to end the national strike. It was accepted by 98 votes to 91. It recognised that there was now, "a drift back to work in all areas", and that, "the Coal Board have no intentions whatsoever to have any discussions with the union unless they sign the document presented to the TUC on Sunday, February 17th. The dispute should therefore be brought to an end without agreement. The National Executive was asked to negotiate an amnesty for those fired during the strike, but this was not a precondition. The treatment of those black-listed would depend on the inclination of local management. Scargill announced that there would be a return to work on Tuesday, and that the fight would continue as far as the union was concerned. Outside the conference there were agitated scenes among the multitude that had gathered. Scargill required a police escort to leave the building. The South Wales delegation, Emlyn Williams, George Reece and Terry Thomas were called "scabs", kicked and spat upon.

## Mardy Marches!

On 5 March 1985, at Mardy on a Tuesday morning, the "march back with dignity" was stage-managed admirably. "Dignity" had been the watchword of the organisers and this they achieved. Flanked all the way by applause, with heads held high and banners flying, the colliery band led the way. Whole families joined up with the singing crowd while those women for whom the hour was still too early watched the carnival from doorways, in nighties and dressing-gowns. On the mountain road between the village and the mine, a heavy smattering of reporters and camera men covered the hillside, scuttling along to the next vantage point as the procession advanced. They were not disappointed, and their media copy went around the world. As the procession arrived at the pit the men moved aside to clap through the women. It all epitomised what the strike was about - solidarity and communities. Rousing speeches were given, about solidarity, fighting spirit, and continuing the struggle. This was just a truce, not a defeat. There was talk of regrouping forces, so as to be able to fight another day. It all flew in the face of MacGregor's scheme of things, that Scargill's beaten men should return to work in obvious defeat, with heads hung low and tail between their legs.

Phil Weekes wrote in his diary, "The men returned to work together, with bands playing, flags flying and with considerable dignity". MacGregor saw it differently, writing later (The Enemy Within), "I don't know what this was going to prove to anyone, beyond demonstrating that these poor loyal men, who had been led such a song and dance for a whole year by Arthur Scargill were still held in vassal thrall by him. It was a pathetic gesture".


## Chaos and Defeat.

Elsewhere during that week there was chaos. Men refused to work with "scabs" and management strove to re-introduce discipline. At Penrikyber, ugly scenes were reported between miners and deputies, which resulted in the latter returning home. Some hard-liners, particularly from Kent, continued to picket. Arthur Scargill himself led one group of Yorkshire miners back to work, only to be stopped by three Kent miners who had come all the way to picket that particular colliery. True to his creed, Scargill turned back and the men did not work that day.

Gradually the men became used to the novel experience of once more having money in their pockets, while the wives had to set priorities as to which debt should be paid off first. In dribs and drabs the miners returned, some scarred in body and mind and some with broken marriages, but all facing a cranking up of the rat race, combined with a calculated elimination of their industrial power. Margaret Thatcher had scored another triumph, of Falklands dimensions. It proved to be a seminal moment, when the left in British politics lost and the right won. The 1980s would indeed prove to be a decade of revolution, but the Thatcher revolution, not the revolution envisaged by the NUM's left wing. She would now get free reign as the strike, after 358 days the longest and bitterest industrial dispute in British history, was finally over.


## SCABS AND KILLERS.

### Strikebreakers.

Within weeks of the dispute ending, both the wage claim and the overtime ban were settled. Still festering was the "scab" problem, for the level of hatred was frightening. In reply to a question by the Western Mail newspaper concerning the future of such people, the dead pan Emlyn Williams, president of the NUM in South Wales, had stated, in his typically humourless style:

"Mr. Scargill has said on behalf of the National Coordinating Committee that if they come back they will be embraced and welcomed back into the fold. The South Wales Area is not that way inclined —— We shall never forgive them. To us they are scabs and no different from 1911 or 1926. They will be treated as scabs when the strike is over".

The union leadership in South Wales were evidently not prepared to forgive individual miners for initiative they had themselves shown by initiating an end to the strike in defiance of the national leadership.

Indeed, the latter were to make more than just a passing reference to "scabs" and "traitors" in reference to none other than the South Wales leadership themselves.

From the first day back at work, strikebreakers were spat at and verbally abused by fellow workers and by women canteen staff. One individual at the phurnacite plant in Mountain Ash found human excreta in his socks and cleaning jelly in his boots. When his wife arrived to collect him, angry workers chased the car, which was pelted with a variety of missiles.

At Ffaldau Colliery in the Garw valley, Monty Morgan, the first man in South Wales to return, was greeted with a wall of silence. The canteen was closed when he walked in for a cup of tea and no one would shower in his vicinity. His colleagues turned their backs all day while, "even my old friends are afraid of talking to me". It was alleged that both the milkman and postman were prevented from making deliveries to his house. Within a short time he would move to Gloucester.

Much later, in 2004, Councillor Derrick Griffiths of Betws would be quoted as saying, "As far as I know, he only came back once for a visit but people heard that he was back and he had to go. Feelings are running high even now and people still talk about it. Memories are long —— I could never understand what he thought he could achieve. He lived in a village with hundreds of striking miners. He got a day's pay but ruined his life".

On 12 March 1985, a letter was sent to Mr. Phillip Weekes, South Wales Area Director, from a miner at Cwm Colliery:

"The sheer intensity of hatred against myself personally, leaves me in fear of my life. Although my work mates and I appreciated that there would be some animosity, the degree of hostility, which has escalated to MURDEROUS pitch, verifies that they are out for blood. —— I am bringing these facts to your attention, as for me to continue work under such circumstances would be suicidal".

Anonymous death threats were received and "vile and degrading substances" pushed through his letterbox. Such incidents were orchestrated by the local lodge, but without their direct involvement. Apparently the local NUM held him, and others like him, responsible for having "broken their revolution". There was to be a follow-up letter from a psychiatric consultant at East Glamorgan Hospital, where the individual concerned was receiving treatment as an outpatient. He was eventually resettled in the South Midlands Area. This particular case was one of those brought to the attention of the Prime Minister, Mrs. Margaret Thatcher.

In May 1985, Margaret Thatcher met Ian MacGregor to emphasise how vital it was that those miners who had worked during the strike and were now suffering should be given the necessary consideration and support.


## Convictions.

It was in this same month that the killers of taxi driver David Wilkie, one aged 21 and the other 20, were sentenced at Cardiff Crown Court. Both were from Rhymney, and each was convicted of murder and sentenced to twenty years. Strict security surrounded the court appearance of both men. Subsequently, the Court of Appeal reduced the conviction to manslaughter and the sentence to eight and a half years.

As a sign of the times, a few days after the trial's end a miners' demonstration and march was organised in Rhymney, home town of the two killers. A dominating placard, held aloft, read "Rhymney a town in mourning", the mourning being, not for the victim, but for those who killed him. Only a police guard diverted the march from the house of the working miner concerned. In the absence of more vigorous action, shouts of "scab" had to suffice, along with the promise that the strike-breaker would be ostracised, made by Lodge Chairman Mr Ivor John, one of the leaders of the march.

One of the speakers, Mr. Edward Rowlands MP, was quite mild in his criticism, "We are not saying that a terrible act was not done —— But what we are saying is that the two lads in our community are not murderers and should not be branded as murderers". For good measure, among the final speeches, Mr Ray Davies, a Labour member of the Mid-Glamorgan County Council was reported as saying, "When that despicable verdict was announced there were shock waves of horror and revulsion that went through the valley". But there was more to come.

Nineteen years later in 2004, firmly ensconced in Westminster with a safe parliamentary seat, the world looked different to Kim Howells, who now appears to show some regret concerning his role in the strike. His justification was that he could see no other option at the time. He would say, "We were prepared to be beguiled by our own rhetoric". Then, as a speaker at the march, his own rhetoric was in full flood:

"They will never be alone, our communities will always be with them and we will do our utmost to ensure that this absurd decision is reversed —— Any one of us that took part in active picketing in the strike could have thrown those rocks because we were forced to protect our communities". (The Sunday Times queried what they were being protected against: an invading army bent on putting the inhabitants to the sword and backed up by flame-throwing tanks?)

According to Mr Howells, there was also a political aspect to the verdicts:

"I am as shocked as everyone else here that this government set out with its whole parliamentary para-phernalia to defeat us as a class". Indeed, the two convicted were merely "the sacrificial lambs of the system".

Mr Llew Smith MP pitched in with the same theme. He said that the sentence was "political —— a warning that anyone who decides to take on the government will not be tolerated".

Peter Heathfield, NUM General Secretary, said elsewhere that for him the killers were the victims of legislation designed to indicate to working people, "That is your lot if you choose to rebel against the establishment".

All in all it would have been no surprise if the two killers had been persuaded to plead self-defence. Others in the country felt that, unlike the two convicted, taxi driver David Wilkie had been the victim of a death sentence for rebelling. His rebellion however had not been against the establishment but against the NUM.

### Redundancy for Strikebreakers.

On 4 July 1985, Ian MacGregor replied to the request of Neil Kinnock, leader of the Labour Party, that miners fired during the course of the strike should be reinstated:

"We had cases of violence and intimidation on a scale never before seen. Management had to fight to keep pits open and to protect their working miners and other employees and their families. This intimida-tion is still continuing —— The Board gave an undertaking during the strike to protect working miners and we will honour that undertaking. It is therefore the Board's policy not to reinstate anyone dismissed on good evidence of involvement in intimidation".

Initially, all requests to be made redundant by those subject to victimisation were turned down. The generous redundancy terms of the NCB applied only when a colliery was closed, not on request.

On 6 November 1985, MacGregor relented, agreeing to redundancy payments for former strikebreakers who were suffering intimidation, and who wished to leave the industry.

Plate 18 Tower Colliery Shaft with Pithead baths on the Right and Breacon beacons in the Background.

# Chapter 15
## NEMESIS.

*"It must be noted that men must be either caressed or annihilated.*
*They will revenge themselves for small injuries*
*but cannot do so for great ones.*
*The injury therefore that we do to a man must be such*
*that we need not fear his vengeance".*
Niccolo Machiavelli

## VENGEANCE.

If statements issuing from the NUM National President subsequent to the strike are judged at face value, vengeance was never very far from his mind. In an interview over a year after the strike's end George Reece, General Secretary of the South Wales NUM, would say (ref SWML AUD/573), "I personally advised Arthur to stay away from the television and stop making stupid statements. If he were to listen to his friends more, his real friends, then we could help him. I don't know who is advising him but whoever it is they're not doing a very good job".

In March 1985 Scargill declared, "All our future struggles will be stronger as a result". The strike had inspired, "hope, effort and solidarity, not only in Britain but throughout the world". In July, during the first post-strike NUM conference, the union, Scargill said, "had challenged the very heart of the capitalist system". The only way, he told the conference, was, "to fight again with the same determination, the same pride". For such a fight, however, his legions would have to be kept intact. In practice they were to be radically whittled down. By the end of the decade, 115,000 members were to be lost. The South Wales labour force had been sliced to 5,000, a far cry indeed from their one-time peak of a quarter of a million. Lancashire and Scotland were down to 3,000 and the three ultra-militant pits in Kent had ceased to exist.

## ALL CHANGE!

### Open Season.

The NUM had returned to work without any agreement whatever, having rejected the NCB's final document. They were now totally exposed, for as a result the Board saw themselves free of any obligation as far as the union was concerned. For MacGregor it would be open season. In words attributed to Oliver Cromwell on an earlier occasion - "The Lord hath delivered them into our hands".

MacGregor was a man in a hurry. Over seventy years of age, he had been appointed for a three-year term to bring the industry into the black. By now, already half of that period had been consumed in facing down Scargillism. Those on his team who advocated magnanimity in victory were given short shrift. The NCB, and the Government, were now free to pursue their policy unhindered. MacGregor was to write:

"Now we had succeeded, we were going to exert our right to manage the enterprise. From now on there didn't have to be a ritual genuflection to the NUM every time we wanted to do anything. If they thought they were marching back to where they had left off they had a very rude shock coming to them".

The NCB's final document, rejected by the NUM, had at least said:

"The parties will concentrate on the future success of the industry and commit themselves to reconciliation and restoration of relationships —— The NCB recognises that the NUM represents and advances the interest of its members and their employment opportunities".

Now, the union would be denied even this. Their previous role as joint regulator of terms and conditions at the pithead had gone for good. Branch officials were sent back down the pit to work. From now on, managers ruled. Future pay negotiations were held without the presence of the NUM, since Scargill refused to sit down with the Union of Democratic Mineworkers.

## Left Wing Waterloo.

Largely as a consequence of the traumatic national strikes, policy objectives emerged for the coal industry that were fundamentally political in purpose. They emerged under the Conservative government in 1979-80 and were adhered to consistently during the period of their rule, which ended in 1997. The strategy was twofold; first to break the power of the NUM permanently, and secondly to demonstrate the superiority of private enterprise over public ownership. The first was seen as an imperative, since the NUM was identified as being the cause of the Heath government's downfall in 1974. The second would be achieved by eventually returning the coal industry to the private sector. Both objectives were mutually consistent and reinforcing. Traditional energy policy considerations were overridden by the political, and associated financial, objectives. In this strategic context, the defeat of the NUM in the 1984-5 strike was a decisive turning point.

In the Battle of Waterloo, it was the defeat of Napoleon's Imperial Guard, the best he had to offer, which finally initiated the French rout. This swept them from the field and led to Napoleon's removal from the scene, changing history and the face of Europe for the next century. In retrospect, the humbling of the NUM, as "shock troops of the labour movement" equivalent to the Imperial Guard, led to the Waterloo of British trade unionism, for British history was also changed. Henceforward, new rules would apply. Trade unions, previously regarded, at least by themselves, as an integral part of British corporate and political life, would more and more come to be seen as yesterday's men, a busted flush.

- In the 1970's 54 per cent of employees were members of a trade union.
- In 1984 it was 50 per cent.
- By 2004 it was 25 per cent.

During the early 1980's, 10 million working days were being lost nationally as a result of strike action. During 1984, 27 million working days had been so lost. Twenty years later, it would be 1:3 million. In an overall strategic context, corporatism was totally rejected. Instead, conventional wisdom would now hold that Britain should strive to become the most USA-like economy in Europe, with flexible labour markets, shareholder-driven corporations and high, debt-fuelled consumer spending. A focus on the long-term as per France and Germany, implied by having to answer to interests other than professional money managers, such as government shareholders, regional banks and strong unions, became decidedly out of fashion. Not for this government the traditional European concepts of a dominant state role, plus international organizations and supranational authority. Equally despised were income redistribution and a wider definition of "rights" including education, free health, plus unemployment benefits. The key to the future would be unlocked by a striving for individual wealth for, in the words of one famous Thatcherism, "There is no such thing as society".

In this sense, the concept of egalitarianism ended in 1985. Statistics showing a growing gap between the rich and poor in society, particularly between 1984-90, bear witness to this. By the 21st Century the concept of a job for life, with real power being in the hands of organised labour, belonged to another age. With no sign of the pendulum returning, indeed with Margaret Thatcher speaking highly of the Labour Party's leader Tony Blair, ostensibly her political enemy, all indications are that her victory is complete.

The Conservatives are proud of the surge of productivity they allege occurred following the defeat of the miners, leading to the current economic strength of the country. A study by the National Institute for Economic and Social Research shows that there was indeed a significant increase in the late 1980s and early 1990s. This has however since slowed down. In a longer term context, in the 1960's, before the miners strike, productivity also made great strides, only to slow down again in the 1970s. Overall, in the 20 years before the strike, UK productivity increased at an average of 2.2 per cent per annum, while in the 20 years afterwards the average figure was 1.9 per cent.

## The Market Rules, OK?

As far as energy was concerned, an unfettered release of market forces replaced strategic planning by the government. Traditionally, the contribution that each fuel should make was determined on the basis of an assessment of what was in the long-term interest of the nation. It was now argued that the nation's true interest lay in letting the market rip, for the blast of competition would surely sweep away inefficiency. This would automatically result in a solution that was the most cost-effective. The four-fuel economy, coal, oil, nuclear power and natural gas, became in effect a five-fuel economy as restrictions were lifted and imported coal was added to the mix. The market would work its magic and sort it all out, subject to some nudging in the right direction.

In practice, competition would push the coal industry to go where mining conditions were optimum. The logic of low cost coal reserves, on a worldwide basis, prevailed. High cost coal was written off. All previous assessments of British coal reserves were effectively trashed for, "If it is not worth digging up then it does not constitute a reserve". Thus disappeared overnight the "300 years of workable reserves", previously quoted by the NCB. Although, in 1993, the UK gas reserves were assessed as running out in a mere 40 years, this was still longer than the economically recoverable British coal reserves.

# NEW BROOM.

## Two Philosophies.

Imperative to all of the above was a concomitant change in the ethos and style of top management. For the NCB the sea change had began already in September 1983, with Ian MacGregor's arrival. Both Lord Robens and his successor, Derek Ezra, had served approximately 11 years as Chairman of the Board. Ezra's successor, Norman Siddall, was another who had come to the forefront under Robens. As Chief Mining Engineer he also had been instrumental in creating the Board as it then was. He was to retire just one year following his appointment. He openly opposed the government's choice as replacement. In his view it was not only unnecessarily provocative to the unions but a slight on the Board's existing managers. The unions and the Board's existing managers were, however, precisely those that the Government, and their instrument MacGregor, were gunning for. In their view, the two parties were in bed with each other. MacGregor and Thatcher were at one in considering the mining industry completely over-unionised, regarding with astonishment that elements of management could even support the aims of strikers. This was a philosophical world apart from NCB Chairman Ezra's view that his co-operation with NUM President Gormley was progressive, and "ahead of its time".

This collective concept, whereby important decisions were hammered out between the whole group of those responsible for their implementation, was alien to MacGregor. In his view it was bureaucratic and inefficient. The open tradition of Lord Robens, Sir Derek Ezra and Norman Siddall was to go. In its place would come an unprecedented concentration of central power. A new creation, the Office of Chairman and Chief Executive, took over all significant responsibility for the industry's affairs; both day-to-day running and long-term policymaking. This boiled down to two people, MacGregor himself and his sidekick Jimmy Cowan, the previous Deputy Chairman. In the former's words, Cowan was the one person in the existing organization he could rely on. A fellow Scot, and also a graduate of Glasgow University, Cowan had worked himself up during a lifetime in the industry. As a mining engineer, and with the same attitude on fundamental issues, Cowan became MacGregor's "window" on the industry, informing him on the nuts and bolts of the organization. This concept of working closely together with a like minded "insider", had also worked for MacGregor at British Steel. Otherwise, the number and influence of full time board members were reduced.

Out of the window was to go any concept of "The brotherhood of mining". Before MacGregor's arrival, seven of the ten Board members were life-long insiders, with an eighth being from the NCB's biggest customer, the Central Electricity Generating Board. In MacGregor's view this was incestuous, with performance being measured by their own organizations' rather low standards. Within twelve months, to blow the cobwebs away and to light up dark corners as he would see it, composition of the Board had been turned on its head. Now seven of the ten members were outsiders. One of them was quoted as saying that they were not so much hard-liners as bottom-liners. Another said that the Board previously had "the flavour of an outfit which has been run for the benefit of its employees".

The British Association of Colliery Management (BACM) was another concept MacGregor had difficulty in comprehending. In his view it was an attempt to run with the hare and the hounds. He had difficulty getting used to a situation where people who clearly were representatives of management could, and did, criticize that management. Even the Area Directors were members of it. BACUM called for abolition of the Office of Chairman and Chief Executive, or at least for a more co-operative style from its two occupants.

## New Faces.

Between October 1984 and February 1985, the NCB lost its four Directors General: of Information, Staff, Industrial Relations and Mining. The Technical Director also resigned. Their replacements had to accept lower status and salary grading, as heads of department only. As management changes and departures multiplied, the atmosphere inside Hobart House, Coal Board Headquarters, became increasingly tense and unhappy.

To further the Cultural Revolution, a number of part-time outsiders, bereft of any coal industry experience, were brought in. Geoff Kirk, head of NCB public relations, was disparaged for holding, "cosy chats with his friends in the media" (read - he understood the press, and he understood his own industry). To Kirk's chagrin Tim Bell, chairman of Saatchi and Saatchi, was brought in to directly advise the chairman in that role. Saatchi and Saatchi had been the PR firm behind the Conservative Party campaigns in 1979 and 1983. Kirk departed, as did Ned Smith in Industrial Relations, not to be replaced. As MacGregor was to write:

"(Ned Smith) told me to my face I could not do these things. I'm afraid he resented my whole style of management. The idea that the Chairman simply said what was going to happen was clearly alien to his and many other people's culture".

This culture was that a publicly owned industry - particularly one blessed with an absence of competing, sectional unions - was able to behave in a civilised manner. Under this concept, union officials and managers could genuinely share a common long-term interest, even though in the short run they fought their corners hard. In an interview with The Sunday Telegraph MacGregor was quoted as saying;

"Ned's a romantic (i.e. Ned Smith of Industrial Relations). As a matter of fact, we had a hell of a lot of people on the Board who were romantic in that way, just not tuned in to the realities we were facing. They loved to be seen as great big magnanimous figures".

In an article in The Guardian on 11 February 1985, John Torode summarised the atmosphere in Hobart House as follows:

"Nobody pretends to know what is happening, nobody can predict the next step to be taken by his own team, nobody wants to defend what is going on. Nobody cares much any more. It has all become something of a sick joke. In public you will go through the motions. In private, you no longer pretend —— In sum, the place is a shambles. Mr MacGregor attempted to reverse thirty years of management by consent in a matter of months. He made a couple of changes at Board level and introduced a Chief Executive. But, below Board level, hundreds of consensus managers have been told to become confrontation men overnight. Cost accounting has replaced social commitment. Union bosses are now to be challenged, not appeased —— It is an impossible burden to place upon managers born of a different school. It will not work without pain and confusion. Kirk and Smith are the first of many who will go over the hill in the months to come".

## Weekes doesn't Play Ball.

In South Wales, Area Director Phil Weekes lost his long-standing board membership. Weekes was highly respected locally for fighting his corner and promoting the coalfield. In the strike's aftermath he had shown his liberal core by agreeing to reinstate almost all the 238 men in his area fired during its course. (Later, on their release, those convicted of killing the taxi driver David Wilkie would not be reinstated. In this case a collection by the union provided these two with a cash donation equivalent to redundancy pay). Such an act of reinstatement was untypical of the otherwise ruthless management ethos that was to prevail.

In contrast, MacGregor's attitude was uncompromising:

"Our first task was to make it clear that we were not going to take back all the men whose thuggery, vandalism and violence had helped shatter so many lives of those who had wished to work, nor those who had done so much damage to NCB and other people's property. We should not forget that we and our working miners had just been through twelve months of the most concentrated mayhem the country had ever seen".

On 22 April 1985, seven weeks after the strike's end, a meeting of the Area Consultative Council was held at Coal House in Llanishen, Cardiff. In this meeting there was no hint of the impending butchery. Area Director Phillip Weekes expressed his extreme pleasure at the coalfield's recovery. He dismissed as groundless, inaccurate and bad for morale, speculation that up to 18 South Wales pits could close. While he felt that four or five pits were coming to the end of their natural lives, production had reached approximately 80 per cent of the pre-strike figure. Three collieries however- Aberpergwm, St. Johns and Mardy- were in serious difficulty, with OMS less than 0.5 tonnes.

Later, he would say in a television interview:

"We made a very quick recovery in South Wales, we picked up our productivity within a few months. I thought, this will really impress people. Then it was made clear to me by Mr. MacGregor that once I was out of the way he would offer every man redundancy, which I had refused to do".

Weekes realised that this would mean the end of the industry. The men were broke after 12 months without pay, with many heavily in debt. Understandably, they would accept large sums of money. The effect would be to bribe them out of the collieries. Aghast, Weekes asked, "You mean everyone, even the profitable pits like Betws colliery"? On receiving an affirmative reply he rejoined, "Well I'm sorry, I refuse to do it", and left the room. There was no more communication from MacGregor; the latter knew that Weekes would shortly resign. He just had to wait a little and then his job would be made easy.

Later that same year, 1985, when Weekes retired, he received neither handshake nor goodbye from MacGregor. It was an inappropriate end to a distinguished career. Phillip Weekes was one of the most senior mining engineers in the country and was highly thought of in the coalfield. He had spent a lifetime in the industry and had been Director General of Mining, as well as NCB Board member. None of this cut any ice with MacGregor. No doubt in the latter's eyes, he was one of the, "hell of a lot of people in the Board who were romantic —— just not tuned in to the realities we were facing. They loved to be seen as great big magnanimous figures". To Weekes, the episode would have been as hurtful as MacGregor's dismissal of Donald Davies's Board membership as being of no real consequence, since he also was shortly to retire. Donald Davies had previously been Director of the NCB West Wales Area and was a former colleague. Weekes commentated that the newspaper report concerned contained one of the most offensive series of comments yet produced by members of this, or any other Board. Such was Mrs Thatcher's "nice man", who would now unleash a reign of industrial slaughter.

## South Wales Slaughter.

In July 1985, three months after the optimistic meeting in April, Phil Weekes retired. Mr. C.J. Davies replaced him as Area Director. The atmosphere changed noticeably, with managers receiving almost daily instructions, phoned through from area or national level. Decision- making at pit level became circumscribed. The older type of colliery manager followed Mr. Weekes into early "retirement", with young men promoted to replace them. These new men were ruthlessly to carry out the dictates of British Coal headquarters, thus doing themselves out of a job, for the closure programme went into high gear. By the end of that same year almost half of the South Wales pits were gone.

## COST RULES.

### "A Great Deal Has Changed".

Due to lack of maintenance, many underground workings had been damaged irreparably during the year of the dispute. In addition, there was still the imperative of bringing the industry onto a sound financial basis. As part of the emergency recovery package to get the show on the road, nearly 40 pits and many more working faces were closed. Some 38,000 people left the industry within a short space of time, in addition to the 12,000 who had already left during the dispute. In the first full year before the strike, national production was 121 Mt. In the first full year after it was 105 Mt. This was a remarkable recovery, bearing in mind the degree of disruption due to flooding and falls of roof, combined with the savage closure programme in the strike's aftermath. In MacGregor's words, "Now we had succeeded, we were going to exert our right to manage the enterprise". Radical thinking became the order of the day, aided by what MacGregor called, "a new spirit of realism and cooperation".

On 11 October 1985, the "New Strategy for Coal" was issued. Drafted by Ken Moses, the then Chief of Mining Operations, it started with the magnificent understatement, "A great deal has changed since the launch of the Plan for Coal in 1974".

The future of the industry would now be built around two interrelated financial goals:

- Phase out the industry's dependence on subsidy, with the aim of breaking even by the decade's end.

- To achieve competitive prices, fixed production targets would be abandoned and a more flexible approach adopted to meeting market requirements.

## Globalisation Rears its Head.

Instead of production targets, mine managers now faced cost targets. It was the price of coal on the international market that, more and more, was casting its shadow. Having already lost out with coking coal, the NCB (now renamed British Coal) was determined to avoid the same fate in the steam coal market for power stations. Between 1973 and 1989, the world trade in steam coal increased from 14 Mt/a to 172 Mt, exceeding that in coking coal. By 1988, three oil companies alone were selling over 100 Mt of steam coal per annum on the international market (Shell-39.6 Mt, Exxon-32 Mt, BP-29 Mt). This began to arrive in Europe in increasing quantities, much of it transhipped through Amsterdam, Rotterdam and Antwerp (the ARA ports). It began to exert a powerful influence over the European coal industry, with the CEGB frequently referring to ARA spot prices. These contrasted sharply with those offered by British Coal, reinforcing the CEGB in their ongoing policy of reducing dependence on indigenous production.

In 1985 the CEGB entered the international spot market, paying £30 per tonne for 120,000 tonnes of Columbian coal. This was delivered to the Fiddlers Ferry power station on the Mersey. The policy continued, with further deliveries to Fiddlers Ferry and to power stations on the Thames.

## We Sell Energy, not Bulk.

To meet the challenge, there was a reformulation of British Coal objectives. Production costs were now allocated to energy content (i.e. per GigaJoule or GJ) of the coal produced, rather than to simple tonnage. This would take into account the differing calorific values of various coals (for example, a typical high calorific value coal could have an energy content of 28 GJ/t. Other coals could have more, or significantly less, energy per tonne). This concept, of selling energy as opposed to just bulk, would enable a true value comparison to be made, not only between different coals but also between alternative fuels. This change in terminology was realistic, and symbolic of the fact that the coal industry was now rooted in an energy market both global and competitive. The target was for all collieries to reduce operating costs (including depreciation but excluding interest charges) to less than £.65 per GigaJoule. Some adjustment was made for collieries producing coal of unusually high market worth, such as the anthracite mines of South Wales. In general however, collieries regularly producing coal in excess of this target were not meeting their capital charges and so were not capable of making "an economic contribution". They would therefore be regarded as targets for early review and possible closure.

In future, investment would only be approved if the overall operating costs for the colliery after investment were less than £1.5 per GigaJoule. For the increased production that resulted directly from such investment, operating costs of less than £1 per GigaJoule would have to apply. At this level of cost, output would not only cover the associated capital charges but could compete on the international market. For all opencast sites, £1 /GJ was set as the target.

**Never Mind Tradition, Lower the Cost.**

With the integration of opencast sites into the overall production system, British Coal distanced itself from the concept that had previously prevailed, namely that opencast production was a mere adjunct to deep mined output. Now, against a background of minimising overall cost, its output would be maximised, along with that from low cost collieries. Increasingly, deep-mined output was replaced by opencast. Such production remained buoyant and throughout the 1980's took a growing share of the British market. Improvements in opencast mining technology allowed deeper and larger workings. It was, however, to run into increasing public protest. Output was heavily concentrated in just a few locations. Three locations (Castle Morpeth, Amber Valley, Cannock Chase) contained 25 per cent of the opencast reserves in England and Wales, whilst 11 districts contained 56 per cent of such reserves. The increase in opencast output, in particular as a proportion of deep-mined output, is shown below.

| Financial Year | Deep mined output (Mt) | Opencast output (Mt) |
|---|---|---|
| 1971-72 | 135.5 | 8.1 |
| 1975-76 | 114.5 | 10.4 |
| 1980-81 | 110.3 | 15.5 |
| 1985-86 | 88.4 | 14.1 |
| 1990-91 | 72.3 | 17.0 |
| 1993-94 (Last full year before privatisation) | 42.7 | 13.5 |
| 1998-99 | 23.7 | 14.9 |

Gradually, through nuclear power, opencast coal and imported coal, the Generating Board was losing its dependence on British deep- mined production. Only the most productive collieries were to remain, and these were further dramatically reorganised. Increasing use was made of heavy-duty faces and a major switch was made to retreat mining, which was now introduced as fast as possible. This method of working enables faults to be located before they can interrupt face operations. Its advantages had been known for decades and were already referred to in the Reid report during the Second World War. It speaks volumes for the conservatism prevailing that the changeover to this method took so long. These changes, the so-called "Wheeler Plan", were pushed through under the aegis of Albert Wheeler, who later became Operations Director and then Joint Deputy Chairman of British Coal.

Total costs for personnel, including those pensioned off, exceeded 50 per cent of the total. At nearly 39 per cent, wages and salaries for existing employees still dominated the direct costs of British Coal. The old formula still applied, cost reduction implied a further increase in the output per man.

## AWAY WITH THEM!

**Lame Ducks?**

Following the strike's conclusion, British Coal would press ahead with their expressed aim, namely the creation of an industry capable of surviving financially in an open and globalised energy market. To meet this objective, assessment was strictly short-term. With the exception of the anthracite area, there was no investment so as to access new reserves. No pit was given the benefit of any doubt. Doubts there certainly were, as units with an impressive record of profit and productivity followed so-called lame ducks into oblivion.

- At Treforgan, Crynant, five boreholes, sunk in 1976, indicated around 19-20 Mt of anthracite present 290-460 metres below the surface. The mine had been one of the most profitable in the UK and the 1974 Plan for Coal had already invested in a new drift and roadways, plus bunkers, 2,230 metres of conveyors, a new rail system for the transport of men and materials, along with additional electrical equipment and pumping. This development should have extended the life of the mine by 20 years and was expected to provide new jobs. The Red Vein seam had been worked out and after the 1984-85 strike the mine was without face capacity. So as to tap an area of anthracite reserves to the east of the drift, twin roadways were to be driven into the area concerned. Despite this, the mine ceased work in September 1985.

- Blaenant, in the Dulais Valley appeared to have all of the pre-requisites necessary for success. A shallow drift mine, working rich fault-free deposits in the anthracite area, it closed on 11 May 1990 having worked from the late 1970's.

- Deep Navigation, Treharris, had consistently been one of the coalfield's best performers. In 1980 it recorded its best ever profit of £2.6 M and in the second week of May 1981 the 780 men employed achieved their best-ever productivity of 3.1 t per man shift. Total saleable output for the week was 9,750 tonnes. In March 1985, immediately after the strike, a single, new high-technology face, equipped with some of the most expensive and massive powered roof supports, cut a saleable weekly output of 9,000 tonnes with a coalface productivity that reached 28 tonnes per man-shift. By 1986 the colliery was producing half a million tonnes of saleable coal per annum. Such good statistics persisted until the end of the decade. Suspiciously, results then deteriorated. Some miners criticised the decision to work with a face height of 9 feet, instead of the previous 5 feet, thus causing problems with the roof. Heavy-duty roof supports at Tower, which had been earmarked for Deep Navigation and which might have alleviated the situation, were left underground when the face at Tower was abandoned early.

Deep Navigation closed in 1991, after a life of 112 years.

## Standard Routine.

Targets were given for outputs that were unrealistic and, if they were attained, higher ones would be set. Closures were often announced within weeks of the shutdown date. To smooth the process, and to mini-mise the public relations damage, every effort was made to manipulate the miners into not initiating any review procedure. A high level (for a working man) of redundancy payment was offered. The lump sum alone, for a man of 49 was as much as £36,480. This was an incredible temptation for men who had gone twelve months without any salary. To subdue resistance, the Board would then announce that the next year's redundancy payments would probably be reduced, thus panicking the men into accepting the inevi-table earlier than was necessary. Eventual redundancy, so the argument went, being based on average wages would be less due to the reduced bonuses that could now be earned. If the men did not accept closure now they would be certain to lose thousands of pounds later when the pit, for certain, would close. The fear of losing out financially was enough to damp out any spark of defiance. Inevitably, the men would agree to closure and inevitably British Coal would move on to the next pit, with the same standard routine.

In practice redundancy payments never were reduced, in fact they increased. Such payments, and other costs arising from colliery closures, were met almost totally by the government, not by British Coal. This meant that management was not subject to any financial restraint in running down the number of mine-workers.

## Defiance.

St. John's Colliery near Maesteg is a rare case of defiance. Here the lodge decided to fight closure and instigate a public enquiry. It was hoped this would set an example that would secure an extended life, not only for St. John's but for all the pits in South Wales and the UK. In practice, British Coal tactics were able to stultify the objective.

On 1 April 1985, C.J.Davies, who at the time was still Deputy Director, descended on the colliery like some angel of death, announcing that he would give his views on the pit's future later that week.

By 7 May 1985, when C.J. Davies again visited the pit, the men were already voting with their feet - 400 had accepted redundancy terms. Nevertheless, the lodge's campaign continued, with the haemorrhaging of manpower not the only obstacle with which they had to contend. A major problem was the speed with which they were being confronted with British Coal initiatives. They and other lodges were being hustled into making rash decisions on vital matters. The Area Executive of the union also complained of not being kept fully informed of developments.

Already before the strike, the South Wales Area of the NUM were preparing a case that St. John's had many years of life in front of it. The key was to drive two new roadways into the proposed Margam take, thus working those attractive reserves from an existing colliery. In September 1985, a national review meeting was held in London. In a detailed presentation, lasting one hour and fifteen minutes, the NUM put their case that the pit should stay open. The Board then made their response. It lasted just a few sentences, and was negative. The Board did agree that St. John's would come under the Modified Review Procedure, the first South Wales pit to which this would apply.

However, the establishment of this independent review body, and agreeing on its nature, was proving to be messy and acrimonious. By the beginning of November British Coal and the NUM at national level still had not agreed, either on a formula as to how the Modified Review Procedure should be operated, or on what basis its decisions should be made. In particular, the Board was resisting any consideration of social hardship. Negotiations were at a stalemate. Meanwhile, at St. John's the Board had been active. Those men who did not want redundancy were enticed to transfer to other pits in South Wales where, "their future would be secure". This was backed up with an ultimatum, whereby 22 November was the last date on which the Board would be prepared to process redundancies. In the absence of such processing, those forced to finish would not receive the social security benefits normally due to them.

On 21 November 1985, at a general meeting, the Area President of the NUM stated that there was no "magic formula", either for solving the conflict over the review procedure or with regard to the latest British Coal ultimatum, due to expire the following day. At the end of the road, with neither hope nor comfort and with all options closed, the men reluctantly agreed to accept closure.

## The Modified Review Procedure.

First; Fudge the Issue.

Against a background of such slaughter, what was actually the position concerning the Modified Review Procedure? Board policy was to manipulate the men so that no review procedure would be invoked. Nevertheless it was there as a possibility. NACODS, the officials union, had reached such an agreement with the Board on 23 October 1984. It had been a key item in their decision not to support the NUM in their hour of need. Some potential weaknesses were noted at the time, critics being led by Arthur Scargill himself. Detailed implementation would, in any event, depend on the agreement of other unions including the NUM, but the NUM had gone back to work without any agreement with the Board at all. In addition, the procedure did not cover closures that the NCB could blame on damage caused by the strike itself.

The Independent Review Body was a key part of the Modified Procedure and was the subject of considerable acrimony. NACODS thought that they had won a form of independent arbitration on NCB actions with regard to pit closures. Their proposal at the time had been:

"The criteria to include social consequences, economics, employment prospects and workable reserves. The decision of the Independent Body would be binding on all parties"

What actually emerged in the final agreement was:

"The Colliery Review Procedure —— will be amended to include an independent body whose function will be to consider a reference from any one of the parties on any matter arising under the above clauses about which there is disagreement. Full weight will be given by the parties to the advice of this independent body"

Second; Minimise its Effect.

The agreement had served its purpose, of fobbing-off NACODS and getting them to withdraw their impending strike. MacGregor had had no intention of negotiating away, as he put it, "the crown jewels". Any restriction which the Review Body put on management freedom of action now had to be minimised The revelation that he had been outmanoeuvered would bring bitter complaints from the NACODS General Secretary, Peter McNestry, who would say that his treatment by the Board had been, "dishonourable and insulting". With Robens, no doubt he would have got a gentleman's agreement. To make such an agreement, however, one has to be dealing with gentlemen.

Issues actually covered by the new procedure were as follows:

- Earlier warning when a new closure came under consideration.

- If union officials wished to prepare a case for opposition, more time and better facilities would be provided, such as access to detailed accounts.

- Adequate notice of the final decision would be given for national officers to consult their members.

- In the case of irreconcilable agreement there would be an "appeal to an independent body".

Crucial questions were left open. Who would be the members of such a body? How would the chairman be appointed? What was its legal status and the detailed terms of reference? What range of matters could be investigated? Could for example these include the social costs involved in depriving a whole community of its livelihood and reason for existence, with all its homes, schools, shops, transport facilities, traditions and job prospects? Nevertheless, in spite of open questions, the option of "appeal to an independent body" was a definite pledge.

Third; Disregard it.

On 27 February 1986, the true worth of this pledge became clear, in an explanation by British Coal of the review procedure as applied at Bates Colliery in Northumberland. No secret was made of the fact that, while British Coal had an obligation to listen to the recommendations of the Independent Review Body (IRB), they had no obligation whatever to accept them, which was the situation that occurred at Bates. NACODS fought the case in the High Court, which found in favour of British Coal. The public relations department of BC explained:

"The IRB has advisory powers only, as agreed by the unions. The Board agreed to give full weight to the IRB's findings, and we have done that. It is the Board's responsibility to manage the industry and everyone is clear that the Board must make the final decision. Because of the various stages of the review procedure, with 2 stages of local discussions, followed by an internal national appeal meeting and ultimately reference to the IRB, it is unlikely that by the time a proposed closure reaches the IRB stage any significant new factors will be identified which could affect the pit's prospects and which have not already been identified in detail by the Board".

As to the social costs involved in a closure, the PR release goes on, "The general social problems of the community at large; these are matters for the government, not the Board". Any improvement in results at the colliery concerned was written off on the basis that, "Experience clearly shows that results improve for only short periods before severe geological problems occur".

There was always coal left in the ground, that was not the issue. The issue was that it was the Board's decision as to where the best return on investment could be obtained, bearing in mind both quality and price as required by the markets available. The PR release refuted any lack of social consciousness as follows:

- The Board offers generous transfer benefits for long and short distance moves for those who wish to stay in the industry.

- The best redundancy benefits in the UK are available for those who wish to leave the industry.

- British Coal Enterprise is a government funded job-creation venture. In all traditional mining areas British Coal Enterprise is regularly in discussion with local authorities, local enterprise agencies and other organizations to see how they can work together to attract new jobs.

# Chapter 16
## E TU BRUTE!

*E Tu Brute (you too Brutus!).*
Exclamation allegedly made by Julius Caesar on seeing that among
the assassins stabbing him to death was Brutus, his closest colleague.

## THE AGENDA.

### Bedfellows.

In 1960, of the 200Mt of coal consumed in the UK, 26 per cent was for electricity generation.

By 1992, with 101Mt of coal consumed, electricity generation was taking by far the lion's share, with 79 per cent.

Electricity generation was not only the biggest market for coal. Coal was also by far the main source of electricity generation. Ipso facto, privatisation of the generators would not only transform the electricity supply industry. It could not fail to have a significant effect upon its traditional bedfellow, with all indications being that this effect would be negative.

In 1990, the UK Electricity Supply Industry (ESI) was privatised and deregulated. At privatisation, the existing 5-year contract between the CEGB and British Coal for deliveries of 70 Mt annually was coming to an end. The two major generators that now appeared on the scene, National Power and Power Gen, agreed to buy 65 Mt of British coal for one year, declining to 60 Mt for the second and third years. After that British Coal would have to take its chance in the marketplace. The writing was on the wall.

There had been no widespread public pressure to remedy shortcomings. Rather it was yet another expression of the government's philosophy that efficiency could be increased and costs cut by exposure to market forces, rather than by policy intervention. In addition, by selling the industry off to shareholders money would be raised for the treasury and future investment could be raised on the stock market or from banks, without adding to the government's borrowing requirements. There was another, more political agenda. Margaret Thatcher in particular saw the privatisation programme as "one of the central means of reversing the corrosive and corrupting effects of socialism" (see her book, "The Downing Street Years").

### Dirty Tricks.

The NUM of course could be guaranteed to oppose the measure with might and main. Unfortunately for the union, in the very same year that this issue came to a head, their energies were diverted in defending Scargill and Heathfield, their President and General Secretary respectively, against charges of embezzlement. These charges first appeared in the Daily Mirror whose owner was, of all people, Robert Maxwell. The self-same Robert Maxwell was subsequently proved to have looted his employees' pension fund to stave off financial embarrassment. Subsequent discussion of Maxwell's involvement with Mossad, the Israeli secret service, implies that he would have been no stranger to dirty tricks. "The Cook Report" on Central Television followed up the attack on Scargill and Heathfield, who went to court.

On 19 June 1991, the court case ended in favour of Scargill and Heathfield. The attempt to get them removed as unsuitable persons to run a trade union had failed. Nevertheless, although the charges had been proven false, the NUM had been diverted during what was a critical period.

# ELECTRICITY PRIVATISATION.

## Selective Virtue.

In their worship of "market forces" the government showed itself to be highly selective. The Social Darwinism of market fundamentalists would be skewed so as to conform with political, not economic, objectives. Even with regard to the coal industry Margaret Thatcher would write:

"I also knew we might have to face another strike. Where would we be if we had closed the pits at which moderate miners would have kept on working, and kept more profitable but more left wing pits open"?

The paramount political need was to find ready purchasers for the state- owned utility. The objective of reducing NUM power also had an important influence on the way in which privatisation of the ESI was carried out.

## Sweeteners.

In May 1992, the National Audit Office stated in their report, "The Government's over-riding objective was to complete the privatisation of the entire industry within the lifetime of a single parliament". Such indecent haste, working to the deadline of a general election, meant a determination to get the deal through as quickly as possible. One consequence of this was the extremely lenient terms offered to investors. A large increase in tariffs, perhaps about 25 per cent, was made prior to privatisation, to ensure its success. The assets of the Central Electricity Generating Board and the Area boards were sold at very low prices, perhaps one-half to two-thirds of their value. Initially, a lower or no return was provided to the government for the portion of the financing that it provided. In spite of the huge cost for lawyers and consultants as a result of privatisation, the result was a disproportionate share of the industry's economic return going to shareholders in the new companies. Levels of profitability and rates of return on capital were widely seen as being excessive.

## The Nuclear Embarrassment.

Government objectives at the time included not only a controlled run-down of the coal industry but also, in stark contrast, the sustaining of nuclear power. With nuclear power, however, even if lionised by Margaret Thatcher, there was a problem. In practice the intention of including it in the initial privatisation had to be abandoned. Although the 90 per cent of total expenditure for research and development in the power industry, which nuclear power had absorbed, had been carried by the government, amortisation of the capital investment incurred formed the largest component in their costs. This form of generation is characterised by very high fixed costs and low variable costs. Plants with high fixed costs will always struggle in competitive markets where, inevitably, prices are volatile. In addition, the cost of processing the radioactive spent fuel elements and of storing the resultant waste, together with the future decommissioning costs of nuclear stations, was a deterrent to any prospective buyer. To the chagrin of the Thatcherites, the City refused to invest in privatised nuclear utilities. Thatcher's predilection for nuclear power ran into a significant setback. Now, the government was stuck with a nuclear industry on its books, generating 20 per cent of the nation's electricity but with no assurance of a market.

At last the truth was out. Even the rabid free-marketeers of the Thatcher administration were forced into making some concession to strategic thinking. The nuclear stations were removed from the sale and kept under state control as Nuclear Electric. To guarantee the nuclear market, albeit at premium prices, the Thatcher government conceived the Non-Fossil Fuel Obligation (NFFO) to prop up the industry. The NFFO obliged Regional Electricity Companies (RECs), which buy and distribute the power, to obtain a portion of their supply from non-fossil sources. At the time of privatisation, this was entirely nuclear energy. The RECs paid a premium price for this portion (initially 10 per cent on top of electricity bills), which was passed on to their customers. The NFFO applied to England and Wales, with special provisions for Scotland.

Between 1990-95, the NFFO raised £7.4 billion. Of this, only £300 M went to renewables. The rest went to nuclear power. In spite of their questionable economics, the nuclear stations were given a guaranteed market for their output. In the event of a future slump in demand, they would be the last to shut down.

The original intention of including nuclear power in the privatisation meant that at least one of the new private companies, National Power, had to be sufficiently large to accommodate the financial risks. Since competition in generation was the bedrock of the whole policy, another company, Power Gen, had to be sufficiently large to compete with National Power. As a consequence, virtually all of the generating capacity was divided between just two companies. Nuclear power was withdrawn from the deal at a relatively late stage and the Government's overriding priority was to irreversibly complete privatisation before the 1992 general election. Consequently, there was no time to unscramble the resultant duopoly of generation in England and Wales. It is generally accepted that, from an economic standpoint, a greater number of smaller companies would have been preferable. With the duopoly providing 80 per cent of market share and subsidised nuclear power providing the great bulk of what was remaining, the concept of a free market was a travesty. Subsequently, the Electricity Regulator would reduce the initial dominance of National Power and Power Gen. By 2000 their combined market share was only 20 per cent. They can no longer control the market price of power.

## The "Dash for Gas".

At privatisation, the UK already had enough generating capacity to meet demand. The fact that in the first two years of privatisation so much was invested in new power stations can only mean that investors must have expected to make good profits with low risks.

In March 1991, the European Commission allowed natural gas to be used for electricity generation. At this time, significant improvements in gas generation efficiencies were being achieved. This was partly due to improvements in turbine design but mainly due to the replacement of "open cycle" with "combined cycle" technology. Efficiencies of 50 per cent were being achieved, compared with 40 per cent for modern coal-fired plants. New independent power producers (IPPs), using such combined cycle gas turbine sets (CCGTs), made their presence felt. These new stations were small, modular and capable of generating cleaner power at an operating cost below many of the coal-fired plants. They came on the market when low capital cost installations were being sought by companies seeking finance from banks and investors. For these, the low risk, relatively low investment, and steady earning streams appeared attractive, particularly when compared with a new coal-fired plant. To the coal- fired stations, concentrated mainly in the English Midlands, a smattering of gas-fired stations were now added, mainly along the East coast. All this occurred at a time when UK gas prices were falling and British Gas began to sell interruptible contracts at a discount.

In 1995, these apparently risk-free investments lost their shine. The gas price collapsed to half its previous level. In addition, technical improvements had not only reduced the amount of gas required to generate each unit of electricity by 20 per cent but also construction costs by 30 per cent. At privatisation, the price of gas had seemed to be as low as it could go. Investors had been confident enough to buy gas on 15-year take-or-pay contracts - they had to buy the gas whether or not they could use it. Now, with the new calculations, far from being the cheapest plants on the market, the initial tranche of gas-fired stations were generating at a price 30 per cent higher than plants ordered after 1995. Since the price of coal had also fallen significantly in this time, the gas-fired plants built immediately following privatisation now became the most expensive. Their owners had to write off billions of dollars in wasted investment costs and in buying out the uneconomic gas contracts.

In the meantime the rush to construct new gas-fired power stations, as opposed to optimising the existing coal-fired capacity, had resulted in an overall excess capacity margin of 40 per cent. This is way above the level regarded as optimal. With almost no growth in load, new capacity was compensated for by the removal from service of coal-burning plant. During the first six years following privatisation, 10,700 MW of such new gas-fired capacity was added. Some of the coal-fired stations shut down were still quite useful. Investment losses resulting from their premature retirement were borne by the public, whose government had sold it to the new owners at very low prices. It is an open question whether the overall environmental benefits of the shift to gas justified the extra capital costs to retire coal-burning plants at an early age, particularly since the price of coal continued to fall significantly.

**A New Culture.**

If the overall financial benefits of privatisation were questionable, what was achieved was that the whole character and culture of the electricity supply industry changed. Instead of engineers, commodities traders and accountants now ruled, with engineers becoming no more than support staff to the latter. The previous, if implicit, energy policy of supporting the twin pillars of indigenous coal plus nuclear power was swept away. Henceforward, only one of those pillars would be supported. For the rest, the assumption was that electricity was just another product like baked beans, whose availability is best left to market forces. Commercial objectives became paramount (at least on a micro-economic, if not on a macro-economic scale, as outlined above). These superseded the previous engineer-dominated management and the considerable influence of trade unions. The previously rigid demarcation between engineering and finance started to break down. Reduced staffing levels led to the management of subcontractors and multi-skilling. Instead of engineering-led projects, market-led projects became the norm, plus packaged deals for customers. Energy marketing businesses emerged, which did not own the distribution infrastructure.

As a nationalised industry there had been no significant pressure to cut costs. The industry saw itself as a public service, with the main driving force being a statutory responsibility to "keep the lights on". Since the monopoly structure had allowed full pass-through of costs, financial parameters were regarded as constraints, rather than objectives. Now there were shareholders expecting a return on their investment.

**Benefits - Real and Imagined.**

Although the pressure was now on to decrease cost, the cost of investment actually increased, due to the larger returns for risk taking required by private investors. In a monopoly market, as previously prevailed, companies might be able to borrow money at a real rate (net of inflation) of 10 per cent. For a risky project they will require at least 5 per cent more. It is often the case that construction cost repayment represents between one and two thirds of the cost of power generated, depending on what type of power station is involved. Consequently, an increase in interest rate of 50 per cent could raise wholesale power prices by up to a third. When opening up electricity generation to competition the gamble for consumers is that market discipline will be so tough - more appropriate choice of plant plus tighter control of costs - as to more than make up for this extra cost.

Whether the whole restructuring and privatisation of the electricity industry was worth it is, to a great extent, a subjective decision. It has proven to be extremely difficult to compare electricity prices with what they would have been had the exercise not been undertaken. For privatisation to be accepted politically it was necessary to show price reductions, and these were indeed achieved. Supporters of privatisation are not slow to point out that not only has atmospheric pollution been reduced, for most UK consumers prices also fell in real terms (approximately 11 per cent reduction in the domestic price of electricity by 1997). However, a true comparison with costs under the old publicly owned model can only be made by including a due consideration of the following:

i)   There was a 25 per cent increase in tariffs prior to privatisation, made to ensure its success.

ii)  The assets of the Central Electricity Generating Board and the Area Boards were sold at very low prices, perhaps one-half to two-thirds of their value. This was a subsidy provided by the public, who owned the facilities being sold.

iii) The private generators did not have to bear the financial burden of nuclear power. Instead, the government carried this.

iv)  Initially a low or no return was provided to the government for the proportion of the financing that it provided.

v)   Subsidies to the coal industry were eliminated.

vi)  The government paid lawyers and consultants, required to execute the changes,, using public funds.

vii) Studies by CIGRE of France show that, in the six years following privatisation, the real generated price for electricity in almost all nations declined by between 15 per cent and 32 per cent. In the UK the reduction claimed in the 1990's was about 20 per cent.

Approximately 40 per cent of the price of electricity generation is made up of the cost of fuel and, during the first years of ESI privatisation, oversupplied markets led to world wide reductions in coal, oil and gas prices. This translated into a concomitant reduction in the price of electricity generated. The same mechanism would have applied in the UK, even without privatisation. After nearly 15 years of privatisation the Financial Times claimed an inflation adjusted drop in UK electricity prices of 28 per cent. This should be compared with the larger 36 per cent drop over the same period, in the almost entirely unregulated USA.

While the advantages for consumers were questionable, commercial advantage for individual companies and shareholders was very real. Most of the economic benefits of privatisation were retained by the new shareholders and not passed on to the customers. While generation costs dropped significantly, retail prices barely changed.

On the basis of the above, and despite all propaganda to the contrary, shake up of the Electricity Supply Industry (ESI) in Britain cannot be regarded as having been a glowing success. All that has been proved is that in economic circumstances manipulated to be extremely favourable, and with severe restrictions on the extent to which competition can operate, the system did not fail and the consumer price for electricity fell marginally. Shareholder profits were enormous.

## Trend Setter UK.

It was an act of faith on the government's part that enough electricity would be available, and at a fair price, without anybody having the statutory obligation of ensuring it. Nevertheless, the Conservative government of the time peddled their privatisation and liberalisation wares by means of conferences in Brussels and throughout Europe.

In 1996, the European Union directive on liberalisation of the electricity market was agreed. The UK model was to be adopted, in some form or other, by other countries seeking to reform their utilities. In the introduction of competitive generation, the UK was followed by Australia, Finland, Norway, Sweden and the United States. At the time of UK privatisation the creation of a competitive pool for electricity was unique in the world. What was not fully appreciated at the time was the necessity of sufficient and sophisticated regulation, so as to avoid market manipulation by dominant players. This was later to be brought home, in particular by the de-regulation disaster in California.

The general philosophy of ESI privatisation was that independent, private consumers, such as large industries or Regional Electricity Companies (RECs), would buy their electricity from Independent Power Producers (IPP's) in accordance with competitive market forces. The infrastructure for long-distance transmission, which served to link the former with the latter, was open to all consumers and generators. This national grid was recognised as being a natural monopoly. After privatisation it was operated as a separate company. Privatisation did not end government involvement in the industry; rather it changed its form. The previous direct interaction with state-owned concerns was replaced by an arms-length relationship, between private companies and the regulatory authorities. The Office of Electricity Regulation (OFFER) was set up to prevent the overcharging of such monopoly services and to oversee the various licence conditions.

## The Concept is Perverted.

Local distribution and local sales were in the hands of the RECs. In a perversion of the independent, private concept, these, however, owned some of the IPPs and were committed to buy from them. In addition, the RECs themselves were subject to incorporation into other concerns. Within a year of the takeover or merger of REC's being allowed, half of them ceased to have an independent existence. The combination of undervalued assets with good, low-risk revenue streams resulted in the REC's becoming "cash cows" attracting mainly foreign predators.

For some years after privatisation, the Regional Electricity Companies maintained a significant local monopoly status. In addition, they were allowed equity participation in the Independent Power Producers (IPP's) that were operating the new gas turbine stations (CCGT's). Such plant was funded on the basis of long-term (usually 15 years) base load operation This meant that virtually all of their output would be sold to one or more of the participating REC's under fixed price contracts. The effect of this was to isolate REC's from the spot market for electricity. The associated gas supply contracts were on a use-or-pay basis, whereby the generators committed themselves to a certain level of gas consumption.

As long as their franchises existed, the REC's were able to pass on the cost of purchasing electricity from their unregulated subsidiaries, the generating companies, to their captive consumers. Although the consumers were captive, the return obtained from their equity shares in such generating companies was unlimited. Consequently, it was almost always more profitable for an REC to take power from an IPP, in which it had a stake, rather than from other sources, even if another source was cheaper. The actual cost of generation was almost irrelevant. Such a book-keeping environment decoupled the profit-and-loss accounts of individual REC's from the overall national picture. As a consequence, coal-fired plant was now being run at much reduced load factors, resulting in a situation where economic coal stations were being displaced by more expensive gas stations.

In April 1996, so as to limit vertical integration of the industry, which was at odds with the original privatisation strategy, the government decided not to allow the bids by Power Gen and National Power for two RECs. Nevertheless, the trend continued. In contrast to what had been expected, there was virtually no horizontal integration.

By mid 1997, only one REC remained independent. The South Wales Electricity Board was one of several to be taken over by US utility companies (Southern Electric International in the SWEB case). Direct or indirect foreign ownership (particularly by US utilities) and integration of electricity with gas supply and other services such as water would become issues.


## The Pool.

An attempt was made to reconcile a competitive market with the impossibility of distinguishing the output of one producer from another, since the product was identical and the transmission system was shared. The UK concept was that generators and distributors feed into, and draw from, a common pool. Since electricity cannot be stored on any large scale, this pool was an accountancy exercise, meant to reflect the balance of supply and demand. In order to keep to the privatisation timetable, the only option then available was to adapt the software used by the old generation and transmission company, the Central Electricity Generating Board (CEGB). The trading price for electricity, or "pool price", between generators and the distributing companies (RECs), was to be set on an half hour by half hour basis, one day beforehand. The intention was to bring generator sets on line in order of increasing costs (i.e. the most expensive set, as required to meet demand, is the last to join the schedule). This theory ran into the practical problem of erratic price signals being given, for example by generating companies manipulating the market by withdrawing plant at key times. This was a strong disincentive for buyers and sellers to trust the pool. In addition, unplanned outages and unforseen sags or surges in demand could also cause great volatility in the "pool price". As an example, the loss of the 2,000 MW supply from France during a strike in the mid-1990s caused the pool price to jump £120 / MWh, peaking at £1,500 / MWh. Between April 1990 and January 1994, pool prices rose by 43 per cent. Such volatility led to the development of companies offering "hedging" contracts. This is a form of insurance whereby the price of electricity to the purchaser is guaranteed. The "hedging" company takes the risk, but charges for the privilege.

The government required retail electricity suppliers to purchase all available output from the nuclear stations, at prices subsidised by consumers. This accounted for 17 per cent of demand, rising by 1994 to 25 per cent. The European Commission required similar treatment for nuclear power imported from Scotland and France, which contributed another 8-10 per cent. In addition, bilateral contracts between generators and large consumers, thus bypassing the pool, were still allowed. As a result of all this, more than 90 per cent of electricity consumption was provided from sources not subject to pool competition.


## Liberalisation, the Flawed Panacea.

A dependable electricity supply is inextricably linked; not only to quality of life but also national security. There is a dichotomy between long-term security of supply/ environmental policies and the requirements

270

of financial markets, with their emphasis on high rates of return and short-term cash flow. The driving force for the companies concerned is to maximise their own profit, not to minimise the total cost of electricity. The long-term welfare of consumers, however, cannot always be measured by economic efficiency. To avoid the prospect of power cuts, capacity must be installed which is only seldom utilised. This is good insurance but not economically optimal from the investor's point of view. Such extra capacity also serves to put a downward pressure on prices, which is also not in the investor's interest.

Large rewards are provided to those with skill in playing the rules of the competitive game, as compared to those with skill in lowering the cost of producing and transmitting electricity. Spot markets can be manipulated by withholding power until prices rise to more profitable levels. Mergers and take-overs can reduce the number of competitors while, on a long term basis, prices can be kept high by failing to build enough power stations to satisfy demand. Rapid expansion in demand results in a premium being placed upon the creation of sufficient infrastructure and generating capacity.

In 2000, problems experienced in the United States following deregulation there, particularly in the state of California, bear witness to the potential for customer exploitation endemic in an inadequately regulated system. In terms of international electricity prices, the United States was already well placed without deregulation, as the following table of residential prices for electricity shows (US Energy Information Administration).

| Country | Residential price per kilowatt-hour, 1999 (in US $) | Compared to United States |
|---|---|---|
| Argentina | 0.141 | 174% |
| Australia (1997) | 0.080 | 99% |
| Brazil (1998) | 0.128 | 158% |
| Chile | 0.090 | 111% |
| Denmark | 0.207 | 256% |
| France (1998) | 0.129 | 159% |
| Germany | 0.152 | 188% |
| Greece | 0.090 | 111% |
| Ireland | 0.117 | 144% |
| Japan | 0.212 | 262% |
| Netherlands | 0.132 | 163% |
| UK | 0.117 | 144% |
| USA | 0.81 | 100% |

In California, the classic case of liberalisation failure, the wholesale price of electricity became more than four times that of the previous year, with occasional price spikes of 50 times normal. Wholesale prices, that were as low as 2.1 cents per kwh in February 1999, spiked to 31.7 cents per kwh in December 2000. News of blackouts and plant closures became routine. State Regulators had been reluctant to allow price flexibility, while preventing suppliers buying power from the generators on long-term contracts. As a result, timely indication of eventual demand and capacity required was not given. The construction of additional generating plant, which proved to be necessary, was not triggered. Unscrupulous traders were able to exploit transmission bottlenecks to drive up electricity prices. Collusion between generators exacerbated shortages and caused prices to rise, e.g. by simultaneous repair work upon a large number of power stations. Electricity was exported to neighbouring states under a contract made when California prices were low, while a subsidiary of the same utility in a neighbouring state would sell electricity, at premium prices, back to Californian clients when shortages there began to bite. The notorious Enron, the epitome of accounting malpractice, proved adept at manipulating the system. To stabilise wholesale prices the state government was forced to intervene, at the cost of incurring debt but halting the power cuts and rampant price instability.

In the UK, in spite of being politically contentious, privatisation/ deregulation was carried through due to the power of the central government under the British system. Differing political, legal and cultural traditions mean that processes in California became dominated by lawyers while, in the UK, civil servants with little technical knowledge strove to make commonsense decisions. Bearing in mind the complexity of the industry and the radical nature of the changes made, it is to the credit of all concerned that in the UK transformation was carried out with no major hitches such as disruption of electricity supplies. Except in Scotland and Northern Ireland the regional dimension was unimportant. In addition, the infrastructure was already established while growth in demand was modest and capacity adequate.

Nevertheless, the first decade of privatisation was characterised by a degree of confusion and over-complication. That the pool as a means of trading electricity did not adequately reflect market forces is shown by the fact that during the 1990's pool prices (as opposed to long-term contracts) actually increased by 10 per cent. During the same period, capital costs for new plant fell by nearly 40 per cent, the efficiency of combined-cycle gas plant increased by more than 10 per cent and spot gas prices fell by 50 per cent.

Later, another factor was to make itself felt. In the first stages of privatisation almost all new plants were designed for base-load operation. As a plethora of private companies came in, each making over-ambitious plans for their share of the market, the result was an excess of such plants and a deficit of peaking plants. Consequently, in the medium term, there was a gross over-supply of capacity. There were just too many power stations. This led to a price collapse, down to a level too low to support nuclear plant. The reduction in profits also led to a departure of American investors from the scene. At first sight advantageous, such low prices act as a strong deterrent to future investment.

## THE EFFECT ON COAL.

### Coal's Last Redoubt.

At the time of electricity privatisation, most of Britain's generation was from fuel supplied under long-term contracts with British Coal. These were initially for three years, to be re-negotiated in 1993 for a further five years. This was intended to provide some stability during the impending privatisation of the coal industry. There was some nuclear, oil and hydro generation. There was no gas generation at all. Indeed, at that time, European law precluded the use of gas for electricity generation purposes.

In 1991, the generation mix was as follows:

- Coal:              63%

- Nuclear:           19%

- Oil:               9%

- Gas:               1% (2 CCGT stations, but a forecasted

                     increase to 25% by 1995/96).

- Imports:           5% (Power imported from France).

- Hydro+Renewables:  3%

Although the amount of coal burnt in power stations had gradually increased over the years, as a result of losing other markets coal generally had been in steady decline. The following table shows the decline of the coal industry nationally, up until 1992. It is based upon NCB/ British Coal statistics:

| Year | Total UK Output (Mt) | Deep Mine Output (Mt) | No. of producing collieries | No. of mineworkers (1,000's) |
|------|------|------|------|------|
| 1955 | 225.2 | 211.3 | 850 | 740.8 |
| 1956/66 | 185.7 | 177.0 | 483 | 495.1 |
| 1975/76 | 125.8 | 114.5 | 241 | 273.2 |
| 1985/86 | 104.5 | 88.4 | 133 | 157.8 |
| 1991/92 | 91.1 | 71.0 | 50 | 48.9 |

On the positive side, the government could illustrate some success:

i) No operating subsidies had been paid to British Coal by the government since March 1990.

ii) Between 1987 and 1992 there had been an overall increase in productivity of 61 per cent. This could be broken down as follows:

- 8% due to closure of inefficient pits.

- 8% due to opening of new pits (Selby complex).

- 45% due to improvements in existing mines.

iii) With an output of 5.95 tonnes/man-shift British deep- mines were by far the most efficient in Europe (to keep this in perspective, in the USA deep mines were clocking up an average productivity of between 20-24 tonnes/man-shift).

The Conservative objective of running down indigenous coal coincided with the grain of market forces and environmental developments current at that time. These were:

- The collapse of oil prices in 1986, from $30 per barrel to $10. This was the result of energy-saving measures, combined with increased production from the North Sea.

- The rise of sterling against the US dollar, reducing the price of imports.

- The emergence of a large international trade in low price steam coal. After the shocks of the 1970's, oil's price went so high that it could no longer compete with coal in the generation of electricity. Governments then included coal as an option for securing future energy supplies. Not all countries possessed coal, and in Europe and Japan the industry had been run down. This was the origin of the latter-day international coal trade, with infrastructure and technology built up in the 1980's.

- In March 1991, the European Union repealed EC Directive 75/404/EEC, which restricted the use of natural gas for electricity generation. This action opened the way for the government to reverse its traditional policy, and proved to be the most critical factor as far as coal was concerned. Previously, gas had always been confined to so-called "premium" users (domestic, petrochemicals etc.). The logic behind this had been to maximise the availability of reserves, and to optimise overall energy usage.

- In 1992, at the Rio Summit Meeting and as a result of increasing concern about global warning, countries pledged to reduce emissions of "greenhouse gases", principally carbon dioxide. Limits on the emission of sulphur dioxide, nitrous oxide and particles were progressively tightened.

## Breathing Space.

At that time, gas was plentiful in the seas around Great Britain. The new Combined Cycle Gas Turbine technology was relatively cheap to install, and plants could be constructed quickly. Thus arose the "Dash for Gas", the large-scale introduction of gas burning into the UK's electricity generation industry, exceeding all expectations. This had been the last great redoubt of indigenous coal. In addition, there was now freedom to import coal as required. Nevertheless, to stabilise the situation during the privatisation process, a breathing space was given to indigenous coal.

In 1990, three-year contracts were signed with the new generating companies in England and Wales (five year contracts in Scotland). All of these contracts were substantially above world market prices. In the course of the next three years while they lasted, the coal industry would have to pull a rabbit out of the hat.

That the coalmining industry itself was a target for privatisation was obvious to everyone. Not all those concerned wanted to travel to this Promised Land. Sir Robert Haslam, Chairman of British Coal is quoted as saying:

"The perception that somehow private industry has some great magic wand and can come in and do something which nationalised industries cannot do has not got a great deal of validity". These were not the kind of sentiments that the government wished to hear and in future they would not hear them, at least not from senior management in British Coal.

On 1 January 1991, Mr. Neil Clark succeeded Lord Haslam as Chairman. The former was an accountant through and through, although he did admit to, "having a certain fascination for engineering". His previous experience included accountancy work with the Anglo-American Mining Corporation of South Africa.

On November 1991, Coal News printed a statement by Mr. Clark:

"You could be forgiven for feeling dismayed and disenchanted at recent media speculation on the diminishing role for British Coal as we progress through the 1990's —— If plans exist to reduce the size of the safest, most efficient and most productive deep-mining business in the whole of Europe to a pitifully small number of collieries, I too might feel like throwing in the towel; THERE ARE NO SUCH PLANS".

## The Nightmare Occurs.

Events would prove that in fact the media were much better informed than Mr. Clark about the prospects facing his industry, perhaps indicative of the respect in which the government held both him and it. Nevertheless, far from throwing in the towel, Mr. Clark would commit himself to pushing through the self-same plans he had initially disparaged and said did not exist. There is no indication that he showed resistance. The next actor to appear on stage would, in any event, cut the ground from under him!

In 1992, after the general election in that year, the nightmare expressed at the NUM annual conference in 1976 by Lawrence Daly, General Secretary at the time, was finally realised. Michael Heseltine was made Secretary of State for Trade and Industry. Known as the Tarzan of the Conservative Party, he had been instrumental in dethroning Margaret Thatcher the previous year, failing nevertheless to occupy her stool. Famous for his grabbing of the speaker's mace during one parliamentary debate and waving it at the opposition, his emotional attitude to mining, and its traditional status, can be summed up by a typically pithy remark:

"I am sick to death of being constantly reminded by people of what their fathers did and what their grandfathers did. I am far more interested in what their children and their grandchildren are going to do" (this from the man who was a leading light in the Tory campaign to preserve fox-hunting and the traditional English countryside).

On the 1984-85 struggle he commented:

"I have never been so confident of the position of a government as I was as a member of that cabinet in 1985. We were fighting in my view a wholly legitimate constitutional battle for the supremacy of the law".

Regarding the accelerated run-down of the mining industry:

"I don't think it's vengeance, its an observation on the consequences of militancy —— It could have been different if there hadn't been militancy and a strike".

## THE 1992 MASSACRE..

### Search and Destroy.

In the autumn of 1992 the blow fell on what was left of UK coal-mining. By that time it was already all but over in South Wales, with Betws, Taff Merthyr and Tower the only pits remaining. As annual contracts between the Electricity Supply Industry and British Coal were renegotiated, immediately the result of government policy made itself felt. By this time long-term contracts had already been signed with gas suppliers for the new CCGTs. Altogether, 15 such stations were expected to come on stream by 1995. As an additional factor, the Sizewell B nuclear station was due to start up in 1994.

This competition from natural gas and nuclear, plus that from imported coal, resulted in a significantly reduced demand by the electricity generators for coal overall and for British coal in particular. The generators were building new bulk terminals at Bristol and Liverpool for handling coal imports. These could handle larger ships thus removing the need for transhipment at a continental port or, alternatively, the use of smaller ships at a higher price. Already, coal could be imported into the Thameside power stations at a price per unit of contained energy at £1.15-1.30 per GigaJoule. Under existing contracts, the average delivered cost of domestic coal was £2 per GigaJoule. Not only was it more expensive, most British coal was of lower quality than its internationally traded counterpart, in terms of sulphur, ash and chlorine content.

In September 1992 the generators did not accept British Coal's final offer. This was for 40Mt/a, at a pithead price of £1,51 /GigaJoule, falling to 30Mt in 1997-98, at a pithead price of £1.33 /GigaJoule. As a result of this rejection by the generators, British Coal foresaw the following consequences:

- From 31 March 1993, there would be an immediate drop in the annual tonnage supplied, from 65 Mt to 40 Mt.

- This implied a drop in deep-mined production from 59 Mt in 1992-93 to 32 Mt

- From 1 April 1994 there would be a further reduction in tonnage supplied, to 30 Mt.

- This meant a deep-mined production of 28 Mt.

- By 1997 the number of coalmines in the UK would be reduced from the current fifty-one to fifteen.

With limited potential for exports, markets for coal other than for electricity generation were also expected to decline, due to:

- Further penetration of gas into industrial and domestic markets.

- Increased use of imported coal (the British steel industry was already importing all of its coking coal).

- A worldwide recession forcing industrial curtailment.

On 13th October 1992, as a reaction to this situation, Michael Hesseltine announced in Parliament the virtual demise of the British coalmining industry.

- In 1947, at nationalisation, there were 980 pits with 700,000 employees in the industry.

- In 1985, at the end of the national miners' strike, there were 169 pits with 221,000 employees.

- In 1992, at the time of the announcement, there were 51 pits (fifty in operation plus Ashfordby, which was under development) with 54,000 employees.

In one fell swoop, almost overnight; thirty-one pits were to be closed, some of them within a matter of days. The remaining 20 pits would require 24,000 employees. The resulting 30,000 job losses was the biggest redundancy in the country's history and would cost one billion pounds. Former Energy Secretary

Tony Benn described it as "a search and destroy mission against the National Union of Mineworkers". He criticised the principle of putting fiscal rectitude above human dignity. It was feared that the knock-on effect on mining firms, coal-fired power stations, railway depots and service trades would add a further 70,000 to the job losses.

## Public Reaction.

This was a shock to the nation, with the general mood not being helped by the fact that "Black Wednesday" had occurred just one month previously. This was when the United Kingdom had to quit the European Exchange Rate Mechanism and devalue the pound. There was a furore. Public reaction was strong and immediate, with the Union of Democratic Miners also feeling betrayed. The Welsh Secretary said on the radio that he had not been informed. Leading Conservatives, such as Edward Heath and Teddy Taylor joined in the attack. Winston Churchill (grandson of the great man) visited a colliery where the UDM was strong. The government's majority in Parliament was not large. A parliamentary vote on the subject of these pit closures resulted in a government majority of just 22, with 6 Conservatives voting against their own party. The standing of Arthur Scargill in public opinion took an immediate jump upwards, with people saying, "He was right after all". Even the tabloids came a long way from the previous "Mine Fuehrer" headline in The Sun.

On 16 October 1992 the Daily Mirror ran a front-page headline, "March with Us" and included articles by left-wingers Tony Benn and Paul Foot. There was a massive national demonstration in London in support of mining communities. An estimated quarter of a million people were in Hyde Park and later Tony Benn presented a petition of about 30,000 signatures to parliament. Such pressure, combined with ongoing protests from MPs from all parties, led to a moratorium on 21 of the 31 pits due for closure. Only ten of them would close immediately. Following a court action these ten became subject to the statutory 90-day consultation period, to end on 29 January 1993. The remaining twenty-one pits would be subject to review.

On 20 October 1992 Hesseltine commissioned an American company of mining and geological engineering consultants, John T. Boyd Co. of Pittsburgh, Pennsylvania, to carry out an independent analysis.

On 21st December 1992, the original pit closure decision was declared illegal by the High Court. Nevertheless, British Coal ceased production at the 10 pits due to close immediately, while continuing to pay the workforce. Their argument was that coal mined there would simply take away the market from pits that were viable.

## The Boyd's Report.

When the Boyd's Report was submitted, it oozed globalisation and survival of the fittest. The following were listed as being the facts of the situation:

- The increase in productivity by British Coal of 234 per cent over the previous seven years was commendable but of little significance in a world context. Current productivity was still only 20-35 per cent of that in the USA and Australia.

- Deep-mine production costs were twice or three times that of major exporting countries, e.g. USA, Australia, Republic of South Africa.

- British Coal would never reach costs as low as the above due to inherent factors such as geological conditions, age of existing collieries, plus operational and statutory limitations.

- Some exports of premium coals were possible, but not on a large scale.

- For power stations situated inland, British Coal could become competitive.

- The high capital cost and increasing difficulty in obtaining planning consent for the construction of major new collieries in the UK would prohibit any new development of large underground mines for the foreseeable future.

- Consequently, attrition in the number of collieries due to the depletion of reserves would result in coal production declining.

British Coal was of the opinion that the collieries now proposed for closure but on hold could achieve the operating costs necessary to be viable. The consultants studied this possibility. In their view it was a question of becoming better with what one had rather than adding a lot of new technology. Boydes stated:

"The quality and commitment of the local management team (i.e. their ability to motivate the labour force) can influence colliery cost by a factor of 30 per cent or more —— Numerous changes are required to existing statutes and British Coal policy to operate in a commercial environment and achieve potential cost reductions —— The ability to extend shift times and implement regular weekend work will assist in providing supplemental tonnage in the medium term —— Enactment of modern mining regulations and the establishment of a strong management organisational structure and authority are essential to achieving maximum production from available colliery capacity —— Pro-active participation of Her Majesty's Inspectorate of Mines in these changes and the implementation of new mining practices is critical to promote safety while accelerating the introduction of modern regulations". Such changes and practices included:

i) A flexible work schedule, so as to allow extended shift times and weekend work.

ii) Compulsory redundancy for all levels of employment.

iii) Restructuring of colliery management, involving the elimination of all statutory positions below the level of colliery manager.

iv) Concentrate management at the colliery, so as to minimise overheads above this level.

v) Modern underground work practices, such as the use of electrical cable splicing and the use of oxy-acetylene cutting torches and welding equipment.

vi) Increased use of roof bolting (that is the clamping of roof strata together by means of a series of glorified rawl plugs) as a means of roadway support, instead of the conventional steel arches.

vii) Multiple-entry development, which is the use of a combined gate road for adjacent faces. In the UK, adjacent coalfaces are usually separated from one another by means of a pillar of coal

viii) In-seam mining, that is a return to the old concept whereby access roadways are always driven in the seam, as opposed to horizons driven straight and level, through rock strata if necessary.

Production and market figures, both recent and projected, were given as follows:

| | Historical | | Estimated | Projected. | | | | |
|---|---|---|---|---|---|---|---|---|
| MARKETS | 1990-91(Mt) | 1991-92(Mt) | 1992-93(Mt) | 1993-94(Mt) | 1994-95(Mt) | 1995-96(Mt) | 1996-97(Mt) | 1997-98(Mt) |
| Electricity Generation | 70 | 69 | 63 | 40 | 30 | 30 | 30 | 30 |
| Others | 19 | 17 | 13 | 10 | 9 | 9 | 9 | 9 |
| TOTAL | 89 | 86 | 76 | 50 | 39 | 39 | 39 | 39 |
| SOURCE OF SUPPLY | | | | | | | | |
| Deep mines | 71 | 70 | 59 | 32 | 28 | 28 | 27 | 27 |
| Opencast | 17 | 17 | 16 | 15 | 14 | 14 | 14 | 12 |
| Coal stocks | 1 | (1) | 1 | 3 | (3) | (3) | (2) | - |

The Boyd consultants said that in the USA and Australia, although geological conditions were generally superior to the UK, even in cases where similar conditions had been encountered, productivity there was still much higher. Significant use was made in their report of the words "modern" and "safety".

Replacing the words "new" and "modern" with "American", what was being proposed was the introduction of hire-and-fire, plus the "rip, tear and bust" of American mining culture. The problem was that catching up with America (or trying to) meant adopting aspects of American society that would prove unpalatable or even impossible. Americans work longer hours than Europeans and face other pressures to perform - often their access to healthcare depends on being employed. People are under greater discipline as a result. Boyd consultants studied two scenarios as a means of improving productivity:

- CASE I: Continuation of current work practices, within existing mining legislation and British Coal policy.

- CASE II: This assumed an unconstrained industry, operating under "modern mining regulations and a commercial setting" (including increasing shift length from 7.25hrs to 8hrs) so as to achieve potential cost reductions.

Boyd's used a price of £1.3 per GigaJoule (GJ) of energy supplied to a power station as a basis for their calculations (in the UK, typically 1 tonne of coal = 24.3 GJ). National Power, one of the main generating companies, considered this as being equivalent to internationally traded prices over the long term. The conclusion reached by Boyd's was that, under CASE II, up to 13 of the 21 collieries being reviewed for closure could, within 3-5 years, reduce the price of energy supplied to £1.2 per GJ (Betws was not one of these). Therefore, if the CASE II conditions were accepted, these 12-13 pits could be considered potentially economic. This was equivalent to 15.9 Mt of additional output. If the working week was increased to 6 days, then the price of energy delivered could be reduced further, to £1.09 per GJ.

In January 1993, the consultant's report was submitted to the Coal Review Team of the Department of Trade and Industry.

In March 1993, and based on this report, the government published their conclusions in a white paper, "The Prospects for Coal, the Conclusions of the Government's Coal Review":

Twelve of the twenty-one pits reviewed (those that showed potential under CASE II as above) would be further assessed for economic viability. The remaining nine would be closed. The white paper stated that the BC Chairman had committed the corporation to halving its overhead costs within the next three years. He was confident of achieving the performance levels set out in the Boyd's report within an even shorter period.

The government's view of the world was spelt out in their conclusions:

"The government believes that the coal industry will be best placed to make these changes when it has been fully returned to the private sector —— In 1979 the government inherited a largely state-owned energy sector. The state-owned energy industries were in many cases significantly subsidised and over-manned, while protected from the disciplines of the marketplace. These elements exemplified and contributed to the failure of the British economy at that time. State- owned industries have often made uneconomical investments, or preserved activities well beyond the time when their commercial rationale ran out, often as a result of political intervention —— Britain's coal industry was shielded for too long from competition under easy arrangements between state-owned monopolies. The move towards a freer market in electricity exposed these arrangements and hastened their demise. At the time of electricity privatisation in 1990, BC was given a further period to adapt, through three-year contracts with the generators substantially above the price at which imported coal was available. BC's failure to take advantage of this opportunity, and its lack of competitiveness in world terms, lie at the heart of the current problem —— Change is inevitable in a modern industrial economy. Companies and industries rise, flourish and decline and others take their place. Mining and its associated activities cannot be exempt from this process, which has been seen many times and in many places".

On 31 March 1993, BC finally agreed new supply contracts with National Power and Power Gen. These would be for a period of 5 years. However, they involved a substantial reduction in deliveries. Only 35 Mt would be delivered in the first financial year, followed by 30 Mt in the remaining years. Private mines were offered contracts totalling 3 Mt for the first 2 years, with a possible increase to 5 Mt for the subsequent 3 years. The generating companies expressed their intention to run down the stocks which had been built up and to concentrate their imports on a few suppliers, mainly Columbian. There would also be occasional spot purchases. As a result of these government conclusions following the Boyd Report, there was a call by Scargill for mass demonstrations and a one- day stoppage of industry as a protest.

On 2 April 1993, all of the NUM manned pits were idle, but not with 100 per cent support. British Coal retaliated swiftly: They stopped automatically deducting union dues on the NUM's behalf. Now they would have to be collected manually and individually. This was a cumbersome and expensive process, which threatened to reduce membership and create a pool of non-union labour.

## The Boyd's Follow-up.

In 1993-94, in a messy and complex series of decisions, the privatisation process started. Some BC collieries were closed and others "mothballed" or offered for sale to the private sector. Subsequently, especially following privatisation, major recommendations in the Boyd's report were tried out, although the UK Mines' Inspectorate rejected any relaxation of controls on the use of oxy-acetylene burning and electric welding underground. Nevertheless:

- There was a major shedding of manpower, with the use of contractors greatly reduced.

- There was a change in legislation, separating the roles of inspection and supervision.

- The multiple-entry system of face development was attempted, but abandoned as being generally impractical under UK mining conditions. Here the mines are deeper and operate under different design parameters to those prevailing in the USA.

- In most mines, roof bolting became the preferred method of support for gate roads, leading to the face. For long-term infrastructure however, steel arches remained the principle system.

The large-scale application of roof bolting had never been supported by the NUM. They regarded a fatal fall of ground at Bilsthorpe Colliery, in February 1994, as being a consequence. It was alleged that Boyd's, who reported based on American experience, had brought pressure to bear on the Health and Safety Executive. The inspector's report rejected this.

At the request of British Coal, who were fully aware of the problems they would experience in attempting to introduce the radical CASE II scenario, Boyd's reassessed the situation, adopting a "more middle of the road approach", that is CASE I, but assuming that existing mining regulations would be modernised gradually. In this event, instead of the 12-13 pits judged to be potentially viable under CASE II, only 3 of the 21 under threat were judged capable of achieving a delivered energy price of less than £1.33 per GJ.

By August 1993, ten months after the initial closure announcement, and as a consequence of this further assessment, only 3 of the threatened 21 remained open. The Conservative government, grateful for the critical support which they had received from the Nottinghamshire miners in breaking the national strike of 1984-85, went on to close most of the pits there also, just has they had done elsewhere. Margaret Thatcher wrote:

"I felt a strong sense of obligation and loyalty to the Nottinghamshire miners who had stayed at work in spite of all the violence the militants threw at them".

She would show some unease when interviewed on the subject at this time, but she was no longer in power. In any event, market forces and globalisation are not static. They can move on, to devour their initial beneficiaries. Now the new Union of Democratic Mineworkers was also calling "foul".

**Second Opinion.**

In its report of 1993, the Parliamentary Trade and Industry Committee was to sum up British Coal's new Holy Writ. Four changes in working practices were seen by the Board as being necessary to improve productivity underground. These would be a final dagger through the heart of the nationalisation spirit. The changes were:

i) Repeal the Coal Mines' Regulation Act of 1908, limiting underground shifts to 7.25 hours.

ii) Reorganise management and supervision within collieries, in particular altering the role of pit deputies.

iii) Repeal section 4G of the Coal Industry Nationalisation Act. This provided for consultation and conciliation arrangements within the industry. Such a repeal would give British Coal, "the flexibility and freedom to manage the industry more effectively"

iv) Authorisation for compulsory redundancies.

The Committee's report expressed an alternative viewpoint to the government's. They criticised the latter's financial analysis, which lay behind the closure of the 31 pits. They stated:

"The cost of the pit closures to the taxpayer and the cost in terms of lost jobs will be substantial, even before less easily quantified aspects such as social costs are taken into account —— We find it disappointing that the Treasury apparently failed to conduct any comparison between the Exchequer costs of closing the 31 pits and the costs of a temporary subsidy to enable British Coal to enlarge its markets —— We also consider it reprehensible both that negotiations with the Treasury over the redundancies were so protracted and that the Treasury then required all the redundancies to take effect within the remainder of the financial year".

The report also said that the benefits of electricity privatisation were not as optimal as the government would have one believe. On this issue it stated:

"One of the underlying principles of electricity privatisation was that greater competition will create downward pressure on costs and prices and ensure that the customer, not the producer or distributor, comes first. In practice, while there has certainly been greater efficiency and downward pressure on costs, these savings have not found their way through to customers. The main contributor to lower electricity prices appears to have been the still nationalised British Coal. The beneficiaries of greater efficiency have been shareholders rather than customers. Figures provided by the NUM, based on company reports and accounts, indicate that whereas the total profits in the electricity supply industry of England and Wales in 1988-89 were £777 M, in 1992 they were £3,380 M, an increase of 335 per cent —— Some of the alternative fuels or alternative sources of generation provide, or may provide, dearer electricity; specifically, at least some CCGT's have higher costs than coal-fired stations operating on base load, and imports from France are more expensive than coal-generated electricity".

The report also made the point that British manufacturers had played only a small part in supplying the new CCGT's while British mining equipment suppliers were threatened by the sudden disappearance of their home market.

The above report of the Parliamentary Trade and Industry Committee was not discussed on the floor of the House of Commons. None of its recommendations were adopted. The die had been cast, with tens of thousands of additional redundancies created in mining districts. NUM membership shrank to 8,000 and the union was in financial crisis. The Miners' Redundancy Scheme was extended to 31 December 1993. As typical figures, payment to an average miner with 15 years' service would be around £23,000 and that to an average non-industrial employee around £27,000.

For areas affected by closures, funding for regeneration measures was increased to £200 M nationally. In Wales, £43 M of public funds were targeted on pit closure areas. A variety of projects were financed and managed by Local Authorities, Training and Enterprise Councils, plus the Welsh Development Agency. Lord Peter Walker was appointed in October 1992 to advise both the President of the Board of Trade and the Secretary of State for Wales on the optimum application of these measures.

Already, during the course of the national strike in 1984, British Coal Enterprise had been inaugurated. This was a subsidiary of BC, formed to create employment opportunities for ex-mining employees. In eight years, according to government statistics, it had helped to create some 83,000 employment opportunities. Its activities included: financial support to job creating businesses, the provision of managed workspace for new or expanding small businesses and the Job and Career Change Scheme (JACCS). This latter was a job resettlement programme for ex-BC employees.

## THE ULTIMATE PRIVATISATION.

### End of the Queue.

In 1994, as a result of the policies outlined above, the whole mining industry had been rendered ripe for privatisation. The government had decided that BC would not be privatised as a single entity. In this way a competitive coal sector would be created in the UK. Whether by intention or design, coal would find itself in an extremely weak position. According to the Independent on Sunday (28 August 1994):

"Left at the end of the queue, the victim of a predatory customer, headed by a supine management reluctant to battle with the Government, it had no chance".

During the early summer there was a pre-qualification process of bidders, to asses their capacity and fitness for the new role. This was followed by a round of bidding.

On 12 October 1994, Michael Hesseltine announced the successful bidders at the Conservative Party Conference.

In November 1994, just before privatisation, a "return to Victorian values" took concrete shape. In line with a Boyd's recommendation, the government repealed legislation dating from the early twentieth century restricting working hours in underground mines. The maximum standard shift was increased from 7.25 to 8 hours.

On privatisation, the Coal Authority, with headquarters at Mansfield, would become the government department responsible for all residual coal-related matters. This Authority would be independent of the industry, being itself prohibited from mining or using any coal mined. Neither could it explore or plan for production. Its function would be to vet and inspect applications to mine and carry out related activities, such as commercial drainage of methane. Liabilities, such as subsidence problems, mine water pollution and gas emission also fell within their remit. All operators would compete for licences under equal terms, including those working the small drift mines in South Wales. These latter were therefore subject to a much more stringent regulatory pressure than had been the case with the nationalised corporation. The NCB/BC had generally been content to receive from them a tonnage royalty.

### Mission Accomplished!

By 31 December 1994, the remaining twenty-three deep mines in the UK, plus opencast workings, had been returned to private enterprise. Government strategic objectives for the coalmining industry had thereby been achieved. To ensure that they were achieved, these apostles of the free market carried out some decidedly non-free market measures. If private interests had been treated generously at nationalisation, upon de-nationalisation they were also treated generously. All residual commitments of British Coal were taken over by the government, in addition to financial support prior to privatisation and the writing-off of assets. At its peak, alone in the financial year 1989-90, such support totalled approximately 9 billion Euros. By 1999, approximately 3 billion Euros for subsequent support was registered at the European Commission and accepted. In contrast, there was no auditing by the Commission of the privatisation of assets well below their market price. There was also no EU involvement in the contracts for coal supply for electricity generation, which were intended to get the newly privatised mining industry off to a good start and were based on a price for coal about 50 per cent above the world market price. According to the International Energy Authority, between 1995 and 1998 these were equivalent to a subsidy in excess of 1 billion Euros.

## No Banners!

In stark contrast to vesting day in 1947, re-privatisation of the industry was not a valedictory moment. No banners were raised in honour of what Cecil Parkinson, the previous Secretary of State for Energy, had called the "jewel in the crown" and "the ultimate privatisation". Rather than the victory of freedom over the dark forces of the state, in general the whole deal came across as rather squalid, belonging to the realm of second-hand car salesmen. Politicians did their best, with their stock-in-trade of fine, heroic, and empty sentiments. On the eve of privatisation Tim Eggar, then Energy Minister, said:

"I believe that by freeing the industry from the constraints of public ownership we are offering a great opportunity to those who work in it and depend on it to take their place within a truly competitive energy market and, by building on the achievements that have already been made, create for themselves a secure and viable future".

British Coal was divided between the following private companies:

1.0) In Scotland:

1.1) <u>Monktonhall Colliery</u>, like Tower Colliery in Wales, was also subject to a brave attempt to continue by means of a workers' buy-out. Unlike Tower, it soon came to grief. Flooding combined with geological problems made the mine unviable.

In early 1997, the mine closed.

1.2) <u>Mining Scotland</u> took over the Longannet complex, near the Firth of Forth.

2.0) In England:

2.1) <u>RJB Mining</u> bought the majority of English mines (14 production units, including 3 within the Selby complex, together with 14 open cast sites) for £815 million, reduced after negotiation from their initial offer of £900 million. During the period prior to privatisation Richard Budge, the owner, had taken a significant political profile, having held a number of discussions with the minister responsible for coal privatisation. The size of his company thereby increased five-fold. It became the big brother of UK coal mining and the largest private mining company in Europe.

In 2001, after the withdrawal of Richard Budge, RJB Mining was renamed UK Coal plc. By the early 2000's, 9 of their mines were still in operation. Among the closures were the new "super mine" at Asfordby in Leicestershire and Selby. Selby was the largest mining complex in Europe.

2.2) <u>Hatfield Coal</u>, with one mine.

2.3) <u>Coal Investments</u> took over 5 mines, mothballed by BC after the coal crisis of 1992. With insufficient capital the company ran into trouble. Huge debts were accumulated, exacerbated by the changes in mining technology that it adopted, all in combination with the low price obtained for its coal.

In 1996, the company declared bankruptcy and shut down all of their mines. A new company, Midlands Mining, reopened 2 of these shortly afterwards, only to close them again after a few years.

3.0) In Wales:

3.1) Also to <u>Coal Investments</u>, Cwmgwili Colliery. Cwmgwili appears in the British Coal list of closures as having closed in 1980. After privatisation it re-opened under the ownership of Coal Investments plc, only to be pulled down by the general collapse of that company.

In 1994, it was subject to a management buy-out. Subsequent to that the mine appears to have worked little or no coal.

By 1995, it had finally closed.

3.2) To <u>Celtic Energy Ltd</u>.

Nine opencast sites plus five opencast disposal points.

3.3) To <u>Betws Anthracite Ltd</u>.

Betws Colliery.

3.4) To <u>Goitre Tower Anthracite Ltd</u>.

Tower Colliery.


## The Buy-out Option.

Two British Coal mines in South Wales, Betws New Mine and Tower Colliery as above, not only managed to survive the BC massacre and move into private ownership but were also able to thrive. Both pits worked the northern outcrop of the coalfield. Here the reserves are more accessible and overall costs are less than is the case with the deeper mines.

It was only in the early 1990's, with few mines remaining, that the buy-out option was presented to the mining industry. The concept had already been recommended in the 1987 report of the Parliamentary Energy Committee. They considered that British Coal's concentration on super-pits and high-technology mining might well mean that smaller pits were not considered for investment and development, although they could have been worked efficiently and profitably by older methods. They recommended that when a pit was closed by BC, the licence to operate at that site should immediately be offered on the open market, with the workforce of the pit being closed having first refusal.

It would have been highly embarrassing to the government and to British Coal if the men or management bought their "uneconomic" pits and then proceeded to make money out of them. It must be said, however, that candidates for such a buy-out would have been few. Being much deeper mines, running costs would have been far higher than is the case with Betws or Tower. In addition, considerable capital investment would have been required, so as to bring them up to competitive levels. The South Wales record concerning a return on such capital investment is not encouraging.

<u>Betws</u> was classed as a small mine and was a drift near Ammanford, in the beautiful Welsh countryside of Carmarthenshire. It was the last mine to be sunk in South Wales, commencing production in 1978 and using mechanised longwall methods in the Red Vein seam. It had access drifts some 3,200 metres long into the Betws Mountain, with an average gradient of 1 in 7. From the bottom of the drifts, 1,500-metre roadways were driven through the Gardner's fault to the production districts. Depth below the surface was 550 metres. When closed by British Coal in 1993 it employed 113 men. The previous year it had produced from the Four Feet seam 126,000t of high-quality anthracite, in short supply in the UK.

In April 1994 it reopened after a buy-out by four ex-managers. From then on, 50-60 miners worked an average seam thickness of 1.4 metres, using a hand-got pillar and stall method.

Betws finally closed in August 2003.

<u>Tower</u> was closed by British Coal in April 1994, the same month that Betws reopened. It was the last British Coal mine to work in South Wales. A workers buy-out reopened the mine at the beginning of 1995. At the time of writing (2004) the colliery is still in operation.

In contrast to the above two mines, which operated from privatisation for some considerable time afterwards, the two following units had already been closed down by the NCB some years before privatisation and only reopened some years afterwards. Their second life would prove to be short-lived.

<u>Pentreclwydau</u> at Glyn Neath, which the NCB had closed in 1967, reopened as a privatised entity in September 1996. Two drifts were developed to access some 70 Mt of prime anthracite available in the thick six feet and nine feet seams. Working depth was 420 m and less, with mechanised room and pillar working together with roof bolting as primary support. Annual production was projected at 264,000 tonnes, mainly for Aberthaw Power Station.

In November 1997, following a production hiatus and change of management it re-started again.

In September 1998, Pentreclwydau finally went into liquidation.

Aberpergwm Drift Mine in the Neath Valley reopened at the beginning of the twenty-first century and was producing about 1,000 t/week with hand working, albeit only for a short period of time before final closure.

## Welsh Remnants.

At the time of writing (2004) Tower still survives, the only underground mine left in Wales. Current production at Tower is 630,000 t/a with 440 employees, using fully mechanised longwall working. Its future is heavily dependent on the 1000 MW Aberthaw Power Station on the coast. This dominates the local market and takes the great bulk of its output. Aberthaw can consume up to 4 Mt of coal per annum. The station was designed to burn low volatile coal that, in the UK, is only available from the local South Wales Coalfield. The station also uses imported coal of the right quality.

In South Wales at privatisation there was also one smaller coal-fired power station, Uskmouth (since shut down), plus the two integrated steel plants of Margam and Llanwern. Steel production at the latter has ceased, while the former now imports all its coal. For coal exports, three terminals are available (a deepwater terminal at Swansea plus Cardiff and Newport). With the exception of Tower, coalmining in South Wales is now confined to the highly profitable, if controversial, opencast working with its minimal employment opportunities.

By 1997, Celtic Energy owned 6 such opencast sites, of which 450 employees worked 2 sites directly, producing 0.4 Mt (the other 4 were operated by contractors). In that year, 2.2 Mt were produced in total, of which 50 per cent went to Aberthaw Power Station, with an anticipated 5-year contract from March 1998. Other markets were high quality anthracite for domestic briquetting and export. Annual turnover was approximately £110 M.

In addition to the above, South Wales has a number of small levels scattered around the rim of the coalfield. In 2002 these were down to four, from 85 in 1992.

Production in Wales is determined to a large extent by local markets, independent of production in England. There is a specialist domestic and industrial market for low volatile coals. Production for the Electricity Supply Industry here is almost entirely linked to Aberthaw Power Station. There was little or no competition with English mines for UK markets outside Wales.

## Honorary Oscar.

On 1 April 1995, after privatisation, the massacre of the industry and with only two pits left operating, the honorary freedom of Cardiff was bestowed on the South Wales miners by Mr. Rickie Ormonde, the "People's Lord Mayor". The freedom ceremony was held at City Hall. George Reece, now South Wales NUM President and accompanied by the Lord Mayor in full regalia, held up the scroll of honour. There was a march through town behind proud lodge banners that were, with the exception of Tower, of historical interest only. It was decades, if not a century, previously that the miners had made Cardiff the greatest coal exporting port in the world and produced the wealth that created, among other things, its rebuilt castle and fine civic centre. Now, with the industry on its death bed, it seemed like an honorary Oscar awarded to a fine actor who had never won one in the whole of his career, but was about to pass away.

## CRISIS YET AGAIN.

### Where the Coal Came From -

In 1977 the NCB had foreseen production at the end of the century as being 170 Mt. Even as late as 1990, with privatisation of the electricity industry, a higher proportion of coal-fired generation was projected than actually was the case.

In 1997, the UK actually produced 32.2 Mt from deep mines and 15.4 Mt from open cast, giving a total of 47.6 Mt. The number of pits was 23 (down from 51 in 1992), with most of these in Yorkshire and the East Midlands. More than a quarter of national coal consumption was imported, with imports totalling 19 Mt. The main suppliers were:

- USA:              6.5 Mt.

- Australia:        4.4 Mt.

- Columbia:         3.3 Mt.

- Canada:           1.6 Mt.

- South Africa:     1.0 Mt.

- Poland:           0.6 Mt.

## -And Where it Went To.

Of the imports, steam coal for electricity generation totalled 10.3 Mt, with the balance (approximately 9 Mt) for the steel industry and coking plants. When the contribution of stocks and small levels is added, total national consumption was about 71 Mt. Of this figure, 50 Mt was for electricity generation, of which 45 per cent was produced by coal. A total of 10,000 miners were employed (down from 41,000 in 1992).

## How the Coal is Won.

In the UK generally, production is by means of retreat longwall mining. This requires high development rates to maintain face replacement. Although the methods and technology of coalmining have remained essentially unchanged over the past 30 years, application has improved considerably. There are continuing marginal improvements in technology and performance. Modern mining methods are sensitive to both seam continuity and structure. Seams currently worked are horizontal or gently inclined. Seam gradients rarely exceed 1 in 10 (6 degrees). The thickness of those worked vary in the range 1-4m, with the majority in the range 1.4-2.2m. While minor faults or changes in seam thickness can be accepted, prior investigation and planning ensure that significant faults, washouts and intrusions are avoided in the course of production.

## RJB Woes.

In the three years following privatisation, RJB Mining spent 1,000 million pounds on capital projects, of which 300 million was on underground development. This increased the reserves available to the company by 138 Mt, to a total of 488 Mt. From that point on, they ran into trouble. The problems were several:

- In its initial share prospectus, RJB forecast an increase in productivity from 2,032 tonnes per man-year in 1992-93 to over 3,300 tonnes per man-year in 2000. Actual productivity achieved was more like 2,500 tones per man-year.

- Costs remained higher than world market prices, exaggerated by the strength of the pound and the worldwide over capacity. For equivalent quality, British coal cost about twice as much.

- While South Wales might be characterised by high quality coal, that from the English Midlands and Yorkshire, where most of the remaining pits were situated, is of poor quality. The sulphur content of British coal averaged 1.6 per cent, against 0.7-0.8 per cent with imports. Ash content lay between 15-20 per cent, higher than coals traded internationally.

- The high sulphur and chlorine content of indigenous coal, combined with out-of-date environmental protection technology at most British power stations, meant that environmental problems with regard to the burning of coal remained unsolved.

- There was easy access to cheap and less polluting natural gas.

- Planning permission for new opencast sites, with their much lower production costs, was difficult to obtain.

At privatisation in 1994, contracts had been negotiated, with government support, for RJB to supply coal to the generators National Power, Power Gen and Eastern Electricity.

In 1997, these were now up for renewal, but the generators wanted lower tonnages and tighter profit margins on the suppliers' side. Power Gen for example insisted on a 15 per cent price reduction. They backed this up by quoting the availability of cheaper coal, both from foreign sources and smaller producers.

The year 1998 was to prove especially difficult for RJB Mining. The effect of the new contracts was to slash annual profit by almost two thirds. The current annual turnover of approximately £822.5 M compared with £1,461 M in 1995, the first year of privatisation. Imports again equalled 19 Mt as in the previous year, but this time out of a total UK consumption of 53 Mt, as opposed to 66,6 Mt (excluding stocks and small levels). The performance of RJB Mining between privatisation and 2002 (in 2001 it was renamed UK Coal) is given below.

The deterioration from 1998 onwards is apparent.

| Year | Pre-tax profit (Loss)-£M | Turnover-£M | Output-Mt | Sales-Mt |
|---|---|---|---|---|
| 1995 | 173 | 1,461 | 37 | 41.9 |
| 1996 | 189 | 1,308 | 34.9 | 37.6 |
| 1997 | 172.5 | 1,124 | 31.8 | 31.2 |
| 1998 | 50 | 822.5 | | 25.9 |
| 1999 | 11 | 700 | | 22.5 |
| 2000 | 17.8 Includes 53.3 from coal operating aid. | 705 | | 24.5 Includes 2.6 from stock. |
| 2001 | (26.5) Deep mine loss of (46.7), plus opencast profit. | 662.5 | 19.6 Deep mines 15.4, plus opencast 4.2. | 20.0 |
| 2002 | (83.1) incl. (60) due to closures. | 596.5 | | 20.0 |

## A Challenge For New Labour.

In 1997, Labour replaced the Conservatives as the party in government. Faced with another potential crisis in coal, the newly elected administration initiated a review of electricity generation policy. In November and December of that year, hundreds of miners lobbied MPs at Westminster, amid growing concern that up to 5,000 mining jobs could be lost before Christmas. Following them might go a further 50,000 in associated manufacturing industries. The lobbyists were disappointed. The Government was not prepared to subsidise a private company such as RJB, particularly since during the previous year profits had totalled £189 M. After 18 years in the political wilderness, non-intervention, respect for market forces and the acceptance of cheap imports was now the agenda of "New Labour".

In March 1998, the generators were persuaded to extend the existing coal delivery contracts by a further three months. This would provide a breathing space in which it was hoped a way could be found out of the crisis.

In June 1998, the "Review of Energy Sources for Power Generation" was published by the government. There would be neither subsidies nor quotas for the use of coal. Instead there would be a three-year moratorium with regard to new natural gas-fired power stations. The review would be followed by a detailed government white paper on the subject.

On 8 October 1998 the white paper was made public under the title "Conclusions of the Review of Energy Sources for Power Generation and Government Response to fourth and fifth Reports of the Trade and Industry Committee". As strategic objectives the white paper quoted:

- Competition in the interest of the consumer.

- No particular fuel or supplier should be in recept of any unfair advantage.

- Diversity and security of supply.

- Long-term availability of the fuels used.

- The role of the Government was to prevent any market distortions, which could jeopardise the above.

The government would work to achieve a level playing field ("fairness not favours"). The nature of the electricity market, however, de-regulated as it now was, limited the government's ability to intervene directly in support of coal. The future of coal lay in its own hands since the decision, which fuel, to use was first and foremost a commercial matter. Nuclear power was recognised as being uneconomic. However, existing stations would continue in service. Oil-fired stations would, on grounds of cost, be confined to peak duty only. The Government intended that by 2010, 10 per cent of British electricity would be generated from renewable sources although for the foreseeable future (i.e. up to 2020) there was no realistic alternative to the large-scale use of fossil fuels. The white paper concentrated therefore mainly on the two fuels, coal and gas.

The advantages of gas had led to a significant increase in gas-fired capacity in recent years and this was not called into question. Nevertheless, there had to be some slowing down in its introduction, so as to maintain the objective of providing a supply that was both diverse and secure. If present trends continued then, by 2020, between 55 per cent and 90 per cent of gas would need to be imported (primarily from Russia but also Algeria). Implicitly, therefore, coal would continue to provide an essential pillar for electricity generation in the UK. The British Government saw no prospect of an increase in the proportion of electricity generated from coal. However, by means of the limited restrictions placed on new gas-fired stations it was hoped that its position could be stabilised.

## Liberalisation Revisited.

Reforms were proposed in the white paper for the electricity market in Great Britain (Northern Ireland was excluded due to its geographical position and much smaller energy requirements). These reforms were general rather than specific. They boiled down to six items:

i)  Attempt to sell off the coal-fired power stations of the large generating companies, so as to increase competition between them.

ii)  Increase competition in the electricity generation market, in combination with the moratorium on new natural gas-fired power stations.

iii)  Independent approval for the generation and distribution activities of the electricity companies. This should increase competition and reduce monopolistic tendencies, whereby consumers were committed to specific generators.

iv)  Reform of trading with the national grid (i.e. the electricity "pool"), so as to ensure "proper competition" in the field of electricity generation.

v)  Negotiate a fair-trading of electricity with European partners (i.e. via the underwater link with France).

vi) In addition to the unit price for energy delivered, all generators should receive fair recompense for the standby and stability service, which they provide to the system.

## Perverse Developments.

Implicit in the above was recognition that the initial British version of electricity market liberalisation, the first in the world and often regarded by other countries as a shining example to be followed, had led to a number of developments that were perverse. The "Dash for Gas" had resulted in an overshoot occurring in the switch to gas-fired generation. Two distortions in particular were identified by the white paper:

a) The pool as operated distorted competition between the various fuels, as it did between existing and new power stations. This resulted in an unfair advantage for natural gas.

b) There was inadequate competition between coal-fired power stations. As a consequence their price for generated power was unduly high. This had attracted an excessive level of entry into the generation industry (by October 2002, the number of companies generating electricity had increased to over thirty).

The report stated that:

"Had the fossil fuel generating capacity of the former Central Electricity Generating Board been distributed among 5-6 competing generators instead of just two, and had the RECs been forbidden to take a stake in the IPPs, it is unlikely that over-investment in CCGTs would have gone as far as it has".

The pool was operated on the basis that power for each 30 minute period of the 24 hours between 5am to 5am was accepted from power stations on the basis of "merit order", i.e. the cheapest offer was accepted first, then the next cheapest, and so on until total demand had been catered for. Generation companies had submitted such offers at 10am the previous day. However, when it came to payment, all units delivered during each period were paid for at the same price. This price was the unit charge of the most expensive station accepted during the period concerned. As a consequence of this, generators could make an offer independent of their actual costs (even down to zero) just to get their power accepted, knowing that the price which they would actually receive would be that charged by the most expensive station on line at the time.

In addition, generators could make contracts directly with large consumers, independent of the pool price. This happened when the companies responsible for local electricity distribution invested in their own power stations. Due to the relative speed and low cost of construction, these stations were invariably gas-fired. In the case of such "sweetheart" arrangements it was in their interest to pass on to the consumer electricity (and the price) from their own power station in which they had invested, rather than from an alternative source even if that alternative source was cheaper. An additional weakness was that the flexibility of coal-fired power stations in adjusting to variations in demand was not financially recognised, which in the event of true competition would have been the case.

The result of all this was advantageous for the smaller scale generator with new gas-fired plant. They could guarantee their market, either by going into partnership with a large consumer and/or by bidding zero into the pool. The large bulk suppliers could not play the same game. Due to the magnitude of their contributions, any cutthroat price that they offered would dominate the system, and would be what they would have to live with. As a consequence, the large "portfolio generators" built their own gas-fired capacity, at the expense of their large coal-fired stations.

## New Electricity trading Arrangements (NETA).

On 27 March 2001 the UK pool was replaced by a system of wholesale traders. Under the so-called New Electricity Trading Arrangements (NETA), such wholesale traders are used by RECs and other large consumers in their dealings with the generators. Payment using NETA is now made on the basis of the individual price as bid, not a standard price for all generators based on the most expensive accepted. There is no official marker price to use as a reference. Confidential, bilateral agreements between generators and large consumers are still allowed, as was the case with the pool. The industry shift to a structure dominated by vertically integrated generator/suppliers, providing power primarily for their own consumers, means that the spot market is even less relevant. Compared with a centrally planned system, it is far from clear that this results in a net economic advantage to consumers.

Using NETA, contracts for the buying and selling of electricity are on the basis of half-hour settlement periods, possibly up to several years ahead. Generators are recompensed for units supplied in excess of their contract and financially penalised for any shortfall. RECs can be financially rewarded for reducing demand. Such adjustments are achieved by means of contact between the grid operator and the generator/ supplier. Ahead of each half-hour settlement period a balancing mechanism is initiated. This is designed to ensure system security and align actual demand with actual supply. One advantage that NETA has compared with its predecessor, the electricity "pool", is the ability to change the rules under which the market operates. One such change was the reduction in "gate closure time", i.e. the deadline by which adjustment decisions have to be made for the buying and selling of power for each settlement period. This was reduced from 3.5 hours in advance to 1 hour. The reduction in lead time benefited renewables, with their sensitivity to the vagaries of wind and weather. In practice, only about 2 per cent of sales occur within such a short-term adjustment mechanism, the remaining 98 per cent being sold on long-term contracts just like any other commodity.

The system has been criticised on the basis that generators are encouraged to run with excess capacity, in the hope of picking up any additional demand. This results in sets being run at below optimum efficiency, thus wasting fuel while increasing emission. In addition, RECs ensure that their contracts exceed their highest estimate of demand, thus obtaining kudos for the inevitable reduction. Nevertheless, NETA's success was widely touted on the basis that in its first year the wholesale price of electricity fell by 30-40 per cent. By the beginning of 2004, this price was still around 15 per cent less. The retail price for domestic consumers did not fall, resulting in corresponding profits for those companies with a significant base of domestic consumption. On a European scale, however, UK domestic electricity is still among the cheapest.

While enthusiasm for liberalisation in Europe is running out of steam, partly due to the en masse departure of the American utilities as a result of low prices and profits, turning the clock back will not be easy. French and German companies now own most of the generating assets in the UK.

## SUE THEM!

### EU Coal.

By 1998, when RJB Mining was in such straits, the situation in the European Union was that, apart from the UK, of the 15 member countries only 3 were producing coal. These were Spain, France and Germany.

Spain produced 17.5 Mt, with 9 Mt being imported, mainly from the USA and South Africa. Again coal is used for electricity generation (24 Mt in 1997) with the steel industry consuming 3.5 Mt. In 1997 there were still 22,500 miners employed but it was expected that this number would decrease by at least 4,000 in the near future. Spain is also a producer of brown coal (9.5 Mt) and this production is stable.

France produced 6.8 Mt in 1997, with the intention of terminating production completely by 2005 (in actual fact the last French coalmine, at Creuzfeld near the German border and employing 400 miners, closed on 23 April 2004. This marked the end of a 300-year history of coalmining in France). The number of miners employed was 5,000. For this domestic production, electricity generation was the prime market. Imports totalled 15.8 Mt, of which 9.5 Mt was for the steel industry, 3 Mt for electricity generation and the remainder for general industry. The proportion of coal used for electricity generation is small since, in 1997, 78.2 per cent of this was produced by nuclear power.

Germany was the major producing country, with output at 52 Mt. In addition, 19.9 Mt were imported (main suppliers: South Africa-7.2 Mt, Poland-4 Mt, Columbia-3.8 Mt, plus the USA and the Czech Republic). Imports, mainly steam coal for power generation, were forecast to increase significantly as domestic production contracted. By 2005, 40 Mt of imports have been estimated. It must not be forgotten that Germany is also a major producer of brown coal (175 Mt in 1997). In contrast to its black coal production, which is deep- mined and heavily subsidised, this is produced in vast opencast sites and is highly competitive.

Coal for coking is processed in the two major coking plants owned by the German steel industry. Coal accounted for 55 per cent of electricity generation. Of this, 28 per cent was black coal and 27 per cent brown coal (lignite). Of primary energy demand, the following proportions applied:

- Coal:                     25%
- Oil:                      41%
- Gas:                      21%
- Nuclear:                  12%
- Renewables (incl. hydro):                                                    1%

The number of miners had reduced to 47,500 in 1997, from 72,000 in 1994.

In 1997, all German coalmines were taken over by Deutsche Steinkohle AG (DSK), a public company in which the German government, along with major corporations, have shares. An agreement was also made between the parties concerned to reduce the subsidy of 4.5 billion Euros to 2.7 billion Euros by 2005. This would result in an industry of about 9 mines and 28 Mt output per annum. Thereafter, further reductions are planned.

## Foul!

In 1998, the British complained to the European Court, opposing subsidies to the coalmining industries of other EU countries (in particular Germany and Spain) on the basis of unfair competition. The justification was that UK production costs were only one third of the German and one quarter of the Spanish. The whole German concept for their coalmining industry was the target of heavy fire from Celtic Energy and, in particular, from RJB Mining. The latter vented their spleen by initiating legal proceedings. The government remained in the background, giving moral support only. The British companies conveniently forgot the massive government underpinning which accompanied privatisation, and which had enabled them to flourish. Having just lost such support, in their newfound virtue they felt outraged that the industry in Germany should still be receiving it.

The reduction in German subsidies notwithstanding, both current and planned, complaints from the UK were directed at the subsidy programme as a whole, plus the incorporation of DSK as owner of all German coalmines. In addition, complaints were made concerning exports of anthracite from Germany. The EU Commission found against Germany in the case of anthracite exports but otherwise supported the German government in their policy. Although British coal was by far the cheapest in the European Union, its marketing difficulties were not the result of continental subsidies but lay elsewhere (the "dash for gas" etc.). In addition, the negative consequences of shutting down the German coal industry would be out of all proportion to any benefit that RJB mining might accrue.

German reaction to the barrage from the UK was one of incomprehension. They had committed themselves to reduce subsidies and hence allow an increase in imports, albeit in a controlled manner so as to minimise social disruption. However, even if the whole German coalmining industry were to disappear this would not be of any benefit to the British, since British coal was not only more expensive than that available on the world market but of lower quality as well. Other countries might well benefit from a German demise but not them. The episode was regarded as a dog-in-the-manger attitude by a fellow industry that should have known better, and which had tried to find a solution to its problems elsewhere.

It remains speculation why the EU did not also investigate the question as to who was actually covering the cost difference between British indigenous coal, which was still being consumed, and the same amount of coal if it had been obtained at the cheaper world market price. It was by now generally recognised that this world market price was not artificially low as the result of subsidies, something that was previously maintained in the UK.

In 1981 there were 211 collieries in the UK, employing just under 300,000 people; by 2003 the number was down to less than 20 pits, employing about 5,000. In spite of such sacrifices and significant price reductions, British production, although the cheapest in Europe, was still unable to match the international price of coal. Since 1998 UK production continued to fall, from 32.2 Mt in that year to 21.8 Mt in 2000 and 16.7 Mt in 2001.

## GERMANY.

### Energy Policy.

In the European Union, Germany is the largest producer of coal and the largest energy market. It is also the fifth largest such market in the world, after the USA, China, Russia and Japan. In 1983, the Monopolies and Mergers Commission Report considered the success of Germany in eliminating inefficient capacity, as opposed to the UK. At that time 38 German pits were operating, producing 95 Mt, against 200 UK mines producing 108.81 Mt. In the intervening period, inefficient capacity has also been eliminated in the UK, but production nevertheless continued to decline. Coalmining in Germany also contracted, to 27.6 Mt of black coal in 2004.

At the turn of the century, brown coal and black coal together accounted for about a quarter of total primary energy production and 52 per cent of electricity generation. Of this, 12 per cent was from black coal, expected to reduce to 10 per cent. In spite of this relatively high contribution from coal, Germany is on track to meet its Kyoto targets. This is due to the virtual collapse of the highly polluting East German economy following reunification.

The country summarises its energy policy as being three times the letter E: Einsparen (energy saving), Effizienz (energy efficiency) and Erneubare (renewable energy). The government is campaigning within the EU for a target reduction in greenhouse gas emission of 30 per cent by 2020, when compared with 1990 levels. Germany's own target for this date is a 40 per cent reduction. By 2020, renewables are expected to provide 20 per cent of total primary energy, oil 16 per cent and natural gas 40 per cent. Long-term contracts with the Netherlands and Russia ensure supply of the latter. Nuclear energy has become politically non-U and will be phased out. With 8,734 megawatts (in 2002), Germany has the world's largest installed capacity of wind turbines, in spite of having some of the worst wind resources in Europe. In 1999 a law was passed guaranteeing, for a period of twenty years, an attractive minimum price for electricity generated from renewable sources.

### Production.

Each German colliery employs typically 3-4,000 employees, which is much larger than the UK norm. With several amalgamations, it consists of 4-6 shafts. Underground transport of coal to the coal-raising shaft can be as long as 20km. Typically 3-4 seams are worked in each colliery, with the main coalfield, the Ruhr, noted for heavy faulting and a series of syn-and anticlines. Depths are greater than the UK, often in excess of 1100 metres. Due to the geothermic gradient, whereby temperature increases with depth, air conditioning is often used to cool the ventilation air. Output per man shift is about 7 tonnes. At the turn of the century, 40,000 employees operated nine collieries. Of these, two are in the Saar area with the remaining seven being north of the Ruhr. Of the latter, six have been paired together, forming three massive production units.

The existence of an indigenous mining industry provides German manufacturers of mining machinery with both development potential and a showcase for their wares. German mining machinery is well placed to participate in the expected worldwide increase in production.

## Brown Coal.

The cheapest form of power generation in Germany is from stations adjacent to the vast opencast workings of brown coal (or lignite). Shallow fields of this substance, halfway between peat and coal itself, are found west of the Rhein between Cologne and Aachen. These comprise the largest such reserves in Europe and produce 95 per cent of domestic output. The remainder comes from East Germany. This is a resource that the UK does not possess. The latest brown coal fired power station in the Rhineland produces electricity at a generation cost of 2.4 EUR cents per kWh. This compares with a national average of 5 EUR cents. This station, at Niederaussem, was commissioned in September 2002 and cost 1,2 billion Euros to build. Of this sum, 400 million Euros, a full one-third, was spent on pollution control. This bears witness, both to the inherently environment-unfriendly nature of the basic fuel, and the determination of the German government that this problem be overcome.

## Efficiency.

While some coal is used in the two coke-works owned by the steel industry, the vast majority of output, as in the UK, is for power generation. As in the UK the domestic market for coal is negligible, having lost out to natural gas.

As well as coal mines, the holding company DSK also owns a number of coal-fired power stations adjacent to some of their mines. In Germany, some of the most expensive coal in the world is burnt in some of the cleanest and most efficient power stations in the world. Since higher efficiency implies less fuel consumption for the same output, if coal-fired power stations everywhere were brought up to German levels of efficiency then this alone would result in an overall reduction in carbon dioxide emission greater than Kyoto requirements (WCI 2003b). A modern German coal-fired power station operates with a typical efficiency of 40 per cent, compared with a world average of 32 per cent and 25 per cent in Russia and China. New stations are planned, having efficiencies of 47 per cent, with 50 per cent regarded as being achievable. Higher efficiencies imply higher temperatures and pressures, which in turn require the development of materials capable of withstanding them.

An additional objective of research and development is in the field of carbon dioxide reduction, the aim being to separate this from the exhaust gases for subsequent use, or long-term storage. As a major coal producing and consuming nation, Germany is in possession of modern technology across the whole spectrum of operations, from production to utilisation.

## Subsidies.

While black coal from Britain is at least within striking distance of the world market price (currently 30 EUR /t), production costs in Germany are approximately 130 EUR/t. Whereas in the UK subsidies to the industry fell by 95 per cent between 1983 and 1995, over the same period German coal subsidies increased by 86 per cent (in Spain, between 1986-1995, coal subsidies increased by 142 per cent). It has been negotiated with the EU that subsidies will be gradually reduced, until they finally terminate in 2012.

In 2004 nevertheless, state subsidies to the German mining industry still totalled EUR 3.3 billion, similar to that for wind energy. This corresponds to EUR 82,500 for every miner employed.

## Closures.

In September 2003, to conform with an EU agreement to reduce subsidies, it was announced that between 2005 and 2007 four mines will close. This will reduce the number of mines to 6. The number of employees in the industry would be reduced from approximately 40,000 to less than 20,000. In contrast to the British massacre, a minimum of 2 years' notice was given of impending closure. This will be carried out in conjunction with a social plan involving financial compensation and/or alternative employment.

Looking further into the future, the decline in black coal production is expected to continue, from 27.6 Mt in 2004 to 16 Mt by 2012, the latter output being produced by five mines. In the once great coalfield of the Ruhr, Germany's largest, currently only 8 per cent of the working population is involved in mining.

In 2004, Werner Mueller, previously Economic Minister and currently head of RAG, a major share-holder in the German mining industry, spoke of the possibility of a new mine. The background to this apparently bizarre concept was the fact that, in spite of imports, shortage of coke had forced some German steelworks to cut back on production. Due largely to the economic boom in China consuming such immense resources, the price of blast furnace coke had increased by a factor of ten within twelve months, to EUR 500/t.

## Drink up Lads!

The most northerly coalmine in Germany is the anthracite mine at Ibbenbueren, west of Osnabrück. At 1,500 metres it is the deepest mine in Europe (the deepest shaft in the UK was at Parsonbage Colliery at Leigh in Greater Manchester, at 1,259 metres, while the deepest in South Wales was at Abernant, at 820 metres. The Western Deep Level at Carltonville, in South Africa is 3,658 metres). Half of Ibbenbueren's output goes to the adjacent power station, also owned by DSK. The mine has a workforce of 2,800 men and enough reserves for 60 years. Forty years ago, 8,000 men were employed in coalmining in this area.

In 2002 the German Chancellor, Gerhard Schröder, visited the mine. In a festival atmosphere further financial support was promised, both for the future of the mine and for the region. Beer was consumed by all while the colliery band, clad in the folklore black dress of the mineworker, played "Glück Auf", based on the traditional underground greeting. It symbolises the best of luck in the common, difficult, environment.

# Chapter 17

## THE SUBLIME - and the RIDICULOUS.

*Compared with the material aspect,
the importance of morale is as three to one.*
Napoleon Bonaparte.

### THE BACKDROP.

### Nature -.

From the circuitous A4061, linking the Heads of the Valleys Road at Hirwaen with the Rhondda, spectacular views can be obtained down the Rhondda Fawr and northwards to the distant panorama of the Brecon Beacons. Here lies the coalfield's most rugged upland scenery. Separating the north crop from the Rhondda Valleys to the south are the rugged ridges of Craig-y-Llyn and Craig Ogwr. At 600 metres these are the highest elevations in Glamorgan. The deep, northward facing, lake-filled cwms, now clothed in forests, fall steeply into the openness of the Hirwaen Common and bear witness to the time when glaciers moulded the upland Glamorgan scenery. North of the ridge is this open section of the north crop, where the seams rise gently to the surface, rendering them suitable for opencast and drift mining. The additional presence of iron-ore influenced location of the great ironworks, which developed in the late eighteenth and nineteenth centuries. The scars and scourings of the north crop, along the A456 Heads of the Valleys Road, can still be seen.

Above, along the flat mountain crests, is a sprawling moorland world bereft of humankind, inhabited by sheep and a few semi-wild ponies. Coarse grass, heather, bilberry and bracken appear to stretch in all directions, the vista sometimes broken by recent forestation. When the mist does not hang low, broad sweeping views can be obtained across the gaping dissections of several valleys. To the north lies the verdant and undulating sweep of the Brecon Beacons and to the south, the gentle Vale of Glamorgan (Bro Morgannwg). From some points, and on exceptional days when a recent shower has cleared the air, the fresh sunshine may extend this view across the blue insertion of the Bristol Channel to the shimmering and hazy coastline of the county of Somerset. From these hilltops, the results of the nineteenth century industrial ravishing lie shielded from view, deep in the valleys that divide the Glamorgan Uplands (Blaenau Morgannwg) into a series of Ridges (Cefn) and Mountains (Mynydd). On this upland crest, only the scar of an occasional colliery waste heap bear witness to this other, unseen world.

### -And Man.

Here in the early 21st century, below that "ridge of horrid rock and precipices" which all those years ago confronted Daniel Defoe on his way from Brecknok into Glamorganshire, and which he had to cross before his descent into "a moist, agreeable vale opening to the south", lie the last deep coal workings left in Wales. The landscape, brooding and Wagnerian, offers an ideal backdrop for such an heroic last stand. Here, where Welsh coalmining began; it reached its politically radical heights and is now coming to a prolonged and radical conclusion, worthy of its history.

In 1831, here at Hirwaen during the so-called Merthyr Rising, was the first known occasion that the red flag was used as a symbol of revolt in Britain. Ironstone miners and skilled puddlers, provoked by wage cuts and political oppression, had taken control of Merthyr Tydfil. Professor Hywel Francis has described how, when the Swansea Yeomanry moved against them, they were ambushed and disarmed at Hirwaen. The rebels sacrificed a calf and washed a flag in its blood, impaled a loaf of bread on the flagstaff and used it as a war banner. The current conclusion to this long story of radicalism and industrial activity is not merely the result of techno-economic forces. It is a microcosm of how people and communities can and should react when confronted with the whims of a market place unconstrained by considerations of human need or of what constitutes a just society.

## Hidden Wealth.

Beneath the massif as described above lay a large area of dry steam coal, extending to semi-anthracite in the west and semi-bituminous in the east. At the time of nationalisation, due to its inaccessibility from the surface and remoteness from surrounding pits, this had remained largely unworked. By then, such virgin areas were rare in South Wales. Inevitably, in accordance with their remit to exploit all of the nation's coal, it would attract the planners' attention. As a basis for development, a handful of collieries already existed at the periphery. Hard up against the ridge, on its north side, is Tower Colliery. This is basically a drift mine, driven downwards into the mountainside. Within the Cwm of Graig-y-Llyn and adjacent to the A4061 before its hairpin climb up and over into the Rhondda Fawr, a shaft has also been sunk. This is nearer to the working faces and facilitates ventilation, plus the transport of men and supplies. As the last mine left in Wales, and as a unique example of a buy-out by the workforce of their own pit, Tower Colliery would achieve international fame.

Subsequent to nationalisation, however, the planners saw not Tower as the main key for opening the considerable reserves available but two other pits. This triangle of collieries, aware of each other's presence but initially isolated and unfamiliar to each other, is a microcosm of the South Wales mining experience. It is in this general area that mining started, reached its peak and, at the time of writing, continues with opencast workings and Tower as the last remaining deep mine. An initial path of separate development would be reconfigured, resulting in the triangle's destiny becoming inextricably intertwined.

## The "Glamour Boys".

Nestling in tightly at the extreme northern cul-de-sacs of their respective valleys, cramped and dominated by the enveloping escarpments, Mardy in the Rhondda Fach (small Rhondda), and Fernhill in the Rhondda Fawr (big Rhondda), were to become the "glamour boys", the two big development pits for the reserves in question. These were to join the list of NCB "super collieries". They were to become the most striking feature of coalmining reorganisation in the Rhondda Valleys since the Second World War, ensuring that valley's vital and valuable contribution to the recovery of Britain's coal industry. In terms of planning effort and the flow of capital investment, Tower, the ultimate winner, would remain a poor relation. Indeed, Towers current reserves could have been worked from Fernhill. As it is, they are partially interleaved with Fernhill workings, similar to the interleaving teeth of two separate combs.

## MARDY.

### "Little Moscow".

Mardy was first off the mark. In 1949 the NCB announced that the first complete colliery development in the South Wales Coalfield was to be carried out on the site of the nos. 3+4 shafts near the village of Maerdy. The shafts were tucked in between steep valley walls, south of the reservoir that supplies the Rhondda Fach with water. If the surroundings are bleak, the past of Maerdy village and pit (the NCB renamed the pit "Mardy" so as to avoid confusion with another Maerdy Colliery in West Wales) was bleaker. The pit went into nationalisation with a reputation behind it. Although much of South Wales Coalfield society could be designated as militant, Mardy went one stage further along the road, becoming known as "Little Moscow". This tag originated during the 1926 lockout and was first used by the South Wales Daily News, with a subtitle, "Lawless Mardy-Red Reign of Terror". Strangers, so the article said, were called "spies" in the streets, the children wore red sashes at funerals and there was even a Communist soccer team. The article continued:

"It is extremely difficult for a person who has not come into contact with the young Communists of Maerdy to form any conception of their extraordinary mentality. The power they have acquired in the town has gone to their heads like wine, and as they have had no experience in any town except Maerdy, they are unable to realise the weight of public opinion against Communism in the country generally, and believe that soon other towns will be controlled by Communists".

# Arthur Horner.

Noah Ablett, involved in the Tonypandy riots and co-author of "The Miners' Next Step", was one of those who had influence upon Maerdy's militant past. The phenomena and duration of "Little Moscow" however, (1919-1934), coincided with Mardy's association with Arthur Horner, a slight, earnest, bespectacled, owl-like, atom bomb of a man. If time and place can mould a person, an exceptional person may mould time and place. As his successor Will Paynter described him, "A man of his times who did much to shape his times".

Arthur Lewis Horner came to Maerdy during the Great War of 1914-18. In his own words, he conducted a fierce struggle against this imperialist butchery of the workers from the day of its inception. At the age of 17 he had been awarded a scholarship to a Baptist college in Birmingham only to leave after 6 months, declaring that politics interested him more than religion.

In 1914, still a practicing Baptist, he preached sermons on the theme, "Thou shalt not kill". He had already been active in the Rhondda Valley in the Standard and Lewis Merthyr lodges of the SWMF. His trade union activities compelled him to adopt an assumed name in order to find work at all. With the miners in a strong bargaining position during the war, and the colliery company satisfied, due to guaranteed profits, he and other militants were able to make inroads. After the introduction of conscription he was sentenced to six months' hard labour at Wormwood Scrubs for avoiding military service. On his release he was turned over to the military who imprisoned him again for "incorrigible misconduct". He declared in the court martial proceedings that whatever side wins, the workers were bound to lose; the war was being waged in capitalist interests and to the detriment of workers in all countries.

On Mayday 1919, when elected as a checkweigher for Mardy Colliery, he was in Cardiff Jail at the time (a checkweigher represented the colliers in confirming the amount of coal produced, and hence the wages due. Apart from their industrial duties they were councillors to the needy, letter writers and conscience of the community). On release from jail, after his election and a hunger strike, he informed his first lodge meeting that he was willing to shoulder a rifle to fight for the working classes but not for the enemy of the workers, the capitalists.

In 1920, at the age of twenty-six, he joined the Communist Party of Great Britain as a founding member. He was to remain a member for the rest of his life. An attempt to stop safetymen working on the pithead boilers during the strike of 1921 lead to a one month prison sentence for unlawful assembly and intimidation.

By 1923 Horner was ensconced on the Central Committee of the British Communist Party. This heralded in an era where the local militants of Mardy were in conflict, not only with the owners but with the South Wales Miners Federation as well. Nevertheless, the year of 1925 saw his election to the Executive Council of that body.

Following the trauma of the 1926 lockout, he wrote of his return to Mardy:

"I was returning with bitterness in my heart to my own people, to tell them that we were beaten, that the sufferings ahead were going to be far worse than those we had endured in the strike and lock-out. But I knew there would be no personal recriminations from the men and women of Maerdy. They would never have given in. Right to the end there was not a whisper of defeatism among —— the members of Mardy lodge. If the whole coalfield had stood as firmly as Mardy we could have won".

In 1927 he played a prominent role in the hunger march to London and became member for South Wales on the Executive Council of the Miners' Federation of Great Britain. As Communist candidate for the Rhondda East constituency in the general election of 1929 he polled over 5,000 votes. .

In 1930 the Mardy lodge was expelled from the SWMF. This was a result of their opposition to the local official Labour Party candidate, plus their attack on the official leadership's "capitulation" to the "Trade Union and Labour bureaucracy" and their reference to "the inevitable treachery of a Labour Government". The expelled lodge continued to function. However, its members were no longer employed at the colliery and the unity of the SWMF had been breached.

In December 1930, when Horner returned from his visit to Russia (he was Secretary of the International Miners Propaganda Committee), he was faced with Byzantine political manoeuvrings by the Communist Party as to the correct way ahead, and also attempts to undermine his own position within it, being accused of developing a "cult of personality". While battling against sectarians within the party he could be openly contemptuous of abstract revolutionary slogans, offered as practical guides to reality. He argued that they served to isolate the Communist Party from the rest of the working class. Defence by him of a worker's house against a bailiff of the Rhondda District Council resulted in a further term of some months hard labour. Police Inspector W.E.Reece told the court that Horner had assumed the role of dictator and was active in his efforts to sow dissention amongst the employees. A plausible speaker, so said the inspector, he was always ready to take the lead in any form of demonstration or procession that had as its object a movement against law and order, for which he had the most utter contempt. Although the source of his income had not been ascertained, it could be assumed that he was being well paid by Russia for his efforts to destroy the peace of this country, which he had apparently determined to undermine. Horner protested that the statement was prejudiced and calculated to do him harm. It contained no reference, he said, to the fact that he had been a member of the Executive Council of the Miners' Federation of Great Britain.

In 1931, the general election of that year saw him increase his vote to over 10,000, short of what was necessary to win the seat but nevertheless massive for a Communist Party candidate in the United Kingdom.

In 1933 he stood again, in a bitterly fought campaign against the official Labour Party candidate, W.H.Mainwaring. Events would convince Horner of the folly of working outside the SWMF and would almost lead to his breaking with the Communist Party. The expelled lodge eventually merged with the replacement lodge in 1934.

In 1936 Horner became president of the SWMF. During the Second World War he served on the Invasion Trade Union Committee for South Wales. This body was responsible for resistance measures in event of a German occupation of the area.

In 1944 he became the first General Secretary of the National Union of Mineworkers, a post that he held until his retirement in 1959. He never gave up his membership of the Communist Party, although reputably shocked by events in Eastern Europe. On his retirement another Communist Rhondda miner, Will Paynter, succeeded him.

In 1968 he died.

**The Pit.**

Due to the highly charged trading and industrial relations situation, the pit itself went through a chequered period of activity. It closed following the general strike of 1926 when the owners, Lockett-Merthyr Co., went out of business. Welsh Associated Collieries reopened the mine in 1932. Of the four colliery shafts, nos. 1+2 were shut down.

In 1935, one year after re-integration of the expelled communist lodge, the company was taken over by Powell Duffryn Ltd. To nullify the lodge they promptly shut the colliery down, only to reopen the remaining Nos. 3+4 shafts the following year, but on the owner's terms. Only 330 men, acceptable to the owners, were re-employed. There was to be no checkweigher. No fixed price list as a basis for wages was agreed to. When they were not ignored, the lodge was deliberately impeded.

In 1940, as a result of losing the export trade following the fall of France, the colliery closed again. At nationalisation, there were 5 men employed underground and 10 on the surface, on a maintenance basis.

**Reconstruction.**

Objectives.

The NCB reconstruction plan was the epitome of everything that was great and good about the nationalisation concept, with its associated strategic planning. With a capital investment budgeted at £5 M (1940's prices), not only would it provide large scale and optimum access to valuable reserves, it would also endow an area characterised by depression and industrial relations strife with a long and secure future. Coal to be worked, the only large reserves remaining in the Rhondda Fach, was sub-bituminous with a volatile percentage of 10-13.5 per cent and an ash content of 6-7 per cent. Little difficulty was anticipated in selling this type of coal, potential markets being industrial steam raising, schools, domestic and phurnacite (a processed smokeless fuel).

South of Mardy the Rhondda Fach Valley, as a very old mining area, had been extensively worked. The Ferndale pits were still in operation, with production confined to the small, remote pillars remaining. Ferndale's workings were already three and a half miles (5.6 km) from pit bottom, with the section of some roadways just large enough to allow the passage of a 30 cwt dram. Apart from some reserves to the east, little coal remained. As these reserves could be more economically worked from the adjacent Cynan Valley, there was no economic future for Ferndale. Manpower for the new project, which was estimated to reach 2,600 by 1956, could therefore be made available by closing the pits at Ferndale and also the Bwllfa Pit at Cwmdare in the Cynan Valley, over the mountain from Maerdy.

Bwllfa itself would have required major investment in stone drivages to continue as an independent unit, since its reserves were hemmed in by geological faults to the west and a syncline to the south. The decision was taken to incorporate Bwllfa into the project, but only as an upcast shaft for the underground ventilation and for additional winding of men and supplies. For this purpose a heading, two and a half miles (4 km) long, was driven between the two pits. The disused Gadlys Pit at Nantmelyn in the Cynan Valley was also linked to the project. This was used for the pumping out of minewater. The boundary between the Mardy take and that of Tower and Fernhill was to be the 55 metre Hirwaun 2A fault in the west, plus the 38 metre Hirwaun 2 fault in the north west. Due to the proximity of the Lluest Wen and Castell Nos reservoirs, blocks of coal would have to be left unworked immediately beyond the colliery shafts so as to avoid subsidence in this area.

## Underground Configuration.

Although the seams were fairly level and did not present the problem of steep measures as on the southern crop of the coalfield, in common with Nantgarw the principle of horizon mining would also be employed at Mardy.

These horizons would be driven in line with each other and initially at three levels. The shafts were deep enough to accommodate a fourth horizon, to be developed at some stage in the future. The horizons were:

- No. 1 (yellow) horizon at a depth of 221.3m.

- No. 2 (red) horizon at a depth of 297.2m.

- No. 3 (blue) horizon at a depth of 373m.

- No. 4 (future) horizon at a depth of 443.4m.

The nos 3+4 shafts would be re-equipped with new cages and guides, plus electric winding engines. Connection with Bwllfa was at the red horizon level. Coal seams would be worked from a higher horizon to the next lower. Underground (i.e. "staple") shafts and spiral chutes, situated in the lateral roadways, were to interconnect the horizons. The horizon roadways were 4.6m at the base and 3.4m high. Below the surface, reference was made to the colliery looking like the London underground system. For transportation of coal to pit bottom, diesel locomotives were to be employed, hauling 3-ton mine cars instead of the usual 30 cwt (1.5t). drams. These mine cars were to be arranged in "journeys" (i.e. trains) of thirty-five. Such transport was used for men and supplies as well as coal.

## Surface Façade.

Due to the fact that the colliery was sited in a steep and narrow valley, confinement of the surface build-ings into as small an area as possible was necessary. The winding engine houses, coal preparation plant, pithead baths, lamp room, offices and canteen were all completely rebuilt in the new cubic style, with concrete, red brick and glass. The electrical substation, plus electrical, mechanical and blacksmiths' workshops, were to be accommodated in one vast building, presenting "a glistening façade against the moorland background". This restricted nature of the surface made it very costly, if not impossible, to dump all pit refuse there. Consequently, all dirt was to be mechanically crushed on the surface then returned underground for stowing. Here it would be blown pneumatically into the waste areas left behind following coal extraction. The need for ugly slag tips above ground would thereby be eliminated. Surface facilities were to be adequate for 2,000 men at Mardy itself and 800 at Bwllfa

## Optimism.

The optimism associated with this first step into a new era radiates forth from the preamble to the technical plans of the NCB:

"The priority associated to the scheme under the divisional development plan is a high one. It is one of eight reorganisation schemes scheduled for immediate development. If all the factors involved have been correctly assessed the productivity obtained should compare favourably with any other mine in the division. The labour in the area is reasonably good and if the present effort is maintained when the men are transferred to Mardy the results obtained will be satisfactory —— Underground conditions are expected to be good and no particular difficulties should be encountered due to faults etc. The 4 feet. and 6 feet seams have been the most productive and, apart from the virgin area now to be worked, these two seams have been almost exhausted in the locality. It is anticipated therefore that very good results should be obtained".

On Saturday, 28 August 1954, the official opening of the redeveloped Mardy Colliery took place. Appropriately, Arthur Horner, now General Secretary of the National Union of Mineworkers, officiated at the ceremony. The Colliery Manager was Mr. D.M "The Hooker" James. By now the new mine was in full operation, with 185 men employed on the surface and 890 underground, working four seams.

Major development work continued into the early 1960's. At this time the contractors, Cementation Construction Ltd., were still employing 64 men at the mine, working on staple shafts, headings and drivages. Double-shift working was intended, with an annual output by 1957 of 947,000t, at an overall output per man-shift of 32.3 cwt (1.6t). Workable reserves, accessible from the original scheme, were estimated at 80 Mt. There would be an additional 33 Mt available from the later development of the 4th (bottom) horizon. The official publicity spoke confidently of an eventual output of 4,000 tons of coal per day being achieved by the mid-1950's. There were at least 100 years of work, with a consequent securing of the valley's future. As a new pit, many of those transferred there found it lacking in esprit-de -corps. It was stuck out in the wilderness and simply too big. This, however, was to be the least of Mardy's problems.

## **Reality.**

Disappointment.

As the pit built up, some actual statistics were:

- In 1954; with manpower of 975, production was 83,000 tons.

- In 1956; with manpower of 901, production was 166,000 tons.

- In 1958; with manpower of 979, production was 177,000 tons.

- In 1960; with manpower of 1,502, production was 313,000 tons.

By the early 1960s, and against the above background, internal NCB annual reviews for the South Western Division make for sober reading. On the subject of Mardy, gone is the initial enthusiasm.

In 1962, such a report stated that the most important factor emerging was the impact of extremely difficult geological conditions on future prospects. As a consequence, planned output had been reduced to

460,000 t per annum (from 947,000t), and overall output per man-shift to 27.2 cwt (1.38t) from 32.3 cwt (1.6t). Estimated profit per ton was reduced to 11sh. 10d.

The 1963 review was even more depressing:

"Results were disappointing in the first half of 1963, but in the latter half productivity increased and averaged 26.9 cwt (1.37t) for the year, at a profit of 8sh. per ton". The report concluded with a negative kind of optimism. Since Mardy produced coals for Phurnacite production, was a contributor to net profit, and since most of the money had been spent anyway, "it was agreed that the project should continue".

The surface installation also had its problems, for the coal preparation plant proved to have been badly designed. As late as 1976 complaints were still being received concerning lack of coal clearance underground due to non-effective operation of the plant. This was causing a backlog in the production chain.

In 1979, Bwllfa Pit closed, with the men being transferred to Mardy proper.

By 1981, four seams were still being worked, on a fully mechanised basis. The 5 feet and 7 feet seams were cut and loaded by ranging drum shearers while the Yard and Gellideg (the deepest seam in the coalfield) were worked by Gleithobel ploughs. Roof supports on the coalfaces were largely of the hydraulic self-advancing type. Expected output per manshift was 28.2 cwt (1.43t) overall, with 5.3 tonnes at the coalface. Manpower deployment was: coalface 200, elsewhere-underground 230, surface 228, and development work 120.


The 1984-85 Strike.

Already before the 1984-85 strike, Mardy had reluctantly become aware that it was destined to take the path that Fernhill had already taken, namely combination with Tower, to which they would be linked underground. As in Fernhill, all production would henceforward emerge at the Tower drift.

The amalgamation would save approximately 200 jobs on Mardy surface. It also replaced the old and troublesome coal preparation plant with the modern one at Tower. There would be a substantial reduction in transport costs to the Phurnacite plant at Aberaman in the Cynon Valley, not far from Tower. This was the main market for Mardy coal (52 per cent, compared with 34 per cent for the domestic market and 14 per cent for power stations). An additional cost saving was the maintenance of the British Rail branch line along the length of the Rhondda Fach. Passenger service had already been terminated and now the line could be shut down completely. It was not lost on the men at Mardy that a similar step had presaged the closure of Fernhill, their equivalent in the Rhondda Fawr. All of the men recognised at the time that this amalgamation would probably lead to the total closure of their own colliery. When the call for strike action came, their commitment to the cause was total.

In Maerdy it was a call to the spirit of the days of old. It was grasped with enthusiasm, for here was the last chance to fight for their pit and they were prepared to see it through to the bitter end. There were many public comments, all on the theme, "We have got to win". Every Sunday morning the strike committee met in the welfare hall to discuss strategy and how to raise funds. Clever, and convinced of the righteousness of their cause, they were very proud of the radical traditions of their lodge. Many joined the itinerant pickets and fund- raising teams. The talk was that, when the strike was won, they would get the passenger rail service to Maerdy reinstated, and see to it that all sections of the social services were improved.

As the strike continued, however, the sense of humour at those Sunday meetings became subject to strain. Depression reigned when the prospect of support from the National Association of Colliery Overmen, Deputies and Shotfirers (NACODS) collapsed. Winter was the low point. Many people were freezing in their homes. In a time warp back to the days of the 1926 lock-out, when armies of men had hacked away at the upper coal measures in the side of the mountains, marking out the coal seams with lines of horizontal scars, in some places still visible today, now people were again out on the icy tips, digging for lumps of coal. Anything that could be burnt was taken away. Old sleepers were chopped up. Sections of fence disappeared in the night. Wooden cable drums were torn apart. Much electricity was tapped off by bypassing the meter. Food was running low.

The macho men of the valleys found their traditional dominance challenged by the women's support groups. It was they who organised the soup kitchens and pressed the local contractors for food and money. Clothes were obtained from all parts of the world. Their formidable presence was even felt on picket duty at the pit, daring anyone to even think about being the first scab in Maerdy. In a quotation from one miner, "Anyone who tried that would get thrown straight down the shaft. Those women would stop a tank". After the nadir of that bitter 1984 winter, however, even here support for the strike began to crumble. The pointlessness of carrying on was becoming more and more apparent. As one miner put it, men wanted to go back to work but, please behind a nimbus of dignity, instead of just creeping in like scabs.

On Tuesday, 26th February 1985, the movement for a return to work without an agreement came to fruition in, of all places Mardy, last pit in the Rhondda, "Little Moscow", and cradle of Communists. That evening 600 or so of the 753 Mardy strikers packed into Ferndale Workingmen's Hall and Institute for perhaps the most significant single lodge meeting in the whole year-long trauma of the strike. Lodge Chairman, Arvon Evans, expressed the general feeling - that there was a clear recognition Thatcher was not going to allow the kind of settlement they could sign and that the best way to stop the NUM being smashed was an orderly return to work. From within this run down, four-story, building came a message that quickly spread across the country. Mardy had thrown in the towel. For the remainder of Britain's suffering coalfields, the die had been cast.

On Tuesday morning 5 March 1985, the decision to march back with heads held high was carried out with all the moving dignity that the organisers intended. With the Tylerstown and Maerdy brass bands leading the way, the whole workforce, fifty-one of whose colleagues had been arrested and not one of whom had abandoned the strike for even a single day, formed up to follow the massed lodge banners. Dozens of foreign cameramen and television crews were not disappointed, for the long, slow, defiant trudge back to work was the epitome of an honourable surrender. The footage went around the world. It was an emotional moment and the Mardy men went back with clenched fists raised. Nothing, however, could hide the bitter truth, that they and Maerdy had been well and truly beaten. On that cold and frosty morning, as they marched out of "Little Moscow", a parallel was drawn with that other retreat, of Napoleon's Grand Army from the real Moscow. That too was to prove the harbinger of final collapse.

The glorious march back to work was not matched by its aftermath. During the strike Mardy had lost two coalfaces. After a month, they could still only reach 37 per cent of the expected output.


Amalgamation with Tower.

In 1986, as previously with Fernhill, the NCB cut their losses at Mardy. Output was diverted by underground roadway to Tower Colliery and the two units merged. Two converging headings were driven, from the vicinity of Tower drift bottom and from the Red Horizon at Mardy. They connected on 14 May 1986, with only 1.3 cm out of point. In the 4 years prior to the merger with Tower there had been no general recruitment at Mardy. The workforce had already been reduced from 850 to 750 during that period and now a further 192 surface jobs would go. When, four years later, the pit's final hour struck, this time there was acceptance.


Closure.

In September 1990, the men voted to accept the decision to close the mine, the main consideration being the magnitude of the redundancy pay-offs, varying between £17,000 and £30,000. A British Coal statement said that by agreement between management and miners the pit would close "because the colliery's economically workable coal is exhausted". The power of the NUM had been broken and virtually every member of the once vigorous Communist party had thrown in his hand. The proud march back to work without any agreement whatsoever, intended to ensure survival of the union, had in fact ensured its downfall. There was no longer any mood for militant talk, let alone action. There was some reference to "NCB lies", implicit in the over 120 Mt reserves and the 100 year life promised in the reconstruction publicity. There were no lies. The euphoria of those early years had simply evaporated. Like atomic power and the dot com revolution which was to follow, the bubble had simply burst and the world was now a different place. Commonwealth trading preferences, energy shortage, lack of shipping and high freight rates had been replaced by globalisation and coal imports, plentiful shipping, low freight rates and a four-fuel economy.

Mardy colliery, at the time of closure employing 310 men with an average age of 34, was the last mine to have worked in the Rhondda Valleys. These were the epitome of the South Wales coalfield and were once probably the most intensively mined area in the world, with fifty-four mines working along their length. At their peak in 1913, a 500 t trainload of coal left the Rhondda every 10 minutes of the working day. Since the original opening of Mardy colliery in 1893 until final closure, a total of 12.8 Mt of coal had been extracted with165 miles (266km) of underground roadways being developed. Total exploitation, on a seam-by-seam basis, is given below (million tonnes):

- Gorllwyn    -    1.9

- 2ft. 9      -    2.0

- 4ft.        -    3.4

- 6ft.        -    0.885

- 9ft.        -    1.0

- Bute        -    0.626

- Yard        -    0.678

- 7ft.        -    0.740

- 5ft.        -    1.38

- Gellideg    -    0.78


In December 1990, Mardy Colliery was closed by British Coal.


There was a second and final march by Mardy miners, this time from, instead of to, the pit. It was as emotional as the procession up the valley in 1985 - but this time there was no pretence that defeat was anything but total. The weather joined in the all-pervading gloom as damp, misty, cloying drizzle hung on the mountain slopes. At the mine a huge crowd of miners, plus their families and supporters, had gathered. They stood, dripping, as dignitaries spoke. Children recited their party pieces and hymns were sung. As the colliery band struck up with "Cwm Rhondda" the sadness reached a pinnacle of intensity as hardened miners fought to hold back tears. In a tribute to yuletide, carols were also sung, but never was the season of good cheer less cheerful.

As the crowd followed the union banner for the last time, back down into the grey, dripping village, threading their way through deep puddles that punctuated the broken, pot-holed track, there was reflection. Gareth Childs, secretary of the Rhondda branch of NALGO, had expressed the sentiments of his union, "If there was any justice, the last pit in the world to close would be in the Rhondda". In the crucible of Noah Ablett and Arthur Horner, the saga of Rhondda coalmining, along with its fifty-three pits and one-time fame, was, after 150 years, finally consigned to history.

In March 1996, over 5 years later, an area on the fringe of Mardy, leading up to the former colliery, was cleared, flattened and landscaped to provide an eight-acre site for a 14,864sq.m factory. Within the scheme boundary, 250,000 tons of spoil were moved. The operating company was Fenner Polymer, producing various products for the automobile industry. A total of 540 jobs were planned. The factory itself cost £7 M to build. Total investment in the whole project was £25 M, contributed by Fenner, Welsh Development Agency, the Welsh Office, County and Borough Councils, plus Mid-Glamorgan Tech.

In December 1997 the official opening was held, during which Mr. Brian Willet, chief executive of the Welsh Development Agency, unveiled a plaque. Fenner's chief executive described the plant as the flagship of the company, saying it was the most advanced facility of its kind in Europe. During the first year, orders lost due to currency fluctuations and a general weakening in the automobile market, all combined with commissioning problems, resulted in 130 redundancies. The directors expressed confidence that with improvements in efficiency and market forces, further investment would be attracted and stability would result.

In 2003, local MP Chris Bryant said in a debate in parliament that Maerdy was one of the most deprived wards in Wales, with many people living in the Rhondda Fach referring to it as the forgotten, or hidden, valley.

In October 2004 the Maerdy factory, now called United Polymers and employing 310 people, announced that it had gone into administration. Less than one month previously, 156 staff at the Chubb fire extinguisher factory in nearby Ferndale had been told their jobs were being moved to China.

## FERNHILL.

### The Crucible.

The saga of Fernhill was to have less flair. Its development came later and its demise earlier than Mardy's. Unlike Mardy, it was not a new entity linked to two valleys and manned by men, most of whom were initially transferred from elsewhere. The workforce at Fernhill came almost exclusively from the upper Rhondda Fawr, especially the village of Treherbert. Nestling in the cul-de-sac of Blaenrhondda, Fernhill is overshadowed by a range of mountains, of medium height but whose effect is nonetheless massive, with gaunt escarpments on three sides. To the west it is dwarfed by the flat topped and grey sandstone fringed massif of "Pen Pych" (the Sentinel), which dominates completely this northern head of the Rhondda Fawr. Its rugged sandstone crown rises precipitously and is a great attraction for climbers. Those who master its difficult and dangerous slopes are rewarded with a panoramic view of great beauty. In winter, this magnificent amphitheatre of rocks and cwms can transform into a world of frost and frozen waterfalls, while mists, damp and penetrating, swathe down from the heights. At such times, on the A4061 mountain road above, drivers inch forward through the murk, with headlight beams penetrating like fingers, lost in the claustrophobic whiteness.

### Militancy.

It was in the 1930's that the Fernhill lodge of the South Wales Miners' Federation spawned a militancy that was to last until the colliery's final closure, some forty years later. This "We stick up for our rights" ethos was to persist, even when their rights were wrong. Among some of the major strikes and disputes at the colliery in the early days were:

- A strike in 1934 against the "scab" South Wales Miners Industrial Union, in which safety men were withdrawn for the first time in the South Wales Coalfield since 1921.

- In 1936 a dispute arose over twelve men who had not received a minimum wage payment for filling small coal. This resulted in 64 men staying down the pit, resulting in a world record for an underground sit-down strike of 12 days (292 hours).

Lodge chairman at the time was Jack Williams, with the local alias of "Jack Down Tools" or, alternatively, "Jack Williams Bolshie". Subsequently he would become Chairman of the Rhondda Council, a post that he held for decades (were the council houses built in "Garden City", directly opposite the dwellings of Fernhill Colliery management and thereby spoiling their view, just coincidence?). Lacking the fame of their colleagues over the mountain in Mardy, nevertheless here too a communist sub-culture existed. This culture would flourish, as more moderate souls would wilt before the fear of being scorned and ridiculed as "boss's men".

### The Pit.

The five shafts at Fernhill were actually an amalgamation of two pits. Shafts nos. 1+2 on the east side of the narrow valley belonged to the original Fernhill Colliery whereas 3+4+5, on the other (west) side, belonged to North Dunraven. In the left-wing view, North Dunraven was always more progressive. The men from 1+2 were written off as "chapel types", who "would always say yes to the undermanager". It was the star of North Dunraven that would prove to be ascendant.

At nationalisation, Fernhill employed 261 men on the surface and 880 underground. Due to its location close to the anthracite area, Fernhill coal differed to some extent from the general nature of Rhondda steam coal. The coal here was classed as "dry steam" which, being almost smokeless and suitable for slow-burning stoves was subject to a big demand.

## Reconstruction.

### The Duke Kicks Off.

On 28 April 1955, the Duke of Edinburgh made a much-publicised visit to the colliery. By this time manpower was 1,031, with 446 at the coalface, 380 elsewhere underground and 205 on the surface. Coal production was by hand. The royal visit emphasised the publicity being given at that time for a wide ranging reconstruction scheme. As the first move in this scheme, a large pithead baths building had recently been completed. This building incorporated not only bathing facilities for 2,000 men but also office accommodation, plus a large modern canteen and medical centre with state registered nurse in charge.

As part of the publicity accompanying the Duke of Edinburgh's visit, the seams at Fernhill with their estimated reserves were given as follows:

| Seam. | Workable reserves (tons). |
|---|---|
| - 2 ft. 9in. | 3,332,000 |
| - 4 ft. | 9,984,000 |
| - 6 ft. | 10,535,000 |
| - Red Vein. | 8,562,000 |
| - 9 ft. | 19,360,000 |
| - Bute. | 8,038,000 |
| - Yard. | 6,279,000 |
| - 7 ft. | 6,460,000 |
| - 5 ft. | 10,018,000 |
| - Gellideg. | 5,973,000 |
| Total: | 88,541,000 |

Seams above the 2ft. 9in. were not regarded as being potential reserves. They had already been worked extensively. The Rhondda No. 2 seam for example had been worked by means of four levels burrowed into the western mountain, for lengths up to 1,372m. To date, the lowest seam worked at Fernhill had been the Bute. Below this the seams were virgin as far as Fernhill was concerned. They were assessed as follows:

Yard: This had a section of approximately 0.84 m. There was a working face in this seam at Tydraw Colliery and, according to borehole information, was workable to the north-east and possibly in the central section.

7 ft.: According to borehole information, this was unworkable in the north and central areas. However, there were reserves to the south.

5 ft.: This had been extensively worked at Tydraw Colliery, where there were two 0.6m sections, separated by a band of shale which varied between 0-0.9m. Boreholes indicated a 0.9m clean coal working section in the Fernhill area.

Gellideg: Boreholes had proven an average section of 0.76m. Indications were that it would be workable in the western part of the north and central areas.

With an investment estimated initially at £5,500,000, the development was to be divided into two phases.

## Phase 1.

In the first and smaller of these phases, which was completed in 1956, all coal raising from the nos. 1 and 4 shafts was terminated and concentrated on no.2. In future the former shafts would be used for men and supplies only (no. 3 shaft was employed for upcast ventilation while no. 5 was no longer used). This concentrated surface operations at the original Fernhill Colliery to the east of the site. To accelerate this raising of coal in no. 2 shaft, skip winding was employed for the first time in the history of the South Wales Coalfield. By this method, coal, instead of being carried in drams by cage to the surface, is loaded at pitbottom into a skip (of 2.5 t capacity in this case). It is then discharged from the skip upon its reaching the surface. This initial development was successful.

In 1957, with a production of 263,000 t, the first year of operation following completion of Phase 1 was considered a boom year. Overall output-per-manshift increased from 18 to 20.9 cwt (0.9-1.06t). However, the benefits resulting from this initial phase were regarded by the NCB as likely to deteriorate by 1964-65. To ensure the long-term future of the colliery, access was required to the lower seams, with bigger shafts for the necessary ventilation. At that time the main underground roadways were in the Gorllwyn seam (not as deep as the seams listed above). In addition to this, the surface plant and equipment were old and required renewal. In particular a new coal preparation plant was necessary since washing capacity was inadequate and the screens (for the separation of rock from coal) were in very poor condition.

## Phase 2.

Consequently, further reconstruction would be necessary. As a result of phase one above, the area around the nos. 3, 4, and 5 shafts (i.e. the original North Dunraven surface) was no longer used for coal handling. It thus became available for work associated with the long-term development of phase 2. The theme of this long-term project was to enlarge the field of operations, while concentrating production channels. Output-per-manshift would be improved and output generally increased. The North Dunraven surface was to be completely rebuilt and nos. 4+5 shafts deepened. No. 4 shaft was also to be widened. After that, the surface of the original Fernhill Colliery, along with the three remaining shafts, nos. 1,2,3, would be decommissioned. Initial coalfaces in the central area should be in production by 1964, with planned output being achieved by the end of that year. Completion of development work was scheduled for 1965.

In 1958, the Headquarters Finance Committee of the National Coal Board approved this phase 2 plan. Its main justifications were as follows:

- Ensure continuity of production and more economic mining of the northern and central areas of the "take" during the next 60 years.

- Utilize manpower from the Tydraw+Glenrhondda Collieries (two smaller mines nearby) when they close. Existing manpower of 946 was to be increased to 1,846. If the above closures proved to be inadequate, then additional manpower could be transferred from Park Colliery.

Specific objectives were:

- Increase production from 1,052t saleable to 2,768t saleable per day.

- Increase overall productivity from 20.9 to 29.9 cwts (1.06-1.5t). per man-shift.

As financial objectives:

- Net capital investment to be £7,354,386.

- Yield on total investment to be 8.9%.

- Operating profit per annum to be £1,045,416 (an increase of £809,976).

- Profit per ton to be 31s 6d (an increase of 20s 5d).

The new surface would be concentrated around shafts nos. 4+5. All coal would be wound in no. 5 with no. 4 being the upcast, reserved for men and supplies. Only these two would be used by the completely reconstructed mine. Shafts 1+2+3 were to be filled in.

Technical Features.

The main technical features of the project are listed below:

- Deepen the 6m diameter no. 5 shaft from 248m to 407m.

- Enlarge the 3.7m diameter no. 4 shaft to 6m. In addition, deepen this shaft to 375m from the maintained depth of 272m. (The original sinking had been 307m to the upper 6 feet seam).

- Install a new main ventilating fan, with new fan drift, to shaft no. 4.

- Develop the reserves in the central and northern areas by driving horizons at different levels. These horizons would be linked with each other by means of underground (staple) shafts. The horizon section would be 4.9m across and 3.7m high. In future there would be a third horizon at the lowest level.

- Introduce battery (later changed to diesel) locomotive haulage on the horizon roadways, hauling trains of 1.5 t mine cars.

- Completely modernise the transport and coal handling system, both surface and underground. This included a skip winding plant for shaft no. 5 (This latter requirement was later changed to cage winding of mine cars, so as to reduce breakage of coal, since Fernhill coal of less than 1.6cm had proved difficult to sell).

- Construct a new coal preparation plant, plus a new aerial ropeway for rubbish disposal.

- Completely electrify the surface (instead of steam and compressed air power).

- Provide new surface buildings (later to be heated by a plant burning unsaleable coal).

The shafts would be configured as follows:

Shaft no. 4 (upcast).

- At 211m, existing pumping station in Gorllwyn seam.

- At 272m, landing for first horizon.

- At 347m, landing for second horizon.

- At 366m, sump cleaning.

Shaft no. 5 (downcast).

- At 281m, first horizon for ventilation.

- At 357m, second horizon for man-riding (later changed to coal winding).

- At 366m, skip loading for coal winding (later deleted).

- At 400m, sump cleaning.

In April 1960, revisions to the plan were submitted and approved during the course of that year. During planning for phase 2, the figure for reserves available in all seams as given during the Duke of Edinburgh's visit, namely 88,541,000 t, was revised downwards, to approximately 77 Mt. This would still be adequate for 115 years at the planned output of 664,440 t (saleable) per annum. Just for the second horizon, reserves of 42 Mt were available in the north and central areas. At the planned output, this alone was sufficient for 63 years work. The additional reserves could be accessed by future development, including the proposed third horizon. The plan was to initially work the north and central areas. Working towards the south would follow at a later date.


Activity.

The late 1950's and early 1960's were dynamic times at Fernhill, as phase 2 of the reconstruction plan was pressed ahead on schedule. With the North Dunraven section of the colliery appearing as much like a building site as a mine, the German mining contractor Thyssen was responsible for the underground development and completed much of the work. Shaft no.5 was deepened as planned and the associated insets constructed. The horizons were driven. Shaft no. 4 was filled in and then its re-sinking commenced, with its diameter now increased from 3.7m to 6m. A fan drift between this shaft and the future main fan for the mine was completed. In addition to the impressive pithead baths building, the surface became endowed with new workshops, plus a 33,000V electric substation and an electric winding engine house for the no. 5 shaft. Technical achievement was to be second to none.


Fighting Fire with Nitrogen.

On 24 July 1962, following shotfiring when driving the first horizon, combustion of gas was noted. Men were immediately withdrawn from the drivage, which was already more than 914m long. No injuries were sustained and initially several conventional methods of extinguishing were tried, including stifling by sand and stonedust, plus extinction by water and carbon dioxide, all to no avail. Due to a slight uphill gradient, it was not possible to flood the chamber. By means of a sandbag barrier, the heading was therefore sealed off, 640m back from the fire. This was completed in two days. It was hoped that thereby the fire would soon be starved of oxygen and go out. In fact, combustion of methane was being well supported by air leaking-in through the loose shale structure around the plug of sandbags and also via old workings through which the new horizon had passed. Cement sprayed onto the sandbags and injected into the strata around the plug failed to stop this leakage of air. After five weeks it was therefore decided to suffocate the fire with nitrogen. A compressed air pipeline, for the use of drilling hand tools, already existed from the surface into the horizon and this was now used for nitrogen supply.

In one night, in darkness, mud, high winds and driving rain, British Oxygen and NCB technicians assembled a nitrogen evaporation plant at the no. 5 shaft pit top. The plant was completed within 16 hours of the first summons being made to British Oxygen. It was calculated that at least 1,699 cu.m of gas per hour would be required to combat the fire successfully. The sealed-off section had a volume of 9,911 cu.m and there were leaks everywhere. Output was built up to the calculated level within a few days of installation. All resources of the British Oxygen's four production plants at their Cardiff works were switched to maximum round-the-clock production of liquid nitrogen to quench the Fernhill fire. Every two hours for twelve weeks a fleet of British oxygen road tankers journeyed from Cardiff to Fernhill Colliery and back. Where other methods had failed nitrogen succeeded; the blaze was checked and held.

This was not the end of the story, however. There were still many crevices where burning methane remained, tiny points of flame that would again burst into full life if the nitrogen was withdrawn, or allowed to disperse. Cautiously, backdraught techniques were introduced which in time drove the last vestiges of fire to extinction. After seventeen weeks, with twelve of them on nitrogen supply, the fire was finally extinguished. During this time, 2,550 tons of liquid nitrogen in 1,150 loads had been delivered. In the rest of the colliery the coal had never stopped coming up and the miners stayed at work. A serious production loss had been avoided. This was the first time that nitrogen gas had been called upon to undertake such a mammoth task, in such large quantities and so effectively.

On 18 November 1962, jubilation over this success was marred by a tragic fatality, incurred as rescue teams entered the sealed area to spray cooling water and to finally confirm the fire's extinction. Twenty-four teams were on site from all over South Wales, to work shifts limited to a duration of 2 hours. The canteen came up trumps with hot meals being served on the completion of each shift. On approval being given by the NCB, Mines Inspectorate and the NUM, rescue team members, with breathing apparatus in action, crawled along the pipe that had been left through the main seal. Awaiting them was an entry into fantasialand, as they emerged into a dark world of high temperature and ethereal hanging vapours, with the very atmosphere deadly. It was an environment such as to disturb the composure of all but the most sanguine of men. As the walls were sprayed, large pools of water accumulated and it was into one such pool that a member of the team was seen to collapse. A surface blacksmith from another colliery, 17 stone and in excess of 6 ft., it would later be ascertained that his rubber mouthpiece had been bitten through. As the team came to the aid of their stricken colleague, in the imbroglio of rescue, a second team member would lose his mouthpiece. He would himself become a casualty. On reaching the surface the first man was already dead, while the second was rushed to Llwynypia hospital, being discharged later in the day. One result of this incident would be a limitation on the size of men accepted into the rescue teams.

## Anarchy.

### Dictatorship of the Proletariat!

Throughout all of this development effort, existing in parallel but never part of it, was another world, that of production and of the communist-inspired lodge. Viewed as isolated and "Indian territory" by much of the union, in the lodge's eyes they were in the forefront, the flame of the socialist movement in South Wales. The rising union star, George Reece, who would later become General Secretary/ Deputy President for South Wales, cut his teeth at this time as craftsman's representative for Fernhill. Far and away more militant than other lodges and their own South Wales leadership, already at the end of the 1950's they were advocating strike action against pit closures. There were other militant and communist lodges, whose deliberations were however always underpinned by an appreciation that, at the end of the day, survival and prosperity of the pit took precedence over communist dogma. Nowhere else does the "Dictatorship of the Proletariat" seem to have been translated into reality to the extent that it was in Fernhill. It was the lodge that determined manpower allocation, as well as overall parameters of work, the management's statutory responsibility notwithstanding. The lodge committee, under Clifford True, their chairman, would effectively veto any work norm, or working method, not in compliance with their own prior concept. With a mission to rectify the capitalist system of society, based upon exploitation for profit, a welter of unofficial strikes, contempt and general aggravation awaited a manager not to the liking of the lodge. Unenviable indeed was the position of such a manager who was neither a local boy, nor had strong nerves, and whose working methods did not meet the lodge's approval. Treated with contempt by the latter, a life of stress, relieved by sick leave, would likely be his lot.

In the late 1950's and early 1960's, when nationally the Robens' era was ensuring harmony and co-operation between the NCB and the NUM, at Fernhill the line between militancy and anarchy was crossed. A strike culture became endemic and part of the normal working routine, with men automatically following a call to down tools, sometimes unaware of the reason why. Hardly a week went by without an unofficial strike, the justification being that only so could instant gratification be achieved. Sometimes individual underground districts were affected, sometimes the pit as a whole. The sickness was contagious, and was getting out of control. Disagreements between the men themselves, or between the men and a lodge decision as to who worked where, would result in meetings on the coalface, followed by a walkout. Frequently the following shift would stay out in sympathy.

With Fernhill arguably the most strike-happy pit in the United Kingdom, there was local pride in their assumed reputation of being "the ruination of management". Problems with coalface mechanisation, resulting from geological conditions, also took their toll. Production figures tell the story:

- 1954: with 934 men an output of 230,000t.

- 1957: with 987 men an output of 263,000t.

- 1958: with 987 men an output of 217,000t.

- 1961: with 1,015 men an output of 183,000t.

(In 1934, with manpower of 1,750, the output had been 500,000 t).

<u>Write-off.</u>

It was at this this time that William Whitehead, NUM South Wales President, stated at a mining forum held at the South Wales Institution of Engineers in Cardiff:

"FERNHILL IS PLANNED TO BECOME ONE OF THE FINEST UNITS IN THE COUNTRY; LET ALONE IN SOUTH WALES".

His local colleagues however hardly seemed interested; they had their own agenda. Regarded as outsiders, the reconstruction team were not immune from the effects of the general ethos. Hence an agitated outburst on the part of the reconstruction manager, "I've never come across a place where officials are treated with such contempt". On the part of the workforce, interest in, and commitment to, the plans and investment being made for their future was noticeable by its absence, a typical comment being, "None of those b——s can tell anyone in Fernhill what to do". There is no future in throwing seed onto barren land and a non-cooperative workforce could stifle investment. The drive behind Fernhill's reconstruction slipped away.

Almost at dead of night, the reconstruction team who had become increasingly reticent slipped away to leave the colliery in peace. The partially sunk no. 4 shaft with its new fan drift was simply filled in, while the exemplary no. 5 shaft never did wind any coal. Slides of its pit-bottom might be shown at mining presentations as an example of technical virtuosity but it remained a folly, unseen except for the occasional individual engaged on shaft or pump inspection. Its superb, concrete lined insets had been driven just a hundred metres or so, into a dead end. At least the first horizon was maintained for diesel locomotive transport, but only for men and supplies. There would be no big splash in the press concerning reduced prospects for the valley, and the money that had been wasted.

Relative peace returned as the union eventually imposed a measure of control on the anarchy and a local ex-collier boy, David John Hughes, became colliery manager. Short and peppery, his standards were high and respected, but latent tensions on the industrial relations front were to remain. There was an intervening period when production was washed at Nantgarw, thereby bypassing the clapped-out old coal preparation plant, but the situation could not remain static and it did not.

## Amalgamation with Tower.

<u>Unfinished Symphony.</u>

In 1964, to the chagrin of David John Hughes who thereby ceased to be king of his own castle, the NCB cut their losses and Fernhill merged with Tower Colliery to form a single streamlined unit. Fernhill's output was diverted to Tower by means of an underground roadway in the Bute seam. The combined production of the two mines was brought out on a single cable belt conveyor via the Tower drift. An annual contribution of 250,000 t was planned for Fernhill, produced by 860 men. At that time the coal produced was semi-anthracite, used for domestic heating and for manufacture of the popular smokeless fuel "Phurnacite".

Along with the partially re-sunk no. 4, nos. 1+2 shafts were also filled in. The associated surface of the original Fernhill Colliery was flattened, while the North Dunraven surface, an intended beacon for Rhondda's future, lived out its last years in dilapidation, a tatty unfinished symphony. The pithead baths/canteen, workshops and no.5 winding engine house stood as isolated monuments to what might have been. Shaft no. 5 was confined to winding men and supplies and no. 3 kept for ventilation purposes. Right up until final closure, no. 3 shaft continued to use its fine museum piece of a twin horizontal cylinder steam winding engine, manufactured by Leighs of Patricroft, Lancashire. Since the boiler plant had shut down, this would now be operated on compressed air.

## A Clash of Cultures.

Marriage between the two pits was to prove uneasy, involving a clash of cultures. Among other things, the Fernhill men regarded the standard of roadways at Tower as being lower than their own. Bottlenecks occurred in coal transportation. A particular bone of contention would be the regular stoppage of conveyor belts taking out Fernhill production. This was a time prior to construction of the new coal preparation plant at Tower. The bottleneck problem was compounded due to the current plant there being overloaded. To ease the situation, road transport was organised to the coal preparation plant at Park Colliery. A less than charitable interpretation was attributed by the Fernhill men, who maintained that Tower men were putting their own interests first and giving priority to their own production. Eventually, following investigation by NCB national headquarters, three underground surge bunkers were installed at Fernhill.

## I Don't Trust Management and I Never Will.

Two anecdotes accompanied the headquarters' staff visit, both indicative of the ethos prevailing at Fernhill. A friendly greeting by a headquarters' visitor to a local man of his acquaintance resulted in the latter being accused by his colleagues, only half jokingly, of being a headquarters' spy. Another half joking remark by the canteen manageress greeted the same visitor when he requested brown sauce on his meal, "What do you think this is, the Ritz?" The feeling of one Tower undermanager that at Fernhill a general mistrust of management existed was confirmed by one individual, who told him, "I don't trust management and I never will". On their part, towards the end, an impression gained ground in Tower that the Fernhill men were not really trying. Self-advancing roof supports at the coalface were given up in Fernhill after some weeks, whereas at that time Tower had been using them for six years or so.

## The Long Road to Closure.

### To Close or Not to Close?

In 1969, the unofficial strike to improve surfacemen's wages broke out. Throughout this conflict, the lodge was in the forefront (as were their colleagues at Tower).

In 1972 came the first of the great national strikes. Fernhill was one of the first pits to withdraw safety cover, against the advice of the NUM. This strike ended on 28 February 1972.

In May 1972, the East Wales area of the NCB prepared a special report for the Regional Chairman of the Board on the subject of Tower/Fernhill. Its conclusions are summarised as follows:

i) The pit had been placed in jeopardy in 1970 and remained in jeopardy.

ii) An ultimatum had been given to the NUM lodges at meetings in early 1971. Following this there had been pledges of full cooperation to make the colliery viable. There was evidence of sincerity inasmuch as there had been a marked improvement in men's attitude, particularly at Tower.

iii) Notwithstanding the improvement in attitude, there was still a marked lack of appreciation as to what comprises optimum performance.

iv) Output from the current and projected four longwall faces would be inadequate to reduce the expected full year loss of £640,000 to break-even level.

v) Based on the clear inability of Tower/Fernhill to achieve acceptable results, the Area found itself unable to recommend any course of action other than closure.

vi) However, the coal from Tower/Fernhill was of special importance for the phurnacite plant at Mountain Ash. In addition, closure would involve severe social consequences, since the scope for effective redeployment was limited to 203 men. This would leave 958 redundant.

On 9 May 1972, a letter to the Staff Manager of the East Wales Area from the NCB Regional Chairman, stated:

"I had my periodic meeting with the (Conservative) Permanent Under Secretary for Wales at the Welsh Office on 26 April when, inter alia, the future of Tower/Fernhill was discussed. The pospect of its closure sometime in the late summer or early autumn of this year naturally dismayed him and his colleagues".

At the time, and in contrast to what was to happen later, social implications of colliery closure were a cause for government concern. It seems to have been such dismay at the social consequences of closure, together with the fact that Tower/Fernhill coal was essential for the phurnacite plant at Mountain Ash (an important supplier of smokeless fuel for the domestic market), which continued to keep the unit alive.

Consultation.

In spite of repeated management requests, the Fernhill lodge was the only one in the area not attending regular consultative committee meetings. These were a pit level forum for discussion between management and unions. Topics included productivity and safety, plus general problems including whether closure loomed and if so what could be done about it.

On 16 October 1974, at a general meeting of the colliery NUM, Lodge Chairman Clifford True dismissed the consultative committee as just a talking shop. He argued that no good would come from attending these meetings. George Reece, by now heavily involved in coalfield-wide responsibilities for the South Wales NUM, was criticised for neglecting his colliery duties. He nevertheless argued that consultative committees were not just talking shops. Reece pointed out that, bearing in mind the critical position of the pit, the lodge should stop burying its head in the sand and attend. Subsequently there was attendance, but for a three-month trial period only. This was followed by renewed withdrawal.

Financial losses and antiquated methods of work at Fernhill, plus the division of investment between Fernhill and Tower, were becoming issues. Power loading had not worked well in Fernhill, in the opinion of management because the men did not want it to work. The colliery was one of the last pits in South Wales to operate a timber supported, hand-orked coalface, being undercut only, using an Anderson Boyes AB15 undercutting machine. This was phased out in the mid-1970's.

Production and Dust.

By the mid-1979s, Fernhill operations were confined to a single face in the 9ft. seam. The final years before closure were characterised by acrimonious debate concerning methods of working this face. Roof conditions were difficult, with a tendency for the strata to break up and fall in upon exposure. This resulted in extra roof support work having to be done, thus slowing down production. To increase production by avoiding such exposure and consequent roof problems, a layer of coal directly below the roof would have to be left. This meant, however that when the roof crashed into the waste as the face advanced, a considerable amount of extra dust was generated. This affected the eyes and was a health hazard. The final saga is outlined below, based on meeting reports of the colliery NUM lodge.

In April 1975, the new 9-10 coalface was due to start production, working the 9 feet seam. This face was mechanised, with power loading by means of a ranging drum shearer. Roof support was by means of hydraulic, self-advancing chocks. Immediately there was disagreement between management and the lodge concerning who was to work the face. Management demanded the right to select the most appropriate men for the team, the lodge countered with their traditional requirement that seniority alone should be the determining factor. The manager said he had received a letter from the Area Deputy Director (Mining) saying that if the 9-10 team was picked from the seniority list it was doomed to failure. The manager also said that if men continued to come out early he would take them to court, or stop the man-iding facility. There were too many unofficial meetings being held on the face and he did not intend to recompense wages for this. Notwithstanding management warnings about jeopardising the future, the lodge, as usual, had their way. In the words of their minute report:

"Unless the manager' list for the 9-10 is altered in accordance with lodge wishes, no further discussions will be held with management".

In March 1976, the Lodge Chairman reported that Tower/Fernhill had made a profit and that the output per manshift was 30 cwt (1.52t). They were now only one of eight South Wales pits within budget. By the end of the year, £80,000 would be invested in a 450-ton underground bunker so as to reduce bottlenecks in coal transportation. However, excessive dust was reported on the 9-10. An inspector had visited the face and said that the men should look after the sheeting between the face and the waste area in the same way that they do in other pits. (In the waste area, left behind as the face advances, much dust is generated as the roof there collapses). The chairman warned that work would be suspended if the manager assigned a specialist in hydraulic supports from another pit to the face, since the lodge had already given 4 names of face workers to be purpose-trained.

By April 1978 the position was that, as a result of dust being produced, the lodge had been refusing to work with a coal roof for approximately one year. Consequently, coal was now being worked up to the overlaying strata, resulting in roof problems. These in turn were holding back production. The Lodge Chairman reported that the pit was in a most critical position. In the previous year £1,500,000 had been lost and in the previous month alone, £250,000 lost.

At this time Fernhill was only one of two lodges that had voted to reject the Board's productivity agreement (that is one of only two lodges in the last coalfield in the country to accept it). As a result of the dayshift deciding to ban weekend overtime, the position on the face had become critical. The committee's recommendation was that work should now return to normal. The meeting then became bitter, with men throwing abuse at the lodge. The statement was made from the floor that the chairman should resign, for suggesting that the power loader make a production cut along the face.

On 11 June 1978, the secretary stated that this was one of the most important meetings ever to be held at Fernhill. The pit had lost over £700,000 in the first quarter and if the trend continued the loss would be £3 M by year's end. The 9-10 coalface would be at its boundary with the Glyncorrwg geological disturbance by Christmas. At this time it was imperative that the new 9-13 face be available for work. The NCB had to be seen to be doing something about the dust, e.g. water infusion, resin the roof, proper barrier sheeting along the edge of the waste, all to be correctly maintained. If the decision was not made to return to working under a coal roof then the board was unlikely to invest £750,000 in six leg, self-advancing hydraulic chocks for roof support on the new 9-13. At the end of the general meeting there was an overwhelming vote for the 9-10 to return to working under a coal roof, but with reservations (although the decision was now made, it would not be acted upon).

On 21 June 1978, the situation at Tower/Fernhill was raised at a general colliery review meeting with the NCB. The full review procedure for Fernhill was being avoided, since it was no longer classed as an independent colliery but just part of the Tower/Fernhill combined unit. In addition, assuming a transfer of manpower to Tower, total redundancies would be less than 50. At the meeting it was made clear that of the combined unit, Fernhill was the problem, with its single low productivity face. A replacement face would be required in 3-4 months' time.

On 9 September 1978, the general meeting was informed of a discussion with the Area Deputy Director (Mining). He had asked whether the 9-10 had returned to working under a coal roof. The reply was negative but that this would be discussed in a general meeting. Mr. Cleaver, the Deputy Director, had stated that even when working under top coal, results on the 9-10 were only 10 cuts/week. He could see no reason to hope for better results on the new 9-13. At a face length of 146m and two cuts/day this would result in a daily production of 320 tons. The same investment in the N21 face at Tower would result in 440 tons/day, which he was sure of getting. In addition £800,000 per annum could be saved by shutting down Fernhill completely (£566,000 on the surface, £100,000 on power consumption plus £130,000 on rates). There was no reason why Fernhill should continue. There was work for every Fernhill man at Tower and the older men could be given redundancy. However, someone else would have to make the final decision. Operating costs for the combined units were £8,500,000 that year, with an expected loss of £2,000,000.

An argument was made from the floor that it would be wrong to sterilize the coal of the 9 feet seam, which had the lowest ash content in the coalfield. The speaker was sure that the lodge officials would agree with him - 3 cuts per day on the face were possible. The two coalface representatives argued against going back under a coal roof, due to their experience of dust conditions prevailing before working directly to the strata. Accordingly, the chairman informed the meeting that the committee's recommendation was that they do not work under a coal roof. The minutes report:

"There were many questions, which were answered by the chairman. When the vote was taken it was unanimously decided not to work under the top coal" (thereby reversing the decision made on 11 June 1978).

On 13 September 1978, it was reported that the manager had expressed his disappointment concerning the decision not to work under top coal. This had led to a safety issue. The pit safety inspector's report had said that sparks were coming off the hard blue stone roof when the machine was cutting the upper part of the seam. The 9 feet seam was gassy and this could lead to an ignition. If the men would not agree to leave top coal, the manager would send them out. Emlyn Williams, NUM President in South Wales, was now attending lodge meetings. He agreed with the safety inspector's report. After long discussion it was decided to recommend to face workers that they work under top coal and that pressure be put on the Board to do everything possible to suppress the dust. Another meeting would not be called since face workers had already agreed to work under top coal at a previous meeting, albeit under protest (a decision made on 11 June - but subsequently reversed on 9 September 1978).

On 20 September 1978, the manager said that at present the face was only producing 40 tons per shift. Unless the men worked under top coal when instructed to do so by the overman, he would send them out. Emlyn Williams, NUM South Wales President, warned that he would have difficulty in getting conference to support Fernhill on this issue since many other pits were already working under top coal (for example, the G.24 coalface at Deep Duffryn Colliery, a so-called "spearhead" face and one of the most productive in the area, had also been working under top coal. Deep Duffryn was characterised by soft coal, with a consequently high dust concentration. It was also characterised by the hard-working nature of its men).

Emlyn Williams said that if strides were not taken at the meeting that weekend to get back under top coal there would be trouble. Someone else expressed the view it would in any event be better to go back under top coal to protect the roof and prevent a fall, before someone had a serious injury. A fall of ground had already occurred, resulting in a 2 metre high cavity in the roof of the face. The decision was made to return to working under top coal and to press the Board to do everything possible in the way of dust suppression.

On 23 September 1978, the general meeting was informed that the Board's threats of closure were not in accordance with normal review procedure. However, since working coal up to the roof there had been no success. The number of cuts had dropped to 5 per week. In addition, under conditions of work now existing there could be a serious accident resulting from a fall of roof, or gas ignition. An alternative opinion given was that in years to come men would die as a result from working under such dust conditions. Another contribution was that if men were transferred to other pits they might well have to work under top coal there. It was preferable to tolerate such conditions while still working in Fernhill. The lodge's recommendation to work under top coal, while pressurising the Board to do everything possible to reduce dust, was accepted (although by no means unanimously, which would become apparent).

On 21 October 1978, at a committee meeting, the chairman reported 3-shift working on the 9-10. He said that on the basis of what had been happening in the pit over the last few weeks, one would not think that the union was trying to keep the pit open. What was happening now between the general body, the lodge committee men and the lodge officials was that everyone was badgering. Whether the committee stood or fell, the rules of this lodge would be carried out. (Discipline as exerted by the lodge, previously effective, was now falling apart).

On 5 November 1978, the chairman told the general meeting that the number of men who had turned up was pathetic, especially since a bus had been laid on for them. It was important that they should know where they were going. The position at the pit was that one section was opposing the other. Every decision taken by the lodge was now being challenged. Anybody doing that should apply for a position on the lodge; the notice would be put up a few weeks later. (The meeting then deteriorated into confusion, with marching and counter-marching as far as shift patterns were concerned, plus individuals making their own decisions as to where they were going to work and when).

On 18 November 1978, the general meeting was informed of a meeting between the union and the Area Director at the NCB offices in Llanishen, Cardiff. On opening the meeting the Area Director, Mr. Phillip Weekes, had asked to confine the discussion to the 9-10 and 9-13 coalfaces.

Mr. Clifford True, the Lodge Chairman, had made the case that for its first two years of operation the 9-10 had given good results. In 1976, its first year of operation, it had made a profit of £10,000. The dust problem had caused them to stop leaving top coal and to work up to the roof strata instead. This had been a failure. They had now returned to working under a coal roof and dust screens of paper mesh between the coalface and the waste had been introduced. This had proven to be successful (author's italics). However, the life of the face was limited since it was now approaching the Glyncorrwg geological disturbance. As a result of their present experience with the 9-10 he did not anticipate a dust problem arising on the 9-13 (author's italics). In addition, he felt that 3 cuts per day were obtainable on the 9-13.

Mr. Cleaver, Deputy Area Director (Mining) was of the opinion that no better results would come from the 9-13 than had come from the 9-10. He wanted the men transferred to Tower where a face, also in the 9 feet seam, was being prepared. He was sure that this would give good results and would make the pit viable. The Director asked if there was now a lack of effort on the 9-10. To this question the reply on the Board side was a defining silence. He said that he would like to visit the pit himself before making a decision.

On 9 December 1978, the chairman reported to the general meeting on the Area Director's visit. The Area Director had said that he wanted the 9-10 to get up to the break-even level of 15 cuts per week within the next month. At that time he would visit the pit again and make a decision. Both the Deputy Director (Mining) and the Area Production Manager were of the opinion that the 9-13 should not be started.

The Lodge Chairman gave the advantages and disadvantages of an Area production incentive scheme to the general meeting and gave the lodge's recommendation that it be accepted. The resolution was carried 9 votes to 1. (The Area Director had previously made clear that such Area incentive schemes were neither NCB nor NUM policy. Such schemes were to be on a pit and not on an Area basis. By this time, the concept had already been accepted nationally).

It was decided that if employees of the firm working on the surface did not have their union cards by 5 January then they would not be allowed on the premises.

On 13 January 1979, at a committee meeting, it was stated that there were conveyor belt problems in Tower and that management were not giving clearance for Fernhill coal.

On 28 March 1979, at a committee meeting, the chairman said the Board was playing for time in not calling a meeting with regard to the 9-13. The 9-10 was now in a disturbance and the hydraulic chocks for roof support were sinking into the floor. The manager had pleaded for 20 men to go to Tower to open a face in the 9 feet seam there. The chairman had replied that this was the manager's problem. He would just have to start recruiting.

On 1 April 1979, the chairman reported to the general meeting on the serious position at the pit. The 9-10 had now reached the Glyncorrwg disturbance. The face should close and the men be transferred to the 9-13 immediately. At a meeting with the Area Director at Llanishen the previous Friday, the latter had said that since his visit to the 9-10 results had been disappointing. They had not got near to the 15 cuts per week necessary to break even. In addition to this, the absentee figures at the pit were 30 per cent overall, with 40 per cent at the coalface. Rather than invest in the 9-13, where he could see there would be no better results than had been achieved with the 9-10 over the past 3 years, it would be better to develop the N21 in Tower.

The Area Director requested that 20 faceworkers and 10 day wagemen be sent to Tower as soon as possible to open the N21. The remaining 200 would follow later. On being asked whether he was saying that Fernhill was to close, Mr. Weekes replied in the affirmative. He said that there would be no review procedure at Fernhill. There would be an inconvenience payment of £1,200 for each man if they went to

Tower. The South Wales NUM president said that it would be wrong to sterilize the reserves left in the Fernhill take. A joint planning meeting would be held to discuss the issue. Reaction from the floor was mixed, examples being:

- "I've had a gutsfull of 9-10. If we can have the £1,200, let's go to Tower".

- "As far as I am concerned, I will not work in the 9-10 on Monday. We're only staying in Fernhill to give some men better jobs".

- "I'm quite prepared to stay in Fernhill since we don't know if the dust conditions would be any better in Tower".

The committee's recommendations were accepted by 62 votes to 16, these were:

- Fight to keep Fernhill open.

- Wait for the results of the planning meeting.

- Hold a further general meeting in two weeks' time.

On14 April 1979, the general meeting was informed that the Fernhill case had been put personally to Joe Gormley, the National President. At a recent planning meeting, the Board maintained that the assessment of reserves made in 1955, at the time of the Duke of Edinburgh's visit, also included the reserves for the Tydraw and Glenrhondda Collieries (since closed). The planners at that time were also not aware of the fault running from Mardy to Glyncorrwg. The conclusion reached by the joint study was that, although the upper seams had been extensively worked, there was a considerable amount of workable reserves remaining in the 9 feet seam, available on the Fernhill side of the Tower/ Fernhill combine. In addition, closure would completely sterilize the extensive area to the south, since there is no other mine with access to this area. The immediate choice was either:

- Write off Fernhill and transfer the men to Tower so as to develop the N21 face in the 9 feet seam there.

- Alternatively, equip and work the 9-13 immediately.

The committee's recommendation that they stay in the 9-10 until after the report of the next meeting with the Area Director was accepted 38 votes to 5.

On 19 May 1979, it was announced to the general meeting that the NCB had decided nationally to spend £1 M on the 9-13. The Board had made the decision as a result of the united stand of the Tower/Fernhill joint lodges. However, there were some provisos made by the Board:

- Three cuts were expected per day.

- The Board would study results after 3 months.

The NUM South Wales President said that the absentee problem would have to be looked into at the pit. Lodge Chairman, Mr. Clifford True, said that now the Board had made a decision on the 9-13, they would have to press the Board on recruitment. Mr. Brian True made the statement that everyone should be rejoicing at the news. He hoped that the men would make every effort on the 9-13.

On 15 August 1979, at a committee meeting, the chairman reported on a meeting with the Area Director, who asked when production would start on the 9-13. This was generally agreed to as being on 1 October. For the present there was insufficient money available to install a bunker to smooth out bottlenecks in coal transportation. The 9-13 would have to prove itself first. Absenteeism had improved since 9 men had been given notice.

In February 1980, at a meeting in the Llanishen office, the performance of the 9-13 face was reviewed. The bottom line was that it had not proved itself. It was agreed that, notwithstanding the considerable efforts made to establish it as a successful operation, the Fernhill section of the combined mine should close at the earliest opportunity.

In Fernhill the will to fight had gone. The lump sum to be received upon transfer to Tower had proved to be an attraction and the production bonuses being earned there were said to be higher. The grass was looking greener on (literally) the other side of the hill. Militant to the last, at a mass meeting the 280 men at Fernhill voted 2 to 1 for a coalfield strike on the issue of pit closures, one of the few pits to do so. They then agreed to the closure of their own pit and to transfer to a new district at Tower "because of dust conditions at the face". Mr. Clifford True, Lodge Chairman, was quoted in the local press as saying that it had not been an easy meeting:

"I have never seen a situation like it before in my life where men have been so decisive in their attitude, even before they have heard the report from the lodge officials". Their efforts to keep the pit open had been defeated by the appalling dust conditions at the 9-13 face. Said Mr. True:

"We are not prepared to work in these conditions any longer. It would be immoral to ask the men to continue working at the pit".

He said that under no circumstances would they have been prepared to accept closure on the basis of profit and loss:

"At the moment output at the pit is on a par with most other pits —— We still regret the fact that there are millions of tonnes of reserves still in the pit which the Coal Board are refusing to exploit".

Indeed, closure surprised everyone familiar with the pit, particularly their colleagues at Tower, who knew that the reserves were there. Sympathy was expressed with those working under conditions of severe dust but the reason given for such dust, namely working under a coal roof, had been standard practice at other collieries for some time.

The lodge had issued exhortations to the Board concerning the dust issue and, on 18 November 1978, the Lodge Chairman had stated that dust screens between the face and the waste had been successful. The fight of the lodge to keep their pit open did not itemise the actual dust counts in the atmosphere or whether the technical possibilities for suppressing dust had been exhausted. Dust suppression is a bread and butter issue for mining engineers. NCB management consisted of mining engineers, as did most of HM Inspectorate. The NUM also employed their own mining engineers. The question remains as to whether such dust conditions were inevitable, and whether all technical means available to ensure suppression had been exhausted. This has not been documented. The use of respirators was not seriously discussed. In the 9 feet seam, excessive water used for dust suppression might have further weakened an already weak roof and floor, but judicious placing of the infusion points and control of water flow can greatly minimise the deleterious effect. The use of wetting agents also tends to reduce the quantity of water necessary for a given result.

Much later, in 1998, the NCB would stand convicted of a general failure to insist on adequate dust suppression measures, in particular where it was thought that production might be compromised. Mr. Justice Tucker said officials had placed coal production above health and safety. They had failed to take reasonable steps to combat the effects of coal dust and had failed to encourage the use of respirators - available from the mid-1960's. So much for management but, on the part of the lodge, at no stage in the saga as recorded by them do they seem to have insisted on a professional presentation of dust counts with regard to regulations, or the use of respirators, or a discussion of the possible dust suppression options, or a propaganda campaign to ensure the constant and diligent application of means of alleviation. In its publication "The Control of Dust in the Mine", the South Wales NUM had stated, "The means of suppression are available; whether or not reasonable health conditions will obtain depends on the attitude of the persons in the mine, whether they be officials responsible for the supervision of suppression activities, the samplers, or the workmen". The consultative committee, as an appropriate starting point for initiating and co-ordinating such action, was boycotted by the lodge and contemptuously dismissed as "just a talking shop", the only case in the area where such an attitude prevailed.

Fernhill had been famous for its unfocused militancy, engendered by the lodge. As the end approached, obstreperousness on the part of the men, to which they had been brought up, would brush aside the lodge itself. Fernhill was closed as a result of its being grossly uneconomic. It would not be the only pit where this was the result of incessant industrial disputes and general "aggro" on the part of lodge officials, influencing the men.

On 23 February 1980, Fernhill Colliery finally closed down as a production unit. The NCB list of closures states the reason as being "Exhaustion of reserves".

On 7 January 1981, the last entry in the lodge minute book was recorded. The lodge recommended staying where they were until the last man had left. Salvage operations for the recovery of re-usable equipment and scrap continued. The site was then demolished by the NCB and the area landscaped.

## Wild West Postscript.

First Attempt.

The story has a bizarre postscript. The wild environment offers its own attractions. The nearby village of Blaencwm, for example, has become popular as a base for pony trekking. In the words of the London-based publicity officer for Texas, Deputy Sheriff Danny Arnold, "It is similar to the foothills of the Rockies in autumn and has a definite Arizona feel".

In 1987, six years after closure, permission was given by the Rhondda Development Services Committee for the erection of "Westernworld", a Western Holiday Theme Park on the Fernhill Colliery site. If Üpper Rhondda's future could not be secured for coalmining by "one of the finest units in the country let alone in South Wales", then why not by the United Kingdom's greatest re-creation of the wild west? With the Rhondda Heritage Park at the other end of the valley, tourism might yet ensure a bright future. The developer was Western Promotions of Birmingham.

With a target of 5,000 visitors in a weekend and ultimately more than 300,000 visitors per annum, Managing Director, Brian Hughes, expressed confidence that it would become the Rhondda's top attraction. An investment estimated at £1 M, would create 55 jobs initially, with more to come. There would be a saloon with daily entertainment, a sheriff's office, gaolhouse, undertaker, gun shop, general store, livery stables, barber's shop, gun shop, courthouse and bank. Live shows and rodeos were planned. Later additions would be a western museum, a mansion house, a reconstruction of the Alamo fort, plus an Indian village complete with Indians. So as to blend in with the environment, the company promised to further landscape the area and to plant 1,000 trees. Where NCB and NUM once engaged in confrontation, now staged fights were to break out, with tables and the bodies of stuntmen flying everywhere. Tourists could volunteer for the fate so often wished by management upon recalcitrant lodge officials, namely to get locked up and spend the night in jail. His mayoral counterpart, Mr. John Davies of the Rhondda, invited Clint Eastwood, Wild West film star and mayor of Carmel, California, to open the project. Apparently otherwise engaged, or perhaps knowing from experience the danger of being bushwhacked in Indian Territory, he declined, thereby neatly sidestepping a catastrophe and preserving his reputation.

On Saturday 2 May 1987, the upper Rhondda Fawr was "en fete" for the grand opening, with a parade setting off from the Pentre Council Offices at 10am. Hundreds turned out along the five-mile route to cheer them on. "The world's finest western style horseman", together with a colleague, formed the equestrian duo leading the parade. Following in an open carriage, Deputy Sheriff Danny Arnold, who was to mastermind entertainment at Westernworld, accompanied the mayor, whose chain of office clashed incongruously with the Stetson hat upon his mayoral head. Behind came an assortment of characters - confederate and union civil war officers and troopers complete with standards flying, along with Mexicans and Indians, all followed by the chrome and fins of a fleet of Studebakers, Buicks and Dodges from the South Wales American Car Club. Backing them up were coachloads of western enthusiast groups in full cowboy and cowgirl gear.

Where previously black-faced colliers, each with his "block" of firewood under his arm, had wound their weary way home, now the Comancheros from Barry, the Wild Bunch from Milton Keynes and the Broken Barrel Boys from Leicester swaggered through the streets. As the parade swung triumphally onto site, hanging on to their Stetsons and thankful for warm underwear in the strong winds, the families accompanying them reeled back in stunned anti-climax as the hooting and hollering were replaced by cries of despair. Managing Director Brian Hughes had previously said:

"The big things look after themselves, it is the little things which sometimes hold you back from the finish".

The "little things" referred to included such details as many of the initial buildings not being complete as promised, or even started. Timber cladding of such concrete block buildings as existed, intended to create the appearance and character of a western town, was noticeable for its absence. Instead of the promised stunt horse riding, shooting displays and various re-enactments, machinery and building material were scattered around, a constant danger to visitors. Questions were asked as to whether half-finished concrete buildings and cement mixers really were typical of "an absolutely genuine western town from about the 1860's", which was what it was promised to be. One of the more generous comments was, "Well, it'll be nice when it's finished". Such a precipient descent from the sublime to the ridiculous was a disaster from which Western Promotions was never able to recover. One month later the company went into liquidation, with debts of half a million pounds.


Second Attempt.

In October 1987, a local businessman took over the site and attempted to salvage something from the wreckage. One of his first acts was to run out of town the eight cowboys who had sold their homes and given up jobs to bring their families to South Wales. Since the initial project bit the dust they had been supported by food aid from the Blaenrhondda Action Group. The new owner said, "I need people who can do construction work about the site as well as play at cowboys". At least the shooting, hard-riding cowgirl member of the team might have been able to get her old job back, as assistant in a local day centre for the elderly. The Golden Garter saloon was refurbished at a cost of £65,000 and the site renamed the Rainbow Valley Ranch. This attempt at establishing a major tourism complex in the area also collapsed. After a period of dereliction, a company called Fernhill Mining Ltd. took over, ostensibly for coal reclamation. A battered sign warned off trespassers from the dismal, dilapidated site, occupied now by an occasional and equally dismal inhabitant.

In 1998, the Wild West buildings (such as they were) were finally demolished. It was an ignominious end for "One of the finest units in the country, let alone in South Wales".

# Chapter 18

## THE MINERS' NEXT STEP - AND THEIR FINAL ONE.

*What will happen to our children?*
*What on earth will they all do?*
*They'll grow up to become vandals!*
*Destroying everything in view!*
G. L. Davies, Llantrisant.

*To provide employment for as long as possible within a safe*
*and accident-free environment and with a disciplined workforce.*
Tower Colliery mission statement.

In 1946, as a prelude to nationalisation, the South Wales Regional Survey initiated by the Ministry of Fuel and Power stated:

"It can be confidently expected that the 1938 level of output (35 Mt) can be maintained for at least a hundred years". No less than 48 pits were regarded as having such prolonged lives in front of them.

In 2004, forty-two years before the expiry of that confident time span, deep mining in Wales consists of a single colliery. In grotesque contrast to the confident predictions made, its annual output is approximately 0.6 Mt.

## TOWER: THE ENVIRONMENT.

Unlike the surroundings of both Fernhill and Mardy, narrow and confined within the heads of their respective Rhondda Valleys, Tower Colliery by contrast, while dominated by the adjacent Mynydd-y-Llyn Mountain, is situated on the fringe of the openness that is Hirwaun Common. Unlike the traditional local, village-oriented pits, nowadays with improved roads and universal car ownership, Tower is cosmopolitan, with employees coming from as far afield as Abergavenny. Its drift penetrates the base of Mynydd-y-Llyn, which separates the common from Fernhill and the Rhondda Fawr to the south.

Dwarfed by the mountain, and almost as an afterthought, the green headgear of the Tower upcast shaft can be seen, adjacent to a small and unprepossessing cluster of ancillary buildings. Major among these is the fan/winding engine house and the pithead baths, both in utilitarian red brick. The Tower shaft is 162 metres deep and is used for return ventilation. Being nearer to the working districts than the drift, it is also used for the winding of men. Stretching out like an elongated black finger from behind the ridge to the east is an extended conveyor gantry, crossing the nineteenth century mining landscape and linking the railhead with the Tower drift and adjacent coal preparation plant. Where the finger pokes at the mountain an inclined tunnel descends to the level of the lower coal measures. This drift serves for intake ventilation. In addition, all production is brought out and supplies taken in this way.

In Tower's southern foreground is the manmade reservoir of "Llyn Fawr", nestling within the precipitous and forested slopes of Mynydd-y-Llyn and providing water for the Rhondda Fawr. Stretched out along the northern horizon and forming the boundary of the plain lies the Brecon Beacons National Park panorama. To east and west are the heads of two valleys, each of which opens out into the common. The Cynon aims southeast at Pontypridd and Cardiff while the Neath aligns itself southwest, towards Neath and Swansea. Within this great vista, gently undulating country is divided between coniferous forestation, farmland, light industry and opencast workings. This is the setting for the drama that was to unfold in the last decade of the twentieth century, in the death throes of the nationalised British coal industry.

# TOWER: THE CULT.

## The Past -.

Tower is a radical pit in a traditionally radical area. One example of such antecedents was Gwilym Richards. Like his contemporary Arthur Horner, he was aa checkweigher. One of the most driven thinkers and activists of the South Wales Miners Federation, he was one of those victimised after the 1921 lockout and was never again able to work in the district. As a second example, Tom Howell Jones, former Lodge Chairman, was killed in 1938 while fighting fascism in the Spanish Civil War as part of the International Brigade.

## -And the Present.

The origin of Tower's current fame, however, is much more recent. The pit remains an unique example of a miners' take-over of their own mine. As a good David-versus-Goliath yarn, the number of documentaries, plays, films and even an opera, which the story has engendered, bear witness to its attraction for the popular imagination,.

On Saturday, 23 October 2000 the opera, by Alun Hodinott, was premiered in the Grand Theatre, Swansea. The story has also been the subject of a cult French documentary film, Charbons Ardents (Burning Coal), by Jean-Michel Carré.

In January 2004 the news broke that next up would be Tower-the film. Colin Welland had already completed the screenplay and casting was due to begin within a month. Producer David Kelly was conjuring with a list of names, including some of Wales's finest - Ioan Gruffudd, Matthew Rhys and Catherine Zeta-Jones as the forceful young accountant who arranged financing of the workers' buy-out. The intention of Welland and Kelly was to complete the film within the year, the tenth anniversary of the legendary events that were to bring Tower onto the world stage. Often lost from view within the grey drizzle clinging to the nearby Mynydd-y-Llyn, there seems nothing about this unprepossessing industrial site that would in any way attract the attention of artists, writers and the media.

# TOWER: THE HISTORY.

## The Mists of Time.

### The Name -.

Since the mid 1700's a large number of workings have operated in this general area, both shafts and drifts.

From 1848, Hirwaun Common was blessed with a local folly "Crawshay`s Tower", Crawshay being one of the famous ironmasters of Merthyr. This actual circular tower has long since disappeared but, being on the hillside high above Hirwaen and dominating the landscape as it then did, its name was perpetuated by local mining activities.

In 1864, the name Tower first surfaced when the drift mine Goitre Colliery was renamed Tower Graig. This lasted until 1896.

In 1878, in the meantime, the Bute Trustees had opened up another entity. This was named simply Tower Colliery. Tower Colliery is the Methuselah of pits. Since closure in 2002 of the Prince of Wales Colliery in Pontefract, Yorkshire, which dated from the 1860's, Tower's position is unchallenged, not only as the oldest mine in the UK but also the oldest in Europe. Although the last deep mine left in Wales, some of the earliest workings in the coalfield are in this area. With the intensity of today's mining, Tower is a phenomenon that will never be repeated.

### -And the Coal.

As a consequence of the coal's proximity to the surface, mining in the Hirwaen Common area, for local and domestic use, started early. Its origin is lost in the mists of time. Significant mining started when the industrial revolution brought great ironworks to this area. The seams of the Lower and Middle coal measures, along with additional veins of the necessary limestone and iron ore, outcrop over a wide area at Hirwaun. This made them easily accessible for exploitation by the ironmasters. The great coal rush into the Cynon Valley started when the Hirwaun Ironworks opened in 1757. A full century before the Rhondda came into eminence, while it still remained a pristine area of clear streams and wooded glades; the Cynon became the greatest coal-producing valley in the world.

Centrally placed along this northern outcrop, and situated on the margin between the steam coal and anthracite sections, the first identifiable mining of coal at Tower was in 1864. Early workings tended to be in the steam coal section. In recent years, workings have been concentrated in the western, or anthracite, "take". Seams worked during the life of the colliery have been, in descending order; Four Feet, Six feet, Red Vein, Nine Feet, Bute, Seven Feet and Five Feet. The current "take" is close to the recognised base of the lower coal measures. It is traversed by three large faults. Traditionally, these have divided the mine into natural sections.

## Nationalisation.

### Concentration.

At the time of nationalisation, approximately 1,000 men were employed (up from 679 in 1918). Under NCB planning the mine was served by three vertical shafts and six cross measure drifts from the surface.

By 1958, the pit was producing 311,357 tons per annum with manpower of 1,340. Of these, 616 were on the coalface. At present, only the no.3 new (intake) drift and no.4 (upcast) shaft remain in operation. This shaft was sunk between 1941 and 1943 while the drift dates from 1959, replacing one originally sunk in 1920. This drift, along with 1,100 metres of overland conveyor between drift mouth and the railhead, was the central point of a reorganisation aimed at concentrating together all of the diverse entities which, at that time, still remained under the Tower umbrella.

By 1962, output had increased to 368,000 tons per annum, with 1,192 persons employed. At this time, the 9 ft., 7 ft. and 5 ft. seams were being worked.

### American Methods.

The 9 feet seam at Tower, in addition to being worked by ploughing techniques was, due to exceptionally good roof conditions in this area, one of the few cases in South Wales where American mining machinery was employed. As well as being used to drive development roadways in the seam, Joy continuous miners worked production headings, in accordance with the "pillar and stall" method.

On 12 April 1962, it was in just such a heading that an explosion occurred, killing nine men. Headings were also worked by shot firing, in combination with gathering arm mechanical loaders.

## New Horizons.

### Link-up with Fernhill.

In 1964 came the link-up with Fernhill and the uneasy marriage began. The latter's coal was diverted to Tower by means of an underground roadway in the Bute seam. In this single streamlined unit the 860 men at Fernhill were to contribute an additional annual output of 250,000 t. Bottlenecks in the transportation system resulted in problems, with accusations from Fernhill that their conveyors were being stopped so as to give Tower priority. Coal produced at this time was semi-anthracite, used for domestic heating and manufacture of the popular smokeless fuel "phurnacite".

Confrontation with the previous capital investment in Fernhill impressed the Tower men, such as the pit bottom ("like an underground station") and the main horizon, with diesel locomotive haulage. At the time, and until 1984, there were still pit ponies at Tower, employed for the transportation of supplies. Also impressive was the canteen at Fernhill with its size, layout and variety of menu. The provision of a range of cooked meals over and above hot pies, and their availability on two weekday evenings when a show was held at the local Tynewidd Labour Club, was luxury indeed. These evening meals meant that those interested in the show could go there directly from work. They would not have to miss thereby a cooked meal, normally eaten at home. Notwithstanding the cleanliness, friendliness and efficiency of the service, and while £1.50 for fish or curry with chips appeals, eating facilities at Tower radiate all of the charm, cosiness and air of permanency of a building-site canteen.

## Militancy Rekindled.

Tower also became a "receiving pit" for miners transferred as a result of closures elsewhere. Tyrone O'Sullivan was one of those so transferred, from the Abergorky Colliery in Mountain Ash. There were other committed socialists and from this period on there was a rekindling of militancy among the miners of Tower.

In 1969 they took a lead in the unofficial strike over surfacemen's hours. There then followed a period of poor financial results. At this time there was NCB criticism to the effect that the lodge was not showing adequate commitment.

Between1970 and1974, manpower at the mine reduced dramatically, from 1,382 to 559.

In 1974, an opencast operation close to the shaft resulted in an inrush of water. This flooded old underground workings in the vicinity and has exacerbated pumping problems at Tower to this day.

## A Clash of Cultures.

### Characters.

In 1981, following Fernhill's closure and the incorporation of its remaining workforce into Tower, manpower increased to 725. Both pits had a tradition of militancy. Underlying that at Tower, however, was always a determination that the pit must survive and that its interests be served, an appreciation not always apparent in the more nihilistic history of their new bedfellows.

Fernhill had always been noted for its real characters, from the pre-war Lodge Chairman "Jack Down Tools" to overman "Big Chief Roaring Bull" et al. On transfer, the Fernhill men had wanted a district of their own and were given the N21 coalface in the 9 feet seam. Integration was not helped by this British Coal policy of keeping them together under their own officials, as opposed to being incorporated as individuals within the existing workforce. Among other things, their overmen were used to a status that seemed "aristocratic" (like little gods), being addressed as "Mr." At Tower this form of address was reserved for those of undermanager status and above. The cosmopolitan nature of the Tower men, drawn from a wide area of South Wales, contrasted with those of Fernhill, all of whom hailed from the upper Rhondda Fawr, mainly Treherbert. A "them and us" ethos developed, with different expectations on the part of the two groups.

### Flexibility, (and Lack of it).

For the, "We stick up for our rights", Fernhill men, Tower did not prove to be the Promised Land. At Fernhill they had complained of the dust. Now, in their opinion, working conditions and underground roadways at Tower were not so good as at Fernhill while, in their view, the lodge was not so active in following up complaints.

At this time the colliery was working the 6 feet seam, at a section of 1.22 metres and the 9 feet seam, at a section of between 1.65 and 1.9 metres. Maximum depth below the surface was 458 metres. All coal production was mechanised, with power loaders of the ranging drum shearer type. Coalface roof supports were self-advancing, with coalface length varying between 137 and 187 metres. Daily output was planned at 900 tonnes, with an output per manshift of 5.47t (coalface) and 1.32 t (overall). A relative lack of experience in coalface mechanisation on the part of the Fernhill men became apparent to those at Tower. Also noticeable was a certain lack of flexibility on the part of their new colleagues. One example was a reluctance to assist in work outside one's own job description. Another was the fact that, previously, a man had not been allowed by the lodge to work on any shift different to the one originally chosen. There was also a fixation on a maximum rate of coalface advance. If this was such as to require the erection of three additional roadway support rings per day instead of two, then this was regarded as excessive by the Fernhill team, who also had a more liberal interpretation of the lunch break than that prevailing at Tower. An additional problem with which the lodge was confronted was administration of the Coal Board owned houses in Blaenrhondda. Although owned by the Board, according to custom and practice they had become in effect a fiefdom of the Fernhill lodge. For some time after Fernhill's closure in 1980 its workings remained interconnected with those of Tower. This necessitated a continual pumping out of minewater from the former. The interconnection was later sealed off and a minimum distance maintained, so as to avoid any flooding of the Tower workings.

## In the Doldrums.

Flooding Again.

In 1982 there was indeed another serious flooding incident, this time in the workings of the 9 feet seam and resulting from an inadvertent incursion into the abandoned workings of the old Rhigos Colliery. These workings were above the northern section of the colliery take. Within two hours, an initial dribble of evil-smelling water into the gate road at one end of the N17 coalface had built up into a small stream. With the flow of water continuing to increase, the district was evacuated. Extra pumps were hurriedly brought into service while men, waist-deep in water, manhandled the steel pipelines into position. As a consequence of this flooding all workings in the 9 feet seam at Tower Colliery were sealed off. As a result, the financial position at this time became extremely unsatisfactory. Over a 12 month period the colliery lost more than £4 M.

Strike.

In 1984 the men of Tower lodge were leading lights in getting the national strike off the ground in the South Wales coalfield, in the face of a general lack of enthusiasm.

In 1985, unlike Mardy, Tower voted to continue the strike, before succumbing to the inevitable. The recovery of production was slow. After one month, only 68 per cent of the target was achieved, with the V28 face operating normally but the V27 giving poor results. Bryn Williams, Colliery Manager and a local boy, resigned following disagreement with Area headquarters on the degree of management severity to be employed. As a cousin of Kim Howells, union militant and research officer of the South Wales NUM, he was an example of nationalisation blurring the social divide. Four "scabs" were sent to Coventry and within eight months the last had resigned.

## Recovery.

Link-up with Mardy.

In May 1986, Mardy's output was diverted to Tower by a new underground roadway, linking with the Mardy blue horizon. In the same year the 6 feet seam had also been abandoned due to exhaustion of easily accessible reserves. Henceforward, all production has been concentrated in the combined 5+7 feet seam. In this part of the coalfield the two are close enough together to be treated as one. From this time onward, production improved. An NCB press release stated that 6,000 saleable tons per week were necessary if the pit was to become financially solvent. To ensure this level of production, £5 M were invested in heavy-duty, high-technology equipment for the V29 coalface. A new generation of double telescopic, powered roof supports, plus a 373 kw power loading machine were installed. The face was of 3-metre section and the twin cutting drums of the power loader were capable of profiling the access roadways at each end of the face, thus reducing the work necessary to create "stable holes". This concept set the trend for all main production systems henceforward used at Tower.

In the late 1980's, a small but efficient new coal preparation plant was erected close to the drift entrance.

## Welcome on Board.

In December 1990, as previously with Fernhill, on Mardy's closure its workforce was incorporated into Tower. Integration of the Mardy men proved to be easier than was the case with Fernhill, notwithstanding banter about "Mardy bullshitters, marching back to work behind a brass band". The average age of the men was much younger (34 years of age) and not least, there had been much more social contact between the two valleys. Bwllfa Pit, which had been part of the Mardy complex, was itself in the Cynan Valley.

Rather than continually having to pump out the Mardy workings, they were allowed to flood. The Mardy workings were much deeper than Tower's (Tower no.4 shaft is 162m deep, whereas Mardy no.4 had a depth of 373m and Mardy no.3 - 391m). Nevertheless, an explosion proof and waterproof dam was constructed, sealing the only connecting roadway between the Mardy and Tower workings. This dam was designed to withstand the maximum conceivable water pressure, even if the level were to rise to the surface of the Bwllfa shaft.

## Survival.

### The Price Must be Right.

In January 1992, "Tower News", the colliery magazine, spoke of survival as being the overriding objective of the pit. By April of the following year new contracts with the power generators would come into force and coal had to be produced at a price that they were prepared to pay. This was £1.40 per GigaJoule. There were a number of positive aspects to report. Absenteeism was down to 5 percent, while the V32 face (which had followed on from the V29 as above) had been the first in South Wales to achieve a production of 2,400 t/day. Some 18 weeks before start-up of the V32, classroom teach-ins for team captains, craftsmen and officials had been held and these had paid off. Characteristics of the new equipment had been explained by manufacturers reps. Currently the V33 was in production and a development plan existed for replacement capacity.

### Transport Revolution.

The time was quickly approaching when all rope haulages would be removed from underground. The long distances now involved meant that large section roadways were necessary so as to minimise ventilation resistance. Such large sections, together with improvements in roadway safety and standards, allowed all supplies for the various worksites underground to be transported along the 18 miles of roadways by means of Freely Steerable Vehicles (FSV's). These can be described as heavy-duty forklift trucks, designed for rugged terrain. FSV's are self-propelled and diesel powered, with large rubber-tyred wheels, designed for minimum roadway penetration. They are operated from a centrally-placed driver's cab. They can carry up to 13 tonnes of materials and equipment to any district underground. They operate to and from a loading bay at the bottom of the drift. Between this point and the surface, transport of supplies is effected by a steel rope haulage.

This sea change in underground transport was epitomised by Tower, with horses eliminated and "humping" by human donkeys, a hated characteristic of traditional pit work, reduced to a minimum. This colliery, the last in South Wales to use pit ponies, was one of the first to introduce FSV's. The ponies finally left in 1984, when the last national miners' strike began. Stables, with their smell of hay and manure, were replaced by a garage, 1 mile from pit bottom, and reeking instead of oil.

# TOWER: CLOSURE AND BUY-OUT.

## Closure.

### No Future - Or Is There?

By 1992, of the underground workings, 85 per cent were less than 3 years old. The remaining 15 per cent had been reorganised and improved. All of this notwithstanding, British Coal came to regard Tower as being surplus to requirements. As on so many previous occasions, plans, ostensibly long-term, were changed. The associated crippling of a local community was of no relevance in the equation. This time, however, the game would be played differently.

In April 1994, Tower Colliery closed. It was the last mine owned by British Coal to work in the South Wales Coalfield. According to BC, the high level of gas emission at the coalface, which jeopardised both production and safety, had justified the closure. In addition it was maintained that reserves were fast depleting and no market existed for the high quality anthracite produced. To cap it all, the pit was geologically faulted. Consequent on all of this, it was not possible to cover the cost of mining there. During the 14-day period that the union was allowed to officially oppose closure, public statements from colliery management continued to emphasise doom and gloom as to the future.

Such a black picture did not convince the workforce. Neither did it convince colliery management. Meanwhile, while in public talking down the pit, secretly they were meeting to plan a management buy-out. This was the era of general re-privatisation and the Thatcher- inspired crusade for "capitalist freedom". Some individuals were making millions out of such buy-outs, the role of employees being that they are made to give of their utmost.

### Tower Does Not Play Ball.

The by now finely honed British Coal routine went into action. An attractive financial deal was offered to anyone who volunteered to leave. For those who did not accept redundancy within one month, the package would of course be withdrawn. As an additional flourish, the redundancy package was upped by nine thousand pounds, provided it was accepted within eight days. Unbelievably, it was not. The local NUM lodge proved highly motivated and emotionally committed to their pit, with a drive to keep it open and to provide employment in the Cynon Valley. Management disinformation and psychological pressure were met with a determination and a planning skill that proved to be unique in the whole saga of the industry's contraction. Publicity was the key and an intense campaign was carried out. There was a march of 280 miles to London.

On 15 April 1994, in the same week as the march, there was a 27-hour stay-down strike by veteran Tower miner Glyn Roberts and Ann Clwyd, local MP for the Cynon Valley. Ten years later, as one of "Blair's babes" and human rights spokesperson for the Labour Government, she would be noted for faithfully repeating the fatuous optimism on Iraq as per her master's voice. At the time of closure she was open to suggestion that authority be defied. Management's clenched-teeth reaction was to agree that the pit could stay open. However, wages would be cut, production targets increased and, when the pit did eventually close, redundancy payments reduced. Under such pressure the men buckled. They agreed that the pit should close, with 70 per cent voting for and 30 per cent against.

## Buy-out.

### No Guarantees.

In the agony of defeat, the germ of an idea took root in lodge thinking. In 1992, when Michael Heseltine had announced the closure of the 31 pits, he had said, quoting an idea that apparently originated with former Chairman of the Conservative Party, Cecil Parkinson, "If the miners want to keep their pits, let them buy them themselves". Tower was a lodge noted for its militancy, one of those who, against the opposition of the majority, had worked and schemed to get the 1984 strike of the ground. Now, the energy involved in the bruiser tactics of earlier confrontations was redirected. In this final confrontation they would eventually come away with a workers buy-out, for a coalmine unique in the world.

The publicity campaign went into high gear with letters to the great and the good. Parliament was lobbied and the Wales Co-operative Development and Training Centre approached for help in preparing a bid. This organization had strong trade union links, being the only co-operative in the UK financed by the TUC.

A meeting was held to bring previous employees on board. To this first meeting 178 men turned up. The suggestion that they should invest £2,000 of their redundancy money in a scheme to buy back the pit was met with an initial incredulous, deafening silence, followed by an almighty row. At the end of it, only one man voted against. Regular meetings were held with all the men and a steering committee of eight elected to work with the Development and Training Centre. The number of miners prepared to put their trust in the lodge subsequently increased to 239. Confronted with management statements that the pit had no future, with no guarantee that they would have a job at the end of it all, or even that the pit if obtained could sell its coal, each individual would nevertheless increase his initial £2,000 investment to a total of £8,000.

## Management Joins The Pickets.

Local management support for, or involvement in, the concept of a workers buy-out was noticeable for its absence. The possibility of such involvement had been brusquely rejected at the start of the buy-back process, no doubt influenced by the evaporation of their own dreams of riches. British Coal would also keep its distance. For an organization that in recent years had made a virtue of "the smack of firm management" and for those individuals with a family background of management in the mining industry, the whole enterprise no doubt seemed like a peasants' revolt. The prospect of making common cause with the revolutionaries of 1984-85 would have gone against the grain. Since by law certain officials having the necessary statutory qualifications are necessary before a mine can be operated, such management rejection potentially meant death for the project. The necessary officials include a manager, a unit electrical engineer, plus a unit mechanical engineer.

Consequently, it was at first sight a bizarre development when Mr. Phillip Weekes, previously Area Director of South Wales under the NCB/British Coal, responded positively to a request. Although well past retirement age and not in the very best of health, he would be prepared to act as Chairman for the new enterprise should it get off the ground, thus showing where his heart lay. Previously Mr. Weekes had been the source of such pre-strike newspaper headlines as, "Sheer Bloody Madness". When an official at Tower wrote to him during the 1984-85 strike, commenting on the lodge's obsession with "revolution" and referring to the "disgusting objects" thrown through his letter-box due to his reluctance to get involved, Mr. Weekes had replied with understanding.

The lodge had not only been instrumental in initiating and maintaining the national strike of 1984-85, they had also voted to continue, even after Mardy had been against. More recently they had played a leading role in ensuring the re-election of Arthur Scargill as President of the NUM, against the inclination of their own coalfield leadership. Nevertheless, and contrary to initial appearances, a basis for rational discussion did exist between a former NCB senior manager on one side and left-wing leading lights on the other. This synergistic relationship between those previously on different sides of the fence was to reap rewards, being an example of a "third way", and in keeping with the valley's collectivist community traditions.

A valley boy himself, Mr. Weekes would reveal himself as being a long-term card-carrying member of the Labour Party. An example of liberally inclined management, so maligned by MacGregor, he had himself been a victim of that era, among other things having lost his Board membership. During the national strike MacGregor had received correspondence criticising Weekes for "drinking tea with strikers". In a word, he epitomised that management style which had produced such incredulity on the part of Margaret Thatcher. Mr. Weekes was to be respected as a fair-minded man, and recognised as someone who understood the Welsh miner. The potential Chairman was now to throw himself into the, as he put it, "new adventure", becoming a figurehead during the campaign and providing invaluable support. His contacts and experience, developed during a lifetime in the industry, proved to be invaluable and gave credibility to the enterprise. His personal experience covered the whole spectrum of post-war mining, from private enterprise with the Tredegar Iron and Coal Company to nationalisation and now, with the wheel turned full circle, back to private enterprise again. The numerous interviews and comments, which he gave to the media during this period, were a major influence in legitimising the bid in the eyes of many professional people and financial institutions. During the initial four years his leadership of the company was of vital importance, with all directors who served under him benefiting from, and being inspired by, his experience and guidance.

He passed away in June 2003.


The New Regime.

On the lodge's side, militancy did not mean an inflexible following of Communist dogma. One aspect of their militancy had always been a determination to ensure that management carry out development work, necessary to ensure the pit's future. Four years after the buy-out, on Mr. Weekes's retirement due to ill-health, this slim, white-haired and droll patrician figure would be replaced as Company Chairman by the blond, ebullient heavyweight, Tyrone O'Sullivan. For twenty-two years a member of the Tower lodge, he had been a major driving force during the workers buy-out. He is also a director of the company and an ideal "front man" for the organization and the hard core of competence behind him. Since then decorated with an OBE ("old broken-down electrician" according to his men) he drove a Vauxhall Vectra and in 2003 earned a salary of £35,000, making him, in his own words, "the lowest paid chairman in Europe". In March 2004 he was voted in as Chairman for an additional 3-year term.

Gradually the management team was built up, as men in possession of the necessary qualifications came on board. Some of the British Coal management team did return, including a number judged to have old-style attitudes. The hard core, however, who had caused aggravation during the buy-back period, did not return, in spite of their wishes to the contrary. The associated reduction in status, which such a return would have involved, proved to be unacceptable to them.


Finance.

With a management team now in existence, financing could be applied for. Specialist advice was required on structuring the bid, since it was to be made in open competition with large and experienced mining companies. Price Waterhouse was selected as financial advisors - ironically the same company the government had used to sequestrate NUM funds during the 1984-85 strike. After four months of work a business plan was produced, incorporating a mining plan, an independent survey and future projections.

Barclays Bank, the only bank prepared to meet the buy-out team, came up with a loan of £2 million, on condition that the team could raise their own £2 million. This they were able to do when individual miners increased their contributions from £2,000 to £8,000. This was mainly redundancy money, although 60 of them took out personal loans to fund the investment. In effect the mine was purchased with an initial down payment of £2 million, followed by a system of deferred payments. A royalty payment to the government for each tonne of coal sold over a period of five years was negotiated. Michael Heseltine, Secretary of State for Trade and Industry, had been unsympathetic but John Redwood, then Secretary of State for Wales, pledged his support.

In October 1994, at the Tory party conference, success of the workers' buy-out was announced. This was not a venue which those involved would regard as being an appropriate culmination of their efforts, but the Tories evidently sensed that some public relations mileage could be made. In any event, vision, initiative and drive had defeated the competition, overcome all obstacles and mastered the learning process in a project completely different to anything which those involved had ever previously attempted. Dyed-in-the-wool socialists had learned how to survive in a hardheaded capitalist world. The deal was officially completed in December.

Triumph.

On 2 January 1995, the mine was re-opened under the name of Goitre Tower Anthracite Limited. Already on the first shift, two and a half cuts were made along the face by the power loader, with the men feeling "as if they were walking on air". In spite of prospects having been talked down by the previous management, the weekly production target was achieved after just 4 days', instead of 5 days' work. Within three months they were in profit. In the first full year, a pre-tax profit of £3,600,000 was achieved, with such success continuing in subsequent years. Coal was provided to Aberthaw Power Station, the steel industry, domestic markets and overseas. The superior quality anthracite is used for households and industry while the lower quality coal goes to Aberthaw in the form of small-grained "duff". Output and manpower, during the first years after the buy-out, are summarised below:

| Year | 1995 | 1996 | 1997 | 1998 |
|------|------|------|------|------|
| Saleable output (t) | 480,000 | 560,000 | 560,000 | 580,000 |
| Manpower | 310 | 342 | 360 | 360 |

Tower had been built up by British Coal to handle an annual production of 1 Mt. Consequently, its infrastructure was more than adequate. As a comparison, in 1990 the budgeted annual output under British Coal for Tower/Mardy had been 600,0000 t, with a manpower of 853 for the combined mine. Some left when Mardy finally closed and not all of those remaining were prepared to put up their money and join the new enterprise. To join retrospectively was not allowed.

**Tower Coal.**

Quality.

The general quality specification of the coal produced at Tower is as follows:

- Thermal Content:     30 GJ/t (British coal on average has 24.3 GJ/t)

- Ash:     4.4% (British coal on average has 15-20%)

- Sulphur:     0.95% (British coal on average has 1.6%)

- Chlorine:     0.03%

- Volatiles:     7.8-8.0%

Markets.

Of the 1998 production, 34 per cent was for British Steel, 26 per cent for Aberthaw Power Station, 26 per cent for the household market and the remainder to general industry. Although the principal requirement of the steel industry is for coking coal, which Tower does not produce, Tower semi-anthracite was mixed with coking coal/coke so as to improve thermal characteristics of the smelting process. The power station coal used at Aberthaw is in the form of a 50/50 blend with other, higher volatile South Wales coals from open cast. The station also imports coal.

Under a contract awarded by the Central Purchasing Consortium of Welsh Local Authorities, Tower delivered direct to over 100 schools and other public buildings in South Wales. The wholly-owned coal pre-packing subsidiary, Welsh Dragon Coal Limited, distributed anthracite that was mined and washed at the colliery. Also available were bituminous house coal and smokeless briquettes. Outside Wales, Evans and Reid Ltd. of Cardiff distribute Tower products. As part of the marketing strategy, expert advice is offered concerning total energy packages including fuel supply, heating equipment, installation and maintenance services, plus ash removal.

In 1995, the first coal exports from Cardiff docks in recent years took place, when Tower coal was exported to Europe, e.g. Spain, Ireland and Germany, for the power station and processed fuel markets.

## TOWER: SURVIVAL.

### Mother Nature.

On 22 October 1999, Mother Nature made herself felt in the form of a recorded earth tremor. Fissures opened up between the underground workings in the combined 5+7 feet seam and the 9 feet seam above. Under pressure, heavy gas ingress from the latter polluted the production district, with 2 per cent being measured in the return airway (by law, men have to be withdrawn at a gas content of 1.25 per cent and above). As a consequence, production was shut down for a period of three months. Methane drainage was extended and resort made to coal stocks on the surface for market supply.

### The Markets Change.

Steel.

In 2001, Tower's skill at survival was again put to the test. In that year a requirement by the South Wales steel industry for a price reduction of 5 per cent, which Tower did not feel able to meet, resulted in the loss of that market. Fortunately, this coincided with an increase in the coal burn by Aberthaw, resulting from higher gas+oil prices. Initially plagued by the generator's reluctance to sign a long-term contract, in the course of that year such a contract was signed.

Electricity.

Ten merry-go-round trains per week depart the railhead for Aberthaw Power Station on the South Wales coast, transporting fine coal or "duff". The remaining coal is shipped out by road. Aberthaw is currently by far the most important market for Tower. The coal burn at Aberthaw involves mixing the semi-anthracite from Tower with other, lower quality coals (the 4 foot seam at Tower, although not worked at present, would be suitable for such mixing). Tower has been supplying Aberthaw on a series of three-year contracts, meeting approximately 25 per cent of its requirements. The decision by Aberthaw in 2003 to install Flue Gas Desulphurisation (FGD) implies a long-term future for the station. It is hoped that Tower will be around to continue supplying part of their requirements.

Briquettes.

There is a continuing decline in the UK domestic and products market. As compensation, the only way forward is to break into the briquette market, with the European continent being its centre of gravity. To this end, Tower bought its own briquette manufacturing plant at Capelhendre in West Wales.

In April 2004 this installation was replaced by a new one, constructed adjacent to the coal preparation plant at Tower. This market is highly lucrative, with export potential such as to France and Ireland. On the continent of Europe, briquettes were once universal for domestic heating. The reduction in overall market size has caused such plants there to shut down. Tower looks forward to supplying the rump market that remains. Currently briquetting is proceeding on two shifts per day, with the intention of increasing this to three shifts.

Statistics.

In 2002, Tower achieved its highest output to date, with 630,000 tonnes. Employment at the mine totalled 440, of which 320 were shareholders. A contracting firm provided other employees. Of the production, Aberthaw used 450,000 t and 140,000 t were consumed as general domestic and industrial products. The remaining 40,000 t were processed in Tower's own plant for briquette manufacture.

By 2004, with a production of approximately 600,000t/a, 70 per cent is sent to the railhead for transport to Aberthaw, 28 per cent is sent out by road as high grade products and 2 per cent as briquettes.

## Modern Mining - as she is done.

### The Seam.

Although in the past up to 14 seams have been worked at Tower and adjacent mines, current production is concentrated on a single 300 m long coalface in the 5+7 feet combined seam. The two seams are very close together in this area, being separated only by a band of "muck". This is loaded out with the coal and rejected at the coal preparation plant. In spite of some local opposition, additional land has been allocated for the tipping of waste. Typically, the mined section is 1.65 m, with 1.3 m of this being coal.

### The System.

The power loader is a type 4LS09 ranging drum shearer from the company Joy, designed to produce 55 tonnes of coal per minute in a seam thickness between 1.4-3.5 metres. The twin cutting drums (one at each end) are of 1.82 metre diameter and each can be raised or lowered hydraulically on its mounting arm. Movement along the face is by means of a chainless (i.e. rack and pinion) haulage. The machine is controlled by radio remote control, enabling the operator to select an optimal position, not necessarily directly adjacent to the machine itself. Supports are self-advancing. The production system represents current state-of-the-art as far as coal mining is concerned.

### Production Philosophy.

The production philosophy at Tower is to work this single longwall face on the retreat method, three shifts per day, five days per week. While the standard shift pattern is 5 x 7.25 hrs per week, at the coalface individuals work 4 x 9 hrs, except on afternoons. Face maintenance is carried out between afternoons and nights.

### Water.

At present water ingress is being experienced on the current V44 coalface. A highly motivated workforce will be instrumental in overcoming this, as well as other challenges such as faulting. Water ingress is having an effect, not only upon production conditions but also upon the coal preparation plant where the product is now received in a wet condition. In the words of Tyrone O'Sullivan, written in the colliery magazine of summer 2004:

"Water does not stop you producing coal. It's how you control the water that counts. In the coldest countries in the world, they don't freeze up every winter. They learn to live with the ice and snow. And we must live with the water at Tower".

### Replacement Capacity.

Simultaneously with the operation of one face, roadways for a replacement face are being driven. This replacement face will also be worked on the retreat and is fitted out with a second set of equipment, before the working coalface reaches its boundary. Continuity of production is therefore ensured. Such coalface development is financed out of profits. For these new drivages, a DOSCO LH1300 heading machine is employed. A metal arm, capped by a rotating cone sprinkled with cutting picks, is manoeuvred hydraulically to chew away at the face of the drivage.

Transport.

Production is transported the entire distance to the coal preparation plant on the surface by means of conveyors. A purpose-built underground bunker, 4.8 km from pit bottom, smooths out dips and surges. Rate of extraction is a function of the rate of sales. With the face being 11.27 km from pit bottom, a to-and-fro travelling time for the face workers of 2.25 hrs. per shift is involved. The conveyors are used for man-riding in addition to coal transportation (top belt for outbye and the return bottom belt for inbye).

## TOWER: THE FUTURE.

### Reserves.

Boundaries.

The Tower "take" is split by a series of faults which throw the level of the seams up or down by varying distances (up to 50 metres). Extent of the take is defined to the north by the boundary of the coal measures; to the south by the waterlogged old workings of Fernhill; to the east by the old workings of Mardy, also waterlogged, and to the west by the Glyncorrwg Fault. Beyond this lie waterlogged workings of the old Glyncorrwg Colliery. Tower operations lie currently to the west and heading more and more in that direction. Experience of working Glyncorrwg indicates a likely increase in fault density, as well as steep local gradients.

The workings at Tower are interleaved with old workings from Fernhill. In addition there were a number of old drift mines in this area and there are extensive remains of iron workings dating back several hundred years. All these need to be considered very carefully when planning new developments. Water ingress from opencast workings in 1974, and inadvertent incursion into the old workings of Rhigos Colliery in 1982, with consequent flooding, are indicative of the danger.

Potential.

In November 1993, prior to Tower's closure by British Coal, an assessment of the reserves remaining was carried out. In the table below, workable seams are given in descending order. Also given is the vertical separation from the previous seam, the estimated quantity of exploitable coal per seam, and the estimated time required to work out those reserves.

| Seam | Approximate vertical separation from previous seam | Estimated reserves (Mt) | Estimated time required to work the reserves. | Remarks |
|---|---|---|---|---|
| 2ft. 9in. | - | - | - | Not assessed |
| 4ft. | 20m | 4.5 | 7 years | |
| 6ft. | 30m | 6.0 | 9 years | Too close together |
| Red Vein | 7m | 5.7 | 8 years | to work both |
| 9ft. | 26m | 3.75 | 6 years | |
| Combined 7ft./5ft. | 62m | 7.5 | 12 | |

- The only seam deeper than the combined 7ft/5ft is the Gellideg.

- The Red Vein had never been worked at Tower and only one face in the 6ft. However, a high intensity of thrust faulting was expected in these two seams and there was no data on the strength of roof or floor. In the extreme west of the "take" these seams were above the flooded 9ft. workings of the old Glyncorrwg Colliery.

- Much of the reserves in the 9ft. had been lost when the workings in this seam were flooded in 1982. In addition, Fernhill had also exploited this seam extensively, with faces from Fernhill having worked right across the V32, V33, V34 and V36 panels in the combined 7ft./5ft. at Tower.

- Between the 9ft. and the combined 7ft./5ft. lie the Bute and the Yard seams. These are not considered workable in this area. The Bute contains extensive and flooded workings from Fernhill. In this seam the P6 face from Fernhill has worked right across the main east-west lateral access roadways, the backbone of Tower's current production.

A review of this assessment regarded the figures quoted as being too optimistic, with a probable reduction in the estimated reserves of greater than 50 per cent. The reasons given for this were likely variability in the seams, plus the probability of washouts and changes in the quality and structure. In addition, natural or man-made hazards had to be planned for, e.g. mine water and gas, plus surface constraints such as the Llyn Fawr Reservoir together with its associated water tunnel, and also the motorway. Even if a reduction of this order of magnitude proved to be the case, this still left the mine with a significant life in front of it. Nevertheless, British Coal's decision was for closure.

### Current Seam.

All future reserves in the seam currently being worked, the composite seven/five feet, lie to the west. In this seam is the backbone of current production, namely the twin trunk roadways running westwards from both shaft and drift into the production districts. Here the panels of coal are worked, one at a time, to the north and to the south of these main roadways. As time goes on, and reserves are extracted, the western boundary looms. This is the Glyncorrwg Fault, with behind it the waterlogged workings of the old Glyncorrwg Colliery.

Unless capital is available to access other seams, life of the pit will be determined by reserves in the current seam. These lie mainly south of the main east-west roadways. Four faces had already been planned by British Coal to work here. Over and above the British Coal plans, Tower Colliery proposed to work up to nine additional faces beyond these, although little exploration data was available at that point in time. North of the main east-west roadways, the panels are even-numbered. South of these they are odd-numbered. Currently, the V44 is being worked and experiencing water ingress.

Generally, reserves north of the main east-west roadways consist of panels having limited extent, due to known or anticipated faulting plus the fact that 45 m above the reserves in the northwest are flooded Fernhill workings in the Bute seam. To work this area, consultants have recommended drilling, with probable dewatering. For the limited reserves available in this area, Tower Colliery does not regard this as being cost-effective. Company projections are at present based on economic mining continuing further and further to the west in the current seam. Reserves to the northeast will be taken at the end of mine life, as they currently protect the main mine drift from subsidence. Five additional panels in the current seam are regarded as capable of being worked. This should ensure continuity of production through to 2008.

### Longer Term.

With regard to a longer-term future, a report on coal production in England and Wales at the turn of the century, by International Mining Consultants (IMC) for the DTI, states that the mine has the potential to access other seams in the mid to long-term, subject to successful exploration and financing of the development work. Although the quality of coal is not regarded as being as good, future potential exists in the 9 feet seam, roughly 100 m above the present level, and in the 6 feet seam, an additional 30 m above that. The future working of these alternative seams, following exhaustion of the composite seven/five feet, is under active consideration. Order of magnitude cost of accessing these seams, either by drivages driven upwards from the existing main roadways or drifts driven downwards from the surface, is assessed as being approximately £20 M.

In March 2003, the UK government announced as part of their white paper on energy a coal investment scheme to help existing pits develop new reserves, where they are economically viable and safeguard jobs. This included up to 30 per cent of the cost of opening new reserves. This 30 per cent of government aid would still leave £14 M of capital that would have to be raised externally, since such a sum is not available from revenue. Tower's long-term future depends upon securing extended sales contracts, so as to warrant the investment involved in accessing other seams.

Mineral rights belong to the state. Under the Coal Privatisation Act, an additional licence would have to be sought from the Coal Authority to work other seams. Following a professionally prepared application, it is unlikely that permission to work other seams would be refused. Project evaluation involves boreholes, to assess not only the marketability of new seams but also whether the two existing sets of coalface equipment (each valued at £20 M) could be used. Should the decision be made to access new reserves, then Tower would hope for a grant from the Welsh Assembly. The latter is prepared to invest such finance in new factories employing 400-500 people so why not in a new coal seam, thereby securing employment for an equivalent number? In this day and age, however, the prevailing wisdom is that private companies must largely look after themselves.

## Speculation.

Tower's Days Numbered?

In 2003, the marketing situation deteriorated to the worst since the company had started, eight years before. As a result, Betws Colliery closed with the loss of 110 jobs. The reduced operating economics resulted in the four managers who had bought the mine selling the surface area as a business park and housing development, thus crowning their overall operating profit with a real estate windfall. As a cooperative Tower had other priorities. As it was, market discipline resulted in a freeze on any pay increase. The Betws closure, combined with limited reserves in the seam currently worked at Tower, encouraged speculation that Tower itself had only a life of one or two years remaining. Under market pressure due to competition combined with mild weather, plus the fact that workings were extending ever further westward into uncertain ground, Tower was described as surviving rather than thriving.

Rejection.

On 1 September 2003, Chairman Tyrone O'Sullivan rejected such speculation. Five-year and seven-year plans were in place and would continue, with the possibility of opening at least two more seams. Business plans were being worked on, with new drifts being an option. Aberthaw Power Station would be around until 2015 or 2018. The proposed opencast mine at nearby Ffos y Fran would not significantly undercut the Tower production costs since they also required investment in planning, development and restoration of the site. This latter proposal, by Miller Argent and called the East Merthyr Reclamation Scheme might also have heightened concern about Tower's future, in spite of the planning objections usual with open cast schemes. This particular scheme aims to extract 10Mt of coal over a 17-year period.

Mr. O'Sullivan said that his company was flexible and geared up for the future, adapting to new markets by developing the production of briquettes for sale to Belgium, France and Ireland. They would however be looking to receive positive support from the UK Government and Welsh Assembly in the years to come. He contrasted the £30 M of government subsidies available to the British coal industry over a period of 3 years with the £2.3 billion available annually to German pits.

## Challenges.

New and Better Ways.

Of necessity, and notwithstanding their antipathy to Ian MacGregor, Tower has taken on board his philosophy for the industry's future, namely; a new approach that is constantly on the search for opportunities to develop the company, plus new and better ways of doing things on the road to high-output and low-cost. MacGregor's hated expressions, "administration", "bureaucracy" and "the status quo", have produced a similar negative resonance at Tower. The forty or so managerial staff under British Coal have been reduced to 14. There are 27 officials. The deputy's responsibilities are confined to safety. An overman, working together with the coalface captain, supervises production. The workforce elects the latter.

The buy-out process itself reduced the core workforce to those prepared to invest their redundancy money. Additional, non-share-holding employees are employed from a contracting company where necessary. The shareholders are multi-skilled, being flexible enough to cover a number of different jobs, and this is recognised with the reward of additional rest days. Whatever the future may bring, there is no resting on laurels. Challenges are seen as opportunities.

## Gas.

The fact that it is the gassiest mine at present operating in the UK has been an incentive to install a methane drainage scheme. In addition to reducing the danger of gas accumulations underground, the methane is used as fuel for six containerised 11,000-volt generator sets, driven by spark ignition gas engines of Deutz manufacture. These were installed on the surface in partnership with United Utilities. They comprise the largest generation plant in Britain to run on gas from a working colliery. A treatment plant on the surface cleans the gas of water and dust. Initial capacity of this plant was up to 1,550 litres/sec of gas. In spite of initial problems resulting from the high moisture content of the gas, each generator set generates up to 1.3 megawatts of electricity. Since the internal electrical load is 5-6 megawatts, not only is the colliery normally self-sufficient in energy but excess energy may be exported to the national grid. The generators are designed for continuous operation at full load, with 90 per cent availability throughout the year. Annual savings are in the range of £700,000 -800,000. Additional sets might well be installed.

In accordance with the emissions trading scheme of the European Union, the generating plant has had allocated to it an acceptable level of carbon dioxide emission. Currently, issue is being taken with a contradiction in this scheme. Whereas electricity generated from methane originating from landfill rubbish sites is classed as a renewable form of energy, this is not the case if the methane originates in a working mine. If it were, Tower would be entitled to Renewable Obligation Certificates (R.O.C.s), worth up to £1.2 M per annum. The only way that the plant could reduce its emission of carbon dioxide is to release more methane directly into the environment, instead of burning it in the generator sets. Since methane is itself a greenhouse gas, 21 times more harmful than carbon dioxide, there is a breakdown in logic here.

## Margam.

In 1998, the announcement was made that Tower Colliery, together with Celtic Energy, would develop the large reserves of coking coal east of and directly adjacent to, the Margam Steelworks on the South Wales coast. In the first new deep-mine in the coalfield for decades, 200 miners would work an estimated 27 Mt of reserves for at least 20 years, at an annual production of 0.4 Mt. In addition to the adjacent steelworks, markets would include cement production and power generation. Such prime coal, of a suitable type and adjacent to its customer, is an attractive concept. Celtic Energy made the appropriate mineral planning and licence applications. As part of the concept, Tower would supply the deep mining know-how. Another company, Modal Mining, made similar applications for an adjacent area, west of the Celtic Energy application.

This project had been simmering in the background for some time. It was first mooted by the NCB in the mid-1970's. British Coal also carried out a deep mine feasibility study in the late 1980's. The NCB's conclusion was that the project was not economically feasible at that time, mainly due to the interest payments that would have been incurred. In 1990 British Coal investigated a smaller scheme, based on a drift access, and two additional boreholes were drilled. At this time and in this area the Gellideg seam in particular was judged by British Steel to be of excellent quality. In total, British Coal considered three seams for possible extraction, all of which are of coking coal grade. Their conclusions were:

- Two foot nine: A consistently clean seam, with thickness varying between 1.5-1.8 m. The structure above the seam, however, was not considered capable of providing a good roof for working under.

- Upper nine feet: A normally clean seam and is expected to vary in thickness between 1.0-2.0 m. The roof is less disturbed than the two foot nine.

- Gellideg: A seam is of very high quality (ash 2.5-4.5%, sulphur 0.4-0.7%, chlorine 0.1%) and varies in thickness between 2.0-2.6 m. The roof and floor strata are strong. There is a possibility of sandstone washouts affecting the seam.

Borehole information shows the following seams (east of area):

| Seam | Depth (metres) |
|------|----------------|
| No. 1 Rhondda | 165 |
| No. 3 Rhondda (already worked out) | 435 |
| Two foot nine. | 785 |
| Upper four feet. | 818 |
| Lower four feet. | 828 |
| Six feet. | 850 |
| Upper nine feet. | 906 |
| Lower nine feet. | 910 |
| Bute. | 920 |
| Five feet. | 985 |
| Gellideg. | 1032 |

Celtic Energy considered 8 Mt of coal available in the Upper Nine Feet, with 1.65 m seam thickness, plus 14 Mt in the Gellideg, with 2.3 m seam thickness.

In the western part of the area the six feet seam may be considered. This is over 2 m thick. However, investigation showed it as being highly disturbed. It is likely to be difficult to work. The strata dips at about 15 degrees to the north-northeast and faulting has broken up the reserves into blocks normally too small for longwall mining. This makes room and pillar working the likely option. The degree of deformation is highest at the southern outcrop, where the seams come to the surface.

The Celtic Energy/Tower proposal was for an underground mine, having drift access from the periphery of the nearby Park Slip opencast site. Celtic Energy operates this. Entry from the base of the highwall at the edge of the opencast excavation offered some reduction in drift drivage costs. However, the major faults anticipated would still require a costly capital scheme. For a capital expenditure of £25 M, two drifts would be driven, at a gradient of 1 in 4. Production thereafter would be by room and pillar methods, with output anticipated at 0.4-0.5 Mt/annum. Since the coal was of prime quality, this should ensure high proceeds, with markets in steel, power generation and general industry. Such high proceeds would counteract the fact that extensive exploration had indicated a disturbed geology, likely to preclude any high productivity mining equipment. Gas problems could prove to be both a nuisance and a safety hazard.

In late 2000, with the increase in the price of foreign coal, confidence in the project was reaffirmed. Not all ideas come up trumps, however, and realisation depended on the willingness of potential investors to invest. This in turn was a function, both of the steel industry's future in South Wales and of the world market price for coking coal.

In 2001 Tower lost the steel industry market that they already had, when CORUS, the plant operators, demanded the lowest prices possible. In addition, the blast furnaces at Llanwern Steelworks in Newport closed down. Thus ended a potentially exciting opportunity, and another chapter in the long-running saga of the Margam coal reserves.

## Making Coal Greener.

On 17 June 2003, a one-day conference was held at the Rhondda Heritage Centre on the subject of Welsh Coal. Included in the presentation by Marketing Director Phil White was a description of the research and development work Tower has engaged upon, among other things in blending coal with biomass - sawdust, household waste etc., as a move towards green energy. In his conclusion, Tyrone O'Sullivan stressed the need for "the greens of this world to shake hands with the coal producers".

## Dreams.

At Tower, visionary thinking is alive. One of Mr. O'Sullivan's more exotic concepts, mooted but as yet on hold, is for an underground tourist centre. In an example of industrial democracy at work the project was voted down by the work force, where hardheaded financial conservatives remain to be convinced. A tourist centre, but with a difference, the concept involves an hotel, but one sited underground. There would be an audio-visual environment where the sights were genuine and the sounds were genuine, since coal would still be won, handled and prepared, albeit on an appropriately small scale. When imagination takes flight the sky's the limit and if the lessons of Fernhill's wild west tourist ranch are learnt, the "lost civilisation" of Welsh coal mining may yet come alive again for future generations, here where it all started.

## TOWER: THE MINERS NEXT STEP?
## Expert Opinions?
### March-Back.

The march-back to work on 2 January 1995, following twenty months' of closure, was as internationally newsworthy and historic as that at Mardy ten years previously. There was, however, a profound difference between the two occasions. This time the triumph was not staged but genuine. It was a socialist triumph, of individuals over an organization judged to be remote and impersonal, and whose prognostications of doom were in the event proven to be ludicrous.

### The Experts' Report.

In 1993, a report by the Parliamentary Trade and Industry Committee assessed Tower's future as being, "either short-life or less able to withstand the rigors of the new ESI" (Electricity Supply Industry). The same report was equally dismissive of Betws, "unlikely to be viable against future markets". In the same year, the John T. Boyd consultant's analysis gave Betws a life of 5-8 years (total reserves of 4 Mt to be worked at a rate of 0.5-0.75 Mt per annum). From that date, its actual life proved to be 10 years. As far as Tower was concerned, Boyds considered its life to be limited to four and a half years (total reserves of 3.6 Mt to be worked at a rate of 0.8 Mt per annum). They quoted one fault in particular as being likely to stop the working face and render the pit uneconomic. This was an argument used by British Coal in their closure decision. In reality, practical mining know-how, combined with determination, enabled the face to work through the fault. Additional and appropriate roof support in the fault's vicinity meant that it was not the pit killer that the international experts had predicted. Conversely, what they did propose for the UK mining industry, in particular double entry faces where adjacent panels use a common gate road, were not practical at Tower.

## Small is Beautiful.

Philosophical Thoughts.

Ironically, the expression" Small is beautiful" originated from a one- time economic advisor to the NCB, Dr. Schumacher, and was in marked contrast to the big pit obsession of the Board. His concept was to be proven at Tower, a left-over remnant of that very organization. With the "super mine" of Selby confined to history, Tower just keeps on chugging along. Difficult though the conditions might be, it was confirmed that the South Wales Coalfield still offered niche opportunities. How many other closures, one wonders, ostensibly on economic grounds, were justified on an equally questionable basis? As far back as 1981-82 Tower was losing £33.2 for every tonne produced. It could have been closed on economic grounds then. How many other pits had latent within them the untapped potential for success? Now, mine owners from Cuba to the former Eastern block travel to see how workers' participation functions. In striving for their community and the welfare of the workforce, it is unlikely that the lodge had any time to spare for philosophical thought. In practice, Manicheanism was the philosophy, with socialists learning to employ capitalist tools.

Shareholder Employees.

In 2004 there were approximately 400 shareholders and 120 contractor's men. At the time of the initial buy-out there were 239 shareholders. During the original buy-out, each employee invested £8,000 in the form of one-pound shares. Shares that were worth £8,000 at the time of the buy-out had, by 2003, appreciated to £36,000. Consequently, a new employee, who on completion of his trial period is also required to invest £8,000, will receive a correspondingly reduced number of shares. An annual dividend is paid on each share. As a consequence, more recent employees receive a lower total dividend. Since they do an equivalent amount of work, this has resulted in heartfelt debate!

On retirement, shares are maintained in possession of the former employee. Otherwise, on leaving the company, shares are cashed in to a company trust. Following the buy-out, the new owners introduced contributory pension rights for all miners for the first time, plus an extra week of annual leave (making it 38 working days). Sickness and accident benefit is first class. There is also concessionary house coal. Employee remuneration remains in the region of 42-48 per cent of total operating costs. Tower's reputation as an employer, in an area where jobs are thin on the ground, is indicated by the fact that a vacancy for three surface labourers resulted in 300 applicants. Unlike British Coal and in stark contrast to the remainder of the UK mining industry, employees are paid a standard salary, with no production bonus. The latter is judged as being detrimental to safety. The equivalent of the British Coal bonus was divided among the workforce and added to basic salary. Overtime working is avoided if possible.

In 2003, face workers were earning £482 per week. This is high compared with other surviving collieries and compared with £340 per week at Bettws, prior to its closure. There is a night shift premium of £70 per week. Weekend work is not subject to any overtime mark-up but is paid at standard rate (or time off in lieu). In NCB days, 150 per cent payment for Saturday and 200 per cent for Sunday was the norm. This is perhaps an indication of different standards accepted when the workforce itself owns the organization. Similarly, when the hot summer of 2003 reduced turnover by £3 M in six weeks and contributed to the absence of any pay rise between April 2002 and 2004, there was no movement for industrial action. Under the NCB this would have been unthinkable.

## Utopia?

The Nationalisation Dream.

In 1910, Thomas Straker, General Secretary of the Northumberland miners, gave his evidence to the Sankey Commission, recommending public ownership of the pits:

"Any administration of the mines under nationalisation must not leave the miner in the position of a mere wage-earner, whose sole energies are directed to the will of another —— he must have a share in the management of the industry —— he must feel that the industry is run by him to produce coal for the use of the community, instead of profit for a few people". When nationalisation eventually came, this lofty aim was not achieved.

## Workers' Control - the Theory.

The idea of miners' ownership originated in South Wales and, after 83 years, was uniquely realised there. The Tower example of reconciliation between the forces of labour and capital, historically in such crass contradiction, was seen by some as a final realisation of "The Miners' Next Step", the 1912 pamphlet produced in the wake of the Tonypandy riots. This had predicted that nationalisation would be a political error and that nothing less than direct ownership should be the miners' next step. The final objective was the achievement of a state where:

"Mankind shall at last have pleasure and inclination to really live as men and not as the beasts which perish". The strategy advocated to achieve this was:

- The old policy of identity of interest between employers and ourselves be abolished and a policy of open hostility be installed.

- With regard to elimination of the employer, the pamphlet states that nationalisation, "docs not lead in this direction but simply makes a national trust with all the force of the Government behind it, whose one concern will be to see that the industry is run in such a way as to pay the interest on the bonds with which the Coalowners are paid out, and to extract as more profit as possible in order to relieve the taxation of other landlords and capitalists".

As an alternative to nationalisation, what was advocated was:

- Our objective be to build up an organization, that will ultimately take over the mining industry, and carry it on in the interest of the workers.

Industrial democracy was advocated, on the following basis:

- To have a vote in determining who shall be your fireman (note: now called a deputy), manager, inspector etc. is to have a vote in determining the conditions, which shall rule your working life. On that vote will depend in a large measure your safety of life and limb, of your freedom of oppression by petty bosses, and would give you an intelligent interest in and control over your conditions of work. To vote for a man to represent you in Parliament, to make rules for, and assist in appointing officials to rule you, is a different proposition altogether.

## Workers' Control - the Practice.

Tower is proud to carry the flag of Welsh trade union militancy but, when eighty-three years later the objective of miners' ownership was finally achieved, albeit for one mine as opposed to the whole industry, there were to be some anomalies between 1912 theory and 1995 practice. Although there is no place for old-style authoritarian attitudes, in a competitive and potentially dangerous environment there is an appreciation that discipline, and a management structure, are necessary. In addition, it is also sometimes necessary to make quick decisions within this management structure, without prior reference to the workforce. Similarly, during the negotiation of commercial agreements, confidentiality has to be maintained. The amount of money set aside as a reserve is also a management decision.

The selection of their management by workers themselves, in an environment where safety requirements and technical know-how result in statutory qualifications being a prerequisite, is not regarded as realistic (an exception is Team Captain on the coalface). Equally unrealistic was an initial justification of pilfering on the basis that, "it belongs to me anyway". Similarly there have been mutterings about individuals abusing the excellent sickness scheme. Utopia is only possible in the event of everyone being a genuine socialist, which in reality few are. Management responsibility includes allocation of personnel (which, interestingly enough, was not the case at Fernhill where union power was the order of the day).

This aspect has even caused a strike. This occurred on a Monday morning when two faceworkers, who had been trained to operate Freely Steerable Vehicles (FSV's), were allocated this task by management without their prior knowledge. On their objections having no effect, they walked out, with others joining in sympathy. The whole affair fizzled away in a couple of days, with no long-term poisoning of the atmosphere.

In spite of all this, there remains a feeling of personal involvement among the workforce. A figure of 0.07 per cent for unauthorised absenteeism gave rise to the remark at the time by Chairman Phillip Weekes, "If I'd had figures like these seventeen years ago I'd be in the House of Lords by now". There is reciprocity on the part of the company. During the three-month production shutdown in 1999, resulting from heavy gas emission, no person was laid off during this period. When market forces in 2003 resulted in the closure of Betws, with the loss of jobs for employees but a significant real estate profit for the owners, those employed at Tower would suffer a pay freeze only. Although in theory the coalface could be operated by a shift of 8 men, in fact the team consists of 15 individuals. Significant changes in working methods are put to the workforce for confirmation, e.g., when roof-bolting techniques were proposed for secondary support instead of the conventional steel rings, a special meeting was held of those shareholders directly involved (the proposal was carried, with 6 of the 150 voting against).

It can be said that, during the four shareholder meetings per annum, everyone is equal. Every shareholder is free to raise issues of concern and vote on resolutions. Otherwise, during a normal day's work, the management structure applies. In practice, most items raised from the floor during shareholder meetings are not big picture issues but result from a worm's eye view of day to day operations.


## Where Does All This Leave The Unions?

The slogan on the banner of the Tower NUM lodge proclaims, "Eternal Vigilance is the Price of Freedom". Tower continues to promote internationalism, and always solidarity. Although nowadays society in general is materialistic and it is difficult to identify any specific enemy, the past can never be forgotten. The pit is still very much NUM-orientated, with the Union of Democratic Mineworkers (UDM) having no chance whatsoever. NACODS represents the officials and BACM the management. The union no longer negotiates wage rates, but will meet with the directors in the event of any other industrial dispute. Tower, at the time of writing, remains the only pit in the United Kingdom where Arthur Scargill is allowed underground.

In 2002, Scargill finally retired from Chairmanship of the NUM, although he continued to be employed as a consultant to that organization. By this time membership was down to approximately 4,000. The sentiments of the pro Scargill camp were expressed in The Morning Star, in an article by Tony Benn, ex-Labour cabinet minister and fellow casualty of the general movement to the right in British politics:

"Arthur Scargill, one of the finest trade union leaders of our generation, retired after a lifetime of service to the National Union of Mineworkers, to the Labour movement and to the ideals of Socialism. No man did more than Arthur to defend his members and their families and the communities in which they lived, to protect the environment or to argue for a rational energy policy that took account of the key role that coal should play in the future economy of this country. For all that we owe him a debt of gratitude".

In February 2003, politically active as ever, Scargill stood (unsuccessfully) in Monmouthshire for the Welsh Assembly, as candidate for his own Socialist Labour Party. This he had launched on 1 May 1996, against the feeling of the ex-activists at Tower who thought that he would be better employed in trying to change the Labour Party from within. There would be no political support from that quarter. Nevertheless, and notwithstanding his Yorkshire roots, his left-wing orientation could not be more at home than in the dying embers of the one-time civilisation that was once coalmining in South Wales.

# Chapter 19

## THE NEW ENERGY - ANTI PORTAS.

*"Folks are sad and disillusioned,*
*No more hope - just only dreams,*
*For alas they see no future,*
*At least that is just what it seems".*
G. L. Davies, Llantrisant.

### QUO VADIS, BRITISH COAL?

A Change in Thinking.

The decline of the British coalmining industry in the last 50 years of the twentieth century, is shown in the following table:

| UK fuel source. | 1950 (%) | 1960 (%) | 1970 (%) | 1980 (%) | 1999 (%) |
|---|---|---|---|---|---|
| Coal | 89.6 | 73.9 | 46.6 | 35.6 | 15.9 |
| Petroleum | 10.0 | 25.5 | 44.6 | 37.6 | 32.3 |
| Natural gas | - | - | 5.3 | 21.8 | 40.8 |
| Nuclear electricity | - | 0.4 | 3.3 | 4.8 | 8.4 |
| Hydro- electricity | 0.4 | 0.2 | 0.2 | 0.2 | 0.2 |
| Electricity imports | - | - | - | - | 0.5 |

By the beginning of the twenty-first century, a sea change had occurred in the general approach to energy questions. Instead of the balance of payments and national independence, in particular by means of indigenous sources so as to ensure security of supply, the main thrust had switched to globalisation, market liberalisation and avoidance of climate change. Where did this leave the remaining rump of the once enormous British coalmining industry?

### British Coal? No -.

In 1992/93, the annual report of British Coal estimated that 190 billion tonnes lie beneath the UK, in seams which are above 0.6m in thickness and less than 1,200m in depth. Of this amount, 45 billion tonnes could be won with existing technology. This was adequate for well over 300 years working. The cost of extraction however was such that, in the present market situation, of the reserves that are technically accessible only a small proportion could be exploited competitively. The report goes on:

"On current expectations, a programme of investment in new mines could not be economically justified. This is likely to remain the case for the foreseeable future. The reserves that can be economically mined are therefore effectively limited to those that can be accessed from present workings. Even at existing mines it is not economic to recover all the coal which could be accessed. Reserves elsewhere will however remain to be exploited by future generations, perhaps with different technology, should it become economic to do so". Decline therefore was predicted to continue.

In 1993, the same year as the above British Coal report, a government white paper was dismissive of the entire indigenous mining industry, while looking with interest at reserves abroad:

"The United Kingdom's coal reserves are small by international standards. For illustration, coal underlines less than 15,000 sq. miles of the nation's land area, compared with more than 450,000 sq. miles in the USA. The general view in the industry is that the UK reserves amount to less than 1 per cent of the world total —— Not included in the world total to date are the probably large undiscovered resources of coal in the southern hemisphere, where only Australia and S. Africa have been explored to any extent".

### -But Foreign Coal? Yes!

International proven reserves of fossil fuels, as given by the London- based World Coal Institute, are listed below, in billion tonnes of oil equivalent (btoe).

| Region. | Oil (btoe). | Gas (btoe). | Coal (btoe). |
|---|---|---|---|
| Middle East. | 95 | 50 | - |
| South & Central America. | 15 | 10 | 12 |
| Africa. | 10 | 10 | 38 |
| Europe. | 4 | 8 | 55 |
| Former Soviet Union. | 10 | 50 | 110 |
| North America. | 10 | 8 | 125 |
| Asia/Pacific. | 12 | 15 | 160 |

Concerning UK access to such unbounded resources, the 1993 white paper stated:

"Coal imports could not be restricted without a serious risk that such action would be incompatible with the UK's EC and GATT obligations. The government recognises the importance of these obligations to the UK's success as a trading nation and has no wish to breach them".

In practice, the world market price for coal was proving to be a hurdle which the British coal industry could not jump. As a consequence, UK production continued to decline, from 32 Mt of deep-mined coal in 1995 to 17 Mt in 2001/02. Opencast production is much cheaper but faces considerable problems with regard to the obtaining of planning permission.

Between 1988 and 1998, while coalmining in the UK was being gutted, North American production and demand both increased by 13 per cent. In the same period, production in the Asia/Pacific region jumped by 35 per cent, with consumption up by 30 per cent (against an overall increase in primary energy demand for the region of 47 per cent).

### What is a Reserve?

This new international competition has resulted in a drastic downward revision as to what constitutes an economically workable reserve, resulting in mine closure and a reassessment of the figures.

In 1991, BP estimated UK reserves as being 9.1 billion tonnes, then 0.8 per cent of the world total.

In 1993, as stated above, British Coal quoted workable reserves as equalling 45 billion tonnes (those being commercially workable were much less)..

By 1998, BP had revised their UK figures downwards to 1.5 billion tonnes (0.2 per cent of world total). This represented a reserve to production ratio of 52 years (BP Amoco 1999). In the same year a government-initiated report by International Mining Consultants Ltd. (IMCL) came up with an estimate of 541 million tonnes. According to their estimate, at the current rate of production this would be adequate for 26 years (as a comparison, in 2003 international reserves were estimated by the World Coal Institute as being adequate for over 200 years at the prevailing rate of world consumption). The IMCL Report said that, of the British reserves, 86 per cent lay in the revere of RJB Mining. At that time (1998), RJB Mining were operating 14 pits and producing 21 Mt/annum. A further 75 Mt of reserves were accessible by the remaining companies producing coal. Each of these operated a single colliery and were Scottish Coal, Midlands Mining, Hatfield Coal, Blenkinsopp Collieries and Goitre Tower Anthracite. Between them they produced 5 Mt/annum.

## British Mining at the Turn of the Century.

Where?

By the turn of the century, large-scale (over 1 Mt/annum per pit) mining was confined to the Nottinghamshire and Yorkshire Coalfields, generally working deeper but thicker seams than in the past.

What?

Of the 17 deep mines currently active in the UK, six had been sunk or effectively rebuilt since 1960. Eleven dated from before the Second World War. For these, access has been made to new seams during the previous two decades, generally by means of steep inclines (drifts) from shaft bottom level to the deeper measures. For deep mines, the shallower deposits were already exhausted. Currently, average depths were greater than 600 metres, with several mines having depths in excess of 1,000 metres.

How?

Access to one of the 17 mines was by drift only, to eight by shaft only and the remainder by a combination of drifts and shafts. Coal was brought out, either through the drift by means of high capacity conveyor belts, or by shaft hoisting systems. The more recent shaft winding systems were of the tower-mounted, multi-rope, friction type. After washing and sorting in the coal preparation plant on the surface, the yield of saleable coal from run-of-mine production may be as low as 60 per cent.

What For?

With the exception of South Wales, all coal currently mined in the UK is bituminous steam coal. The saleable product is generally a blended power station fuel, having an energy content of about 24 GJ/tonne, with 16 per cent ash and 12 per cent moisture. By the year 2000, the market for such coal had sunk to 20 Mt. This was down from 50 Mt in 1996 and 80 Mt in 1990.

The Dominant Market.

Electricity generation dominates the market for UK coal. By now, the concept of this industry as a state monopoly, closely tied to indigenous coal and dominated by the engineering challenge of keeping the lights on, has been confined to history. Multiple, privately owned generating companies, many of then international and involved in products and services other than electricity, compete with each other for market share. Traders and risk managers, all dedicated to the commercial objective of attracting customers and making profit, set the tone.

In 1998, of UK generation, gas-firing accounted for 31 per cent (there was none in 1990). Coal-fired generation accounted to 34 per cent (as against 72 per cent in 1990). An increasing proportion of the coal burned came from UK opencast sources and the world market. When the long-term contracts for domestic coal were re-negotiated in that year, coal costs for British power stations decreased still further. More recently, increases in the price of gas have increased the coal burn, which in 2000 was as low as 20 per cent.

By 2003, the contribution of the various fuels towards UK electricity generation was as follows:

| Fuel | Contribution towards electricity generation (%) |
|---|---|
| Coal | 33 |
| Gas | 33 |
| Nuclear | 23 |
| Oil | 4-6 |
| Renewables, hydro and imports from France. | 5-7 |

As a comparison, the coal contribution towards electricity generation in some other countries is as follows:

| Country | Coal's contribution towards electricity generation (%) |
|---|---|
| Poland | 94 |
| Greece | 67 |
| Germany | 50 |
| Denmark | 47 |
| USA | 50 |
| China | 75 |

## The Vagaries of Trade.

Blown Hither and Thither!

Financial pressure on the coal industry continued, not only as a result of competition from gas. The strong increase in the value of the pound at the turn of the century resulted in a three-year low of $25 per tonne in the internationally traded price for coal. At $40 per tonne, British coal was easily undercut by imports, in spite of their transport costs. This forced the closure of additional pits.

At the end of that same millennium year, however, the vagaries of exchange rates and international trade again resulted in an up-beat mood. Oil and gas prices once more rose, while foreign coal now cost $35 per tonne before transport. RJB Mining stated that every tonne they produced could now be sold. The City remained cautious, however, and investment for the future continued to be tight.

In 2001, UK total deep mined output was 15.5 Mt.

In 2002, the opencast position was as follows:

| Region | Manpower | Output (tonnes) |
|---|---|---|
| England | 1,149 | 5,111,000 |
| Scotland | 1,260 | 8,186,000 |
| Wales | 306 | 1,178,000 |
| Total | 2,715 | 14,475,000 |

In 2002, Longannet, the last mine in Scotland, was subject to a break-in of water and closed. The same year, UK Coal announced the end of the Prince of Wales Colliery in Pontefract, Yorkshire. That year also saw the demise of the coke works at Cwm. This latter had been operated by Coal Products Ltd. and was the last in South Wales.

<u>Selby.</u>

Also in 2002, and particularly newsworthy, was the closure announcement of Selby, the north Yorkshire "super pit" employing 2,100 men. Selby was expected to close in August 2004. In 1999 RJB mining had given the complex a life up to the year 2009. Selby was the flagship of the UK mining industry. It epitomised what modern mining was supposed to be all about. It had taken 20 years to plan and bring the complex into full production. At its peak in 1993-94 it broke UK output and productivity records by producing 12 Mt of coal per annum from the single Barnsley seam it was authorised to work. Now its output was down to 4.4 Mt per annum. Originally consisting of five integrated mines, it possessed a combined coal handling and processing facility on the surface at Gascoigne Wood. Here the entire output was processed and dispatched to Drax, Eggborough and other major power stations. Now, by the turn of the century, the most productive areas had already been worked.

The original five production units had since been reduced to three, Stillingfleet, Riccall and Winstow. The remaining two, Whitemoor and North Selby, had "merged" with the others. The easiest, most accessible coal was exhausted and investors did not see the working of faults and disturbances as conforming with the current money-making strategy. Only fault free areas were of interest. The company's assessment, supported by independent consultants, saw no prospect of viable mining from the limited resources remaining. Combined with falling coal prices, the company claimed that adverse geology had resulted in £30 M per annum being lost during the previous 4 years. In addition, water ingress into areas about to be mined had sterilised potential reserves.

Millions of tonnes of untapped reserves were now walked away from and abandoned without a fight. The whole exercise was derided by some as a "smash and grab raid" on the part of the new coalowners, interested only in "get rich quick" schemes. For the Yorkshire pit villages the experience was painful. Typically, 2-3 years after closure of their mine, about 50 per cent of the miners remained unemployed, while those in employment earn just 50 per cent of their previous wage.

Selby Mine finally closed on 26 October 2004.

## SO WHAT REMAINS OF UK COAL?

By 2004, the position was as follows:

- In Scotland, following the closure of Longannet in 2002, there are no more deep mines left.

- In Wales, with the closure of Betws in 2003, only Tower remains.

- In England, after Selby and the closure in 2003 of Clipstone colliery near Mansfield in Nottinghamshire, 9 deep mines survive.

<u>UK Coal.</u>

With the exception of Hatfield Colliery at Doncaster in Yorkshire, all of the English mines are owned by UK Coal Ltd. (previously RJB Mining). They are:

| Mine | Location | Manpower | Annual output in 2001 (Mt) |
|------|----------|----------|----------------------------|
| Thoresby | Edwinstowe, Notts. | 476 | 1.5 |
| Welbeck | Nr. Mansfield, Notts. | 504 | 1.5 |
| Daw Mill | Nr. Coventry, West Midlands. | 481 | 1.2 |
| Ellington | Nr. Morpeth, Northumbria. | 391 | 0.6 |
| Harworth | Nr. Doncaster, Yorks. | 481 | 1.1 |
| Rossington | Nr. Doncaster, Yorks. | 338 | 0.4 |
| Maltby | Nr. Rotherham, Yorks. | 456 | 1.6 |
| Kellingley | Nr. Rotherham, Yorks. | 456 | 1.6 |

The Ellington complex in Northeast England consists of three interconnected units, working up to 15 km under the North Sea. In 2000, RJB Mining wanted to shut it down but this was avoided by means of government financial support.

Non-UK Coal.

The non-UK Coal deep mines remaining in Great Britain (2004) are:

| Mine | Location | Manpower | Annual output in 2001 (Mt) |
|------|----------|----------|----------------------------|
| Hatfield | Doncaster, Yorks. | 200 | 0.5 |
| Tower | Aberdare, Mid Glam. | 250 | 0.5 |

In August 2001, Hatfield Colliery had been closed by its then owner, the Hatfield Coal Company. At the time it employed over 220 staff.

In October 2001, Coalpower Ltd. took the colliery over. This was Richard Budge's new company after he gave up control of RJB Mining.

In 2002, long-term plans for the colliery were released, including the building of a power station and a business park (see below, under "Coal, the Way Ahead").

**Government Aid.**

In March 2003, notwithstanding the earlier deriding of European state support for indigenous mining, the UK government announced a 3-year coal investment scheme. While not nearly as generous as the German scheme, it at least accepted the principle. It allowed £60 million of state funds to be invested in "demonstrably viable" deep mine production. This included up to 30 per cent of the cost of opening new reserves.

- Hatfield colliery was able to receive such government aid for its proposed scheme, since the pit was deemed to have a viable long-term future in front of it.

- Tower Colliery is currently studying the development of new reserves due to impending exhaustion of the current seam. This is foreseen within the next few years.

**The Maintenance of Production.**

If UK production levels after 2008 are to be maintained at or above 15 Mt per annum then either investment is required in new mines or, alternatively, less attractive reserves in existing mines have to be worked. In either case, a higher cost scenario is involved. If production is to be maintained, then the latest date for introducing new mine capacity is 2012/2015.

**WHERE DOES ENERGY GO FROM HERE?**

**Planning versus Market Forces.**

The theoretical arguments of planning versus market forces in determining the optimum energy mix are only part of the story. Unforeseen political and military events can turn out to be as much, if not more, relevant than economic factors. The shattering oil price increases of the 1970's are examples of this. The Yom Kippur War played an important role in triggering the first oil shock. In the case of gas, supplies may be dependent upon pipelines and events thousands of kilometres away, be it terrorism or operational failure.

In 2003 for example, the inadvertent closing of a valve in Indonesia resulted in extensive power cuts in Singapore. There was a repeat performance in June 2004, the valve on this occasion being at the Singapore end of the pipeline. There is also the issue that in severe cold weather, the peak in gas demand coincides with the peak in electricity demand. To reduce the contract price, gas is sometimes provided on a basis that allows for an interruption in supply. The situation could arise where a choice would have to be made between power stations and industrial/domestic consumers. In such a case it would be technically and contractually easier to cut off the power stations.

All of the energy industries fight their corner. The energy mix proposed by the nuclear industry is proposed below, compared with an approximate diversity index developed by Stirling in 1994. This is a statistical attempt to give an optimum generation mix in the UK, bearing in mind not only economic factors but also the chance of unforeseen events:

| Fuel | Nuclear proposal (%) | Stirling (%) |
| --- | --- | --- |
| Nuclear | 25 | 14 |
| Coal | 15 | 27 |
| Oil | - | 7 |
| Gas | 40 | 20 |
| Renewables:<br>Intermittent (e.g.wind+sun)<br>Continuous (e.g. biomass) | 20 | 13<br>17 |

## Gas.

Gas The Invisible.

The media coverage of the energy scene includes subsidies for atomic power, as well as miners' strikes, the ongoing OPEC saga and protests about petrol prices. The nuclear industry lobbies continually, with an array of highly vocal academics writing articles and giving interviews. Gas in contrast, at least ever since the "Bonanza" days of the late 1960's, never seems to make the front page. Natural gas from the North Sea has been a good luck story for the UK. One positive aspect of this development is that the emission of carbon dioxide as a result of electricity generation has been reduced by 30 per cent over the previous 10 years. The UK seems on track to meet its commitments under the Kyoto objectives for the environment.

Gas is sold by a large number of different producers, under a variety of contract terms, and in a competitive market. Its consumption is set for ongoing growth. Nevertheless, it still accounts for a significantly lower proportion of the market than coal did, as recently as the early 1990's. This situation is set to change.

- In 1967, known UK reserves of natural gas totalled 775 billion cu. metres (bcm). That corresponded to 25 years at the current rate of consumption.

- By 1997, reserves available were estimated as being 1,590 bcm (Wood Mackenzie). That corresponded to 17 years' supply at the current rate of consumption.

- By 2002, it was calculated that total reserves remaining in the UK lie between 2,030-3,175 bcm, if the standard statistical probability of the Department of Trade and Industry (DTI) is incorporated. This was estimated to be adequate for a period of between 18 and 28 years. Proven reserves were much less than that, at about 6 years.

Gas, the Dominant.

At the beginning of the twenty-first century, Britain is one of only two G7 countries that are self-sufficient in energy (the other being Canada). This golden age is coming to an end. Transco, the operator of Britain's gas distribution system, predicts a 12 per cent annual increase in UK gas demand up to 2013. With such an increase, UK North Sea reserves will be hard pressed. Transco forecasts that UK gas production could fall from 108 bcm in 2000 to under 50 bcm by 2013. With North Sea prospects now less appealing, fewer wells are being drilled each year. In addition, the average amount of gas found per well is also less.

In 2000, the UK Offshore Operators Association summed up the position in their economic report:

"What is clear is that the development of the remaining oil and gas will be more difficult, given the combination of smaller field sizes, higher development costs, ageing infrastructure and lower real product prices".

With UK production set to fall, demand nevertheless continues to increase. The country will become a net importer and, with gas supplies getting tighter, prices will rise. William Hastings, Chairman and Managing Director of Marathon International (GB), a major gas producer, said that by 2010 the UK and Ireland could have to import 85 bcm of gas per annum. In energy content, this is equivalent to approximately 91 Mt of coal. At least one new pipeline is desperately needed.

A new pipeline from Norway would cost £600 M and take over two years to build. Plentiful supplies are also available from Russia, the Middle East and North Africa. Politically desirable or not, the UK will have to rely on these regions for the lion's share of its total gas supply. Forecasts for the amount of gas to be imported by 2020 have varied between 55 per cent and 90 per cent of requirements. There is a government commitment to increase the contribution of renewable energy to 20 per cent by the year 2020. This still means that gas would account for 70-75 per cent of electrical power generated, thus replacing coal as by far the dominant fuel. Unlike gas, however, coal is either indigenous or imported from stable countries (e.g. USA, Australia, South Africa).


Foreign Fields.

In addition to connections with its own North Sea gas fields, by the early twenty-first century Britain was linked to the continent by two major gas pipelines:

   i) One runs from the Norwegian North Sea to St. Fergus in Scotland. This has an annual capacity of 9 bcm and will be used by Norway's Statoil to deliver the 5 bcm per annum it has contracted to deliver from 2005 to Centrica, a company that markets under the British Gas brand.

   ii) The second pipeline is larger. This links Bacton in Norfolk with Zeebrugge in Belgium. Originally built to export gas from Britain, modifications are underway to enable it to import instead, up to 24 bcm by 2005.


These two pipelines together can deliver about one third of UK gas demand, but more import capacity is needed. With insufficient capacity, prices will rise even more. Reinforcements to the system, at present foreseen, are as follows:

   a) Also to Bacton in Norfolk, an additional pipeline is under construction by the Dutch Gasunie. From 2005, 8 bcm of gas will be supplied to Centrica from Den Helder under a ten-year contract. It is likely that this gas will originate in Siberia. Russia's Taproom plans to build a 3,000 km pipeline from Siberia to supply Finland, Sweden, Germany and the Netherlands, along with the UK. Construction is due to commence in 2005. By 2007, up to 30 bcm of Siberian gas per annum could be flowing into Western Europe by this means.

   b) Norsk Hydro and Partners are developing the Ormen Lange Field, lying deep under the Norwegian North Sea. The field is huge, even by Norwegian standards, and could be producing 15-20 bcm per annum when it starts up in 2007, ramping up to 20 per cent of total UK gas demand by the decade's end. This gas will be brought ashore at Easington on the east coast, with a boosting station at the Sleipner platform, half way between Britain and Norway.

   c) An alternative way of transporting gas over very long distances is to liquefy it and send it by purpose-built ships. Japan and Korea are major importers of Liquefied Natural Gas (LNG) from Australia and South East Asia. In the 1970's, Britain also imported small quantities from Algeria. With the large-scale introduction of North Sea gas these ceased. Capital costs are high, since highly specialised tankers are required, along with a purpose-built landing terminal and a regasification plant. However, with the market price for gas rising and capital costs falling, LNG could experience a renaissance in the UK. Three companies have projects on the drawing board to deliver a total of up to 24 bcm before 2010 using this method.

For the European Union as a whole, in 1995 around two-thirds of its gas requirements came from indigenous sources, mainly the UK and Netherlands. The remaining 35 per cent was imported, from Norway, Russia and Algeria. By the year 2020, the International Energy Authority predicts that the region will be importing 70 per cent of its requirements.

## Whatever Happened to Cheap Gas?

In October 2004, the Parliamentary Trade and Industry Select Committee started an investigation into gas pricing. Ofgem, the energy regulator, had already been looking into the issue for nine months. Currently, in spite of competition, plus indigenous supplies from the North Sea, gas prices in the UK are 30 percent higher than in Continental Europe. Questions have also been raised there, however, as to the justification of linking the price of gas to that for heating oil. Thus it was in 2004 that, although the cost of incoming gas at the German border went down by 6.4 percent, the selling price was subject to a 13 percent increase. Before politicians can control the cartels there is still much work to be done. With the UK price being so much higher than on the continent it is obvious that either energy companies have been colluding to keep prices high - a suggestion which they fiercely deny - or the continentals are in recept of hidden subsidies. As a foretaste of the future, wholesale gas prices in the UK increased by 45 percent in 2004, with a further 30 percent rise predicted for 2005.

## A Policy Review- At Last.

### Who Is Steering The Ship?

The policy of aiming for the lowest achievable prices in electricity generation, using the panacea of "Market Forces", was initiated by the Thatcher government and not seriously questioned by their "New Labour" replacement. Why then did the latter, this business-friendly, non-interventionist government, decide to carry out an energy policy review? The fact of the matter is, when only the cheapest type of power generation is constructed, the eventual effect is to produce a "monoculture" with all of its ramifications regarding security and the potential for future price increases. The "Dash for Gas" in the United Kingdom is an example of cost minimisation as the prevailing culture in electricity generation.

With the future uncertain and a 10-year lead-time to construct a major power station, it is open to question how the country can optimally meet its energy requirements in the middle of the twenty-first century. The strategic objective is to protect the environment and to ensure security/diversity/economy of supply, but, "Who is steering the ship?" Can these objectives be met simply by letting the market rip? Short-term shareholder expectation sits uneasily with the investment required for long-term market security.

### All Our Eggs In One Basket?

With all significant new investment going into gas and none into either nuclear power or coal, in 20 years or so virtually all existing coal and nuclear power stations will have reached the end of their working lives. Most of the magnox stations from the first nuclear power programme are due to close by 2010. Unless this policy changes, by the year 2020 the nuclear contribution will have reduced from 25 per cent to 3 per cent, with only one nuclear power station left by 2025. Coal's position is similar to nuclear, with a reduction from 30 per cent to 6 per cent staring it in the face. European measures to limit carbon emissions and improve air quality will force either modernisation or closure on most of the older coal-fired power stations. In the absence of new mines, much of the UK's economically viable deep-mined coal is likely to be exhausted by 2013. Already almost half of the coal used is imported.

## LOW CARBON ECONOMY.

### Things Are Warming Up!

There was another reason for the sudden surge in government interest regarding energy supply. Protection of the environment had now shifted to centre stage. In the twentieth century, the earth had warmed up by about 0.6 °C, largely due to increased greenhouse gas emissions resulting from human activities. Without action to reduce emissions, the earth's temperature is likely to rise at a faster rate than at any time in the last 10,000 years or more.

In 2002, after years of being accused of drift and lack of interest, even the non-interventionist, market-orientated New Labour Party felt called upon to explain and justify its energy philosophy in a review, published by the Performance and Innovation Unit of the Cabinet Office. This was a discussion document, to be followed by a government white paper. Its main emphasis was on the need to limit climate change, combined with the provision of adequate, economic and secure supplies of energy.

### Domestic Supplies Are Not Secure Supplies!

The Energy Review was sanguine with regard to the increased dependence on gas, including gas imported from overseas. It saw no pressing problems with this and pointed out that 70 per cent of the world reserves lay in regions peripheral to Europe and thus could be easily accessed (North Africa, Middle East, Former Soviet Union). These were adequate for 100 years at the current European consumption rate. With regard to security of supply, the key lay in developing strong links with trading partners, that is, those nations involved in production and transit. The Review said:

"Energy imports allow access to cheaper and more diverse sources than if energy were produced solely at home. Experience with coal in the 1970's and 80's, and with the fuel protests of 2000 suggest that the equation of "domestic" and "secure" does not always apply".

The review concluded with the following clarion call for action:

"The nation must not be lulled into inaction by long timescales and a future which will belong mainly to our grandchildren. The time for action is now. Given that there is considerable inertia in the system and that low carbon technologies are not part of the conventional energy system, a change of direction will be difficult to achieve. It will require clarity of purpose in all parts of government".

### The White Paper.

The Vision.

In March 2003 the government white paper, Our Energy Future-Creating a Low carbon Economy, was issued as a follow-up to the above review. If the review concluded with a clarion call, the white paper started with one:

"We believe we need to prepare for an energy system that is likely to be quite different from today —— Innovation will give us options we cannot even imagine now. The scenario will need to be updated in the light of experience".

The challenges would be met by the achievement of four goals:

    i)  Cut carbon dioxide emissions.

    ii)  Maintain the reliability of energy supplies.

    iii) Promote competitive markets in the UK and beyond.

    iv) Ensure every home is adequately and affordably heated.

The Problem.

To emphasise the gravity of the situation the white paper pointed out that, in the UK, economic losses to communities and businesses resulting from weather conditions had increased ten-fold over the last forty years. Usage of the Thames barrier, erected to prevent flooding in Central London, had also increased from once every two years in the 1980's to an average of six times per annum in the period 1997-2002. The 1990's were the warmest decade since records began. The level of atmospheric carbon dioxide was one third above that prevailing before the industrial revolution and was now growing faster than ever. The effects of this could already be seen:

- Ice caps are retreating from many mountain peaks, like Kilimanjaro.

- Global mean sea level rose by an average of 1.2 mm per annum during the twentieth century.

- In the Arctic, summer and autumn sea ice has thinned by 40 per cent in recent decades.

- Global snow cover had reduced by 10 per cent since the 1960's.

- El N_no events (a change in weather patterns around the Central Pacific, resulting in unusually wet or dry conditions) have become more frequent and intense during the last 20-30 years.


We Will Exceed Kyoto!

Foreseen was a brave new world in which the UK would curb its appetite for energy and show leadership in tackling climate change. Although the UK produces only 2 per cent of the total global emissions, a key announcement, mentioned specifically in the Prime Minister's foreword, was that a recommendation made by the Royal Commission on Climate Change in 2000 would be accepted. The UK was thus committed to a 60 per cent reduction in carbon dioxide emissions by 2050. This far exceeds the target of the Kyoto Protocol, which requires an overall cut in greenhouse gas emissions by 2012 of 12.5 per cent below 1990 levels. The target set for 2050 implies 20-30 per cent of electricity from renewables, with 10 per cent by 2010 being a milestone along the way.


Welcome to the Importers' Club!

It was accepted that by 2006, the country would become a net importer of gas and by 2010 a net importer of oil. By 2020, Britain would be dependant on imports for three-quarters of its total primary energy consumption. The current energy independence was an exception among major industrial countries, however. Canada was the only other example. The way ahead was to maintain energy reliability through diversity, with many sources of energy, many suppliers and many supply routes.


Energy And Foreign Policy Now Intertwined.

Renewables would assist in reducing the dependence on imports, but the foreign policy dimension implicit in the new situation was spelt out:

- "Securing reliable energy supplies will need to be an increasingly important part of our European and foreign policy".

- "We need to give greater prominence to strategic energy issues in foreign policy".

- "The Foreign and Commonwealth Office will work more closely with other government departments to achieve common objectives in international energy security".

- "In promoting diversity we will also work to minimise the risk of disruption to supplies from regional disputes or local instability".

## No Intervention?

The government would not decide the composition of fuel mix. Non-intervention was stated as a principle, although since April 2002 the so-called Renewables Obligation was already requiring suppliers to obtain an increasing proportion of their electricity from renewable sources. A subsidy was being given for the increasing use of such energy. Nevertheless, it was maintained that liberalised and competitive markets would continue to be a cornerstone of energy policy:

"Vigorous competition improves efficiency and drives down prices. This has already been seen in energy markets. For domestic consumers, average prices in real terms fell by 10 per cent for gas and 19% for electricity between 1997 and 2002. For industrial users, between 1997 and 2001, electricity prices fell by 22 per cent in real terms".

The cheapest and safest way ahead was energy efficiency. Since 1970 the size of the UK economy had doubled, while overall energy consumption had increased by only 15 per cent. The government would support research, including international research, into clean coal technology plus carbon capture and storage. A new National Energy Research Centre would be established.

## Domestic Coal - Along With Others.

Domestic coal production was likely to decline as existing pits reached the end of their geological and economic lives. Within ten years most of our existing deep mines were likely to have exhausted their economic reserves. However, an investment aid scheme would be introduced to help existing pits develop new reserves, where they were economically viable and safeguard jobs. The white paper says:

"If ways could be found cost-effectively to handle the carbon, keeping coal-fired generation in the fuel mix would offer significant energy security and diversity benefits. Coal is easy to store and transport and can be secured from diverse and stable suppliers, both domestically and worldwide. Loads in coal-fired stations can also be varied relatively easily, so coal-fired generation is particularly useful in meeting peak demand or covering for supply intermittencies in other fuels. —— Coal, like oil and increasingly gas, is an internationally traded commodity —— Given this relatively mature and flexible market, there do not appear to be strong economic grounds for supporting UK coal production as a hedge against import prices or security of electricity supply —— We recognise that coal producers can make positive contributions to areas that are often economically and socially disadvantaged, by providing well-paid and skilled jobs. The UK's coal industry is the most efficient in Europe. It has made great strides in improving productivity and has shown itself able, except in unfavourable market conditions, to compete successfully both with other fuels and with exports".

## Not So Grand Finale!

The finale of the white paper commences in thundering style:

"We have set out a challenging long-term agenda for change. We need to make sure we have the institutions in government to deliver it".

It then descends into anticlimax. As to what the institutions charged with recasting the entire energy strategy of the country might be it goes on:

"We do not believe we need a new organization for this —— The DTI's Energy Strategy Unit will provide the focal point of a network - a Sustainable Energy Policy Network - of departmental policy units that will be involved in delivering the white paper commitments".

There follows an "Uncle Tom Cobbley and all" list of departments involved in this network.

- Department of Trade and Industry (DTI).

- Department of Environment, Food and Rural Affairs (DEFRA).

- Foreign and Commonwealth Office (FCO).

- The Treasury.

- Office of the Deputy Prime Minister (ODPM).

- Department of Transport (DfT).

- The Scotland Office.

- The Wales Office.

- The devolved administrations.

- The Environment Agency.

- Office of Gas and Electricity Markets.


## The New Organization - Which Is Not Needed!

Having asserted that a new organization was not needed, the white paper then proceeds to describe what it calls a new organization, "to provide a clear line of accountability for the network".

i) An ad hoc ministerial group will oversee the delivery of commitments made in the white paper. The Secretary of State for Trade and Industry will chair this group jointly with the Secretary of State for the Environment, Food and Rural Affairs.

ii) Another new creation, the Sustainable Energy Policy Advisory Board, comprising senior and independent experts and stakeholders will support the above group. Their role will be to provide well-informed, independent advice on the approach and work of the network as a whole.

iii) "To ensure the transparency" of progress being made towards the aims set out in the white paper, an annual report by the Sustainable Energy Network will be issued.

iv) The extensive range of government energy indicators, already published annually, will continue to be published. However, indicators are required giving a broad overview as to whether energy policy objectives are being achieved. What these indicators might be was not yet clear and views would be sought.


## Flavour of the Month?

### A Bland and Weak Report!

Time will tell whether this latest white paper is the preface to significant historical change, or whether it is just another "flavour of the month", as per the post-World War 2 calls to maximise coal production and the 1960's "white hot technological revolution".

On 3 April 2003, the Science and Technology Committee of the House of Commons, chaired by Ian Gibson MP, criticised the white paper as being heavy on principles but light on the practical means of achieving them. The whole document was dismissed as "a bland and weak report", with "no prospect" of meeting its own targets of carbon dioxide reduction and renewable source contribution. The energy policy proposed was just "too fragmented".

In the committee's view the white paper offered extensive analysis but few practical proposals. Investment, in comparison with other countries, was "pitiful". They came to a more robust conclusion as to what form the follow-up should take. Nothing less than a new ministry, dedicated to renewable energy, would be capable of pulling all of the diverse groups together. In their view, renewable sources were not coming on-stream fast enough and only nuclear power could fill the gap:

"The sums invested in public research and development lack focus and are wholly insufficient in helping the UK met its renewables targets".

The committee proposed a radical taxation system, distinguishing between fossil fuel and carbon-free or carbon neutral sources.

The government rejected the committee's report. In their view, the new authority as proposed would "divert effort into the creation of structures and possibly new silos separate from the main stream of energy policy". According to the government:

"The Renewables Obligation, exemption from the Climate Change Levy, the EU Emissions Trading Scheme, combined with capital grants and support for research and development provide a huge package of support for renewables which will be worth around £1 billion a year by 2010 from the Renewables Obligation and Climate Change Levy alone, and which is bringing forward very substantial investment".

The Institution of Civil Engineers also pitched in against the white paper. They called for the creation of a chief engineering advisor, similar to the existing chief medical officer. The current energy plans they said "lack diversity and security of supply", with the result that the UK could face blackouts in a few years time. The current mix of approximately 32 per cent coal, 38 per cent gas, 23 per cent nuclear, 4 per cent oil and 3 per cent renewables would be superseded by new gas-fired power stations coming on-stream. This would mean becoming reliant on "energy sources supplied via pipelines from politically unstable countries thousand of miles away". Unlike other European countries, Britain's gas storage facilities were extremely limited, being adequate for less than two weeks. A call was made for the government to increase investment in energy storage and in "the full range of available fuels". There should be research into new nuclear stations and into carbon sequestration.

## Where's The Money Coming From?

That the programme is associated with a price tag is obvious. The white paper estimated that the increased use of renewable energy, including the trading of carbon emissions, would cost £1 billion per annum by 2010. This equates to an estimated 5 per cent real increase in household energy prices.

On 28 April 2003, the Financial Times quoted the Energy Minister, Brian Wilson, as citing the price increase as being up to 10 per cent. This latter figure includes the cost of "rewiring Britain". A major shift to renewables implies breaking the monopoly of massive power stations, transmitting energy in bulk down through the network. A multitude of scattered renewable generators, connected to local distribution systems, will have a profound change on the electrical system of the UK. A constant question raised by critics of the white paper is, "Where will the money come from"? Such significant increases in renewables as have been achieved, for example in Denmark, have been the result of generous government subsidies. Competitive markets, so eulogised in the white paper, discourage the very plants necessary to provide diversity and reduce greenhouse gas emissions. In Britain the government, in spite of its professed non-intervention, is prepared to guarantee a purchase price for renewable energy up to a level that currently lies between 7.3-9.7 EUR cents per kwh (normal price for a generated kwh is about 4-5 cents). This level of subsidy finds its way into long-term contracts for the generators. These can be up to ten years. It has been argued that, in the UK, subsidies are not sufficiently long-term to persuade investors to commit the kind of money that is necessary.

## It's A Breeze!

In terms of self-sustaining commercial development, renewable energy is still in its infancy. "Biomass" generation, using fuel such as waste or specifically planted trees, is in its gestation period but is not forecast to become commercially viable on a large scale until about 2010. An even longer timescale applies to wave and tidal technologies, with the large-scale commercial exploitation of solar power being even further down the road. This leaves wind power as the great renewables hope for the immediate future. The UK's wind resources are in fact the best in Europe, particularly in Scotland, where the average wind speed is 8.5 m/s.

In 2003, offshore wind generation capacity in the UK totalled 4 MW but, according to the British Wind Energy Association, to achieve the 10 per cent target by 2010, 8,000 MW of turbine capacity will need to be installed, half onshore and half offshore.

By 2004, the government had chosen developers for 15 offshore sites. These are concentrated in the Thames Estuary, the greater Wash and the North Wales coast. Such offshore wind power was flagged by the white paper as being a big contributor. Onshore wind farms are plagued by planning problems, understandably, since just to replace the ageing magnox nuclear reactors by wind power would mean covering an area the size of Lincolnshire with turbines. Although nuclear power is unattractive economically, this is why the government still keeps the option open as a fallback position.

Energy And The Royal Coach.

At least the foreign policy imperatives of the white paper are making their presence felt, in different ways at different places.

In June 2003, the visit by President Putin was the first Russian state visit to the UK for over 130 years and was a follow-up to the contract, worth over £6 billion and signed by British Petroleum, for development in the Russian Far East. To date, this was the largest ever signed by Russia with a foreign company. In addition, discussions were held between the two governments concerning the construction of a pipeline, destined to bring Russian gas directly to the UK.

The trip in the golden, horse-drawn, coach with the Queen as company, together with his photo opportunity with the royals while dressed in tails (his first such photograph ever), were public proof that the occasion was important enough for the Russians finally to have been forgiven for the assassination of their own royal family by the Bolsheviks. The ill-fitting nature of the evening dress specially, and inadequately, tailored for Putin on that occasion cannot be attributed to a lingering royal grudge on the issue.

## COAL, THE WAY AHEAD.

### Gasification By The User.

While the nuclear industry is lobbying for the replacement of existing nuclear stations with new capacity, the coal lobby is arguing for more research into the clean burning of coal and a more appropriate use of this important national resource. As to which type of clean coal technology should be introduced, the mining industry's own preference is for Integrated Gasification Combined Cycle (IGCC), using on-site gasification by the user. The reasons are:

i)   By offering an alternative gas supply it effectively puts a cap on gas prices.

ii)   IGCC builds on the success of gas turbines for power generation. Gas so generated is also fully compatible with fuel cells.

iii)   Such gasification technology need not be confined to coal. Gasification offers a clean disposal for many difficult wastes, such as municipal solid wastes, sewage sludge, plastics and refinery residues.

iv)   Fuel flexibility and security of supply would be enhanced, and not only by keeping coal in the energy mix. A single such plant may have a possible choice between coal, petcoke, orimulsion, natural gas and waste.

v)   The process is already 40-45 per cent efficient, with the potential to reach 50 per cent in the near term and >60 per cent in the longer term. This depends on higher inlet temperatures to the gas turbine being achieved (current efficiency of a gas turbine combined cycle plant, using natural gas, is 55 per cent).

At present, the gas cleaning stage for sulphur and particles can only operate at relatively low temperatures. This restricts the overall efficiency obtainable. However, even now, when the system operates as a combined heat and power plant, with local utilisation of the waste heat produced, overall efficiencies of around 80 per cent are possible. The modular nature of IGCC component construction, combined with the likelihood of mass production, gives the potential for significant cost reductions after a number of such plants have been built.

## First Steps.

A Derisory Sum.

In 1993, prior to privatising the Coal Research Establishment at Cheltenham along with the rest of British Coal, the Government announced a grant of £12 M for such clean coal application, a derisory sum when compared with the hundreds of millions spent on developing and researching nuclear energy, along with the excessively large building programmes for such a new technology. British Coal had expressed confidence that before the end of the decade, but subject to funding, their topping cycle would be a candidate for new coal-fired generation in the UK. This system combined gasification with combustion of the remaining, non-gasified, coal. However, with the death of the coalmines and the consequent emasculation of the mining lobby, clean coal technologies, once pursued, were put on a back burner in the UK.

Progress Abroad.

Elsewhere during 1993, the world's first ICGCC plant was started up at Bruggenum, near Maastricht in the Netherlands. This 250 mw project was commenced in 1989, following a new government policy that required a balanced diversification of energy supply. The Dutch government of the time saw coal as supplying one-third of the country's electricity requirements, but only if this was compatible with strict environmental standards.

By 2003, over 1,500 megawatts of coal-fired IGCC were operating worldwide, in the Netherlands, Spain and the US where, due to that country's enormous coal reserves, it is the subject of much research and investment. An additional 2,200 megawatts was in the process of design.

## The UK Gets On Board.

The Hatfield Solution.

On 6 August 2003, the first application of the technology in the UK was announced. It will also be one of the first power plants to be built in the country for 5 years. The 40 per cent drop in wholesale energy prices had forced producers to close or mothball plants. Coalpower Ltd., Richard Budge's new company on his exit from RJB Mining, won government approval for the first phase of a £350 M scheme to build a 430MW IGCC plant at Hatfield Colliery in Yorkshire. This beat UK Coal, which has plans to build a similar plant next to its Kellingley Colliery in West Yorkshire. The Hatfield plant was developed by Jacobs Consultancy and will consume coal direct from the colliery. Completion is expected in 2006. The estimated price for electricity generated is competitive, at 3p/kwh. This is less than onshore wind power and the plant will operate at full load for 95 per cent of the time, as opposed to a typical 27 per cent in the wind power case. To be economically viable the plant must operate constantly at or near full load, with just short shutdown periods for annual maintenance.

Material In And Material Out.

The initial plant at Hatfield will consume some 934,000 t/a of coal. A second, future plant is foreseen. The colliery currently produces 600,000 t/a and has access to 100 Mt of reserves. Coalpower has applied for government aid to extend underground capacity. The aim is not just to safeguard the 200 jobs currently at the colliery but also to develop a so-called "Power Park". Eighty per cent of the site will consist of industrial units and twenty per cent commercial. The intention is to bring jobs to the area and provide a market for the electricity, waste heat and other products emanating from the new plant.

In addition to the gas itself, by-products produced by the gasification process are:

- Pure sulphur.

- Inert slag as construction material.

- Export oxygen, nitrogen and argon.

- Export hydrogen for fuel cells and/or internal combustion engines.

- Carbon dioxide for oilfield injection, resulting in enhanced recovery.

Sulphur will be sold to chemical companies in the UK. The slag will be a non-leachable glassy substance that will find a market among local concrete block manufacturers. Smaller quantities of other solid wastes will be disposed of at licensed landfills. In addition, Richard Budge aims to capture hydrogen and carbon dioxide in commercial volumes. With regard to the former, up to 5t per hour could be exported at over 99 per cent purity. This could be supplied at low pressure via a pipeline to supply more than 2,000 buses with non-polluting fuel.

The captured carbon dioxide will be used in enhanced oil and gas recovery techniques (EOR). Hatfield Colliery is just 16 km from a North Sea access that would allow it to reach the Forties Field. This is a good candidate for EOR as the field is expected to reach the end of normal extraction in 4-5 years. Injected $CO_2$ will displace more of the oil/gas, thus improving yield by up to 10 per cent. The carbon dioxide so injected remains "sequestered" underground. The concept is not cheap. A single carbon dioxide pipeline from a medium coal-fired power station, together with onshore compression plus wellhead injection and handling facilities, would cost around £1-1.5 billion. The additional oil recovered would justify this investment but might not cover the cost of capturing and storing carbon dioxide at the power station.

Elsewhere in the North Sea the Danish energy company ELSAM, together with Kinder Morgan from the US, is looking to establish a network of carbon dioxide pipelines linking power plants in Denmark, Norway and the UK to offshore oilfields. When complete, 1,500 km of offshore pipelines and 900 km of onshore pipelines will connect 10 power plants to 12 oilfields. They are planned to supply 700 Mt of $CO_2$ over the eight-year life of the project.

In 2004, Valleys Energy was due to begin work on a 460 MW IGCC plant on the site of the former Drym opencast site, near Onllwyn in the Neath Valley of South Wales. It was expected to go on line in 2007, but without associated carbon capture and sequestration.

### The US Does It Big.

In February 2003, the United States launched "FutureGen", the most ambitious IGCC project to date. Led by a consortium from the coal and power industries it involves a research power plant with integrated sequestration and hydrogen production. One billion dollars of public and private money will be invested in a plant intended, within 10 years, to produce electricity at no more than 10 per cent above the cost of a high-tech conventional coal plant. Totally free of pollution and greenhouse gases, it will be associated with carbon dioxide capture and storage. It will also produce clean hydrogen for down-stream, pollution free, usage.

In May 2003, in a related initiative, the US brought together ministers from 14 countries for the Carbon Sequestration Leadership Forum. This aimed to advance technologies for the separation and storage of carbon dioxide resulting from the burning of coal before it enters the atmosphere. Such projects will remove uncertainties surrounding the cost of large-scale capture and storage. If successful they will put ultra-low emission, coal-based generation within reach, at an affordable price. The associated gasification technology is also an abundant potential source for huge quantities of manufactured hydrogen. Such quantities would be required for widespread application of hydrogen-based, emission-free energy systems.

### Has the Horse Bolted?

For Coal - The End In Sight.

To date all IGCC plants are subsidised and significant technical challenges remain, such as catering for rapid changes in load. However, this is a technology that is now reaching its technical and economic potential. Developments regarded as inevitable, such as an increase in gas prices and reliance on foreign supply, will serve as an incentive that this potential be tapped. In addition, oil prices remain volatile, subject in particular to political instability. By October 2004 the price of crude in New York had reached $55 a barrel, a 13-year high and still climbing. These developments must call into question the wisdom of the "dash for gas", when reserves of this premium fuel were depleted by an unrestrained foray into power generation.

With China now massively importing and restricting coal exports, this commodity also experienced a significant price hike. At the end of 2004, the internationally traded price of coal had doubled in the previous 12 months, to EUR 60/t for power station coal and EUR 120/t for coking coal. Nevertheless, coal remains the cheapest option for electricity generation - typically 1.6p/kwh for existing plant and 2-2.5p/kwh for a new plant with emission control equipment to the latest stringent standards. With coal-fired power stations, loads can also be varied relatively quickly to meet demand.

All of these developments may call into question the short-sighted massacre of British coalmining, but the horse has now bolted. There is little prospect of new mines in the UK for the foreseeable future. Consequently, and according to the government, much of the UK's economically viable deep-mined coal is likely to be exhausted by 2013.

A Clean Coal Levy?

In an effort to save what remains, UK Coal is lobbying the government to support the commercial demonstration of cleaner coal technologies and to encourage their widespread adoption. In a debate on energy policy in the House of Lords the Liberal Peer Lord Ezra, former Chairman of the National Coal Board, argued for the introduction of a "Clean Coal Levy" on electricity prices. If nuclear energy benefited from the Climate Change Levy, and the Renewables Obligation benefits renewable energy, the concept of a Clean Coal Obligation is only logical. Electricity suppliers would be obliged to purchase specified quantities of energy generated from clean coal sources. The consumer would thus pay a very modest price to protect the security and diversity of energy supplies. Without such encouragement the UK risks losing not only coal's contribution to the security and diversity of fuel supplies for power generation, which it provided for so long, but also the experience to develop such power stations in other parts of the world - a potentially valuable export business.

No More Political Clout.

Planning for a future based upon optimising the use of indigenous coal is not a concept that evokes enthusiasm in the corridors of British power. Mining in Britain is virtually finished, and with it the political clout that the miners once had. In contrast, nuclear power may be discredited, but the nuclear lobby can still muster an impressive array of doctors and professors to argue their case.

Should the government have got it wrong the option of unblocking the chimney and tracking down a chimney sweep hardly exists anymore, although in South Wales Tower Colliery is still there (2004). In the short term at least, one can still put a dragon on the fire.

# Chapter 20

## MEMORIES

*"What has happened to our miners?*
*We don't have them as of yore,*
*Are they lost and gone forever,*
*Will we see them anymore?".*
G. L. Davies, Llantrisant.

Tower Colliery might have been a success, but the miners' fight for their valley communities was lost.

## SOUTH WALES REINVENTED.

### The Vale - Backwater To Productive Backbone.

Industrial South Wales of but recent memory has been turned on its head. Once a multitude of railways transhipped wealth generated in the upland valleys to the greedy ports or steelworks on the coast. Between those two areas of intense activity lay the gentle Vale of Glamorgan. Encompassed by the never-ending streams of coal trundling down from the Western Valleys to Swansea and from the Eastern Valleys to Cardiff, Barry and Newport, "The Vale" remained an unaffected backwater, still primarily agricultural and a place to escape. The clanking, rattling coal trains, every ten minutes from the Rhondda Valley alone, circumvented this rural area, characterised by isolated villages, small market towns and quiet country pubs. Now the slash of the M4 across that bucolic landscape has attracted a corridor of hi-tech industry, accompanied by a fringe of repetitive housing estates.

The M4 has become South Wales' main economic asset, having long replaced steel and coal as its productive backbone. The policies of the Welsh Assembly and of Westminster appeared to be working as hundreds of foreign companies, European, North American and Asian moved in, to produce one of the fastest regional growth rates in the UK. As a social follow-on, shift work and second jobs have become normal, along with a large increase in the number of women in work. In the last 20 years the incidence of strikes has also reduced dramatically, from 300 days per annum per 1000 workers, to 10 days.

### The New And The Old.

<u>High Tech.</u>

By the early twenty-first century and for the first time in living memory, unemployment in Wales was lower than the national average. The aircraft maintenance base of British Airways at Cardiff (Roose) Airport and the major development at Llantrisant by the German engineering company Bosch are two of the early flagship examples of this development. Further west, the Baglan Energy Park is a further, on-going example. In a joint scheme between BP, Neath/Port Talbot Council and the Welsh Development Agency, a gas turbine based power station, commissioned at the turn of the century, will provide electricity and steam to the adjacent BP Chemicals plant as well as the Energy Park. This latter, a 200 acre site, is intended to house manufacturing, information technology and call centres, all attracted by the low cost power and heat. The 2000MW of electrical power, which South Wales imports from outside the region, will be reduced by up to 25 per cent as a result of this additional local generation.

In contrast, the dock areas are pale shadows of their illustrious past, looking to "yuppie" development and services for their present and future glory. Of those employed in Cardiff, 80 per cent now work in the service industries. Whereas before the 1984-85 miners' strike 32 per cent of the working population in Wales were active in mining and manufacturing, that figure is now 18 per cent.

What's Left Of Steel And Coal?

The steel industry, in spite of massive layoffs, is Wales' largest manufacturing employer, with 7,800 staff. With all of its coal imported and output per man at previously undreamed-of heights, it struggles to survive against intense global competition.

In 2004 steelmaker Corus was able to announce its first profit since formation of the group, when British Steel and the Dutch Hoogovens merged in 1999. This improvement in results was thanks to the rapidly growing Chinese economy, combined with painful restructuring that included total closure of the steelworks at Ebbw Vale, plus cessation of steel making at Llanwern.

The coal industry has shrivelled to less than it was 200 years ago and is insignificant in the general economy. Where the massed coal trains once headed south along the valleys a single-track railway, with its hourly service of twin diesel railcars, has replaced the triple or quadruple tracks of yesteryear. The railway line previously dedicated to coal transportation from the Cambrian Colliery has been converted into a road, partially financed by the European Union and linking previously isolated communities to the M4. The valleys, once dominated by waste tips and the spinning wheels of pit headgear, now nestle beneath serried ranks of Forestry Commission conifers. They are green again, with the Rhondda once more stunningly beautiful. Apart from limited work at modest pay in one of the occasional "screw driver assembly" factories, they offer themselves as dormitory areas for Cardiff, Swansea and the M4 corridor. However, although housing in the valleys is much cheaper, there has been little up-valley migration of commuters. The valleys have not experienced any significant knock-on effect from the M4 corridor and Cardiff Bay developments.

## Isolation.

A specific geographical problem is that the valley communities were built where coal was found, not because people would otherwise have chosen to live there, to access work in the wider economy. With no equivalent to the vibrant but now defunct mining industry, they remain isolated from the positive economic statistics, unable to escape their past. This was a past characterised by united and living communities, struggling in the face of exploitation and deprivation. Under the slogan "Close a pit and kill a community" it was for the survival of these communities that the mammoth struggle of 1984-85 was fought. This self same unity was what enabled it to be fought. Since that struggle failed miserably, have the apocalyptic visions of that time come to pass?

## DEPRESSION LIVES ON.
### No More Open Doors.
We Can't Do It.

The brutal butchering of the industry has indeed left a legacy. Some indication of the social cost involved is given by the fact that the coalfields nationally are home to 5 million people - 8 per cent of the total UK population. In the valleys, social and health problems are part of this inheritance while the spirit of, "We cannot do it, someone else will do it better" remains deeply imbibed. The passion and fire that produced Aneurin Bevin, A.J.Cook, Arthur Horner, Will Paynter, Noah Ablett of Ton-y-Pandy riot fame and all the rest, are now as quiescent and as remote as those of the great nonconformist religious revivals. The coal industry was hard and dangerous, but nothing has come along to replace it. Coal meant real work, hard but honest, and with solidarity throughout the community. The optimum exploitation of seams meant thinking long-term. Defence by senior politicians of the current job market fails to impress many, who see it as being characterised by an excess of so-called "Mickey-Mouse McJobs", short-term, part-time and low paid.

One thesis is that, in the knowledge economy, the ability to add value does not result from the possession of land or raw materials or capital, not even of "information", which itself is a form of raw material.

Added value now results from innovation, which is the use of know-how or, in other words, creativity. Just as industrial and office workers pushed farmers away from their central place in the economic scheme of things, new creative stars in the world of work will in turn replace them.

## Drugs.

In the valleys, of all this there is no sign. Drug dependency is growing. On 13 September 2004, at Merthyr Crown Court, when sentencing 13 members of a Merthyr drug gang to prison terms ranging from 2 to 9 years, Judge John Curran said:

"During the 14 years I have sat in this court I have watched with horror at the rising tide of drug addiction that has swept South Wales, Merthyr Tydfil in particular, and the crime committed as a result of it". Referring to the Gurnos estate, he said, "Drug dealing had reached monumental proportions. Life was becoming intolerable".

Even in the 1980's the valleys were largely crime-free, at least with the exception of petty crime. Now, the memory of permanently opened front doors, with neighbours confidently walking in with no more than a shouted announcement of their entry, has been confined to history. Bolts and chain locks on the front doors and an increasing number of burglar alarm boxes bear witness to a different ethos.

## Another Canary Wharf?

In 1987, the Parliamentary Energy Committee called for a higher level of resources and the, "commitment of energy, imagination, and purpose at least comparable to that required by such major schemes as the redevelopment of London's dockland areas". In reality the mining valleys did not become another Canary Wharf.

In 1988 there was a "Valleys' Initiative". This was launched by the Secretary of State for Wales, re-sponding to a report on the South Wales Valleys. This found mass unemployment, low incomes, social deprivation, run-down urban areas and a poor image.

In 1990, Mardy, the last pit in the Rhondda, closed. By then the valleys' population had sunk from its 1924 peak of 169,000 to 81,000. At the time of closure, twenty-five percent of the valleys' menfolk were unemployed.

In 1992, a 51-page report ("Rebuilding our Communities: A New Agenda for the Valleys" by Kevin Morgan and Adam Price) called the Valleys' Initiative "a flop", branding it as "essentially a marketing exercise". It found that, despite £800 M having been spent, less than half of the people of working age were in full-time employment, while of the 50 worst off parts of Wales, most were in the valleys. Tips had been greened and thousands of daffodils planted but economically the valleys had not been incorporated into a "Greater Cardiff". The Tory dream of a new, individualistic, entrepreneurial culture had sputtered and gone out. According to the University of Southampton's "Atlas of Mortality", published in the early 1990`s, the valleys had the highest premature death rate in Europe. The main illnesses were cancer, heart attacks, hypertension and respiratory diseases caused by lung infections.

In 1998, Aberfan's legacy continued, with an independent inquiry in October of that year showing that severe flooding had been exacerbated by spoil dumped from the removed tips. The inheritance left behind by that lost civilisation of Welsh coal is not just confined, however to physical manifestation, or even social deprivation; the medical and mental trauma left in its wake continues.

In 2003, a study published in the British Journal of Psychiatry said that nearly one in three survivors of the Aberfan disaster was still suffering from post-traumatic stress disorder. Of the 145 children who sur-vived, many said they still suffered from flashbacks and had difficulty in sleeping because of the event. Much schooling had been lost, which most never really made up:

"We were a generation that lost out. We lost out on our education and on our futures. I can't think of any of us who ever did really well and most of us just stayed and grew up in the village. We haven't gone far at all" (Pantglas pupil, quoted in Is it still raining in Aberfan?).

# IDLENESS.

## Unemployment By Another Name.

In contrast to the apparent litany of doom as above, statistics, at least at first sight, tell a different story. With its record of depression, many would guess that unemployment in the Rhondda would lie in the range of 30, 40, or even 50 percent. Surprisingly, in mid-2003 it was a mere 4.2%. This was marginally ahead of the Welsh average. It is said, however, that while figures can't lie, liars can figure! With such an apparent improvement in the valleys' fortunes, why did Rhondda's Member of Parliament, Chris Bryant, press for a parliamentary debate on the problems of ex-mining communities? This was nearly twelve and a half years after closure of the last mine in his constituency. The kernel of the problem dealt with in the debate was the masking of unemployment, now called economic inactivity, by incapacity benefit.

In 2003, in Britain as a whole, the official dole queue had fallen to 850,000, but the number of people drawing incapacity benefit had almost quadrupled since the 1970s, to more than 2.7 million. Many of these say that they would like to work. The regional breakdown is as follows:

- South-East England  - 2.3%

- London  - 2.5%

- North East England  - 7.3%

- Wales  - 7.9%

With a national unemployment rate of just 4.8 per cent, the UK is regarded as exemplary in this regard, but a leading article in the Financial Times of July 28, 2004 expressed a similar concern to Mr. Bryant's:

"Many without work were encouraged onto sickness benefits during the 1990s as a way of massaging unemployment figures, such that over the course of two decades the number quadrupled to reach 2.7M a decade ago. But while the number claiming unemployment has fallen since the mid 1990s, the number of those claiming incapacity benefit has hardly budged. In many areas of the country it has therefore effectively replaced jobseekers' allowance as the primary form of unemployment relief. —— A study conducted by Sheffield Hallam University found jobless figures would double were this effect taken into account".

The article also pointed out that within semi-skilled service sector jobs there is already vast underemployment, with over a quarter of UK employees now working less than 30 hours a week.

## The Debate.

Opening Address.

On 20 May 2003 (Tuesday) the parliamentary debate was held. It dealt with a national problem. It was, however, the valleys of South Wales which provided the main thrust of the discussion. In his opening address Mr. Bryant pointed out that the 4.2 per cent unemployment figure for his constituency masked in truth an enormous amount of hidden unemployment, mainly in the form of those claiming some form of sickness benefit. This masking of the true unemployment figures was worst in mining areas.

Quoting the interim report "Employment for All", which had been issued earlier in the year by the Work and Pensions Committee, Mr. Bryant said that more than 10 of the top 20 districts for male sickness in August 2001 were former mining constituencies. Top of the list was Merthyr Tydfil. Here, 26.9 per cent of males between 16 and 64 years of age were on sickness benefit. In Rhondda Cynon Taff the figure was 18.2 per cent. This latter figure, however, did not convey the true extent of the problem. As well as many of the poorest wards in Wales, this area also includes some of the wealthiest, thus reducing the overall average. If the figure for the Rhondda were viewed in isolation, Merthyr's 26.9 per cent would be far exceeded. In reality, well over one quarter of working-age men in the Rhondda were on some form of sickness benefit.

## Problem Valleys.

Mr. Wayne David MP (Caerphilly) reinforced the argument. Five out of the eight areas with the highest number of claimants for incapacity benefit in the United Kingdom were in South Wales: Blaenau Gwent, Rhondda Cynon Taff, Neath and Port Talbot, Caerphilly and, top of the list, Merthyr Tydfil and Rhymney. If the figures are broken down even more, they show a concentration in a relatively small area at the heads of the valleys. In a situation without parallel in the United Kingdom, in some wards as many as one in four people of working age are claiming incapacity benefit while, of males between 16 and 60, up to 40 per cent are idle. A particularly worrying concomitant of this is that young people are growing up, regarding this as a perfectly natural thing to do.

It was pointed out that in the tight valleys there is little flat land on which to create large new concerns. There will never again be a business there employing tens of thousands of men. When a mine closed, the local economy collapsed and the community lost its focus. Not only the mine but also the businesses dependant on the mine followed it into oblivion. All too often, miners were dumped onto the benefits system and then forgotten, a situation inherited by their children and grandchildren. In the early 1990's incapacity benefit was offered where no employment was available. If people left the pit the day before it closed and then signed on immediately for incapacity benefit, this served government interests. Those concerned were thereby removed from the unemployment statistics.

## Benefit Culture.

Such massaging of the statistics created a side effect, namely a benefit culture. It is a culture and a frame of mind into which a hard core remains locked. Mr. Llew Smith MP (Blaenau Gwent) said that the jobs that have come along are almost invariably part-time, low-paid and soul-destroying. The real problem was that there were no worthwhile jobs. According to a survey of school children in coalfield communities, conducted by the Coalfields Regeneration Trust, by far the most popular choice as an ideal job was the armed forces. People's understanding of work has had to change dramatically. Up until the recent past work was manual and on the doorstep, or close to it. It was predominantly for men, and mostly for life. If they developed medical problems they would simply be moved from the coalface to a lighter task in another part of the mine. In essence the mine provided its own system for rehabilitating people with health problems, since they would still have work. All of these things no longer apply.

## Transport The Key.

The communities were not developed to have easy access to places further afield. The workplace in an adjacent valley might be just 3 or 5km distant as the crow flies. Getting there, however, might entail taking a bus down one valley and a second bus up another valley, often with poor connections. Without a car one cannot get to a job, but without a job one cannot afford a car. In addition, there is a mismatch between the skills available and the needs of employers. Public transport must be at the heart of policy and the infrastructure must be in place to get those who want to work to employers with vacancies for people with skills. Chris Bryant MP quoted numerous employers who expressed the desire to employ more people, if only they could find someone to answer the phone without sounding grumpy and surly.

## Work And Health.

Many aspects of the regeneration lie with the Welsh Assembly. The government green paper, Pathways to Work: Helping People into Employment, sets out their strategy for enabling those with health problems to move into work. The original taskforce report said that, "the coalfields have a unique combination of concentrated joblessness, physical isolation, poor infrastructure and severe health problems". One pilot study is underway in Bridgend. The object is to bring home to people that it now pays to take what can be the difficult step back into work, especially if they have been idle for many years. The government insist that this not about forcing sick people into jobs.

The gap between the healthiest and those with the worst health mirrors that between the wealthiest and those with the least disposable income. Many such problems are the result of poor nutrition, while many others are residual, the result of men having worked in the pits. At the beginning of the twenty-first century, hundreds of men were still fighting for compensation for the coal dust in their lungs, a relic of the years they spent working underground. Widows of men who died from the killer dust were also seeking payments.

## DUST.

### Dust Or Smoking?

It had been a hard fight, but pneumoconiosis and silicosis have long been recognised as occupational diseases, justifying compensation. The former involves the presence of coal dust in the lungs and the latter the harder, more abrasive, stone dust. Other chest complaints may have their origins elsewhere, particularly in smoking. This had enabled British Coal to reject any charge of culpability in such cases. The diseases concerned are emphysema and chronic bronchitis. Both of them have little chance of cure. Treatment is aimed at relieving symptoms.

Emphysema is a lung disease involving damage to the air sacs or alveoli. The lungs lose their elasticity and become less able to expand and contract. Since the alveoli cannot deflate completely, less oxygen is taken into the lungs, resulting in breathing difficulties.

Cigarette smoking is the most frequent cause but it was argued that coal dust causes the release of chemicals that damage the walls of the air sacs. The damage worsens over time, affecting the exchange of oxygen and carbon dioxide, the process by which we breathe.

Chronic Bronchitis is an inflammation of the bronchi, the main air passages to the lungs. It occurs over a long period, recurring over several years. It is characterised by excessive bronchial mucus, with a cough that lasts for three months or more in at least two consecutive years. Severity of the disease depends to a great extent on whether the sufferer smokes, and on the amount and duration of the exposure to coal dust.

### The Board Is Called To Book.

Landmark Judgement.

In 1998, in a landmark judgement, Mr Justice Turner of the High Court awarded average damages of £18,000 to the six miners who, since 1991, had been involved in litigation with their former employer, British Coal. The case set a precedent for the hundreds of thousands of miners, former miners and their widows, waiting in the wings with similar claims. Each case would have to be made through a solicitor and would take three or more years to assess. They are assessed by respiratory specialists, using all available British Coal plus Department of Health and Social Security medical records. Living claimants have breathing tests and a full medical. Deceased claims are based on notes only. In the biggest compensation scheme against a single employer ever awarded, by 2004 the government was paying out approximately £2 M every working day, with a final bill estimated as being over £7 billion.

Deadline.

March 1, 2004, was the deadline for such cases. Previously, Peter Evans, partner and head of claimant litigation at Hugh James Solicitors, had made a public statement to the effect that there were still thousands of ex-miners and their families who had not yet registered to claim the compensation to which they were entitled. Less than half of the 100,000 plus miners who worked in South Wales mines since the mid-1950's had registered. All the signs were that a large band of people was unaware of their right to claim compensation. Mr. Evans said:

"The biggest problem is that relatives of deceased miners are not sure if they can claim. Close relatives of deceased miners have as much right to claim under the scheme as living former miners. Many people mistakenly believe that they cannot claim if respiratory problems such as emphysema, bronchitis and industrial asthma were not the cause of death or listed on the death certificate. That is simply not the case".

Statistics.

By the above deadline, 557,000 claims had been received from former pitmen in the UK for lung problems or Vibration White Finger (VWF). This latter is a numbing of the fingers resulting from the use of machinery (pneumatic picks being a prime cause). For lung disease, over £1 billion compensation had already been paid out, plus £959 M for VWF.

By June 2004, the position nationally concerning respiratory claimants alone was as follows:

| | |
|---|---|
| Claims Registered. | 566,000 |
| Claims Settled in Full. | 138,000 |
| Interim Payments. | 74,000 |
| Total Damages Paid to date. | £1.1 billion |

Of the 89,254 claims submitted in Wales, only 34,456 of the claimants were still alive. Full settlements had been made to 13,052 claimants in Wales and to 9,700 families of applicants who had already died.

Also by June 2004, damages awarded for respiratory disease plus VWF in example constituencies is given below:

| CONSTITUENCY | DAMAGES AWARDED (£ million). |
|---|---|
| Berwick-upon-Tweed | 11.4 |
| Burnley | 3.5 |
| Edinburgh East & Musselburgh | 2.0 |
| Kirkcaldy | 6.2 |
| Makerfield | 11.4 |
| Merthyr Tydfil & Rhymney | 48.8 |
| North West Durham | 11.6 |
| Pontypridd | 19.2 |
| St. Helen's North | 7.9 |
| Wentworth | 30.2 |

# REMNANTS.
## Burying The Industry.
Open Spaces -

Many regarded the loss of jobs as a price worth paying for an end to the terrible toll in human life and suffering, as well as the desecration of a once beautiful landscape. These were hallmarks of the era when coal was king. Legacies remain, although far less physical than the detritus left behind after industrial contractions in the past.

In contrast to the policy of the old private coalowners, when British Coal closed a mine towards the end of the twentieth century, little that was obvious remained to tell the tale. Open spaces and smoothed out waste heaps served to bury the numerous corpses of a once great industry. On departure of the last miner, bulldozers were in action, reducing the surface buildings to rubble. The headgear was dismantled and shafts filled in, leaving millions of pounds worth of valuable equipment underground. To take just one example, it took only three weeks to seal off Celynen South Colliery. In this period, 30,000 tonnes of shale, 18,000 tonnes of hardcore, plus 2,500 tonnes of clay were poured down the three shafts. The cleared and flattened surfaces were left to await a new reputable tenant, who would bring prosperity and employment. When no such tenant transpired (which all too often was the case) the sites were converted into playing fields or covered with cosmetic grass.

## -And Parks.

In 2000, five years of land reclamation work at a cost of £4.5 m were completed on the site of the former Deep Navigation Colliery at Trelewis. Also incorporated in the scheme were the adjacent Trelewis Drift and Taff Merthyr Collieries. The resultant Taff Bargoed Community Park, 2.4 km long, includes a series of picturesque lakes, Britain's biggest reed bed, "organic" pollution cleansing system and a rock-climbing centre that attracts 70,000 visitors per annum. Future plans include Britain's first ice climbing wall (indoors, since Welsh weather is wet but not Arctic), plus a man-made caving system, a canoeing centre and several sports fields. The project was funded by the Welsh Development Agency and managed by Merthyr Tydfil County Borough Council.

## Subsidence.

Where shallow seams have been mined and future building is required in the area, the past does not allow itself to be so easily extirpated. It comes back to haunt the developer and local council in the form of an extensive system of boring and then filling, all necessary to stabilize the potential building site against subsidence.

## Ghosts.

### Dinas Rescue Station.

At Dinas in the Lower Rhondda is the only mines rescue station left in Wales. The rescue station at Dinas is itself an inheritance of the past, albeit still a living entity. Sited in the Lower Rhondda Fawr where the valley is at its narrowest, it is set back off the road and a mere 183 metres from where in 1812 Walter Coffin, the local coal czar, sunk the first Rhondda shaft. A long liturgy of drama commenced in 1911 when the Coal Mines Act of that year made provision for colliery owners to provide central rescue stations.

On 27 June 1912, King George V and Queen Mary made the first entry in the visitors' book of the newly inaugurated rescue station. Since then, over 200 emergency calls have been responded to. Each, with a succinct hand-written description of the incident, is listed at the station.

On 20 December 1997, the last entry (up to 2002) was made in the logbook of emergency call-outs. It was also one of the most bizarre and illustrates that, elimination of physical artefacts notwithstanding; ghosts of the past can still intrude without warning to confound the living.

Two members of the public were walking a dog on the one-time site of the Lady Margaret Colliery at Treherbert in the upper Rhondda Fawr. This mine had already ceased production prior to the Second World War. Their pre-Christmas deliberations, accompanied by a quiet smoke, were savagely interrupted by the blue flame of a methane ignition, which sprang out from the seal of a nearby shaft, seeking them out. One of the two was himself an ex-underground worker and, showing presence of mind, their jump over an adjacent embankment saved them from serious injury and perhaps death. The shaft seal, obviously not gas-tight and further damaged by the explosion, was subsequently repaired, with work being completed on Christmas Eve. The dog never forgot this incident, showing signs of stress on any attempt to repeat that fateful walk.

The rapid decline in the coal industry locally was not reflected in the operation of the Dinas Rescue Station, as it had to take the place of those other South Wales rescue stations that successively closed:

- Abercynon          Closed 1929.

- Aberaman           Closed 1947.

- New Tredegar       Closed 1956.

- Brynmenin (Maesteg)  Closed 1980.

- Crumlin            Closed 1986.


Rescue as Private Enterprise.

Nowadays, together with five in the English Midlands, the station forms part of Mines Rescue Service Ltd., a private but non-profit making company.

In 1995, on privatisation, this company replaced British Coal in providing an emergency escape and rescue service to the UK coal-mining industry. The Dinas Station survives due to a statutory requirement that all mines must have the services of such a rescue station available to them within 60 minutes of an incident occurring. Primarily it serves Tower, along with small levels and the remnants of British Coal operations. The company as a whole is sustained by a levy on the colliery companies for each ton of coal produced (10p/t in 1995, 14p/t in 2001). In addition there is association with a number of non-coal mines in the UK, plus diversification into health and safety related issues for all types of industry.

At Dinas, 4 officers, 12 brigadesmen and 21 part-timers continue the tradition. Among the specialised equipment owned and maintained by Mines Rescue Service Ltd. are five emergency mobile winder sets, kept in case regular shaft winders should fail. One of these is kept at the Big Pit Mining Museum.


# HERITAGE.

## Big Pit.

This is at Blaenavon (tel. 01495 790311; open March to November daily) and is the National Mining Museum of Wales. Blaenavon was designated at the turn of the millennium as a World Heritage Site of "outstanding universal value".

In 1782 its industrial history commenced when three industrialists, Hill, Hopkins and Pratt opened the first coalmine there.

In 1789, they started iron production at the North Street furnaces.

In 1878 the problem of large-scale steel-making from iron that originated from other than low phosphoric ores was solved at Blaenavon. The patents, by Sidney Gilchrist Thomas and his cousin Percy Gilchrist, were later sold to the American industrialist Andrew Carnegie. At the old ironworks are preserved the furnaces where once ironstone, coal and limestone were devoured to produce the glowing pigs of iron. Visitors can also see the houses where workers lived.

By 1914, Blaenavon was in decline. The use of imported ore resulted in the steel industry moving to the coast.

In 1938, the last furnace was dismantled.

Big Pit is based on a colliery that closed in 1980. Previous discussions with the National Coal Board regarding the preservation of various collieries after closure had been unsuccessful for a number of reasons, such as excessive depth, plus drainage and/or ventilation problems.

At the end of 1972, the possibility of preserving the shaft and surface buildings at Big Pit seemed promising. A development scheme was under way to replace the shaft with a drift for coal raising purposes. Especially the shallow depth made it a suitable choice for a coalmine museum.

In 1975, the first formal meetings were held between representatives of the NCB, National Museum of Wales, Welsh Tourist Board, local authorities and other bodies. The Coal Board carried out conservation work on the surface buildings as well as repair work underground around pit bottom and along possible visitor routes. Legally it is still a mine, for its unique attraction is the descent by cage through one of the original shafts to the level of actual underground workings. The underground visit lasts about an hour and gives some feel for the environment. An audio-visual gallery plus extensive surface installations complement the underground visit. These installations include the familiar pithead gear and winding engine house, plus pithead baths, lamp room, workshops and a reconstructed miner's cottage.

## Afan Argoed.

This country park in the Afan Valley houses the South Wales Miners' Museum (tel. 01639 850564; open April to September daily). This was a pioneering effort as far as mining museums are concerned. The last pit in the valley closed in 1970 and the museum was created to tell the story of South Wales mining and the mining communities. It has a collection of early mining machinery and a simulated coalface.

## Cefn Coed.

At this colliery museum in Crynant (tel. 01639 750556; open April to October daily) are the surface remains of a latecomer to the valleys. With a shaft depth of 732 metres, it was the deepest anthracite mine in the world when mining began in 1930. It closed in 1968, but important machinery was saved, including the horizontal steam-winding engine installed in1927 plus Lancashire boilers and the compressor that supplied compressed air to power underground machinery. A shallow gallery has been specially created to allow visitors to see underground working methods. An unusual feature of the colliery is that no mining village ever developed around it.

## Elliot Colliery.

Here, in New Tredegar, the winding house with its magnificent example of a steam winding engine now stands alone. It is possible to experience the winding engine in motion and discover the story of Elliot Colliery and the local coal industry. There is a souvenir shop and refreshment facilities (tel. 01443 822666; www.caerphilly.gov.uk/visiting; open /Easter to October: Wednesday/Thursday/Friday 11am-4pm, Saturday/Sunday/Bank Holidays 2-5pm. - October to Easter: Wednesday/Thursday/Friday 11am-4pm).

## The Hetty Shaft.

This shaft of the old Great Western Colliery, at Trehafod in the Lower Rhondda, is still equipped with pithead gear and winding engine house. It was closed as an operating mine before the Second World War. However, the Hetty Shaft was maintained as ventilation for the nearby Tymawr Colliery, which closed in 1983. Adjacent to the winding engine house, the fan house can also be seen. The reciprocating, steam winding engine was originally built in 1875 by Barker and Cope at Kidsgrove, Staffordshire,. The drum is 4.9 m in diameter and originally held flat rope. After years of being neglected and vandalised, the Pontypridd Historical Society has renovated both winding house and engine. It can now operate again, using compressed air instead of steam.

## Kidwelly Industrial Museum.

This museum (tel. 01554 891084; open Spring Bank Holiday to September, all day weekdays and weekend afternoons) concentrates on the tinplate industry, which was a feature of this part of Wales. However, remains of the former Morlais Colliery, with its pithead gear, are on the same site.

## Penallta Colliery.

Here, in Gelligaer, the pithead gears are still to be seen. This was one of the later closures, with the pit remaining in operation until 1991.

## Rhondda Heritage Park.

This centre (tel. 01443 682036; open Easter to October every day - during winter open every day except Monday) is close to the Hetty Shaft mentioned above. The Lewis Merthyr Colliery surface has been converted into an experience, showing not only the technicalities involved in winning the high quality steam coal of the Rhondda, but also the unique society which developed there. Whereas other museums present the story simply and with few frills, this one makes extensive use of multi-media displays and simulations of the underground environment. In the vicinity are riverside and forest walks. A pleasant restaurant, a bookshop, plus fun facilities for the kids complete the family outing.

In the year 2000, the local actor Glyn Houston officially inaugurated one of the few memorials to the many victims of the fight to win coal. This is a replica of an oil safety lamp, 2 metres high, and situated at the Heritage Park entrance. Some miles away, at Llwynypia in the central Rhondda Fawr, the Rhondda Civil Society sponsored another memorial commemorating Rhondda's past. Viscount Tonypandy inaugurated this in 1993. On a 2.4 metre high plinth a collier, of similar height, stands together with his wife, who nurses a baby Welsh-style in the traditional shawl wrapped around her. Adjacent to the main road, it stands on the site of the former Glamorgan Colliery. Close by is the derelict engine house where police and strikers once fought it out, starting the 1911 Ton-y-Pandy riots.

## Senghenydd.

The Pit Disaster Memorial Exhibition may be viewed by appointment only (tel. 01222 832061 for Aber Valley Community Council, or 01222 832192 for Mrs. L. Smith - Secretary of the Community Centre). The disasters of 1901 and 1913 are dealt with, the latter being the worst in British mining history.

## Tower Colliery.

This, the only remaining deep-mine left in Wales, has its own visitor centre (advisable to phone in advance: tel. 01685 811199). It offers a range of videos, diagrams, posters and press cuttings relative to the drama of the workers' take-over and the subsequent operation of the mine.

THE END.

# TECHNICAL TERMS AND ABBREVIATIONS:

## ABBREVIATIONS.

BACM: British Association of Colliery Management.

BC: British Coal (In 1986, the NCB was so renamed).

BP: British Petroleum.

bcm: billion cubic meters.

CCGT: Combined Cycle Gas Turbine (A gas turbine driven electrical generator whereby the heat of the gas turbine exhaust is used to produce steam. This in turn powers an additional, steam turbo-generator).

CEGB: Central Electricity Generating Board.

CHP: Combined Heat and Power (Electrical generation where the waste heat of the driving machine is utilised; typically for an industrial process or for district heating).

$CO_2$: Carbon Dioxide.

Cwt: hundredweight (i.e. one twentieth of a ton); may be either singular or plural.

DSK: Deutsche SteinKohle (the Germany company, part private and part state owned, which currently owns and operates all deep coal mines in that country).

EOR: Enhanced Oil Recovery (the recovery of additional oil from a field by the injection of gas, such as carbon dioxide, so as to force up extra oil).

GJ: GigaJoule (See under "Technical Terms" below).

EOR: Enhanced Oil Recovery (The injection of gas or water into depleted oil fields, thus forcing up additional oil).

ESI: Electricity Supply Industry.

EU: European Union.

FGD: Flue Gas Desulphurisation.

GATT: General Agreement on Tariffs and Trade.

GW: Gigawatt (See under "Technical Terms" below).

ICGCC: Integrated Coal Gasification Combined Cycle (A combined cycle gas turbine, as under CCGT above, where the fuel is obtained from coal. This is gasified in the vicinity of the set).

IPP: Independent Power Producer.

IRB: Independent Review Body.

JCM: Joy Continuous Miner (A coal-winning machine, manufactured by the company Joy Mining, designed to advance on a narrow front. Used for the pillar and stall method of working and for driving development headings in coal).

LNG: Liquefied Natural Gas.

MFGB: Miners Federation of Great Britain.

m: metre (or metres).

Mt; million tonnes.

MW: Megawatt (See under "Technical Terms" below).

NACODS: National Association of Colliery Overmen, Deputies and Shotfirers.

NCB: National Coal Board.

Nox: Nitrous Oxide.

NUM: National Union of Mineworkers.

OECD: Organisation for Economic Cooperation and Development.

OFFER: Office of Electricity Regulation.

OMS (Output per Man-Shift); Standard method of measuring productivity in the mining industry. Average tonnage produced for each individual shift worked.

OPEC: Organisation of Petroleum Exporting Countries.

RECs: Regional Electrical Companies (Since privatisation, responsible for local distribution and consumer sales).

SO2: Sulphur Dioxide.

SWMF: South Wales Miners Federation.

t: tonne (or tonnes).

UDM : Union of Democratic Mineworkers.

## TECHNICAL TERMS:

Anticline: A dome-like formation of the strata, which reaches a high point before descending again.

Armoured Flexible Conveyor (AFC): A shallow, floor-mounted conveyor along the length of mechanised coalfaces. It is used to mount and guide the power loader in its travel along the face and to transport production off the face to the first of the roadway conveyors. Coal transport is by means of a scraping effect, resulting from metal bars or "flights" at regular intervals, connected between two chains running in slots on either side of the conveyor. As its name suggests it is manufactured of armour steel and its constituent pans can move relative to each other, allowing it to "snake over", behind the power loader. It is powered by one or several electric motors.

Deputy: Mining official responsible for a district underground. Charged with the statutory duty of ensuring safety within that district, e.g. checking for gas, adequacy of roof support etc.

Drift: An inclined main roadway, sometimes between two different depths underground but usually linking underground workings with the surface. This method is used instead of shafts in the case of shallow mines.

Drivage: An underground roadway in the process of construction (see also heading).

Duff: A term used in South Wales for small coal.

Fault: A geological discontinuity, due to prehistoric disturbance, whereby the seam and adjacent layers have been thrown upwards or downwards, relative to adjacent strata.

Gate-road: Underground roadway between the end of a coalface and one of the main trunk roadways of the pit. Each coalface has an intake-gate and a return-gate. An intake-gate (or main-gate) is used as an intake airway for coalface ventilation and for the transportation of outgoing coal. A return-gate (or tail-gate) is the return airway and is used to bring up supplies.

GigaJoule (GJ): A unit of energy equal to a thousand million joules. One joule is the amount of energy consumed when a power of one watt is applied for one second. Coal is not as uniform a substance as natural gas. It is customary to convert coal to energy content on the basis of coal equivalent energy as follows: 1 tonne = 29.3 GJ.

Gigawatt: A unit of power equal to a thousand megawatts.

Heading: An underground roadway in the process of construction (see also drivage), or one of the main (i.e. trunk) roadways of the pit.

Horizon: A large-section roadway, driven straight and level through the strata, as opposed to just following the ups and downs coal seam, which only rarely is in a horizontal plane. Such a roadway may therefore be used for locomotive haulage. It may be connected to the coalseams and other, parallel, horizons by means of lateral roadways. Horizons at different levels may be connected by means of underground shafts, called "staple" shafts.

Horizon mining: A method of working inclined coal seams by driving horizons at different levels from the shafts to intersect with and gain access to the seams.

Inbye: Towards the coalfaces and away from the shafts.

Journey: A train of 30 cwt. trams or, alternatively, mine cars. These latter may be of 1.5 tonnes or, more usually, 3 tonnes capacity. The journey is moved by steel rope haulage, or by locomotive haulage if the roadway is sufficiently straight and level as per "horizon" standards.

Level: A small private mine, consisting of a penetration into the mountainside where the coal seam is exposed.

Megawatt: A unit of power equal to a million watts.

Outbye: Away from the coalfaces and towards the shafts.

Overman: Mining official in charge of several underground districts. He fits into the management structure between the level of deputy and the undermanager. The latter is responsible for the complete underground workings within a particular seam.

Panel: The oblong-shaped area of coal extracted during the total lifetime of a particular longwall coalface.

Power Loading Machine: A machine that traverses the coalface, cutting off the coal from the seam while simultaneously loading it onto the Armoured Flexible conveyor (AFC).

Ripping lip: The vertical face of rock formed where a roadway of greater height connects with a space of lower height, typically a coalface. As the face advances, this lip must be brought down so as to advance the roadway. This is frequently done with explosives.

Roadway: Underground tunnel, linking the shafts with the working faces. They may be divided into main (or trunk) roadways that lead directly to the shafts or secondary roadways off the main (see gate road).

Shaft (upcast): This is the shaft by means of which the ventilation air, returning from the underground workings, is exhausted. A "fan drift" links the shaft, near its top, with the large ventilation fan for the mine. Access to the pit top is via an air lock, to prevent short-circuiting of the air. This shaft is usually employed to wind men and supplies only, due to the problem of bringing coal continuously through the air lock.

Shaft (downcast): This is the shaft used as intake for the ventilation air required by the underground workings. It is used for the continuous winding of coal since there is no pit-top airlock, which would otherwise obstruct operation.

Shotfiring: The use of explosives to move ground.

Skip/Skip winding: A tank-like container dedicated to the winding of coal in a shaft. This is opposed to a cage, for winding the drams or mine cars in which coal is transported. In the latter case, the cage may also be used for winding men and supplies.

Stable holes: A recess at each end of the face, such as to enable the cutting element of the power loader to be moved over, in preparation for the next cut. They are sometimes worked as short extensions to the gate roads.

Staple shaft: This is a shaft between two levels (usually horizons) underground. It is normally employed to bring coal down to the lower horizon, by means of a spiral chute within the shaft. Locomotive transportation will then take it to pit-bottom.

Syncline: A basin-like formation of the strata, which reaches a deepest point before rising again.

Washout: An area in a coal seam where the coal has simply disappeared. Thought to be caused by the original vegetation, from which the coal was originally formed, being washed away during the process of its transformation.

# *Acknowledgements*

First and foremost I am indebted to my friend and colleague George Tan, whose good offices and practical support enabled this book to be published.

Invaluable input was provided by Glyn Roberts and Ken Davies of Tower colliery. I thank them for their co-operation.

Roy Green and Harry Pearce provided input on practical mining and the social background.

Dr. I. W. Fawcett is a consultant involved in miners' respiratory diseases and associated claims for compensation. He was good enough to talk to me on this subject.

The Rescue Centre at Dinas provided information, both historical and on the current state of the industry.

Staff at the South Wales Miners Library, plus those at Glamorgan Records Office, Big Pit Mining Museum and the Nantgarw Collection all proved co-operative and helpful. I am indebted to Clare Boucher of the former, for obtaining permission to quote from the South Wales Coalfield Collection, and to Peter Bennet of the latter for his assistance in the selection of photographs.

A special thanks is due to my brother-in-law, Cyril Bevis, for his uncomplaining service as my chauffeur, his periods of waiting for me to finish my research, plus his general hospitality during my visits to South Wales.

Last but not least I would like to thank my wife Carin for her indispensable proof reading of the manuscript and also for her understanding and tolerance of my frequent absences. These were either away from home in the course of research or bent over my computer while hidden away in my "den" at home.

The opinions expressed, and any mistakes made, are my own.

Mike Thomas,
Ratingen,
November 2004

## Documentary Sources

Prime among the documentary sources for this book have been the South Wales Miners Library (SWML) and South Wales Coalfield Archive, both at the University of Wales Swansea, plus in addition the Glamorgan Records Office in Cardiff.

In addition to providing specific documentation, the South Wales Miners Library was most useful for overall background information, including the excellent South Wales Coalfield Directory by Ray Lawrence (Blackwood 1998).

What went on behind the governmental scenes during the 1972 strike, and the run-up to the 1974 strike, was obtained from cabinet papers accessible at the National Archives at Kew in London.

The Nantgarw Collection of the National Museum of Wales made available their Photographic Collection for illustration purposes.

Documents relevant to specific chapters are listed in the Bibliography, under the chapter's title.

# Bibliography

In addition to general documentatary and personal sources, the following includes main material drawn upon in my research for specific chapters. As well as archive documents and newspaper articles published literature is also included. These works provide suggestions for further reading, as well as acknowledging my debt to their authors.

1) The Last Explosion.
- Glamorgan Records D/D NCB 67/7/1 and 2; Cambrian Colliery reorganisation.
- Glamorgan Records D/D NCB 67/4/10 to 12 & 67/4/148; Cambrian Colliery explosion.
- HMSO; Inspector's report - Explosion at Cambrian colliery Glamorgan.
- Rhondda Leader 21 & 28 May 1965.

2) Why Coal?
- International Energy Agency; World Energy Outlook 1998.
- International Energy Agency; The Link Between Energy and Human Activity 1997.
- International Energy Agency; The Future Role of Coal 1998.
- International Energy Agency; Coal Information 2000.
- International Energy Agency; Projected Costs of Generating Electricity 1998.
- International Energy Agency; Regional trends in Energy-Efficient, Coal-Fired, power generation Technologies 1998.
- Financial Times International Coal reports September - October 2000.
- Financial Times 3 February 2003.

3) The Legacy.
- Glamorgan records D/D NCB 6-14; Current newscuttings on Tonypandy Riots.
- "The Rhondda Valleys" by E. D. Lewis; University College Cardiff Press 1959.
- "Rhondda Anthology" by Meic Stephens; Cromwell Press 1993.
- "Capitalism, Community and Conflict" by Chris Williams; University of Wales Press 1998.
- "The Fed" by Hywel Francis & Dai Smith; University of Wales Press 1998.
- "Coal Society" by David Egan; Gomer Press 1987.
- "Wynford Vaughan-Thomas Wales"; Michael Joseph 1981.
- "A Tour Through the Island of Great Britain"; completed in 1726, Daniel Defoe

4) Brave New World.
- Glamorgan Records D/D NCB 67/11/1 to 7; Press Digest (1947-58)
- SWML AUD/65; Interview with Phillip Weekes (1979-82).
- Ministry of Fuel and Power; Report of Technical Advisory Committee on Coal Mining 1945.
- Ministry of Fuel and Power; South Wales Coalfield. Regional Survey report.
- "The Fed" by Hywel Francis & Dai Smith; University of Wales Press 1998.

5) Money, Money. Money.
   - Glamorgan Records D/D NCB 67/12/40; SW Division Output in 1947.
   - SWML AUD/65; Interview with Phillip Weekes (1979-82).
   - "The Fed" by Hywel Francis & Dai Smith; University of Wales Press 1998.
   - "Im Wandel der Zeit" by Thyssen (Great Britain) Ltd. Article on the companies 40th anniversary of its UK operations.
   - "Ten Year Stint" by Lord Robens; Cassell 1972.

6) White Hot Heat.
   - Parliamentary Select Committee on the Nationalised Industries; Report on the Exploitation of North sea Gas 1968.
   - Parliamentary Energy Committee Fourth Report; The Cost of Nuclear power 1989-90.
   - DTI Report; British Energy Policy and the Coal Industry 1993.

7) The Odyssey of Decline.
   - Glamorgan Records D/D NCB 67/5/11; Proposed Closure of Cambrian and Glyncastle Collieries.

8) Why Us?
   - Glamorgan Records D/D NCB 67/5/1 and 2; Colliery Closures.
   - G lamorgan Records D/D NCB 67/5/17 to 20; Colliery Closures.
   - Glamorgan Records D/D NCB 67/7/44 to 47; Reorganisation Schemes.
   - Glamorgan Records D/D NCB 67/7/66; Reorganisation Schemes.
   - Glamorgan Records D/D NCB 67/7/69; Penallta Underground Reorganisation.
   - Glamorgan Records 67/8/1 to 4; Colliery Review Procedure.
   - Glamorgan Records D/D NCB 67/12/1 to 35 and 37; NCB Public Relations.
   - "Rhondda Past and Future" by K. S. Hopkins; Rhondda Borough Council 1980.

9) Dust and Disaster.
   - Glamorgan Records D/D NCB 67/3/9 to 17; Inspectorates Reports on explosions in South Wales (1956-71).
   - Glamorgan Records D/D NCB 67/4/141 to 143; Pneumoconiosis.
   - DTI Report; Outburst of coal and firedamp at Cynheidre/Pentremawr Colliery.
   - "The Control of Dust in Mines"; Cymric Federation Press 1959.
   - "Aberfan, Government and Disasters" by Iain McLean & Martin Johnes; Welsh Academic Press 2000.
   - "Senghennydd" by Michael Lieven; Gomer Press 1994.
   - Colliery Guardian 22 November 1962.

10) Fighting Retreat.
   - "Ten Year Stint" by Lord Robens; Cassell 1972.
   - SWML AUD/110; Interview with Brian Williams (31/1/80).
   - AMEME Journal, diverse articles throughout the 1960s.
   - Colliery Guardian, diverse articles throughout the 1960s.

11) Militancy - and Triumph.
   - Glamorgan Records D/D NCB 67/1/9; National Strike.
   - Glamorgan Records D/D NCB 67/12/41 and 42; Pit Profiles.
   - SWML AUD/415 Interviews with Dai Frances and George Reece; (8/2/74).
   - SWML AUD/60; Interview with Tyrone O'Sullivan (22/1/81).
   - DTI; The Plan for Coal 1974.
   - National Archives; Cabinet papers 1972-73.
   - Electronics and Power April 1979.
   - "Ten Year Stint" by Lord Robens; Cassell 1972.
   - "The Fed" by Hywel Francis & Dai Smith; University of Wales Press 1998.
   - Financial Times 3 February 1974.

12) Ate.
   - Glamorgan Records D/D NCB 67/6/1 and 2; Planning and Development.
   - DTI Consultative Document; Energy Policy 1978.
   - "The Benn Diaries" by Tony Benn; Arrow Books 1996.
   - "Strike" by the Sunday Times Insight Team; Coronet 1985.

13) Deus Ex Machina - but Delayed.
   - Glamorgan Records D/D NCB 67/1/10; South Wales Strike.
   - Glamorgan Records D/D NCB 67/6/3; Planning and Development.
   - SWML AUD/65; Interview with Phillip Weekes (1979-82).
   - SWML AUD/60; Interview with Tyrone O'Sullivan (22/1/81).
   - NCB South Wales Area; Anthracite Strategy Review.
   - Monopolies and Mergers Commission; Report on the Coal Mining Industry 1983.
   - "The Downing Street Years" by Margaret Thatcher; HarperCollins 1993.

14) Hubris.
   - Glamorgan Records D/D NCB 67/1/11; NUM Strike.
   - Glamorgan Records D/D NCB 67/1/17; Area Directors Strike Correspondence.
   - Glamorgan Records D/D NCB 67/1/32 to 34; Industrial Relations Issues in South Wales.
   - SWML AUD/573; Interview with George Reece (6/1/86).
   - SWML AUD/60; Interview with Tyrone O'Sullivan (22/1/81).
   - "The Enemy Within, the Secret War against the Miners" by Shamus Milne; Verso 1994.
   - "Strike" by the Sunday Times Insight Team; Coronet 1985.

- IEE Review January 1955.
- "The Downing Street Years" by Margaret Thatcher; HarperCollins 1993.
- "The Coal War"; BBC TV documentary 2004.
- "Rock and a Hard Place"; ITV documentary 2004.
- "Strike; when Britain went to war"; TV4 documentary 2004.

15) Nemesis.
- Glamorgan Records D/D NCB 67/6/3; Planning and Development.
- Glamorgan Records D/D NCB 67/9/2; Capital Expenditure Allocations (1984-85).
- Glamorgan Records D/D NCB 67/12/43; British Coal, South Wales Group News (1986).
- Glamorgan Records 67/12/48; British Coal Activities (1991-92).
- SWML AUD/573; Interview with George Reece (6/1/86).
- "The Enemy Within" by Ian MacGregor.

16) E Tu Brute!
- White Paper on Coal Industry 1993.
- DTI Report; Review of the Energy Sources for Power Generation.
- "The Downing Street Years" by Margaret Thatcher; HarperCollins 1993.
- Energie magazine, first quarter 1992.
- Glueckauf magazine, diverse articles between 1996 and 2002.

17) The Sublime - and the Ridiculous.
- Glamorgan Records D/D NCB 67/5/13; Tower No.1 and Fernhill closures.
- Glamorgan Records D/D NCB 67/7/113 to 117; Fernhill reconstruction.
- Glamorgan Records D/D NCB 67/9/1; Reports on Completed Capital Projects in SW Division (1956-65).
- Glamorgan Records D/D NCB 67/1/45; Mardy Colliery, meetings between management and NUM (1967-81).
- Glamorgan Records D/D NCB 67/7/107 to 110; Mardy Colliery performance and closure.
- Glamorgan Records D/D NCB 67/12/36; Souvenir of last pit in the Rhondda.
- SWML AUD/140 Interview with George Reece; (22/10/80).
- SWML; Fernhill Lodge Minute Books; ref nos. MNC/NUM/L/17/1 to 9 (1957-80).
- "The Fed" by Hywel Francis & Dai Smith; University of Wales Press 1998.
- "Arthur Horner: a Political Biography" by Nina Fishman; Lawrence & Wishart 2004.
- The Times Saturday Review 29 September 1990.
- Western Mail 5 Jan 1987, 2 & 4 May 1987
- Rhondda Leader 30 April 1987,
- South Wales Echo 15 August 1987.

18) The Miner's Next Step - and Their final One.
- Glamorgan Records D/D NCB 67/7/118 to 124; Tower Colliery Face Design, Assessment of Reserves and Reorganisation.
- Glamorgan Records D/D NCB 67/12/45 to 47; Tower and Mardy News.
- DTI report, prepared by International Mining Consultants (IMC); Prospects for Coal Production in England, Scotland and Wales 1999.
- "Tower of Strength" by Tyrone O'Sullivan; Mainstream 2001.
- "The Tower Story" by Professor Hywel Francis; Commissioned by Tower colliery.
- Tower Colliery Magazine summer 2003 edition.
- Tower Colliery Magazine summer 2004 edition.
- "Tower", a mainly photographic work by Roger Tiley.

19) The New Energy - Anti Portas.
- DTI report, prepared by International Mining Consultants (IMC); Prospects for Coal Production in England, Scotland and Wales 1999.
- World Coal Institute; The Role of Coal as an Energy Source.
- Royal Commission on Environmental Pollution; Report on Energy - the Changing Climate.
- Cabinet Office Performance and innovation Unit; The Energy Review 2002.
- DTI White Paper; Our Energy future - Creating a Low carbon Economy 2003.
- Financial Times 28 April 2003.

20) Memories.
- House of Commons Hansard Debates for 20 May 2003.
- "How Real is My Valley"? by John Evans; Underground Press 1994.
- Mines Rescue Service annual report 2001.
- Dinas Mines Rescue Station incident book.
- Western Mail 27 December 2000.

Other Books to be recommended, and used as background reading:
- "Collieries of South Wales" (1 & 2) by John Cornwell; Landmark 2001 & 2002.
- "A Photographic History of mining in South Wales" by John O'Sullivan; W. H. Smith 2001.
- "Images of the South Wales Mines" by David Bellamy; Sutton Publishing 1993.

# H

# I

# K

# L

# M

# N

# O

# P

# R

# S